MW01034252

# THE FIREFLY MINI
# SPANISH/ENGLISH
# VISUAL DICTIONARY

Jean-Claude **Corbeil**
Ariane **Archambault**

FIREFLY BOOKS

# A FIREFLY BOOK

Published by Firefly Books Ltd. 2009
Copyright © 2006 QA International

First printing

Publisher Cataloging-in-Publication Data  (U.S.)
Corbeil, Jean-Claude.
    The Firefly mini Spanish English visual dictionary / Jean-Claude Corbeil ; Ariane Archambault.
[600] p. : col. ill. ; cm.
Includes index.
Summary: A general reference visual dictionary featuring terms in English and Spanish. Includes sections on astronomy, geography, the animal and vegetable kingdoms, human biology, the home, clothing and accessories, art and architecture, communication, transportation, energy, science, society and sports.
ISBN-13: 978-1-55407-494-5 (pbk.)
ISBN-10: 1-55407-494-0  (pbk.)
1. Picture dictionaries, Spanish.  2. Picture dictionaries, English. 3. Spanish language – Dictionaries – English.  4. English language – Dictionaries – Spanish.  I. Archambault, Ariane.  II. Title.
463.21 dc22    PC4629.C6736 2006

Library and Archives Canada Cataloguing in Publication
Corbeil, Jean-Claude, 1932-
    The Firefly mini Spanish/English visual dictionary / Jean-Claude Corbeil, Ariane Archambault.
Includes index.
ISBN-13: 978-1-55407-494-5
ISBN-10: 1-55407-494-0
    1. Picture dictionaries, Spanish.  2. Picture dictionaries, English. 3. Spanish language-Dictionaries-English.  4. English language-Dictionaries-Spanish.  I. Archambault, Ariane, 1936-  II. Title.
AG250.C66375 2006    463'.21    C2006-900746-2

Published in the United States by
Firefly Books (U.S.) Inc.
P.O. Box 1338, Ellicott Station
Buffalo, New York 14205

Published in Canada by
Firefly Books Ltd.
66 Leek Crescent
Richmond Hill, Ontario L4B 1H1

Cover design: Gareth Lind

Printed in Singapore
11 10 9 8 7 6 5 4 3 2   12 11 10 09
Version 3.5.1

ACKNOWLEDGMENTS

Our deepest gratitude to the individuals, institutions, companies and businesses that have provided us with the latest technical documentation for use in preparing The Firefly Mini Spanish/English Visual Dictionary.

Arcand, Denys (réalisateur); Association Internationale de Signalisation Maritime; Association canadienne des paiements (Charlie Clarke); Association des banquiers canadiens (Lise Provost); Automobiles Citroën; Automobiles Peugeot; Banque du Canada (Lyse Brousseau); Banque Royale du Canada (Raymond Chouinard, Francine Morel, Carole Trottier); Barrett Xplore inc.; Bazarin, Christine;Bibliothèque du Parlement canadien (Service de renseignements); Bibliothèque nationale du Québec (Jean-François Palomino); Bluechip Kennels (Olga Gagne); Bombardier Aéronautique; Bridgestone-Firestone; Brother (Canada); Canadien National; Casavant Frères ltée; C.O.J.O. ATHENES 2004 (Bureau des Médias Internationaux); Centre Eaton de Montréal; Centre national du Costume (Recherche et de Diffusion); Cetacean Society International (William R. Rossiter); Chagnon, Daniel (architecte D.E.S. – M.E.Q.); Cohen et Rubin Architectes (Maggy Cohen); Commission Scolaire de Montréal (École St-Henri); Compagnie de la Baie d'Hudson (Nunzia Iavarone, Ron Oyama); Corporation d'hébergement du Québec (Céline Drolet); École nationale de théâtre du Canada (Bibliothèque); Élevage Le Grand Saphir (Stéphane Ayotte); Énergie atomique du Canada ltée; Eurocopter; Famous Players; Fédération bancaire française (Védi Hékiman); Fontaine, PierreHenry (biologiste); Future Shop; Garaga; Groupe Jean Coutu; Hôpital du Sacré-Cœur de Montréal; Hôtel Inter-Continental; Hydro-Québec; I.P.I.Q. (Serge Bouchard); IGA Barcelo; International Entomological Society (Dr. Michael Geisthardt); Irisbus; Jérôme, Danielle (O.D.); La Poste (Colette Gouts); Le Groupe Canam Manac inc.; Lévesque, Georges (urgentologue); Lévesque, Robert (chef machiniste); Manutan; Marriot Spring Hill suites; MATRA S.A.; Métro inc.; ministère canadien de la Défense nationale (Affaires publiques); ministère de la Défense, République Française; ministère de la Justice du Québec (Service de la gestion immobilière – Carol Sirois); ministère de l'Éducation du Québec (Direction de l'équipement scolaire- Daniel Chagnon); Muse Productions (Annick Barbery); National Aeronautics and Space Administration; National Oceanic and Atmospheric Administration; Nikon Canada inc.; Normand, Denis (consultant en télécommunications); Office de la langue française du Québec (Chantal Robinson); Paul Demers & Fils inc.; Phillips (France); Pratt & Whitney Canada inc.; Prévost Car inc.; Radio Shack Canada ltée; Réno-Dépôt inc.; Robitaille, Jean-François (Département de biologie, Université Laurentienne); Rocking T Ranch and Poultry Farm (Pete and Justine Theer); RONA inc.; Sears Canada inc.; Secrétariat d'État du Canada : Bureau de la traduction ; Service correctionnel du Canada; Société d'Entomologie Africaine (Alain Drumont); Société des musées québécois (Michel Perron); Société Radio-Canada; Sony du Canada ltée; Sûreté du Québec; Théâtre du Nouveau Monde; Transports Canada (Julie Poirier); Urgences-Santé (Éric Berry); Ville de Longueuil (Direction de la Police); Ville de Montréal (Service de la prévention des incendies); Vimont Lexus Toyota; Volvo Bus Corporation; Yamaha Motor Canada Ltd.

QA International wishes to extend a special thank you to the following people for their contribution to The Firefly Mini Spanish/English Visual Dictionary:

Jean-Louis Martin, Marc Lalumière, Jacques Perrault, Stéphane Roy, Alice Comtois, Michel Blais, Christiane Beauregard, Mamadou Togola, Annie Maurice, Charles Campeau, Mivil Deschênes, Jonathan Jacques, Martin Lortie, Frédérick Simard, Yan Tremblay, Mathieu Blouin, Sébastien Dallaire, Hoang Khanh Le, Martin Desrosiers, Nicolas Oroc, François Escalmel, Danièle Lemay, Pierre Savoie, Benoît Bourdeau, Marie-Andrée Lemieux, Caroline Soucy, Yves Chabot, Anne-Marie Ouellette, Anne-Marie Villeneuve, Anne-Marie Brault, Nancy Lepage, Daniel Provost, François Vézina, Brad Wilson, Michael Worek, Lionel Koffler, Maraya Raduha, Dave Harvey, Mike Parkes, George Walker, Anna Simmons, Sophie Pellerin, Kien Tang, Guylaine Houle, Tony O'Riley.

The Firefly Mini Spanish/English Visual Dictionary was created and produced by
QA International
329, rue de la Commune Ouest, 3e étage
Montréal (Québec) H2Y 2E1 Canada
T 514.499.3000  F 514.499.3010
www.qa-international.com

EDITORIAL STAFF

Publisher: Jacques Fortin

Authors: Jean-Claude Corbeil and Ariane Archambault

Editorial Director: François Fortin

Editor-in-Chief: Serge D'Amico

Graphic Design: Anne Tremblay

PRODUCTION

Nathalie Fréchette

Cynthia Morneau

TERMINOLOGICAL RESEARCH

Jean Beaumont

Catherine Briand

Nathalie Guillo

Anne Rouleau

ILLUSTRATIONS

Art Direction: Jocelyn Gardner, Anouk Noël

Jean-Yves Ahern

Rielle Lévesque

Alain Lemire

Mélanie Boivin

Yan Bohler

Claude Thivierge

Pascal Bilodeau

Michel Rouleau

Carl Pelletier

Raymond Martin

LAYOUT

Pascal Goyette

Janou-Ève LeGuerrier

Véronique Boisvert

Karine Raymond

Geneviève Théroux Béliveau

DOCUMENTATION

Gilles Vézina

Kathleen Wynd

Stéphane Batigne

Sylvain Robichaud

Jessie Daigle

DATA MANAGEMENT

Programmer: Éric Gagnon

Daniel Beaulieu

REVISION

Marie-Nicole Cimon

Liliane Michaud

Véronica Schami

PREPRESS

Karine Lévesque

François Hénault

Julien Brisebois

Patrick Mercure

**Jean-Claude Corbeil** is an expert in linguistic planning, with a world-wide reputation in the fields of comparative terminology and socio-linguistics. He serves as a consultant to various international organizations and governments.

**Ariane Archambault**, a specialist in applied linguistics, has taught foreign languages and is now a terminologist and editor of dictionaries and reference books.

# Introduction to

## *The Firefly Mini Spanish/English Visual Dictionary*

### A DICTIONARY FOR ONE AND ALL

*The Firefly Mini Spanish/English Visual Dictionary* uses pictures to define words. With thousands of illustrations and thousands of specialist and general terms, it provides a rich source of knowledge about the world around you.

Designed for the general reader and students of language, *The Firefly Mini Spanish/English Visual Dictionary* responds to the needs of anyone seeking precise, correct terms for a wide range of objects. Using illustrations enables you to "see" immediately the meaning of each term.

You can use *The Firefly Mini Spanish/English Visual Dictionary* in several ways:

**By going from an idea to a word.** If you are familiar with an object but do not know the correct name for it, you can look up the object in the dictionary and you will find the various parts correctly named.

**By going from a word to an idea.** If you want to check the meaning of a term, refer to the index where you will find the term and be directed to the appropriate illustration that defines the term.

**For sheer pleasure.** You can flip from one illustration to another or from one word to another, for the sole purpose of enjoying the illustrations and enriching your knowledge of the world around us.

### STRUCTURE

*The Firefly Mini Spanish/English Visual Dictionary* is divided into THEMES, outlining subjects from astronomy to sports.

More complex subjects are divided into SUB-THEMES; for example, the Animal Kingdom chapter is divided into themes including insects and arachnids, mollusks, and crustaceans.

The TITLES name the object and, at times, the chief members of a class of objects are brought together under the same SUBTITLE.

The ILLUSTRATIONS show an object, a process or a phenomenon, and the most significant details from which they are constructed. It serves as a visual definition for each of the terms presented.

### TERMINOLOGY

Each word in *The Firefly Mini Spanish/English Visual Dictionary* has been carefully chosen and verified. Sometimes different words are used to name the same object, and in these cases the word most commonly used was chosen.

**COLOR REFERENCE**

On the spine and back of the book this identifies and accompanies each theme to facilitate quick access to the corresponding section in the book.

**TITLE**

It is highlighted in English, and the Spanish equivalent is placed underneath in smaller characters. If the title runs over a number of pages, it is printed in gray on the pages subsequent to the first page on which it appears.

**SUB-THEME**

Most themes are subdivided into sub-themes. The sub-theme is given both in English and in Spanish.

**NARROW LINES**

These link the word to the item indicated. Where too many lines would make reading difficult, they have been replaced by color codes with captions or, in rare cases, by numbers.

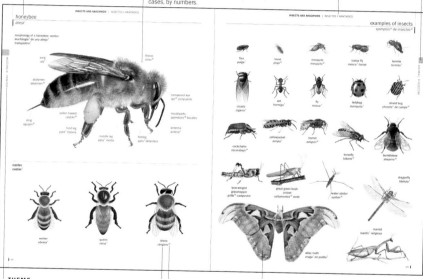

**THEME**

It is always unilingual, in English.

**TERM**

Each term appears in the index with a reference to the pages on which it appears. It is given in both languages, with English as the main index entry.

**GENDER INDICATION**

F: feminine M: masculine N: neuter

The gender of each word in a term is indicated.

The characters shown in the dictionary are men or women when the function illustrated can be fulfilled by either. In these cases, the gender assigned to the word depends on the illustration; in fact, the word is either masculine or feminine depending on the sex of the person.

**ILLUSTRATION**

It serves as the visual definition for the terms associated with it.

# Contents

# List of chapters

ASTRONOMY

# solar system
*sistema$^M$ solar*

**outer planets**
***planetas$^M$ externos***

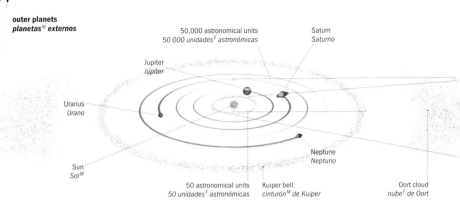

50,000 astronomical units
*50 000 unidades$^F$ astronómicas*

Saturn
*Saturno*

Jupiter
*Júpiter*

Uranus
*Urano*

Sun
*Sol$^M$*

Neptune
*Neptuno*

50 astronomical units
*50 unidades$^F$ astronómicas*

Kuiper belt
*cinturón$^M$ de Kuiper*

Oort cloud
*nube$^F$ de Oort*

# planets and satellites
*planetas$^M$ y satélites$^M$*

Phobos
*Fobos*

Ceres
*Ceres*

Moon
*Luna$^F$*

Deimos
*Deimos*

Venus
*Venus*

Jupiter
*Júpiter*

Mercury
*Mercurio*

Earth
*Tierra$^F$*

Mars
*Marte*

Io
*Io*

Callisto
*Calisto*

Europa
*Europa*

Ganymede
*Ganimedes*

Sun
*Sol$^M$*

ASTRONOMY

solar system

**inner planets**
*planetas<sup>M</sup> internos*

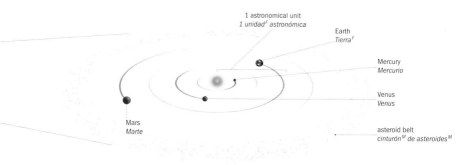

1 astronomical unit
*1 unidad<sup>F</sup> astronómica*

Earth
*Tierra<sup>F</sup>*

Mercury
*Mercurio*

Venus
*Venus*

Mars
*Marte*

asteroid belt
*cinturón<sup>M</sup> de asteroides<sup>M</sup>*

planets and satellites

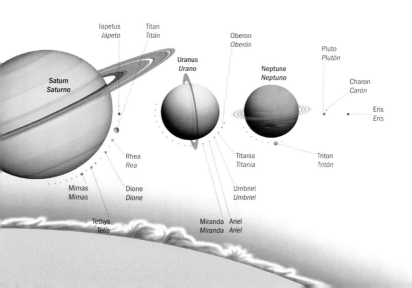

Iapetus
*Jápeto*

Titan
*Titán*

Oberon
*Oberón*

Pluto
*Plutón*

Uranus
*Urano*

Neptune
*Neptuno*

Charon
*Carón*

Saturn
*Saturno*

Eris
*Eris*

Rhea
*Rea*

Titania
*Titania*

Triton
*Tritón*

Mimas
*Mimas*

Dione
*Dione*

Umbriel
*Umbriel*

Tethys
*Tetis*

Miranda   Ariel
*Miranda   Ariel*

3

ASTRONOMY

# Sun
*Sol*[M]

**structure of the Sun**
*estructura*[F] *del Sol*[M]

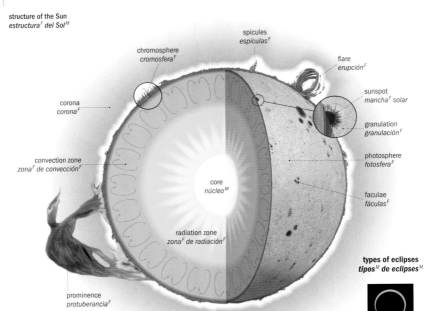

chromosphere
*cromosfera*[F]

spicules
*espículas*[F]

flare
*erupción*[F]

sunspot
*mancha*[F] *solar*

corona
*corona*[F]

granulation
*granulación*[F]

convection zone
*zona*[F] *de convección*[F]

photosphere
*fotosfera*[F]

core
*núcleo*[M]

faculae
*fáculas*[F]

radiation zone
*zona*[F] *de radiación*[F]

prominence
*protuberancia*[F]

**types of eclipses**
*tipos*[M] *de eclipses*[M]

annular eclipse
*eclipse*[M] *anular*

**solar eclipse**
*eclipse*[M] *solar*

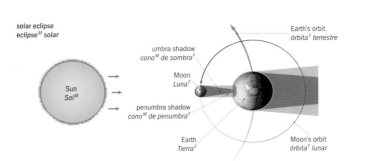

Earth's orbit
*órbita*[F] *terrestre*

umbra shadow
*cono*[M] *de sombra*[F]

Moon
*Luna*[F]

Sun
*Sol*[M]

penumbra shadow
*cono*[M] *de penumbra*[F]

Earth
*Tierra*[F]

Moon's orbit
*órbita*[F] *lunar*

partial eclipse
*eclipse*[M] *parcial*

total eclipse
*eclipse*[M] *total*

# Moon
*Luna*[F]

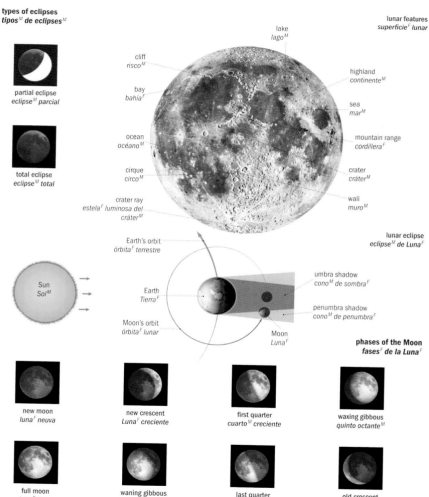

**types of eclipses**
***tipos***[M] ***de eclipses***[M]

partial eclipse
*eclipse*[M] *parcial*

total eclipse
*eclipse*[M] *total*

lunar features
*superficie*[F] *lunar*

lake
*lago*[M]

cliff
*risco*[M]

bay
*bahía*[F]

highland
*continente*[M]

sea
*mar*[M]

ocean
*océano*[M]

mountain range
*cordillera*[F]

cirque
*circo*[M]

crater
*cráter*[M]

crater ray
*estela*[F] *luminosa del cráter*[M]

wall
*muro*[M]

lunar eclipse
*eclipse*[M] *de Luna*[F]

Earth's orbit
*órbita*[F] *terrestre*

Sun
*Sol*[M]

Earth
*Tierra*[F]

Moon's orbit
*órbita*[F] *lunar*

umbra shadow
*cono*[M] *de sombra*[F]

penumbra shadow
*cono*[M] *de penumbra*[F]

Moon
*Luna*[F]

**phases of the Moon**
***fases***[F] ***de la Luna***[F]

new moon
*luna*[F] *neuva*

new crescent
*Luna*[F] *creciente*

first quarter
*cuarto*[M] *creciente*

waxing gibbous
*quinto octante*[M]

full moon
*luna*[F] *llena*

waning gibbous
*tercer octante*[M]

last quarter
*cuarto*[M] *menguante*

old crescent
*Luna*[F] *menguante*

ASTRONOMY

# galaxy
*galaxia*$^F$

**Milky Way**
*Vía*$^F$ *Láctea*

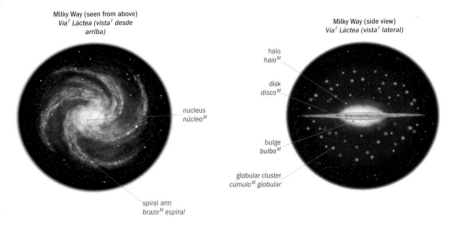

Milky Way (seen from above)
*Vía*$^F$ *Láctea (vista*$^F$ *desde arriba)*

Milky Way (side view)
*Vía*$^F$ *Láctea (vista*$^F$ *lateral)*

halo
*halo*$^M$

disk
*disco*$^M$

nucleus
*núcleo*$^M$

bulge
*bulbo*$^M$

globular cluster
*cúmulo*$^M$ *globular*

spiral arm
*brazo*$^M$ *espiral*

# comet
*cometa*$^M$

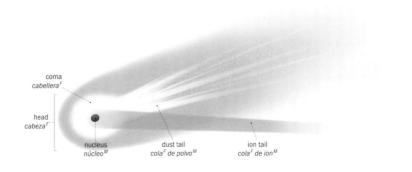

coma
*cabellera*$^F$

head
*cabeza*$^F$

nucleus
*núcleo*$^M$

dust tail
*cola*$^F$ *de polvo*$^M$

ion tail
*cola*$^F$ *de ion*$^M$

# Hubble space telescope
*telescopio*[M] *espacial Hubble*

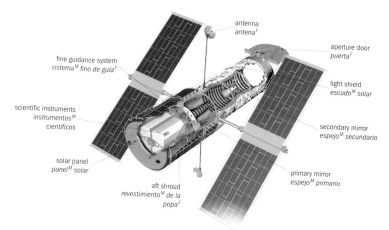

antenna
*antena*[F]

aperture door
*puerta*[F]

fine guidance system
*sistema*[M] *fino de guía*[F]

light shield
*escudo*[M] *solar*

scientific instruments
*instrumentos*[M]
*científicos*

secondary mirror
*espejo*[M] *secundario*

solar panel
*panel*[M] *solar*

primary mirror
*espejo*[M] *primario*

aft shroud
*revestimiento*[M] *de la*
*popa*[F]

# astronomical observatory
*observatorio*[M] *astronómico*

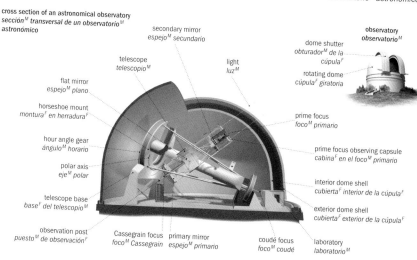

cross section of an astronomical observatory
*sección*[F] *transversal de un observatorio*[M]
*astronómico*

secondary mirror
*espejo*[M] *secundario*

observatory
*observatorio*[M]

dome shutter
*obturador*[M] *de la*
*cúpula*[F]

telescope
*telescopio*[M]

light
*luz*[M]

rotating dome
*cúpula*[F] *giratoria*

flat mirror
*espejo*[M] *plano*

horseshoe mount
*montura*[F] *en herradura*[F]

prime focus
*foco*[M] *primario*

hour angle gear
*ángulo*[M] *horario*

prime focus observing capsule
*cabina*[F] *en el foco*[M] *primario*

polar axis
*eje*[M] *polar*

interior dome shell
*cubierta*[F] *interior de la cúpula*[F]

telescope base
*base*[F] *del telescopio*[M]

exterior dome shell
*cubierta*[F] *exterior de la cúpula*[F]

observation post
*puesto*[M] *de observación*[F]

Cassegrain focus
*foco*[M] *Cassegrain*

primary mirror
*espejo*[M] *primario*

coudé focus
*foco*[M] *coudé*

laboratory
*laboratorio*[M]

# refracting telescope
*telescopio<sup>M</sup> refractor*

finderscope
*anteojo<sup>M</sup> buscador*

cradle
*abrazadera<sup>F</sup>*

main tube
*tubo<sup>M</sup> principal*

dew shield
*parasol<sup>M</sup>*

eyepiece
*ocular<sup>M</sup>*

eyepiece holder
*portaocular<sup>M</sup>*

star diagonal
*ocular<sup>M</sup> acodado*

focusing knob
*botón<sup>M</sup> de enfoque<sup>M</sup>*

declination setting scale
*círculo<sup>M</sup> graduado de declinación<sup>F</sup>*

azimuth clamp
*palanca<sup>F</sup> de bloqueo<sup>M</sup> del acimut<sup>M</sup>*

altitude clamp
*palanca<sup>F</sup> de bloqueo<sup>M</sup> de la altura<sup>F</sup>*

right ascension setting scale
*anillo<sup>M</sup> graduado<sup>M</sup> de ascensión<sup>F</sup> recta*

counterweight
*contrapeso<sup>M</sup>*

azimuth fine adjustment
*ajuste<sup>M</sup> fino del acimut<sup>M</sup>*

altitude fine adjustment
*ajuste<sup>M</sup> fino de la altura<sup>F</sup>*

fork
*horquilla<sup>F</sup>*

tripod accessories shelf
*repisa<sup>F</sup> para accesorios<sup>M</sup>*

tripod
*trípode<sup>M</sup>*

cross section of a refracting telescope
*sección<sup>F</sup> transversal de un telescopio<sup>M</sup> refractor*

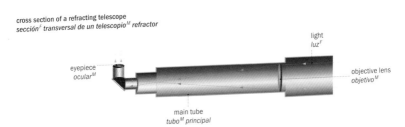

light
*luz<sup>F</sup>*

eyepiece
*ocular<sup>M</sup>*

objective lens
*objetivo<sup>M</sup>*

main tube
*tubo<sup>M</sup> principal*

# reflecting telescope
*telescopio ᴹ reflector*

finderscope
*anteojo ᴹ buscador*

eyepiece
*ocular ᴹ*

cradle
*abrazadera ᶠ*

support
*soporte ᴹ*

main tube
*tubo ᴹ principal*

focusing knob
*botón ᴹ de enfoque ᴹ*

declination setting scale
*anillo ᴹ graduado de declinación ᶠ*

right ascension setting scale
*anillo ᴹ graduado de ascensión ᶠ recta*

azimuth fine adjustment
*ajuste ᴹ fino del acimut ᴹ*

azimuth clamp
*palanca ᶠ de bloqueo ᴹ del acimut ᴹ*

altitude fine adjustment
*ajuste ᴹ fino de la altura ᶠ*

altitude clamp
*palanca ᶠ de bloqueo ᴹ de la altura ᶠ*

cross section of a reflecting telescope
*sección ᶠ transversal de un telecopio ᴹ reflector*

eyepiece
*ocular ᴹ*

secondary mirror
*espejo ᴹ secundario*

concave primary mirror
*espejo ᴹ cóncavo primario*

light
*luz ᶠ*

main tube
*tubo ᴹ principal*

ASTRONOMY

# space shuttle
*transbordador$^M$ espacial*

space shuttle at takeoff
*transbordador$^M$ espacial en posición$^F$ de lanzamiento$^M$*

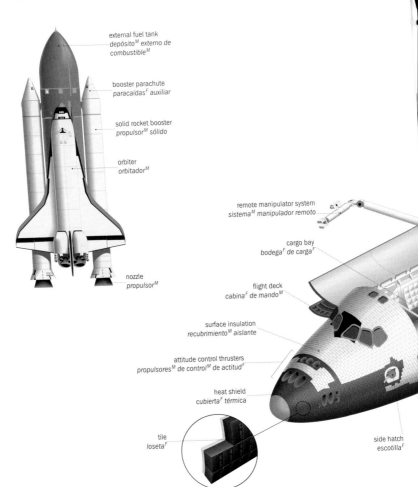

external fuel tank
*depósito$^M$ externo de combustible$^M$*

booster parachute
*paracaídas$^F$ auxiliar*

solid rocket booster
*propulsor$^M$ sólido*

orbiter
*orbitador$^M$*

remote manipulator system
*sistema$^M$ manipulador remoto*

cargo bay
*bodega$^F$ de carga$^F$*

nozzle
*propulsor$^M$*

flight deck
*cabina$^F$ de mando$^M$*

surface insulation
*recubrimiento$^M$ aislante*

attitude control thrusters
*propulsores$^M$ de control$^M$ de actitud$^F$*

heat shield
*cubierta$^F$ térmica*

tile
*loseta$^F$*

side hatch
*escotilla$^F$*

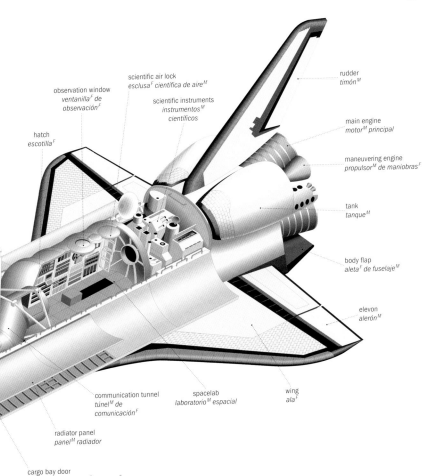

orbiter
*orbitador*<sup>M</sup>

scientific air lock
*esclusa*<sup>F</sup> *científica de aire*<sup>M</sup>

observation window
*ventanilla*<sup>F</sup> *de*
*observación*<sup>F</sup>

scientific instruments
*instrumentos*<sup>M</sup>
*científicos*

hatch
*escotilla*<sup>F</sup>

rudder
*timón*<sup>M</sup>

main engine
*motor*<sup>M</sup> *principal*

maneuvering engine
*propulsor*<sup>M</sup> *de maniobras*<sup>F</sup>

tank
*tanque*<sup>M</sup>

body flap
*aleta*<sup>F</sup> *de fuselaje*<sup>M</sup>

elevon
*alerón*<sup>M</sup>

communication tunnel
*túnel*<sup>M</sup> *de*
*comunicación*<sup>F</sup>

spacelab
*laboratorio*<sup>M</sup> *espacial*

wing
*ala*<sup>F</sup>

radiator panel
*panel*<sup>M</sup> *radiador*

cargo bay door
*puerta*<sup>F</sup> *de la bodega*<sup>F</sup> *de carga*<sup>F</sup>

# configuration of the continents

*configuración^F de los continentes^M*

EARTH

**planisphere**
*planisferio^M*

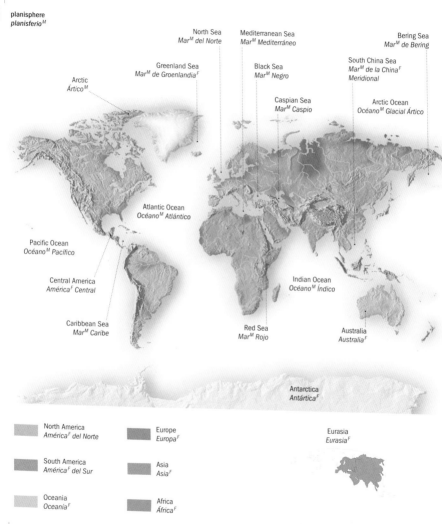

North Sea
*Mar^M del Norte*

Mediterranean Sea
*Mar^M Mediterráneo*

Bering Sea
*Mar^M de Bering*

Greenland Sea
*Mar^M de Groenlandia^F*

Black Sea
*Mar^M Negro*

South China Sea
*Mar^M de la China^F
Meridional*

Arctic
*Ártico^M*

Caspian Sea
*Mar^M Caspio*

Arctic Ocean
*Océano^M Glacial Ártico*

Atlantic Ocean
*Océano^M Atlántico*

Pacific Ocean
*Océano^M Pacífico*

Central America
*América^F Central*

Indian Ocean
*Océano^M Índico*

Caribbean Sea
*Mar^M Caribe*

Red Sea
*Mar^M Rojo*

Australia
*Australia^F*

Antarctica
*Antártica^F*

North America
*América^F del Norte*

Europe
*Europa^F*

Eurasia
*Eurasia^F*

South America
*América^F del Sur*

Asia
*Asia^F*

Oceania
*Oceanía^F*

Africa
*África^F*

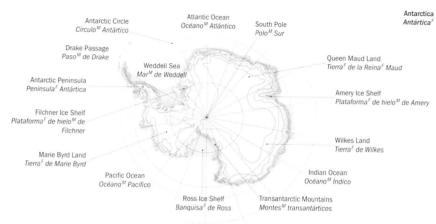

Antarctica
*Antártica*[F]

Antarctic Circle
*Círculo*[M] *Antártico*

Atlantic Ocean
*Océano*[M] *Atlántico*

South Pole
*Polo*[M] *Sur*

Drake Passage
*Paso*[M] *de Drake*

Queen Maud Land
*Tierra*[F] *de la Reina*[F] *Maud*

Weddell Sea
*Mar*[M] *de Weddell*

Antarctic Peninsula
*Península*[F] *Antártica*

Amery Ice Shelf
*Plataforma*[F] *de hielo*[M] *de Amery*

Filchner Ice Shelf
*Plataforma*[F] *de hielo*[M] *de Filchner*

Wilkes Land
*Tierra*[F] *de Wilkes*

Marie Byrd Land
*Tierra*[F] *de Marie Byrd*

Indian Ocean
*Océano*[M] *Índico*

Pacific Ocean
*Océano*[M] *Pacífico*

Ross Ice Shelf
*Banquisa*[F] *de Ross*

Transantarctic Mountains
*Montes*[M] *transantárticos*

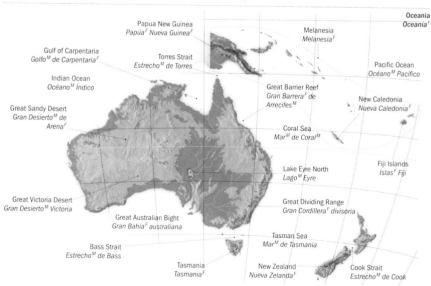

Oceania
*Oceanía*[F]

Papua New Guinea
*Papúa*[F] *Nueva Guinea*[F]

Melanesia
*Melanesia*[F]

Gulf of Carpentaria
*Golfo*[M] *de Carpentaria*[F]

Torres Strait
*Estrecho*[M] *de Torres*

Pacific Ocean
*Océano*[M] *Pacífico*

Indian Ocean
*Océano*[M] *Índico*

Great Barrier Reef
*Gran Barrera*[F] *de Arrecifes*[M]

New Caledonia
*Nueva Caledonia*[F]

Great Sandy Desert
*Gran Desierto*[M] *de Arena*[F]

Coral Sea
*Mar*[M] *de Coral*[M]

Fiji Islands
*Islas*[F] *Fiji*

Lake Eyre North
*Lago*[M] *Eyre*

Great Victoria Desert
*Gran Desierto*[M] *Victoria*

Great Dividing Range
*Gran Cordillera*[F] *divisoria*

Great Australian Bight
*Gran Bahía*[F] *australiana*

Bass Strait
*Estrecho*[M] *de Bass*

Tasman Sea
*Mar*[M] *de Tasmania*

Tasmania
*Tasmania*[F]

New Zealand
*Nueva Zelanda*[F]

Cook Strait
*Estrecho*[M] *de Cook*

North America
*América<sup>F</sup> del Norte*

Bering Strait
*Estrecho<sup>M</sup> de Bering*

Beaufort Sea
*Mar<sup>M</sup> de Beaufort*

Mackenzie River
*Río<sup>M</sup> Mackenzie*

Hudson Bay
*Bahía<sup>F</sup> de Hudson*

Baffin Island
*Bahía<sup>F</sup> de Baffin*

Greenland
*Groenlandia<sup>F</sup>*

Gulf of Alaska
*Golfo<sup>M</sup> de Alaska<sup>F</sup>*

Great Lakes
*Grandes Lagos<sup>M</sup>*

Aleutian Islands
*Islas<sup>F</sup> Aleutianas*

Newfoundland Island
*Isla<sup>F</sup> de Terranova<sup>F</sup>*

Rocky Mountains
*Montañas<sup>F</sup> Rocosas*

Saint Lawrence River
*Río<sup>M</sup> San Lorenzo*

Grand Canyon
*Gran Cañón<sup>M</sup>*

Appalachian Mountains
*Montes<sup>M</sup> Apalaches<sup>M</sup>*

Mississippi River
*Río<sup>M</sup> Mississippi*

Gulf of California
*Golfo<sup>M</sup> de California<sup>F</sup>*

Gulf of Mexico
*Golfo<sup>M</sup> de México<sup>M</sup>*

West Indies
*Antillas<sup>F</sup>*

Yucatan Peninsula
*Península<sup>F</sup> del
Yucatán<sup>M</sup>*

Caribbean Sea
*Mar<sup>M</sup> de Caribe<sup>M</sup>*

Central America
*América<sup>F</sup> Central*

Isthmus of Panama
*Istmo<sup>M</sup> de Panamá<sup>M</sup>*

**South America**
*América<sup>F</sup> del Sur*

Orinoco River
*Río<sup>M</sup> Orinoco*

Amazon River
*Río<sup>M</sup> Amazonas*

Equator
*ecuador<sup>M</sup>*

Gulf of Panama
*Golfo<sup>M</sup> de Panamá<sup>M</sup>*

Andes Cordillera
*Cordillera<sup>F</sup> de los Andes<sup>M</sup>*

Lake Titicaca
*Lago<sup>M</sup> Titicaca*

Atacama Desert
*Desierto<sup>M</sup> de Atacama*

Paraná River
*Río<sup>M</sup> Paraná*

Patagonia
*Patagonia<sup>F</sup>*

Falkland Islands
*Islas<sup>F</sup> Malvinas*

Tierra del Fuego
*Tierra<sup>F</sup> del Fuego<sup>M</sup>*

Cape Horn
*Cabo<sup>M</sup> de Hornos*

Drake Passage
*Paso<sup>M</sup> de Drake*

Europe
*Europa*[F]

Barents Sea
*Mar*[M] *de Barents*

Ural Mountains
*Montes*[M] *Urales*[M]

Lake Ladoga
*Lago*[M] *Ladoga*

Kola Peninsula
*Península*[F] *de Kola*

Volga River
*Río*[M] *Volga*

Gulf of Bothnia
*Golfo*[M] *de Botnia*[F]

Norwegian Sea
*Mar*[M] *de Noruega*[F]

Dnieper River
*Río*[M] *Dniéper*

Iceland
*Islandia*[F]

Baltic Sea
*Mar*[M] *Báltico*

North Sea
*Mar*[M] *del Norte*

Scandinavian Peninsula
*Península*[F] *Escandinava*

Irish Sea
*Mar*[M] *de Irlanda*[F]

Atlantic Ocean
*Océano*[M] *Atlántico*

English Channel
*Canal*[M] *de la Mancha*[F]

Vistula River
*Río*[M] *Vístula*

Alps
*Alpes*[M]

Black Sea
*Mar*[M] *Negro*

Iberian Peninsula
*Península*[F] *Ibérica*

Strait of Gibraltar
*Estrecho*[M] *de Gibraltar*[M]

Pyrenees
*Pirineos*[M]

Danube River
*Río*[M] *Danubio*

Balkan Peninsula
*Península*[F] *de los Balcanes*[M]

Carpathian Mountains
*Montes*[M] *Cárpatos*[M]

Mediterranean Sea
*Mar*[M] *Mediterráneo*

Adriatic Sea
*Mar*[M] *Adriático*

Aegean Sea
*Mar*[M] *Egeo*

Asia
*Asia*[F]

EARTH

Aral Sea
*Mar*[M] *de Aral*

Lake Baikal
*Lago*[M] *Baikal*

Gobi Desert
*Desierto*[M] *de Gobi*

Kamchatka Peninsula
*Península*[F] *de Kamchatka*

Caspian Sea
*Mar*[M] *Caspio*

Sea of Japan
*Mar*[M] *de Japón*[M]

Black Sea
*Mar*[M] *Negro*

Pacific Ocean
*Océano*[M] *Pacífico*

Red Sea
*Mar*[M] *Rojo*

Japan
*Japón*[M]

Korean Peninsula
*Península*[F] *de Corea*[F]

East China Sea
*Mar*[M] *de la China*[F] *Oriental*

Philippines
*Filipinas*[F]

Gulf of Aden
*Golfo*[M] *de Adén*

Himalayas
*Himalaya*[M]

Arabian Peninsula
*Península*[F] *de Arabia*[F]

Gulf of Oman
*Golfo*[M] *de Omán*

South China Sea
*Mar*[M] *de la China*[F] *Meridional*

Persian Gulf
*Golfo*[M] *Pérsico*

Arabian Sea
*Mar*[M] *Arábigo*

Indonesia
*Indonesia*[F]

Indian Ocean
*Océano*[M] *Índico*

Bay of Bengal
*Bahía*[F] *de Bengala*

19

**Africa**
*África*[F]

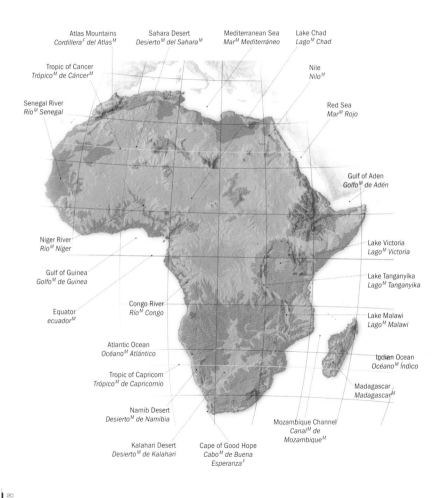

Atlas Mountains
*Cordillera*[F] *del Atlas*[M]

Sahara Desert
*Desierto*[M] *del Sahara*[M]

Mediterranean Sea
*Mar*[M] *Mediterráneo*

Lake Chad
*Lago*[M] *Chad*

Tropic of Cancer
*Trópico*[M] *de Cáncer*[M]

Nile
*Nilo*[M]

Senegal River
*Río*[M] *Senegal*

Red Sea
*Mar*[M] *Rojo*

Gulf of Aden
*Golfo*[M] *de Adén*

Niger River
*Río*[M] *Níger*

Lake Victoria
*Lago*[M] *Victoria*

Gulf of Guinea
*Golfo*[M] *de Guinea*

Lake Tanganyika
*Lago*[M] *Tanganyika*

Equator
*ecuador*[M]

Congo River
*Río*[M] *Congo*

Lake Malawi
*Lago*[M] *Malawi*

Atlantic Ocean
*Océano*[M] *Atlántico*

Indian Ocean
*Océano*[M] *Índico*

Tropic of Capricorn
*Trópico*[M] *de Capricornio*

Madagascar
*Madagascar*[M]

Namib Desert
*Desierto*[M] *de Namibia*

Mozambique Channel
*Canal*[M] *de Mozambique*[M]

Kalahari Desert
*Desierto*[M] *de Kalahari*

Cape of Good Hope
*Cabo*[M] *de Buena Esperanza*[F]

## cartography
*cartografía*[F]

Earth coordinate system
*sistema*[M] *de coordenadas*[F]
*terrestres*

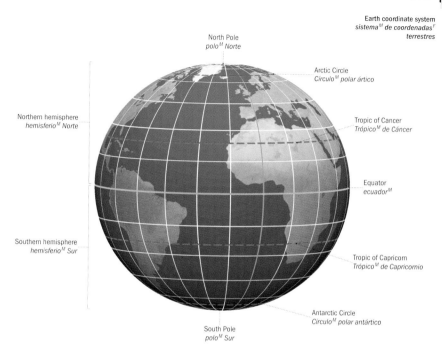

North Pole
*polo*[M] *Norte*

Arctic Circle
*Círculo*[M] *polar ártico*

Tropic of Cancer
*Trópico*[M] *de Cáncer*

Northern hemisphere
*hemisferio*[M] *Norte*

Equator
*ecuador*[M]

Southern hemisphere
*hemisferio*[M] *Sur*

Tropic of Capricorn
*Trópico*[M] *de Capricornio*

Antarctic Circle
*Círculo*[M] *polar antártico*

South Pole
*polo*[M] *Sur*

**hemispheres**
***hemisferios***[M]

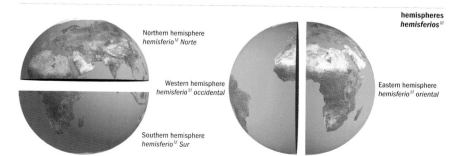

Northern hemisphere
*hemisferio*[M] *Norte*

Western hemisphere
*hemisferio*[M] *occidental*

Eastern hemisphere
*hemisferio*[M] *oriental*

Southern hemisphere
*hemisferio*[M] *Sur*

cartography

EARTH

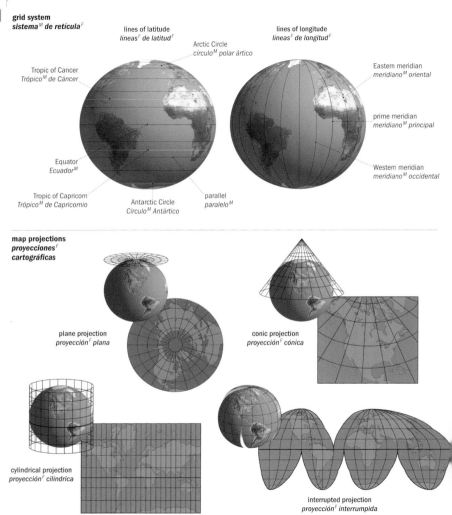

**grid system**
*sistema* <sup>M</sup> *de retícula* <sup>F</sup>

lines of latitude
*líneas* <sup>F</sup> *de latitud* <sup>F</sup>

Arctic Circle
*círculo* <sup>M</sup> *polar ártico*

Tropic of Cancer
*Trópico* <sup>M</sup> *de Cáncer*

Equator
*Ecuador* <sup>M</sup>

Tropic of Capricorn
*Trópico* <sup>M</sup> *de Capricornio*

Antarctic Circle
*Círculo* <sup>M</sup> *Antártico*

parallel
*paralelo* <sup>M</sup>

lines of longitude
*líneas* <sup>F</sup> *de longitud* <sup>F</sup>

Eastern meridian
*meridiano* <sup>M</sup> *oriental*

prime meridian
*meridiano* <sup>M</sup> *principal*

Western meridian
*meridiano* <sup>M</sup> *occidental*

**map projections**
*proyecciones* <sup>F</sup>
*cartográficas*

plane projection
*proyección* <sup>F</sup> *plana*

conic projection
*proyección* <sup>F</sup> *cónica*

cylindrical projection
*proyección* <sup>F</sup> *cilíndrica*

interrupted projection
*proyección* <sup>F</sup> *interrumpida*

**compass rose**
*rosa<sup>F</sup> de los vientos<sup>M</sup>*

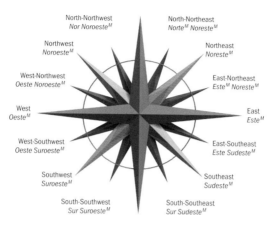

North
*Norte<sup>M</sup>*

North-Northwest
*Nor Noroeste<sup>M</sup>*

North-Northeast
*Norte<sup>M</sup> Noreste<sup>M</sup>*

Northwest
*Noroeste<sup>M</sup>*

Northeast
*Noreste<sup>M</sup>*

West-Northwest
*Oeste Noroeste<sup>M</sup>*

East-Northeast
*Este<sup>M</sup> Noreste<sup>M</sup>*

West
*Oeste<sup>M</sup>*

East
*Este<sup>M</sup>*

West-Southwest
*Oeste Suroeste<sup>M</sup>*

East-Southeast
*Este Sudeste<sup>M</sup>*

Southwest
*Suroeste<sup>M</sup>*

Southeast
*Sudeste<sup>M</sup>*

South-Southwest
*Sur Suroeste<sup>M</sup>*

South-Southeast
*Sur Sudeste<sup>M</sup>*

South
*Sur<sup>M</sup>*

**political map**
*mapa<sup>M</sup> político*

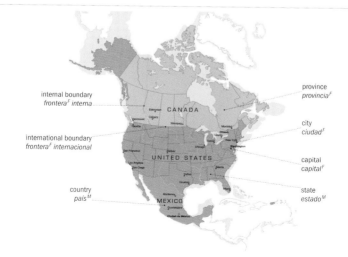

internal boundary
*frontera<sup>F</sup> interna*

province
*provincia<sup>F</sup>*

city
*ciudad<sup>F</sup>*

international boundary
*frontera<sup>F</sup> internacional*

capital
*capital<sup>F</sup>*

country
*país<sup>M</sup>*

state
*estado<sup>M</sup>*

CANADA

UNITED STATES

MEXICO

**physical map**
*mapa^M físico*

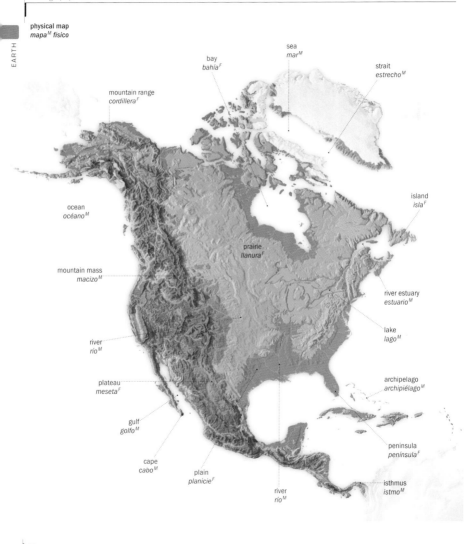

bay
*bahía^F*

sea
*mar^M*

strait
*estrecho^M*

mountain range
*cordillera^F*

island
*isla^F*

ocean
*océano^M*

prairie
*llanura^F*

mountain mass
*macizo^M*

river estuary
*estuario^M*

lake
*lago^M*

river
*río^M*

archipelago
*archipiélago^M*

plateau
*meseta^F*

gulf
*golfo^M*

peninsula
*península^F*

cape
*cabo^M*

plain
*planicie^F*

isthmus
*istmo^M*

river
*río^M*

## urban map
### mapa<sup>M</sup> urbano

railroad line
vía<sup>F</sup> férrea

railroad station
estación<sup>F</sup> del ferrocarril<sup>M</sup>

bridge
puente<sup>M</sup>

suburbs
zona<sup>F</sup> residencial (de las afueras<sup>F</sup>)

park
parque<sup>M</sup>

river
río<sup>M</sup>

cemetery
cementerio<sup>M</sup>

woods
bosques<sup>M</sup>

monument
monumento<sup>M</sup>

circular route
circunvalación<sup>F</sup>

traffic circle
rotonda<sup>F</sup>

highway
autopista<sup>F</sup>

district
distrito<sup>M</sup>

street
calle<sup>F</sup>

avenue
avenida<sup>F</sup>

public building
edificio<sup>M</sup> público

boulevard
bulevar<sup>M</sup>

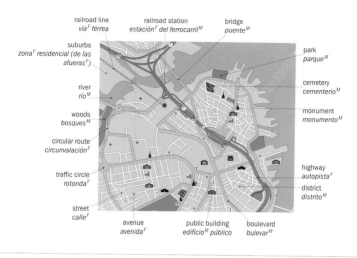

## road map
### mapa<sup>M</sup> de carreteras<sup>F</sup>

highway number
número<sup>M</sup> de la autopista<sup>F</sup>

road
carretera<sup>F</sup>

highway
autopista<sup>F</sup>

road number
número<sup>M</sup> de la carretera<sup>F</sup>

rest area
área<sup>F</sup> de descanso<sup>M</sup>

airport
aeropuerto<sup>M</sup>

service area
área<sup>F</sup> de servicio<sup>M</sup>

national park
parque<sup>M</sup> nacional

belt highway
carretera<sup>F</sup> de circunvalación<sup>F</sup>

scenic route
ruta<sup>F</sup> pintoresca

secondary road
carretera<sup>F</sup> secundaria

point of interest
punto<sup>M</sup> de interés<sup>M</sup>

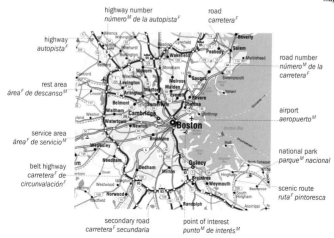

EARTH

## section of the Earth's crust
*corte<sup>M</sup> de la corteza<sup>F</sup> terrestre*

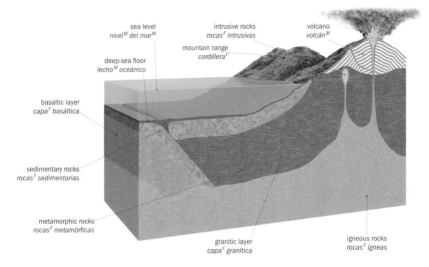

sea level
*nivel<sup>M</sup> del mar<sup>M</sup>*

intrusive rocks
*rocas<sup>F</sup> intrusivas*

volcano
*volcán<sup>M</sup>*

mountain range
*cordillera<sup>F</sup>*

deep-sea floor
*lecho<sup>M</sup> oceánico*

basaltic layer
*capa<sup>F</sup> basáltica*

sedimentary rocks
*rocas<sup>F</sup> sedimentarias*

metamorphic rocks
*rocas<sup>F</sup> metamórficas*

granitic layer
*capa<sup>F</sup> granítica*

igneous rocks
*rocas<sup>F</sup> ígneas*

## structure of the Earth
*estructura<sup>F</sup> de la Tierra<sup>F</sup>*

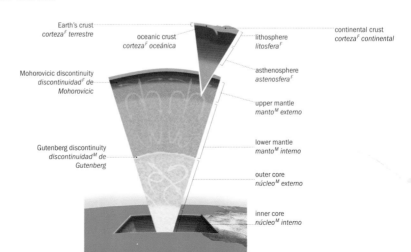

Earth's crust
*corteza<sup>F</sup> terrestre*

oceanic crust
*corteza<sup>F</sup> oceánica*

lithosphere
*litosfera<sup>F</sup>*

continental crust
*corteza<sup>F</sup> continental*

Mohorovicic discontinuity
*discontinuidad<sup>F</sup> de Mohorovicic*

asthenosphere
*astenosfera<sup>F</sup>*

upper mantle
*manto<sup>M</sup> externo*

Gutenberg discontinuity
*discontinuidad<sup>M</sup> de Gutenberg*

lower mantle
*manto<sup>M</sup> interno*

outer core
*núcleo<sup>M</sup> externo*

inner core
*núcleo<sup>M</sup> interno*

EARTH

## tectonic plates
*placas<sup>F</sup> tectónicas*

North American Plate
*placa<sup>F</sup> norteamericana*

Cocos Plate
*placa<sup>F</sup> de Cocos*

Caribbean Plate
*placa<sup>F</sup> del Caribe*

Pacific Plate
*placa<sup>F</sup> del Pacífico*

Nazca Plate
*placa<sup>F</sup> de Nazca*

Scotia Plate
*placa<sup>F</sup> de Escocia*

South American Plate
*placa<sup>F</sup> sudamericana*

African Plate
*placa<sup>F</sup> africana*

Eurasian Plate
*placa<sup>F</sup> euroasiática*

Philippine Plate
*placa<sup>F</sup> de Filipinas*

Australian-Indian Plate
*placa<sup>F</sup> indoaustraliana*

Antarctic Plate
*placa<sup>F</sup> antártica*

subduction
*subducción<sup>M</sup>*

divergent plate boundaries
*placas<sup>F</sup> divergentes*

convergent plate boundaries
*placas<sup>F</sup> convergentes*

transform plate boundaries
*fallas<sup>F</sup> transformantes*

## earthquake
*terremoto<sup>M</sup>*

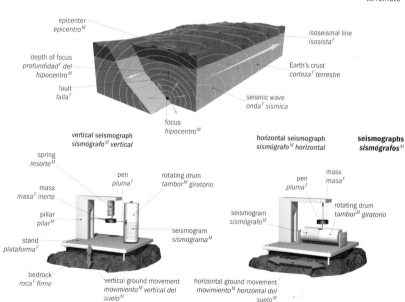

epicenter
*epicentro<sup>M</sup>*

depth of focus
*profundidad<sup>F</sup> del hipocentro<sup>M</sup>*

fault
*falla<sup>F</sup>*

focus
*hipocentro<sup>M</sup>*

isoseismal line
*isosista<sup>F</sup>*

Earth's crust
*corteza<sup>F</sup> terrestre*

seismic wave
*onda<sup>F</sup> sísmica*

vertical seismograph
*sismógrafo<sup>M</sup> vertical*

horizontal seismograph
*sismógrafo<sup>M</sup> horizontal*

**seismographs**
***sismógrafos<sup>M</sup>***

spring
*resorte<sup>M</sup>*

mass
*masa<sup>F</sup> inerte*

pillar
*pilar<sup>M</sup>*

stand
*plataforma<sup>F</sup>*

bedrock
*roca<sup>F</sup> firme*

pen
*pluma<sup>F</sup>*

rotating drum
*tambor<sup>M</sup> giratorio*

seismogram
*sismograma<sup>M</sup>*

vertical ground movement
*movimiento<sup>M</sup> vertical del suelo<sup>M</sup>*

mass
*masa<sup>F</sup>*

pen
*pluma<sup>F</sup>*

rotating drum
*tambor<sup>M</sup> giratorio*

seismogram
*sismógrafo<sup>M</sup>*

horizontal ground movement
*movimiento<sup>M</sup> horizontal del suelo<sup>M</sup>*

EARTH

# volcano
*volcán<sup>M</sup>*

**volcano during eruption**
*volcán<sup>M</sup> en erupción<sup>F</sup>*

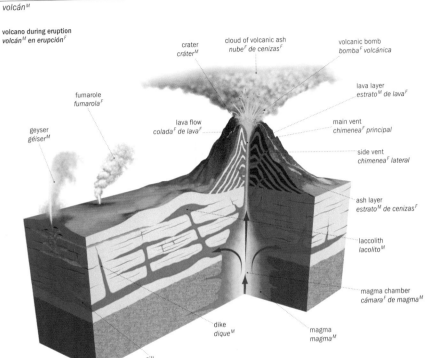

crater
*cráter<sup>M</sup>*

cloud of volcanic ash
*nube<sup>F</sup> de cenizas<sup>F</sup>*

volcanic bomb
*bomba<sup>F</sup> volcánica*

lava layer
*estrato<sup>M</sup> de lava<sup>F</sup>*

fumarole
*fumarola<sup>F</sup>*

lava flow
*colada<sup>F</sup> de lava<sup>F</sup>*

main vent
*chimenea<sup>F</sup> principal*

geyser
*géiser<sup>M</sup>*

side vent
*chimenea<sup>F</sup> lateral*

ash layer
*estrato<sup>M</sup> de cenizas<sup>F</sup>*

laccolith
*lacolito<sup>M</sup>*

magma chamber
*cámara<sup>F</sup> de magma<sup>M</sup>*

dike
*dique<sup>M</sup>*

magma
*magma<sup>M</sup>*

sill
*filón-capa<sup>M</sup>*

**examples of volcanoes**
*ejemplos<sup>M</sup> de volcanes<sup>M</sup>*

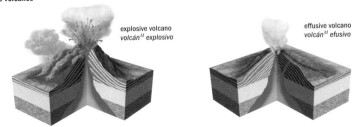

explosive volcano
*volcán<sup>M</sup> explosivo*

effusive volcano
*volcán<sup>M</sup> efusivo*

# mountain
*montaña*[F]

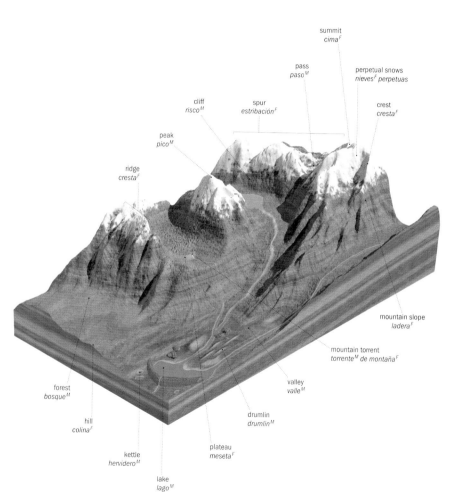

summit
*cima*[F]

pass
*paso*[M]

perpetual snows
*nieves*[F] *perpetuas*

cliff
*risco*[M]

spur
*estribación*[F]

crest
*cresta*[F]

peak
*pico*[M]

ridge
*cresta*[F]

mountain slope
*ladera*[F]

mountain torrent
*torrente*[M] *de montaña*[F]

forest
*bosque*[M]

valley
*valle*[M]

hill
*colina*[F]

drumlin
*drumlin*[M]

kettle
*hervidero*[M]

plateau
*meseta*[F]

lake
*lago*[M]

# glacier
*glaciar*<sup>M</sup>

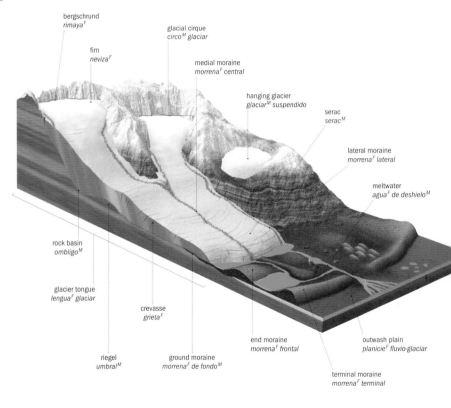

bergschrund
*rimaya*<sup>F</sup>

firn
*neviza*<sup>F</sup>

glacial cirque
*circo*<sup>M</sup> *glaciar*

medial moraine
*morrena*<sup>F</sup> *central*

hanging glacier
*glaciar*<sup>M</sup> *suspendido*

serac
*serac*<sup>M</sup>

lateral moraine
*morrena*<sup>F</sup> *lateral*

meltwater
*agua*<sup>F</sup> *de deshielo*<sup>M</sup>

rock basin
*ombligo*<sup>M</sup>

glacier tongue
*lengua*<sup>F</sup> *glaciar*

crevasse
*grieta*<sup>F</sup>

end moraine
*morrena*<sup>F</sup> *frontal*

outwash plain
*planicie*<sup>F</sup> *fluvio-glaciar*

riegel
*umbral*<sup>M</sup>

ground moraine
*morrena*<sup>F</sup> *de fondo*<sup>M</sup>

terminal moraine
*morrena*<sup>F</sup> *terminal*

# cave
*gruta* [F]

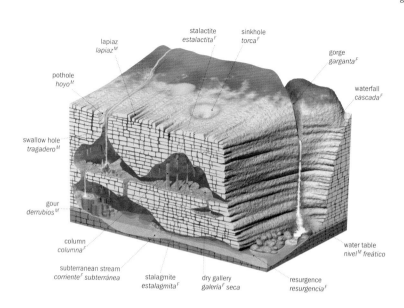

pothole
*hoyo* [M]

lapiaz
*lapiaz* [M]

stalactite
*estalactita* [F]

sinkhole
*torca* [F]

gorge
*garganta* [F]

waterfall
*cascada* [F]

swallow hole
*tragadero* [M]

gour
*derrubios* [M]

column
*columna* [F]

subterranean stream
*corriente* [F] *subterránea*

stalagmite
*estalagmita* [F]

dry gallery
*galería* [F] *seca*

resurgence
*resurgencia* [F]

water table
*nivel* [M] *freático*

# landslides
*desprendimientos* [M] *de tierras* [F]

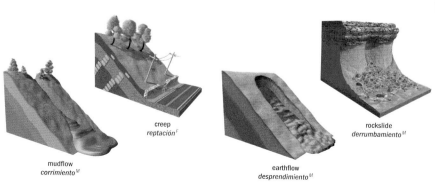

mudflow
*corrimiento* [M]

creep
*reptación* [F]

earthflow
*desprendimiento* [M]

rockslide
*derrumbamiento* [M]

EARTH

# watercourse
*corriente<sup>F</sup> de agua<sup>F</sup>*

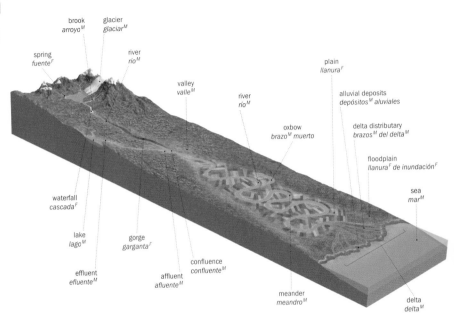

brook
*arroyo<sup>M</sup>*

glacier
*glaciar<sup>M</sup>*

spring
*fuente<sup>F</sup>*

river
*río<sup>M</sup>*

valley
*valle<sup>M</sup>*

river
*río<sup>M</sup>*

oxbow
*brazo<sup>M</sup> muerto*

plain
*llanura<sup>F</sup>*

alluvial deposits
*depósitos<sup>M</sup> aluviales*

delta distributary
*brazos<sup>M</sup> del delta<sup>M</sup>*

floodplain
*llanura<sup>F</sup> de inundación<sup>F</sup>*

sea
*mar<sup>M</sup>*

waterfall
*cascada<sup>F</sup>*

lake
*lago<sup>M</sup>*

gorge
*garganta<sup>F</sup>*

confluence
*confluente<sup>M</sup>*

effluent
*efluente<sup>M</sup>*

affluent
*afluente<sup>M</sup>*

meander
*meandro<sup>M</sup>*

delta
*delta<sup>M</sup>*

# lakes
*lagos<sup>M</sup>*

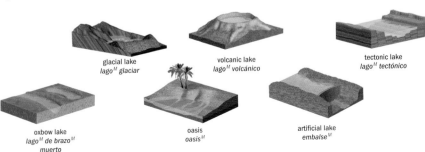

glacial lake
*lago<sup>M</sup> glaciar*

volcanic lake
*lago<sup>M</sup> volcánico*

tectonic lake
*lago<sup>M</sup> tectónico*

oxbow lake
*lago<sup>M</sup> de brazo<sup>M</sup>
muerto*

oasis
*oasis<sup>M</sup>*

artificial lake
*embalse<sup>M</sup>*

# wave
*ola<sup>F</sup>*

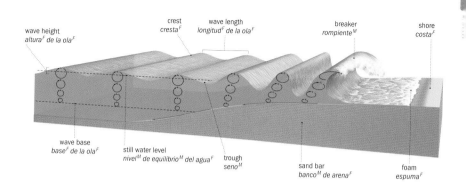

wave height
*altura<sup>F</sup> de la ola<sup>F</sup>*

crest
*cresta<sup>F</sup>*

wave length
*longitud<sup>F</sup> de la ola<sup>F</sup>*

breaker
*rompiente<sup>M</sup>*

shore
*costa<sup>F</sup>*

wave base
*base<sup>F</sup> de la ola<sup>F</sup>*

still water level
*nivel<sup>M</sup> de equilibrio<sup>M</sup> del agua<sup>F</sup>*

trough
*seno<sup>M</sup>*

sand bar
*banco<sup>M</sup> de arena<sup>F</sup>*

foam
*espuma<sup>F</sup>*

# ocean floor
*fondo<sup>M</sup> oceánico*

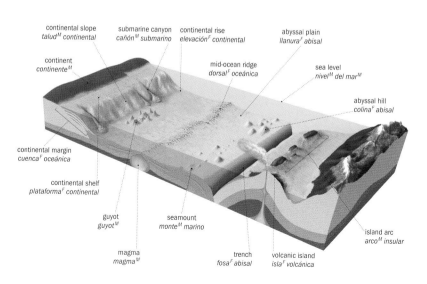

continental slope
*talud<sup>M</sup> continental*

submarine canyon
*cañón<sup>M</sup> submarino*

continental rise
*elevación<sup>F</sup> continental*

abyssal plain
*llanura<sup>F</sup> abisal*

continent
*continente<sup>M</sup>*

mid-ocean ridge
*dorsal<sup>F</sup> oceánica*

sea level
*nivel<sup>M</sup> del mar<sup>M</sup>*

abyssal hill
*colina<sup>F</sup> abisal*

continental margin
*cuenca<sup>F</sup> oceánica*

continental shelf
*plataforma<sup>F</sup> continental*

guyot
*guyot<sup>M</sup>*

seamount
*monte<sup>M</sup> marino*

trench
*fosa<sup>F</sup> abisal*

volcanic island
*isla<sup>F</sup> volcánica*

island arc
*arco<sup>M</sup> insular*

magma
*magma<sup>M</sup>*

# ocean trenches and ridges

*fosas^F y dorsales^F oceánicas*

EARTH

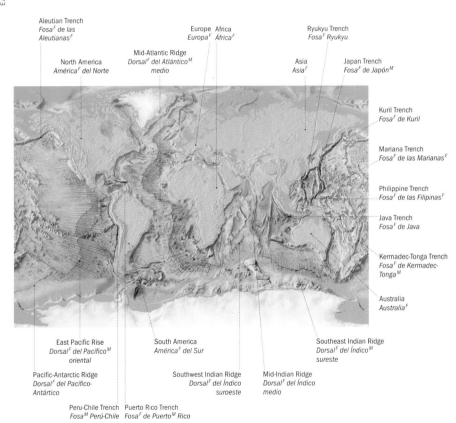

Aleutian Trench
*Fosa^F de las
Aleutianas^F*

North America
*América^F del Norte*

Mid-Atlantic Ridge
*Dorsal^F del Atlántico^M
medio*

Europe  Africa
*Europa^F  África^F*

Asia
*Asia^F*

Ryukyu Trench
*Fosa^F Ryukyu*

Japan Trench
*Fosa^F de Japón^M*

Kuril Trench
*Fosa^F de Kuril*

Mariana Trench
*Fosa^F de las Marianas^F*

Philippine Trench
*Fosa^F de las Filipinas^F*

Java Trench
*Fosa^F de Java*

Kermadec-Tonga Trench
*Fosa^F de Kermadec-
Tonga^M*

Australia
*Australia^F*

East Pacific Rise
*Dorsal^F del Pacífico^M
oriental*

South America
*América^F del Sur*

Southeast Indian Ridge
*Dorsal^F del Índico^M
sureste*

Pacific-Antarctic Ridge
*Dorsal^F del Pacífico-
Antártico*

Southwest Indian Ridge
*Dorsal^F del Índico
suroeste*

Mid-Indian Ridge
*Dorsal^F del Índico
medio*

Peru-Chile Trench
*Fosa^M Perú-Chile*

Puerto Rico Trench
*Fosa^F de Puerto^M Rico*

# common coastal features
*configuración<sup>F</sup> del litoral<sup>M</sup>*

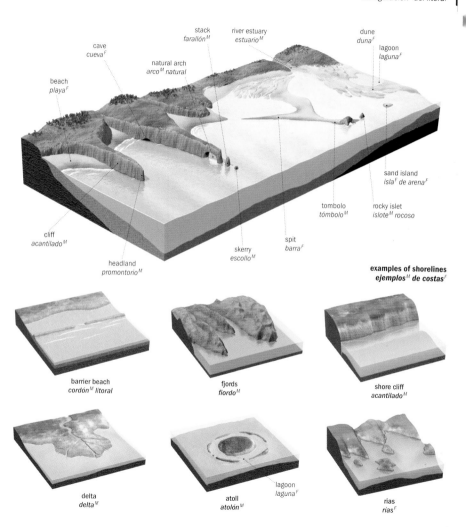

beach
*playa<sup>F</sup>*

cave
*cueva<sup>F</sup>*

natural arch
*arco<sup>M</sup> natural*

stack
*farallón<sup>M</sup>*

river estuary
*estuario<sup>M</sup>*

dune
*duna<sup>F</sup>*

lagoon
*laguna<sup>F</sup>*

sand island
*isla<sup>F</sup> de arena<sup>F</sup>*

rocky islet
*islote<sup>M</sup> rocoso*

tombolo
*tómbolo<sup>M</sup>*

spit
*barra<sup>F</sup>*

skerry
*escollo<sup>M</sup>*

headland
*promontorio<sup>M</sup>*

cliff
*acantilado<sup>M</sup>*

**examples of shorelines**
*ejemplos<sup>M</sup> de costas<sup>F</sup>*

barrier beach
*cordón<sup>M</sup> litoral*

fjords
*fiordo<sup>M</sup>*

shore cliff
*acantilado<sup>M</sup>*

delta
*delta<sup>M</sup>*

atoll
*atolón<sup>M</sup>*

lagoon
*laguna<sup>F</sup>*

rias
*rías<sup>F</sup>*

EARTH

# desert
*desierto*<sup>M</sup>

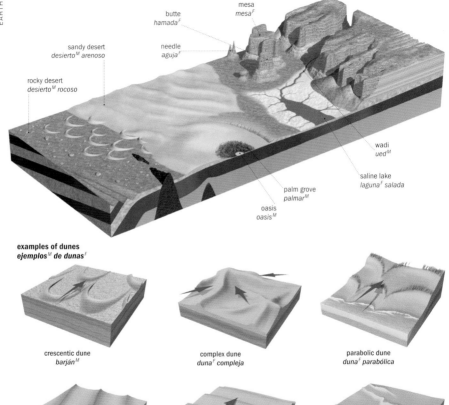

mesa
*mesa*<sup>F</sup>

butte
*hamada*<sup>F</sup>

sandy desert
*desierto*<sup>M</sup> *arenoso*

needle
*aguja*<sup>F</sup>

rocky desert
*desierto*<sup>M</sup> *rocoso*

wadi
*ued*<sup>M</sup>

saline lake
*laguna*<sup>F</sup> *salada*

palm grove
*palmar*<sup>M</sup>

oasis
*oasis*<sup>M</sup>

**examples of dunes**
**ejemplos**<sup>M</sup> **de dunas**<sup>F</sup>

crescentic dune
*barján*<sup>M</sup>

complex dune
*duna*<sup>F</sup> *compleja*

parabolic dune
*duna*<sup>F</sup> *parabólica*

longitudinal dunes
*dunas*<sup>F</sup> *longitudinales*

transverse dunes
*dunas*<sup>F</sup> *transversales*

chain of dunes
*cadena*<sup>F</sup> *de dunas*<sup>F</sup>

# profile of the Earth's atmosphere
*corte$^M$ de la atmósfera$^F$ terrestre*

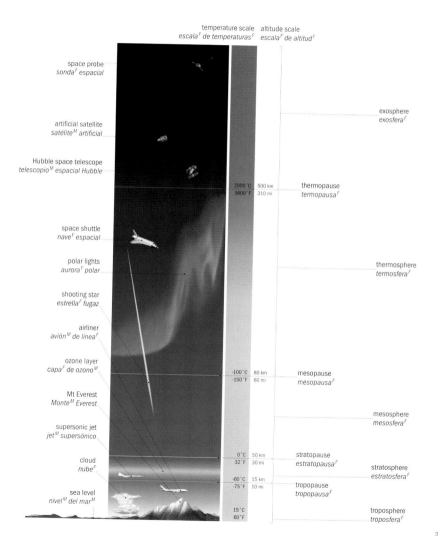

temperature scale
*escala$^F$ de temperaturas$^F$*

altitude scale
*escala$^F$ de altitud$^F$*

space probe
*sonda$^F$ espacial*

artificial satellite
*satélite$^M$ artificial*

exosphere
*exosfera$^F$*

Hubble space telescope
*telescopio$^M$ espacial Hubble*

| 2000°C | 500 km |
| 3600°F | 310 mi |

thermopause
*termopausa$^F$*

space shuttle
*nave$^F$ espacial*

polar lights
*aurora$^F$ polar*

thermosphere
*termosfera$^F$*

shooting star
*estrella$^F$ fugaz*

airliner
*avión$^M$ de línea$^F$*

ozone layer
*capa$^F$ de ozono$^M$*

| -100°C | 80 km |
| -150°F | 60 mi |

mesopause
*mesopausa$^F$*

Mt Everest
*Monte$^M$ Everest*

mesosphere
*mesosfera$^F$*

supersonic jet
*jet$^M$ supersónico*

cloud
*nube$^F$*

| 0°C | 50 km |
| 32°F | 30 mi |

stratopause
*estratopausa$^F$*

stratosphere
*estratosfera$^F$*

| -60°C | 15 km |
| -75°F | 10 mi |

tropopause
*tropopausa$^F$*

sea level
*nivel$^M$ del mar$^M$*

| 15°C |
| 60°F |

troposphere
*troposfera$^F$*

# seasons of the year
*estaciones<sup>F</sup> del año<sup>M</sup>*

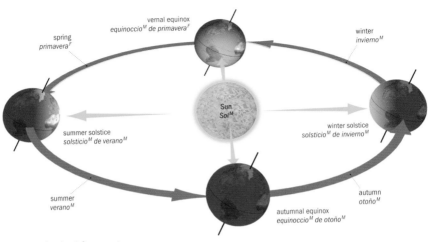

vernal equinox
*equinoccio<sup>M</sup> de primavera<sup>F</sup>*

spring
*primavera<sup>F</sup>*

winter
*invierno<sup>M</sup>*

Sun
*Sol<sup>M</sup>*

summer solstice
*solsticio<sup>M</sup> de verano<sup>M</sup>*

winter solstice
*solsticio<sup>M</sup> de invierno<sup>M</sup>*

summer
*verano<sup>M</sup>*

autumn
*otoño<sup>M</sup>*

autumnal equinox
*equinoccio<sup>M</sup> de otoño<sup>M</sup>*

# meteorological forecast
*previsión<sup>F</sup> meteorológica*

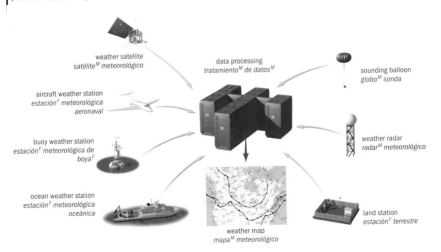

weather satellite
*satélite<sup>M</sup> meteorológico*

data processing
*tratamiento<sup>M</sup> de datos<sup>M</sup>*

sounding balloon
*globo<sup>M</sup> sonda*

aircraft weather station
*estación<sup>F</sup> meteorológica
aeronaval*

buoy weather station
*estación<sup>F</sup> meteorológica de
boya<sup>F</sup>*

weather radar
*radar<sup>M</sup> meteorológico*

ocean weather station
*estación<sup>F</sup> meteorológica
oceánica*

land station
*estación<sup>F</sup> terrestre*

weather map
*mapa<sup>M</sup> meteorológico*

## weather map
*mapa<sup>M</sup> meteorológico*

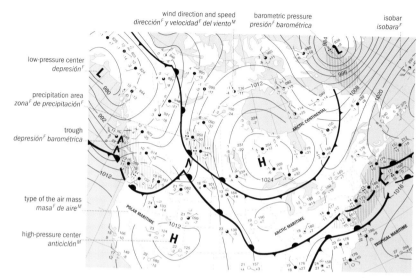

wind direction and speed
*dirección<sup>F</sup> y velocidad<sup>F</sup> del viento<sup>M</sup>*

barometric pressure
*presión<sup>F</sup> barométrica*

isobar
*isobara<sup>F</sup>*

low-pressure center
*depresión<sup>F</sup>*

precipitation area
*zona<sup>F</sup> de precipitación<sup>F</sup>*

trough
*depresión<sup>F</sup> barométrica*

type of the air mass
*masa<sup>F</sup> de aire<sup>M</sup>*

high-pressure center
*anticiclón<sup>M</sup>*

## station model
*modelo<sup>M</sup> de estación<sup>F</sup>*

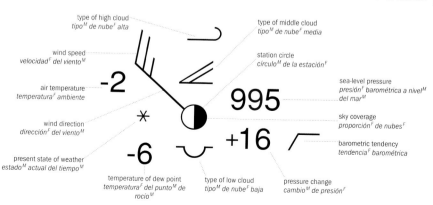

type of high cloud
*tipo<sup>M</sup> de nube<sup>F</sup> alta*

type of middle cloud
*tipo<sup>M</sup> de nube<sup>F</sup> media*

wind speed
*velocidad<sup>F</sup> del viento<sup>M</sup>*

station circle
*círculo<sup>M</sup> de la estación<sup>F</sup>*

air temperature
*temperatura<sup>F</sup> ambiente*

sea-level pressure
*presión<sup>F</sup> barométrica a nivel<sup>M</sup> del mar<sup>M</sup>*

wind direction
*dirección<sup>F</sup> del viento<sup>M</sup>*

sky coverage
*proporción<sup>F</sup> de nubes<sup>F</sup>*

present state of weather
*estado<sup>M</sup> actual del tiempo<sup>M</sup>*

barometric tendency
*tendencia<sup>F</sup> barométrica*

temperature of dew point
*temperatura<sup>F</sup> del punto<sup>M</sup> de rocío<sup>M</sup>*

type of low cloud
*tipo<sup>M</sup> de nube<sup>F</sup> baja*

pressure change
*cambio<sup>M</sup> de presión<sup>F</sup>*

# climates of the world

*climas<sup>M</sup> del mundo<sup>M</sup>*

*(world map)*

**tropical climates**
*climas<sup>M</sup> tropicales*

 tropical rain forest
*tropical<sup>M</sup> lluvioso*

 tropical wet-and-dry (savanna)
*tropical<sup>M</sup> húmedo y seco (sabana<sup>F</sup>)*

**dry climates**
*climas<sup>M</sup> áridos*

steppe
*estepario*

desert
*desértico*

**cold temperate climates**
*climas<sup>M</sup> templados fríos*

 humid continental—hot summer
*continental<sup>M</sup> húmedo - verano<sup>M</sup> tórrido*

 humid continental—warm summer
*continental<sup>M</sup> húmedo - verano<sup>M</sup> fresco*

 subarctic
*subártico<sup>M</sup>*

**warm temperate climates**
*climas<sup>M</sup> templados cálidos*

 humid subtropical
*subtropical húmedo*

 Mediterranean subtropical
*subtropical mediterráneo*

 marine
*marítimo*

**polar climates**
*climas<sup>M</sup> polares*

 polar tundra
*tundra<sup>F</sup>*

polar ice cap
*hielos<sup>M</sup> perpetuos*

**highland climates**
*climas<sup>M</sup> de alta montaña<sup>F</sup>*

 highland
*climas<sup>M</sup> de montaña<sup>F</sup>*

# precipitation
*precipitaciones*<sup>F</sup>

**winter precipitation**
***precipitaciones*<sup>F</sup>
*invernales***

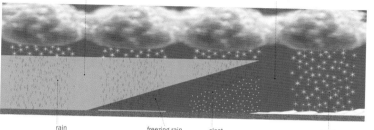

warm air
*aire*<sup>M</sup> *caliente*

cold air
*aire*<sup>M</sup> *frío*

rain
*lluvia*<sup>F</sup>

freezing rain
*lluvia*<sup>F</sup> *helada*

sleet
*aguanieve*<sup>M</sup>

snow
*nieve*<sup>M</sup>

stormy sky
*cielo*<sup>M</sup> *turbulento*

cloud
*nube*<sup>F</sup>

lightning
*rayo*<sup>M</sup>

rainbow
*arco*<sup>M</sup> *iris*

rain
*lluvia*<sup>F</sup>

dew
*rocío*<sup>M</sup>

mist
*neblina*<sup>F</sup>

fog
*niebla*<sup>F</sup>

rime
*escarcha*<sup>F</sup>

frost
*hielo*<sup>M</sup>

# clouds
*nubes* F

**high clouds**
***nubes* F *altas***

cirrostratus
*cirrostratos* M

cirrocumulus
*cirrocúmulos* M

cirrus
*cirros* M

**middle clouds**
***nubes* F *medias***

altostratus
*altostratos* M

altocumulus
*altocúmulos* M

**low clouds**
***nubes* F *bajas***

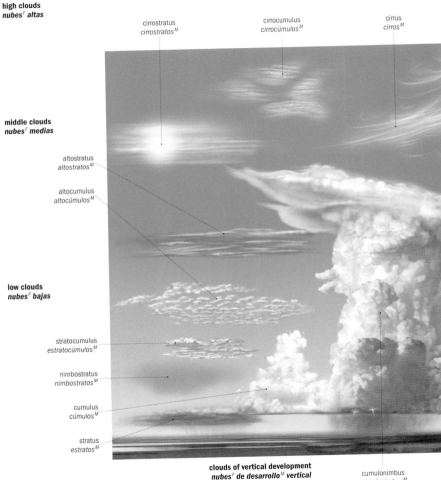

stratocumulus
*estratocúmulos* M

nimbostratus
*nimbostratos* M

cumulus
*cúmulos* M

stratus
*estratos* M

**clouds of vertical development**
***nubes* F *de desarrollo* M *vertical***

cumulonimbus
*cumulonimbos* M

## tornado and waterspout
*tornado<sup>M</sup> y tromba<sup>F</sup> marina*

waterspout
*tromba<sup>F</sup> marina*

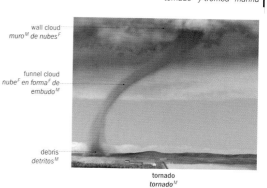

wall cloud
*muro<sup>M</sup> de nubes<sup>F</sup>*

funnel cloud
*nube<sup>F</sup> en forma<sup>F</sup> de embudo<sup>M</sup>*

debris
*detritos<sup>M</sup>*

tornado
*tornado<sup>M</sup>*

## tropical cyclone
*ciclón<sup>M</sup> tropical*

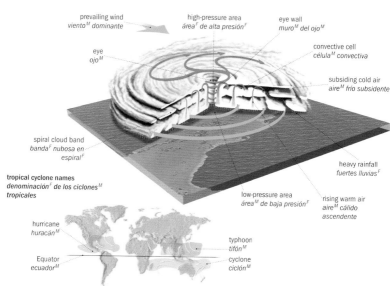

prevailing wind
*viento<sup>M</sup> dominante*

high-pressure area
*área<sup>F</sup> de alta presión<sup>F</sup>*

eye wall
*muro<sup>M</sup> del ojo<sup>M</sup>*

eye
*ojo<sup>M</sup>*

convective cell
*célula<sup>M</sup> convectiva*

subsiding cold air
*aire<sup>M</sup> frío subsidente*

spiral cloud band
*banda<sup>F</sup> nubosa en espiral<sup>F</sup>*

heavy rainfall
*fuertes lluvias<sup>F</sup>*

tropical cyclone names
*denominación<sup>F</sup> de los ciclones<sup>M</sup> tropicales*

low-pressure area
*área<sup>M</sup> de baja presión<sup>F</sup>*

rising warm air
*aire<sup>M</sup> cálido ascendente*

hurricane
*huracán<sup>M</sup>*

typhoon
*tifón<sup>M</sup>*

Equator
*ecuador<sup>M</sup>*

cyclone
*ciclón<sup>M</sup>*

# vegetation and biosphere
*vegetación<sup>F</sup> y biosfera<sup>F</sup>*

## vegetation regions
**distribución<sup>F</sup> de la vegetación<sup>F</sup>**

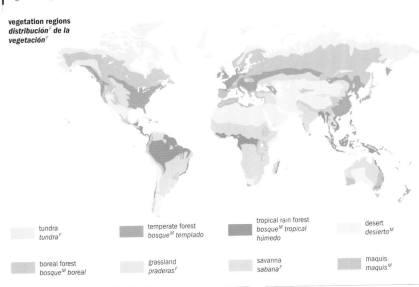

tundra
*tundra<sup>F</sup>*

temperate forest
*bosque<sup>M</sup> templado*

tropical rain forest
*bosque<sup>M</sup> tropical húmedo*

desert
*desierto<sup>M</sup>*

boreal forest
*bosque<sup>M</sup> boreal*

grassland
*praderas<sup>F</sup>*

savanna
*sabana<sup>F</sup>*

maquis
*maquis<sup>M</sup>*

## elevation zones and vegetation
**altitud<sup>F</sup> y vegetación<sup>F</sup>**

glacier
*glaciar<sup>M</sup>*

tundra
*tundra<sup>F</sup>*

coniferous forest
*bosque<sup>M</sup> de coníferas<sup>F</sup>*

mixed forest
*bosque<sup>M</sup> mixto*

deciduous forest
*bosque<sup>M</sup> de hoja<sup>F</sup> caduca*

tropical forest
*bosque<sup>M</sup> tropical*

## structure of the biosphere
**estructura<sup>F</sup> de la biosfera<sup>F</sup>**

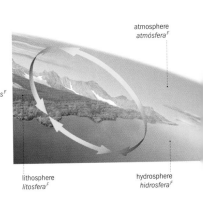

atmosphere
*atmósfera<sup>F</sup>*

lithosphere
*litosfera<sup>F</sup>*

hydrosphere
*hidrosfera<sup>F</sup>*

## food chain
### cadena<sup>F</sup> alimentaria

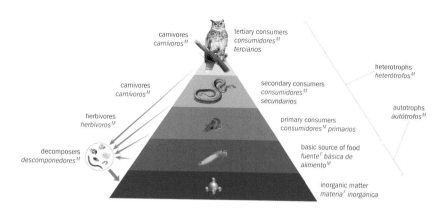

carnivores
carnívoros<sup>M</sup>

tertiary consumers
consumidores<sup>M</sup>
terciarios

heterotrophs
heterótrofos<sup>M</sup>

carnivores
carnívoros<sup>M</sup>

secondary consumers
consumidores<sup>M</sup>
secundarios

autotrophs
autótrofos<sup>M</sup>

herbivores
herbívoros<sup>M</sup>

primary consumers
consumidores<sup>M</sup> primarios

decomposers
descomponedores<sup>M</sup>

basic source of food
fuente<sup>F</sup> básica de
alimento<sup>M</sup>

inorganic matter
materia<sup>F</sup> inorgánica

## hydrologic cycle
### ciclo<sup>M</sup> hidrológico

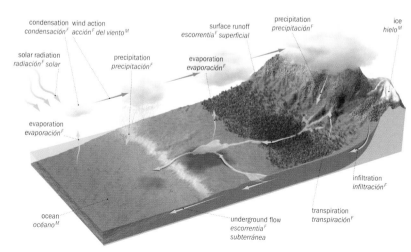

condensation
condensación<sup>F</sup>

wind action
acción<sup>F</sup> del viento<sup>M</sup>

surface runoff
escorrentía<sup>F</sup> superficial

precipitation
precipitación<sup>F</sup>

ice
hielo<sup>M</sup>

solar radiation
radiación<sup>F</sup> solar

precipitation
precipitación<sup>F</sup>

evaporation
evaporación<sup>F</sup>

evaporation
evaporación<sup>F</sup>

infiltration
infiltración<sup>F</sup>

ocean
océano<sup>M</sup>

underground flow
escorrentía<sup>F</sup>
subterránea

transpiration
transpiración<sup>F</sup>

# greenhouse effect

*efecto^M invernadero^M*

EARTH

**natural greenhouse effect**
*efecto^M invernadero^M natural*

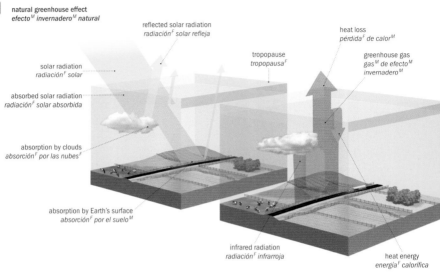

reflected solar radiation
*radiación^F solar refleja*

heat loss
*pérdida^F de calor^M*

tropopause
*tropopausa^F*

greenhouse gas
*gas^M de efecto^M invernadero^M*

solar radiation
*radiación^F solar*

absorbed solar radiation
*radiación^F solar absorbida*

absorption by clouds
*absorción^F por las nubes^F*

absorption by Earth's surface
*absorción^F por el suelo^M*

infrared radiation
*radiación^F infrarroja*

heat energy
*energía^F calorífica*

**enhanced greenhouse effect**
*aumento^M del efecto^M invernadero^M*

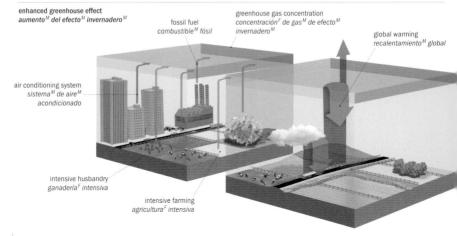

fossil fuel
*combustible^M fósil*

greenhouse gas concentration
*concentración^F de gas^M de efecto^M invernadero^M*

global warming
*recalentamiento^M global*

air conditioning system
*sistema^M de aire^M acondicionado*

intensive husbandry
*ganadería^F intensiva*

intensive farming
*agricultura^F intensiva*

EARTH

## air pollution
*contaminación^F del aire^M*

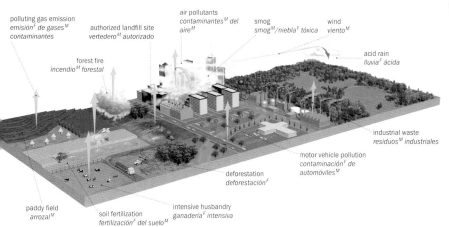

polluting gas emission
*emisión^F de gases^M
contaminantes*

authorized landfill site
*vertedero^M autorizado*

air pollutants
*contaminantes^M del
aire^M*

smog
*smog^M/niebla^F tóxica*

wind
*viento^M*

acid rain
*lluvia^F ácida*

forest fire
*incendio^M forestal*

industrial waste
*residuos^M industriales*

motor vehicle pollution
*contaminación^F de
automóviles^M*

deforestation
*deforestación^F*

paddy field
*arrozal^M*

soil fertilization
*fertilización^F del suelo^M*

intensive husbandry
*ganadería^F intensiva*

## land pollution
*contaminación^F del suelo^M*

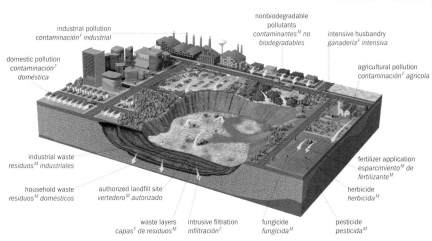

industrial pollution
*contaminación^F industrial*

nonbiodegradable
pollutants
*contaminantes^M no
biodegradables*

intensive husbandry
*ganadería^F intensiva*

domestic pollution
*contaminación^F
doméstica*

agricultural pollution
*contaminación^F agrícola*

industrial waste
*residuos^M industriales*

household waste
*residuos^M domésticos*

authorized landfill site
*vertedero^M autorizado*

waste layers
*capas^F de residuos^M*

intrusive filtration
*infiltración^F*

fungicide
*fungicida^M*

pesticide
*pesticida^M*

fertilizer application
*esparcimiento^M de
fertilizante^M*

herbicide
*herbicida^M*

EARTH

# water pollution
*contaminación<sup>F</sup> del agua<sup>F</sup>*

industrial waste
*residuos<sup>M</sup> industriales*

nuclear waste
*residuos<sup>M</sup> nucleares*

intensive farming
*agricultura<sup>F</sup> intensiva*

oil pollution
*contaminación<sup>F</sup> de
petróleo<sup>M</sup>*

waste water
*aguas<sup>F</sup> residuales*

household waste
*residuos<sup>M</sup> domésticos*

water table
*manto<sup>M</sup> freático*

septic tank
*fosa<sup>F</sup> séptica*

pesticide
*pesticida<sup>M</sup>*

oil spill
*vertido<sup>M</sup> de
hidrocarburos<sup>M</sup>*

animal dung
*excrementos<sup>M</sup> de
animales<sup>M</sup>*

# acid rain
*lluvia<sup>F</sup> ácida*

nitric acid emission
*emisión<sup>F</sup> de ácido<sup>M</sup>
nítrico*

nitrogen oxide emission
*emisión<sup>F</sup> de óxido<sup>M</sup> de
nitrógeno<sup>M</sup>*

atmosphere
*atmósfera<sup>F</sup>*

wind
*viento<sup>M</sup>*

cloudwater
*agua<sup>F</sup> de nubes<sup>F</sup>*

acid rain
*lluvia<sup>F</sup> ácida*

acid snow
*nieve<sup>F</sup> ácida*

sulfuric acid emission
*emisión<sup>F</sup> de ácido<sup>M</sup> sulfúrico*

sulfur dioxide emission
*emisión<sup>F</sup> de dióxido<sup>M</sup> de sulfuro<sup>M</sup>*

fossil fuel
*combustible<sup>M</sup> fósil*

watercourse
*corriente<sup>F</sup> de agua<sup>F</sup>*

leaching
*lixiviación<sup>F</sup>*

soil
*suelo<sup>M</sup>*

water table
*manto<sup>M</sup> freático*

lake acidification
*acidificación<sup>F</sup> de los
lagos<sup>M</sup>*

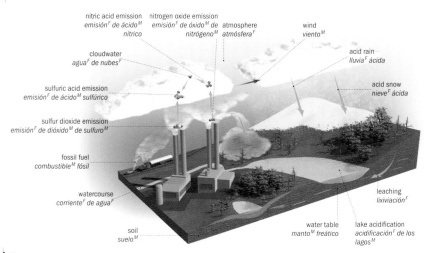

# selective sorting of waste

*separación<sup>F</sup> selectiva de residuos<sup>M</sup>*

EARTH

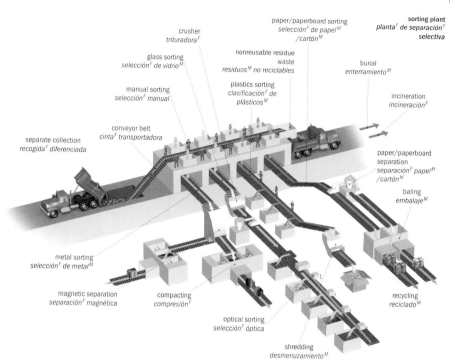

crusher
*trituradora<sup>F</sup>*

glass sorting
*selección<sup>F</sup> de vidrio<sup>M</sup>*

manual sorting
*selección<sup>F</sup> manual*

conveyor belt
*cinta<sup>F</sup> transportadora*

separate collection
*recogida<sup>F</sup> diferenciada*

paper/paperboard sorting
*selección<sup>F</sup> de papel<sup>M</sup>/cartón<sup>M</sup>*

sorting plant
*planta<sup>F</sup> de separación<sup>F</sup> selectiva*

nonreusable residue waste
*residuos<sup>M</sup> no reciclables*

plastics sorting
*clasificación<sup>F</sup> de plásticos<sup>M</sup>*

burial
*enterramiento<sup>M</sup>*

incineration
*incineración<sup>F</sup>*

paper/paperboard separation
*separación<sup>F</sup> papel<sup>M</sup>/cartón<sup>M</sup>*

baling
*embalaje<sup>M</sup>*

metal sorting
*selección<sup>F</sup> de metal<sup>M</sup>*

magnetic separation
*separación<sup>F</sup> magnética*

compacting
*compresión<sup>F</sup>*

optical sorting
*selección<sup>F</sup> óptica*

shredding
*desmenuzamiento<sup>M</sup>*

recycling
*reciclado<sup>M</sup>*

**recycling containers
*contenedores<sup>M</sup> de reciclaje<sup>M</sup>***

paper recycling container
*contenedor<sup>M</sup> de reciclado<sup>M</sup> de papel<sup>M</sup>*

glass recycling container
*contenedor<sup>M</sup> de reciclado<sup>M</sup> de vidrio<sup>M</sup>*

aluminum recycling container
*contenedor<sup>M</sup> de reciclado<sup>M</sup> de aluminio<sup>M</sup>*

paper collection unit
*contenedor<sup>M</sup> de recogida<sup>M</sup> de papel<sup>M</sup>*

glass collection unit
*contenedor<sup>M</sup> de recogida<sup>M</sup> de vidrio<sup>M</sup>*

recycling bin
*cubo<sup>M</sup> de basura<sup>F</sup> reciclable*

# plant cell
*célula<sup>F</sup> vegetal*

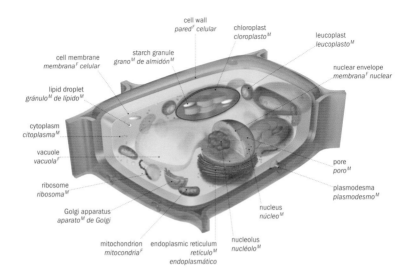

cell wall
*pared<sup>F</sup> celular*

chloroplast
*cloroplasto<sup>M</sup>*

leucoplast
*leucoplasto<sup>M</sup>*

cell membrane
*membrana<sup>F</sup> celular*

starch granule
*grano<sup>M</sup> de almidón<sup>M</sup>*

nuclear envelope
*membrana<sup>F</sup> nuclear*

lipid droplet
*gránulo<sup>M</sup> de lípido<sup>M</sup>*

cytoplasm
*citoplasma<sup>M</sup>*

vacuole
*vacuola<sup>F</sup>*

pore
*poro<sup>M</sup>*

ribosome
*ribosoma<sup>M</sup>*

plasmodesma
*plasmodesmo<sup>M</sup>*

Golgi apparatus
*aparato<sup>M</sup> de Golgi*

nucleus
*núcleo<sup>M</sup>*

mitochondrion
*mitocondria<sup>F</sup>*

endoplasmic reticulum
*retículo<sup>M</sup>
endoplasmático*

nucleolus
*nucléolo<sup>M</sup>*

# lichen
*liquen<sup>M</sup>*

**structure of a lichen**
*estructura<sup>F</sup> de un
liquen<sup>M</sup>*

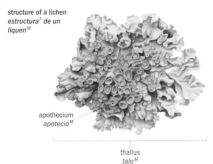

apothecium
*apotecio<sup>M</sup>*

thallus
*talo<sup>M</sup>*

**examples of lichens**
*ejemplos<sup>M</sup> de líquenes<sup>M</sup>*

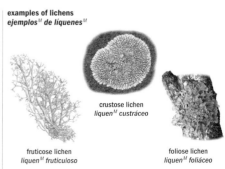

crustose lichen
*liquen<sup>M</sup> custráceo*

fruticose lichen
*liquen<sup>M</sup> fruticuloso*

foliose lichen
*liquen<sup>M</sup> foliáceo*

# moss
*musgo<sup>M</sup>*

## structure of a moss
*estructura<sup>F</sup> de un musgo<sup>M</sup>*

## examples of mosses
*ejemplos<sup>M</sup> de musgos<sup>M</sup>*

capsule
*cápsula<sup>F</sup>*

stalk
*pedúnculo<sup>M</sup>*

leaf
*hoja<sup>F</sup>*

stem
*tallo<sup>M</sup>*

rhizoid
*rizoide<sup>M</sup>*

prickly sphagnum
*esfagno<sup>M</sup>*

common hair cap moss
*politrico<sup>M</sup>*

# algae
*alga<sup>F</sup>*

## structure of an alga
*estructura<sup>F</sup> de un alga<sup>F</sup>*

## examples of algae
*ejemplos<sup>M</sup> de algas<sup>F</sup>*

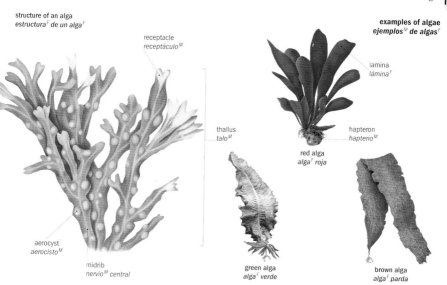

receptacle
*receptáculo<sup>M</sup>*

lamina
*lámina<sup>F</sup>*

thallus
*talo<sup>M</sup>*

hapteron
*hapterio<sup>M</sup>*

red alga
*alga<sup>F</sup> roja*

aerocyst
*aerocisto<sup>M</sup>*

midrib
*nervio<sup>M</sup> central*

green alga
*alga<sup>F</sup> verde*

brown alga
*alga<sup>F</sup> parda*

# mushroom

*hongo* [M]

**structure of a mushroom**
*anatomía* [F] *de un hongo* [M]

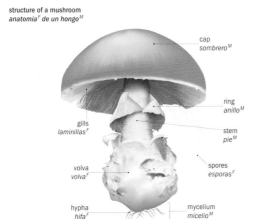

cap
*sombrero* [M]

ring
*anillo* [M]

gills
*laminillas* [F]

stem
*pie* [M]

volva
*volva* [F]

spores
*esporas* [F]

hypha
*hifa* [F]

mycelium
*micelio* [M]

**deadly poisonous
mushroom**
*hongo* [M] *mortal*

**poisonous
mushroom**
*hongo* [M] *venenoso*

destroying angel
*amanita* [F] *virosa*

fly agaric
*falsa oronja* [F]

# fern

*helecho* [M]

**structure of a fern**
*estructura* [F] *de un
helecho* [M]

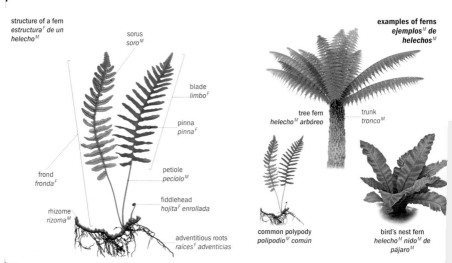

sorus
*soro* [M]

blade
*limbo* [F]

pinna
*pinna* [F]

frond
*fronda* [F]

petiole
*peciolo* [M]

fiddlehead
*hojita* [F] *enrollada*

rhizome
*rizoma* [M]

adventitious roots
*raíces* [F] *adventicias*

**examples of ferns**
*ejemplos* [M] *de
helechos* [M]

tree fern
*helecho* [M] *arbóreo*

trunk
*tronco* [M]

common polypody
*polipodio* [M] *común*

bird's nest fern
*helecho* [M] *nido* [M] *de
pájaro* [M]

# plant
*planta*<sup>F</sup>

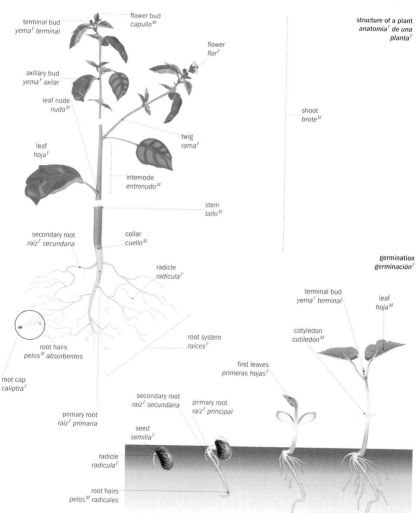

**structure of a plant**
*anatomía*<sup>F</sup> *de una planta*<sup>F</sup>

terminal bud
*yema*<sup>F</sup> *terminal*

flower bud
*capullo*<sup>M</sup>

flower
*flor*<sup>F</sup>

axillary bud
*yema*<sup>F</sup> *axilar*

leaf node
*nudo*<sup>M</sup>

shoot
*brote*<sup>M</sup>

leaf
*hoja*<sup>F</sup>

twig
*rama*<sup>F</sup>

internode
*entrenudo*<sup>M</sup>

stem
*tallo*<sup>M</sup>

secondary root
*raíz*<sup>F</sup> *secundaria*

collar
*cuello*<sup>M</sup>

radicle
*radícula*<sup>F</sup>

germination
*germinación*<sup>F</sup>

terminal bud
*yema*<sup>F</sup> *terminal*

leaf
*hoja*<sup>M</sup>

cotyledon
*cotiledón*<sup>M</sup>

root hairs
*pelos*<sup>M</sup> *absorbentes*

first leaves
*primeras hojas*<sup>F</sup>

root cap
*caliptra*<sup>F</sup>

root system
*raíces*<sup>F</sup>

primary root
*raíz*<sup>F</sup> *primaria*

secondary root
*raíz*<sup>F</sup> *secundaria*

primary root
*raíz*<sup>F</sup> *principal*

seed
*semilla*<sup>F</sup>

radicle
*radícula*<sup>F</sup>

root hairs
*pelos*<sup>M</sup> *radicales*

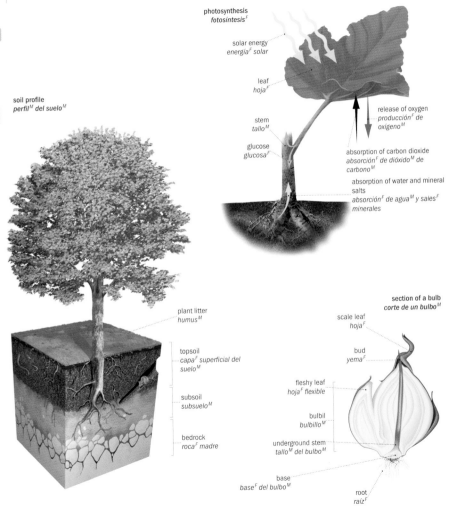

**photosynthesis**
*fotosíntesis*<sup>F</sup>

solar energy
*energía*<sup>F</sup> *solar*

leaf
*hoja*<sup>F</sup>

stem
*tallo*<sup>M</sup>

glucose
*glucosa*<sup>F</sup>

release of oxygen
*producción*<sup>F</sup> *de*
*oxígeno*<sup>M</sup>

absorption of carbon dioxide
*absorción*<sup>F</sup> *de dióxido*<sup>M</sup> *de*
*carbono*<sup>M</sup>

absorption of water and mineral
salts
*absorción*<sup>F</sup> *de agua*<sup>M</sup> *y sales*<sup>F</sup>
*minerales*

**soil profile**
*perfil*<sup>M</sup> *del suelo*<sup>M</sup>

plant litter
*humus*<sup>M</sup>

topsoil
*capa*<sup>F</sup> *superficial del*
*suelo*<sup>M</sup>

subsoil
*subsuelo*<sup>M</sup>

bedrock
*roca*<sup>F</sup> *madre*

**section of a bulb**
*corte de un bulbo*<sup>M</sup>

scale leaf
*hoja*<sup>F</sup>

bud
*yema*<sup>F</sup>

fleshy leaf
*hoja*<sup>F</sup> *flexible*

bulbil
*bulbillo*<sup>M</sup>

underground stem
*tallo*<sup>M</sup> *del bulbo*<sup>M</sup>

base
*base*<sup>F</sup> *del bulbo*<sup>M</sup>

root
*raíz*<sup>F</sup>

## simple leaves
*hojas*<sup>F</sup> *simples*

reniform
*reniforme*

cordate
*acorazonada*

orbiculate
*orbicular*

spatulate
*espatulada*

linear
*acicular*

hastate
*astada*

ovate
*aovada*

lanceolate
*lanceolada*

peltate
*peltada*

### structure of a leaf
*estructura*<sup>F</sup> *de una hoja*<sup>F</sup>

tip
*punta*<sup>F</sup>

vein
*nervadura*<sup>F</sup> *secundaria*

margin
*borde*<sup>M</sup>

blade
*hoja*<sup>F</sup>

midrib
*nervadura*<sup>F</sup> *principal*

petiole
*pecíolo*<sup>M</sup>

stipule
*estípula*<sup>F</sup>

sheath
*vaina*<sup>F</sup>

leaf axil
*axila*<sup>F</sup> *de la hoja*<sup>F</sup>

## compound leaves
*hojas*<sup>F</sup> *compuestas*

trifoliolate
*trifoliada*

palmate
*palmeada*

pinnatifid
*pinatifida*

abruptly pinnate
*paripinnada*

odd pinnate
*imparipinnada*

## leaf margins
*la hoja*<sup>F</sup> *según su borde*<sup>M</sup>

dentate
*dentada*

doubly dentate
*doble dentada*

crenate
*festoneada*

ciliate
*ciliada*

entire
*entera*

lobate
*lobulada*

# flower

flor<sup>F</sup>

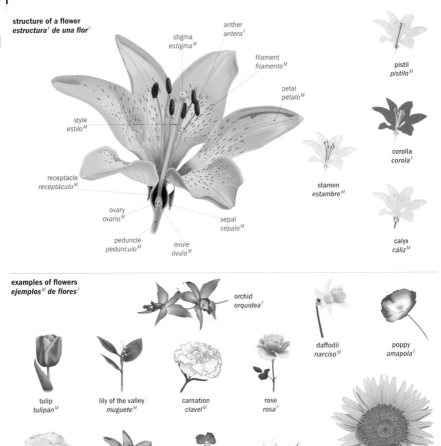

**structure of a flower**
*estructura<sup>F</sup> de una flor<sup>F</sup>*

stigma
estigma<sup>M</sup>

anther
antera<sup>F</sup>

filament
filamento<sup>M</sup>

petal
pétalo<sup>M</sup>

style
estilo<sup>M</sup>

receptacle
receptáculo<sup>M</sup>

ovary
ovario<sup>M</sup>

sepal
sépalo<sup>M</sup>

peduncle
pedúnculo<sup>M</sup>

ovule
óvulo<sup>M</sup>

pistil
pistilo<sup>M</sup>

corolla
corola<sup>F</sup>

stamen
estambre<sup>M</sup>

calyx
cáliz<sup>M</sup>

**examples of flowers**
*ejemplos<sup>M</sup> de flores<sup>F</sup>*

orchid
orquídea<sup>F</sup>

daffodil
narciso<sup>M</sup>

poppy
amapola<sup>F</sup>

tulip
tulipán<sup>M</sup>

lily of the valley
muguete<sup>M</sup>

carnation
clavel<sup>M</sup>

rose
rosa<sup>F</sup>

begonia
begonia<sup>F</sup>

lily
azucena<sup>F</sup>

violet
violeta<sup>F</sup>

crocus
croco<sup>M</sup>

sunflower
girasol<sup>M</sup>

## types of inflorescences
*variedades*<sup>F</sup> *de inflorescencias*<sup>F</sup>

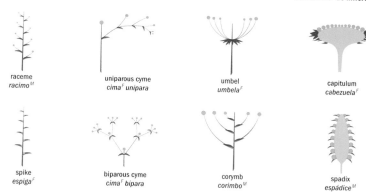

raceme
*racimo*<sup>M</sup>

uniparous cyme
*cima*<sup>F</sup> *unipara*

umbel
*umbela*<sup>F</sup>

capitulum
*cabezuela*<sup>F</sup>

spike
*espiga*<sup>F</sup>

biparous cyme
*cima*<sup>F</sup> *bipara*

corymb
*corimbo*<sup>M</sup>

spadix
*espádice*<sup>M</sup>

# fruit
*frutos*<sup>M</sup>

### fleshy fruit: stone fruit
*drupa*<sup>F</sup>

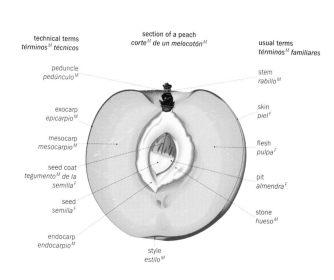

technical terms
*términos*<sup>M</sup> *técnicos*

section of a peach
*corte*<sup>M</sup> *de un melocotón*<sup>M</sup>

usual terms
*términos*<sup>M</sup> *familiares*

peduncle
*pedúnculo*<sup>M</sup>

exocarp
*epicarpio*<sup>M</sup>

mesocarp
*mesocarpio*<sup>M</sup>

seed coat
*tegumento*<sup>M</sup> *de la semilla*<sup>F</sup>

seed
*semilla*<sup>F</sup>

endocarp
*endocarpio*<sup>M</sup>

style
*estilo*<sup>M</sup>

stem
*rabillo*<sup>M</sup>

skin
*piel*<sup>F</sup>

flesh
*pulpa*<sup>F</sup>

pit
*almendra*<sup>F</sup>

stone
*hueso*<sup>M</sup>

VEGETABLE KINGDOM

**fleshy fruit: pome fruit**
*pomo<sup>M</sup> carnoso*

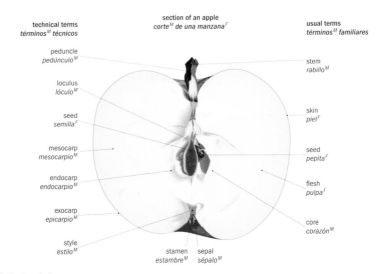

technical terms
*términos<sup>M</sup> técnicos*

section of an apple
*corte<sup>M</sup> de una manzana<sup>F</sup>*

usual terms
*términos<sup>M</sup> familiares*

peduncle
*pedúnculo<sup>M</sup>*

loculus
*lóculo<sup>M</sup>*

seed
*semilla<sup>F</sup>*

mesocarp
*mesocarpio<sup>M</sup>*

endocarp
*endocarpio<sup>M</sup>*

exocarp
*epicarpio<sup>M</sup>*

style
*estilo<sup>M</sup>*

stamen
*estambre<sup>M</sup>*

sepal
*sépalo<sup>M</sup>*

stem
*rabillo<sup>M</sup>*

skin
*piel<sup>F</sup>*

seed
*pepita<sup>F</sup>*

flesh
*pulpa<sup>F</sup>*

core
*corazón<sup>M</sup>*

**fleshy fruit: citrus fruit**
*fruto<sup>M</sup> carnoso: cítrico<sup>M</sup>*

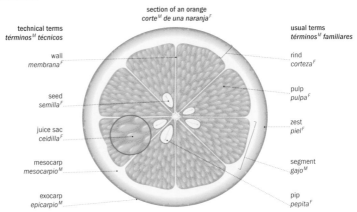

technical terms
*términos<sup>M</sup> técnicos*

section of an orange
*corte<sup>M</sup> de una naranja<sup>F</sup>*

usual terms
*términos<sup>M</sup> familiares*

wall
*membrana<sup>F</sup>*

seed
*semilla<sup>F</sup>*

juice sac
*ceidilla<sup>F</sup>*

mesocarp
*mesocarpio<sup>M</sup>*

exocarp
*epicarpio<sup>M</sup>*

rind
*corteza<sup>F</sup>*

pulp
*pulpa<sup>F</sup>*

zest
*piel<sup>F</sup>*

segment
*gajo<sup>M</sup>*

pip
*pepita<sup>F</sup>*

**fleshy fruit: berry fruit**
*fruto* F *carnoso: baya* F

VEGETABLE KINGDOM

technical terms
*términos* M *técnicos*

section of a grape
*corte* M *de una uva* F

usual terms
*términos* M *familiares*

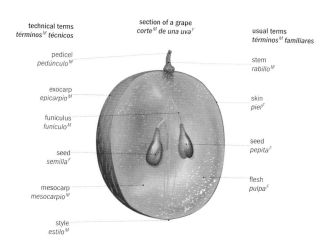

pedicel
*pedúnculo* M

exocarp
*epicarpio* M

funiculus
*funículo* M

seed
*semilla* F

mesocarp
*mesocarpio* M

style
*estilo* M

stem
*rabillo* M

skin
*piel* F

seed
*pepita* F

flesh
*pulpa* F

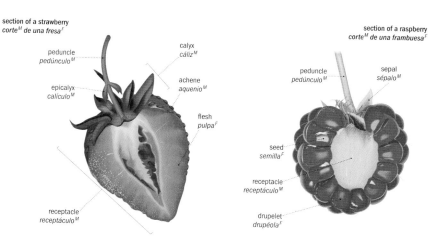

section of a strawberry
*corte* M *de una fresa* F

peduncle
*pedúnculo* M

epicalyx
*calículo* M

receptacle
*receptáculo* M

calyx
*cáliz* M

achene
*aquenio* M

flesh
*pulpa* F

section of a raspberry
*corte* M *de una frambuesa* F

peduncle
*pedúnculo* M

sepal
*sépalo* M

seed
*semilla* F

receptacle
*receptáculo* M

drupelet
*drupéola* F

VEGETABLE KINGDOM

## dry fruits
*frutos*<sup>M</sup> *secos*

husk
*cáscara*<sup>F</sup>

section of a follicle: star anise
*corte*<sup>M</sup> *de un folículo*<sup>M</sup> *: anís*<sup>M</sup>
*estrellado*

seed
*semilla*<sup>F</sup>

follicle
*folículo*<sup>M</sup>

suture
*sutura*<sup>F</sup>

section of a silique: mustard
*corte*<sup>M</sup> *de una silicua*<sup>F</sup> *: mostaza*<sup>F</sup>

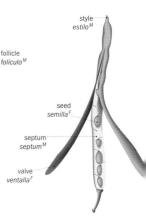

style
*estilo*<sup>M</sup>

seed
*semilla*<sup>F</sup>

septum
*septum*<sup>M</sup>

valve
*ventalla*<sup>F</sup>

section of a hazelnut
*corte*<sup>M</sup> *de una avellana*<sup>F</sup>

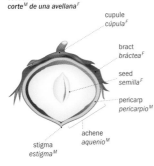

cupule
*cúpula*<sup>F</sup>

bract
*bráctea*<sup>F</sup>

seed
*semilla*<sup>F</sup>

pericarp
*pericarpio*<sup>M</sup>

achene
*aquenio*<sup>M</sup>

stigma
*estigma*<sup>M</sup>

section of a legume: pea
*corte*<sup>M</sup> *de una legumbre*<sup>F</sup> *:*
*guisante*<sup>M</sup>

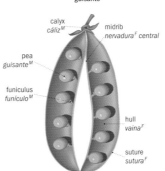

calyx
*cáliz*<sup>M</sup>

midrib
*nervadura*<sup>F</sup> *central*

pea
*guisante*<sup>M</sup>

funiculus
*funículo*<sup>M</sup>

hull
*vaina*<sup>F</sup>

suture
*sutura*<sup>F</sup>

style
*estilo*<sup>M</sup>

section of a capsule: poppy
*corte*<sup>M</sup> *de una cápsula*<sup>F</sup> *:*
*amapola*<sup>F</sup>

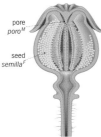

pore
*poro*<sup>M</sup>

seed
*semilla*<sup>F</sup>

section of a walnut
*corte*<sup>M</sup> *de una nuez*<sup>F</sup>

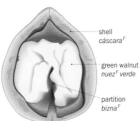

shell
*cáscara*<sup>F</sup>

green walnut
*nuez*<sup>F</sup> *verde*

partition
*bizna*<sup>F</sup>

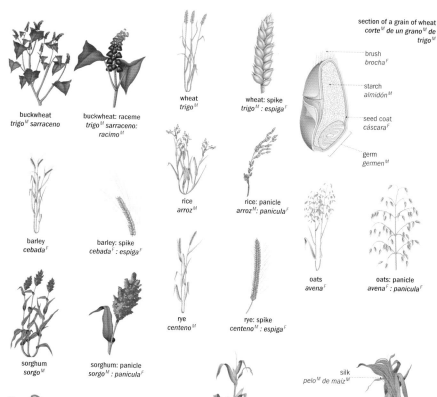

buckwheat
*trigo* <sup>M</sup> *sarraceno*

buckwheat: raceme
*trigo* <sup>M</sup> *sarraceno:*
*racimo* <sup>M</sup>

wheat
*trigo* <sup>M</sup>

wheat: spike
*trigo* <sup>M</sup> : *espiga* <sup>F</sup>

section of a grain of wheat
*corte* <sup>M</sup> *de un grano* <sup>M</sup> *de*
*trigo* <sup>M</sup>

brush
*brocha* <sup>F</sup>

starch
*almidón* <sup>M</sup>

seed coat
*cáscara* <sup>F</sup>

germ
*germen* <sup>M</sup>

barley
*cebada* <sup>F</sup>

barley: spike
*cebada* <sup>F</sup> : *espiga* <sup>F</sup>

rice
*arroz* <sup>M</sup>

rice: panicle
*arroz* <sup>M</sup>: *panícula* <sup>F</sup>

oats
*avena* <sup>F</sup>

oats: panicle
*avena* <sup>F</sup> : *panícula* <sup>F</sup>

rye
*centeno* <sup>M</sup>

rye: spike
*centeno* <sup>M</sup> : *espiga* <sup>F</sup>

sorghum
*sorgo* <sup>M</sup>

sorghum: panicle
*sorgo* <sup>M</sup> : *panícula* <sup>F</sup>

millet
*mijo* <sup>M</sup>

millet: spike
*mijo* <sup>M</sup> : *espiga* <sup>F</sup>

corn
*maíz* <sup>M</sup>

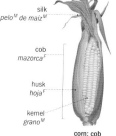

silk
*pelo* <sup>M</sup> *de maíz* <sup>M</sup>

cob
*mazorca* <sup>F</sup>

husk
*hoja* <sup>F</sup>

kernel
*grano* <sup>M</sup>

corn: cob
*maíz* <sup>M</sup> : *mazorca* <sup>F</sup>

# grape
*uva<sup>F</sup>*

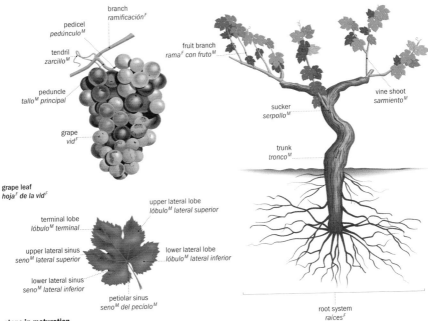

**bunch of grapes**
*racimo<sup>M</sup> de uvas<sup>F</sup>*

branch
*ramificación<sup>F</sup>*

pedicel
*pedúnculo<sup>M</sup>*

tendril
*zarcillo<sup>M</sup>*

peduncle
*tallo<sup>M</sup> principal*

grape
*vid<sup>F</sup>*

**vine stock**
*cepa<sup>F</sup> de vid<sup>F</sup>*

fruit branch
*rama<sup>F</sup> con fruto<sup>M</sup>*

vine shoot
*sarmiento<sup>M</sup>*

sucker
*serpollo<sup>M</sup>*

trunk
*tronco<sup>M</sup>*

**grape leaf**
*hoja<sup>F</sup> de la vid<sup>F</sup>*

upper lateral lobe
*lóbulo<sup>M</sup> lateral superior*

terminal lobe
*lóbulo<sup>M</sup> terminal*

upper lateral sinus
*seno<sup>M</sup> lateral superior*

lower lateral lobe
*lóbulo<sup>M</sup> lateral inferior*

lower lateral sinus
*seno<sup>M</sup> lateral inferior*

petiolar sinus
*seno<sup>M</sup> del pecíolo<sup>M</sup>*

root system
*raíces<sup>F</sup>*

**steps in maturation**
*etapas<sup>F</sup> de la maduración<sup>F</sup>*

flowering
*floración<sup>F</sup>*

fruition
*fructificación<sup>F</sup>*

ripening
*envero<sup>M</sup>*

ripeness
*madurez<sup>F</sup>*

structure of a tree
*anatomía*<sup>F</sup> *de un*
*árbol*<sup>M</sup>

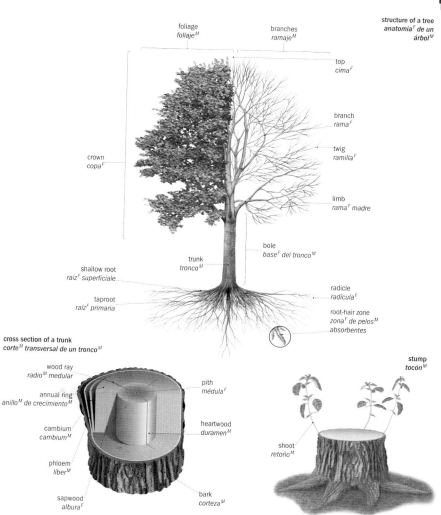

foliage
*follaje*<sup>M</sup>

branches
*ramaje*<sup>M</sup>

top
*cima*<sup>F</sup>

branch
*rama*<sup>F</sup>

twig
*ramilla*<sup>F</sup>

crown
*copa*<sup>F</sup>

limb
*rama*<sup>F</sup> *madre*

bole
*base*<sup>F</sup> *del tronco*<sup>M</sup>

trunk
*tronco*<sup>M</sup>

shallow root
*raíz*<sup>F</sup> *superficial*

radicle
*radícula*<sup>F</sup>

taproot
*raíz*<sup>F</sup> *primaria*

root-hair zone
*zona*<sup>F</sup> *de pelos*<sup>M</sup>
*absorbentes*

cross section of a trunk
*corte*<sup>M</sup> *transversal de un tronco*<sup>M</sup>

wood ray
*radio*<sup>M</sup> *medular*

pith
*médula*<sup>F</sup>

annual ring
*anillo*<sup>M</sup> *de crecimiento*<sup>M</sup>

cambium
*cambium*<sup>M</sup>

heartwood
*duramen*<sup>M</sup>

phloem
*líber*<sup>M</sup>

sapwood
*albura*<sup>F</sup>

bark
*corteza*<sup>M</sup>

stump
*tocón*<sup>M</sup>

shoot
*retoño*<sup>M</sup>

63

**examples of broadleaved trees**
*ejemplos*<sup>M</sup> *de latifolios*<sup>M</sup>

oak
*roble*<sup>M</sup>

birch
*abedul*<sup>M</sup>

weeping willow
*sauce*<sup>M</sup> *llorón*

poplar
*álamo*<sup>M</sup>

palm tree
*palmera*<sup>F</sup>

maple
*arce*<sup>M</sup>

beech
*haya*<sup>F</sup>

walnut
*nogal*<sup>M</sup>

# conifer
*conífera*<sup>F</sup>

branch
*rama*<sup>F</sup>

male cone
*cono*<sup>M</sup> *masculino*

female cone
*cono*<sup>M</sup> *femenino*

pinecone
*piña*<sup>F</sup>

pine seed
*piñón*<sup>M</sup>

**examples of leaves**
*ejemplos*<sup>M</sup> *de hojas*<sup>F</sup>

fir needles
*agujas*<sup>F</sup> *del abeto*<sup>M</sup>

pine needles
*agujas*<sup>F</sup> *del pino*<sup>M</sup>

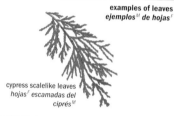

cypress scalelike leaves
*hojas*<sup>F</sup> *escamadas del*
*ciprés*<sup>M</sup>

**examples of conifers**
*ejemplos*<sup>M</sup> *de coníferas*<sup>F</sup>

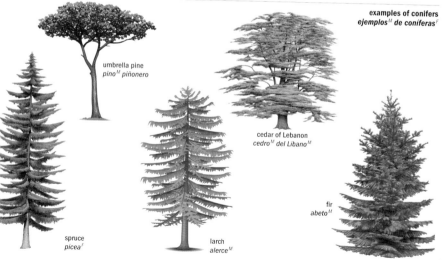

umbrella pine
*pino*<sup>M</sup> *piñonero*

cedar of Lebanon
*cedro*<sup>M</sup> *del Líbano*<sup>M</sup>

spruce
*picea*<sup>F</sup>

larch
*alerce*<sup>M</sup>

fir
*abeto*<sup>M</sup>

# animal cell
*célula^F animal*

ANIMAL KINGDOM

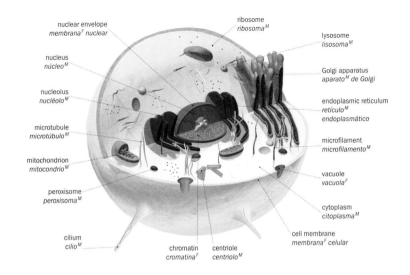

nuclear envelope
*membrana^F nuclear*

ribosome
*ribosoma^M*

lysosome
*lisosoma^M*

nucleus
*núcleo^M*

Golgi apparatus
*aparato^M de Golgi*

nucleolus
*nucléolo^M*

endoplasmic reticulum
*retículo^M endoplasmático*

microtubule
*microtúbulo^M*

microfilament
*microfilamento^M*

mitochondrion
*mitocondrio^M*

vacuole
*vacuola^F*

peroxisome
*peroxisoma^M*

cytoplasm
*citoplasma^M*

cilium
*cilio^M*

cell membrane
*membrana^F celular*

chromatin
*cromatina^F*

centriole
*centriolo^M*

# unicellulars
*unicelulares^M*

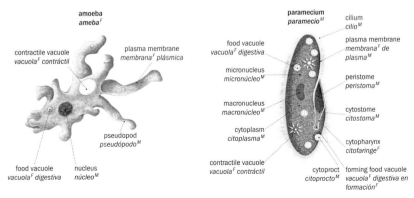

amoeba
*ameba^F*

paramecium
*paramecio^M*

cilium
*cilio^M*

contractile vacuole
*vacuola^F contráctil*

plasma membrane
*membrana^F plásmica*

food vacuole
*vacuola^F digestiva*

plasma membrane
*membrana^F de plasma^M*

micronucleus
*micronúcleo^M*

peristome
*peristoma^M*

macronucleus
*macronúcleo^M*

cytostome
*citostoma^M*

cytoplasm
*citoplasma^M*

cytopharynx
*citofaringe^F*

pseudopod
*pseudópodo^M*

food vacuole
*vacuola^F digestiva*

nucleus
*núcleo^M*

contractile vacuole
*vacuola^F contráctil*

cytoproct
*citoprocto^M*

forming food vacuole
*vacuola^F digestiva en formación^F*

# butterfly
*mariposa*[F]

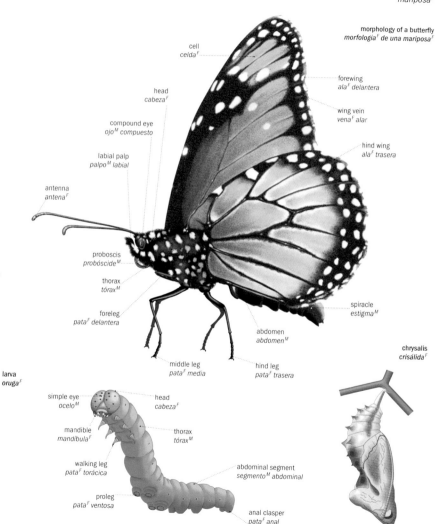

morphology of a butterfly
*morfología*[F] *de una mariposa*[F]

cell
*celda*[F]

forewing
*ala*[F] *delantera*

head
*cabeza*[F]

wing vein
*vena*[F] *alar*

compound eye
*ojo*[M] *compuesto*

hind wing
*ala*[F] *trasera*

labial palp
*palpo*[M] *labial*

antenna
*antena*[F]

proboscis
*proboscide*[M]

thorax
*tórax*[M]

spiracle
*estigma*[M]

foreleg
*pata*[F] *delantera*

abdomen
*abdomen*[M]

middle leg
*pata*[F] *media*

hind leg
*pata*[F] *trasera*

chrysalis
*crisálida*[F]

larva
*oruga*[F]

simple eye
*ocelo*[M]

head
*cabeza*[F]

mandible
*mandíbula*[F]

thorax
*tórax*[M]

walking leg
*pata*[F] *torácica*

abdominal segment
*segmento*[M] *abdominal*

proleg
*pata*[F] *ventosa*

anal clasper
*pata*[F] *anal*

67

# honeybee
*abeja*<sup>F</sup>

**morphology of a honeybee: worker**
*morfología*<sup>F</sup> *de una abeja*<sup>F</sup>
*trabajadora*<sup>F</sup>

wing
*ala*<sup>F</sup>

thorax
*tórax*<sup>M</sup>

abdomen
*abdomen*<sup>M</sup>

compound eye
*ojo*<sup>M</sup> *compuesto*

pollen basket
*cestillo*<sup>M</sup>

mouthparts
*apéndices*<sup>M</sup> *bucales*

sting
*aguijón*<sup>M</sup>

antenna
*antena*<sup>F</sup>

hind leg
*pata*<sup>F</sup> *trasera*

middle leg
*pata*<sup>F</sup> *media*

foreleg
*pata*<sup>F</sup> *delantera*

**castes**
*castas*<sup>F</sup>

worker
*obrera*<sup>F</sup>

queen
*reina*<sup>F</sup>

drone
*zángano*<sup>M</sup>

# examples of insects
*ejemplos<sup>M</sup> de insectos<sup>M</sup>*

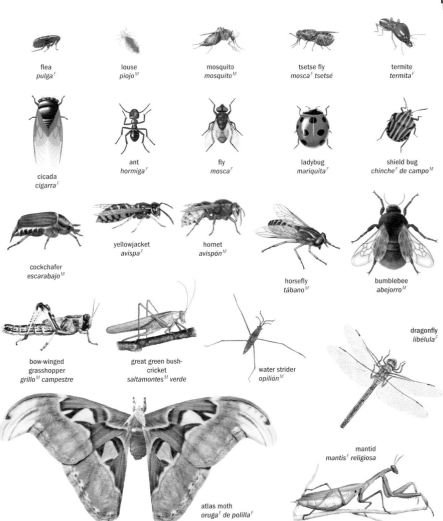

flea
*pulga<sup>F</sup>*

louse
*piojo<sup>M</sup>*

mosquito
*mosquito<sup>M</sup>*

tsetse fly
*mosca<sup>F</sup> tsetsé*

termite
*termita<sup>F</sup>*

cicada
*cigarra<sup>F</sup>*

ant
*hormiga<sup>F</sup>*

fly
*mosca<sup>F</sup>*

ladybug
*mariquita<sup>F</sup>*

shield bug
*chinche<sup>F</sup> de campo<sup>M</sup>*

cockchafer
*escarabajo<sup>M</sup>*

yellowjacket
*avispa<sup>F</sup>*

hornet
*avispón<sup>M</sup>*

horsefly
*tábano<sup>M</sup>*

bumblebee
*abejorro<sup>M</sup>*

bow-winged
grasshopper
*grillo<sup>M</sup> campestre*

great green bush-
cricket
*saltamontes<sup>M</sup> verde*

water strider
*opilión<sup>M</sup>*

dragonfly
*libélula<sup>F</sup>*

mantid
*mantis<sup>F</sup> religiosa*

atlas moth
*oruga<sup>F</sup> de polilla<sup>F</sup>*

# spider
*araña^F*

**spider web**
*tela^F de araña^F*

**morphology of a spider**
*morfología^F de una araña^F*

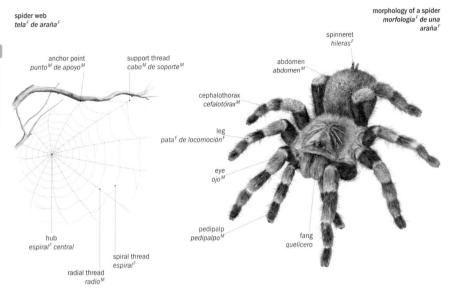

anchor point
*punto^M de apoyo^M*

support thread
*cabo^M de soporte^M*

spinneret
*hileras^F*

abdomen
*abdomen^M*

cephalothorax
*cefalotórax^M*

leg
*pata^F de locomoción^F*

eye
*ojo^M*

pedipalp
*pedipalpo^M*

fang
*quelícero^M*

hub
*espiral^F central*

spiral thread
*espiral^F*

radial thread
*radio^M*

# examples of arachnids
*ejemplos^M de arácnidos^M*

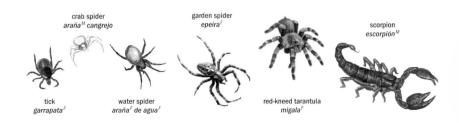

crab spider
*araña^M cangrejo*

garden spider
*epeira^F*

scorpion
*escorpión^M*

tick
*garrapata^F*

water spider
*araña^F de agua^F*

red-kneed tarantula
*migala^F*

# lobster
*bogavante*<sup>M</sup>

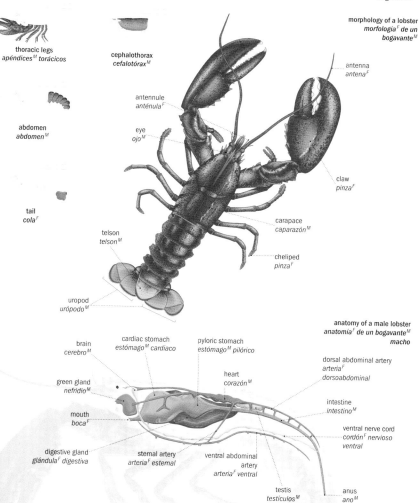

thoracic legs
*apéndices*<sup>M</sup> *torácicos*

cephalothorax
*cefalotórax*<sup>M</sup>

morphology of a lobster
*morfología*<sup>F</sup> *de un*
*bogavante*<sup>M</sup>

antenna
*antena*<sup>F</sup>

antennule
*anténula*<sup>F</sup>

eye
*ojo*<sup>M</sup>

abdomen
*abdomen*<sup>M</sup>

claw
*pinza*<sup>F</sup>

carapace
*caparazón*<sup>M</sup>

tail
*cola*<sup>F</sup>

cheliped
*pinza*<sup>F</sup>

telson
*telson*<sup>M</sup>

uropod
*urópodo*<sup>M</sup>

anatomy of a male lobster
*anatomía*<sup>F</sup> *de un bogavante*<sup>M</sup>
*macho*

brain
*cerebro*<sup>M</sup>

cardiac stomach
*estómago*<sup>M</sup> *cardiaco*

pyloric stomach
*estómago*<sup>M</sup> *pilórico*

heart
*corazón*<sup>M</sup>

dorsal abdominal artery
*arteria*<sup>F</sup>
*dorsoabdominal*

green gland
*nefridio*<sup>M</sup>

intestine
*intestino*<sup>M</sup>

mouth
*boca*<sup>F</sup>

ventral nerve cord
*cordón*<sup>F</sup> *nervioso*
*ventral*

digestive gland
*glándula*<sup>F</sup> *digestiva*

sternal artery
*arteria*<sup>F</sup> *esternal*

ventral abdominal
artery
*arteria*<sup>F</sup> *ventral*

testis
*testículos*<sup>M</sup>

anus
*ano*<sup>M</sup>

# snail

*caracol*<sup>M</sup>

morphology of a snail
*morfología*<sup>F</sup> *de un caracol*<sup>M</sup>

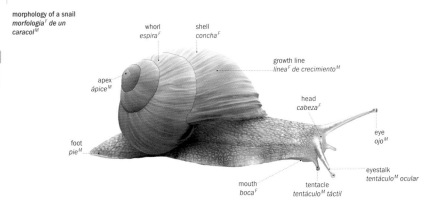

whorl
*espira*<sup>F</sup>

shell
*concha*<sup>F</sup>

growth line
*línea*<sup>F</sup> *de crecimiento*<sup>M</sup>

apex
*ápice*<sup>M</sup>

head
*cabeza*<sup>F</sup>

eye
*ojo*<sup>M</sup>

foot
*pie*<sup>M</sup>

eyestalk
*tentáculo*<sup>M</sup> ocular

mouth
*boca*<sup>F</sup>

tentacle
*tentáculo*<sup>M</sup> táctil

# octopus

*pulpo*<sup>M</sup>

morphology of an octopus
*morfología*<sup>F</sup> *de un pulpo*<sup>M</sup>

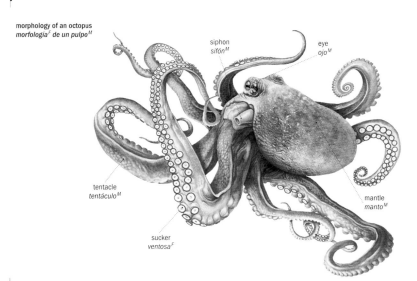

siphon
*sifón*<sup>M</sup>

eye
*ojo*<sup>M</sup>

tentacle
*tentáculo*<sup>M</sup>

mantle
*manto*<sup>M</sup>

sucker
*ventosa*<sup>F</sup>

# univalve shell
*concha<sup>F</sup> univalva*

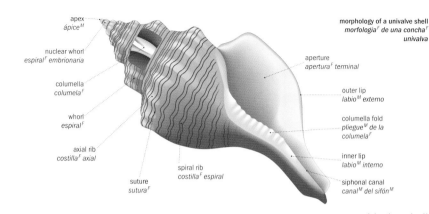

morphology of a univalve shell
*morfología<sup>F</sup> de una concha<sup>F</sup>
univalva*

apex
*ápice<sup>M</sup>*

nuclear whorl
*espiral<sup>F</sup> embrionaria*

columella
*columela<sup>F</sup>*

whorl
*espiral<sup>F</sup>*

axial rib
*costilla<sup>F</sup> axial*

suture
*sutura<sup>F</sup>*

spiral rib
*costilla<sup>F</sup> espiral*

aperture
*apertura<sup>F</sup> terminal*

outer lip
*labio<sup>M</sup> externo*

columella fold
*pliegue<sup>M</sup> de la
columela<sup>F</sup>*

inner lip
*labio<sup>M</sup> interno*

siphonal canal
*canal<sup>M</sup> del sifón<sup>M</sup>*

# bivalve shell
*concha<sup>F</sup> bivalva*

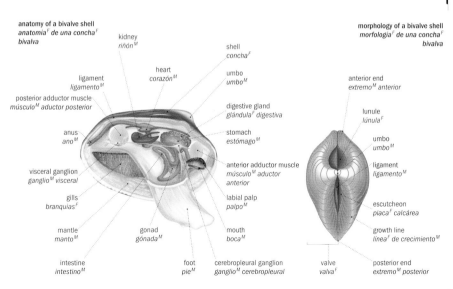

anatomy of a bivalve shell
*anatomía<sup>F</sup> de una concha<sup>F</sup>
bivalva*

kidney
*riñón<sup>M</sup>*

heart
*corazón<sup>M</sup>*

ligament
*ligamento<sup>M</sup>*

posterior adductor muscle
*músculo<sup>M</sup> aductor posterior*

anus
*ano<sup>M</sup>*

visceral ganglion
*ganglio<sup>M</sup> visceral*

gills
*branquias<sup>F</sup>*

mantle
*manto<sup>M</sup>*

intestine
*intestino<sup>M</sup>*

gonad
*gónada<sup>M</sup>*

foot
*pie<sup>M</sup>*

cerebropleural ganglion
*ganglio<sup>M</sup> cerebropleural*

shell
*concha<sup>F</sup>*

umbo
*umbo<sup>M</sup>*

digestive gland
*glándula<sup>F</sup> digestiva*

stomach
*estómago<sup>M</sup>*

anterior adductor muscle
*músculo<sup>M</sup> aductor
anterior*

labial palp
*palpo<sup>M</sup>*

mouth
*boca<sup>M</sup>*

morphology of a bivalve shell
*morfología<sup>F</sup> de una concha<sup>F</sup>
bivalva*

anterior end
*extremo<sup>M</sup> anterior*

lunule
*lúnula<sup>F</sup>*

umbo
*umbo<sup>M</sup>*

ligament
*ligamento<sup>M</sup>*

escutcheon
*piaca<sup>F</sup> calcárea*

growth line
*línea<sup>F</sup> de crecimiento<sup>M</sup>*

valve
*valva<sup>F</sup>*

posterior end
*extremo<sup>M</sup> posterior*

# cartilaginous fish
*pez^M cartilaginoso*

**morphology of a female shark**
*morfología^F de un tiburón^M hembra*

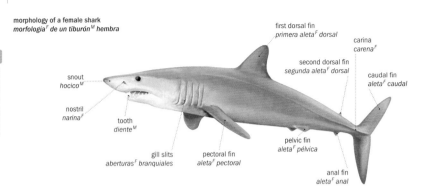

snout
*hocico^M*

nostril
*narina^F*

tooth
*diente^M*

gill slits
*aberturas^F branquiales*

pectoral fin
*aleta^F pectoral*

first dorsal fin
*primera aleta^F dorsal*

second dorsal fin
*segunda aleta^F dorsal*

carina
*carena^F*

caudal fin
*aleta^F caudal*

pelvic fin
*aleta^F pélvica*

anal fin
*aleta^F anal*

# bony fish
*pez^M óseo*

**morphology of a perch**
*morfología^F de una perca^F*

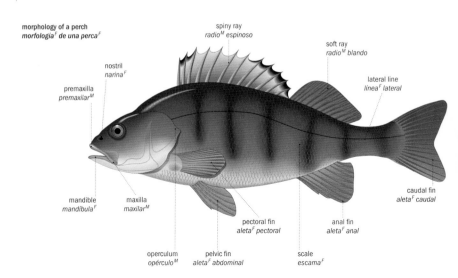

spiny ray
*radio^M espinoso*

soft ray
*radio^M blando*

lateral line
*línea^F lateral*

nostril
*narina^F*

premaxilla
*premaxilar^M*

mandible
*mandíbula^F*

maxilla
*maxilar^M*

operculum
*opérculo^M*

pelvic fin
*aleta^F abdominal*

pectoral fin
*aleta^F pectoral*

scale
*escama^F*

anal fin
*aleta^F anal*

caudal fin
*aleta^F caudal*

# frog
*rana[F]*

## morphology of a frog
*morfología[F] de una rana[F]*

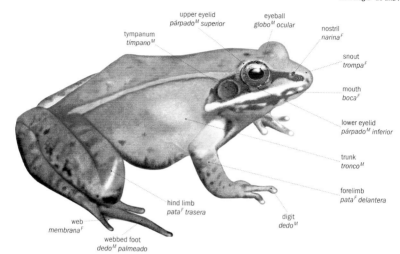

upper eyelid
*párpado[M] superior*

eyeball
*globo[M] ocular*

nostril
*narina[F]*

tympanum
*tímpano[M]*

snout
*trompa[F]*

mouth
*boca[F]*

lower eyelid
*párpado[M] inferior*

trunk
*tronco[M]*

forelimb
*pata[F] delantera*

hind limb
*pata[F] trasera*

digit
*dedo[M]*

web
*membrana[F]*

webbed foot
*dedo[M] palmeado*

## examples of amphibians
*ejemplos[M] de anfibios[M]*

salamander
*salamandra[F]*

wood frog
*rana[F] de bosque[M]*

newt
*tritón[M]*

common frog
*rana[F] bermeja*

common toad
*sapo[M] común*

Northern leopard frog
*rana[F] leopardo*

tree frog
*rana[F] arborícola*

adhesive disk
*ventosa[F]*

# snake
*serpiente*<sup>F</sup>

**morphology of a venomous snake: head**
*morfología*<sup>F</sup> *de una serpiente*<sup>F</sup> *venenosa:*
*cabeza*<sup>F</sup>

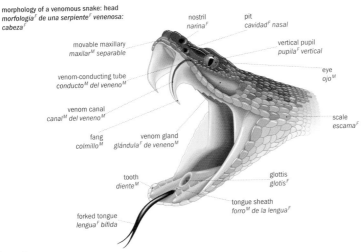

movable maxillary
*maxilar*<sup>M</sup> *separable*

venom-conducting tube
*conducto*<sup>M</sup> *del veneno*<sup>M</sup>

venom canal
*canal*<sup>M</sup> *del veneno*<sup>M</sup>

fang
*colmillo*<sup>M</sup>

venom gland
*glándula*<sup>F</sup> *de veneno*<sup>M</sup>

tooth
*diente*<sup>M</sup>

forked tongue
*lengua*<sup>F</sup> *bífida*

nostril
*narina*<sup>F</sup>

pit
*cavidad*<sup>F</sup> *nasal*

vertical pupil
*pupila*<sup>F</sup> *vertical*

eye
*ojo*<sup>M</sup>

scale
*escama*<sup>F</sup>

glottis
*glotis*<sup>F</sup>

tongue sheath
*forro*<sup>M</sup> *de la lengua*<sup>F</sup>

# turtle
*tortuga*<sup>F</sup>

**morphology of a turtle**
*morfología*<sup>F</sup> *de una tortuga*<sup>F</sup>

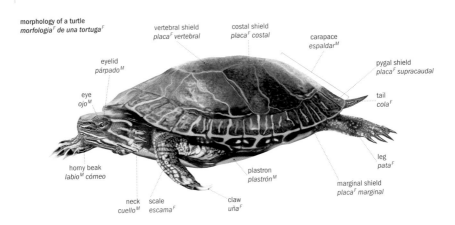

vertebral shield
*placa*<sup>F</sup> *vertebral*

costal shield
*placa*<sup>F</sup> *costal*

carapace
*espaldar*<sup>M</sup>

eyelid
*párpado*<sup>M</sup>

pygal shield
*placa*<sup>F</sup> *supracaudal*

eye
*ojo*<sup>M</sup>

tail
*cola*<sup>F</sup>

horny beak
*labio*<sup>M</sup> *córneo*

leg
*pata*<sup>F</sup>

neck
*cuello*<sup>M</sup>

scale
*escama*<sup>F</sup>

claw
*uña*<sup>F</sup>

plastron
*plastrón*<sup>M</sup>

marginal shield
*placa*<sup>F</sup> *marginal*

# examples of reptiles
*ejemplos<sup>M</sup> de reptiles<sup>M</sup>*

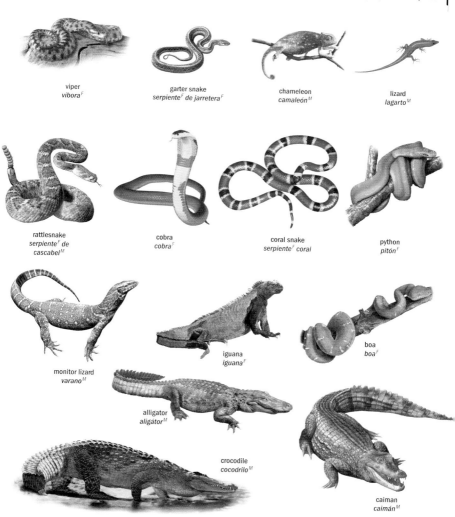

viper
*víbora<sup>F</sup>*

garter snake
*serpiente<sup>F</sup> de jarretera<sup>F</sup>*

chameleon
*camaleón<sup>M</sup>*

lizard
*lagarto<sup>M</sup>*

rattlesnake
*serpiente<sup>F</sup> de
cascabel<sup>M</sup>*

cobra
*cobra<sup>F</sup>*

coral snake
*serpiente<sup>F</sup> coral*

python
*pitón<sup>F</sup>*

monitor lizard
*varano<sup>M</sup>*

iguana
*iguana<sup>F</sup>*

boa
*boa<sup>F</sup>*

alligator
*aligátor<sup>M</sup>*

crocodile
*cocodrilo<sup>M</sup>*

caiman
*caimán<sup>M</sup>*

# bird
*ave*<sup>F</sup>

## morphology of a bird
*morfología*<sup>F</sup> *de un pájaro*<sup>M</sup>

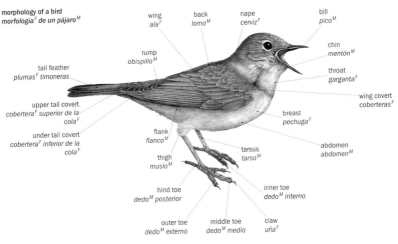

wing
*ala*<sup>F</sup>

back
*lomo*<sup>M</sup>

nape
*cerviz*<sup>F</sup>

bill
*pico*<sup>M</sup>

chin
*mentón*<sup>M</sup>

rump
*obispillo*<sup>M</sup>

throat
*garganta*<sup>F</sup>

tail feather
*plumas*<sup>F</sup> *timoneras*

wing covert
*coberteras*<sup>F</sup>

upper tail covert
*cobertera*<sup>F</sup> *superior de la cola*<sup>F</sup>

breast
*pechuga*<sup>F</sup>

under tail covert
*cobertera*<sup>F</sup> *inferior de la cola*<sup>F</sup>

flank
*flanco*<sup>M</sup>

abdomen
*abdomen*<sup>M</sup>

thigh
*muslo*<sup>M</sup>

tarsus
*tarso*<sup>M</sup>

hind toe
*dedo*<sup>M</sup> *posterior*

inner toe
*dedo*<sup>M</sup> *interno*

outer toe
*dedo*<sup>M</sup> *externo*

middle toe
*dedo*<sup>M</sup> *medio*

claw
*uña*<sup>F</sup>

## head
*cabeza*<sup>F</sup>

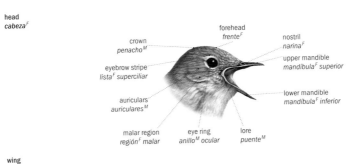

forehead
*frente*<sup>F</sup>

crown
*penacho*<sup>M</sup>

nostril
*narina*<sup>F</sup>

eyebrow stripe
*lista*<sup>F</sup> *superciliar*

upper mandible
*mandíbula*<sup>F</sup> *superior*

auriculars
*auriculares*<sup>M</sup>

lower mandible
*mandíbula*<sup>F</sup> *inferior*

malar region
*región*<sup>F</sup> *malar*

eye ring
*anillo*<sup>M</sup> *ocular*

lore
*puente*<sup>M</sup>

## wing
*ala*<sup>F</sup>

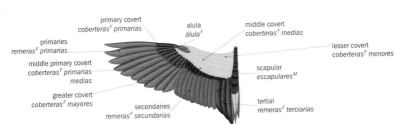

primary covert
*coberteras*<sup>F</sup> *primarias*

alula
*álula*<sup>F</sup>

middle covert
*coberteras*<sup>F</sup> *medias*

primaries
*remeras*<sup>F</sup> *primarias*

lesser covert
*coberteras*<sup>F</sup> *menores*

middle primary covert
*coberteras*<sup>F</sup> *primarias medias*

scapular
*escapulares*<sup>M</sup>

greater covert
*coberteras*<sup>F</sup> *mayores*

secondaries
*remeras*<sup>F</sup> *secundarias*

tertial
*remeras*<sup>F</sup> *terciarias*

bird

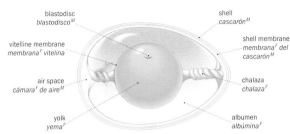

egg
*huevo*$^M$

blastodisc
*blastodisco*$^M$

vitelline membrane
*membrana*$^F$ *vitelina*

air space
*cámara*$^F$ *de aire*$^M$

yolk
*yema*$^F$

shell
*cascarón*$^M$

shell membrane
*membrana*$^F$ *del
cascarón*$^M$

chalaza
*chalaza*$^F$

albumen
*albúmina*$^F$

ANIMAL KINGDOM

**examples of bills**
***ejemplos***$^M$ ***de picos***$^M$

aquatic bird
*ave*$^F$ *acuática*

granivorous bird
*ave*$^F$ *granivora*

bird of prey
*ave*$^F$ *de rapiña*$^F$

insectivorous bird
*ave*$^F$ *insectivora*

wading bird
*ave*$^F$ *zancuda*

**examples of feet**
***ejemplos***$^M$ ***de patas***$^F$

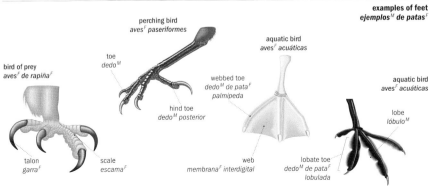

perching bird
*aves*$^F$ *paseriformes*

aquatic bird
*aves*$^F$ *acuáticas*

bird of prey
*aves*$^F$ *de rapiña*$^F$

toe
*dedo*$^M$

hind toe
*dedo*$^M$ *posterior*

webbed toe
*dedo*$^M$ *de pata*$^F$
*palmipeda*

aquatic bird
*aves*$^F$ *acuáticas*

lobe
*lóbulo*$^M$

talon
*garra*$^F$

scale
*escama*$^F$

web
*membrana*$^F$ *interdigital*

lobate toe
*dedo*$^M$ *de pata*$^F$
*lobulada*

# examples of birds

*ejemplos* M *de pájaros* M

ANIMAL KINGDOM

hummingbird
*colibrí* M

European robin
*petirrojo* M

finch
*pinzón* M

kingfisher
*martín* M *pescador*

nightingale
*ruiseñor* M

sparrow
*gorrión* M

swallow
*golondrina* F

starling
*estornino* M

jay
*arrendajo* M

cardinal
*cardenal* M

swift
*vencejo* M

partridge
*perdiz* F

condor
*cóndor* M

macaw
*guacamayo* M

woodpecker
*pájaro* M *carpintero*

raven
*cuervo* M

toucan
*tucán* M

vulture
*buitre* M

penguin
*pingüino* M

albatross
*albatros* M

heron
*garza* F

pelican
*pelicano* M

stork
*cigüeña* F

pheasant
*faisán*<sup>M</sup>

great horned owl
*búho*<sup>M</sup> *real*

falcon
*halcón*<sup>M</sup>

quail
*codorniz*<sup>F</sup>

eagle
*águila*<sup>F</sup>

hen
*gallina*<sup>F</sup>

duck
*pato*<sup>M</sup>

pigeon
*paloma*<sup>F</sup>

goose
*oca*<sup>F</sup>

rooster
*gallo*<sup>M</sup>

turkey
*pavo*<sup>M</sup>

guinea fowl
*pintada*<sup>F</sup>

ostrich
*avestruz*<sup>F</sup>

peacock
*pavo*<sup>M</sup> *real*

flamingo
*flamenco*<sup>M</sup>

# rodent
*roedor*<sup>M</sup>

**morphology of a rat**
*morfología*<sup>F</sup> *de una rata*<sup>F</sup>

pinna
*pabellón*<sup>M</sup> *de la oreja*<sup>F</sup>

whisker
*vibrisas*<sup>F</sup>

nose
*nariz*<sup>F</sup>

digit
*dedo*<sup>M</sup>

claw
*garra*<sup>F</sup>

fur
*pelaje*<sup>M</sup>

tail
*cola*<sup>F</sup>

## examples of rodents
*ejemplos*<sup>M</sup> *de roedores*<sup>M</sup>

field mouse
*ratón*<sup>M</sup> *de campo*<sup>M</sup>

chipmunk
*ardilla*<sup>F</sup> *listada*

jerboa
*jerbo*<sup>M</sup>

hamster
*hámster*<sup>M</sup>

squirrel
*ardilla*<sup>F</sup>

rat
*rata*<sup>F</sup>

guinea pig
*cobaya*<sup>F</sup>

porcupine
*puerco*<sup>M</sup> *espín*

groundhog
*marmota*<sup>F</sup>

beaver
*castor*<sup>M</sup>

## examples of lagomorphs
*ejemplos*<sup>M</sup> *de lagomorfos*<sup>M</sup>

pika
*pica*<sup>F</sup>

rabbit
*conejo*<sup>M</sup>

hare
*liebre*<sup>F</sup>

# horse
*caballo*<sup>M</sup>

ANIMAL KINGDOM

morphology of a horse
*morfología*<sup>F</sup> *de un*
*caballo*<sup>M</sup>

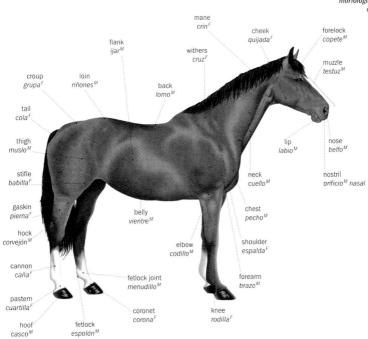

mane
*crin*<sup>F</sup>

cheek
*quijada*<sup>F</sup>

forelock
*copete*<sup>M</sup>

flank
*ijar*<sup>M</sup>

withers
*cruz*<sup>F</sup>

muzzle
*testuz*<sup>M</sup>

croup
*grupa*<sup>F</sup>

loin
*riñones*<sup>M</sup>

back
*lomo*<sup>M</sup>

tail
*cola*<sup>F</sup>

lip
*labio*<sup>M</sup>

nose
*belfo*<sup>M</sup>

thigh
*muslo*<sup>M</sup>

neck
*cuello*<sup>M</sup>

nostril
*orificio*<sup>M</sup> *nasal*

stifle
*babilla*<sup>F</sup>

gaskin
*pierna*<sup>F</sup>

belly
*vientre*<sup>M</sup>

chest
*pecho*<sup>M</sup>

hock
*corvejón*<sup>M</sup>

elbow
*codillo*<sup>M</sup>

shoulder
*espalda*<sup>F</sup>

cannon
*caña*<sup>F</sup>

fetlock joint
*menudillo*<sup>M</sup>

forearm
*brazo*<sup>M</sup>

pastern
*cuartilla*<sup>F</sup>

coronet
*corona*<sup>F</sup>

knee
*rodilla*<sup>F</sup>

hoof
*casco*<sup>M</sup>

fetlock
*espolón*<sup>M</sup>

**gaits**
*andaduras*<sup>F</sup>

walk
*paso*<sup>M</sup>

pace
*portante*<sup>M</sup>

trot
*trote*<sup>M</sup>

canter
*galope*<sup>M</sup>

# examples of ungulate mammals
*ejemplos<sup>M</sup> de mamíferos<sup>M</sup> ungulados*

peccary
*pécari<sup>M</sup>*

wild boar
*jabalí<sup>M</sup>*

pig
*cerdo<sup>M</sup>*

goat
*cabra<sup>F</sup>*

antelope
*antilope<sup>M</sup>*

sheep
*oveja<sup>F</sup>*

calf
*ternero<sup>M</sup>*

white-tailed deer
*ciervo<sup>M</sup> de Virginia<sup>F</sup>*

mouflon
*muflón<sup>M</sup>*

caribou
*reno<sup>M</sup>*

wapiti (elk)
*uapiti<sup>M</sup> (elk<sup>M</sup>)*

okapi
*okapi<sup>M</sup>*

donkey
*asno<sup>M</sup>*

mule
*mula<sup>F</sup>*

cow
*vaca<sup>F</sup>*

zebra
*cebra<sup>F</sup>*

llama
*llama<sup>F</sup>*

bison
*bisonte<sup>M</sup>*

buffalo
*búfalo<sup>M</sup>*

ox
*buey*[M]

yak
*yak*[M]

horse
*caballo*[M]

moose
*alce*[M]

bactrian camel
*camello*[M]

dromedary camel
*dromedario*[M]

rhinoceros
*rinoceronte*[M]

hippopotamus
*hipopótamo*[M]

giraffe
*jirafa*[F]

elephant
*elefante*[M]

ANIMAL KINGDOM

# dog
perro<sup>M</sup>

**morphology of a dog**
*morfología<sup>F</sup> de un perro<sup>M</sup>*

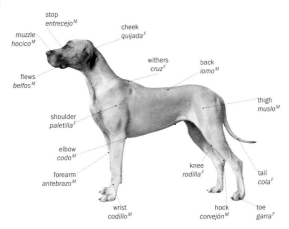

stop
*entrecejo<sup>M</sup>*

cheek
*quijada<sup>F</sup>*

muzzle
*hocico<sup>M</sup>*

withers
*cruz<sup>F</sup>*

back
*lomo<sup>M</sup>*

flews
*belfos<sup>M</sup>*

thigh
*muslo<sup>M</sup>*

shoulder
*paletilla<sup>F</sup>*

elbow
*codo<sup>M</sup>*

knee
*rodilla<sup>F</sup>*

tail
*cola<sup>F</sup>*

forearm
*antebrazo<sup>M</sup>*

wrist
*codillo<sup>M</sup>*

hock
*corvejón<sup>M</sup>*

toe
*garra<sup>F</sup>*

# examples of dog breeds
*razas<sup>F</sup> de perros<sup>M</sup>*

bulldog
*buldog<sup>M</sup>*

collie
*collie<sup>M</sup>*

Dalmatian
*dálmata<sup>M</sup>*

poodle
*caniche<sup>M</sup>*

schnauzer
*schnauzer<sup>M</sup>*

Great Dane
*gran danés<sup>M</sup>*

German shepherd
*pastor<sup>M</sup> alemán*

Saint Bernard
*San Bernardo<sup>M</sup>*

## cat
*gato<sup>M</sup> doméstico*

ANIMAL KINGDOM

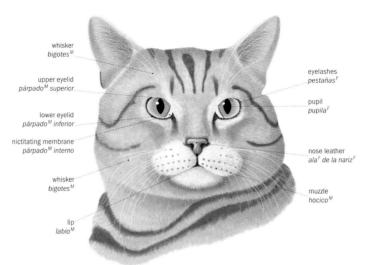

cat's head
*cabeza<sup>F</sup>*

whisker
*bigotes<sup>M</sup>*

upper eyelid
*párpado<sup>M</sup> superior*

lower eyelid
*párpado<sup>M</sup> inferior*

nictitating membrane
*párpado<sup>M</sup> interno*

whisker
*bigotes<sup>M</sup>*

lip
*labio<sup>M</sup>*

eyelashes
*pestañas<sup>F</sup>*

pupil
*pupila<sup>F</sup>*

nose leather
*ala<sup>F</sup> de la nariz<sup>F</sup>*

muzzle
*hocico<sup>M</sup>*

## examples of cat breeds
*razas<sup>F</sup> de gatos<sup>M</sup>*

Siamese
*siamés<sup>M</sup>*

Abyssinian
*abisinio<sup>M</sup>*

Persian
*persa<sup>M</sup>*

Maine coon
*Maine coon<sup>M</sup>*

Manx
*Manx<sup>M</sup>*

# examples of carnivorous mammals
*ejemplos<sup>M</sup> de mamíferos<sup>M</sup> carnívoros*

ANIMAL KINGDOM

weasel
*comadreja<sup>F</sup>*

mink
*visón<sup>M</sup>*

stone marten
*garduña<sup>F</sup>*

marten
*marta<sup>F</sup>*

fox
*zorro<sup>M</sup>*

raccoon
*mapache<sup>M</sup>*

fennec
*fenec<sup>M</sup>*

mongoose
*mangosta<sup>F</sup>*

river otter
*nutria<sup>F</sup> de rio<sup>M</sup>*

badger
*tejón<sup>M</sup>*

skunk
*mofeta<sup>M</sup>*

hyena
*hiena<sup>F</sup>*

lynx
*lince<sup>M</sup>*

wolf
*lobo<sup>M</sup>*

cougar
*puma<sup>M</sup>*

cheetah
*guepardo*<sup>M</sup>

leopard
*leopardo*<sup>M</sup>

lion
*león*<sup>M</sup>

jaguar
*jaguar*<sup>M</sup>

tiger
*tigre*<sup>M</sup>

polar bear
*oso*<sup>M</sup> *polar*

black bear
*oso*<sup>M</sup> *negro*

ANIMAL KINGDOM

# dolphin
*delfín*<sup>M</sup>

**morphology of a dolphin**
*morfología*<sup>F</sup> *de un delfín*<sup>M</sup>

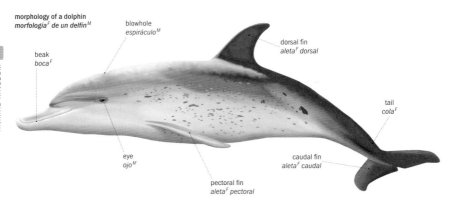

blowhole
*espiráculo*<sup>M</sup>

dorsal fin
*aleta*<sup>F</sup> *dorsal*

beak
*boca*<sup>F</sup>

tail
*cola*<sup>F</sup>

eye
*ojo*<sup>M</sup>

caudal fin
*aleta*<sup>F</sup> *caudal*

pectoral fin
*aleta*<sup>F</sup> *pectoral*

## examples of marine mammals
*ejemplos*<sup>M</sup> *de mamíferos*<sup>M</sup> *marinos*

killer whale
*orca*<sup>F</sup>

seal
*foca*<sup>F</sup>

humpback whale
*rorcual*<sup>M</sup>

northern right whale
*ballena*<sup>F</sup> *boréale*

sperm whale
*cachalote*<sup>M</sup>

sea lion
*otaria*<sup>F</sup>

# gorilla
*gorila^M*

morphology of a gorilla
*morfología^F de un gorila^M*

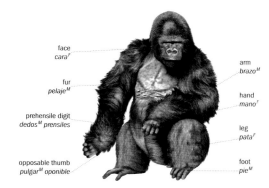

face
*cara^F*

fur
*pelaje^M*

prehensile digit
*dedos^M prensiles*

opposable thumb
*pulgar^M oponible*

arm
*brazo^M*

hand
*mano^F*

leg
*pata^F*

foot
*pie^M*

ANIMAL KINGDOM

# examples of primates
*ejemplos^M de primates^M*

tamarin
*tamarino^M*

marmoset
*tití^M*

baboon
*babuino^M*

macaque
*macaco^M*

orangutan
*orangután^M*

chimpanzee
*chimpancé^M*

lemur
*lémur^M*

gibbon
*gibón^M*

# man
*hombre* M

HUMAN BEING

**anterior view**
*vista* F *anterior*

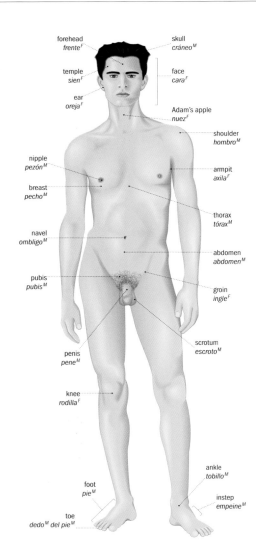

forehead
*frente* F

skull
*cráneo* M

temple
*sien* F

face
*cara* F

ear
*oreja* F

Adam's apple
*nuez* F

shoulder
*hombro* M

nipple
*pezón* M

armpit
*axila* F

breast
*pecho* M

thorax
*tórax* M

navel
*ombligo* M

abdomen
*abdomen* M

pubis
*pubis* M

groin
*ingle* F

scrotum
*escroto* M

penis
*pene* M

knee
*rodilla* F

ankle
*tobillo* M

foot
*pie* M

instep
*empeine* M

toe
*dedo* M *del pie* M

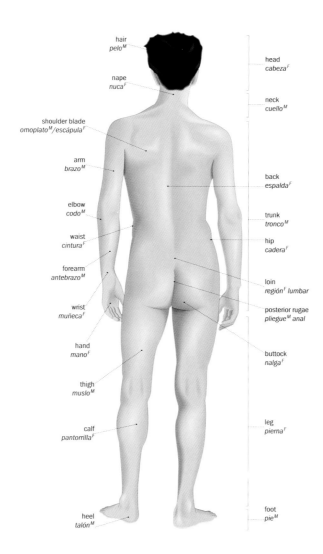

posterior view
vista<sup>F</sup> posterior

hair
pelo<sup>M</sup>

nape
nuca<sup>F</sup>

shoulder blade
omoplato<sup>M</sup>/escápula<sup>F</sup>

arm
brazo<sup>M</sup>

elbow
codo<sup>M</sup>

waist
cintura<sup>F</sup>

forearm
antebrazo<sup>M</sup>

wrist
muñeca<sup>F</sup>

hand
mano<sup>F</sup>

thigh
muslo<sup>M</sup>

calf
pantorrilla<sup>F</sup>

heel
talón<sup>M</sup>

head
cabeza<sup>F</sup>

neck
cuello<sup>M</sup>

back
espalda<sup>F</sup>

trunk
tronco<sup>M</sup>

hip
cadera<sup>F</sup>

loin
región<sup>F</sup> lumbar

posterior rugae
pliegue<sup>M</sup> anal

buttock
nalga<sup>F</sup>

leg
pierna<sup>F</sup>

foot
pie<sup>M</sup>

# woman
*mujer<sup>F</sup>*

**anterior view**
*vista<sup>F</sup> anterior*

HUMAN BEING

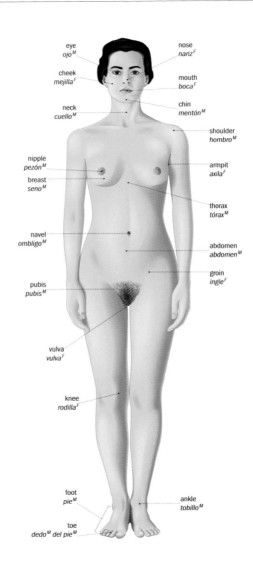

eye
*ojo<sup>M</sup>*

nose
*nariz<sup>F</sup>*

cheek
*mejilla<sup>F</sup>*

mouth
*boca<sup>F</sup>*

neck
*cuello<sup>M</sup>*

chin
*mentón<sup>M</sup>*

shoulder
*hombro<sup>M</sup>*

nipple
*pezón<sup>M</sup>*

armpit
*axila<sup>F</sup>*

breast
*seno<sup>M</sup>*

thorax
*tórax<sup>M</sup>*

navel
*ombligo<sup>M</sup>*

abdomen
*abdomen<sup>M</sup>*

groin
*ingle<sup>F</sup>*

pubis
*pubis<sup>M</sup>*

vulva
*vulva<sup>F</sup>*

knee
*rodilla<sup>F</sup>*

foot
*pie<sup>M</sup>*

ankle
*tobillo<sup>M</sup>*

toe
*dedo<sup>M</sup> del pie<sup>M</sup>*

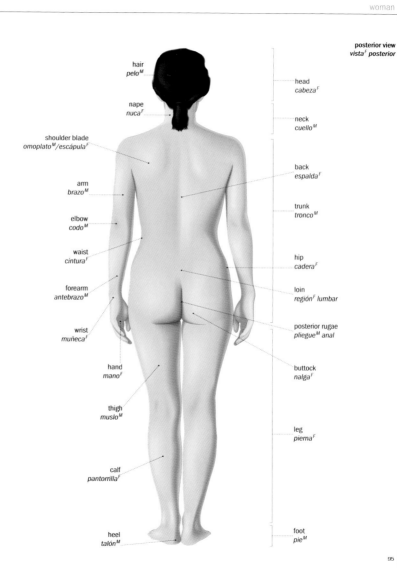

posterior view
*vista* ᶠ *posterior*

HUMAN BEING

hair
*pelo* ᴹ

nape
*nuca* ᶠ

shoulder blade
*omoplato* ᴹ/*escápula* ᶠ

arm
*brazo* ᴹ

elbow
*codo* ᴹ

waist
*cintura* ᶠ

forearm
*antebrazo* ᴹ

wrist
*muñeca* ᶠ

hand
*mano* ᶠ

thigh
*muslo* ᴹ

calf
*pantorrilla* ᶠ

heel
*talón* ᴹ

head
*cabeza* ᶠ

neck
*cuello* ᴹ

back
*espalda* ᶠ

trunk
*tronco* ᴹ

hip
*cadera* ᶠ

loin
*región* ᶠ *lumbar*

posterior rugae
*pliegue* ᴹ *anal*

buttock
*nalga* ᶠ

leg
*pierna* ᶠ

foot
*pie* ᴹ

95

# muscles
*músculos* <sup>M</sup>

**anterior view**
*vista* <sup>F</sup> *anterior*

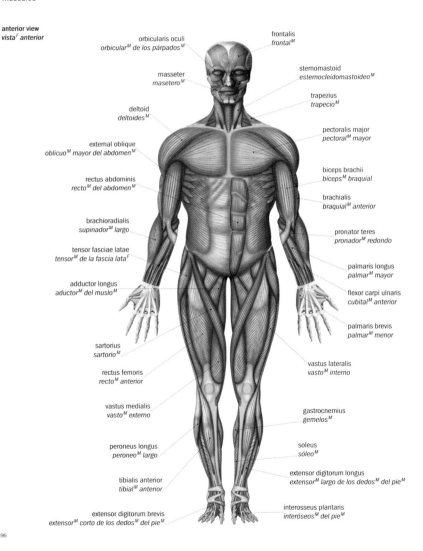

orbicularis oculi
*orbicular* <sup>M</sup> *de los párpados* <sup>M</sup>

frontalis
*frontal* <sup>M</sup>

masseter
*masetero* <sup>M</sup>

sternomastoid
*esternocleidomastoideo* <sup>M</sup>

deltoid
*deltoides* <sup>M</sup>

trapezius
*trapecio* <sup>M</sup>

external oblique
*oblicuo* <sup>M</sup> *mayor del abdomen* <sup>M</sup>

pectoralis major
*pectoral* <sup>M</sup> *mayor*

rectus abdominis
*recto* <sup>M</sup> *del abdomen* <sup>M</sup>

biceps brachii
*bíceps* <sup>M</sup> *braquial*

brachialis
*braquial* <sup>M</sup> *anterior*

brachioradialis
*supinador* <sup>M</sup> *largo*

pronator teres
*pronador* <sup>M</sup> *redondo*

tensor fasciae latae
*tensor* <sup>M</sup> *de la fascia lata* <sup>F</sup>

palmaris longus
*palmar* <sup>M</sup> *mayor*

adductor longus
*aductor* <sup>M</sup> *del muslo* <sup>M</sup>

flexor carpi ulnaris
*cubital* <sup>M</sup> *anterior*

palmaris brevis
*palmar* <sup>M</sup> *menor*

sartorius
*sartorio* <sup>M</sup>

vastus lateralis
*vasto* <sup>M</sup> *interno*

rectus femoris
*recto* <sup>M</sup> *anterior*

vastus medialis
*vasto* <sup>M</sup> *externo*

gastrocnemius
*gemelos* <sup>M</sup>

peroneus longus
*peroneo* <sup>M</sup> *largo*

soleus
*sóleo* <sup>M</sup>

tibialis anterior
*tibial* <sup>M</sup> *anterior*

extensor digitorum longus
*extensor* <sup>M</sup> *largo de los dedos* <sup>M</sup> *del pie* <sup>M</sup>

extensor digitorum brevis
*extensor* <sup>M</sup> *corto de los dedos* <sup>M</sup> *del pie* <sup>M</sup>

interosseus plantaris
*interóseos* <sup>M</sup> *del pie* <sup>M</sup>

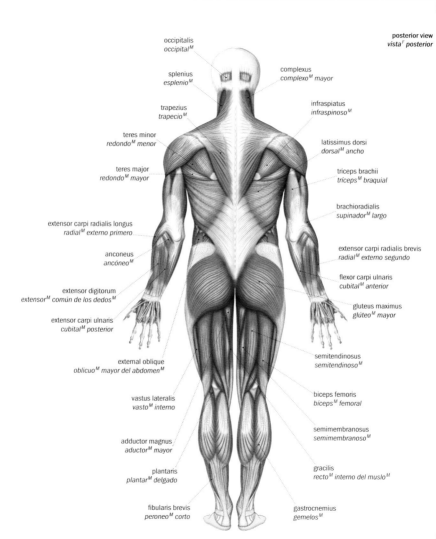

posterior view
*vista*<sup>F</sup> *posterior*

occipitalis
*occipital*<sup>M</sup>

complexus
*complexo*<sup>M</sup> *mayor*

splenius
*esplenio*<sup>M</sup>

infraspiatus
*infraspinoso*<sup>M</sup>

trapezius
*trapecio*<sup>M</sup>

teres minor
*redondo*<sup>M</sup> *menor*

latissimus dorsi
*dorsal*<sup>M</sup> *ancho*

teres major
*redondo*<sup>M</sup> *mayor*

triceps brachii
*tríceps*<sup>M</sup> *braquial*

brachioradialis
*supinador*<sup>M</sup> *largo*

extensor carpi radialis longus
*radial*<sup>M</sup> *externo primero*

extensor carpi radialis brevis
*radial*<sup>M</sup> *externo segundo*

anconeus
*ancóneo*<sup>M</sup>

flexor carpi ulnaris
*cubital*<sup>M</sup> *anterior*

extensor digitorum
*extensor*<sup>M</sup> *común de los dedos*<sup>M</sup>

gluteus maximus
*glúteo*<sup>M</sup> *mayor*

extensor carpi ulnaris
*cubital*<sup>M</sup> *posterior*

external oblique
*oblicuo*<sup>M</sup> *mayor del abdomen*<sup>M</sup>

semitendinosus
*semitendinoso*<sup>M</sup>

vastus lateralis
*vasto*<sup>M</sup> *interno*

biceps femoris
*biceps*<sup>M</sup> *femoral*

semimembranosus
*semimembranoso*<sup>M</sup>

adductor magnus
*aductor*<sup>M</sup> *mayor*

plantaris
*plantar*<sup>M</sup> *delgado*

gracilis
*recto*<sup>M</sup> *interno del muslo*<sup>M</sup>

fibularis brevis
*peroneo*<sup>M</sup> *corto*

gastrocnemius
*gemelos*<sup>M</sup>

HUMAN BEING

# skeleton
*esqueleto* [M]

**anterior view**
*vista* [F] *anterior*

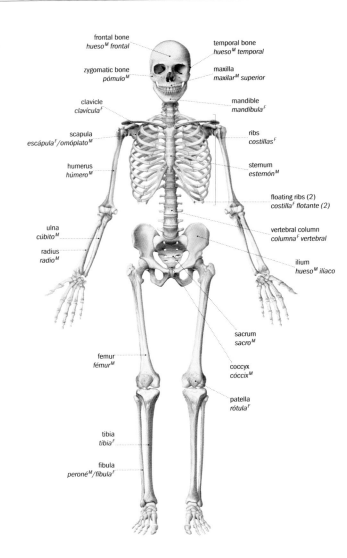

frontal bone
*hueso* [M] *frontal*

temporal bone
*hueso* [M] *temporal*

zygomatic bone
*pómulo* [M]

maxilla
*maxilar* [M] *superior*

clavicle
*clavícula* [F]

mandible
*mandíbula* [F]

scapula
*escápula* [F] / *omóplato* [M]

ribs
*costillas* [F]

humerus
*húmero* [M]

sternum
*esternón* [M]

floating ribs (2)
*costilla* [F] *flotante (2)*

ulna
*cúbito* [M]

vertebral column
*columna* [F] *vertebral*

radius
*radio* [M]

ilium
*hueso* [M] *ilíaco*

sacrum
*sacro* [M]

femur
*fémur* [M]

coccyx
*cóccix* [M]

patella
*rótula* [F]

tibia
*tibia* [F]

fibula
*peroné* [M] / *fíbula* [F]

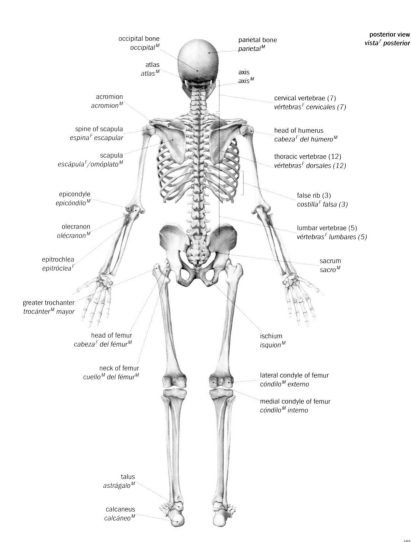

posterior view
*vista$^F$ posterior*

occipital bone
*occipital$^M$*

parietal bone
*parietal$^M$*

atlas
*atlas$^M$*

axis
*axis$^M$*

acromion
*acromion$^M$*

cervical vertebrae (7)
*vértebras$^F$ cervicales (7)*

spine of scapula
*espina$^F$ escapular*

head of humerus
*cabeza$^F$ del húmero$^M$*

scapula
*escápula$^F$/omóplato$^M$*

thoracic vertebrae (12)
*vértebras$^F$ dorsales (12)*

epicondyle
*epicóndilo$^M$*

false rib (3)
*costilla$^F$ falsa (3)*

olecranon
*olécranon$^M$*

lumbar vertebrae (5)
*vértebras$^F$ lumbares (5)*

epitrochlea
*epitróclea$^F$*

sacrum
*sacro$^M$*

greater trochanter
*trocánter$^M$ mayor*

head of femur
*cabeza$^F$ del fémur$^M$*

ischium
*isquion$^M$*

neck of femur
*cuello$^M$ del fémur$^M$*

lateral condyle of femur
*cóndilo$^M$ externo*

medial condyle of femur
*cóndilo$^M$ interno*

talus
*astrágalo$^M$*

calcaneus
*calcáneo$^M$*

skeleton

HUMAN BEING

**lateral view of adult skull**
*vista^F lateral del cráneo^M*
*adulto*

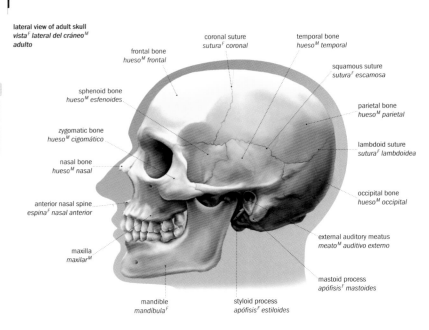

coronal suture
*sutura^F coronal*

temporal bone
*hueso^M temporal*

frontal bone
*hueso^M frontal*

squamous suture
*sutura^F escamosa*

sphenoid bone
*hueso^M esfenoides*

parietal bone
*hueso^M parietal*

zygomatic bone
*hueso^M cigomático*

lambdoid suture
*sutura^F lambdoidea*

nasal bone
*hueso^M nasal*

occipital bone
*hueso^M occipital*

anterior nasal spine
*espina^F nasal anterior*

maxilla
*maxilar^M*

external auditory meatus
*meato^M auditivo externo*

mandible
*mandíbula^F*

styloid process
*apófisis^F estiloides*

mastoid process
*apófisis^F mastoides*

**lateral view of child's skull**
*vista^F lateral del cráneo^M*
*de un niño^M*

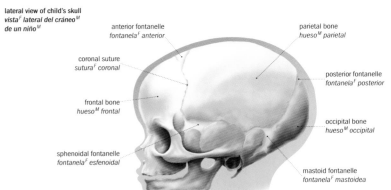

anterior fontanelle
*fontanela^F anterior*

parietal bone
*hueso^M parietal*

coronal suture
*sutura^F coronal*

posterior fontanelle
*fontanela^F posterior*

frontal bone
*hueso^M frontal*

occipital bone
*hueso^M occipital*

sphenoidal fontanelle
*fontanela^F esfenoidal*

mastoid fontanelle
*fontanela^F mastoidea*

# teeth
*dientes*<sup>M</sup>

HUMAN BEING

**human denture**
*dentadura*<sup>F</sup> *humana*

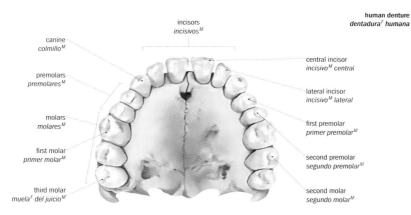

incisors
*incisivos*<sup>M</sup>

canine
*colmillo*<sup>M</sup>

premolars
*premolares*<sup>M</sup>

molars
*molares*<sup>M</sup>

first molar
*primer molar*<sup>M</sup>

third molar
*muela*<sup>F</sup> *del juicio*<sup>M</sup>

central incisor
*incisivo*<sup>M</sup> *central*

lateral incisor
*incisivo*<sup>M</sup> *lateral*

first premolar
*primer premolar*<sup>M</sup>

second premolar
*segundo premolar*<sup>M</sup>

second molar
*segundo molar*<sup>M</sup>

**cross section of a molar**
*corte*<sup>M</sup> *transversal de un*
*molar*<sup>M</sup>

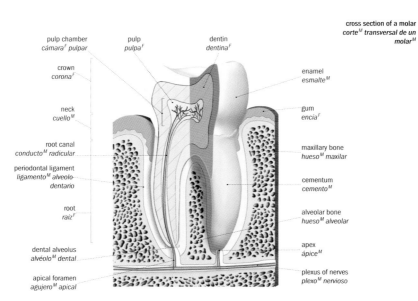

pulp chamber
*cámara*<sup>F</sup> *pulpar*

pulp
*pulpa*<sup>F</sup>

dentin
*dentina*<sup>F</sup>

crown
*corona*<sup>F</sup>

neck
*cuello*<sup>M</sup>

root canal
*conducto*<sup>M</sup> *radicular*

periodontal ligament
*ligamento*<sup>M</sup> *alveolo*
*dentario*

root
*raíz*<sup>F</sup>

dental alveolus
*alvéolo*<sup>M</sup> *dental*

apical foramen
*agujero*<sup>M</sup> *apical*

enamel
*esmalte*<sup>M</sup>

gum
*encía*<sup>F</sup>

maxillary bone
*hueso*<sup>M</sup> *maxilar*

cementum
*cemento*<sup>M</sup>

alveolar bone
*hueso*<sup>M</sup> *alveolar*

apex
*ápice*<sup>M</sup>

plexus of nerves
*plexo*<sup>M</sup> *nervioso*

# blood circulation
*circulación<sup>F</sup> sanguínea*

**principal veins and arteries**
*principales venas<sup>F</sup> y
arterias<sup>F</sup>*

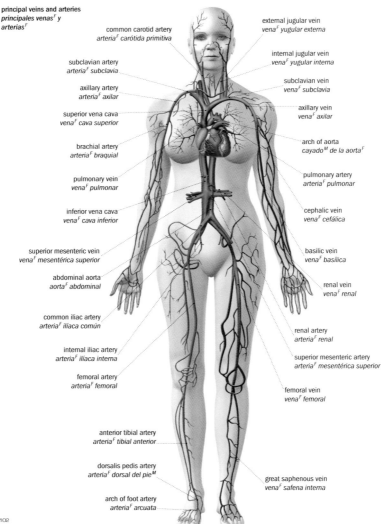

common carotid artery
*arteria<sup>F</sup> carótida primitiva*

subclavian artery
*arteria<sup>F</sup> subclavia*

axillary artery
*arteria<sup>F</sup> axilar*

superior vena cava
*vena<sup>F</sup> cava superior*

brachial artery
*arteria<sup>F</sup> braquial*

pulmonary vein
*vena<sup>F</sup> pulmonar*

inferior vena cava
*vena<sup>F</sup> cava inferior*

superior mesenteric vein
*vena<sup>F</sup> mesentérica superior*

abdominal aorta
*aorta<sup>F</sup> abdominal*

common iliac artery
*arteria<sup>F</sup> ilíaca común*

internal iliac artery
*arteria<sup>F</sup> ilíaca interna*

femoral artery
*arteria<sup>F</sup> femoral*

anterior tibial artery
*arteria<sup>F</sup> tibial anterior*

dorsalis pedis artery
*arteria<sup>F</sup> dorsal del pie<sup>M</sup>*

arch of foot artery
*arteria<sup>F</sup> arcuata*

external jugular vein
*vena<sup>F</sup> yugular externa*

internal jugular vein
*vena<sup>F</sup> yugular interna*

subclavian vein
*vena<sup>F</sup> subclavia*

axillary vein
*vena<sup>F</sup> axilar*

arch of aorta
*cayado<sup>M</sup> de la aorta<sup>F</sup>*

pulmonary artery
*arteria<sup>F</sup> pulmonar*

cephalic vein
*vena<sup>F</sup> cefálica*

basilic vein
*vena<sup>F</sup> basílica*

renal vein
*vena<sup>F</sup> renal*

renal artery
*arteria<sup>F</sup> renal*

superior mesenteric artery
*arteria<sup>F</sup> mesentérica superior*

femoral vein
*vena<sup>F</sup> femoral*

great saphenous vein
*vena<sup>F</sup> safena interna*

HUMAN BEING

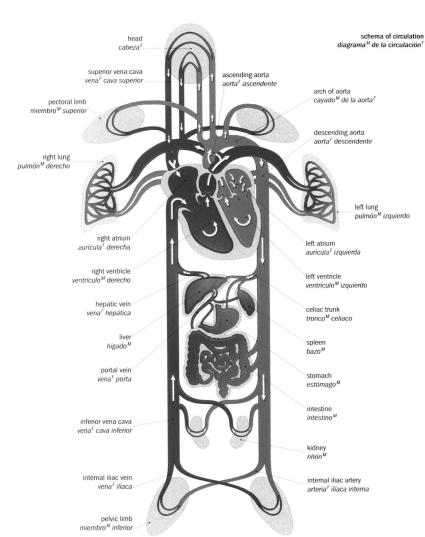

schema of circulation
*diagrama^M de la circulación^F*

head
*cabeza^F*

superior vena cava
*vena^F cava superior*

ascending aorta
*aorta^F ascendente*

arch of aorta
*cayado^M de la aorta^F*

pectoral limb
*miembro^M superior*

descending aorta
*aorta^F descendente*

right lung
*pulmón^M derecho*

left lung
*pulmón^M izquierdo*

right atrium
*aurícula^F derecha*

left atrium
*aurícula^F izquierda*

right ventricle
*ventrículo^M derecho*

left ventricle
*ventrículo^M izquierdo*

hepatic vein
*vena^F hepática*

celiac trunk
*tronco^M celiaco*

liver
*hígado^M*

spleen
*bazo^M*

portal vein
*vena^F porta*

stomach
*estómago^M*

intestine
*intestino^M*

inferior vena cava
*vena^F cava inferior*

kidney
*riñón^M*

internal iliac vein
*vena^F ilíaca*

internal iliac artery
*arteria^F ilíaca interna*

pelvic limb
*miembro^M inferior*

blood circulation

HUMAN BEING

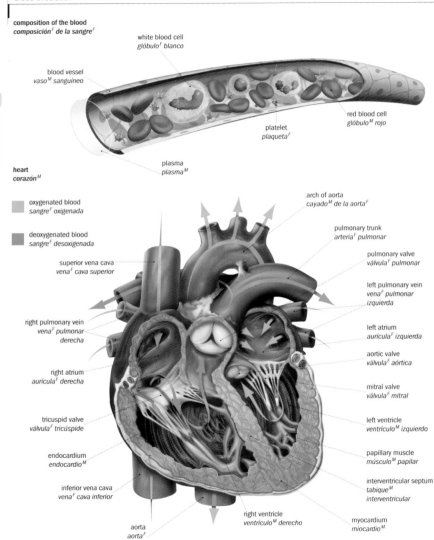

**composition of the blood**
*composición<sup>F</sup> de la sangre<sup>F</sup>*

white blood cell
*glóbulo<sup>F</sup> blanco*

blood vessel
*vaso<sup>M</sup> sanguíneo*

red blood cell
*glóbulo<sup>M</sup> rojo*

platelet
*plaqueta<sup>F</sup>*

plasma
*plasma<sup>M</sup>*

**heart**
*corazón<sup>M</sup>*

oxygenated blood
*sangre<sup>F</sup> oxigenada*

deoxygenated blood
*sangre<sup>F</sup> desoxigenada*

arch of aorta
*cayado<sup>M</sup> de la aorta<sup>F</sup>*

pulmonary trunk
*arteria<sup>F</sup> pulmonar*

superior vena cava
*vena<sup>F</sup> cava superior*

pulmonary valve
*válvula<sup>F</sup> pulmonar*

left pulmonary vein
*vena<sup>F</sup> pulmonar izquierda*

right pulmonary vein
*vena<sup>F</sup> pulmonar derecha*

left atrium
*aurícula<sup>F</sup> izquierda*

right atrium
*aurícula<sup>F</sup> derecha*

aortic valve
*válvula<sup>F</sup> aórtica*

tricuspid valve
*válvula<sup>F</sup> tricúspide*

mitral valve
*válvula<sup>F</sup> mitral*

endocardium
*endocardio<sup>M</sup>*

left ventricle
*ventrículo<sup>M</sup> izquierdo*

papillary muscle
*músculo<sup>M</sup> papilar*

inferior vena cava
*vena<sup>F</sup> cava inferior*

interventricular septum
*tabique<sup>M</sup> interventricular*

aorta
*aorta<sup>F</sup>*

right ventricle
*ventrículo<sup>M</sup> derecho*

myocardium
*miocardio<sup>M</sup>*

# respiratory system
*aparato<sup>M</sup> respiratorio*

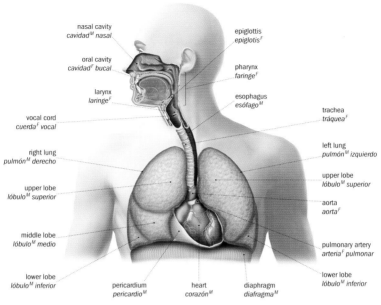

nasal cavity
*cavidad<sup>M</sup> nasal*

oral cavity
*cavidad<sup>F</sup> bucal*

larynx
*laringe<sup>F</sup>*

vocal cord
*cuerda<sup>F</sup> vocal*

right lung
*pulmón<sup>M</sup> derecho*

upper lobe
*lóbulo<sup>M</sup> superior*

middle lobe
*lóbulo<sup>M</sup> medio*

lower lobe
*lóbulo<sup>M</sup> inferior*

epiglottis
*epiglotis<sup>F</sup>*

pharynx
*faringe<sup>F</sup>*

esophagus
*esófago<sup>M</sup>*

trachea
*tráquea<sup>F</sup>*

left lung
*pulmón<sup>M</sup> izquierdo*

upper lobe
*lóbulo<sup>M</sup> superior*

aorta
*aorta<sup>F</sup>*

pulmonary artery
*arteria<sup>F</sup> pulmonar*

lower lobe
*lóbulo<sup>M</sup> inferior*

pericardium
*pericardio<sup>M</sup>*

heart
*corazón<sup>M</sup>*

diaphragm
*diafragma<sup>M</sup>*

**lungs**
***pulmones<sup>M</sup>***

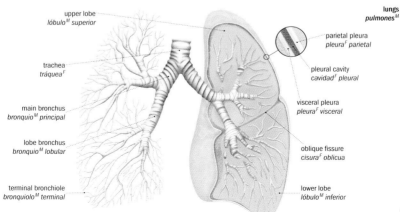

upper lobe
*lóbulo<sup>M</sup> superior*

trachea
*tráquea<sup>F</sup>*

main bronchus
*bronquio<sup>M</sup> principal*

lobe bronchus
*bronquio<sup>M</sup> lobular*

terminal bronchiole
*bronquiolo<sup>M</sup> terminal*

parietal pleura
*pleura<sup>F</sup> parietal*

pleural cavity
*cavidad<sup>F</sup> pleural*

visceral pleura
*pleura<sup>F</sup> visceral*

oblique fissure
*cisura<sup>F</sup> oblicua*

lower lobe
*lóbulo<sup>M</sup> inferior*

# digestive system

*aparato<sup>M</sup> digestivo*

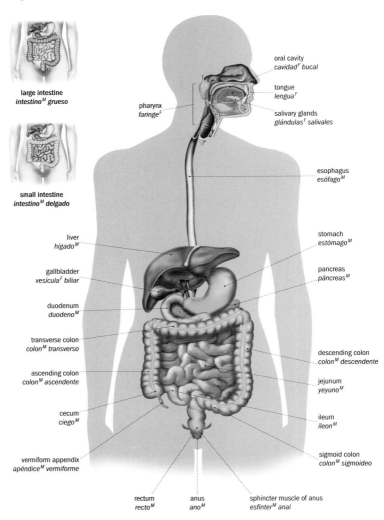

**large intestine**
*intestino<sup>M</sup> grueso*

**small intestine**
*intestino<sup>M</sup> delgado*

oral cavity
*cavidad<sup>F</sup> bucal*

tongue
*lengua<sup>F</sup>*

pharynx
*faringe<sup>F</sup>*

salivary glands
*glándulas<sup>F</sup> salivales*

esophagus
*esófago<sup>M</sup>*

liver
*hígado<sup>M</sup>*

stomach
*estómago<sup>M</sup>*

gallbladder
*vesícula<sup>F</sup> biliar*

pancreas
*páncreas<sup>M</sup>*

duodenum
*duodeno<sup>M</sup>*

transverse colon
*colon<sup>M</sup> transverso*

descending colon
*colon<sup>M</sup> descendente*

ascending colon
*colon<sup>M</sup> ascendente*

jejunum
*yeyuno<sup>M</sup>*

cecum
*ciego<sup>M</sup>*

ileum
*íleon<sup>M</sup>*

vermiform appendix
*apéndice<sup>M</sup> vermiforme*

sigmoid colon
*colon<sup>M</sup> sigmoideo*

rectum
*recto<sup>M</sup>*

anus
*ano<sup>M</sup>*

sphincter muscle of anus
*esfínter<sup>M</sup> anal*

# urinary system
*aparato^M urinario*

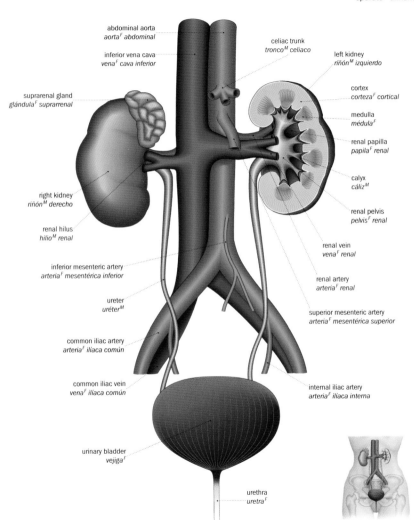

abdominal aorta
*aorta^F abdominal*

inferior vena cava
*vena^F cava inferior*

celiac trunk
*tronco^M celiaco*

left kidney
*riñón^M izquierdo*

suprarenal gland
*glándula^F suprarrenal*

cortex
*corteza^F cortical*

medulla
*médula^F*

renal papilla
*papila^F renal*

calyx
*cáliz^M*

right kidney
*riñón^M derecho*

renal hilus
*hilio^M renal*

renal pelvis
*pelvis^F renal*

renal vein
*vena^F renal*

inferior mesenteric artery
*arteria^F mesentérica inferior*

renal artery
*arteria^F renal*

ureter
*uréter^M*

superior mesenteric artery
*arteria^F mesentérica superior*

common iliac artery
*arteria^F ilíaca común*

common iliac vein
*vena^F ilíaca común*

internal iliac artery
*arteria^F ilíaca interna*

urinary bladder
*vejiga^F*

urethra
*uretra^F*

# nervous system
*sistema^M nervioso*

**peripheral nervous system**
*sistema^M nervioso periférico*

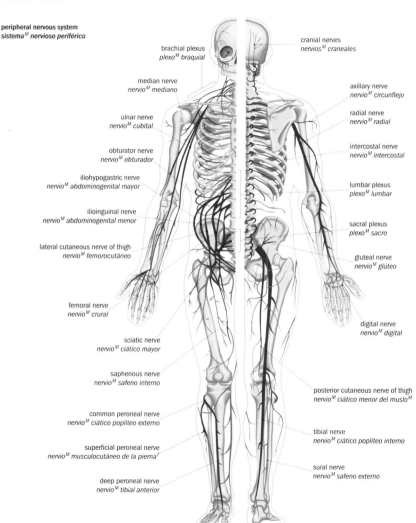

brachial plexus
*plexo^M braquial*

median nerve
*nervio^M mediano*

ulnar nerve
*nervio^M cubital*

obturator nerve
*nervio^M obturador*

iliohypogastric nerve
*nervio^M abdominogenital mayor*

ilioinguinal nerve
*nervio^M abdominogenital menor*

lateral cutaneous nerve of thigh
*nervio^M femorocutáneo*

femoral nerve
*nervio^M crural*

sciatic nerve
*nervio^M ciático mayor*

saphenous nerve
*nervio^M safeno interno*

common peroneal nerve
*nervio^M ciático poplíteo externo*

superficial peroneal nerve
*nervio^M musculocutáneo de la pierna^F*

deep peroneal nerve
*nervio^M tibial anterior*

cranial nerves
*nervios^M craneales*

axillary nerve
*nervio^M circunflejo*

radial nerve
*nervio^M radial*

intercostal nerve
*nervio^M intercostal*

lumbar plexus
*plexo^M lumbar*

sacral plexus
*plexo^M sacro*

gluteal nerve
*nervio^M glúteo*

digital nerve
*nervio^M digital*

posterior cutaneous nerve of thigh
*nervio^M ciático menor del muslo^M*

tibial nerve
*nervio^M ciático poplíteo interno*

sural nerve
*nervio^M safeno externo*

HUMAN BEING

**central nervous system**
*sistema^M nervioso central*

cerebrum
*cerebro^M*

cerebrum
*cerebro^M*

body of fornix
*cuerpo^M del fórnix^M*

cerebellum
*cerebelo^M*

septum pellucidum
*septum^M pellucidum*

corpus callosum
*cuerpo^M calloso*

optic chiasm
*quiasma^M óptico*

vertebral column
*columna^F vertebral*

cerebellum
*cerebelo^M*

pituitary gland
*hipófisis^F*

pineal body
*epífisis^F*

medulla oblongata
*bulbo^M raquídeo*

pons Varolii
*puente^M de Varolio*

spinal cord
*médula^F espinal*

sensitive root
*raíz^F sensitiva*

**structure of the spinal cord**
*estructura^F de la médula^F espinal*

gray matter
*sustancia^F gris*

spinal ganglion
*ganglio^M espinal*

posterior horn
*cuerno^M posterior*

internal filum terminale
*filum^M terminal interno*

white matter
*sustancia^F blanca*

anterior horn
*cuerno^M anterior*

spinal cord
*médula^F espinal*

dura mater
*duramadre^F*

motor root
*raíz^F motora*

spinal nerve
*nervio^M espinal*

terminal filament
*filum^M terminal*

arachnoid
*aracnoides^M*

dura mater
*duramadre^F*

sympathetic ganglion
*ganglio^M simpático*

meninges
*meninges^F*

pia mater
*piamadre^F*

HUMAN BEING

**chain of neurons**
*cadena<sup>F</sup> de neuronas<sup>F</sup>*

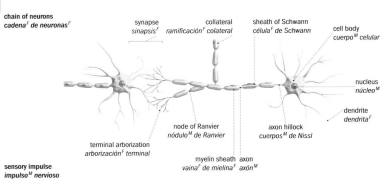

synapse
*sinapsis<sup>F</sup>*

collateral
*ramificación<sup>F</sup> colateral*

sheath of Schwann
*célula<sup>F</sup> de Schwann*

cell body
*cuerpo<sup>M</sup> celular*

nucleus
*núcleo<sup>M</sup>*

dendrite
*dendrita<sup>F</sup>*

node of Ranvier
*nódulo<sup>M</sup> de Ranvier*

axon hillock
*cuerpos<sup>M</sup> de Nissl*

terminal arborization
*arborización<sup>F</sup> terminal*

myelin sheath   axon
*vaina<sup>F</sup> de mielina<sup>F</sup>   axón<sup>M</sup>*

**sensory impulse**
*impulso<sup>M</sup> nervioso*

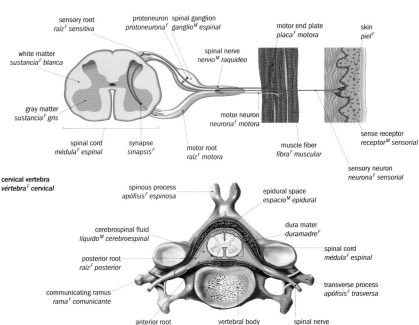

sensory root
*raíz<sup>F</sup> sensitiva*

protoneuron   spinal ganglion
*protoneurona<sup>F</sup>   ganglio<sup>M</sup> espinal*

spinal nerve
*nervio<sup>M</sup> raquídeo*

motor end plate
*placa<sup>F</sup> motora*

skin
*piel<sup>F</sup>*

white matter
*sustancia<sup>F</sup> blanca*

gray matter
*sustancia<sup>F</sup> gris*

spinal cord
*médula<sup>F</sup> espinal*

synapse
*sinapsis<sup>F</sup>*

motor root
*raíz<sup>F</sup> motora*

motor neuron
*neurona<sup>F</sup> motora*

muscle fiber
*fibra<sup>F</sup> muscular*

sense receptor
*receptor<sup>M</sup> sensorial*

sensory neuron
*neurona<sup>F</sup> sensorial*

**cervical vertebra**
*vértebra<sup>F</sup> cervical*

spinous process
*apófisis<sup>F</sup> espinosa*

epidural space
*espacio<sup>M</sup> epidural*

cerebrospinal fluid
*líquido<sup>M</sup> cerebroespinal*

dura mater
*duramadre<sup>F</sup>*

posterior root
*raíz<sup>F</sup> posterior*

spinal cord
*médula<sup>F</sup> espinal*

communicating ramus
*rama<sup>F</sup> comunicante*

transverse process
*apófisis<sup>F</sup> trasversa*

anterior root
*raíz<sup>F</sup> anterior*

vertebral body
*cuerpo<sup>M</sup> vertebral*

spinal nerve
*nervio<sup>M</sup> raquídeo*

# male reproductive organs
*órganos^M genitales masculinos*

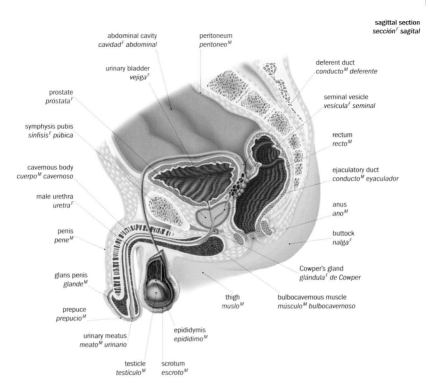

sagittal section
*sección^F sagital*

abdominal cavity
*cavidad^F abdominal*

peritoneum
*peritoneo^M*

urinary bladder
*vejiga^F*

deferent duct
*conducto^M deferente*

prostate
*próstata^F*

seminal vesicle
*vesícula^F seminal*

symphysis pubis
*sínfisis^F púbica*

rectum
*recto^M*

cavernous body
*cuerpo^M cavernoso*

ejaculatory duct
*conducto^M eyaculador*

male urethra
*uretra^F*

anus
*ano^M*

penis
*pene^M*

buttock
*nalga^F*

glans penis
*glande^M*

Cowper's gland
*glándula^F de Cowper*

prepuce
*prepucio^M*

thigh
*muslo^M*

bulbocavernous muscle
*músculo^M bulbocavernoso*

urinary meatus
*meato^M urinario*

epididymis
*epidídimo^M*

testicle
*testículo^M*

scrotum
*escroto^M*

spermatozoon
*espermatozoide^M*

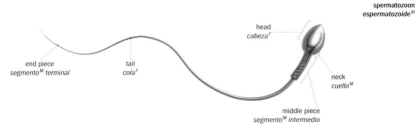

head
*cabeza^F*

end piece
*segmento^M terminal*

tail
*cola^F*

neck
*cuello^M*

middle piece
*segmento^M intermedio*

# female reproductive organs
*órganos<sup>M</sup> genitales femeninos*

HUMAN BEING

**sagittal section**
*sección<sup>F</sup> sagital*

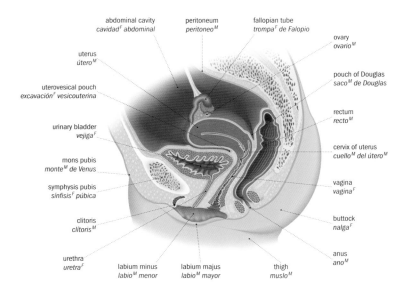

abdominal cavity
*cavidad<sup>F</sup> abdominal*

peritoneum
*peritoneo<sup>M</sup>*

fallopian tube
*trompa<sup>F</sup> de Falopio*

ovary
*ovario<sup>M</sup>*

uterus
*útero<sup>M</sup>*

pouch of Douglas
*saco<sup>M</sup> de Douglas*

uterovesical pouch
*excavación<sup>F</sup> vesicouterina*

rectum
*recto<sup>M</sup>*

urinary bladder
*vejiga<sup>F</sup>*

cervix of uterus
*cuello<sup>M</sup> del útero<sup>M</sup>*

mons pubis
*monte<sup>M</sup> de Venus*

vagina
*vagina<sup>F</sup>*

symphysis pubis
*sínfisis<sup>F</sup> púbica*

buttock
*nalga<sup>F</sup>*

clitoris
*clítoris<sup>M</sup>*

anus
*ano<sup>M</sup>*

urethra
*uretra<sup>F</sup>*

labium minus
*labio<sup>M</sup> menor*

labium majus
*labio<sup>M</sup> mayor*

thigh
*muslo<sup>M</sup>*

**egg**
*óvulo<sup>M</sup>*

corona radiata
*corona<sup>F</sup> radiata*

cytoplasm
*citoplasma<sup>M</sup>*

nucleolus
*nucléolo<sup>M</sup>*

zona pellucida
*zona<sup>F</sup> pelúcida*

nucleus
*núcleo<sup>M</sup>*

HUMAN BEING

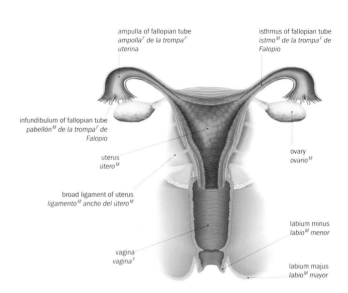

posterior view
*vista*<sup>F</sup> *posterior*

ampulla of fallopian tube
*ampolla*<sup>F</sup> *de la trompa*<sup>F</sup>
*uterina*

isthmus of fallopian tube
*istmo*<sup>M</sup> *de la trompa*<sup>F</sup> *de
Falopio*

infundibulum of fallopian tube
*pabellón*<sup>M</sup> *de la trompa*<sup>F</sup> *de
Falopio*

ovary
*ovario*<sup>M</sup>

uterus
*útero*<sup>M</sup>

broad ligament of uterus
*ligamento*<sup>M</sup> *ancho del útero*<sup>M</sup>

labium minus
*labio*<sup>M</sup> *menor*

vagina
*vagina*<sup>F</sup>

labium majus
*labio*<sup>M</sup> *mayor*

fallopian tubes
*trompas*<sup>F</sup> *de Falopio*

vulva
*vulva*<sup>F</sup>

# breast
*seno*<sup>M</sup>

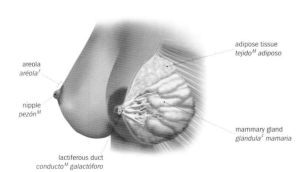

adipose tissue
*tejido*<sup>M</sup> *adiposo*

areola
*aréola*<sup>F</sup>

nipple
*pezón*<sup>M</sup>

mammary gland
*glándula*<sup>F</sup> *mamaria*

lactiferous duct
*conducto*<sup>M</sup> *galactóforo*

# touch
*tacto*<sup>M</sup>

HUMAN BEING

**skin**
*piel*<sup>F</sup>

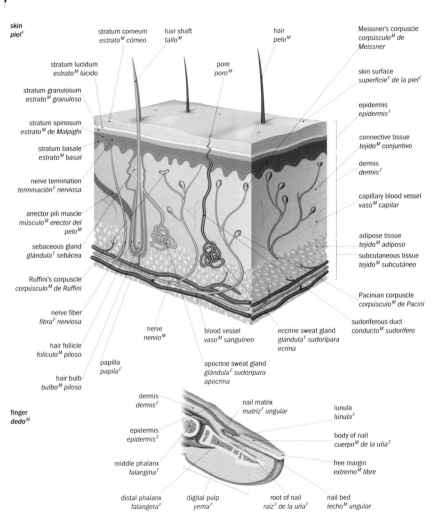

stratum corneum
*estrato*<sup>M</sup> *córneo*

hair shaft
*tallo*<sup>M</sup>

pore
*poro*<sup>M</sup>

hair
*pelo*<sup>M</sup>

Meissner's corpuscle
*corpúsculo*<sup>M</sup> *de Meissner*

stratum lucidum
*estrato*<sup>M</sup> *lúcido*

skin surface
*superficie*<sup>F</sup> *de la piel*<sup>F</sup>

stratum granulosum
*estrato*<sup>M</sup> *granuloso*

epidermis
*epidermis*<sup>F</sup>

stratum spinosum
*estrato*<sup>M</sup> *de Malpighi*

connective tissue
*tejido*<sup>M</sup> *conjuntivo*

stratum basale
*estrato*<sup>M</sup> *basal*

dermis
*dermis*<sup>F</sup>

nerve termination
*terminación*<sup>F</sup> *nerviosa*

capillary blood vessel
*vaso*<sup>M</sup> *capilar*

arrector pili muscle
*músculo*<sup>M</sup> *erector del pelo*<sup>M</sup>

adipose tissue
*tejido*<sup>M</sup> *adiposo*

sebaceous gland
*glándula*<sup>F</sup> *sebácea*

subcutaneous tissue
*tejido*<sup>M</sup> *subcutáneo*

Ruffini's corpuscle
*corpúsculo*<sup>M</sup> *de Ruffini*

Pacinian corpuscle
*corpúsculo*<sup>M</sup> *de Pacini*

nerve fiber
*fibra*<sup>F</sup> *nerviosa*

sudoriferous duct
*conducto*<sup>M</sup> *sudorífero*

nerve
*nervio*<sup>M</sup>

blood vessel
*vaso*<sup>M</sup> *sanguíneo*

eccrine sweat gland
*glándula*<sup>F</sup> *sudorípara ecrina*

hair follicle
*folículo*<sup>M</sup> *piloso*

papilla
*papila*<sup>F</sup>

apocrine sweat gland
*glándula*<sup>F</sup> *sudorípara apocrina*

hair bulb
*bulbo*<sup>M</sup> *piloso*

**finger**
*dedo*<sup>M</sup>

dermis
*dermis*<sup>F</sup>

nail matrix
*matriz*<sup>F</sup> *ungular*

lunula
*lúnula*<sup>F</sup>

epidermis
*epidermis*<sup>F</sup>

body of nail
*cuerpo*<sup>M</sup> *de la uña*<sup>F</sup>

middle phalanx
*falangina*<sup>F</sup>

free margin
*extremo*<sup>M</sup> *libre*

distal phalanx
*falangeta*<sup>F</sup>

digital pulp
*yema*<sup>F</sup>

root of nail
*raíz*<sup>F</sup> *de la uña*<sup>F</sup>

nail bed
*lecho*<sup>M</sup> *ungular*

touch

**hand**
***mano***<sup>F</sup>

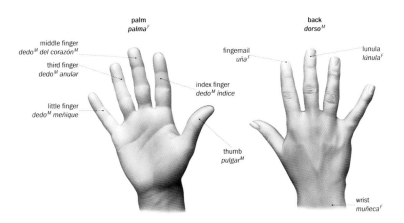

palm
*palma*<sup>F</sup>

back
*dorso*<sup>M</sup>

middle finger
*dedo*<sup>M</sup> *del corazón*<sup>M</sup>

third finger
*dedo*<sup>M</sup> *anular*

little finger
*dedo*<sup>M</sup> *meñique*

index finger
*dedo*<sup>M</sup> *índice*

thumb
*pulgar*<sup>M</sup>

fingernail
*uña*<sup>F</sup>

lunula
*lúnula*<sup>F</sup>

wrist
*muñeca*<sup>F</sup>

HUMAN BEING

hearing
*oído*<sup>M</sup>

**auricle**
***pabellón***<sup>M</sup> ***auricular***

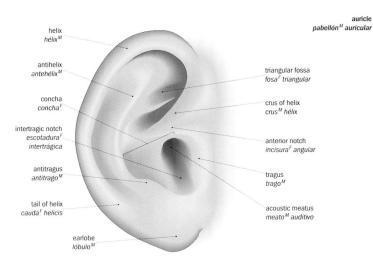

helix
*hélix*<sup>M</sup>

antihelix
*antehélix*<sup>M</sup>

concha
*concha*<sup>F</sup>

intertragic notch
*escotadura*<sup>F</sup>
*intertrágica*

antitragus
*antitrago*<sup>M</sup>

tail of helix
*cauda*<sup>F</sup> *helicis*

earlobe
*lóbulo*<sup>M</sup>

triangular fossa
*fosa*<sup>F</sup> *triangular*

crus of helix
*crus*<sup>M</sup> *hélix*

anterior notch
*incisura*<sup>F</sup> *angular*

tragus
*trago*<sup>M</sup>

acoustic meatus
*meato*<sup>M</sup> *auditivo*

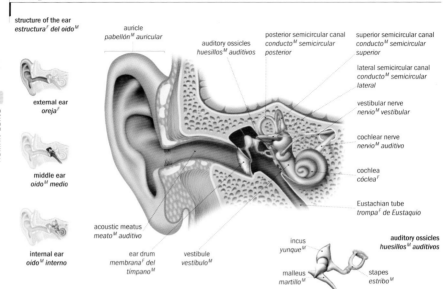

structure of the ear
*estructura$^F$ del oído$^M$*

external ear
*oreja$^F$*

middle ear
*oído$^M$ medio*

internal ear
*oído$^M$ interno*

auricle
*pabellón$^M$ auricular*

auditory ossicles
*huesillos$^M$ auditivos*

posterior semicircular canal
*conducto$^M$ semicircular posterior*

superior semicircular canal
*conducto$^M$ semicircular superior*

lateral semicircular canal
*conducto$^M$ semicircular lateral*

vestibular nerve
*nervio$^M$ vestibular*

cochlear nerve
*nervio$^M$ auditivo*

cochlea
*cóclea$^F$*

Eustachian tube
*trompa$^F$ de Eustaquio*

acoustic meatus
*meato$^M$ auditivo*

ear drum
*membrana$^F$ del tímpano$^M$*

vestibule
*vestíbulo$^M$*

incus
*yunque$^M$*

malleus
*martillo$^M$*

auditory ossicles
*huesillos$^M$ auditivos*

stapes
*estribo$^M$*

# smell and taste
*olfato$^M$ y gusto$^M$*

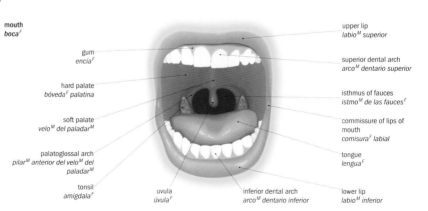

mouth
*boca$^F$*

gum
*encía$^F$*

hard palate
*bóveda$^F$ palatina*

soft palate
*velo$^M$ del paladar$^M$*

palatoglossal arch
*pilar$^M$ anterior del velo$^M$ del paladar$^M$*

tonsil
*amígdala$^F$*

uvula
*úvula$^F$*

inferior dental arch
*arco$^M$ dentario inferior*

upper lip
*labio$^M$ superior*

superior dental arch
*arco$^M$ dentario superior*

isthmus of fauces
*istmo$^M$ de las fauces$^F$*

commissure of lips of mouth
*comisura$^F$ labial*

tongue
*lengua$^F$*

lower lip
*labio$^M$ inferior*

HUMAN BEING

external nose
nariz^F

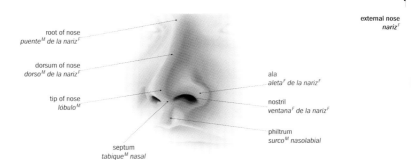

root of nose
puente^M de la nariz^F

dorsum of nose
dorso^M de la nariz^F

tip of nose
lóbulo^M

septum
tabique^M nasal

ala
aleta^F de la nariz^F

nostril
ventana^F de la nariz^F

philtrum
surco^M nasolabial

nasal fossae
fosas^F nasales

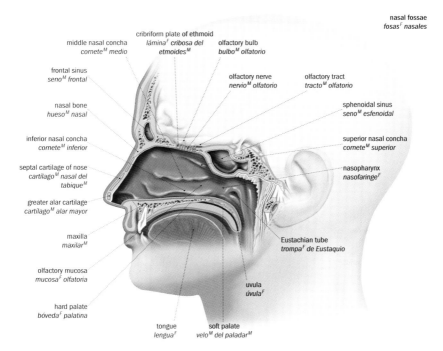

middle nasal concha
cornete^M medio

cribriform plate of ethmoid
lámina^F cribosa del
etmoides^M

olfactory bulb
bulbo^M olfatorio

frontal sinus
seno^M frontal

nasal bone
hueso^M nasal

inferior nasal concha
cornete^M inferior

septal cartilage of nose
cartílago^M nasal del
tabique^M

greater alar cartilage
cartílago^M alar mayor

maxilla
maxilar^M

olfactory mucosa
mucosa^F olfatoria

hard palate
bóveda^F palatina

olfactory nerve
nervio^M olfatorio

olfactory tract
tracto^M olfatorio

sphenoidal sinus
seno^M esfenoidal

superior nasal concha
cornete^M superior

nasopharynx
nasofaringe^F

Eustachian tube
trompa^F de Eustaquio

uvula
úvula^F

tongue
lengua^F

soft palate
velo^M del paladar^M

smell and taste

**dorsum of tongue**
*lengua<sup>F</sup>*

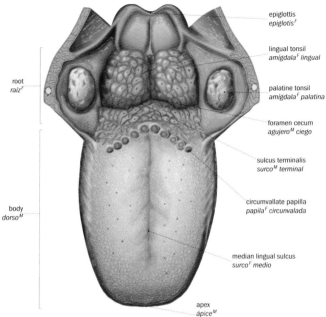

epiglottis
*epiglotis<sup>F</sup>*

lingual tonsil
*amígdala<sup>F</sup> lingual*

palatine tonsil
*amígdala<sup>F</sup> palatina*

root
*raíz<sup>F</sup>*

foramen cecum
*agujero<sup>M</sup> ciego*

sulcus terminalis
*surco<sup>M</sup> terminal*

circumvallate papilla
*papila<sup>F</sup> circunvalada*

body
*dorso<sup>M</sup>*

median lingual sulcus
*surco<sup>F</sup> medio*

apex
*ápice<sup>M</sup>*

**taste receptors**
*receptores<sup>M</sup> gustativos*

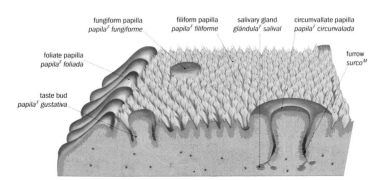

fungiform papilla
*papila<sup>F</sup> fungiforme*

filiform papilla
*papila<sup>F</sup> filiforme*

salivary gland
*glándula<sup>F</sup> salival*

circumvallate papilla
*papila<sup>F</sup> circunvalada*

foliate papilla
*papila<sup>F</sup> foliada*

furrow
*surco<sup>M</sup>*

taste bud
*papila<sup>F</sup> gustativa*

# sight
*vista* F

**eye**
*ojo* M

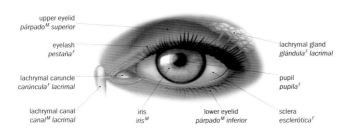

upper eyelid
*párpado* M *superior*

eyelash
*pestaña* F

lachrymal caruncle
*carúncula* F *lacrimal*

lachrymal canal
*canal* M *lacrimal*

iris
*iris* M

lower eyelid
*párpado* M *inferior*

lachrymal gland
*glándula* F *lacrimal*

pupil
*pupila* F

sclera
*esclerótica* F

**eyeball**
*globo* M *ocular*

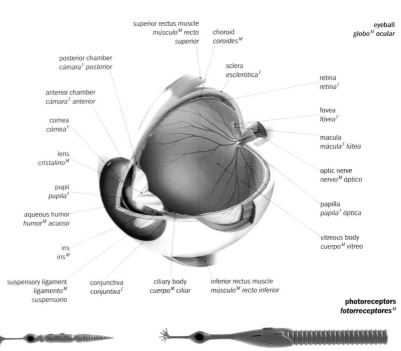

superior rectus muscle
*músculo* M *recto superior*

choroid
*coroides* M

posterior chamber
*cámara* F *posterior*

sclera
*esclerótica* F

anterior chamber
*cámara* F *anterior*

cornea
*córnea* F

lens
*cristalino* M

pupil
*pupila* F

aqueous humor
*humor* M *acuoso*

iris
*iris* M

suspensory ligament
*ligamento* M *suspensorio*

conjunctiva
*conjuntiva* F

ciliary body
*cuerpo* M *ciliar*

inferior rectus muscle
*músculo* M *recto inferior*

retina
*retina* F

fovea
*fóvea* F

macula
*mácula* F *lútea*

optic nerve
*nervio* M *óptico*

papilla
*papilla* F *óptica*

vitreous body
*cuerpo* M *vítreo*

**photoreceptors**
*fotorreceptores* M

cone
*cono* M

rod
*bastoncillo* M

# supermarket

*supermercado* M

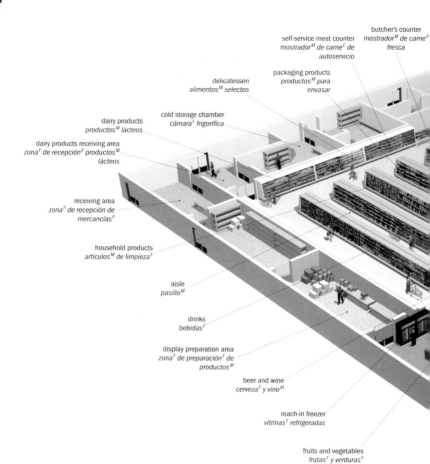

butcher's counter
*mostrador* M *de carne* F
*fresca*

self-service meat counter
*mostrador* M *de carne* F *de*
*autoservicio*

packaging products
*productos* M *para*
*envasar*

delicatessen
*alimentos* M *selectos*

cold storage chamber
*cámara* F *frigorífica*

dairy products
*productos* M *lácteos*

dairy products receiving area
*zona* F *de recepción* F *productos* M
*lácteos*

receiving area
*zona* F *de recepción de*
*mercancías* F

household products
*artículos* M *de limpieza* F

aisle
*pasillo* M

drinks
*bebidas* F

display preparation area
*zona* F *de preparación* F *de*
*productos* M

beer and wine
*cerveza* F *y vino* M

reach-in freezer
*vitrinas* F *refrigeradas*

fruits and vegetables
*frutas* F *y verduras* F

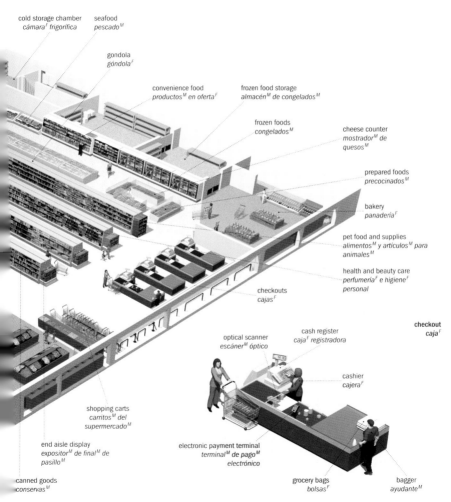

cold storage chamber
*cámara$^F$ frigorífica*

seafood
*pescado$^M$*

gondola
*góndola$^F$*

convenience food
*productos$^M$ en oferta$^F$*

frozen food storage
*almacén$^M$ de congelados$^M$*

frozen foods
*congelados$^M$*

cheese counter
*mostrador$^M$ de
quesos$^M$*

prepared foods
*precocinados$^M$*

bakery
*panadería$^F$*

pet food and supplies
*alimentos$^M$ y artículos$^M$ para
animales$^M$*

health and beauty care
*perfumería$^F$ e higiene$^F$
personal*

checkouts
*cajas$^F$*

checkout
*caja$^F$*

optical scanner
*escáner$^M$ óptico*

cash register
*caja$^F$ registradora*

cashier
*cajera$^F$*

shopping carts
*carritos$^M$ del
supermercado$^M$*

end aisle display
*expositor$^M$ de final$^M$ de
pasillo$^M$*

electronic payment terminal
*terminal$^M$ de pago$^M$
electrónico*

grocery bags
*bolsas$^F$*

bagger
*ayudante$^M$*

canned goods
*conservas$^M$*

# farmstead
*granja<sup>F</sup>*

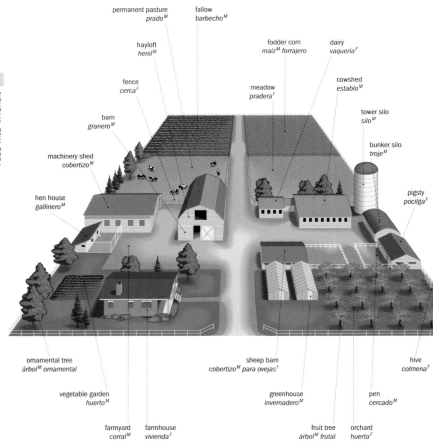

permanent pasture
*prado<sup>M</sup>*

fallow
*barbecho<sup>M</sup>*

hayloft
*henil<sup>M</sup>*

fodder corn
*maíz<sup>M</sup> forrajero*

dairy
*vaquería<sup>F</sup>*

fence
*cerca<sup>F</sup>*

meadow
*pradera<sup>F</sup>*

cowshed
*establo<sup>M</sup>*

barn
*granero<sup>M</sup>*

tower silo
*silo<sup>M</sup>*

machinery shed
*cobertizo<sup>M</sup>*

bunker silo
*troje<sup>M</sup>*

hen house
*gallinero<sup>M</sup>*

pigsty
*pocilga<sup>F</sup>*

ornamental tree
*árbol<sup>M</sup> ornamental*

sheep barn
*cobertizo<sup>M</sup> para ovejas<sup>F</sup>*

hive
*colmena<sup>F</sup>*

vegetable garden
*huerto<sup>M</sup>*

greenhouse
*invernadero<sup>M</sup>*

pen
*cercado<sup>M</sup>*

farmyard
*corral<sup>M</sup>*

farmhouse
*vivienda<sup>F</sup>*

fruit tree
*árbol<sup>M</sup> frutal*

orchard
*huerta<sup>F</sup>*

## mushrooms
*hongos*<sup>M</sup>

truffle
*trufa*<sup>F</sup>

wood ear
*oreja*<sup>F</sup> *de Judas*

royal agaric
*oronja*<sup>F</sup>

delicious lactarius
*mizcalo*<sup>M</sup>

enoki
*seta*<sup>F</sup> *enoki*

oyster
*orellana*<sup>F</sup>

cultivated mushrooms
*champiñón*<sup>M</sup>

green russula
*rusula*<sup>F</sup> *verde*

morels
*morilla*<sup>F</sup>

edible boletus
*boleto*<sup>M</sup> *comestible*

shitake
*shiitake*<sup>M</sup>

chanterelles
*rebozuelo*<sup>M</sup>

FOOD AND KITCHEN

## seaweed
*algas*<sup>F</sup>

arame
*arame*<sup>M</sup>

wakame
*wakame*<sup>M</sup>

kombu
*kombu*<sup>M</sup>

spirulina
*espirulina*<sup>F</sup>

Irish moss
*Irish moss*<sup>M</sup>

hijiki
*hijiki*<sup>M</sup>

sea lettuce
*lechuga*<sup>F</sup> *marina*

agar-agar
*agar-agar*<sup>M</sup>

nori
*nori*<sup>M</sup>

dulse
*dulse*<sup>M</sup>

# vegetables
*hortalizas*<sup>F</sup>

## bulb vegetables
**bulbos**<sup>M</sup>

shallot
*chalote*<sup>M</sup>

water chestnut
*castaña*<sup>F</sup> *de agua*

green onion
*cebolla*<sup>F</sup> *tierna*

scallion
*cebolla*<sup>F</sup> *tierna*

garlic
*ajo*<sup>M</sup>

chives
*cebollino*<sup>M</sup>

leeks
*puerros*<sup>M</sup>

yellow onion
*cebolla*<sup>F</sup> *amarilla*

red onion
*cebolla*<sup>F</sup> *roja*

white onion
*cebolla*<sup>F</sup> *blanca*

pickling onions
*cebolletas*<sup>M</sup>

## tuber vegetables
**tubérculos**<sup>M</sup>

cassava
*mandioca*<sup>F</sup>

crosne
*crosne*<sup>M</sup>

taro
*taro*<sup>M</sup>

jicama
*jicama*<sup>F</sup>

tropical yam
*batata*<sup>F</sup>

Jerusalem artichoke
*aguaturma*<sup>F</sup>

sweet potato
*batata*<sup>F</sup>

potatoes
*patatas*<sup>F</sup>

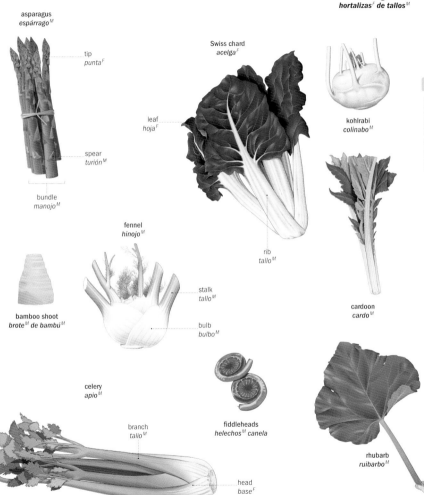

**stalk vegetables**
*hortalizas<sup>F</sup> de tallos<sup>M</sup>*

asparagus
*espárrago<sup>M</sup>*

tip
*punta<sup>F</sup>*

spear
*turión<sup>M</sup>*

bundle
*manojo<sup>M</sup>*

Swiss chard
*acelga<sup>F</sup>*

leaf
*hoja<sup>F</sup>*

rib
*tallo<sup>M</sup>*

kohlrabi
*colinabo<sup>M</sup>*

fennel
*hinojo<sup>M</sup>*

stalk
*tallo<sup>M</sup>*

bulb
*bulbo<sup>M</sup>*

bamboo shoot
*brote<sup>M</sup> de bambú<sup>M</sup>*

cardoon
*cardo<sup>M</sup>*

celery
*apio<sup>M</sup>*

branch
*tallo<sup>M</sup>*

fiddleheads
*helechos<sup>M</sup> canela*

head
*base<sup>F</sup>*

rhubarb
*ruibarbo<sup>M</sup>*

FOOD AND KITCHEN

125

# leaf vegetables
*verduras<sup>F</sup> de hojas<sup>F</sup>*

leaf lettuce
*lechuga<sup>F</sup> rizada*

romaine lettuce
*lechuga<sup>F</sup> romana*

celtuce
*lechuga<sup>F</sup> de tallo<sup>M</sup>*

sea kale
*col<sup>F</sup> marina*

collards
*berza<sup>F</sup>*

escarole
*escarola<sup>F</sup>*

butter lettuce
*lechuga<sup>F</sup> de cogollo<sup>M</sup>*

iceberg lettuce
*lechuga<sup>F</sup> iceberg*

radicchio
*achicoria<sup>F</sup> de Treviso*

ornamental kale
*col<sup>F</sup> ornamental*

curly kale
*col<sup>F</sup> rizada*

grape leaves
*hoja<sup>F</sup> de parra<sup>F</sup>*

brussels sprouts
*coles<sup>F</sup> de Bruselas*

red cabbage
*col<sup>F</sup> lombarda*

white cabbage
*col<sup>F</sup>/repollo<sup>M</sup>*

savoy cabbage
*col<sup>F</sup> rizada de otoño<sup>M</sup>*

green cabbage
*col<sup>F</sup> verde/repollo<sup>M</sup> verde*

pe-tsai
*col<sup>F</sup> china*

bok choy
*pak-choi<sup>M</sup>*

purslane
*verdolaga*<sup>F</sup>

nettle
*ortiga*<sup>F</sup>

watercress
*berro*<sup>M</sup>

dandelion
*diente*<sup>M</sup> *de león*

corn salad
*colleja*<sup>F</sup>

arugula
*ruqueta*<sup>F</sup>

spinach
*espinaca*<sup>F</sup>

garden cress
*berros*<sup>M</sup> *de jardín*

garden sorrel
*acedera*<sup>F</sup>

curly endive
*escarola*<sup>F</sup> *rizada*

Belgian endive
*endivia*<sup>F</sup>

FOOD AND KITCHEN

**inflorescent vegetables**
*inflorescencias*<sup>F</sup>

cauliflower
*coliflor*<sup>F</sup>

broccoli
*brécol*<sup>M</sup>

Gai-lohn
*brécol*<sup>M</sup> *chino*

broccoli rabe
*nabiza*<sup>F</sup>

artichoke
*alcachofa*<sup>F</sup>

FOOD AND KITCHEN

**fruit vegetables**
*hortalizas<sup>F</sup> de fruto<sup>M</sup>*

avocado
*aguacate<sup>M</sup>*

tomato
*tomate<sup>M</sup>*

currant tomatoes
*tomates<sup>M</sup> en rama<sup>F</sup>*

tomatillos
*tomatillos<sup>M</sup>*

olives
*aceitunas<sup>F</sup>*

yellow sweet pepper
*pimiento<sup>M</sup> dulce
amarillo*

green sweet pepper
*pimiento<sup>M</sup> dulce verde*

red sweet pepper
*pimiento<sup>M</sup> dulce rojo*

hot pepper
*chile<sup>M</sup>*

okra
*gombo<sup>M</sup>, quingombó<sup>M</sup>*

gherkin
*pepinillo<sup>M</sup>*

cucumber
*pepino<sup>M</sup>*

seedless cucumber
*pepino<sup>M</sup> sin pepitas<sup>F</sup>*

wax gourd (winter
melon)
*calabaza<sup>F</sup> de China*

eggplant
*berenjena<sup>F</sup>*

summer squash
*calabacín<sup>M</sup>*

zucchini
*calabacín<sup>M</sup>*

bitter melon
*pepino<sup>M</sup> amargo*

pattypan squash
*calabaza<sup>F</sup> bonetera
amarilla*

crookneck squash
*calabaza<sup>F</sup> de cuello
retorcido*

straightneck squash
*calabaza<sup>F</sup> de cuello largo*

chayote
*chayote<sup>M</sup>*

pumpkin
*calabaza<sup>F</sup> común*

spaghetti squash
*calabaza<sup>F</sup> romana*

acorn squash
*calabaza<sup>F</sup> bonetera*

autumn squash
*cidra<sup>F</sup> cayote*

FOOD AND KITCHEN

**root vegetables**
*raíces<sup>F</sup>*

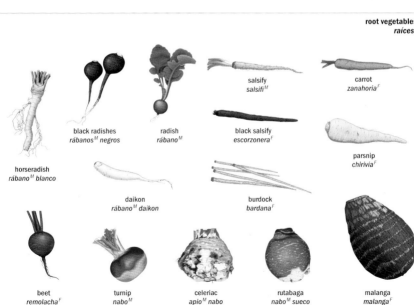

horseradish
*rábano<sup>M</sup> blanco*

black radishes
*rábanos<sup>M</sup> negros*

radish
*rábano<sup>M</sup>*

salsify
*salsifi<sup>M</sup>*

black salsify
*escorzonera<sup>F</sup>*

carrot
*zanahoria<sup>F</sup>*

parsnip
*chirivía<sup>F</sup>*

daikon
*rábano<sup>M</sup> daikon*

burdock
*bardana<sup>F</sup>*

beet
*remolacha<sup>F</sup>*

turnip
*nabo<sup>M</sup>*

celeriac
*apio<sup>M</sup> nabo*

rutabaga
*nabo<sup>M</sup> sueco*

malanga
*malanga<sup>F</sup>*

# legumes
*legumbres*<sup>F</sup>

FOOD AND KITCHEN

alfalfa sprouts
*alfalfa*<sup>F</sup>

lupines
*altramuz*<sup>M</sup>

lentils
*lentejas*<sup>F</sup>

peanut
*cacahuete*<sup>M</sup>

broad beans
*habas*<sup>F</sup>

**peas**
**guisantes**<sup>M</sup>

**dolichos beans**
**dolichos**<sup>M</sup>

chick peas
*garbanzos*<sup>M</sup>

split peas
*guisantes*<sup>M</sup> *partidos*

black-eyed peas
*judía*<sup>F</sup> *de ojo*

lablab beans
*judía*<sup>F</sup> *de Egipto*

green peas
*guisantes*<sup>M</sup>

snow peas
*guisantes*<sup>M</sup> *mollares*

yard-long beans
*judía*<sup>F</sup> *china larga*

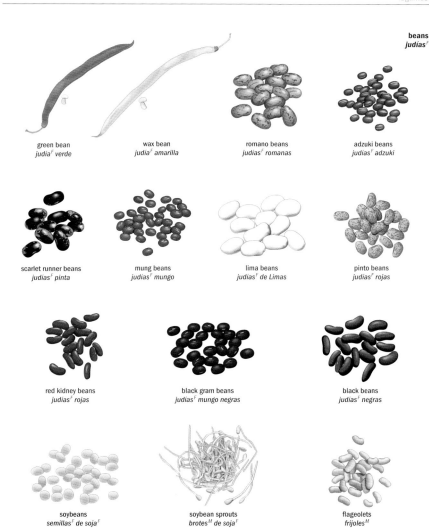

beans
*judías*<sup>F</sup>

green bean
*judía*<sup>F</sup> *verde*

wax bean
*judía*<sup>F</sup> *amarilla*

romano beans
*judías*<sup>F</sup> *romanas*

adzuki beans
*judías*<sup>F</sup> *adzuki*

scarlet runner beans
*judías*<sup>F</sup> *pinta*

mung beans
*judías*<sup>F</sup> *mungo*

lima beans
*judías*<sup>F</sup> *de Limas*

pinto beans
*judías*<sup>F</sup> *rojas*

red kidney beans
*judías*<sup>F</sup> *rojas*

black gram beans
*judías*<sup>F</sup> *mungo negras*

black beans
*judías*<sup>F</sup> *negras*

soybeans
*semillas*<sup>F</sup> *de soja*<sup>F</sup>

soybean sprouts
*brotes*<sup>M</sup> *de soja*<sup>F</sup>

flageolets
*frijoles*<sup>M</sup>

# fruits
*frutas*$^F$

**berries**
*bayas*$^F$

currants
*grosellas*$^F$

black currants
*grosellas*$^F$ *negras*

gooseberries
*grosellas*$^F$ *espinosas*

grapes
*uvas*$^F$

blueberries
*arándanos*$^M$

bilberries
*arándanos*$^M$ *negros*

red whortleberries
*arándanos*$^M$ *rojos*

alkekengi
*alquequenje*$^M$

cranberries
*arándanos*$^M$ *agrios*

raspberries
*frambuesas*$^F$

blackberries
*moras*$^F$

strawberries
*fresas*$^F$

**stone fruits**
*drupas*$^F$

plums
*ciruelas*$^F$

peach
*melocotón*$^M$

nectarine
*nectarina*$^F$

apricot
*albaricoque*$^M$

cherries
*cerezas*$^F$

dates
*dátiles*$^M$

**dry fruits**
*frutas*<sup>F</sup> *secas*

macadamia nuts
*nuezes*<sup>F</sup> *de*
*macadamia*<sup>F</sup>

ginkgo nuts
*nuezes*<sup>F</sup> *de ginkgo*

pistachio nuts
*pistachos*<sup>M</sup>

pine nuts
*piñones*<sup>M</sup>

cola nuts
*nuezes*<sup>F</sup> *de cola*

pecan nuts
*pecanas*<sup>F</sup>

cashews
*anacardos*<sup>M</sup>

almonds
*almendras*<sup>F</sup>

hazelnuts
*avellanas*<sup>F</sup>

walnut
*nuez*<sup>F</sup>

coconut
*coco*<sup>M</sup>

chestnuts
*castañas*<sup>M</sup>

beechnut
*hayuco*<sup>M</sup>

Brazil nuts
*neuzes*<sup>F</sup> *del Brasil*<sup>M</sup>

**pome fruits**
*frutas*<sup>F</sup> *pomo*

pear
*pera*<sup>F</sup>

quince
*membrillo*<sup>M</sup>

apple
*manzana*<sup>F</sup>

Japanese plums
*nísperos*<sup>M</sup>

FOOD AND KITCHEN

**citrus fruits**
*cítricos*$^M$

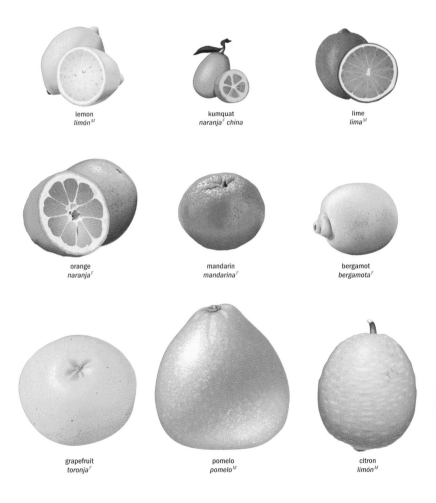

lemon
*limón*$^M$

kumquat
*naranja*$^F$ *china*

lime
*lima*$^M$

orange
*naranja*$^F$

mandarin
*mandarina*$^F$

bergamot
*bergamota*$^F$

grapefruit
*toronja*$^F$

pomelo
*pomelo*$^M$

citron
*limón*$^M$

**melons**
*melones*<sup>M</sup>

cantaloupe
*melón*<sup>M</sup> *cantalupo*

casaba melon
*melón*<sup>M</sup> *invernal*

honeydew melon
*melón*<sup>M</sup> *de miel*

muskmelon
*melón*<sup>M</sup> *escrito*

canary melon
*melón*<sup>M</sup> *amarillo*

watermelon
*sandía*<sup>F</sup>

Ogen melon
*melón*<sup>M</sup> *de Ogen*

fruits

**tropical fruits**
*frutas*<sup>F</sup> **tropicales**

plantain
*plátano*<sup>M</sup>

banana
*banana*<sup>F</sup>

longan
*longan*<sup>M</sup>

tamarillo
*tamarillo*<sup>M</sup>

passion fruit
*fruta*<sup>F</sup> *de la pasión*<sup>F</sup>

horned melon
*kiwano*<sup>M</sup>

mangosteen
*mangostán*<sup>M</sup>

kiwi
*kiwi*<sup>M</sup>

pomegranate
*granada*<sup>F</sup>

cherimoya
*chirimoya*<sup>F</sup>

jackfruit
*fruta*<sup>F</sup> *de jack*

pineapple
*piña*<sup>F</sup>

jaboticabas
*jaboticaba*<sup>F</sup>

litchi
*lichi*<sup>M</sup>

fig
*higo*<sup>M</sup>

Chinese dates
*jojoba*<sup>F</sup>

sapodilla
*zapote*<sup>M</sup>

guava
*guayaba*<sup>F</sup>

rambutan
*rambután*<sup>M</sup>

Japanese persimmon
*caqui*<sup>M</sup>

prickly pear
*higo*<sup>M</sup> *chumbo*

carambola
*carambola*<sup>F</sup>

Asian pear
*pera*<sup>F</sup> *asiática*

mango
*mango*<sup>M</sup>

durian
*durión*<sup>M</sup>

papaya
*papaya*<sup>F</sup>

pepino
*pepino*<sup>M</sup> *dulce*

feijoa
*feijoa*<sup>F</sup>

# spices
*especias^F*

juniper berries
*bayas^F de enebro^M*

cloves
*clavos^M*

allspice
*pimienta^F de Jamaica*

white mustard
*mostaza^F blanca*

black mustard
*mostaza^F negra*

black pepper
*pimienta^F negra*

white pepper
*pimienta^F blanca*

pink pepper
*pimienta^F rosa*

green pepper
*pimienta^F verde*

nutmeg
*nuez^F moscada*

caraway
*alcaravea^F*

cardamom
*cardamomo^M*

cinnamon
*canela^F*

saffron
*azafrán^M*

cumin
*comino^M*

curry
*curry^M*

turmeric
*cúrcuma^F*

fenugreek
*fenogreco^M*

jalapeño chile
*chile^M jalapeño*

bird's eye chile
*guindilla^F*

crushed chiles
*guindilla^F triturada*

dried chiles
*guindilla^F seca^M*

cayenne pepper
*pimienta^F de cayena^F*

paprika
*pimentón^M*

ajowan
*ajowán^M*

asafetida
*asafétida^F*

garam masala
*garam masala^M*

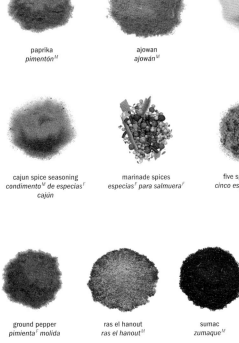

cajun spice seasoning
*condimento^M de especias^F cajún*

marinade spices
*especias^F para salmuera^F*

five spice powder
*cinco especias^F chinas*

chili powder
*guindilla^F molida*

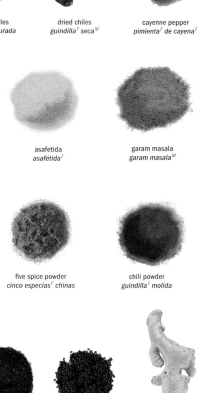

ground pepper
*pimienta^F molida*

ras el hanout
*ras el hanout^M*

sumac
*zumaque^M*

poppy seeds
*semillas^F de adormidera^F*

ginger
*jengibre^M*

# condiments
*condimentos*<sup>M</sup>

Tabasco® sauce
*salsa*<sup>F</sup> *Tobasco*<sup>®M</sup>

Worcestershire sauce
*salsa*<sup>F</sup> *Worcertershire*

tamarind paste
*salsa*<sup>F</sup> *de tamarindo*<sup>M</sup>

vanilla extract
*extracto*<sup>M</sup> *de vainilla*<sup>F</sup>

tomato paste
*concentrado*<sup>M</sup> *de
tomate*<sup>M</sup>

tomato sauce
*salsa*<sup>F</sup> *de tomate*<sup>M</sup>

hummus
*hummus*<sup>M</sup>

tahini
*tajin*<sup>M</sup>

hoisin sauce
*salsa*<sup>F</sup> *hoisin*

soy sauce
*salsa*<sup>F</sup> *de soja*<sup>F</sup>

powdered mustard
*mostaza*<sup>F</sup> *en polvo*<sup>M</sup>

wholegrain mustard
*mostaza*<sup>F</sup> *en grano*<sup>M</sup>

Dijon mustard
*mostaza*<sup>F</sup> *de Dijon*

German mustard
*mostaza*<sup>F</sup> *alemana*

English mustard
*mostaza*<sup>F</sup> *inglesa*

American mustard
*mostaza*<sup>F</sup> *americana*

plum sauce
*salsa^F de ciruelas^F*

mango chutney
*chutney^M de mango^M*

harissa
*harissa^F*

sambal oelek
*sambal oelek^M*

ketchup
*ketchup^M*

wasabi
*wasabi^M*

table salt
*sal^F de mesa^F*

coarse salt
*sal^F gorda*

sea salt
*sal^F marina*

balsamic vinegar
*vinagre^M balsámico*

rice vinegar
*vinagre^M de arroz^M*

apple cider vinegar
*vinagre^M de manzana^F*

malt vinegar
*vinagre^M de malta^F*

wine vinegar
*vinagre^M de vino^M*

FOOD AND KITCHEN

# herbs
*hierbas$^F$ aromáticas*

dill
*eneldo$^M$*

anise
*anis$^M$*

sweet bay
*laurel$^M$*

oregano
*orégano$^M$*

tarragon
*estragón$^M$*

basil
*albahaca$^F$*

sage
*salvia$^F$*

thyme
*tomillo$^M$*

mint
*hierbabuena$^F$*

parsley
*perejii$^M$*

chervil
*perifollo$^M$*

coriander
*cilantro$^M$*

rosemary
*romero$^M$*

hyssop
*hisopo$^M$*

borage
*borraja$^F$*

lovage
*alheña$^F$*

savory
*ajedrea$^F$*

lemon balm
*melisa$^F$*

# cereal
*cereales* $^M$

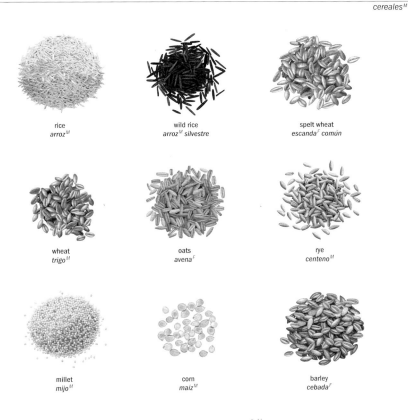

rice
*arroz* $^M$

wild rice
*arroz* $^M$ *silvestre*

spelt wheat
*escanda* $^F$ *común*

wheat
*trigo* $^M$

oats
*avena* $^F$

rye
*centeno* $^M$

millet
*mijo* $^M$

corn
*maíz* $^M$

barley
*cebada* $^F$

buckwheat
*trigo* $^M$ *sarraceno*

quinoa
*quinua* $^F$

amaranth
*amaranto* $^M$

triticale
*triticale* $^M$

# cereal products
*cereales*<sup>M</sup>

## flour and semolina
**harina*<sup>F</sup> y sémola*<sup>F</sup>**

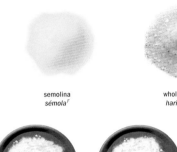

semolina
*sémola*<sup>F</sup>

whole-wheat flour
*harina*<sup>F</sup> *integral*

couscous
*cuscús*<sup>M</sup>

all-purpose flour
*harina*<sup>F</sup> *común*

unbleached flour
*harina*<sup>F</sup> *sin blanquear*

oat flour
*harina*<sup>F</sup> *de avena*<sup>F</sup>

corn flour
*harina*<sup>F</sup> *de maíz*<sup>M</sup>

## bread
*pan*<sup>M</sup>

croissant
*cruasán*<sup>M</sup>

black rye bread
*pan*<sup>M</sup> *de centeno*<sup>M</sup>
*negro*

bagel
*rosquilla*<sup>F</sup>

Greek bread
*pan*<sup>M</sup> *griego*

baguette
*barra*<sup>F</sup> *de pan*<sup>M</sup>

ear loaf
*pan*<sup>M</sup> *espiga*<sup>F</sup>

French bread
*baguette*<sup>F</sup>

chapati
*pan^M indio chapati*

tortillas
*tortillas^F*

pita bread
*pan^M de pita^F*

naan
*pan^M indio naan*

unleavened bread
*pan^M ácimo*

cracked rye bread
*galleta^F de centeno^M*

Scandinavian cracked bread
*galleta^F escandinava*

phyllo dough
*pasta^F de hojaldre^M*

Danish rye bread
*pan^M danés de centeno^M*

American corn bread
*pan^M americano de maíz^M*

multigrain bread
*pan^M multicereales*

Russian pumpernickel
*pan^M negro ruso*

German rye bread
*pan^M alemán de centeno^M*

challah
*pan^M judío hallah*

white bread
*pan^M blanco*

wholemeal bread
*pan^M integral*

farmhouse bread
*pan^M campesino*

Irish soda bread
*pan^M irlandés*

English loaf
*pan^M de flor^F*

**pasta**
*pasta*<sup>F</sup>

rigatoni
*rigatoni*<sup>M</sup>

rotini
*sacacorchos*<sup>M</sup>

conchiglie
*conchitas*<sup>F</sup>

fusilli
*fusilli*<sup>M</sup>

spaghetti
*espagueti*<sup>M</sup>

ditali
*dedalitos*<sup>M</sup>

gnocchi
*ñoquis*<sup>M</sup>

tortellini
*tortellini*<sup>M</sup>

spaghettini
*fideos*<sup>M</sup>

elbows
*tiburones*<sup>M</sup>

penne
*macarrones*<sup>M</sup>

cannelloni
*canelones*<sup>M</sup>

lasagna
*lasañas*<sup>F</sup>

ravioli
*raviolis*<sup>M</sup>

spinach tagliatelle
*tallarines*<sup>M</sup> *de espinacas*<sup>F</sup>

fettucine
*fetuchinas*<sup>F</sup>

**Asian noodles**
*fideos*$^M$ *asiáticos*

soba noodles
*fideos*$^M$ *de soba*$^F$

somen noodles
*fideos*$^M$ *de somen*$^M$

udon noodles
*fideos*$^M$ *de udon*$^M$

rice paper
*galletas*$^F$ *de arroz*$^M$

rice noodles
*fideos*$^M$ *de arroz*$^M$

bean thread cellophane noodles
*fideos*$^M$ *de judías*$^F$ *mungo*

egg noodles
*fideos*$^M$ *de huevo*$^M$

rice vermicelli
*vermicelli*$^M$ *de arroz*$^M$

won ton skins
*pasta*$^F$ *won ton*

**rice**
*arroz*$^M$

white rice
*arroz*$^M$ *blanco*

brown rice
*arroz*$^M$ *integral*

parboiled rice
*arroz*$^M$ *vaporizado*

basmati rice
*arroz*$^M$ *basmati*

# coffee and infusions
*café^M y infusionnes^F*

**coffee**
*café^M*

green coffee beans
*granos^M verdes de café^M*

roasted coffee beans
*granos^M torrefactos de café^M*

**herbal teas**
*tisanas^F*

linden
*tila^F*

chamomile
*manzanilla^F*

verbena
*verbena^F*

**tea**
*té^M*

green tea
*té^M verde*

black tea
*té^M negro*

oolong tea
*té^M oolong*

tea bag
*bolsita^F de té^M*

# chocolate
*chocolate^M*

dark chocolate
*chocolate^M amargo*

milk chocolate
*chocolate^M con leche^F*

cocoa
*cacao^M*

white chocolate
*chocolate^M blanco*

# sugar
*azúcar^M*

granulated sugar
*azúcar^M granulado*

powdered sugar
*azúcar^M glas*

brown sugar
*azúcar^M moreno*

rock candy
*azúcar^M candi*

molasses
*melazas^F*

corn syrup
*jarabe^M de maíz^M*

maple syrup
*jarabe^M de arce^M*

honey
*miel^M*

# fats and oils
*grasas^F y aceites^M*

corn oil
*aceite^M de maíz^M*

olive oil
*aceite^M de oliva^F*

sunflower-seed oil
*aceite^M de girasol^M*

peanut oil
*aceite^M de cacahuete^M*

sesame oil
*aceite^M de sésamo^M*

shortening
*grasa^F para cocinar*

lard
*manteca^F de cerdo^M*

margarine
*margarina^F*

# dairy products
*productos^M lácteos*

yogurt
*yogur^M*

ghee
*mantequilla^F clarificada*

butter
*mantequilla^M*

## cream
*nata^F*

whipping cream
*nata^F de montar*

sour cream
*nata^F agria*

## milk
*leche^M*

homogenized milk
*leche^F homogeneizada*

goat's milk
*leche^F de cabra*

evaporated milk
*leche^F evaporada*

buttermilk
*suero^M de la leche^F*

powdered milk
*leche^F en polvo^M*

## fresh cheeses
*quesos^M frescos*

cottage cheese
*queso^M cottage*

mozzarella
*mozzarella^F*

ricotta
*ricotta^F*

cream cheese
*queso^M cremoso*

## goat's-milk cheeses
*quesos^M de cabra^F*

chèvre cheese
*queso^M chèvre*

Crottin de Chavignol
*Crottin^M de Chavignol*

dairy products

FOOD AND KITCHEN

**pressed cheeses**
*quesos*<sup>M</sup> *prensados*

Jarlsberg
*jarlsberg*<sup>M</sup>

Emmenthal
*emmenthal*<sup>M</sup>

raclette
*raclette*<sup>F</sup>

Parmesan
*parmesano*<sup>M</sup>

Gruyère
*gruyère*<sup>M</sup>

Romano
*pecorino romano*<sup>M</sup>

**blue-veined cheeses**
*quesos*<sup>M</sup> *azules*

Roquefort
*roquefort*<sup>M</sup>

Stilton
*stilton*<sup>M</sup>

Gorgonzola
*gorgonzola*<sup>M</sup>

Danish Blue
*azul danés*<sup>M</sup>

**soft cheeses**
*quesos*<sup>M</sup> *blandos*

Pont-l'Évêque
*Pont-l'Éveque*<sup>M</sup>

Coulommiers
*coulommiers*<sup>M</sup>

Camembert
*camembert*<sup>M</sup>

Brie
*brie*<sup>M</sup>

Munster
*munster*<sup>M</sup>

# meat
*carne*<sup>F</sup>

**cuts of beef**
***cortes*<sup>M</sup> *de vacuno*<sup>M</sup>**

steak
*bistec*<sup>M</sup>

beef cubes
*carne*<sup>F</sup> *de vacuno*<sup>M</sup> *troceada*

ground beef
*carne*<sup>F</sup> *picada*

shank
*morcillo*<sup>M</sup>

tenderloin roast
*lomo*<sup>M</sup>

rib roast
*chuletón*<sup>M</sup>

back ribs
*costillar*<sup>M</sup>

**cuts of veal**
***cortes*<sup>M</sup> *de ternera*<sup>F</sup>**

veal cubes
*carne*<sup>F</sup> *de ternera*<sup>F</sup> *troceada*

ground veal
*carne*<sup>F</sup> *picada de ternera*<sup>F</sup>

shank
*paleta*<sup>F</sup>

roast
*asado*<sup>M</sup>

steak
*bistec*<sup>M</sup>

chop
*chuleta*<sup>F</sup>

**cuts of lamb**
*cortes<sup>M</sup> de cordero<sup>M</sup>*

chop
*chuleta<sup>F</sup>*

ground lamb
*carne<sup>F</sup> picada de cordero<sup>M</sup>*

lamb cubes
*carne<sup>F</sup> de cordero<sup>M</sup> troceada*

roast
*pierna<sup>F</sup> de cordero<sup>M</sup>*

shank
*paletilla<sup>F</sup>*

**cuts of pork**
*cortes<sup>M</sup> de cerdo<sup>M</sup>*

spareribs
*costillar<sup>M</sup>*

ground pork
*carne<sup>F</sup> picada de cerdo<sup>M</sup>*

hock
*codillo<sup>M</sup>*

loin chop
*chuleta<sup>F</sup>*

smoked ham
*jamón<sup>M</sup> ahumado*

roast
*asado<sup>M</sup> de cerdo<sup>M</sup>*

# organ meat
*despojos*<sup>M</sup>

sweetbreads
*mollejas*<sup>F</sup>

heart
*corazón*<sup>M</sup>

liver
*hígado*<sup>M</sup>

marrow
*médula*<sup>F</sup>

tongue
*lengua*<sup>F</sup>

kidney
*riñones*<sup>M</sup>

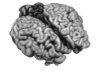

brains
*sesos*<sup>M</sup>

tripe
*tripa*<sup>F</sup>

# game
*caza*<sup>F</sup>

quail
*codorniz*<sup>F</sup>

pigeon
*pichón*<sup>M</sup>

guinea fowl
*pintada*<sup>F</sup>

pheasant
*faisán*<sup>M</sup>

hare
*liebre*<sup>F</sup>

rabbit
*conejo*<sup>M</sup>

## poultry
*aves<sup>F</sup> de corral<sup>M</sup>*

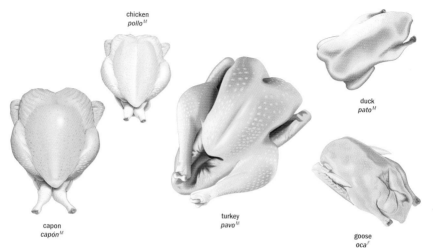

chicken
*pollo<sup>M</sup>*

duck
*pato<sup>M</sup>*

capon
*capón<sup>M</sup>*

turkey
*pavo<sup>M</sup>*

goose
*oca<sup>F</sup>*

## eggs
*huevos<sup>M</sup>*

ostrich egg
*huevo<sup>M</sup> de avestruz<sup>M</sup>*

goose egg
*huevo<sup>M</sup> de oca<sup>F</sup>*

quail egg
*huevo<sup>M</sup> de codorniz<sup>F</sup>*

pheasant egg
*huevo<sup>M</sup> de faisán<sup>M</sup>*

duck egg
*huevo<sup>M</sup> de pato<sup>M</sup>*

hen egg
*huevo<sup>M</sup> de gallina<sup>F</sup>*

# delicatessen
*charcutería*<sup>F</sup>

rillettes
*rillettes*<sup>F</sup>

foie gras
*foie-gras*<sup>M</sup>

prosciutto
*jamón*<sup>M</sup> *serrano*

kielbasa sausage
*salchicha*<sup>F</sup> *kielbasa*

mortadella
*mortadela*<sup>F</sup>

blood sausage
*morcilla*<sup>F</sup>

chorizo
*chorizo*<sup>M</sup>

pepperoni
*pepperoni*<sup>M</sup>

Genoa salami
*salami*<sup>M</sup> *de Génova*

German salami
*salami*<sup>M</sup> *alemán*

Toulouse sausages
*salchicha*<sup>F</sup> *de Toulouse*

merguez sausages
*salchicha*<sup>F</sup> *merguez*

andouillette
*andouillete*<sup>F</sup>

chipolata sausage
*salchicha*<sup>F</sup> *chipolata*

frankfurters
*salchicha*<sup>F</sup> *de Frankfurt*

pancetta
*panceta*<sup>F</sup>

cooked ham
*jamón*<sup>M</sup> *de York*

American bacon
*bacón*<sup>M</sup> *americano*

Canadian bacon
*bacón*<sup>M</sup> *canadiense*

FOOD AND KITCHEN

# mollusks
*moluscos*<sup>M</sup>

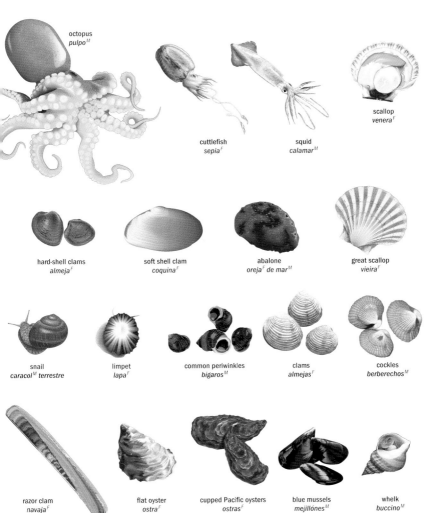

octopus
*pulpo*<sup>M</sup>

cuttlefish
*sepia*<sup>F</sup>

squid
*calamar*<sup>M</sup>

scallop
*venera*<sup>F</sup>

hard-shell clams
*almeja*<sup>F</sup>

soft shell clam
*coquina*<sup>F</sup>

abalone
*oreja*<sup>F</sup> *de mar*<sup>M</sup>

great scallop
*vieira*<sup>F</sup>

snail
*caracol*<sup>M</sup> *terrestre*

limpet
*lapa*<sup>F</sup>

common periwinkles
*bigaros*<sup>M</sup>

clams
*almejas*<sup>F</sup>

cockles
*berberechos*<sup>M</sup>

razor clam
*navaja*<sup>F</sup>

flat oyster
*ostra*<sup>F</sup>

cupped Pacific oysters
*ostras*<sup>F</sup>

blue mussels
*mejillónes*<sup>M</sup>

whelk
*buccino*<sup>M</sup>

# crustaceans
*crustáceos*<sup>M</sup>

FOOD AND KITCHEN

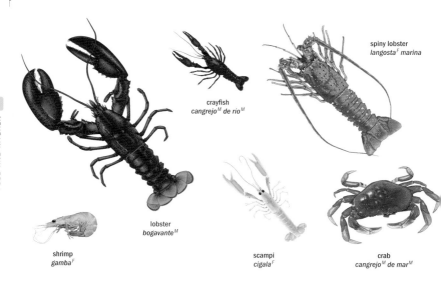

spiny lobster
*langosta*<sup>F</sup> *marina*

crayfish
*cangrejo*<sup>M</sup> *de rio*<sup>M</sup>

lobster
*bogavante*<sup>M</sup>

shrimp
*gamba*<sup>F</sup>

scampi
*cigala*<sup>F</sup>

crab
*cangrejo*<sup>M</sup> *de mar*<sup>M</sup>

# cartilaginous fishes
*peces*<sup>M</sup> *cartilaginosos*

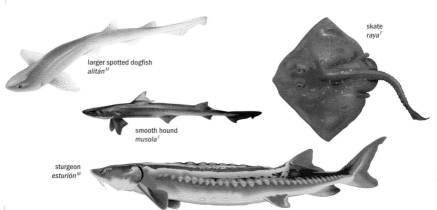

skate
*raya*<sup>F</sup>

larger spotted dogfish
*alitán*<sup>M</sup>

smooth hound
*musola*<sup>F</sup>

sturgeon
*esturión*<sup>M</sup>

# bony fishes
*peces*<sup>M</sup> *óseos*

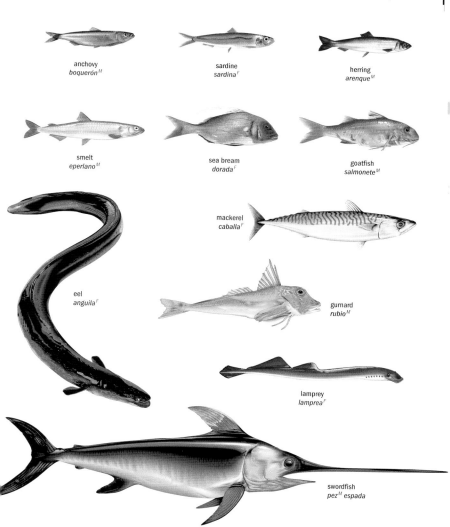

anchovy
*boquerón*<sup>M</sup>

sardine
*sardina*<sup>F</sup>

herring
*arenque*<sup>M</sup>

smelt
*eperlano*<sup>M</sup>

sea bream
*dorada*<sup>F</sup>

goatfish
*salmonete*<sup>M</sup>

mackerel
*caballa*<sup>F</sup>

eel
*anguila*<sup>F</sup>

gurnard
*rubio*<sup>M</sup>

lamprey
*lamprea*<sup>F</sup>

swordfish
*pez*<sup>M</sup> *espada*

bony fishes

bass
*róbalo*<sup>M</sup>

mullet
*mújol*<sup>M</sup>

carp
*carpa*<sup>F</sup>

perch
*perca*<sup>F</sup>

shad
*sábalo*<sup>M</sup>

pike
*lucio*<sup>M</sup>

pike perch
*lucioperca*<sup>M</sup>

bluefish
*anjova*<sup>F</sup>

sea bass
*lubina*<sup>F</sup>

monkfish
*rape*<sup>M</sup>

tuna
*atún*<sup>M</sup>

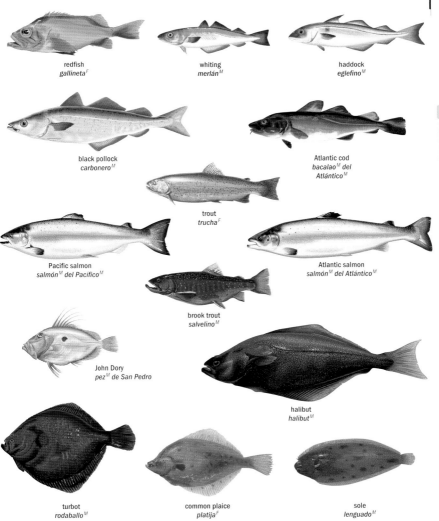

redfish
gallineta[F]

whiting
merlán[M]

haddock
eglefino[M]

black pollock
carbonero[M]

Atlantic cod
bacalao[M] del
Atlántico[M]

trout
trucha[F]

Pacific salmon
salmón[M] del Pacifico[M]

Atlantic salmon
salmón[M] del Atlántico[M]

brook trout
salvelino[M]

John Dory
pez[M] de San Pedro

halibut
halibut[M]

turbot
rodaballo[M]

common plaice
platija[F]

sole
lenguado[M]

FOOD AND KITCHEN

# packaging
*envases<sup>M</sup>*

pouch
*bolsa<sup>F</sup>*

parchment paper
*papel<sup>M</sup> para el horno<sup>M</sup>*

aluminum foil
*papel<sup>M</sup> de aluminio<sup>M</sup>*

freezer bag
*bolsa<sup>F</sup> para congelados<sup>M</sup>*

waxed paper
*papel<sup>M</sup> encerado*

plastic film (cellophane)
*papel<sup>M</sup> de celofán*

mesh bag
*bolsa<sup>F</sup> de malla<sup>F</sup>*

canisters
*botes<sup>M</sup> herméticos*

egg carton
*caja<sup>F</sup> de cartón<sup>M</sup> para huevos<sup>M</sup>*

food tray
*barqueta<sup>F</sup>*

small crate
*caja<sup>F</sup> pequeña*

small open crate
*caja<sup>F</sup> abierta*

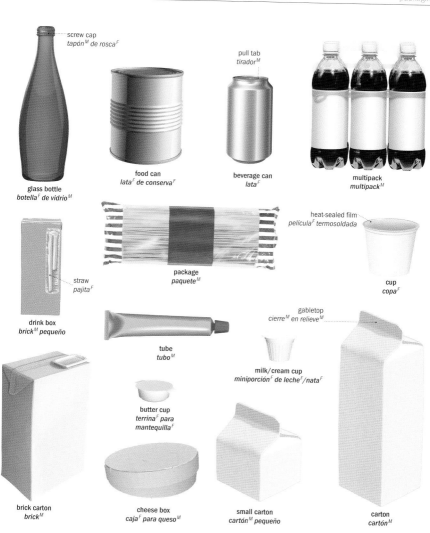

screw cap
*tapón*$^M$ *de rosca*$^F$

glass bottle
*botella*$^F$ *de vidrio*$^M$

food can
*lata*$^F$ *de conserva*$^F$

pull tab
*tirador*$^M$

beverage can
*lata*$^F$

multipack
*multipack*$^M$

straw
*pajita*$^F$

drink box
*brick*$^M$ *pequeño*

package
*paquete*$^M$

heat-sealed film
*película*$^F$ *termosoldada*

cup
*copa*$^F$

tube
*tubo*$^M$

gabletop
*cierre*$^M$ *en relieve*$^M$

milk/cream cup
*miniporción*$^F$ *de leche*$^F$/*nata*$^F$

butter cup
*terrina*$^F$ *para*
*mantequilla*$^F$

brick carton
*brick*$^M$

cheese box
*caja*$^F$ *para queso*$^M$

small carton
*cartón*$^M$ *pequeño*

carton
*cartón*$^M$

# kitchen
*cocina*<sup>F</sup>

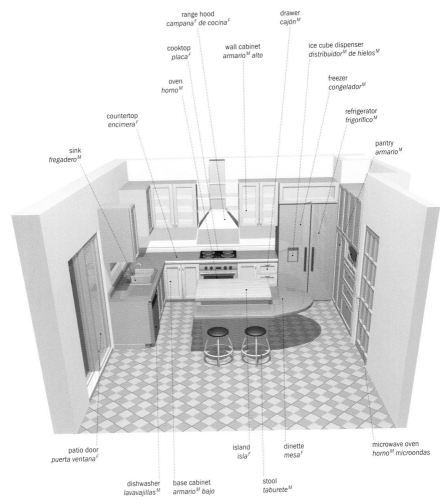

range hood
*campana*<sup>F</sup> *de cocina*<sup>F</sup>

drawer
*cajón*<sup>M</sup>

cooktop
*placa*<sup>F</sup>

wall cabinet
*armario*<sup>M</sup> *alto*

ice cube dispenser
*distribuidor*<sup>M</sup> *de hielos*<sup>M</sup>

oven
*horno*<sup>M</sup>

freezer
*congelador*<sup>M</sup>

countertop
*encimera*<sup>F</sup>

refrigerator
*frigorífico*<sup>M</sup>

sink
*fregadero*<sup>M</sup>

pantry
*armario*<sup>M</sup>

patio door
*puerta ventana*<sup>F</sup>

island
*isla*<sup>F</sup>

dinette
*mesa*<sup>F</sup>

microwave oven
*horno*<sup>M</sup> *microondas*

dishwasher
*lavavajillas*<sup>M</sup>

base cabinet
*armario*<sup>M</sup> *bajo*

stool
*taburete*<sup>M</sup>

# glassware
*cristalería*<sup>F</sup>

liqueur glass
*copa<sup>F</sup> para licores<sup>M</sup>*

port glass
*copa<sup>F</sup> para oporto<sup>M</sup>*

sparkling wine glass
*copa<sup>F</sup> de champaña<sup>F</sup>*

brandy snifter
*copa<sup>F</sup> para brandy<sup>M</sup>*

Alsace glass
*copa<sup>F</sup> para vino<sup>M</sup> de Alsacia*

burgundy glass
*copa<sup>F</sup> para vino<sup>M</sup> de Borgoña*

bordeaux glass
*copa<sup>F</sup> para vino<sup>M</sup> de Burdeos*

white wine glass
*copa<sup>F</sup> para vino<sup>M</sup> blanco*

water goblet
*copa<sup>F</sup> de agua<sup>F</sup>*

cocktail glass
*copa<sup>F</sup> de cóctel<sup>M</sup>*

highball glass
*vaso<sup>M</sup> largo*

old-fashioned glass
*vaso<sup>M</sup> corto*

beer mug
*jarra<sup>M</sup> de cerveza<sup>F</sup>*

champagne flute
*copa<sup>F</sup> de flauta<sup>F</sup>*

small decanter
*decantador<sup>M</sup>*

decanter
*garrafa<sup>F</sup>*

FOOD AND KITCHEN

# dinnerware
*vajilla<sup>F</sup> y servicio<sup>M</sup> de mesa<sup>F</sup>*

demitasse
*tacita<sup>F</sup> de café<sup>M</sup>*

cup
*taza<sup>F</sup>*

coffee mug
*jarra<sup>F</sup> para café<sup>M</sup>*

creamer
*jarrita<sup>F</sup> de leche<sup>F</sup>*

sugar bowl
*azucarero<sup>M</sup>*

salt shaker
*salero<sup>M</sup>*

pepper shaker
*pimentero<sup>M</sup>*

gravy boat
*salsera<sup>F</sup>*

butter dish
*mantequera<sup>F</sup>*

ramekin
*cuenco<sup>M</sup> de queso<sup>M</sup>
blando*

soup bowl
*escudilla<sup>F</sup>*

rim soup bowl
*plato<sup>M</sup> sopero*

dinner plate
*plato<sup>M</sup> llano*

salad plate
*plato<sup>M</sup> de postre<sup>M</sup>*

bread and butter plate
*platito<sup>M</sup> para el pan<sup>M</sup>*

teapot
*tetera<sup>F</sup>*

platter
*fuente<sup>F</sup> de servir*

vegetable bowl
*fuente<sup>F</sup> de verdura<sup>F</sup>*

fish platter
*fuente<sup>F</sup> para pescado<sup>M</sup>*

hors d'oeuvre dish
*bandeja<sup>F</sup> para los
entremeses<sup>M</sup>*

water pitcher
*jarra<sup>F</sup> de agua<sup>F</sup>*

salad bowl
*ensaladera<sup>F</sup>*

salad dish
*bol<sup>M</sup> para ensalada<sup>F</sup>*

soup tureen
*sopera<sup>F</sup>*

# silverware
*cubertería*<sup>F</sup>

**knife**
***cuchillo***<sup>M</sup>

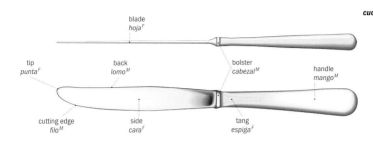

blade
*hoja*<sup>F</sup>

tip
*punta*<sup>F</sup>

back
*lomo*<sup>M</sup>

bolster
*cabezal*<sup>M</sup>

handle
*mango*<sup>M</sup>

cutting edge
*filo*<sup>M</sup>

side
*cara*<sup>F</sup>

tang
*espiga*<sup>F</sup>

**fork**
***tenedor***<sup>M</sup>

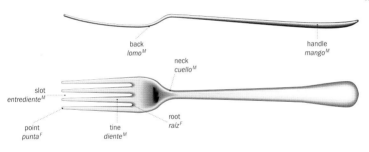

back
*lomo*<sup>M</sup>

handle
*mango*<sup>M</sup>

neck
*cuello*<sup>M</sup>

slot
*entrediente*<sup>M</sup>

point
*punta*<sup>F</sup>

tine
*diente*<sup>M</sup>

root
*raíz*<sup>F</sup>

**spoon**
***cuchara***<sup>F</sup>

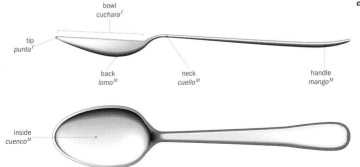

bowl
*cuchara*<sup>F</sup>

tip
*punta*<sup>F</sup>

back
*lomo*<sup>M</sup>

neck
*cuello*<sup>M</sup>

handle
*mango*<sup>M</sup>

inside
*cuenco*<sup>M</sup>

silverware

FOOD AND KITCHEN

**examples of forks**
*ejemplos*<sup>M</sup> *de tenedores*<sup>F</sup>

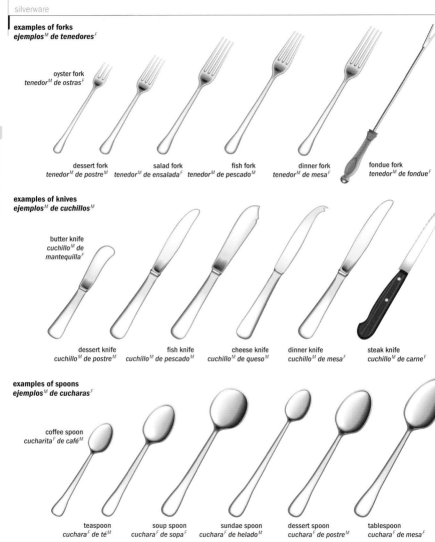

oyster fork
*tenedor*<sup>M</sup> *de ostras*<sup>F</sup>

dessert fork
*tenedor*<sup>M</sup> *de postre*<sup>M</sup>

salad fork
*tenedor*<sup>M</sup> *de ensalada*<sup>F</sup>

fish fork
*tenedor*<sup>M</sup> *de pescado*<sup>M</sup>

dinner fork
*tenedor*<sup>M</sup> *de mesa*<sup>F</sup>

fondue fork
*tenedor*<sup>M</sup> *de fondue*<sup>F</sup>

**examples of knives**
*ejemplos*<sup>M</sup> *de cuchillos*<sup>M</sup>

butter knife
*cuchillo*<sup>M</sup> *de mantequilla*<sup>F</sup>

dessert knife
*cuchillo*<sup>M</sup> *de postre*<sup>M</sup>

fish knife
*cuchillo*<sup>M</sup> *de pescado*<sup>M</sup>

cheese knife
*cuchillo*<sup>M</sup> *de queso*<sup>M</sup>

dinner knife
*cuchillo*<sup>M</sup> *de mesa*<sup>F</sup>

steak knife
*cuchillo*<sup>M</sup> *de carne*<sup>F</sup>

**examples of spoons**
*ejemplos*<sup>M</sup> *de cucharas*<sup>F</sup>

coffee spoon
*cucharita*<sup>F</sup> *de café*<sup>M</sup>

teaspoon
*cuchara*<sup>F</sup> *de té*<sup>M</sup>

soup spoon
*cuchara*<sup>F</sup> *de sopa*<sup>F</sup>

sundae spoon
*cuchara*<sup>F</sup> *de helado*<sup>M</sup>

dessert spoon
*cuchara*<sup>F</sup> *de postre*<sup>M</sup>

tablespoon
*cuchara*<sup>F</sup> *de mesa*<sup>F</sup>

# kitchen utensils
*utensilios<sup>M</sup> de cocina<sup>F</sup>*

**kitchen knife**
*cuchillo<sup>M</sup> de cocina<sup>F</sup>*

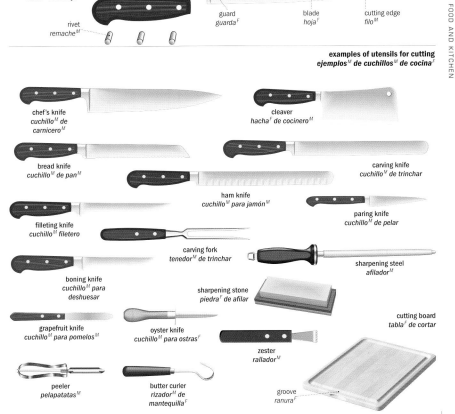

**examples of utensils for cutting**
*ejemplos<sup>M</sup> de cuchillos<sup>M</sup> de cocina<sup>F</sup>*

kitchen utensils

## for opening
### para abrir y descorchar

can opener
abrelatas<sup>M</sup>

bottle opener
abrebotellas<sup>M</sup>

waiter's corkscrew
sacacorchos<sup>M</sup>

lever corkscrew
sacacorchos<sup>M</sup> con
brazos<sup>M</sup>

## for grinding and grating
### para moler y rallar

nutcracker
cascanueces<sup>M</sup>

mortar
almirez<sup>M</sup>

pestle
mano<sup>M</sup>

meat grinder
picadora<sup>F</sup> de carne<sup>F</sup>

garlic press
triturador<sup>M</sup> de ajos<sup>M</sup>

citrus juicer
exprimidor<sup>M</sup>

nutmeg grater
rallador<sup>M</sup> de nuez<sup>F</sup>
moscada

grater
rallador<sup>M</sup>

rotary cheese grater
rallador<sup>M</sup> cilíndrico de
queso<sup>M</sup>

pusher
empujador<sup>M</sup>

crank
manivela<sup>F</sup>

drum
tambor<sup>M</sup>

handle
mango<sup>M</sup>

pasta maker
máquina<sup>F</sup> para hacer pasta<sup>F</sup>
italiana

food mill
pasapurés<sup>M</sup>

mandoline
mandolina<sup>F</sup>

FOOD AND KITCHEN

**for measuring**
*utensilios<sup>M</sup> para medir*

measuring spoons
*cucharas<sup>F</sup>
dosificadoras*

measuring cups
*tazas<sup>F</sup> medidoras*

candy thermometer
*termómetro<sup>M</sup> de
azúcar<sup>M</sup>*

instant-read thermometer
*termómetro<sup>M</sup> de medida<sup>F</sup>
instantánea*

measuring cup
*jarra<sup>F</sup> medidora*

meat thermometer
*termómetro<sup>M</sup> para
carne<sup>F</sup>*

oven thermometer
*termómetro<sup>M</sup> de
horno<sup>M</sup>*

measuring beaker
*vaso<sup>M</sup> medidor*

kitchen timer
*minutero<sup>M</sup>*

egg timer
*reloj<sup>M</sup> de arena<sup>F</sup>*

kitchen scale
*báscula<sup>F</sup> de cocina<sup>F</sup>*

**for straining and draining**
*coladores<sup>M</sup> y escurridores<sup>M</sup>*

mesh strainer
*colador<sup>M</sup> fino*

muslin
*muselina<sup>F</sup>*

chinois
*chino<sup>M</sup>*

funnel
*embudo<sup>M</sup>*

colander
*escurridor<sup>M</sup>*

fry basket
*cesta<sup>F</sup> de freir*

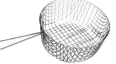

sieve
*tamiz<sup>M</sup>*

salad spinner
*secadora<sup>F</sup> de
ensalada<sup>F</sup>*

FOOD AND KITCHEN

## baking utensils
### utensilios<sup>M</sup> para repostería

icing syringe
jeringa<sup>F</sup> de
decoración<sup>F</sup>

pastry cutting wheel
cortapastas<sup>M</sup>

pastry brush
pincel<sup>M</sup> de repostería<sup>F</sup>

egg beater
batidor<sup>M</sup> mecánico

whisk
batidor<sup>M</sup>

pastry bag and nozzles
manga<sup>F</sup> y boquillas<sup>F</sup>

sifter
tamiz<sup>M</sup>

cookie cutters
moldes<sup>M</sup> de pastas<sup>F</sup>

dredger
espolvoreador<sup>M</sup>

pastry blender
mezclador<sup>M</sup> de
pastelería<sup>F</sup>

baking sheet
bandeja<sup>F</sup> de pastelería<sup>F</sup>

mixing bowls
boles<sup>M</sup> para batir

rolling pin
rodillo<sup>M</sup>

muffin pan
molde<sup>M</sup> para
magdalenas<sup>F</sup>

soufflé dish
molde<sup>M</sup> de soufflé<sup>M</sup>

charlotte mold
molde<sup>M</sup> de carlota<sup>F</sup>

spring-form pan
molde<sup>M</sup> redondo con muelles<sup>M</sup>

pie pan
molde<sup>M</sup> para tartas<sup>F</sup>

quiche plate
molde<sup>M</sup> acanalado

cake pan
molde<sup>M</sup> para
bizcocho<sup>M</sup>

**set of utensils**
*juego*<sup>M</sup> *de utensilios*<sup>M</sup>

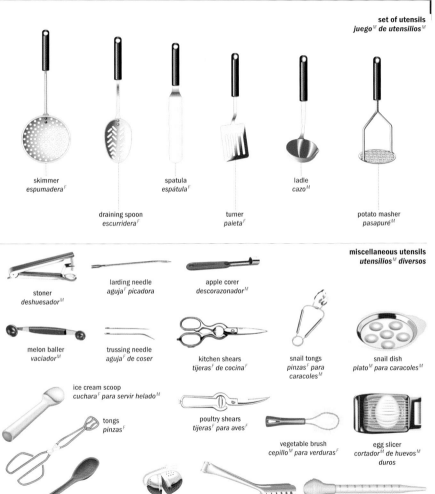

skimmer
*espumadera*<sup>F</sup>

draining spoon
*escurridera*<sup>F</sup>

spatula
*espátula*<sup>F</sup>

turner
*paleta*<sup>F</sup>

ladle
*cazo*<sup>M</sup>

potato masher
*pasapuré*<sup>M</sup>

**miscellaneous utensils**
*utensilios*<sup>M</sup> *diversos*

stoner
*deshuesador*<sup>M</sup>

larding needle
*aguja*<sup>F</sup> *picadora*

apple corer
*descorazonador*<sup>M</sup>

melon baller
*vaciador*<sup>M</sup>

trussing needle
*aguja*<sup>F</sup> *de coser*

kitchen shears
*tijeras*<sup>F</sup> *de cocina*<sup>F</sup>

snail tongs
*pinzas*<sup>F</sup> *para
caracoles*<sup>M</sup>

snail dish
*plato*<sup>M</sup> *para caracoles*<sup>M</sup>

ice cream scoop
*cuchara*<sup>F</sup> *para servir helado*<sup>M</sup>

tongs
*pinzas*<sup>F</sup>

poultry shears
*tijeras*<sup>F</sup> *para aves*<sup>F</sup>

vegetable brush
*cepillo*<sup>M</sup> *para verduras*<sup>F</sup>

egg slicer
*cortador*<sup>M</sup> *de huevos*<sup>M</sup>
*duros*

tasting spoon
*cuchara*<sup>F</sup> *de
degustación*<sup>F</sup>

tea ball
*esfera*<sup>F</sup> *de té*<sup>M</sup>

spaghetti tongs
*pinzas*<sup>F</sup> *para
espagueti*<sup>M</sup>

baster
*engrasador*<sup>M</sup>

# cooking utensils
*utensilios^M de cocina^F*

**wok set**
*wok^M*

lid
*tapa^F*

rack
*rejilla^F*

wok
*wok^M*

burner ring
*quemador^M*

**tagine**
*tajina^F*

**fish poacher**
*besuguera^F*

rack
*rejilla^F*

lid
*tapa^F*

**fondue set**
*servicio^M para fondue^F*

fondue pot
*cacerola^F para fondue^F*

stand
*soporte^M*

burner
*quemador^M*

**terrine**
*terrina^F*

**dripping pan**
*grasera^F*

**roasting pans**
*asadores^M*

**pressure cooker**
*olla^F a presión^F*

pressure regulator
*regulador^M de presión^F*

safety valve
*válvula^F de seguridad^F*

Dutch oven
*cacerola<sup>F</sup> refractaria*

stock pot
*olla<sup>F</sup>*

couscous kettle
*olla<sup>F</sup> para cuscús<sup>M</sup>*

frying pan
*sartén<sup>F</sup>*

steamer
*cazuela<sup>F</sup> vaporera*

egg poacher
*escalfador<sup>M</sup> de huevos<sup>M</sup>*

sauté pan
*sartén<sup>F</sup> honda*

small saucepan
*sartén<sup>F</sup> pequeña*

diable
*sartén<sup>F</sup> doble*

crêpe pan
*sartén<sup>F</sup> para crepes<sup>M</sup>*

steamer basket
*cesto<sup>M</sup> de cocción<sup>F</sup> al vapor<sup>M</sup>*

double boiler
*cacerola<sup>F</sup> para baño<sup>M</sup> María*

saucepan
*cacerola<sup>F</sup>*

# domestic appliances
*aparatos<sup>M</sup> electrodomésticos*

**for mixing and blending**
*para mezclar y batir*

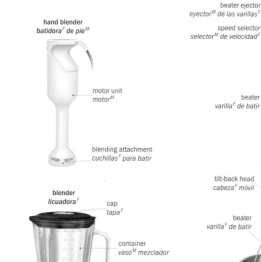

hand mixer
*batidora<sup>F</sup> de mano<sup>F</sup>*

beater ejector
*eyector<sup>M</sup> de las varillas<sup>F</sup>*

speed selector
*selector<sup>M</sup> de velocidad<sup>F</sup>*

handle
*asa<sup>F</sup>*

hand blender
*batidora<sup>F</sup> de pie<sup>M</sup>*

motor unit
*motor<sup>M</sup>*

beater
*varilla<sup>F</sup> de batir*

heel rest
*talón<sup>M</sup> de apoyo<sup>M</sup>*

blending attachment
*cuchillas<sup>F</sup> para batir*

beater ejector
*eyector<sup>M</sup> de las varillas<sup>F</sup>*

table mixer
*batidora<sup>F</sup> de mesa<sup>F</sup>*

speed control
*selector<sup>M</sup> de velocidades<sup>F</sup>*

tilt-back head
*cabeza<sup>F</sup> móvil*

beater
*varilla<sup>F</sup> de batir*

blender
*licuadora<sup>F</sup>*

cap
*tapa<sup>F</sup>*

container
*vaso<sup>M</sup> mezclador*

mixing bowl
*bol<sup>M</sup> mezclador*

cutting blade
*cuchilla<sup>F</sup>*

motor unit
*motor<sup>M</sup>*

control button
*botón<sup>M</sup> de control<sup>M</sup>*

turntable
*disco<sup>M</sup> giratorio*

stand
*pie<sup>M</sup>*

**beaters**
*tipos<sup>M</sup> de varillas<sup>F</sup>*

four blade beater
*varilla de aspas<sup>F</sup>*

spiral beater
*varilla en espiral<sup>F</sup>*

wire beater
*varilla circular*

dough hook
*varilla de gancho<sup>M</sup>*

FOOD AND KITCHEN

FOOD AND KITCHEN

**food processor**
*robot<sup>M</sup> de cocina<sup>F</sup>*

feed tube
*tubo<sup>M</sup> de entrada<sup>F</sup>*

lid
*tapa<sup>F</sup>*

bowl
*bol<sup>M</sup>*

spindle
*eje<sup>M</sup>*

blade
*cuchilla<sup>F</sup>*

handle
*asa<sup>F</sup>*

motor unit
*motor<sup>M</sup>*

**for cutting**
*para cortar*

disks
*discos<sup>M</sup>*

**electric knife**
*cuchillo<sup>M</sup> eléctrico*

power cord
*cordón<sup>M</sup> de alimentación<sup>F</sup>*

blade
*cuchilla<sup>F</sup>*

on-off switch
*interruptor<sup>M</sup>*

**for juicing**
*para exprimir*

citrus juicer
*exprimidor<sup>M</sup> de cítricos<sup>M</sup>*

reamer
*exprimidor<sup>M</sup>*

strainer
*colador<sup>M</sup>*

bowl with serving spout
*recipiente<sup>M</sup> con vertedor<sup>M</sup>*

motor unit
*motor<sup>M</sup>*

domestic appliances

**for cooking**
*para cocinar*

microwave oven
*horno<sup>M</sup> microondas*

door
*puerta<sup>F</sup>*

window
*ventana<sup>F</sup>*

clock timer
*reloj<sup>M</sup> programador*

control panel
*panel<sup>M</sup> de mandos<sup>M</sup>*

latch
*seguro<sup>M</sup>*

FOOD AND KITCHEN

waffle iron
*gofrera<sup>F</sup>*

handle
*asa<sup>F</sup>*

lid
*plancha<sup>F</sup> superior*

hinge
*bisagra<sup>F</sup>*

plate
*parrilla<sup>F</sup>*

temperature selector
*selector<sup>M</sup> de
temperatura<sup>F</sup>*

plate
*parrilla<sup>F</sup>*

toaster
*tostador<sup>M</sup>*

slot
*ranura<sup>F</sup> para el pan<sup>M</sup>*

bread guide
*rejilla<sup>F</sup>*

lever
*palanca<sup>F</sup>*

temperature control
*selector<sup>M</sup> de tostado<sup>M</sup>*

deep fryer
*freidora<sup>F</sup>*

basket
*canastilla<sup>F</sup>*

handle
*empuñadura<sup>F</sup>*

lid
*tapa<sup>F</sup>*

thermostat
*termostato<sup>M</sup>*

signal lamp
*piloto<sup>M</sup>*

timer
*reloj<sup>M</sup>*

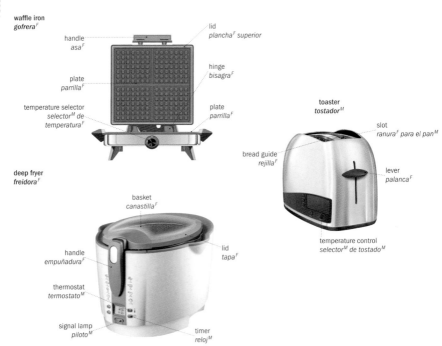

raclette with grill
*raclette-grill*<sup>M</sup>

dish
*bandeja*<sup>F</sup>

cooking plate
*placa*<sup>F</sup> *de cocción*<sup>F</sup>

base
*base*<sup>F</sup>

electric steamer
*vaporera*<sup>F</sup> *eléctrica*

cooking dishes
*platos*<sup>M</sup> *de cocción*<sup>F</sup>

water level indicator
*indicador*<sup>M</sup> *del nivel*<sup>M</sup> *del agua*<sup>F</sup>

signal lamp
*indicador*<sup>M</sup> *luminoso*

timer
*minutero*<sup>M</sup>

indoor electric grill
*parrilla*<sup>F</sup> *eléctrica*

insulated handle
*asa*<sup>F</sup> *aislante*

drip pan
*grasera*<sup>F</sup>

cooking surface
*superficie*<sup>F</sup> *de cocción*<sup>F</sup>

adjustable thermostat
*termostato*<sup>M</sup> *regulable*

bread machine
*amasadora*<sup>F</sup>

lid
*tapa*<sup>F</sup>

control panel
*panel*<sup>M</sup> *de mandos*<sup>M</sup>

window
*ventana*<sup>F</sup>

loaf pan
*molde*<sup>M</sup> *de pan*<sup>M</sup>

electric griddle
*plancha*<sup>F</sup> *eléctrica*

cooking surface
*plancha*<sup>F</sup>

handle
*asa*<sup>F</sup>

detachable control
*enchufe*<sup>M</sup> *y selector*<sup>M</sup>
*desmontables*

grease well
*colector*<sup>M</sup> *de grasa*<sup>F</sup>

FOOD AND KITCHEN

# miscellaneous domestic appliances
*varios aparatos<sup>M</sup> electrodomésticos*

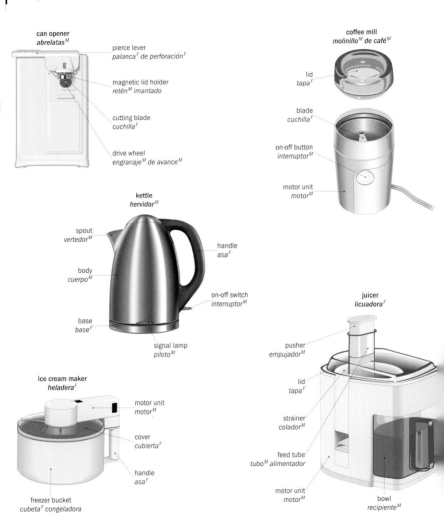

**can opener**
*abrelatas<sup>M</sup>*

pierce lever
*palanca<sup>F</sup> de perforación<sup>F</sup>*

magnetic lid holder
*retén<sup>M</sup> imantado*

cutting blade
*cuchilla<sup>F</sup>*

drive wheel
*engranaje<sup>M</sup> de avance<sup>M</sup>*

**coffee mill**
*molinillo<sup>M</sup> de café<sup>M</sup>*

lid
*tapa<sup>F</sup>*

blade
*cuchilla<sup>F</sup>*

on-off button
*interruptor<sup>M</sup>*

motor unit
*motor<sup>M</sup>*

**kettle**
*hervidor<sup>M</sup>*

spout
*vertedor<sup>M</sup>*

handle
*asa<sup>F</sup>*

body
*cuerpo<sup>M</sup>*

on-off switch
*interruptor<sup>M</sup>*

base
*base<sup>F</sup>*

signal lamp
*piloto<sup>M</sup>*

**juicer**
*licuadora<sup>F</sup>*

pusher
*empujador<sup>M</sup>*

lid
*tapa<sup>F</sup>*

strainer
*colador<sup>M</sup>*

feed tube
*tubo<sup>M</sup> alimentador*

motor unit
*motor<sup>M</sup>*

bowl
*recipiente<sup>M</sup>*

**ice cream maker**
*heladera<sup>F</sup>*

motor unit
*motor<sup>M</sup>*

cover
*cubierta<sup>F</sup>*

handle
*asa<sup>F</sup>*

freezer bucket
*cubeta<sup>F</sup> congeladora*

# coffee makers
*cafeteras*<sup>F</sup>

automatic drip coffee maker
*cafetera*<sup>F</sup> *de filtro*<sup>M</sup> *automática*

reservoir
*depósito*<sup>M</sup> *de agua*<sup>F</sup>

water level
*nivel*<sup>M</sup> *de agua*<sup>F</sup>

signal lamp
*piloto*<sup>M</sup>

on-off switch
*interruptor*<sup>M</sup>

lid
*tapa*<sup>F</sup>

basket
*filtro*<sup>M</sup>

carafe
*cafetera*<sup>F</sup>

warming plate
*placa*<sup>F</sup> *térmica*

Neapolitan coffee maker
*cafetera*<sup>F</sup> *napolitana*

espresso machine
*máquina*<sup>F</sup> *de café*<sup>M</sup> *exprés*

on-off switch
*interruptor*<sup>M</sup>

tamper
*prensa-café*<sup>M</sup>

drip tray
*ubeta*<sup>F</sup> *colectora de gotas*<sup>F</sup>

steam nozzle
*tubo*<sup>M</sup> *de vapor*<sup>M</sup>

steam control knob
*manecilla*<sup>F</sup> *de vapor*<sup>M</sup>

filter holder
*porta-filtro*<sup>M</sup>

water tank
*depósito*<sup>M</sup> *de agua*<sup>F</sup>

vacuum coffee maker
*cafetera*<sup>F</sup> *de infusión*<sup>F</sup>

upper bowl
*recipiente*<sup>M</sup> *superior*

stem
*tubo*<sup>M</sup> *de subida*<sup>F</sup> *del agua*<sup>F</sup>

lower bowl
*recipiente*<sup>M</sup> *inferior*

French press
*cafetera*<sup>F</sup> *de émbolo*<sup>M</sup>

espresso maker
*cafetera*<sup>F</sup> *italiana*

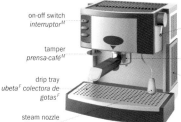

percolator
*percoladora*<sup>F</sup>

spout
*pitorro*<sup>M</sup>

signal light
*piloto*<sup>M</sup>

# exterior of a house

*exterior$^M$ de una casa$^F$*

HOUSE

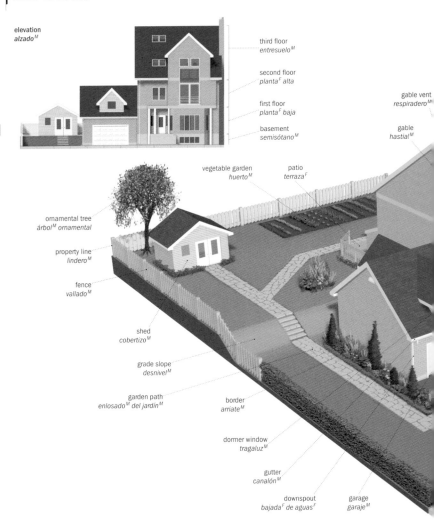

elevation
*alzado$^M$*

third floor
*entresuelo$^M$*

second floor
*planta$^F$ alta*

first floor
*planta$^F$ baja*

basement
*semisótano$^M$*

gable vent
*respiradero$^M$*

gable
*hastial$^M$*

vegetable garden
*huerto$^M$*

patio
*terraza$^F$*

ornamental tree
*árbol$^M$ ornamental*

property line
*lindero$^M$*

fence
*vallado$^M$*

shed
*cobertizo$^M$*

grade slope
*desnivel$^M$*

garden path
*enlosado$^M$ del jardín$^M$*

border
*arriate$^M$*

dormer window
*tragaluz$^M$*

gutter
*canalón$^M$*

downspout
*bajada$^F$ de aguas$^F$*

garage
*garaje$^M$*

light
*mario*<sup>M</sup>

lightning rod
*pararrayos*<sup>M</sup>

chimney pot
*caperuza*<sup>F</sup> *de la chimenea*<sup>F</sup>

chimney
*chimenea*<sup>F</sup>

roof
*tejado*<sup>M</sup>

cornice
*cornisa*<sup>F</sup>

steps
*escalinata*<sup>F</sup>

basement window
*ventana*<sup>F</sup> *del semisótano*<sup>M</sup>

hedge
*seto*<sup>M</sup>

lawn
*césped*<sup>M</sup>

flower bed
*cuadro*<sup>M</sup>

sidewalk
*acera*<sup>F</sup>

porch
*porche*<sup>M</sup>

driveway
*entrada*<sup>F</sup> *del garaje*<sup>M</sup>

site plan
*plano*<sup>M</sup> *del terreno*<sup>M</sup>

HOUSE

# pool
*piscina*<sup>F</sup>

hot tub
*spa*<sup>M</sup>

above-ground swimming pool
*piscina*<sup>F</sup> *elevada*

skimmer
*skimmer*<sup>M</sup>

filter
*filtro*<sup>M</sup>

pump
*bomba*<sup>F</sup>

upright
*montante*<sup>M</sup>

wall
*muro*<sup>M</sup>

in-ground swimming pool
*piscina*<sup>F</sup> *enterrada*

underwater light
*foco*<sup>M</sup> *subacuático*

main drain
*desagüe*<sup>M</sup> *de fondo*<sup>M</sup>

diving board
*trampolín*<sup>M</sup>

discharge outlet
*boquilla*<sup>F</sup> *de vertido*<sup>M</sup>

ladder
*escalera*<sup>F</sup>

steps
*escalones*<sup>M</sup>

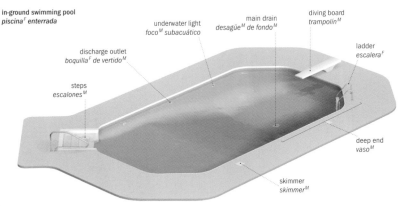

deep end
*vaso*<sup>M</sup>

skimmer
*skimmer*<sup>M</sup>

# exterior door
*puerta$^F$ de entrada$^F$*

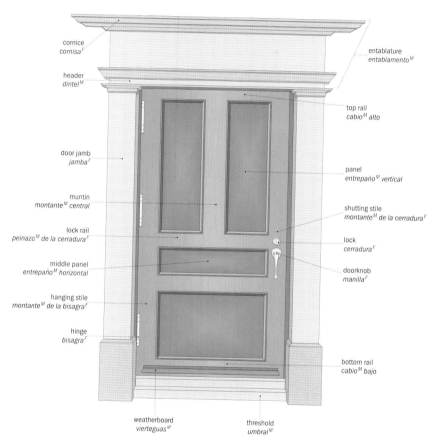

cornice
*cornisa$^F$*

entablature
*entablamento$^M$*

header
*dintel$^M$*

top rail
*cabio$^M$ alto*

door jamb
*jamba$^F$*

panel
*entrepaño$^M$ vertical*

muntin
*montante$^M$ central*

shutting stile
*montante$^M$ de la cerradura$^F$*

lock rail
*peinazo$^M$ de la cerradura$^F$*

lock
*cerradura$^F$*

middle panel
*entrepaño$^M$ horizontal*

doorknob
*manilla$^F$*

hanging stile
*montante$^M$ de la bisagra$^F$*

hinge
*bisagra$^F$*

bottom rail
*cabio$^M$ bajo*

weatherboard
*vierteguas$^M$*

threshold
*umbral$^M$*

HOUSE

# lock
*cerrajería*<sup>F</sup>

**general view**
*vista*<sup>F</sup> *general*

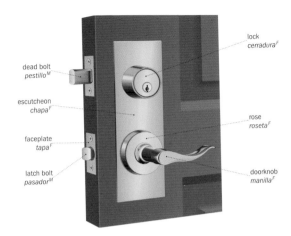

dead bolt
*pestillo*<sup>M</sup>

escutcheon
*chapa*<sup>F</sup>

faceplate
*tapa*<sup>F</sup>

latch bolt
*pasador*<sup>M</sup>

lock
*cerradura*<sup>F</sup>

rose
*roseta*<sup>F</sup>

doorknob
*manilla*<sup>F</sup>

# window
*ventana*<sup>F</sup>

**structure**
*estructura*<sup>F</sup>

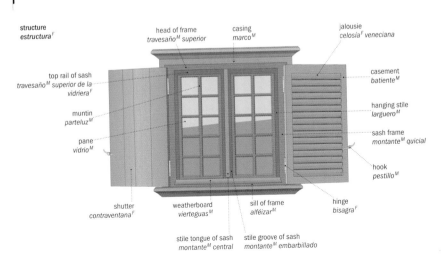

head of frame
*travesaño*<sup>M</sup> *superior*

casing
*marco*<sup>M</sup>

jalousie
*celosía*<sup>F</sup> *veneciana*

top rail of sash
*travesaño*<sup>M</sup> *superior de la vidriera*<sup>F</sup>

muntin
*parteluz*<sup>M</sup>

pane
*vidrio*<sup>M</sup>

casement
*batiente*<sup>M</sup>

hanging stile
*larguero*<sup>M</sup>

sash frame
*montante*<sup>M</sup> *quicial*

hook
*pestillo*<sup>M</sup>

shutter
*contraventana*<sup>F</sup>

weatherboard
*vierteguas*<sup>M</sup>

stile tongue of sash
*montante*<sup>M</sup> *central*

stile groove of sash
*montante*<sup>M</sup> *embarbillado*

sill of frame
*alféizar*<sup>M</sup>

hinge
*bisagra*<sup>F</sup>

# frame
*armazón*[M]

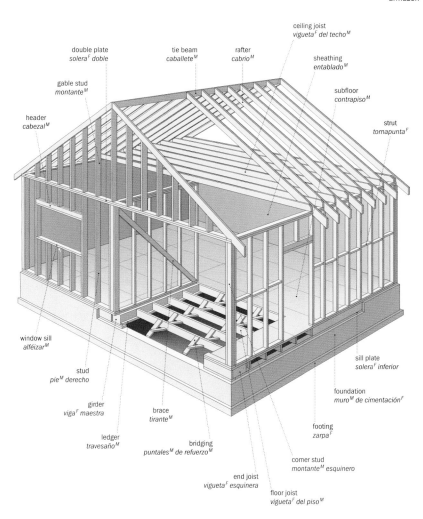

ceiling joist
*vigueta*[F] *del techo*[M]

double plate
*solera*[F] *doble*

tie beam
*caballete*[M]

rafter
*cabrio*[M]

sheathing
*entablado*[M]

gable stud
*montante*[M]

subfloor
*contrapiso*[M]

header
*cabezal*[M]

strut
*tornapunta*[F]

window sill
*alféizar*[M]

sill plate
*solera*[F] *inferior*

stud
*pie*[M] *derecho*

foundation
*muro*[M] *de cimentación*[F]

girder
*viga*[F] *maestra*

brace
*tirante*[M]

footing
*zarpa*[F]

ledger
*travesaño*[M]

bridging
*puntales*[M] *de refuerzo*[M]

corner stud
*montante*[M] *esquinero*

end joist
*vigueta*[F] *esquinera*

floor joist
*vigueta*[F] *del piso*[M]

# main rooms
*habitaciones^F principales*

**first floor**
*planta^F baja*

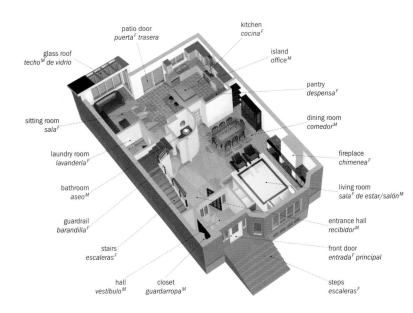

patio door
*puerta^F trasera*

kitchen
*cocina^F*

island
*office^M*

glass roof
*techo^M de vidrio*

pantry
*despensa^F*

sitting room
*sala^F*

dining room
*comedor^M*

laundry room
*lavandería^F*

fireplace
*chimenea^F*

bathroom
*aseo^M*

living room
*sala^F de estar/salón^M*

guardrail
*barandilla^F*

entrance hall
*recibidor^M*

stairs
*escaleras^F*

front door
*entrada^F principal*

hall
*vestíbulo^M*

closet
*guardarropa^M*

steps
*escaleras^F*

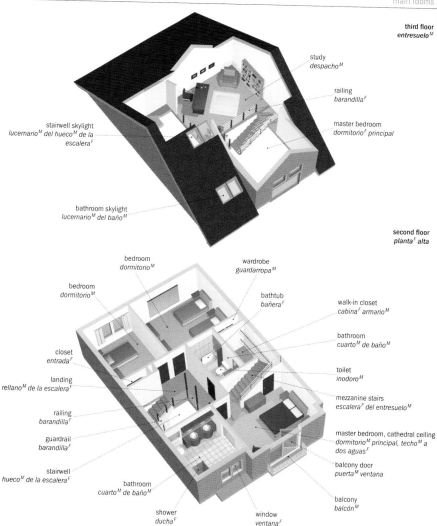

third floor
*entresuelo<sup>M</sup>*

study
*despacho<sup>M</sup>*

railing
*barandilla<sup>F</sup>*

stairwell skylight
*lucernario<sup>M</sup> del hueco<sup>M</sup> de la escalera<sup>F</sup>*

master bedroom
*dormitorio<sup>F</sup> principal*

bathroom skylight
*lucernario<sup>M</sup> del baño<sup>M</sup>*

second floor
*planta<sup>F</sup> alta*

bedroom
*dormitorio<sup>M</sup>*

wardrobe
*guardarropa<sup>M</sup>*

bedroom
*dormitorio<sup>M</sup>*

bathtub
*bañera<sup>F</sup>*

walk-in closet
*cabina<sup>F</sup> armario<sup>M</sup>*

closet
*entrada<sup>F</sup>*

bathroom
*cuarto<sup>M</sup> de baño<sup>M</sup>*

landing
*rellano<sup>M</sup> de la escalera<sup>F</sup>*

toilet
*inodoro<sup>M</sup>*

railing
*barandilla<sup>F</sup>*

mezzanine stairs
*escalera<sup>F</sup> del entresuelo<sup>M</sup>*

guardrail
*barandilla<sup>F</sup>*

master bedroom, cathedral ceiling
*dormitorio<sup>M</sup> principal, techo<sup>M</sup> a dos aguas<sup>F</sup>*

stairwell
*hueco<sup>M</sup> de la escalera<sup>F</sup>*

balcony door
*puerta<sup>M</sup> ventana*

bathroom
*cuarto<sup>M</sup> de baño<sup>M</sup>*

shower
*ducha<sup>F</sup>*

window
*ventana<sup>F</sup>*

balcony
*balcón<sup>M</sup>*

# wood flooring
*pisos<sup>M</sup> de madera<sup>F</sup>*

HOUSE

**wood flooring on cement screed**
*parqué<sup>M</sup> sobre base<sup>F</sup> de cemento<sup>M</sup>*

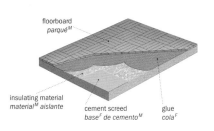

floorboard
*parqué<sup>M</sup>*

insulating material
*material<sup>M</sup> aislante*

cement screed
*base<sup>F</sup> de cemento<sup>M</sup>*

glue
*cola<sup>F</sup>*

**wood flooring on wooden structure**
*entarimado<sup>M</sup> sobre estructura<sup>F</sup> de madera<sup>F</sup>*

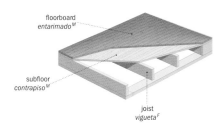

floorboard
*entarimado<sup>M</sup>*

subfloor
*contrapiso<sup>M</sup>*

joist
*vigueta<sup>F</sup>*

**wood flooring arrangements**
*tipos<sup>M</sup> de parqué<sup>M</sup>*

inlaid parquet
*parqué<sup>M</sup> de mosaico*

overlay flooring
*parqué<sup>M</sup> sobrepuesto*

strip flooring with alternate joints
*parqué<sup>M</sup> alternado a la inglesa*

herringbone parquet
*parqué<sup>M</sup> espinapez<sup>M</sup>*

herringbone pattern
*parqué<sup>M</sup> en punta<sup>F</sup> de Hung*

basket weave pattern
*parqué<sup>M</sup> de cestería<sup>F</sup>*

Arenberg parquet
*parqué<sup>M</sup> Arenberg*

Chantilly parquet
*parqué<sup>M</sup> Chantilly*

Versailles parquet
*parqué<sup>M</sup> Versalles*

# textile floor coverings
*revestimientos<sup>M</sup> textiles del suelo<sup>M</sup>*

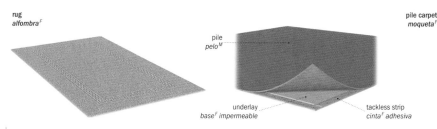

rug
*alfombra<sup>F</sup>*

pile carpet
*moqueta<sup>F</sup>*

pile
*pelo<sup>M</sup>*

underlay
*base<sup>F</sup> impermeable*

tackless strip
*cinta<sup>F</sup> adhesiva*

## stairs
*escalera* F

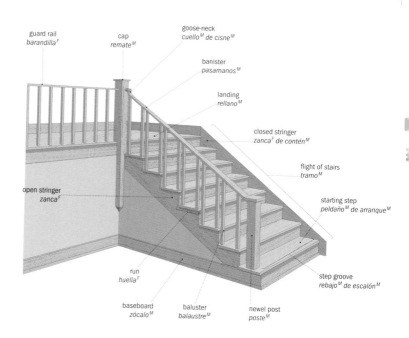

guard rail
*barandilla* F

cap
*remate* M

goose-neck
*cuello* M *de cisne* M

banister
*pasamanos* M

landing
*rellano* M

closed stringer
*zanca* F *de contén* M

flight of stairs
*tramo* M

open stringer
*zanca* F

starting step
*peldaño* M *de arranque* M

run
*huella* F

step groove
*rebajo* M *de escalón* M

baseboard
*zócalo* M

baluster
*balaustre* M

newel post
*poste* M

## step
*peldaño* M

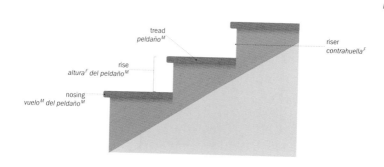

tread
*peldaño* M

riser
*contrahuella* F

rise
*altura* F *del peldaño* M

nosing
*vuelo* M *del peldaño* M

HOUSE

# wood burning
*calefacción^F de leña^F*

**fireplace**
*chimenea^F*

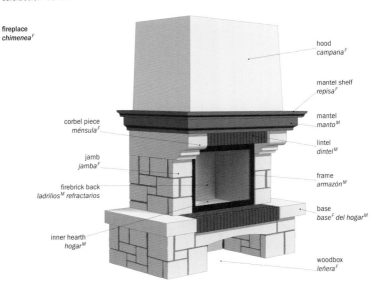

hood
*campana^F*

mantel shelf
*repisa^F*

mantel
*manto^M*

lintel
*dintel^M*

frame
*armazón^M*

base
*base^F del hogar^M*

woodbox
*leñera^F*

corbel piece
*ménsula^F*

jamb
*jamba^F*

firebrick back
*ladrillos^M refractarios*

inner hearth
*hogar^M*

**slow-burning wood stove**
*estufa^F de leña^F a fuego^M lento*

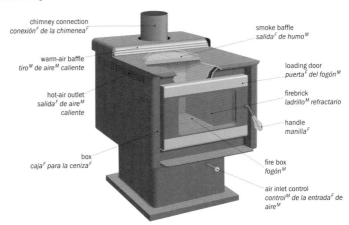

chimney connection
*conexión^F de la chimenea^F*

warm-air baffle
*tiro^M de aire^M caliente*

hot-air outlet
*salida^F de aire^M
caliente*

box
*caja^F para la ceniza^F*

smoke baffle
*salida^F de humo^M*

loading door
*puerta^F del fogón^M*

firebrick
*ladrillo^M refractario*

handle
*manilla^F*

fire box
*fogón^M*

air inlet control
*control^M de la entrada^F de
aire^M*

192

chimney
*chimenea*<sup>F</sup>

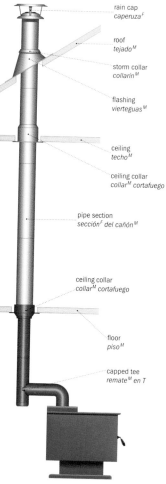

rain cap
*caperuza*<sup>F</sup>

roof
*tejado*<sup>M</sup>

storm collar
*collarín*<sup>M</sup>

flashing
*vierteguas*<sup>M</sup>

ceiling
*techo*<sup>M</sup>

ceiling collar
*collar*<sup>M</sup> *cortafuego*

pipe section
*sección*<sup>F</sup> *del cañón*<sup>M</sup>

ceiling collar
*collar*<sup>M</sup> *cortafuego*

floor
*piso*<sup>M</sup>

capped tee
*remate*<sup>M</sup> *en T*

**fire irons**
***utensilios*** <sup>M</sup> ***para la chimenea*** <sup>F</sup>

log tongs
*tenazas*<sup>F</sup>

poker
*atizador*<sup>M</sup>

shovel
*pala*<sup>F</sup>

broom
*escobilla*<sup>F</sup>

andirons
*morillos*<sup>M</sup>

log carrier
*portaleños*<sup>M</sup>

fireplace screen
*pantalla*<sup>F</sup>

# plumbing system

*cañerías<sup>F</sup>*

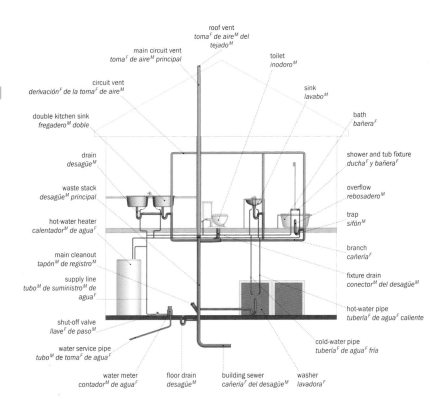

roof vent
*toma<sup>F</sup> de aire<sup>M</sup> del tejado<sup>M</sup>*

main circuit vent
*toma<sup>F</sup> de aire<sup>M</sup> principal*

circuit vent
*derivación<sup>F</sup> de la toma<sup>F</sup> de aire<sup>M</sup>*

toilet
*inodoro<sup>M</sup>*

sink
*lavabo<sup>M</sup>*

double kitchen sink
*fregadero<sup>M</sup> doble*

bath
*bañera<sup>F</sup>*

drain
*desagüe<sup>M</sup>*

shower and tub fixture
*ducha<sup>F</sup> y bañera<sup>F</sup>*

waste stack
*desagüe<sup>M</sup> principal*

overflow
*rebosadero<sup>M</sup>*

hot-water heater
*calentador<sup>M</sup> de agua<sup>F</sup>*

trap
*sifón<sup>M</sup>*

main cleanout
*tapón<sup>M</sup> de registro<sup>M</sup>*

branch
*cañería<sup>F</sup>*

supply line
*tubo<sup>M</sup> de suministro<sup>M</sup> de agua<sup>F</sup>*

fixture drain
*conector<sup>M</sup> del desagüe<sup>M</sup>*

hot-water pipe
*tubería<sup>F</sup> de agua<sup>F</sup> caliente*

shut-off valve
*llave<sup>F</sup> de paso<sup>M</sup>*

water service pipe
*tubo<sup>M</sup> de toma<sup>F</sup> de agua<sup>F</sup>*

cold-water pipe
*tubería<sup>F</sup> de agua<sup>F</sup> fría*

water meter
*contador<sup>M</sup> de agua<sup>F</sup>*

floor drain
*desagüe<sup>M</sup>*

building sewer
*cañería<sup>F</sup> del desagüe<sup>M</sup>*

washer
*lavadora<sup>F</sup>*

ventilating circuit
*circuito<sup>M</sup> de ventilación<sup>F</sup>*

draining circuit
*circuito<sup>M</sup> de desagüe<sup>M</sup>*

cold-water circuit
*circuito<sup>M</sup> de agua<sup>F</sup> fría*

hot-water circuit
*circuito<sup>M</sup> de agua<sup>F</sup> caliente*

HOUSE

# bathroom
*cuarto$^M$ de baño$^M$*

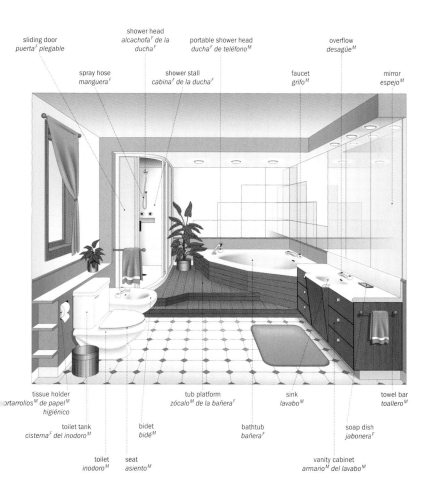

sliding door
*puerta$^F$ plegable*

shower head
*alcachofa$^F$ de la ducha$^F$*

portable shower head
*ducha$^F$ de teléfono$^M$*

overflow
*desagüe$^M$*

spray hose
*manguera$^F$*

shower stall
*cabina$^F$ de la ducha$^F$*

faucet
*grifo$^M$*

mirror
*espejo$^M$*

tissue holder
*portarrollos$^M$ de papel$^M$ higiénico*

tub platform
*zócalo$^M$ de la bañera$^F$*

sink
*lavabo$^M$*

towel bar
*toallero$^M$*

toilet tank
*cisterna$^F$ del inodoro$^M$*

bidet
*bidé$^M$*

bathtub
*bañera$^F$*

soap dish
*jabonera$^F$*

toilet
*inodoro$^M$*

seat
*asiento$^M$*

vanity cabinet
*armario$^M$ del lavabo$^M$*

# toilet
*inodoro*<sup>M</sup>

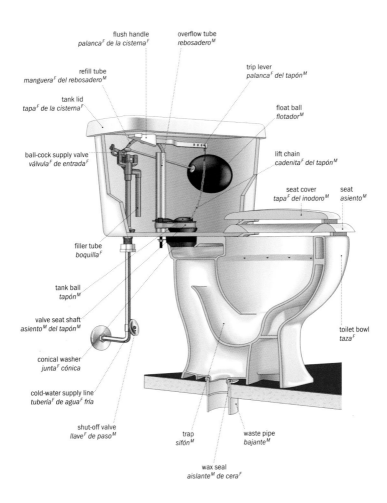

flush handle
*palanca*<sup>F</sup> *de la cisterna*<sup>F</sup>

overflow tube
*rebosadero*<sup>M</sup>

refill tube
*manguera*<sup>F</sup> *del rebosadero*<sup>M</sup>

trip lever
*palanca*<sup>F</sup> *del tapón*<sup>M</sup>

tank lid
*tapa*<sup>F</sup> *de la cisterna*<sup>F</sup>

float ball
*flotador*<sup>M</sup>

ball-cock supply valve
*válvula*<sup>F</sup> *de entrada*<sup>F</sup>

lift chain
*cadenita*<sup>F</sup> *del tapón*<sup>M</sup>

seat cover
*tapa*<sup>F</sup> *del inodoro*<sup>M</sup>

seat
*asiento*<sup>M</sup>

filler tube
*boquilla*<sup>F</sup>

tank ball
*tapón*<sup>M</sup>

valve seat shaft
*asiento*<sup>M</sup> *del tapón*<sup>M</sup>

toilet bowl
*taza*<sup>F</sup>

conical washer
*junta*<sup>F</sup> *cónica*

cold-water supply line
*tubería*<sup>F</sup> *de agua*<sup>F</sup> *fría*

shut-off valve
*llave*<sup>F</sup> *de paso*<sup>M</sup>

trap
*sifón*<sup>M</sup>

waste pipe
*bajante*<sup>M</sup>

wax seal
*aislante*<sup>M</sup> *de cera*<sup>F</sup>

# examples of branching
*ejemplos<sup>M</sup> de conexiones<sup>F</sup>*

garbage disposal sink
*fregadero<sup>M</sup> con triturador<sup>M</sup> de basura<sup>F</sup>*

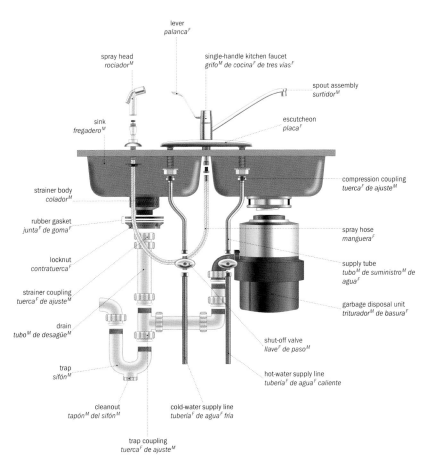

lever
*palanca<sup>F</sup>*

spray head
*rociador<sup>M</sup>*

single-handle kitchen faucet
*grifo<sup>M</sup> de cocina<sup>F</sup> de tres vías<sup>F</sup>*

spout assembly
*surtidor<sup>M</sup>*

sink
*fregadero<sup>M</sup>*

escutcheon
*placa<sup>F</sup>*

compression coupling
*tuerca<sup>F</sup> de ajuste<sup>M</sup>*

strainer body
*colador<sup>M</sup>*

rubber gasket
*junta<sup>F</sup> de goma<sup>F</sup>*

spray hose
*manguera<sup>F</sup>*

locknut
*contratuerca<sup>F</sup>*

supply tube
*tubo<sup>M</sup> de suministro<sup>M</sup> de agua<sup>F</sup>*

strainer coupling
*tuerca<sup>F</sup> de ajuste<sup>M</sup>*

garbage disposal unit
*triturador<sup>M</sup> de basura<sup>F</sup>*

drain
*tubo<sup>M</sup> de desagüe<sup>M</sup>*

shut-off valve
*llave<sup>F</sup> de paso<sup>M</sup>*

trap
*sifón<sup>M</sup>*

hot-water supply line
*tubería<sup>F</sup> de agua<sup>F</sup> caliente*

cleanout
*tapón<sup>M</sup> del sifón<sup>M</sup>*

cold-water supply line
*tubería<sup>F</sup> de agua<sup>F</sup> fría*

trap coupling
*tuerca<sup>F</sup> de ajuste<sup>M</sup>*

HOUSE

# network connection
*conexión<sup>F</sup> a la red<sup>F</sup>*

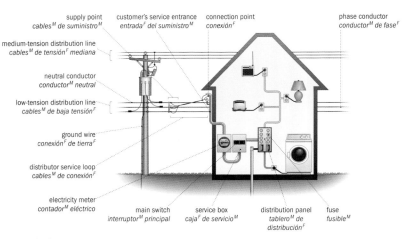

supply point
*cables<sup>M</sup> de suministro<sup>M</sup>*

customer's service entrance
*entrada<sup>F</sup> del suministro<sup>M</sup>*

connection point
*conexión<sup>F</sup>*

phase conductor
*conductor<sup>M</sup> de fase<sup>F</sup>*

medium-tension distribution line
*cables<sup>M</sup> de tensión<sup>F</sup> mediana*

neutral conductor
*conductor<sup>M</sup> neutral*

low-tension distribution line
*cables<sup>M</sup> de baja tensión<sup>F</sup>*

ground wire
*conexión<sup>F</sup> de tierra<sup>F</sup>*

distributor service loop
*cables<sup>M</sup> de conexión<sup>F</sup>*

electricity meter
*contador<sup>M</sup> eléctrico*

main switch
*interruptor<sup>M</sup> principal*

service box
*caja<sup>F</sup> de servicio<sup>M</sup>*

distribution panel
*tablero<sup>M</sup> de distribución<sup>F</sup>*

fuse
*fusible<sup>M</sup>*

# contact devices
*dispositivos<sup>M</sup> de contacto<sup>M</sup>*

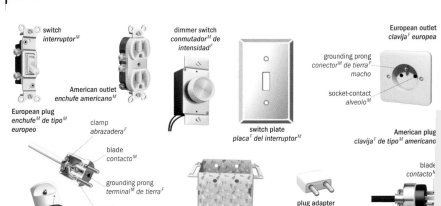

switch
*interruptor<sup>M</sup>*

American outlet
*enchufe americano<sup>M</sup>*

European plug
*enchufe<sup>M</sup> de tipo<sup>M</sup> europeo*

clamp
*abrazadera<sup>F</sup>*

blade
*contacto<sup>M</sup>*

grounding prong
*terminal<sup>M</sup> de tierra<sup>F</sup>*

terminal
*terminal<sup>M</sup>*

cover
*tapa<sup>F</sup>*

dimmer switch
*conmutador<sup>M</sup> de intensidad<sup>F</sup>*

switch plate
*placa<sup>F</sup> del interruptor<sup>M</sup>*

electrical box
*caja<sup>F</sup> de conexiones<sup>F</sup>*

plug adapter
*adaptador<sup>M</sup> de enchufes<sup>M</sup>*

European outlet
*clavija<sup>F</sup> europea*

grounding prong
*conector<sup>M</sup> de tierra<sup>F</sup> macho*

socket-contact
*alveolo<sup>M</sup>*

American plug
*clavija<sup>F</sup> de tipo<sup>M</sup> americano*

blade
*contacto<sup>M</sup>*

grounding prong
*contacto<sup>M</sup> de conexión<sup>F</sup> a tierra<sup>F</sup>*

HOUSE

## incandescent lightbulb
*bombilla<sup>F</sup> incandescente*

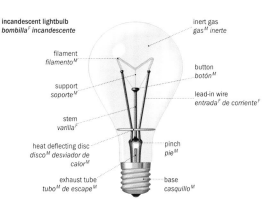

inert gas
*gas<sup>M</sup> inerte*

filament
*filamento<sup>M</sup>*

button
*botón<sup>M</sup>*

support
*soporte<sup>M</sup>*

lead-in wire
*entrada<sup>F</sup> de corriente<sup>F</sup>*

stem
*varilla<sup>F</sup>*

heat deflecting disc
*disco<sup>M</sup> desviador de calor<sup>M</sup>*

pinch
*pie<sup>M</sup>*

exhaust tube
*tubo<sup>M</sup> de escape<sup>M</sup>*

base
*casquillo<sup>M</sup>*

lamp socket
*portalámparas<sup>M</sup>*

bulb
*ampolla<sup>F</sup> de vidrio<sup>M</sup>*

## energy-saving bulb
*bombilla<sup>F</sup> de bajo consumo*

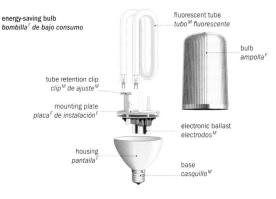

fluorescent tube
*tubo<sup>M</sup> fluorescente*

bulb
*ampolla<sup>F</sup>*

tube retention clip
*clip<sup>M</sup> de ajuste<sup>M</sup>*

mounting plate
*placa<sup>F</sup> de instalación<sup>F</sup>*

electronic ballast
*electrodos<sup>M</sup>*

housing
*pantalla<sup>F</sup>*

base
*casquillo<sup>M</sup>*

screw base
*bombilla<sup>F</sup> de rosca<sup>F</sup>*

bayonet base
*bombilla<sup>F</sup> de bayoneta<sup>F</sup>*

tungsten-halogen lamp
*lámpara<sup>F</sup> halógena*

pin
*contacto<sup>M</sup>*

## fluorescent tube
*tubo<sup>M</sup> fluorescente*

phosphorescent coating
*revestimiento<sup>M</sup> de fósforo<sup>M</sup>*

pin base
*base<sup>F</sup> del tubo<sup>M</sup>*

bulb
*tubo<sup>M</sup>*

pin
*pata<sup>F</sup>*

HOUSE

# armchair
*silla<sup>F</sup> de brazos<sup>M</sup>*

HOUSE

parts
*partes<sup>F</sup>*

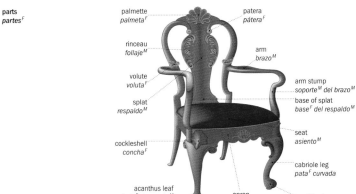

palmette
*palmeta<sup>F</sup>*

patera
*pátera<sup>F</sup>*

rinceau
*follaje<sup>M</sup>*

arm
*brazo<sup>M</sup>*

volute
*voluta<sup>F</sup>*

arm stump
*soporte<sup>M</sup> del brazo<sup>M</sup>*

splat
*respaldo<sup>M</sup>*

base of splat
*base<sup>F</sup> del respaldo<sup>M</sup>*

seat
*asiento<sup>M</sup>*

cockleshell
*concha<sup>F</sup>*

cabriole leg
*pata<sup>F</sup> curvada*

acanthus leaf
*hoja<sup>F</sup> de acanto<sup>M</sup>*

apron
*cortina<sup>F</sup>*

scroll foot
*pie<sup>M</sup> de voluta<sup>F</sup>*

**examples of armchairs**
***ejemplos<sup>M</sup> de divanes<sup>M</sup> y butacas<sup>F</sup>***

Wassily chair
*silla<sup>F</sup> Wassily*

director's chair
*silla<sup>F</sup> plegable de lona<sup>F</sup>*

rocking chair
*mecedora<sup>F</sup>*

cabriolet
*silla<sup>F</sup> cabriolé*

méridienne
*meridiana<sup>F</sup>*

récamier
*sofá<sup>M</sup> tipo<sup>M</sup> imperio*

club chair
*butaca<sup>F</sup>*

bergère
*silla<sup>F</sup> poltrona*

sofa
*sofá<sup>M</sup>*

love seat
*sofá<sup>M</sup> de dos plazas<sup>F</sup>*

chesterfield
*chesterfield<sup>M</sup>*

# side chair
*silla*<sup>F</sup> *sin brazos*<sup>M</sup>

**parts**
***partes***<sup>F</sup>

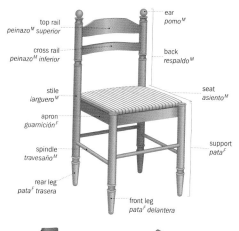

top rail
*peinazo*<sup>M</sup> *superior*

cross rail
*peinazo*<sup>M</sup> *inferior*

stile
*larguero*<sup>M</sup>

apron
*guarnición*<sup>F</sup>

spindle
*travesaño*<sup>M</sup>

rear leg
*pata*<sup>F</sup> *trasera*

ear
*pomo*<sup>M</sup>

back
*respaldo*<sup>M</sup>

seat
*asiento*<sup>M</sup>

support
*pata*<sup>F</sup>

front leg
*pata*<sup>F</sup> *delantera*

**examples of chairs**
***ejemplos***<sup>M</sup> ***de sillas***<sup>F</sup>

rocking chair
*mecedora*<sup>F</sup>

stacking chairs
*sillas*<sup>F</sup> *apilables*

folding chairs
*sillas*<sup>F</sup> *plegables*

chaise longue
*tumbona*<sup>F</sup>

# seats
*asientos*<sup>M</sup>

ottoman
*puf*<sup>M</sup>

bean bag chair
*silla*<sup>F</sup> *cojin*<sup>M</sup>

step chair
*silla*<sup>F</sup> *escalera*<sup>F</sup>

bench
*banco*<sup>M</sup>

banquette
*banqueta*<sup>F</sup>

footstool
*escabel*<sup>M</sup>

bar stool
*taburete*<sup>M</sup>

# table
*mesa*$^F$

**gate-leg table**
*mesa*$^F$ *de hojas*$^F$ *abatibles*

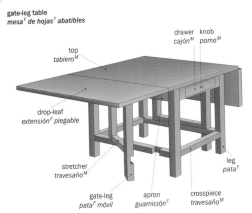

drawer
*cajón*$^M$

knob
*pomo*$^M$

top
*tablero*$^M$

drop-leaf
*extensión*$^F$ *plegable*

stretcher
*travesaño*$^M$

gate-leg
*pata*$^F$ *móvil*

apron
*guarnición*$^F$

crosspiece
*travesaño*$^M$

leg
*pata*$^F$

**examples of tables**
*ejemplos*$^M$ *de mesas*$^F$

**extension table**
*mesa*$^F$ *plegable*

top
*tablero*$^M$

extension
*extensión*$^F$

**nest of tables**
*juego*$^M$ *de mesas*$^F$

**serving cart**
*mesita*$^F$ *de servicio*$^M$

# storage furniture
*muebles*$^M$ *contenedores*

**armoire**
*armario*$^M$

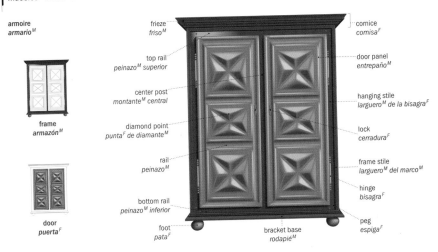

**frame**
*armazón*$^M$

**door**
*puerta*$^F$

frieze
*friso*$^M$

top rail
*peinazo*$^M$ *superior*

center post
*montante*$^M$ *central*

diamond point
*punta*$^F$ *de diamante*$^M$

rail
*peinazo*$^M$

bottom rail
*peinazo*$^M$ *inferior*

foot
*pata*$^F$

bracket base
*rodapié*$^M$

cornice
*cornisa*$^F$

door panel
*entrepaño*$^M$

hanging stile
*larguero*$^M$ *de la bisagra*$^F$

lock
*cerradura*$^F$

frame stile
*larguero*$^M$ *del marco*$^M$

hinge
*bisagra*$^F$

peg
*espiga*$^F$

HOUSE

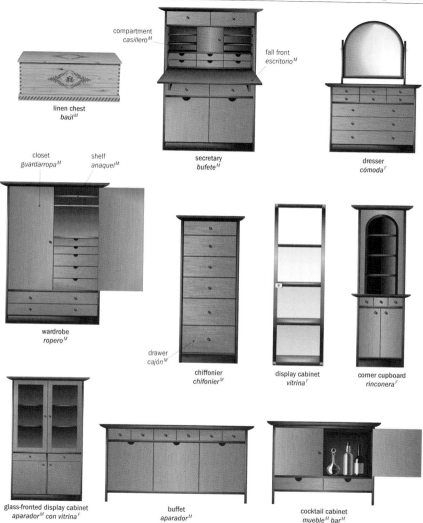

linen chest
baúl<sup>M</sup>

compartment
casillero<sup>M</sup>

fall front
escritorio<sup>M</sup>

secretary
bufete<sup>M</sup>

dresser
cómoda<sup>F</sup>

closet
guardarropa<sup>M</sup>

shelf
anaquel<sup>M</sup>

wardrobe
ropero<sup>M</sup>

drawer
cajón<sup>M</sup>

chiffonier
chifonier<sup>M</sup>

display cabinet
vitrina<sup>F</sup>

corner cupboard
rinconera<sup>F</sup>

glass-fronted display cabinet
aparador<sup>M</sup> con vitrina<sup>F</sup>

buffet
aparador<sup>M</sup>

cocktail cabinet
mueble<sup>M</sup> bar<sup>M</sup>

# bed
*cama*<sup>F</sup>

HOUSE

**sofa bed**
*sofá cama*<sup>M</sup>

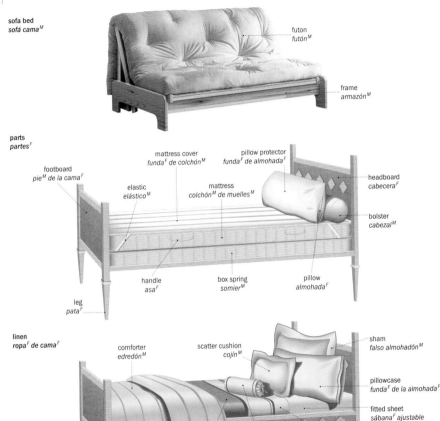

futon
*futón*<sup>M</sup>

frame
*armazón*<sup>M</sup>

**parts**
*partes*<sup>F</sup>

footboard
*pie*<sup>M</sup> *de la cama*<sup>F</sup>

mattress cover
*funda*<sup>F</sup> *de colchón*<sup>M</sup>

pillow protector
*funda*<sup>F</sup> *de almohada*<sup>F</sup>

elastic
*elástico*<sup>M</sup>

mattress
*colchón*<sup>M</sup> *de muelles*<sup>M</sup>

headboard
*cabecera*<sup>F</sup>

bolster
*cabezal*<sup>M</sup>

handle
*asa*<sup>F</sup>

box spring
*somier*<sup>M</sup>

pillow
*almohada*<sup>F</sup>

leg
*pata*<sup>F</sup>

**linen**
*ropa*<sup>F</sup> *de cama*<sup>F</sup>

comforter
*edredón*<sup>M</sup>

scatter cushion
*cojín*<sup>M</sup>

sham
*falso almohadón*<sup>M</sup>

pillowcase
*funda*<sup>F</sup> *de la almohada*<sup>F</sup>

fitted sheet
*sábana*<sup>F</sup> *ajustable*

flat sheet
*sábana*<sup>F</sup>

blanket
*manta*<sup>F</sup>

neck roll
*cojín*<sup>M</sup>

dust ruffle
*faldón*<sup>M</sup>

# children's furniture
*muebles<sup>M</sup> infantiles*

**playpen**
*cuna<sup>F</sup> plegable*

**booster seat**
*silla<sup>F</sup> alzadora*

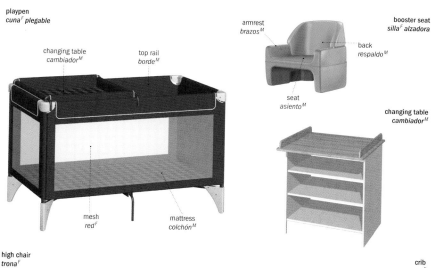

changing table
*cambiador<sup>M</sup>*

top rail
*borde<sup>M</sup>*

armrest
*brazos<sup>M</sup>*

back
*respaldo<sup>M</sup>*

seat
*asiento<sup>M</sup>*

changing table
*cambiador<sup>M</sup>*

mesh
*red<sup>F</sup>*

mattress
*colchón<sup>M</sup>*

**high chair**
*trona<sup>F</sup>*

**crib**
*cuna<sup>F</sup>*

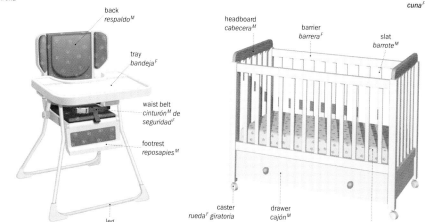

back
*respaldo<sup>M</sup>*

tray
*bandeja<sup>F</sup>*

waist belt
*cinturón<sup>M</sup> de seguridad<sup>F</sup>*

footrest
*reposapies<sup>M</sup>*

leg
*pata<sup>F</sup>*

headboard
*cabecera<sup>M</sup>*

barrier
*barrera<sup>F</sup>*

slat
*barrote<sup>M</sup>*

caster
*rueda<sup>F</sup> giratoria*

drawer
*cajón<sup>M</sup>*

mattress
*colchón<sup>M</sup>*

# lights
*lámparas*<sup>F</sup>

ceiling fixture
*plafón*<sup>M</sup>

hanging pendant
*lámpara*<sup>F</sup> *de techo*<sup>M</sup>

clamp spotlight
*lámpara*<sup>F</sup> *de pinza*<sup>F</sup>

halogen desk lamp
*lámpara*<sup>F</sup> *de despacho*<sup>M</sup>
*halógena*

arm
*brazo*<sup>M</sup>

base
*base*<sup>M</sup>

adjustable lamp
*flexo*<sup>M</sup>

on-off switch
*interruptor*<sup>M</sup>

arm
*brazo*<sup>M</sup>

shade
*pantalla*<sup>F</sup>

spring
*resorte*<sup>M</sup>

adjustable clamp
*tornillo*<sup>M</sup> *de ajuste*<sup>M</sup>

reading lamp
*lámpara*<sup>F</sup> *de cabecera*<sup>F</sup>

shade
*pantalla*<sup>F</sup>

base
*base*<sup>F</sup>

stand
*pedestal*<sup>M</sup>

floor lamp
*lámpara*<sup>F</sup> *de pie*<sup>M</sup>

table lamp
*lámpara*<sup>F</sup> *de mesa*<sup>F</sup>

desk lamp
*lámpara*<sup>F</sup> *de
escritorio*<sup>M</sup>

HOUSE

chandelier
*araña*[F]

bobeche
*arandela*[F]

crystal drop
*colgante*[M]

crystal button
*gota*[F]

column
*columna*[F]

track lighting
*riel*[M] *de iluminación*[F]

bar frame
*armazón*[M]

contact lever
*interruptor*[M]

transformer
*transformador*[M]

spot
*foco*[M]

wall lantern
*farol*[M]

swivel wall lamp
*lámpara*[F] *orientable de pared*[F]

wall sconce
*aplique*[M]

strip lights
*lámparas*[F] *en serie*[F]

post lantern
*farola*[F]

# domestic appliances
*aparatos*[M] *electrodomésticos*

**steam iron**
*plancha*[F] *de vapor*[M]

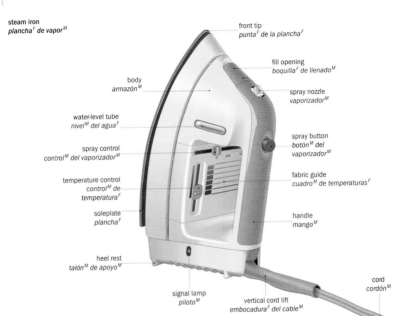

front tip
*punta*[F] *de la plancha*[F]

fill opening
*boquilla*[F] *de llenado*[M]

body
*armazón*[M]

spray nozzle
*vaporizador*[M]

water-level tube
*nivel*[M] *del agua*[F]

spray button
*botón*[M] *del
vaporizador*[M]

spray control
*control*[M] *del vaporizador*[M]

temperature control
*control*[M] *de
temperatura*[F]

fabric guide
*cuadro*[M] *de temperaturas*[F]

soleplate
*plancha*[F]

handle
*mango*[M]

heel rest
*talón*[M] *de apoyo*[M]

cord
*cordón*[M]

signal lamp
*piloto*[M]

vertical cord lift
*embocadura*[F] *del cable*[M]

**hand held vacuum cleaner**
*aspirador*[M] *manual*

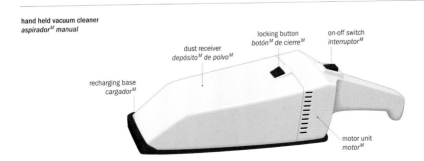

locking button
*botón*[M] *de cierre*[M]

on-off switch
*interruptor*[M]

dust receiver
*depósito*[M] *de polvo*[M]

recharging base
*cargador*[M]

motor unit
*motor*[M]

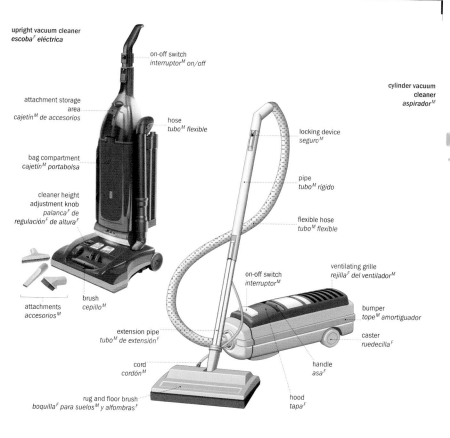

upright vacuum cleaner
*escoba^F eléctrica*

on-off switch
*interruptor^M on/off*

attachment storage
area
*cajetín^M de accesorios*

hose
*tubo^M flexible*

bag compartment
*cajetín^M portabolsa*

cleaner height
adjustment knob
*palanca^F de
regulación^F de altura^F*

attachments
*accesorios^M*

brush
*cepillo^M*

cylinder vacuum
cleaner
*aspirador^M*

locking device
*seguro^M*

pipe
*tubo^M rígido*

flexible hose
*tubo^M flexible*

ventilating grille
*rejilla^F del ventilador^M*

on-off switch
*interruptor^M*

bumper
*tope^M amortiguador*

caster
*ruedecilla^F*

extension pipe
*tubo^M de extensión^F*

cord
*cordón^M*

handle
*asa^F*

rug and floor brush
*boquilla^F para suelos^M y alfombras^F*

hood
*tapa^F*

**vacuum cleaner attachments**
*accesorios^M*

upholstery nozzle
*boquilla^F para tapicería^F*

dusting brush
*cepillo^M-plumero^M*

crevice tool
*boquilla^F rinconera*

floor brush
*cepillo^M para suelos^M*

**range hood**
*campana*<sup>F</sup>

**electric range**
*cocina*<sup>F</sup> *eléctrica*

cooking element
*elemento*<sup>M</sup> *de cocción*<sup>F</sup>

clock timer
*reloj*<sup>M</sup>

cooktop
*encimera*<sup>F</sup>

control panel
*panel*<sup>M</sup> *de mandos*<sup>M</sup>

control knob
*botón*<sup>M</sup> *de mando*<sup>M</sup>

filter
*filtro*<sup>M</sup>

cooktop edge
*borde*<sup>M</sup>

oven
*horno*<sup>M</sup>

handle
*asa*<sup>F</sup>

window
*visor*<sup>M</sup>

**surface element**
*placa*<sup>F</sup> *eléctrica*

tubular element
*resistencia*<sup>F</sup>

terminal
*enchufe*<sup>M</sup>

rack
*parrilla*<sup>F</sup>

drawer
*cajón*<sup>M</sup> *calientaplatos*

**drip bowl**
*protector*<sup>M</sup>

**trim ring**
*arandela*<sup>F</sup>

**gas range**
*cocina*<sup>F</sup> *de gas*<sup>M</sup>

grate
*rejilla*<sup>F</sup>

burner
*quemador*<sup>M</sup>

burner control knobs
*mandos*<sup>M</sup> *de los quemadores*<sup>M</sup>

cooktop
*encimera*<sup>F</sup>

control panel
*panel*<sup>M</sup> *de mandos*<sup>M</sup>

oven
*horno*<sup>M</sup>

handle
*tirador*<sup>M</sup>

window
*visor*<sup>M</sup>

rack
*parrilla*<sup>F</sup>

door
*puerta*<sup>F</sup>

**chest freezer**
*arcón$^M$ congelador*

lock
*cierre$^M$*

lid
*tapa$^F$*

basket
*cesto$^M$*

cabinet
*cuba$^F$*

defrost drain
*válvula$^F$ de drenaje$^M$*

temperature control
*termostato$^M$*

**refrigerator**
*frigorífico$^M$*

switch
*interruptor$^M$*

door stop
*tope$^M$ de la puerta$^F$*

magnetic gasket
*imán$^M$*

butter compartment
*compartimiento$^M$ para mantequilla$^F$*

shelf
*rejilla$^F$*

handle
*manilla$^F$*

meat keeper
*cajón$^M$ para carnes$^F$*

water dispenser
*dispensador$^M$ de agua$^F$*

shelf channel
*riel$^M$ para las rejillas$^F$*

freezer compartment
*congelador$^M$ incorporado*

refrigerator compartment
*espacio$^M$ interior*

storage door
*puerta$^F$ del refrigerador$^M$*

guard rail
*listón$^M$*

dairy compartment
*compartimiento$^M$ para lácteos$^M$*

crisper
*cesto$^M$ para verdura$^F$*

domestic appliances

HOUSE

**front-loading washer**
*lavadora<sup>F</sup> de carga<sup>F</sup> frontal*

control knob
*programador<sup>M</sup>*

temperature selector
*selector<sup>M</sup> de temperatura<sup>F</sup>*

water-level selector
*selector<sup>M</sup> de nivel<sup>M</sup> de agua<sup>F</sup>*

control panel
*panel<sup>M</sup> de control<sup>M</sup>*

door
*puerta<sup>F</sup>*

**top-loading washer**
*lavadora<sup>F</sup> de carga<sup>F</sup> vertical*

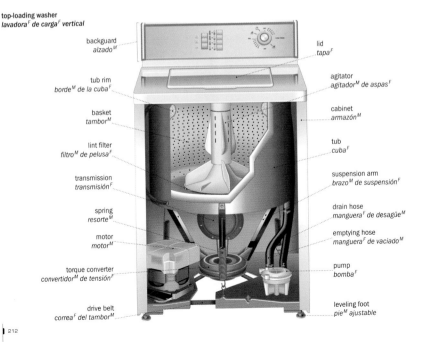

backguard
*alzado<sup>M</sup>*

lid
*tapa<sup>F</sup>*

tub rim
*borde<sup>M</sup> de la cuba<sup>F</sup>*

agitator
*agitador<sup>M</sup> de aspas<sup>F</sup>*

basket
*tambor<sup>M</sup>*

cabinet
*armazón<sup>M</sup>*

lint filter
*filtro<sup>M</sup> de pelusa<sup>F</sup>*

tub
*cuba<sup>F</sup>*

transmission
*transmisión<sup>F</sup>*

suspension arm
*brazo<sup>M</sup> de suspensión<sup>F</sup>*

spring
*resorte<sup>M</sup>*

drain hose
*manguera<sup>F</sup> de desagüe<sup>M</sup>*

motor
*motor<sup>M</sup>*

emptying hose
*manguera<sup>F</sup> de vaciado<sup>M</sup>*

torque converter
*convertidor<sup>M</sup> de tensión<sup>F</sup>*

pump
*bomba<sup>F</sup>*

drive belt
*correa<sup>F</sup> del tambor<sup>M</sup>*

leveling foot
*pie<sup>M</sup> ajustable*

domestic appliances

dryer
*secadora<sup>F</sup> de ropa<sup>F</sup>*

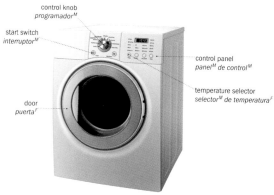

control knob
*programador<sup>M</sup>*

start switch
*interruptor<sup>M</sup>*

control panel
*panel<sup>M</sup> de control<sup>M</sup>*

temperature selector
*selector<sup>M</sup> de temperatura<sup>F</sup>*

door
*puerta<sup>F</sup>*

HOUSE

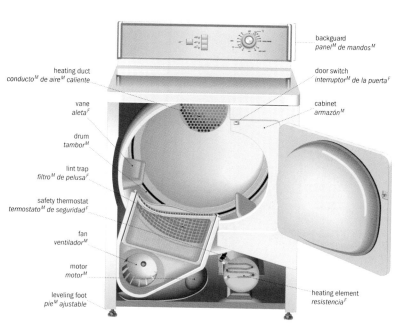

backguard
*panel<sup>M</sup> de mandos<sup>M</sup>*

heating duct
*conducto<sup>M</sup> de aire<sup>M</sup> caliente*

door switch
*interruptor<sup>M</sup> de la puerta<sup>F</sup>*

vane
*aleta<sup>F</sup>*

cabinet
*armazón<sup>M</sup>*

drum
*tambor<sup>M</sup>*

lint trap
*filtro<sup>M</sup> de pelusa<sup>F</sup>*

safety thermostat
*termostato<sup>M</sup> de seguridad<sup>F</sup>*

fan
*ventilador<sup>M</sup>*

motor
*motor<sup>M</sup>*

leveling foot
*pie<sup>M</sup> ajustable*

heating element
*resistencia<sup>F</sup>*

domestic appliances

HOUSE

**control panel: dishwasher**
*panel<sup>M</sup> de control<sup>M</sup>*

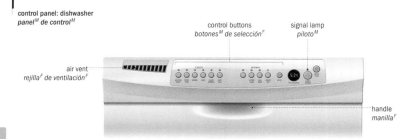

control buttons
*botones<sup>M</sup> de selección<sup>F</sup>*

signal lamp
*piloto<sup>M</sup>*

air vent
*rejilla<sup>F</sup> de ventilación<sup>F</sup>*

handle
*manilla<sup>F</sup>*

**dishwasher**
*lavavajillas<sup>M</sup>*

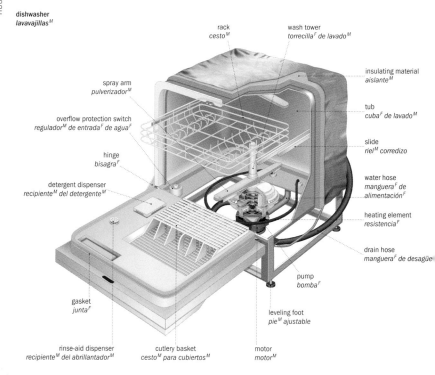

rack
*cesto<sup>M</sup>*

wash tower
*torrecilla<sup>F</sup> de lavado<sup>M</sup>*

insulating material
*aislante<sup>M</sup>*

spray arm
*pulverizador<sup>M</sup>*

tub
*cuba<sup>F</sup> de lavado<sup>M</sup>*

overflow protection switch
*regulador<sup>M</sup> de entrada<sup>F</sup> de agua<sup>F</sup>*

slide
*riel<sup>M</sup> corredizo*

hinge
*bisagra<sup>F</sup>*

water hose
*manguera<sup>F</sup> de alimentación<sup>F</sup>*

detergent dispenser
*recipiente<sup>M</sup> del detergente<sup>M</sup>*

heating element
*resistencia<sup>F</sup>*

drain hose
*manguera<sup>F</sup> de desagüe*

gasket
*junta<sup>F</sup>*

pump
*bomba<sup>F</sup>*

leveling foot
*pie<sup>M</sup> ajustable*

rinse-aid dispenser
*recipiente<sup>M</sup> del abrillantador<sup>M</sup>*

cutlery basket
*cesto<sup>M</sup> para cubiertos<sup>M</sup>*

motor
*motor<sup>M</sup>*

# household equipment
*artículos<sup>M</sup> de limpieza<sup>F</sup>*

tea towel
*bayeta<sup>F</sup> de cocina<sup>F</sup>*

scouring pad
*estropajo<sup>M</sup> con esponja<sup>F</sup>*

dustpan
*recogedor<sup>M</sup>*

broom
*escoba<sup>F</sup>*

mop
*fregona<sup>F</sup>*

HOUSE

handle
*palo<sup>M</sup>*

brush
*cepillo<sup>M</sup>*

block
*lomo<sup>M</sup>*

fibers
*cerdas<sup>F</sup>*

garbage can
*cubo<sup>M</sup> de basura<sup>F</sup>*

lid
*tapa<sup>F</sup>*

handle
*asa<sup>F</sup>*

fibers
*cerdas<sup>F</sup>*

pail
*cubo<sup>M</sup>*

pouring spout
*pitorro<sup>M</sup>*

handle
*asa<sup>F</sup>*

215

DO-IT-YOURSELF AND GARDENING

## plumbing tools
*fontería^F : herramientas^F*

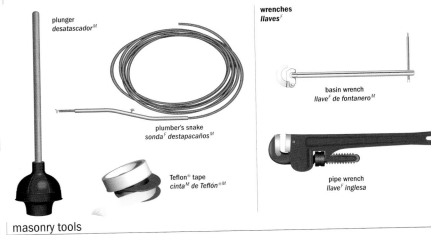

plunger
*desatascador^M*

plumber's snake
*sonda^F destapacaños^M*

Teflon® tape
*cinta^M de Teflón^®M*

**wrenches**
***llaves^F***

basin wrench
*llave^F de fontanero^M*

pipe wrench
*llave^F inglesa*

## masonry tools
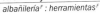
*albañilería^F : herramientas^F*

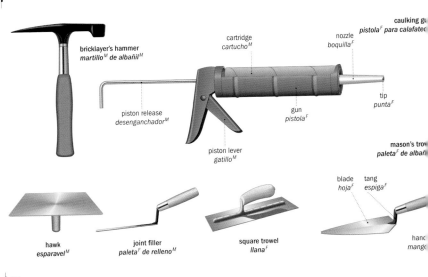

bricklayer's hammer
*martillo^M de albañil^M*

piston release
*desenganchador^M*

piston lever
*gatillo^M*

caulking gu
*pistola^F para calafatec*

cartridge
*cartucho^M*

nozzle
*boquilla^F*

gun
*pistola^F*

tip
*punta^F*

mason's tro
*paleta^F de albañ*

blade
*hoja^F*

tang
*espiga^F*

han
*mang*

hawk
*esparavel^M*

joint filler
*paleta^F de relleno^M*

square trowel
*llana^F*

## electricity tools
*electricidad<sup>F</sup> : herramientas<sup>F</sup>*

op light
terna<sup>F</sup> movible

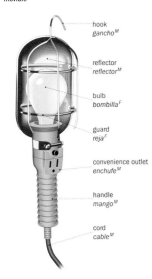

hook
*gancho<sup>M</sup>*

reflector
*reflector<sup>M</sup>*

bulb
*bombilla<sup>F</sup>*

guard
*reja<sup>F</sup>*

convenience outlet
*enchufe<sup>M</sup>*

handle
*mango<sup>M</sup>*

cord
*cable<sup>M</sup>*

neon tester
*lámpara<sup>F</sup> de prueba<sup>F</sup> de neón<sup>M</sup>*

voltage tester
*detector<sup>M</sup> de tensión<sup>F</sup>*

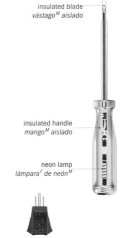

insulated blade
*vástago<sup>M</sup> aislado*

insulated handle
*mango<sup>M</sup> aislado*

neon lamp
*lámpara<sup>F</sup> de neón<sup>M</sup>*

wire nut
*capuchón<sup>M</sup> de plástico<sup>M</sup>*

receptacle analyzer
*probador<sup>M</sup> de contactos<sup>M</sup> con tierra<sup>F</sup>*

ltipurpose tool
nzas<sup>F</sup> multiuso

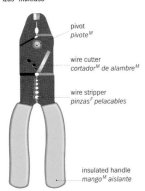

pivot
*pivote<sup>M</sup>*

wire cutter
*cortador<sup>M</sup> de alambre<sup>M</sup>*

wire stripper
*pinzas<sup>F</sup> pelacables*

insulated handle
*mango<sup>M</sup> aislante*

needle-nose pliers
*alicates<sup>M</sup> de punta<sup>F</sup>*

lineman's pliers
*alicates<sup>M</sup> de electricista<sup>M</sup>*

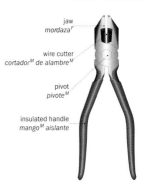

jaw
*mordaza<sup>F</sup>*

wire cutter
*cortador<sup>M</sup> de alambre<sup>M</sup>*

pivot
*pivote<sup>M</sup>*

insulated handle
*mango<sup>M</sup> aislante*

# soldering and welding tools

*herramientas<sup>F</sup> de soldadura<sup>F</sup>*

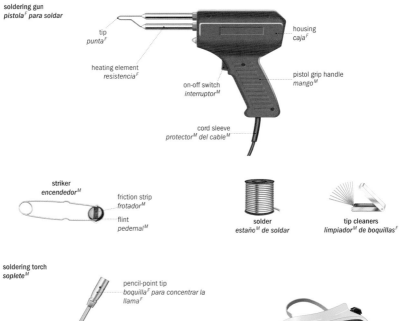

soldering gun
*pistola<sup>F</sup> para soldar*

tip
*punta<sup>F</sup>*

housing
*caja<sup>F</sup>*

heating element
*resistencia<sup>F</sup>*

pistol grip handle
*mango<sup>M</sup>*

on-off switch
*interruptor<sup>M</sup>*

cord sleeve
*protector<sup>M</sup> del cable<sup>M</sup>*

striker
*encendedor<sup>M</sup>*

friction strip
*frotador<sup>M</sup>*

flint
*pedernal<sup>M</sup>*

solder
*estaño<sup>M</sup> de soldar*

tip cleaners
*limpiador<sup>M</sup> de boquillas<sup>F</sup>*

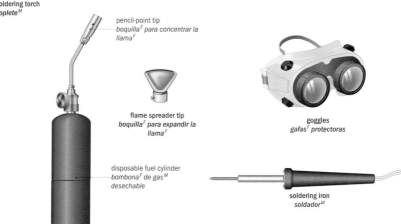

soldering torch
*soplete<sup>M</sup>*

pencil-point tip
*boquilla<sup>F</sup> para concentrar la llama<sup>F</sup>*

flame spreader tip
*boquilla<sup>F</sup> para expandir la llama<sup>F</sup>*

goggles
*gafas<sup>F</sup> protectoras*

disposable fuel cylinder
*bombona<sup>F</sup> de gas<sup>M</sup> desechable*

soldering iron
*soldador<sup>M</sup>*

## painting
*mantenimiento<sup>M</sup> de pinturas<sup>F</sup>*

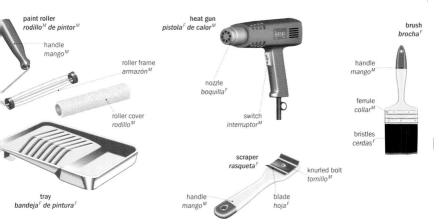

paint roller
*rodillo<sup>M</sup> de pintor<sup>M</sup>*

handle
*mango<sup>M</sup>*

roller frame
*armazón<sup>M</sup>*

roller cover
*rodillo<sup>M</sup>*

tray
*bandeja<sup>F</sup> de pintura<sup>F</sup>*

heat gun
*pistola<sup>F</sup> de calor<sup>M</sup>*

nozzle
*boquilla<sup>F</sup>*

switch
*interruptor<sup>M</sup>*

brush
*brocha<sup>F</sup>*

handle
*mango<sup>M</sup>*

ferrule
*collar<sup>M</sup>*

bristles
*cerdas<sup>F</sup>*

scraper
*rasqueta<sup>F</sup>*

handle
*mango<sup>M</sup>*

knurled bolt
*tornillo<sup>M</sup>*

blade
*hoja<sup>F</sup>*

## ladders and stepladders
*escaleras<sup>F</sup> de mano<sup>F</sup>*

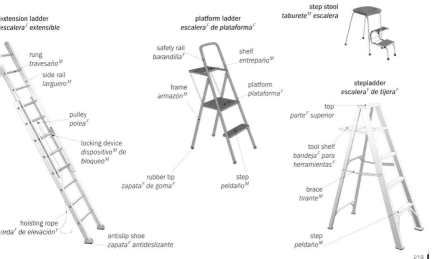

extension ladder
*escalera<sup>F</sup> extensible*

rung
*travesaño<sup>M</sup>*

side rail
*larguero<sup>M</sup>*

pulley
*polea<sup>F</sup>*

locking device
*dispositivo<sup>M</sup> de
bloqueo<sup>M</sup>*

hoisting rope
*cuerda<sup>F</sup> de elevación<sup>F</sup>*

antislip shoe
*zapata<sup>F</sup> antideslizante*

platform ladder
*escalera<sup>F</sup> de plataforma<sup>F</sup>*

safety rail
*barandilla<sup>F</sup>*

frame
*armazón<sup>M</sup>*

rubber tip
*zapata<sup>F</sup> de goma<sup>F</sup>*

shelf
*entrepaño<sup>M</sup>*

platform
*plataforma<sup>F</sup>*

step
*peldaño<sup>M</sup>*

step stool
*taburete<sup>M</sup> escalera*

stepladder
*escalera<sup>F</sup> de tijera<sup>F</sup>*

top
*parte<sup>F</sup> superior*

tool shelf
*bandeja<sup>F</sup> para
herramientas<sup>F</sup>*

brace
*tirante<sup>M</sup>*

step
*peldaño<sup>M</sup>*

# carpentry: nailing tools
*carpintería: herramientas$^F$ para clavar*

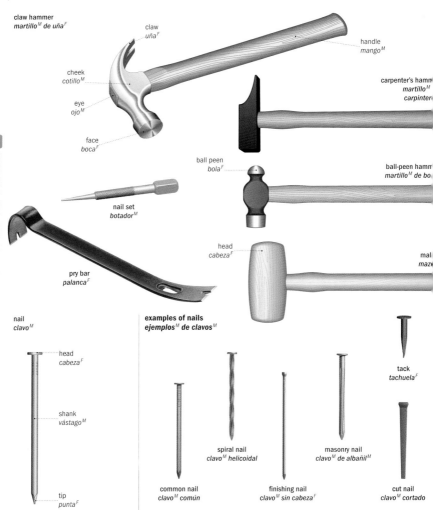

claw hammer
*martillo$^M$ de uña$^F$*

claw
*uña$^F$*

handle
*mango$^M$*

cheek
*cotillo$^M$*

eye
*ojo$^M$*

face
*boca$^F$*

carpenter's hamm
*martillo$^M$*
*carpinter*

nail set
*botador$^M$*

ball peen
*bola$^F$*

ball-peen hamm
*martillo$^M$ de bo*

head
*cabeza$^F$*

mal
*maze*

pry bar
*palanca$^F$*

nail
*clavo$^M$*

**examples of nails**
*ejemplos$^M$ de clavos$^M$*

head
*cabeza$^F$*

shank
*vástago$^M$*

tip
*punta$^F$*

tack
*tachuela$^F$*

spiral nail
*clavo$^M$ helicoidal*

masonry nail
*clavo$^M$ de albañil$^M$*

common nail
*clavo$^M$ común*

finishing nail
*clavo$^M$ sin cabeza$^F$*

cut nail
*clavo$^M$ cortado*

# carpentry: screw-driving tools
*carpintería<sup>F</sup> : herramientas<sup>F</sup> para atornillar*

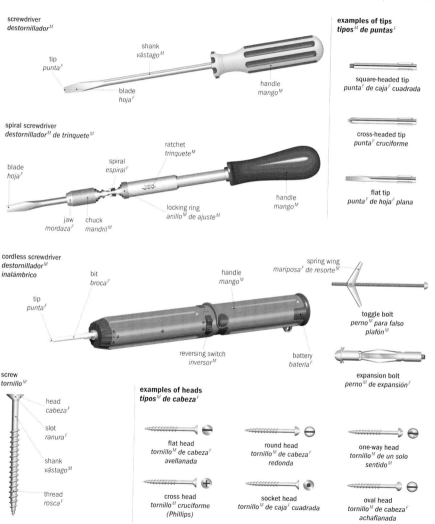

screwdriver
*destornillador<sup>M</sup>*

tip
*punta<sup>F</sup>*

shank
*vástago<sup>M</sup>*

handle
*mango<sup>M</sup>*

blade
*hoja<sup>F</sup>*

spiral screwdriver
*destornillador<sup>M</sup> de trinquete<sup>M</sup>*

blade
*hoja<sup>F</sup>*

spiral
*espiral<sup>F</sup>*

ratchet
*trinquete<sup>M</sup>*

handle
*mango<sup>M</sup>*

locking ring
*anillo<sup>M</sup> de ajuste<sup>M</sup>*

jaw
*mordaza<sup>F</sup>*

chuck
*mandril<sup>M</sup>*

cordless screwdriver
*destornillador<sup>M</sup> inalámbrico*

bit
*broca<sup>F</sup>*

tip
*punta<sup>F</sup>*

handle
*mango<sup>M</sup>*

spring wing
*mariposa<sup>F</sup> de resorte<sup>M</sup>*

reversing switch
*inversor<sup>M</sup>*

battery
*batería<sup>F</sup>*

toggle bolt
*perno<sup>M</sup> para falso plafón<sup>M</sup>*

expansion bolt
*perno<sup>M</sup> de expansión<sup>F</sup>*

screw
*tornillo<sup>M</sup>*

head
*cabeza<sup>F</sup>*

slot
*ranura<sup>F</sup>*

shank
*vástago<sup>M</sup>*

thread
*rosca<sup>F</sup>*

**examples of tips**
**tipos<sup>M</sup> de puntas<sup>F</sup>**

square-headed tip
*punta<sup>F</sup> de caja<sup>F</sup> cuadrada*

cross-headed tip
*punta<sup>F</sup> cruciforme*

flat tip
*punta<sup>F</sup> de hoja<sup>F</sup> plana*

**examples of heads**
**tipos<sup>M</sup> de cabeza<sup>F</sup>**

flat head
*tornillo<sup>M</sup> de cabeza<sup>F</sup> avellanada*

round head
*tornillo<sup>M</sup> de cabeza<sup>F</sup> redonda*

one-way head
*tornillo<sup>M</sup> de un solo sentido<sup>M</sup>*

cross head
*tornillo<sup>M</sup> cruciforme (Phillips)*

socket head
*tornillo<sup>M</sup> de caja<sup>F</sup> cuadrada*

oval head
*tornillo<sup>M</sup> de cabeza<sup>F</sup> achaflanada*

# carpentry: gripping and tightening tools

*carpintería<sup>F</sup> : herramientas<sup>F</sup> para apretar*

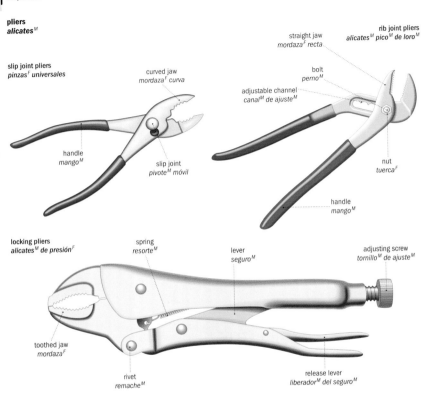

**pliers**
*alicates<sup>M</sup>*

**rib joint pliers**
*alicates<sup>M</sup> pico<sup>M</sup> de loro<sup>M</sup>*

straight jaw
*mordaza<sup>F</sup> recta*

**slip joint pliers**
*pinzas<sup>F</sup> universales*

curved jaw
*mordaza<sup>F</sup> curva*

bolt
*perno<sup>M</sup>*

adjustable channel
*canal<sup>M</sup> de ajuste<sup>M</sup>*

handle
*mango<sup>M</sup>*

slip joint
*pivote<sup>M</sup> móvil*

nut
*tuerca<sup>F</sup>*

handle
*mango<sup>M</sup>*

**locking pliers**
*alicates<sup>M</sup> de presión<sup>F</sup>*

spring
*resorte<sup>M</sup>*

lever
*seguro<sup>M</sup>*

adjusting screw
*tornillo<sup>M</sup> de ajuste<sup>M</sup>*

toothed jaw
*mordaza<sup>F</sup>*

rivet
*remache<sup>M</sup>*

release lever
*liberador<sup>M</sup> del seguro<sup>M</sup>*

**washers**
*arandelas<sup>F</sup>*

flat washer
*arandela<sup>F</sup> plana*

lock washer
*arandela<sup>F</sup> de presión<sup>F</sup>*

external tooth lock washer
*arandela<sup>F</sup> de presión<sup>F</sup> de dientes<sup>M</sup> externos*

internal tooth lock washer
*arandela<sup>F</sup> de presión<sup>F</sup> de dientes<sup>M</sup> internos*

**wrenches**
*llaves*<sup>F</sup>

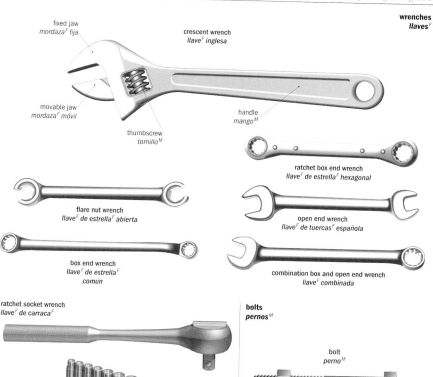

fixed jaw
*mordaza*<sup>F</sup> *fija*

crescent wrench
*llave*<sup>F</sup> *inglesa*

movable jaw
*mordaza*<sup>F</sup> *móvil*

handle
*mango*<sup>M</sup>

thumbscrew
*tornillo*<sup>M</sup>

ratchet box end wrench
*llave*<sup>F</sup> *de estrella*<sup>F</sup> *hexagonal*

flare nut wrench
*llave*<sup>F</sup> *de estrella*<sup>F</sup> *abierta*

open end wrench
*llave*<sup>F</sup> *de tuercas*<sup>F</sup> *española*

box end wrench
*llave*<sup>F</sup> *de estrella*<sup>F</sup>
*común*

combination box and open end wrench
*llave*<sup>F</sup> *combinada*

ratchet socket wrench
*llave*<sup>F</sup> *de carraca*<sup>F</sup>

socket set
*juego*<sup>M</sup> *de casquillos*<sup>M</sup>

**bolts**
*pernos*<sup>M</sup>

bolt
*perno*<sup>M</sup>

nut
*tuerca*<sup>F</sup>

head
*cabeza*<sup>F</sup>

shoulder bolt
*perno*<sup>M</sup> *con collarín*<sup>M</sup>

threaded rod
*rosca*<sup>F</sup>

shoulder
*collarín*<sup>M</sup>

**nuts**
*tuercas*<sup>F</sup>

hexagon nut
*tuerca*<sup>F</sup> *hexagonal*

acorn nut
*tuerca*<sup>F</sup> *cerrada*

wing nut
*tuerca*<sup>F</sup> *de mariposa*<sup>F</sup>

DO-IT-YOURSELF AND GARDENING

**C-clamp**
*prensa^M en C*

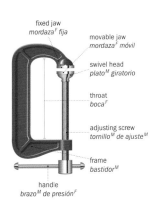

fixed jaw
*mordaza^F fija*

movable jaw
*mordaza^F móvil*

swivel head
*plato^M giratorio*

throat
*boca^F*

adjusting screw
*tornillo^M de ajuste^M*

frame
*bastidor^M*

handle
*brazo^M de presión^F*

**vise**
*torno^M de banco^M*

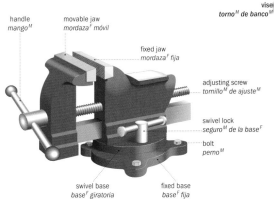

handle
*mango^M*

movable jaw
*mordaza^F móvil*

fixed jaw
*mordaza^F fija*

adjusting screw
*tornillo^M de ajuste^M*

swivel lock
*seguro^M de la base^F*

bolt
*perno^M*

swivel base
*base^F giratoria*

fixed base
*base^F fija*

**pipe clamp**
*sargento^M*

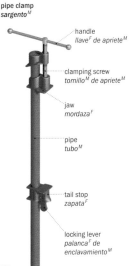

handle
*llave^F de apriete^M*

clamping screw
*tornillo^M de apriete^M*

jaw
*mordaza^F*

pipe
*tubo^M*

tail stop
*zapata^F*

locking lever
*palanca^F de enclavamiento^M*

**work bench and vise**
*banco^M de trabajo^M*

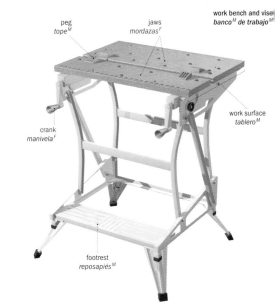

peg
*tope^M*

jaws
*mordazas^F*

work surface
*tablero^M*

crank
*manivela^F*

footrest
*reposapiés^M*

# carpentry: measuring and marking tools
*carpintería<sup>F</sup> : instrumentos<sup>M</sup> de trazado<sup>M</sup> y de medición<sup>F</sup>*

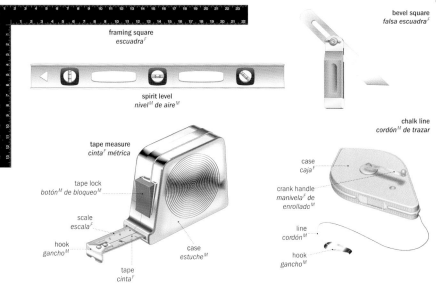

framing square
*escuadra<sup>F</sup>*

bevel square
*falsa escuadra<sup>F</sup>*

spirit level
*nivel<sup>M</sup> de aire<sup>M</sup>*

chalk line
*cordón<sup>M</sup> de trazar*

tape measure
*cinta<sup>F</sup> métrica*

tape lock
*botón<sup>M</sup> de bloqueo<sup>M</sup>*

scale
*escala<sup>F</sup>*

hook
*gancho<sup>M</sup>*

tape
*cinta<sup>F</sup>*

case
*estuche<sup>M</sup>*

case
*caja<sup>F</sup>*

crank handle
*manivela<sup>F</sup> de enrollado<sup>M</sup>*

line
*cordón<sup>M</sup>*

hook
*gancho<sup>M</sup>*

# carpentry: miscellaneous material
*carpintería<sup>F</sup> : materiales<sup>M</sup> varios*

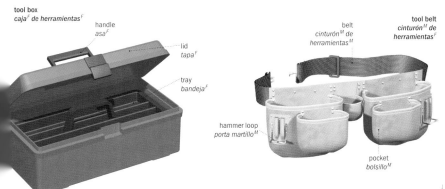

tool box
*caja<sup>F</sup> de herramientas<sup>F</sup>*

handle
*asa<sup>F</sup>*

lid
*tapa<sup>F</sup>*

tray
*bandeja<sup>F</sup>*

belt
*cinturón<sup>M</sup> de herramientas<sup>M</sup>*

tool belt
*cinturón<sup>M</sup> de herramientas<sup>F</sup>*

hammer loop
*porta martillo<sup>M</sup>*

pocket
*bolsillo<sup>M</sup>*

# carpentry: sawing tools
*carpintería^F : herramientas^F para serrar*

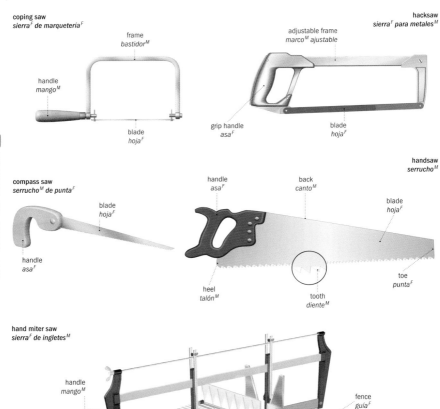

**coping saw**
*sierra^F de marquetería^F*

**hacksaw**
*sierra^F para metales^M*

frame
*bastidor^M*

adjustable frame
*marco^M ajustable*

handle
*mango^M*

grip handle
*asa^F*

blade
*hoja^F*

blade
*hoja^F*

**compass saw**
*serrucho^M de punta^F*

**handsaw**
*serrucho^M*

blade
*hoja^F*

handle
*asa^F*

back
*canto^M*

blade
*hoja^F*

handle
*asa^F*

heel
*talón^M*

tooth
*diente^M*

toe
*punta^F*

**hand miter saw**
*sierra^F de ingletes^M*

handle
*mango^M*

fence
*guía^F*

miter box
*caja^F de ingletes^M*

end stop
*final^M de carrera^F*

blade
*cuchilla^F*

miter latch
*pestillo^M de ingletes^M*

miter scale
*escala^F de ingletes*

clamp
*mordaza^F*

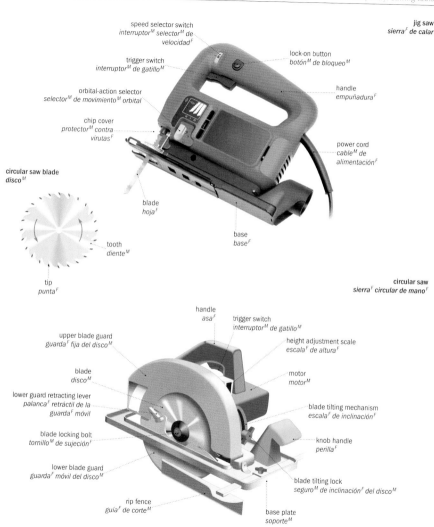

jig saw
*sierra*<sup>F</sup> *de calar*

speed selector switch
*interruptor*<sup>M</sup> *selector*<sup>M</sup> *de velocidad*<sup>F</sup>

lock-on button
*botón*<sup>M</sup> *de bloqueo*<sup>M</sup>

trigger switch
*interruptor*<sup>M</sup> *de gatillo*<sup>M</sup>

handle
*empuñadura*<sup>F</sup>

orbital-action selector
*selector*<sup>M</sup> *de movimiento*<sup>M</sup> *orbital*

chip cover
*protector*<sup>M</sup> *contra virutas*<sup>F</sup>

power cord
*cable*<sup>M</sup> *de alimentación*<sup>F</sup>

circular saw blade
*disco*<sup>M</sup>

blade
*hoja*<sup>F</sup>

base
*base*<sup>F</sup>

tooth
*diente*<sup>M</sup>

tip
*punta*<sup>F</sup>

circular saw
*sierra*<sup>F</sup> *circular de mano*<sup>F</sup>

handle
*asa*<sup>F</sup>

trigger switch
*interruptor*<sup>M</sup> *de gatillo*<sup>M</sup>

upper blade guard
*guarda*<sup>F</sup> *fija del disco*<sup>M</sup>

height adjustment scale
*escala*<sup>F</sup> *de altura*<sup>F</sup>

blade
*disco*<sup>M</sup>

motor
*motor*<sup>M</sup>

lower guard retracting lever
*palanca*<sup>F</sup> *retráctil de la guarda*<sup>F</sup> *móvil*

blade tilting mechanism
*escala*<sup>F</sup> *de inclinación*<sup>F</sup>

blade locking bolt
*tornillo*<sup>M</sup> *de sujeción*<sup>F</sup>

knob handle
*perilla*<sup>F</sup>

lower blade guard
*guarda*<sup>F</sup> *móvil del disco*<sup>M</sup>

blade tilting lock
*seguro*<sup>M</sup> *de inclinación*<sup>F</sup> *del disco*<sup>M</sup>

rip fence
*guía*<sup>F</sup> *de corte*<sup>M</sup>

base plate
*soporte*<sup>M</sup>

# carpentry: drilling tools
*carpintería^F : herramientas^F percutoras*

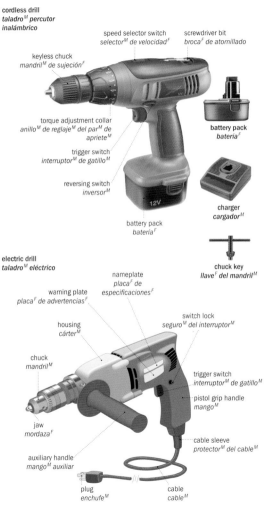

**cordless drill**
*taladro^M percutor*
*inalámbrico*

speed selector switch
*selector^M de velocidad^F*

screwdriver bit
*broca^F de atornillado*

keyless chuck
*mandril^M de sujeción^F*

torque adjustment collar
*anillo^M de reglaje^M del par^M de*
*apriete^M*

trigger switch
*interruptor^M de gatillo^M*

reversing switch
*inversor^M*

battery pack
*batería^F*

battery pack
*batería^F*

charger
*cargador^M*

chuck key
*llave^F del mandril^M*

**electric drill**
*taladro^M eléctrico*

nameplate
*placa^F de*
*especificaciones^F*

warning plate
*placa^F de advertencias^F*

switch lock
*seguro^M del interruptor^M*

housing
*cárter^M*

chuck
*mandril^M*

trigger switch
*interruptor^M de gatillo^M*

pistol grip handle
*mango^M*

jaw
*mordaza^F*

cable sleeve
*protector^M del cable^M*

auxiliary handle
*mango^M auxiliar*

plug
*enchufe^M*

cable
*cable^M*

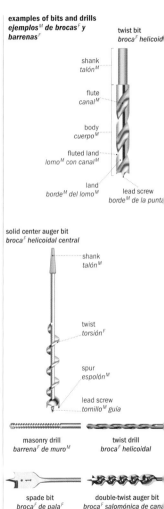

**examples of bits and drills**
**ejemplos^M de brocas^F y**
**barrenas^F**

twist bit
*broca^F helicoid*

shank
*talón^M*

flute
*canal^M*

body
*cuerpo^M*

fluted land
*lomo^M con canal^M*

land
*borde^M del lomo^M*

lead screw
*borde^M de la punta*

solid center auger bit
*broca^F helicoidal central*

shank
*talón^M*

twist
*torsión^F*

spur
*espolón^M*

lead screw
*tornillo^M guía*

masonry drill
*barrena^F de muro^M*

twist drill
*broca^F helicoidal*

spade bit
*broca^F de pala^F*

double-twist auger bit
*broca^F salomónica de canal*
*angosto*

# carpentry: shaping tools
*carpintería$^F$ : herramientas$^F$ de perfilado$^M$*

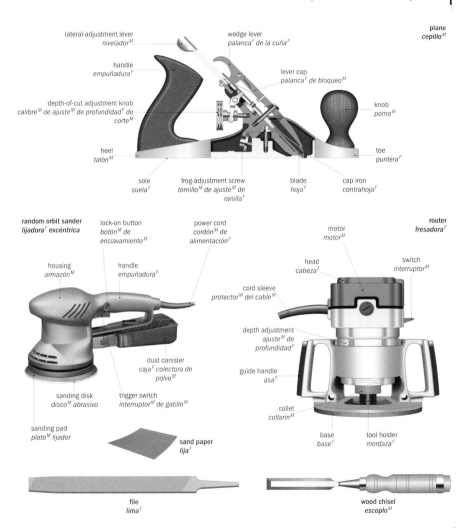

lateral-adjustment lever
*nivelador$^M$*

wedge lever
*palanca$^F$ de la cuña$^F$*

plane
*cepillo$^M$*

handle
*empuñadura$^F$*

lever cap
*palanca$^F$ de bloqueo$^M$*

depth-of-cut adjustment knob
*calibre$^M$ de ajuste$^M$ de profundidad$^F$ de corte$^M$*

knob
*pomo$^M$*

heel
*talón$^M$*

toe
*puntera$^F$*

sole
*suela$^F$*

frog-adjustment screw
*tornillo$^M$ de ajuste$^M$ de ranilla$^F$*

blade
*hoja$^F$*

cap iron
*contrahoja$^F$*

**random orbit sander**
*lijadora$^F$ excéntrica*

lock-on button
*botón$^M$ de enclavamiento$^M$*

power cord
*cordón$^M$ de alimentación$^F$*

motor
*motor$^M$*

router
*fresadora$^F$*

housing
*armazón$^M$*

handle
*empuñadura$^F$*

head
*cabeza$^F$*

switch
*interruptor$^M$*

cord sleeve
*protector$^M$ del cable$^M$*

depth adjustment
*ajuste$^M$ de profundidad$^F$*

dust canister
*caja$^F$ colectora de polvo$^M$*

guide handle
*asa$^F$*

sanding disk
*disco$^M$ abrasivo*

trigger switch
*interruptor$^M$ de gatillo$^M$*

collet
*collarín$^M$*

sanding pad
*plato$^M$ lijador*

base
*base$^F$*

tool holder
*mordaza$^F$*

**sand paper**
*lija$^F$*

file
*lima$^F$*

wood chisel
*escoplo$^M$*

# pleasure garden
*jardín*<sup>M</sup>

DO-IT-YOURSELF AND GARDENING

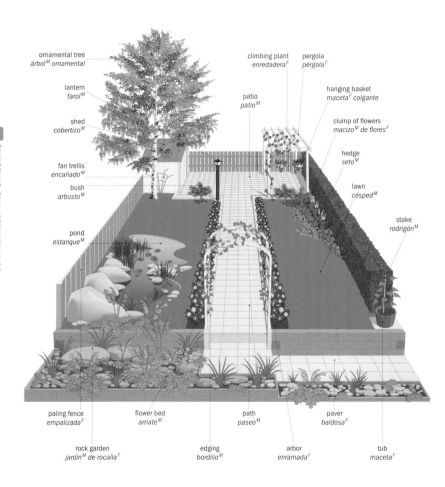

ornamental tree
*árbol*<sup>M</sup> *ornamental*

lantern
*farol*<sup>M</sup>

shed
*cobertizo*<sup>M</sup>

fan trellis
*encañado*<sup>M</sup>

bush
*arbusto*<sup>M</sup>

pond
*estanque*<sup>M</sup>

climbing plant
*enredadera*<sup>F</sup>

patio
*patio*<sup>M</sup>

pergola
*pérgola*<sup>F</sup>

hanging basket
*maceta*<sup>F</sup> *colgante*

clump of flowers
*macizo*<sup>M</sup> *de flores*<sup>F</sup>

hedge
*seto*<sup>M</sup>

lawn
*césped*<sup>M</sup>

stake
*rodrigón*<sup>M</sup>

paling fence
*empalizada*<sup>F</sup>

flower bed
*arriate*<sup>M</sup>

path
*paseo*<sup>M</sup>

paver
*baldosa*<sup>F</sup>

rock garden
*jardín*<sup>M</sup> *de rocalla*<sup>F</sup>

edging
*bordillo*<sup>M</sup>

arbor
*enramada*<sup>F</sup>

tub
*maceta*<sup>F</sup>

## miscellaneous equipment
*equipamiento<sup>M</sup> vario*

compost bin
*cajón<sup>M</sup> de abono<sup>M</sup>
compuesto*

tray
*caja<sup>F</sup>*

wheelbarrow
*carretilla<sup>F</sup>*

handle
*brazo<sup>M</sup>*

leg
*pata<sup>F</sup>*

wheel
*rueda<sup>F</sup>*

## seeding and planting tools
*herramientas<sup>F</sup> para sembrar y plantar*

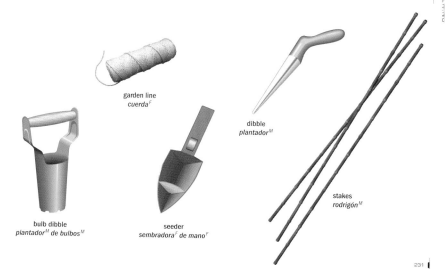

garden line
*cuerda<sup>F</sup>*

dibble
*plantador<sup>M</sup>*

bulb dibble
*plantador<sup>M</sup> de bulbos<sup>M</sup>*

seeder
*sembradora<sup>F</sup> de mano<sup>F</sup>*

stakes
*rodrigón<sup>M</sup>*

# hand tools
*juego<sup>M</sup> de pequeñas herramientas<sup>F</sup>*

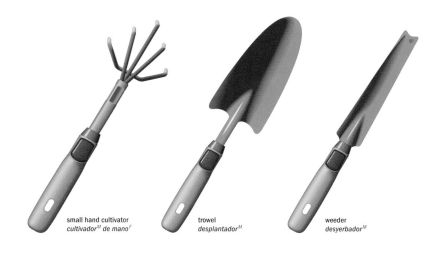

small hand cultivator
*cultivador<sup>M</sup> de mano<sup>F</sup>*

trowel
*desplantador<sup>M</sup>*

weeder
*desyerbador<sup>M</sup>*

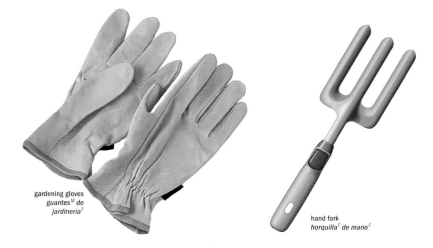

gardening gloves
*guantes<sup>M</sup> de
jardinería<sup>F</sup>*

hand fork
*horquilla<sup>F</sup> de mano<sup>F</sup>*

## tools for loosening the earth
*herramientas<sup>F</sup> para remover la tierra<sup>F</sup>*

weeding hoe
*cultivador<sup>M</sup>*

hoe-fork
*azuela<sup>F</sup>*

draw hoe
*azada<sup>F</sup>*

scuffle hoe
*azada<sup>F</sup> de doble filo<sup>M</sup>*

spade
*laya<sup>F</sup>*

shovel
*pala<sup>F</sup>*

garden fork
*horca<sup>F</sup>*

rake
*rastrillo<sup>M</sup>*

hoe
*azadón<sup>M</sup>*

pick
*pico<sup>M</sup>*

lawn edger
*cuchilla<sup>F</sup> para delimitar el
césped<sup>M</sup>*

# pruning and cutting tools
*herramientas<sup>F</sup> para cortar*

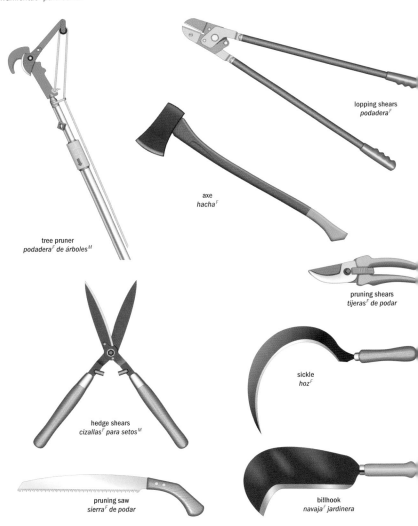

lopping shears
*podadera<sup>F</sup>*

axe
*hacha<sup>F</sup>*

tree pruner
*podadera<sup>F</sup> de árboles<sup>M</sup>*

pruning shears
*tijeras<sup>F</sup> de podar*

sickle
*hoz<sup>F</sup>*

hedge shears
*cizallas<sup>F</sup> para setos<sup>M</sup>*

pruning saw
*sierra<sup>F</sup> de podar*

billhook
*navaja<sup>F</sup> jardinera*

pruning and cutting tools

hedge trimmer
*cortasetos$^{M}$ eléctrico*

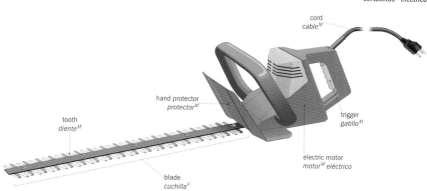

cord
*cable$^{M}$*

hand protector
*protector$^{M}$*

trigger
*gatillo$^{M}$*

tooth
*diente$^{M}$*

electric motor
*motor$^{M}$ eléctrico*

blade
*cuchilla$^{F}$*

chainsaw
*sierra$^{F}$ de cadena$^{F}$*

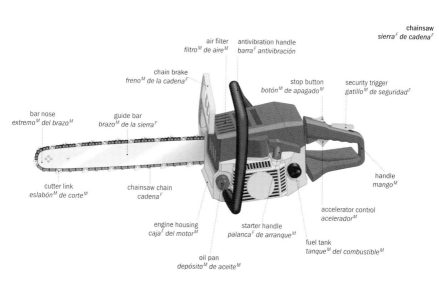

air filter
*filtro$^{M}$ de aire$^{M}$*

antivibration handle
*barra$^{F}$ antivibración*

chain brake
*freno$^{M}$ de la cadena$^{F}$*

stop button
*botón$^{M}$ de apagado$^{M}$*

security trigger
*gatillo$^{M}$ de seguridad$^{F}$*

bar nose
*extremo$^{M}$ del brazo$^{M}$*

guide bar
*brazo$^{M}$ de la sierra$^{F}$*

handle
*mango$^{M}$*

cutter link
*eslabón$^{M}$ de corte$^{M}$*

chainsaw chain
*cadena$^{F}$*

accelerator control
*acelerador$^{M}$*

engine housing
*caja$^{F}$ del motor$^{M}$*

starter handle
*palanca$^{F}$ de arranque$^{M}$*

fuel tank
*tanque$^{M}$ del combustible$^{M}$*

oil pan
*depósito$^{M}$ de aceite$^{M}$*

# watering tools

*herramientas<sup>F</sup> para regar*

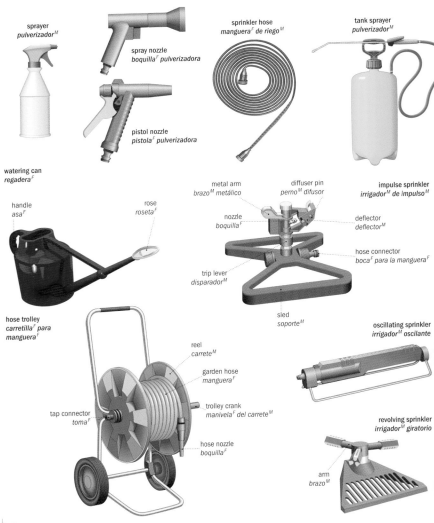

sprayer
*pulverizador<sup>M</sup>*

spray nozzle
*boquilla<sup>F</sup> pulverizadora*

pistol nozzle
*pistola<sup>F</sup> pulverizadora*

sprinkler hose
*manguera<sup>F</sup> de riego<sup>M</sup>*

tank sprayer
*pulverizador<sup>M</sup>*

watering can
*regadera<sup>F</sup>*

handle
*asa<sup>F</sup>*

rose
*roseta<sup>F</sup>*

metal arm
*brazo<sup>M</sup> metálico*

diffuser pin
*perno<sup>M</sup> difusor*

nozzle
*boquilla<sup>F</sup>*

trip lever
*disparador<sup>M</sup>*

impulse sprinkler
*irrigador<sup>M</sup> de impulso<sup>M</sup>*

deflector
*deflector<sup>M</sup>*

hose connector
*boca<sup>F</sup> para la manguera<sup>F</sup>*

sled
*soporte<sup>M</sup>*

hose trolley
*carretilla<sup>F</sup> para manguera<sup>F</sup>*

reel
*carrete<sup>M</sup>*

garden hose
*manguera<sup>F</sup>*

trolley crank
*manivela<sup>F</sup> del carrete<sup>M</sup>*

tap connector
*toma<sup>F</sup>*

hose nozzle
*boquilla<sup>F</sup>*

oscillating sprinkler
*irrigador<sup>M</sup> oscilante*

revolving sprinkler
*irrigador<sup>M</sup> giratorio*

arm
*brazo<sup>M</sup>*

# lawn care
*cuidado<sup>M</sup> del césped<sup>M</sup>*

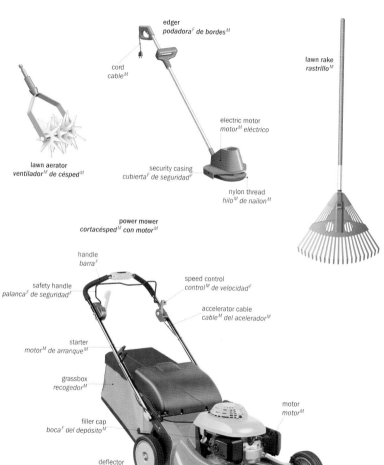

edger
*podadora<sup>F</sup> de bordes<sup>M</sup>*

cord
*cable<sup>M</sup>*

lawn rake
*rastrillo<sup>M</sup>*

electric motor
*motor<sup>M</sup> eléctrico*

lawn aerator
*ventilador<sup>M</sup> de césped<sup>M</sup>*

security casing
*cubierta<sup>F</sup> de seguridad<sup>F</sup>*

nylon thread
*hilo<sup>M</sup> de nailon<sup>M</sup>*

power mower
*cortacésped<sup>M</sup> con motor<sup>M</sup>*

handle
*barra<sup>F</sup>*

speed control
*control<sup>M</sup> de velocidad<sup>F</sup>*

safety handle
*palanca<sup>F</sup> de seguridad<sup>F</sup>*

accelerator cable
*cable<sup>M</sup> del acelerador<sup>M</sup>*

starter
*motor<sup>M</sup> de arranque<sup>M</sup>*

grassbox
*recogedor<sup>M</sup>*

motor
*motor<sup>M</sup>*

filler cap
*boca<sup>F</sup> del depósito<sup>M</sup>*

deflector
*deflector<sup>M</sup>*

casing
*caja<sup>F</sup>*

CLOTHING

**men's headgear**
***sombreros*<sup>M</sup> *de hombre*<sup>M</sup>**

felt hat
*sombrero*<sup>M</sup> *de fieltro*<sup>M</sup>

hatband
*cinta*<sup>F</sup>

binding
*ribete*<sup>M</sup>

crown
*copa*<sup>F</sup>

brim
*ala*<sup>F</sup>

bow
*lazo*<sup>M</sup>

boater
*canotier*<sup>M</sup>

skullcap
*solideo*<sup>M</sup>

derby
*sombrero*<sup>M</sup> *de hongo*<sup>M</sup>

garrison cap
*gorra*<sup>F</sup> *de cuartel*<sup>M</sup>

top hat
*chistera*<sup>F</sup>

shapka
*chapka*<sup>F</sup>

hunting cap
*gorra*<sup>F</sup> *noruega*

ear flap
*orejera*<sup>F</sup>

cap
*gorra*<sup>F</sup>

panama
*panamá*<sup>M</sup>

peak
*visera*<sup>F</sup>

pillbox hat
*sombrero*<sup>M</sup> *sin alas*<sup>F</sup>

cartwheel hat
*pamela*<sup>F</sup>

cloche
*sombrero*<sup>M</sup> *de campana*<sup>F</sup>

toque
*toca*<sup>F</sup>

gob hat
*gorro*<sup>M</sup> *de marinero*<sup>M</sup>

crown
*copa*<sup>F</sup>

sou'wester
*sueste*<sup>M</sup>

turban
*turbante*<sup>M</sup>

brim
*ala*<sup>F</sup>

balaclava
*pasamontañas*<sup>M</sup>

beret
*boina*<sup>F</sup>

stocking cap
*gorro*<sup>M</sup> *de punto*<sup>M</sup> *con*
*borla*<sup>F</sup>

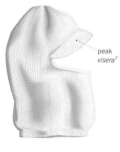

peak
*visera*<sup>F</sup>

felt hat
*sombrero*<sup>M</sup> *de fieltro*<sup>M</sup>

# shoes
*calzados*<sup>M</sup>

**men's shoes**
**zapatos*<sup>M</sup> de hombre*<sup>M</sup>

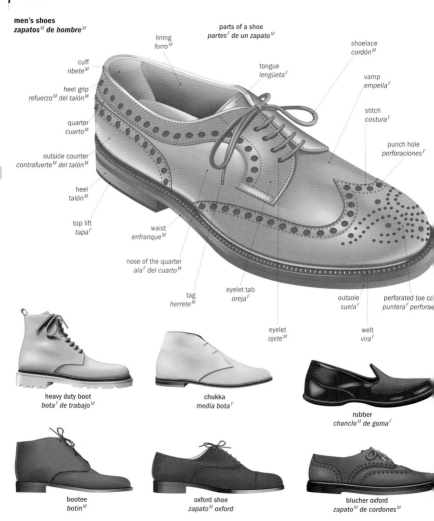

lining
*forro*<sup>M</sup>

parts of a shoe
*partes*<sup>F</sup> de un zapato*<sup>M</sup>

cuff
*ribete*<sup>M</sup>

shoelace
*cordón*<sup>M</sup>

heel grip
*refuerzo*<sup>M</sup> del talón*<sup>M</sup>

tongue
*lengüeta*<sup>F</sup>

vamp
*empella*<sup>F</sup>

quarter
*cuarto*<sup>M</sup>

stitch
*costura*<sup>F</sup>

outside counter
*contrafuerte*<sup>M</sup> del talón*<sup>M</sup>

punch hole
*perforaciones*<sup>F</sup>

heel
*talón*<sup>M</sup>

top lift
*tapa*<sup>F</sup>

waist
*enfranque*<sup>M</sup>

nose of the quarter
*ala*<sup>F</sup> del cuarto*<sup>M</sup>

tag
*herrete*<sup>M</sup>

eyelet tab
*oreja*<sup>F</sup>

outsole
*suela*<sup>F</sup>

perforated toe cap
*puntera*<sup>F</sup> perfora...

eyelet
*ojete*<sup>M</sup>

welt
*vira*<sup>F</sup>

heavy duty boot
*bota*<sup>F</sup> de trabajo*<sup>M</sup>

chukka
*media bota*<sup>F</sup>

rubber
*chanclo*<sup>M</sup> de goma*<sup>F</sup>

bootee
*botín*<sup>M</sup>

oxford shoe
*zapato*<sup>M</sup> oxford

blucher oxford
*zapato*<sup>M</sup> de cordones*<sup>M</sup>

**women's shoes**
*zapatos*<sup>M</sup> **de mujer**<sup>F</sup>

sandal
*sandalia*<sup>F</sup>

ballerina slipper
*bailarina*<sup>F</sup>

sling back shoe
*zapato*<sup>M</sup> *de talón abierto*

pump
*zapato*<sup>M</sup> *de salón*<sup>M</sup>

one-bar shoe
*zapato*<sup>M</sup> *de tacón*<sup>M</sup> *con correa*<sup>F</sup>

T-strap shoe
*zapato*<sup>M</sup> *de correa*<sup>F</sup>

casual shoe
*zapato*<sup>M</sup> *con cordones*<sup>M</sup>

thigh-boot
*bota*<sup>F</sup> *de medio muslo*<sup>M</sup>

boot
*bota*<sup>F</sup>

ankle boot
*botín*<sup>M</sup>

CLOTHING

## unisex shoes
### *calzados* <sup>M</sup> *unisex*

mule
*pantufla* <sup>F</sup>

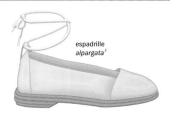

espadrille
*alpargata* <sup>F</sup>

tennis shoe
*zapatilla* <sup>F</sup> *de tenis* <sup>M</sup>

loafer
*mocasin* <sup>M</sup>

sandal
*sandalia* <sup>F</sup>

moccasin
*mocasin* <sup>M</sup>

thong
*chancleta* <sup>F</sup> *playera*

clog
*chancleta* <sup>F</sup>

sandal
*sandalia* <sup>F</sup>

hiking boot
*bota* <sup>F</sup> *de montaña*

## men's gloves
***guantes*<sup>M</sup> *de hombre*<sup>M</sup>**

back of a glove
*dorso*<sup>M</sup> *de un guante*<sup>M</sup>

palm of a glove
*palma*<sup>F</sup> *de un guante*<sup>M</sup>

fourchette
*horquilla*<sup>F</sup>

glove finger
*dedo*<sup>M</sup>

thumb
*pulgar*<sup>M</sup>

palm
*palma*<sup>F</sup>

stitching
*pespunte*<sup>M</sup>

seam
*costura*<sup>F</sup>

snap fastener
*botón*<sup>M</sup> *de presión*<sup>F</sup>

opening
*aberturas*<sup>F</sup> *para los nudillos*<sup>M</sup>

perforation
*perforaciones*<sup>F</sup>

driving glove
*guante*<sup>M</sup> *para conducir*

mitten
*manopla*<sup>F</sup>

## women's gloves
***guantes*<sup>M</sup> *de mujer*<sup>F</sup>**

short glove
*guante*<sup>M</sup> *corto*

wrist-length glove
*guante*<sup>M</sup> *a la muñeca*<sup>F</sup>

gauntlet
*manopla*<sup>F</sup>

evening glove
*guante*<sup>M</sup> *largo*

mitt
*mitón*<sup>M</sup> *largo*

gauntlet
*brazo*<sup>M</sup>

CLOTHING

CLOTHING

## jackets
*chaquetas<sup>F</sup> y chalecos<sup>M</sup>*

**double-breasted jacket**
*chaqueta<sup>F</sup> cruzada*

collar
*cuello<sup>M</sup>*

peaked lapel
*solapa<sup>F</sup> puntiaguda*

lining
*forro<sup>M</sup>*

breast welt pocket
*bolsillo<sup>M</sup> de ojal<sup>M</sup>*

sleeve
*manga<sup>F</sup>*

flap
*solapa<sup>F</sup>*

outside ticket pocket
*bolsillo<sup>M</sup> del cambio<sup>M</sup>*

patch pocket
*bolsillo<sup>M</sup> de parche<sup>M</sup>*

side back vent
*abertura<sup>F</sup> trasera lateral*

**vest**
*chaleco<sup>M</sup>*

V-neck
*cuello<sup>M</sup> en V*

lining
*forro<sup>M</sup>*

welt
*ribete<sup>M</sup>*

front
*delantero<sup>M</sup>*

seam
*costura<sup>F</sup>*

welt pocket
*bolsillo<sup>M</sup> de ribete<sup>M</sup>*

adjustable waist tab
*trincha<sup>F</sup>*

**single-breasted jacket**
*chaqueta<sup>F</sup> recta*

lapel
*solapa<sup>F</sup>*

notch
*muesca<sup>F</sup>*

front
*delantero<sup>M</sup>*

lining
*forro<sup>M</sup>*

pocket handkerchief
*pañuelo<sup>M</sup> de bolsillo<sup>M</sup>*

back
*espalda<sup>F</sup>*

sleeve
*manga<sup>F</sup>*

flap pocket
*bolsillo<sup>M</sup> con cartera<sup>F</sup>*

center back vent
*abertura<sup>F</sup> trasera central*

**shirt**
*camisa*[F]

collar
*cuello*[M]

yoke
*canesú*[M]

set-in sleeve
*manga*[F] *empotrada*

collar point
*punta*[F] *del cuello*[M]

breast pocket
*bolsillo*[M] *superior*

buttoned placket
*tirilla*[F]

front
*delantero*[M]

pointed tab end
*abertura*[F] *con tirilla*[F]

button
*botón*[M]

cuff
*puño*[M]

shirttail
*faldón*[M] *de la camisa*[F]

buttondown collar
*cuello*[M] *con botones*[M]

ascot tie
*corbata*[F] *inglesa*

collar stay
*ballena*[F]

bow tie
*pajarita*[F]

spread collar
*cuello*[M] *italiano*

**necktie**
*corbata*[F]

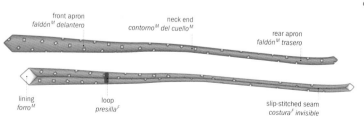

front apron
*faldón*[M] *delantero*

neck end
*contorno*[M] *del cuello*[M]

rear apron
*faldón*[M] *trasero*

lining
*forro*[M]

loop
*presilla*[F]

slip-stitched seam
*costura*[F] *invisible*

CLOTHING

CLOTHING

**pants**
*pantalones^M*

waistband extension
*trabilla^F de la pretina^F*

knife pleat
*pinza^F*

fly
*bragueta^F*

belt loop
*trabilla^F*

front top pocket
*bolsillo^M delantero*

waistband
*pretina^F*

crease
*raya^F*

cuff
*vuelta^F*

**back pocket**
*bolsillo^M trasero*

**suspender clip**
*pinza^F*

**suspenders**
*tirantes^M*

elastic webbing
*banda^F elástica*

adjustment slide
*corredera^F de ajuste^M*

leather end
*lengüeta^F de cuero^M*

button loop
*presilla^F*

**belt**
*cinturón^M*

top stitching
*pespunte^M*

panel
*cuero^M*

tongue
*pasador^M*

buckle
*hebilla^F*

tip
*punta^F*

punch hole
*ojete^M*

belt loop
*trabilla^F*

**underwear**
*ropa<sup>F</sup> interior*

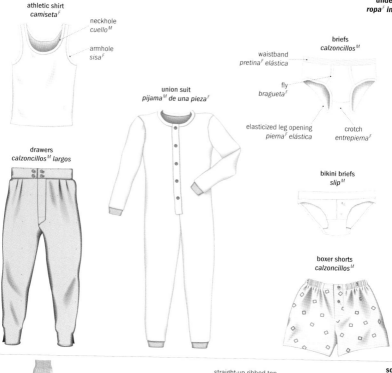

athletic shirt
*camiseta<sup>F</sup>*

neckhole
*cuello<sup>M</sup>*

armhole
*sisa<sup>F</sup>*

briefs
*calzoncillos<sup>M</sup>*

waistband
*pretina<sup>F</sup> elástica*

fly
*bragueta<sup>F</sup>*

union suit
*pijama<sup>M</sup> de una pieza<sup>F</sup>*

elasticized leg opening
*pierna<sup>F</sup> elástica*

crotch
*entrepierna<sup>F</sup>*

drawers
*calzoncillos<sup>M</sup> largos*

bikini briefs
*slip<sup>M</sup>*

boxer shorts
*calzoncillos<sup>M</sup>*

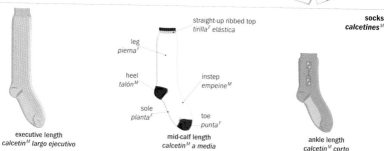

**socks**
*calcetines<sup>M</sup>*

straight-up ribbed top
*tirilla<sup>F</sup> elástica*

leg
*pierna<sup>F</sup>*

heel
*talón<sup>M</sup>*

instep
*empeine<sup>M</sup>*

sole
*planta<sup>F</sup>*

toe
*punta<sup>F</sup>*

executive length
*calcetín<sup>M</sup> largo ejecutivo*

mid-calf length
*calcetín<sup>M</sup> a media
pantorrilla<sup>F</sup>*

ankle length
*calcetín<sup>M</sup> corto*

CLOTHING

## coats
*abrigos*^M *e impermeables*^F

### raincoat
*impermeable*^M

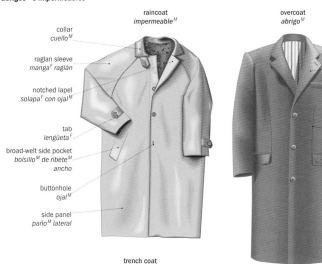

collar
*cuello*^M

raglan sleeve
*manga*^F *raglán*

notched lapel
*solapa*^F *con ojal*^M

tab
*lengüeta*^F

broad-welt side pocket
*bolsillo*^M *de ribete*^M
*ancho*

buttonhole
*ojal*^M

side panel
*paño*^M *lateral*

### overcoat
*abrigo*^M

notched lapel
*solapa*^F *con ojal*^M

breast pocket
*bolsillo*^M *superior*

breast dart
*pinza*^F

flap pocket
*bolsillo*^M *con carte*

### trench coat
*trinchera*^F

two-way collar
*cuello*^M *de doble vista*^F

gun flap
*protector*^M

double-breasted
buttoning
*botonadura*^F *cruzada*

belt
*cinturón*^M

belt loop
*presilla*^F *del cinturón*^M

frame
*hebilla*^F

epaulet
*hombrera*^F

raglan sleeve
*manga*^F *raglán*

sleeve strap loop
*presilla*^F *de la manga*^F

sleeve strap
*correa*^F *de la manga*^F

broad-welt side pocket
*bolsillo*^M *de ribete*^M
*ancho*

### three-quarter coat
*abrigo*^M *de tres cuartos*

parka
*parka*<sup>F</sup>

snap-fastening tab
*botón*<sup>M</sup> *de presión*<sup>F</sup>

zipper
*cremallera*<sup>F</sup>

sheepskin jacket
*zamarra*<sup>F</sup>

duffle coat
*trenca*<sup>F</sup>

hood
*capucha*<sup>F</sup>

yoke
*hombrillo*<sup>M</sup>

frog
*alamar*<sup>M</sup>

patch pocket
*bolsillo*<sup>M</sup> *de parche*<sup>M</sup>

toggle fastening
*botón*<sup>M</sup> *de madera*<sup>F</sup>

jacket
*cazadora*<sup>F</sup>

snap fastener
*botón*<sup>M</sup> *de presión*<sup>M</sup>

windbreaker
*cazadora*<sup>F</sup>

waistband
*pretina*<sup>F</sup>

drawstring
*cordón*<sup>M</sup>

hand-warmer pocket
*bolsillo*<sup>M</sup> *de ojal*<sup>M</sup>

elastic waistband
*pretina*<sup>F</sup> *elástica*

CLOTHING

249

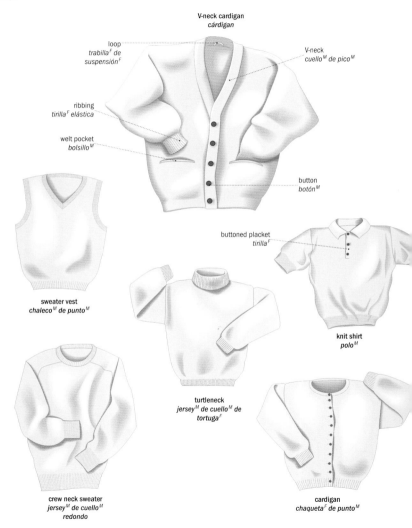

**V-neck cardigan**
*cárdigan*

loop
*trabilla* F *de suspensión* F

V-neck
*cuello* M *de pico* M

ribbing
*tirilla* F *elástica*

welt pocket
*bolsillo* M

button
*botón* M

buttoned placket
*tirilla* F

**sweater vest**
*chaleco* M *de punto* M

**knit shirt**
*polo* M

**turtleneck**
*jersey* M *de cuello* M *de tortuga* F

**crew neck sweater**
*jersey* M *de cuello* M *redondo*

**cardigan**
*chaqueta* F *de punto* M

**suit**
*traje<sup>M</sup> de chaqueta<sup>F</sup>*

jacket
*chaqueta<sup>F</sup>*

skirt
*falda<sup>F</sup>*

**raglan**
*abrigo<sup>M</sup> raglán*

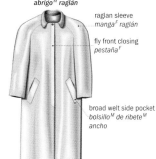

raglan sleeve
*manga<sup>F</sup> raglán*

fly front closing
*pestaña<sup>F</sup>*

broad welt side pocket
*bolsillo<sup>M</sup> de ribete<sup>M</sup> ancho*

**coats**
*chaquetones<sup>M</sup> y abrigos<sup>M</sup>*

top coat
*abrigo<sup>M</sup> redingote*

CLOTHING

**pelerine**
*abrigo<sup>M</sup> con esclavina<sup>F</sup>*

pelerine
*esclavina<sup>F</sup>*

seam pocket
*bolsillo<sup>M</sup> disimulado*

**cape**
*capa<sup>F</sup>*

arm slit
*abertura<sup>F</sup> para el brazo<sup>M</sup>*

**pea jacket**
*chaquetón<sup>M</sup> marinero*

tailored collar
*cuello<sup>M</sup> hechura<sup>F</sup> sastre<sup>M</sup>*

hand-warmer pocket
*bolsillo<sup>M</sup> de ojal<sup>M</sup>*

mock pocket
*bolsillo<sup>M</sup> simulado*

overcoat
*abrigo<sup>M</sup>*

**car coat**
*chaquetón<sup>M</sup> de tres cuartos*

**jacket**
*chaquetón<sup>M</sup>*

**poncho**
*poncho<sup>M</sup>*

**examples of dresses**
*ejemplos$^M$ de vestidos$^M$*

sheath dress
*recto$^M$ entallado*

princess-seamed dress
*corte$^M$ princesa$^F$*

coat dress
*traje$^M$ cruzado*

polo dress
*vestido$^M$ de camiseta$^F$*

housedress
*vestido$^M$ camisero sin mangas*

shirtwaist dress
*vestido$^M$ camisero*

drop-waist dress
*vestido de talle$^M$ bajo*

trapeze dress
*vestido$^M$ acampanado*

sundress
*vestido$^M$ de tirantes$^M$*

wraparound dress
*vestido$^M$ cruzado*

tunic dress
*túnica$^F$*

jumper
*pichi$^M$*

## examples of skirts
### ejemplos<sup>M</sup> de faldas<sup>F</sup>

CLOTHING

gored skirt
falda<sup>F</sup> de piezas<sup>F</sup>

kilt
falda<sup>F</sup> escocesa

sarong
falda<sup>F</sup> sarong<sup>M</sup>

wraparound skirt
falda<sup>F</sup> cruzada

sheath skirt
falda<sup>F</sup> de tubo<sup>M</sup>

ruffled skirt
falda<sup>F</sup> de volantes<sup>M</sup>

straight skirt
falda<sup>F</sup> recta

yoked skirt
falda<sup>F</sup> acampanada

gathered skirt
falda<sup>F</sup> fruncida

culottes
falda<sup>F</sup> pantalón<sup>M</sup>

## examples of pleats
### ejemplos<sup>M</sup> de tablas<sup>F</sup>

inverted pleat
tabla<sup>F</sup> delantera

kick pleat
tabla<sup>F</sup> abierta

accordion pleat
plisada

top-stitched pleat
pespunteada

knife pleat
tablas<sup>F</sup>

CLOTHING

**examples of pants**
*ejemplos* M *de pantalones* M

shorts
*pantalóns* M *cortos*

Bermuda shorts
*bermudas* M

knickers
*bombachos* M

pedal pushers
*pirata* M

jeans
*vaqueros* M

ski pants
*pantalones* M *de tubo* M

footstrap
*trabilla* F

jumpsuit
*buzo* M

overalls
*pantalón* M *peto* M

bell bottoms
*pantalones* M *acampanados*

**jackets, vest and sweaters**
*chaleco* M *, jerseys* M *y chaquetas* F

bolero
*bolero* M

spencer
*bolero* M *con botones* M

blazer
*americana* F

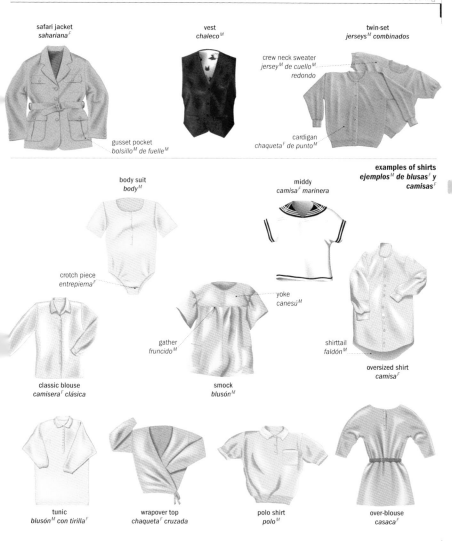

safari jacket
*sahariana*<sup>F</sup>

vest
*chaleco*<sup>M</sup>

twin-set
*jerseys*<sup>M</sup> *combinados*

crew neck sweater
*jersey*<sup>M</sup> *de cuello*<sup>M</sup>
*redondo*

cardigan
*chaqueta*<sup>F</sup> *de punto*<sup>M</sup>

gusset pocket
*bolsillo*<sup>M</sup> *de fuelle*<sup>M</sup>

**examples of shirts**
***ejemplos*<sup>M</sup> *de blusas*<sup>F</sup> y
*camisas*<sup>F</sup>**

body suit
*body*<sup>M</sup>

middy
*camisa*<sup>F</sup> *marinera*

crotch piece
*entrepierna*<sup>F</sup>

yoke
*canesú*<sup>M</sup>

gather
*fruncido*<sup>M</sup>

shirttail
*faldón*<sup>M</sup>

classic blouse
*camisera*<sup>F</sup> *clásica*

smock
*blusón*<sup>M</sup>

oversized shirt
*camisa*<sup>F</sup>

tunic
*blusón*<sup>M</sup> *con tirilla*<sup>F</sup>

wrapover top
*chaqueta*<sup>F</sup> *cruzada*

polo shirt
*polo*<sup>M</sup>

over-blouse
*casaca*<sup>F</sup>

**nightwear**
*lencería*<sup>F</sup>

nightgown
*camisón*<sup>M</sup>

baby doll
*picardía*<sup>M</sup>

kimono
*kimono*<sup>M</sup>

pajamas
*pijama*<sup>M</sup>

negligee
*bata*<sup>F</sup>

bathrobe
*albornoz*<sup>M</sup>

CLOTHING

**hose**
*medias*<sup>F</sup>

panty hose
*pantis*<sup>M</sup>/*medias*<sup>F</sup>

knee-high sock
*calcetin*<sup>M</sup> *largo*

sock
*calcetin*<sup>M</sup>

ankle sock
*tobillera*<sup>F</sup>

short sock
*calcetin*<sup>M</sup>

stocking
*media*<sup>F</sup>

thigh-high stocking
*media*<sup>F</sup> *antideslizante*

fish net stocking
*media*<sup>F</sup> *de malla*<sup>F</sup>

CLOTHING

**underwear**
*ropa^F interior*

corselette
*faja^F con sostén^M*

camisole
*camisola^F*

teddy
*canesú^M*

body suit
*body^M*

panty corselette
*faja^F corsé^M*

half-slip
*falda^F combinación^F*

princess seams
*costura^F de corte^M*
*princesa^F*

foundation slip
*combinación^F*

slip
*combinación^F con*
*sujetador^M*

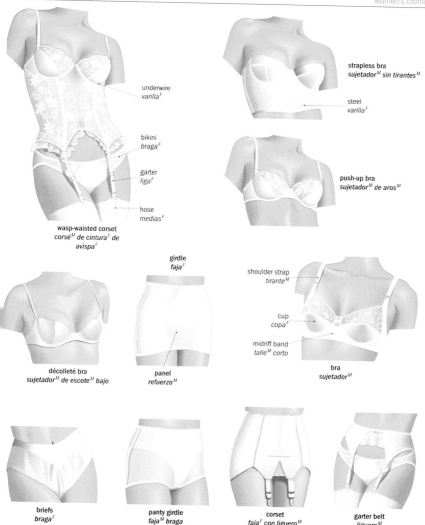

underwire
*varilla*<sup>F</sup>

bikini
*braga*<sup>F</sup>

garter
*liga*<sup>F</sup>

hose
*medias*<sup>F</sup>

wasp-waisted corset
**corsé**<sup>M</sup> **de cintura**<sup>F</sup> **de avispa**<sup>F</sup>

strapless bra
*sujetador*<sup>M</sup> *sin tirantes*<sup>M</sup>

steel
*varilla*<sup>F</sup>

push-up bra
*sujetador*<sup>M</sup> *de aros*<sup>M</sup>

girdle
*faja*<sup>F</sup>

shoulder strap
*tirante*<sup>M</sup>

cup
*copa*<sup>F</sup>

midriff band
*talle*<sup>M</sup> *corto*

décolleté bra
**sujetador**<sup>M</sup> **de escote**<sup>M</sup> **bajo**

panel
*refuerzo*<sup>M</sup>

bra
**sujetador**<sup>M</sup>

briefs
*braga*<sup>F</sup>

panty girdle
**faja**<sup>M</sup> **braga**

corset
**faja**<sup>F</sup> **con liguero**<sup>M</sup>

garter belt
**liguero**<sup>M</sup>

# newborn children's clothing
*ropa<sup>F</sup> de bebé<sup>M</sup>*

CLOTHING

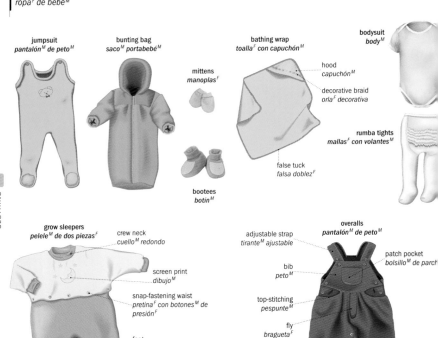

**jumpsuit**
*pantalón<sup>M</sup> de peto<sup>M</sup>*

**bunting bag**
*saco<sup>M</sup> portabebé<sup>M</sup>*

**mittens**
*manoplas<sup>F</sup>*

**bathing wrap**
*toalla<sup>F</sup> con capuchón<sup>M</sup>*

hood
*capuchón<sup>M</sup>*

decorative braid
*orla<sup>F</sup> decorativa*

**bodysuit**
*body<sup>M</sup>*

**rumba tights**
*mallas<sup>F</sup> con volantes<sup>M</sup>*

false tuck
*falsa doblez<sup>F</sup>*

**bootees**
*botín<sup>M</sup>*

**grow sleepers**
*pelele<sup>M</sup> de dos piezas<sup>F</sup>*

crew neck
*cuello<sup>M</sup> redondo*

screen print
*dibujo<sup>M</sup>*

snap-fastening waist
*pretina<sup>F</sup> con botones<sup>M</sup> de presión<sup>F</sup>*

foot
*pie<sup>M</sup>*

**overalls**
*pantalón<sup>M</sup> de peto<sup>M</sup>*

adjustable strap
*tirante<sup>M</sup> ajustable*

bib
*peto<sup>M</sup>*

top-stitching
*pespunte<sup>M</sup>*

fly
*bragueta<sup>F</sup>*

patch pocket
*bolsillo<sup>M</sup> de parche*

inside-leg snap-fastening
*botón<sup>M</sup> de presión<sup>F</sup>*

**shirt**
*camiseta<sup>F</sup>*

**diaper**
*pañal<sup>M</sup>*

**ruffled rumba pants**
*braga<sup>F</sup> de volantes<sup>M</sup>*

ruching
*volantes<sup>M</sup>*

**bib**
*babero<sup>M</sup>*

**disposable diaper**
*pañal<sup>M</sup> desechable*

Velcro closure
*tirita<sup>F</sup> Velcro®*

waterproof pants
*material<sup>M</sup> impermeable*

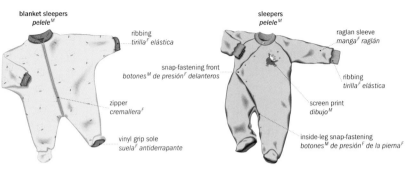

**blanket sleepers**
*pelele^M*

ribbing
*tirilla^F elástica*

snap-fastening front
*botones^M de presión^F delanteros*

zipper
*cremallera^F*

vinyl grip sole
*suela^F antiderrapante*

**sleepers**
*pelele^M*

raglan sleeve
*manga^F raglán*

ribbing
*tirilla^F elástica*

screen print
*dibujo^M*

inside-leg snap-fastening
*botones^M de presión^F de la pierna^F*

## children's clothing
*ropa^F de niños^M*

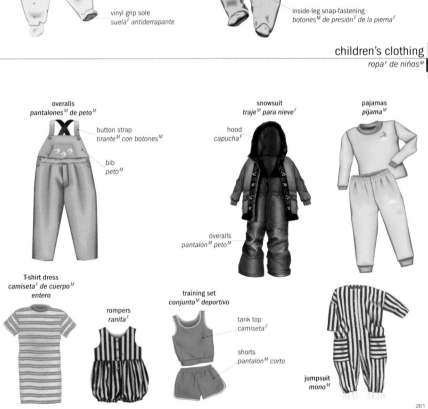

**overalls**
*pantalones^M de peto^M*

button strap
*tirante^M con botones^M*

bib
*peto^M*

**snowsuit**
*traje^M para nieve^F*

hood
*capucha^F*

overalls
*pantalón^M peto^M*

**pajamas**
*pijama^M*

**T-shirt dress**
*camiseta^F de cuerpo^M entero*

**rompers**
*ranita^F*

**training set**
*conjunto^M deportivo*

tank top
*camiseta^F*

shorts
*pantalón^M corto*

**jumpsuit**
*mono^M*

# sportswear

*ropa<sup>F</sup> deportiva*

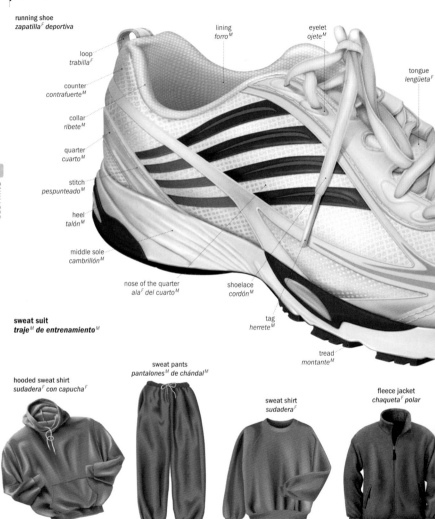

**running shoe**
*zapatilla<sup>F</sup> deportiva*

CLOTHING

loop
*trabilla<sup>F</sup>*

counter
*contrafuerte<sup>M</sup>*

collar
*ribete<sup>M</sup>*

quarter
*cuarto<sup>M</sup>*

stitch
*pespunteado<sup>M</sup>*

heel
*talón<sup>M</sup>*

middle sole
*cambrillón<sup>M</sup>*

nose of the quarter
*ala<sup>F</sup> del cuarto<sup>M</sup>*

lining
*forro<sup>M</sup>*

eyelet
*ojete<sup>M</sup>*

tongue
*lengüeta<sup>F</sup>*

shoelace
*cordón<sup>M</sup>*

tag
*herrete<sup>M</sup>*

tread
*montante<sup>M</sup>*

**sweat suit**
*traje<sup>M</sup> de entrenamiento<sup>M</sup>*

hooded sweat shirt
*sudadera<sup>F</sup> con capucha<sup>F</sup>*

sweat pants
*pantalones<sup>M</sup> de chándal<sup>M</sup>*

sweat shirt
*sudadera<sup>F</sup>*

fleece jacket
*chaqueta<sup>F</sup> polar*

swimming trunks
*traje$^M$ de baño$^M$*

swimsuit
*traje$^M$ de baño$^M$*

footless tights
*mallas$^F$*

**exercise wear**
***ropa$^F$ para ejercicio$^M$***

leotard
*body$^M$*

vamp
*empella$^F$*

punch hole
*perforación$^F$*

tank top
*camiseta$^F$*

T-shirt
*camiseta$^F$*

leg-warmer
*calentador$^M$ de pierna$^F$*

outsole
*suela$^F$*

pants
*pantalones$^M$*

anorak
*anorak$^M$*

boxer shorts
*pantalón$^M$ de boxeo$^M$*

shorts
*pantalón$^M$ ciclista$^M$*

# jewelry
*joyería*<sup>F</sup>

## earrings
*pendientes*<sup>M</sup>

**clip earrings**
*pendientes*<sup>M</sup> *de clip*<sup>M</sup>

**screw earring**
*pendientes*<sup>M</sup> *de tornillo*<sup>M</sup>

**pierced earrings**
*pendientes*<sup>M</sup> *de espiga*<sup>F</sup>

**drop earrings**
*pendientes*<sup>M</sup>

**hoop earrings**
*pendientes*<sup>M</sup> *de aro*<sup>M</sup>

## necklaces
*collares*<sup>M</sup>

**rope necklace**
*lazo*<sup>M</sup>

**opera-length necklace**
*collar*<sup>M</sup> *de una vuelta*<sup>F</sup> , *ópera*<sup>F</sup>

**matinee-length necklace**
*collar*<sup>M</sup> *de una vuelta*<sup>F</sup> , *matinée*<sup>F</sup>

**bib necklace**
*collar*<sup>M</sup> *de 5 vueltas*<sup>M</sup> , *peto*<sup>M</sup>

**velvet-band choker**
*gargantilla*<sup>F</sup> *de terciopelo*<sup>M</sup>

**choker**
*gargantilla*<sup>F</sup>

**pendant**
*pendiente*<sup>M</sup>

**locket**
*medallón*<sup>M</sup>

## bracelets
*brazaletes*<sup>M</sup>

**identification bracelet**
*brazalete*<sup>M</sup> *de identificación*<sup>F</sup>

**charm bracelet**
*pulsera*<sup>F</sup> *de dijes*<sup>M</sup>

**bangle**
*brazalete*<sup>M</sup> *tubular*

## rings
*anillos*<sup>M</sup>

**band ring**
*alianza*<sup>F</sup>

**signet ring**
*sortija*<sup>F</sup> *de sello*<sup>M</sup>

**solitaire ring**
*solitario*<sup>M</sup>

**engagement ring**
*anillo*<sup>M</sup> *de compromiso*<sup>M</sup>

**wedding ring**
*alianza*<sup>F</sup>

# nail care
*manicura<sup>F</sup>*

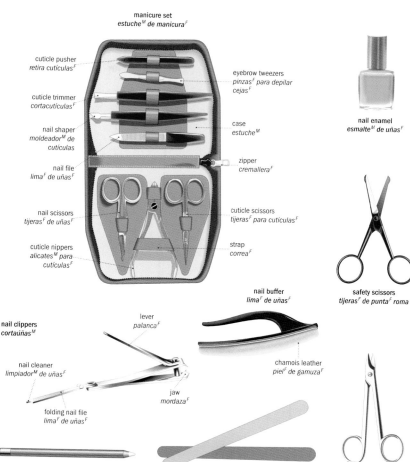

manicure set
*estuche<sup>M</sup> de manicura<sup>F</sup>*

cuticle pusher
*retira cutículas<sup>F</sup>*

cuticle trimmer
*cortacutículas<sup>F</sup>*

nail shaper
*moldeador<sup>M</sup> de cutículas*

nail file
*lima<sup>F</sup> de uñas<sup>F</sup>*

nail scissors
*tijeras<sup>F</sup> de uñas<sup>F</sup>*

cuticle nippers
*alicates<sup>M</sup> para cutículas<sup>F</sup>*

eyebrow tweezers
*pinzas<sup>F</sup> para depilar cejas<sup>F</sup>*

case
*estuche<sup>M</sup>*

zipper
*cremallera<sup>F</sup>*

cuticle scissors
*tijeras<sup>F</sup> para cutículas<sup>F</sup>*

strap
*correa<sup>F</sup>*

nail enamel
*esmalte<sup>M</sup> de uñas<sup>F</sup>*

safety scissors
*tijeras<sup>F</sup> de punta<sup>F</sup> roma*

nail clippers
*cortaúñas<sup>M</sup>*

nail cleaner
*limpiador<sup>M</sup> de uñas<sup>F</sup>*

folding nail file
*lima<sup>F</sup> de uñas<sup>F</sup>*

lever
*palanca<sup>F</sup>*

jaw
*mordaza<sup>F</sup>*

nail buffer
*lima<sup>F</sup> de uñas<sup>F</sup>*

chamois leather
*piel<sup>F</sup> de gamuza<sup>F</sup>*

nail whitener pencil
*lápiz<sup>M</sup> blanco para uñas<sup>F</sup>*

emery boards
*lima<sup>F</sup> de uñas<sup>F</sup>*

toenail scissors
*tijeras<sup>F</sup> de pedicura<sup>F</sup>*

PERSONAL ADORNMENT AND ARTICLES

# makeup
*maquillaje*M

**facial makeup**
*maquillaje*M *facial*

compact
*polvera*F

blusher brush
*brocha*F *aplicadora de colorete*M

pressed powder
*polvo*M *compacto*

powder puff
*borla*F

powder blusher
*colorete*M *en polvo*M

synthetic sponge
*esponja*F *sintética*

loose powder
*polvos*M *sueltos*

loose powder brush
*brocha*F

fan brush
*brocha*F *en forma*F *de abanico*M

liquid foundation
*base*F *líquida*

**eye makeup**
*maquillaje*M *para ojos*M

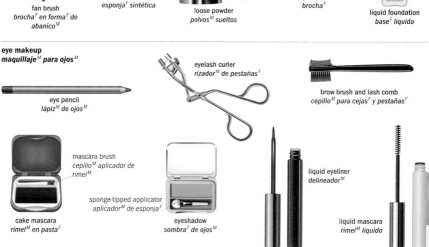

eyelash curler
*rizador*M *de pestañas*F

brow brush and lash comb
*cepillo*M *para cejas*F *y pestañas*F

eye pencil
*lápiz*M *de ojos*M

mascara brush
*cepillo*M *aplicador de rímel*M

sponge-tipped applicator
*aplicador*M *de esponja*F

cake mascara
*rímel*M *en pasta*F

eyeshadow
*sombra*F *de ojos*M

liquid eyeliner
*delineador*M

liquid mascara
*rímel*M *líquido*

**lip makeup**
*maquillaje*M *labial*

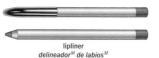

lip brush
*pincel*M *para labios*M

lipliner
*delineador*M *de labios*M

lipstick
*pintalabios*M

# body care
*cuidado<sup>M</sup> personal*

stopper
*tapón<sup>M</sup>*

bottle
*botella<sup>F</sup>*

eau de parfum
*agua<sup>F</sup> de perfume<sup>M</sup>*

toilet soap
*jabón<sup>M</sup> de tocador<sup>M</sup>*

hair conditioner
*acondicionador<sup>M</sup>*

shampoo
*champú<sup>M</sup>*

eau de toilette
*agua<sup>F</sup> de colonia<sup>F</sup>*

bubble bath
*gel<sup>M</sup> de baño<sup>M</sup>*

haircolor
*tinte<sup>M</sup> para el cabello<sup>M</sup>*

deodorant
*desodorante<sup>M</sup>*

washcloth
*manopla<sup>F</sup> de baño<sup>M</sup>*

washcloth
*toalla<sup>F</sup> para la cara<sup>F</sup>*

massage glove
*guante<sup>M</sup> de crin<sup>M</sup>*

vegetable sponge
*esponja<sup>F</sup> vegetal*

bath sheet
*toalla<sup>F</sup> de baño<sup>M</sup>*

bath towel
*toalla<sup>F</sup> de lavabo<sup>M</sup>*

bath brush
*cepillo<sup>M</sup> de baño<sup>M</sup>*

natural sponge
*esponja<sup>F</sup> natural*

back brush
*cepillo<sup>M</sup> de espalda<sup>F</sup>*

# hairdressing
*peinado<sup>M</sup>*

**hairbrushes**
***cepillos<sup>M</sup>***

flat-back brush
*cepillo<sup>M</sup> con base<sup>F</sup> de goma<sup>F</sup>*

round brush
*cepillo<sup>M</sup> redondo*

quill brush
*cepillo<sup>M</sup> de púas<sup>F</sup>*

vent brush
*cepillo<sup>M</sup> de esqueleto<sup>M</sup>*

**combs**
***peines<sup>M</sup>***

Afro pick
*peine<sup>M</sup> afro*

teaser comb
*peine<sup>M</sup> de cardar*

tail comb
*peine<sup>M</sup> de mango<sup>M</sup>*

barber comb
*peine<sup>M</sup> de peluquero<sup>M</sup>*

pitchfork comb
*peine<sup>M</sup> combinado*

rake comb
*peine<sup>M</sup> para desenredar*

hair roller
*rulo<sup>M</sup> para el cabello<sup>M</sup>*
roller
*rulo<sup>M</sup>*
hair roller pin
*alfiler<sup>M</sup>*

wave clip
*pinza<sup>F</sup> para rizar*

hairpin
*horquilla<sup>F</sup> de moño<sup>M</sup>*

hair clip
*pinza<sup>F</sup> para el cabello<sup>M</sup>*

bobby pin
*horquilla<sup>F</sup>*

barrette
*pasador<sup>M</sup>*

PERSONAL ADORNMENT AND ARTICLES

hairdressing

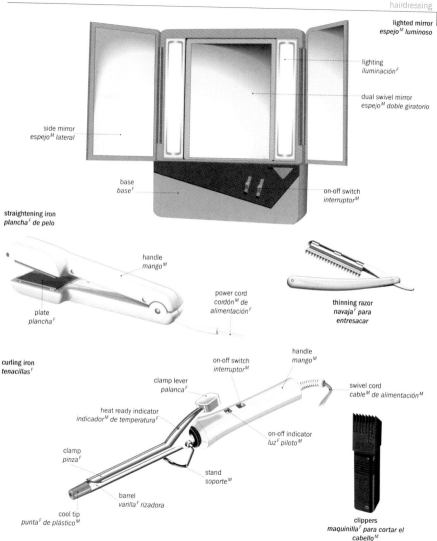

lighted mirror
espejo^M luminoso

lighting
iluminación^F

dual swivel mirror
espejo^M doble giratorio

side mirror
espejo^M lateral

base
base^F

on-off switch
interruptor^M

**straightening iron**
plancha^F de pelo

handle
mango^M

power cord
cordón^M de
alimentación^F

plate
plancha^F

**thinning razor**
navaja^F para
entresacar

**curling iron**
tenacillas^F

on-off switch
interruptor^M

handle
mango^M

clamp lever
palanca^F

swivel cord
cable^M de alimentación^M

heat ready indicator
indicador^M de temperatura^F

on-off indicator
luz^F piloto^M

clamp
pinza^F

stand
soporte^M

barrel
vanilla^F rizadora

cool tip
punta^F de plástico^M

**clippers**
maquinilla^F para cortar el
cabello^M

hairdressing

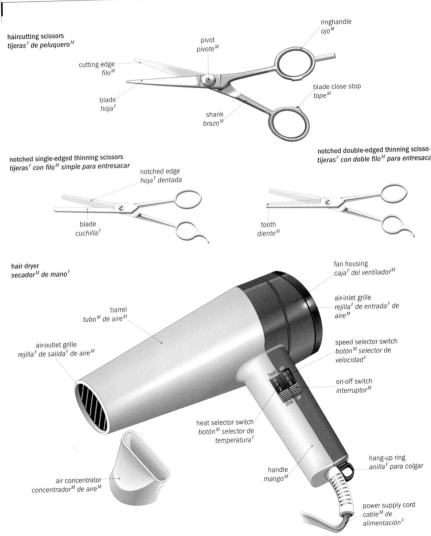

**haircutting scissors**
*tijeras^F de peluquero^M*

pivot
*pivote^M*

ringhandle
*ojo^M*

cutting edge
*filo^M*

blade
*hoja^F*

blade close stop
*tope^M*

shank
*brazo^M*

**notched single-edged thinning scissors**
*tijeras^F con filo^M simple para entresacar*

notched edge
*hoja^F dentada*

blade
*cuchilla^F*

**notched double-edged thinning scisso**
*tijeras^F con doble filo^M para entresaca*

tooth
*diente^M*

**hair dryer**
*secador^M de mano^F*

fan housing
*caja^F del ventilador^M*

air-inlet grille
*rejilla^F de entrada^F de aire^M*

barrel
*tubo^M de aire^M*

speed selector switch
*botón^M selector de velocidad^F*

air-outlet grille
*rejilla^F de salida^F de aire^M*

on-off switch
*interruptor^M*

heat selector switch
*botón^M selector de temperatura^F*

hang-up ring
*anilla^F para colgar*

air concentrator
*concentrador^M de aire^M*

handle
*mango^M*

power supply cord
*cable^M de alimentación^F*

# shaving
*afeitado* M

electric razor
*máquina* F *de afeitar eléctrica*

floating head
*cabezal* M *flotante*

trimmer
*cortapatillas* M

screen
*peine* M *y cuchilla* F

closeness setting
*selector* M *de corte* M

cleaning brush
*escobilla* F *limpiadora*

housing
*caja* F

charge indicator
*indicador* M *de recarga* F

charging light
*luz* F *de encendido* M

on-off switch
*interruptor* M

charging plug
*enchufe* M *de recarga* F

shaving foam
*espuma* F *de afeitar*

power cord
*cable* M *de alimentación* F

shaving brush
*brocha* F *de afeitar*

plug adapter
*adaptador* M

bristle
*cerdas* F

aftershave
*loción* F *para después del afeitado* M

straight razor
*navaja* F *de barbero* M

blade
*hoja* F

handle
*mango* M

pivot
*eje* M

double-edged razor
*maquinilla* F *de afeitar*

disposable razor
*maquinilla* F *desechable*

head
*cabeza* F

collar
*anillo* M

shaving mug
*jabonera* F

blade injector
*distribuidor* M *de hojas* F *de afeitar*

double-edged blade
*hoja* F *de afeitar*

handle
*mango* M

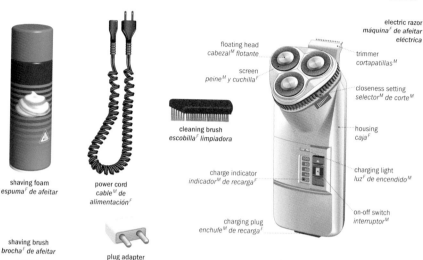
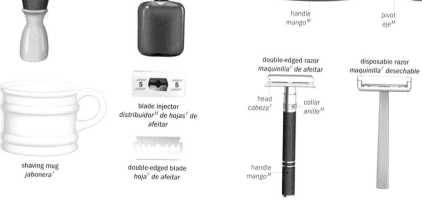

PERSONAL ADORNMENT AND ARTICLES

PERSONAL ADORNMENT AND ARTICLES

# dental care
*higiene<sup>F</sup> dental*

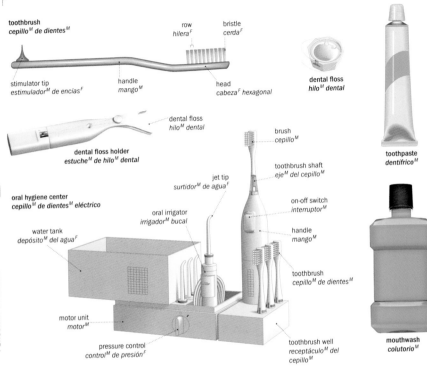

toothbrush
*cepillo<sup>M</sup> de dientes<sup>M</sup>*

row
*hilera<sup>F</sup>*

bristle
*cerda<sup>F</sup>*

stimulator tip
*estimulador<sup>M</sup> de encías<sup>F</sup>*

handle
*mango<sup>M</sup>*

head
*cabeza<sup>F</sup> hexagonal*

dental floss
*hilo<sup>M</sup> dental*

dental floss
*hilo<sup>M</sup> dental*

dental floss holder
*estuche<sup>M</sup> de hilo<sup>M</sup> dental*

brush
*cepillo<sup>M</sup>*

toothbrush shaft
*eje<sup>M</sup> del cepillo<sup>M</sup>*

jet tip
*surtidor<sup>M</sup> de agua<sup>F</sup>*

on-off switch
*interruptor<sup>M</sup>*

toothpaste
*dentífrico<sup>M</sup>*

oral hygiene center
*cepillo<sup>M</sup> de dientes<sup>M</sup> eléctrico*

oral irrigator
*irrigador<sup>M</sup> bucal*

handle
*mango<sup>M</sup>*

water tank
*depósito<sup>M</sup> del agua<sup>F</sup>*

toothbrush
*cepillo<sup>M</sup> de dientes<sup>M</sup>*

motor unit
*motor<sup>M</sup>*

pressure control
*control<sup>M</sup> de presión<sup>F</sup>*

toothbrush well
*receptáculo<sup>M</sup> del cepillo<sup>M</sup>*

mouthwash
*colutorio<sup>M</sup>*

# contact lenses
*lentes<sup>F</sup> de contacto<sup>M</sup>*

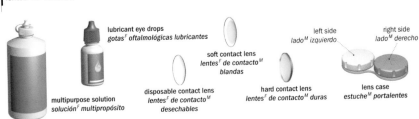

lubricant eye drops
*gotas<sup>F</sup> oftalmológicas lubricantes*

soft contact lens
*lentes<sup>F</sup> de contacto<sup>M</sup> blandas*

left side
*lado<sup>M</sup> izquierdo*

right side
*lado<sup>M</sup> derecho*

disposable contact lens
*lentes<sup>F</sup> de contacto<sup>M</sup> desechables*

hard contact lens
*lentes<sup>F</sup> de contacto<sup>M</sup> duras*

lens case
*estuche<sup>M</sup> portalentes*

multipurpose solution
*solución<sup>F</sup> multipropósito*

# eyeglasses
*gafas<sup>F</sup>*

**eyeglasses parts**
*gafas<sup>F</sup> : partes<sup>F</sup>*

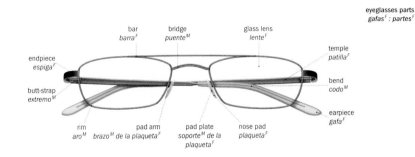

bar
*barra<sup>F</sup>*

bridge
*puente<sup>M</sup>*

glass lens
*lente<sup>F</sup>*

temple
*patilla<sup>F</sup>*

endpiece
*espiga<sup>F</sup>*

bend
*codo<sup>M</sup>*

butt-strap
*extremo<sup>M</sup>*

earpiece
*gafa<sup>F</sup>*

rim
*aro<sup>M</sup>*

pad arm
*brazo<sup>M</sup> de la plaqueta<sup>F</sup>*

pad plate
*soporte<sup>M</sup> de la plaqueta<sup>F</sup>*

nose pad
*plaqueta<sup>F</sup>*

**examples of eyeglasses**
*ejemplos<sup>M</sup> de gafas<sup>F</sup>*

opera glasses
*gemelos<sup>M</sup> de teatro<sup>M</sup>*

sunglasses
*gafas<sup>F</sup> de sol<sup>M</sup>*

half-glasses
*media luna<sup>F</sup>*

# umbrellas and stick
*paraguas<sup>M</sup> y bastones<sup>M</sup>*

**umbrellas**
*paraguas<sup>M</sup>*

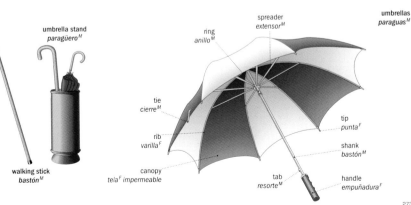

umbrella stand
*paragüero<sup>M</sup>*

spreader
*extensor<sup>M</sup>*

ring
*anillo<sup>M</sup>*

tie
*cierre<sup>M</sup>*

tip
*punta<sup>F</sup>*

rib
*varilla<sup>F</sup>*

shank
*bastón<sup>M</sup>*

canopy
*tela<sup>F</sup> impermeable*

tab
*resorte<sup>M</sup>*

handle
*empuñadura<sup>F</sup>*

walking stick
*bastón<sup>M</sup>*

# leather goods
*artículos<sup>M</sup> de marroquinería<sup>F</sup>*

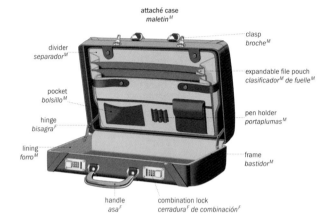

**attaché case** / *maletín<sup>M</sup>*
- divider / separador<sup>M</sup>
- clasp / broche<sup>M</sup>
- expandable file pouch / clasificador<sup>M</sup> de fuelle<sup>M</sup>
- pocket / bolsillo<sup>M</sup>
- pen holder / portaplumas<sup>M</sup>
- hinge / bisagra<sup>F</sup>
- lining / forro<sup>M</sup>
- frame / bastidor<sup>M</sup>
- handle / asa<sup>F</sup>
- combination lock / cerradura<sup>F</sup> de combinación<sup>F</sup>

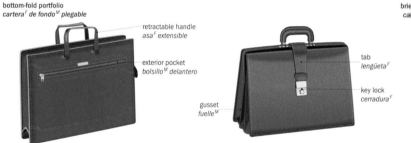

**bottom-fold portfolio** / *cartera<sup>F</sup> de fondo<sup>M</sup> plegable*
- retractable handle / asa<sup>F</sup> extensible
- exterior pocket / bolsillo<sup>M</sup> delantero
- gusset / fuelle<sup>M</sup>

**brie... / ca...**
- tab / lengüeta<sup>F</sup>
- key lock / cerradura<sup>F</sup>

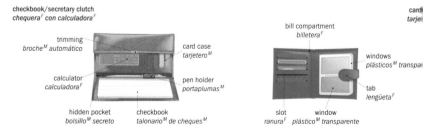

**checkbook/secretary clutch** / *chequera<sup>F</sup> con calculadora<sup>F</sup>*
- trimming / broche<sup>M</sup> automático
- card case / tarjetero<sup>M</sup>
- calculator / calculadora<sup>F</sup>
- pen holder / portaplumas<sup>M</sup>
- hidden pocket / bolsillo<sup>M</sup> secreto
- checkbook / talonario<sup>M</sup> de cheques<sup>M</sup>

**card... / tarje...**
- bill compartment / billetera<sup>F</sup>
- windows / plásticos<sup>M</sup> transpa...
- tab / lengüeta<sup>F</sup>
- slot / ranura<sup>F</sup>
- window / plástico<sup>M</sup> transparente

leather goods

wallet
*billetero*<sup>M</sup>

coin purse
*portamonedas*<sup>M</sup>

key case
*llavero*<sup>M</sup>

purse
*monedero*<sup>M</sup>

passport case
*porta pasaportes*<sup>M</sup>

billfold
*billetera*<sup>F</sup>

writing case
*agenda*<sup>F</sup>

checkbook
*talonario*<sup>M</sup> *de cheques*<sup>M</sup>

eyeglasses case
*funda*<sup>F</sup> *de gafas*<sup>F</sup>

underarm portfolio
*cartera*<sup>F</sup>
*portadocumentos*<sup>M</sup>

## handbags
*bolsos*<sup>M</sup>

drawstring bag
*bolso*<sup>M</sup> *tipo cubo*<sup>M</sup>

satchel bag
*bolso*<sup>M</sup> *clásico*

eyelet
*ojal*<sup>M</sup>

drawstring
*cordón*<sup>M</sup>

front pocket
*bolsillo*<sup>M</sup> *exterior*

handle
*asa*<sup>F</sup>

flap
*ala*<sup>F</sup>

clasp
*broche*<sup>M</sup>

lock
*cierre*<sup>M</sup>

## handbags

box bag
*bolso$^M$ de vestir*

drawstring bag
*bolso$^M$ saco*

shoulder bag
*bolso$^M$ de bandolera$^F$*

buckle
*hebilla$^F$*

shoulder strap
*bandolera$^F$*

muff
*bolso$^M$ manguito$^M$*

hobo bag
*morral$^M$*

accordion bag
*bolso$^M$ de fuelle$^M$*

gusset
*fuelle$^M$*

tote bag
*bolsa$^F$ de lona$^F$*

men's bag
*bolso$^M$ de hombre*

sea bag
*saco$^M$ de marinero$^M$*

duffel bag
*bolso$^M$ de viaje$^M$*

carrier bag
*bolso$^M$ de la compra$^F$*

shopping bag
*capazo$^M$*

# luggage
*equipaje$^M$*

utility case
*neceser$^M$*

carry-on bag
*bolso$^M$ de viaje$^M$*

handle
*asa$^F$*

tote bag
*maletín$^M$*

exterior pocket
*bolsillo$^M$ exterior*

shoulder strap
*bandolera$^F$*

garment bag
*portatrajes*^M

zipper
*cremallera*^F

luggage carrier
*carrito*^M *portamaletas*^M

frame
*armazón*^M

luggage elastic
*correa*^F *elástica*

stand
*soporte*^M

backpack
*mochila*^F

retractable handle
*mango*^M *retractable*

upright suitcase
*maleta*^F *vertical*

Pullman case
*maleta*^F *clásica*

handle
*asa*^F

identification tag
*etiqueta*^F *de
identificación*^F

frame
*bastidor*^M

pull strap
*correa*^F

wheel
*ruedecilla*^F

trim
*guarnición*^F

weekender
*maleta*^F *de fin*^M *de semana*^F

trunk
*baúl*^M

hasp
*aldabilla*^F

tray
*bandeja*^F

interior pocket
*bolso*^M *interior*

curtain
*panel*^M *de separación*^F

latch
*abrazadera*^F

cornerpiece
*contera*^F

fittings
*herraje*^M

handle
*asa*^F

garment strap
*correa*^F *de retención*^F

lock
*cerradura*^F

shell
*tapa*^F

PERSONAL ADORNMENT AND ARTICLES

# pyramid
*pirámide*<sup>F</sup>

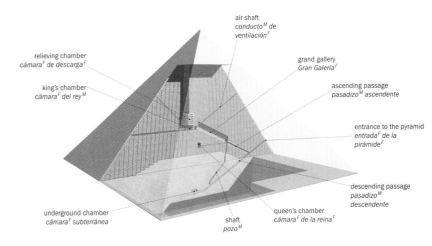

air shaft
*conducto*<sup>M</sup> *de ventilación*<sup>F</sup>

relieving chamber
*cámara*<sup>F</sup> *de descarga*<sup>F</sup>

grand gallery
*Gran Galería*<sup>F</sup>

king's chamber
*cámara*<sup>F</sup> *del rey*<sup>M</sup>

ascending passage
*pasadizo*<sup>M</sup> *ascendente*

entrance to the pyramid
*entrada*<sup>F</sup> *de la pirámide*<sup>F</sup>

descending passage
*pasadizo*<sup>M</sup> *descendente*

underground chamber
*cámara*<sup>F</sup> *subterránea*

shaft
*pozo*<sup>M</sup>

queen's chamber
*cámara*<sup>F</sup> *de la reina*<sup>F</sup>

# Greek theater
*teatro*<sup>M</sup> *griego*

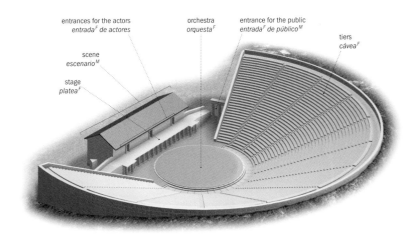

entrances for the actors
*entrada*<sup>F</sup> *de actores*

orchestra
*orquesta*<sup>F</sup>

entrance for the public
*entrada*<sup>F</sup> *de público*<sup>M</sup>

tiers
*cávea*<sup>F</sup>

scene
*escenario*<sup>M</sup>

stage
*platea*<sup>F</sup>

# Greek temple
*templo^M griego*

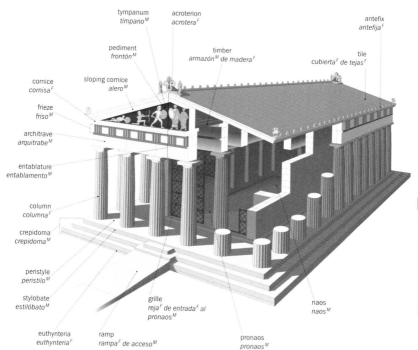

tympanum
*tímpano^M*

acroterion
*acrotera^F*

antefix
*antefija^F*

pediment
*frontón^M*

timber
*armazón^M de madera^F*

tile
*cubierta^F de tejas^F*

cornice
*cornisa^F*

sloping cornice
*alero^M*

frieze
*friso^M*

architrave
*arquitrabe^M*

entablature
*entablamento^M*

column
*columna^F*

crepidoma
*crepidoma^M*

peristyle
*peristilo^M*

stylobate
*estilóbato^M*

grille
*reja^F de entrada^F al pronaos^M*

naos
*naos^M*

euthynteria
*euthynteria^F*

ramp
*rampa^F de acceso^M*

pronaos
*pronaos^M*

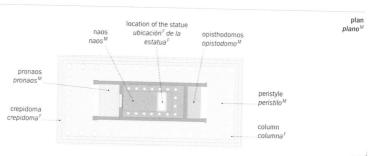

plan
*plano^M*

naos
*naos^M*

location of the statue
*ubicación^F de la estatua^F*

opisthodomos
*opistodomo^M*

pronaos
*pronaos^M*

peristyle
*peristilo^M*

crepidoma
*crepidoma^F*

column
*columna^F*

# Roman house
*casa<sup>F</sup> romana*

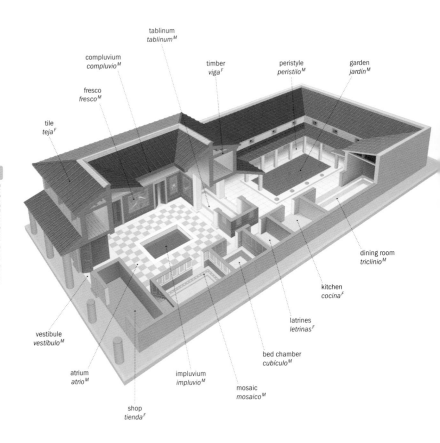

tablinum
*tablinum<sup>M</sup>*

compluvium
*compluvio<sup>M</sup>*

timber
*viga<sup>F</sup>*

peristyle
*peristilo<sup>M</sup>*

garden
*jardín<sup>M</sup>*

fresco
*fresco<sup>M</sup>*

tile
*teja<sup>F</sup>*

dining room
*triclinio<sup>M</sup>*

kitchen
*cocina<sup>F</sup>*

latrines
*letrinas<sup>F</sup>*

vestibule
*vestíbulo<sup>M</sup>*

bed chamber
*cubículo<sup>M</sup>*

atrium
*atrio<sup>M</sup>*

impluvium
*impluvio<sup>M</sup>*

mosaic
*mosaico<sup>M</sup>*

shop
*tienda<sup>F</sup>*

# Roman amphitheater
*anfiteatro^M romano*

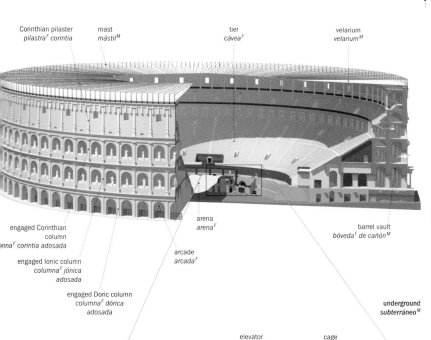

Corinthian pilaster
*pilastra^F corintia*

mast
*mástil^M*

tier
*cávea^F*

velarium
*velarium^M*

engaged Corinthian
column
*columna^F corintia adosada*

engaged Ionic column
*columna^F jónica
adosada*

engaged Doric column
*columna^F dórica
adosada*

arena
*arena^F*

arcade
*arcada^F*

barrel vault
*bóveda^F de cañón^M*

underground
*subterráneo^M*

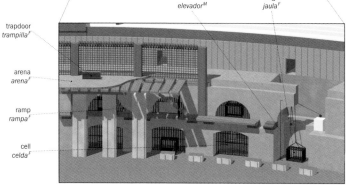

elevator
*elevador^M*

cage
*jaula^F*

trapdoor
*trampilla^F*

arena
*arena^F*

ramp
*rampa^F*

cell
*celda^F*

# castle
castillo<sup>M</sup>

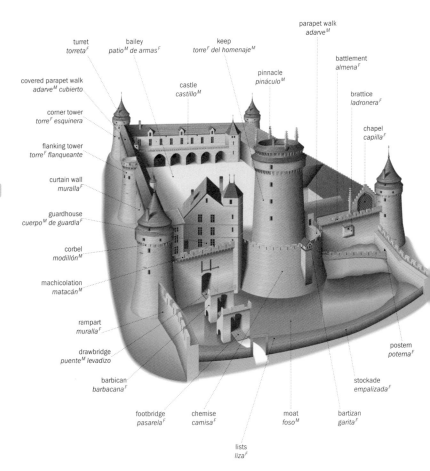

parapet walk
adarve<sup>M</sup>

turret
torreta<sup>F</sup>

bailey
patio<sup>M</sup> de armas<sup>F</sup>

keep
torre<sup>F</sup> del homenaje<sup>M</sup>

battlement
almena<sup>F</sup>

pinnacle
pináculo<sup>M</sup>

covered parapet walk
adarve<sup>M</sup> cubierto

castle
castillo<sup>M</sup>

brattice
ladronera<sup>F</sup>

corner tower
torre<sup>F</sup> esquinera

chapel
capilla<sup>F</sup>

flanking tower
torre<sup>F</sup> flanqueante

curtain wall
muralla<sup>F</sup>

guardhouse
cuerpo<sup>M</sup> de guardia<sup>F</sup>

corbel
modillón<sup>M</sup>

machicolation
matacán<sup>M</sup>

rampart
muralla<sup>F</sup>

postern
poterna<sup>F</sup>

drawbridge
puente<sup>M</sup> levadizo

barbican
barbacana<sup>F</sup>

stockade
empalizada<sup>F</sup>

footbridge
pasarela<sup>F</sup>

chemise
camisa<sup>F</sup>

moat
foso<sup>M</sup>

bartizan
garita<sup>F</sup>

lists
liza<sup>F</sup>

# pagoda
*pagoda*<sup>F</sup>

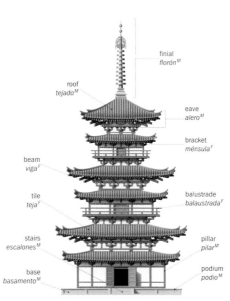

finial
*florón*<sup>M</sup>

roof
*tejado*<sup>M</sup>

eave
*alero*<sup>M</sup>

bracket
*ménsula*<sup>F</sup>

beam
*viga*<sup>F</sup>

balustrade
*balaustrada*<sup>F</sup>

tile
*teja*<sup>F</sup>

stairs
*escalones*<sup>M</sup>

pillar
*pilar*<sup>M</sup>

base
*basamento*<sup>M</sup>

podium
*podio*<sup>M</sup>

# Aztec temple
*templo*<sup>M</sup> *azteca*

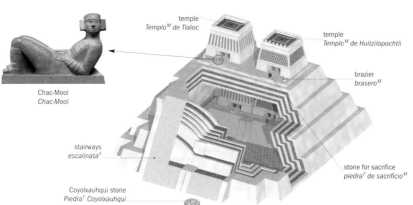

temple
*Templo*<sup>M</sup> *de Tlaloc*

temple
*Templo*<sup>M</sup> *de Huitzilopochtli*

brazier
*brasero*<sup>M</sup>

Chac-Mool
*Chac-Mool*

stairways
*escalinata*<sup>F</sup>

stone for sacrifice
*piedra*<sup>F</sup> *de sacrificio*<sup>M</sup>

Coyolxauhqui stone
*Piedra*<sup>F</sup> *Coyolxauhqui*

# cathedral
*catedral*<sup>F</sup>

**Gothic cathedral**
*catedral*<sup>F</sup> *gótica*

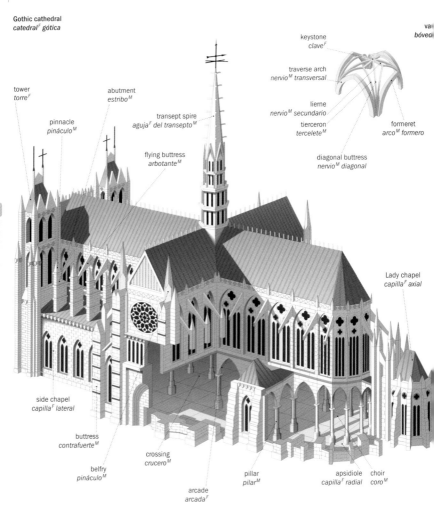

va⟨
*bóve⟨*

keystone
*clave*<sup>F</sup>

traverse arch
*nervio*<sup>M</sup> *transversal*

lierne
*nervio*<sup>M</sup> *secundario*

tierceron
*tercelete*<sup>M</sup>

formeret
*arco*<sup>M</sup> *formero*

diagonal buttress
*nervio*<sup>M</sup> *diagonal*

tower
*torre*<sup>F</sup>

abutment
*estribo*<sup>M</sup>

transept spire
*aguja*<sup>F</sup> *del transepto*<sup>M</sup>

pinnacle
*pináculo*<sup>M</sup>

flying buttress
*arbotante*<sup>M</sup>

Lady chapel
*capilla*<sup>F</sup> *axial*

side chapel
*capilla*<sup>F</sup> *lateral*

buttress
*contrafuerte*<sup>M</sup>

crossing
*crucero*<sup>M</sup>

belfry
*pináculo*<sup>M</sup>

pillar
*pilar*<sup>M</sup>

apsidiole
*capilla*<sup>F</sup> *radial*

choir
*coro*<sup>M</sup>

arcade
*arcada*<sup>F</sup>

ARTS AND ARCHITECTURE

cathedral

façade
*fachada*<sup>F</sup>

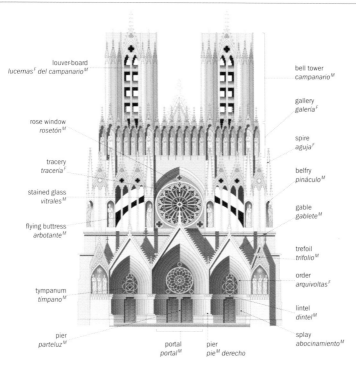

louver-board
*lucernas*<sup>F</sup> *del campanario*<sup>M</sup>

bell tower
*campanario*<sup>M</sup>

gallery
*galería*<sup>F</sup>

rose window
*rosetón*<sup>M</sup>

spire
*aguja*<sup>F</sup>

tracery
*tracería*<sup>F</sup>

belfry
*pináculo*<sup>M</sup>

stained glass
*vitrales*<sup>M</sup>

gable
*gablete*<sup>M</sup>

flying buttress
*arbotante*<sup>M</sup>

trefoil
*trifolio*<sup>M</sup>

order
*arquivoltas*<sup>F</sup>

tympanum
*tímpano*<sup>M</sup>

lintel
*dintel*<sup>M</sup>

pier
*parteluz*<sup>M</sup>

splay
*abocinamiento*<sup>M</sup>

portal
*portal*<sup>M</sup>

pier
*pie*<sup>M</sup> *derecho*

plan
*plano*<sup>M</sup>

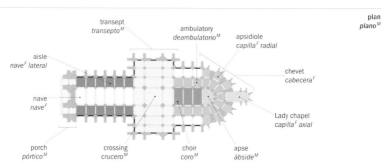

transept
*transepto*<sup>M</sup>

ambulatory
*deambulatorio*<sup>M</sup>

apsidiole
*capilla*<sup>F</sup> *radial*

aisle
*nave*<sup>F</sup> *lateral*

chevet
*cabecera*<sup>F</sup>

nave
*nave*<sup>F</sup>

Lady chapel
*capilla*<sup>F</sup> *axial*

porch
*pórtico*<sup>M</sup>

crossing
*crucero*<sup>M</sup>

choir
*coro*<sup>M</sup>

apse
*ábside*<sup>M</sup>

285

# elements of architecture

*elementos<sup>M</sup> arquitectónicos*

**examples of doors**
*ejemplos<sup>M</sup> de puertas<sup>F</sup>*

**manual revolving door**
*puerta<sup>F</sup> giratoria manual*

canopy
*tambor<sup>M</sup>*

wing
*hoja<sup>F</sup>*

enclosure
*estructura<sup>F</sup> interior*

push bar
*tirador<sup>M</sup>*

compartment
*compartimiento<sup>M</sup>*

automatic sliding door
*puerta<sup>F</sup> corredera automática*

motion detector
*sensor<sup>M</sup> de movimiento*

wing
*hoja<sup>F</sup>*

**conventional door**
*puerta<sup>F</sup> convencional*

**folding door**
*puerta<sup>F</sup> plegable*

strip
*tira<sup>F</sup>*

**strip door**
*puerta<sup>F</sup> de tiras<sup>F</sup>*

**fire door**
*puerta<sup>F</sup> cortafuego*

**sliding folding door**
*puerta<sup>F</sup> de librillo<sup>M</sup>*

**sliding door**
*puerta<sup>F</sup> corredera*

**sectional garage door**
*puerta<sup>F</sup> de garaje<sup>M</sup> seccional*

**up and over garage door**
*puerta<sup>F</sup> basculante de garaje<sup>M</sup>*

ARTS AND ARCHITECTURE

## examples of windows
### ejemplos<sup>M</sup> de ventanas<sup>F</sup>

sliding folding window
ventana<sup>F</sup> de librillo<sup>M</sup>

French window
ventana<sup>F</sup> a la francesa<sup>F</sup>

casement window
ventana<sup>F</sup> a la inglesa<sup>F</sup>

louvered window
ventana<sup>F</sup> de celosía<sup>F</sup>

sliding window
ventana<sup>F</sup> corredera

sash window
ventana<sup>F</sup> de guillotina<sup>F</sup>

horizontal pivoting window
ventana<sup>F</sup> basculante

vertical pivoting window
ventana<sup>F</sup> pivotante

## elevator
### ascensor<sup>M</sup>

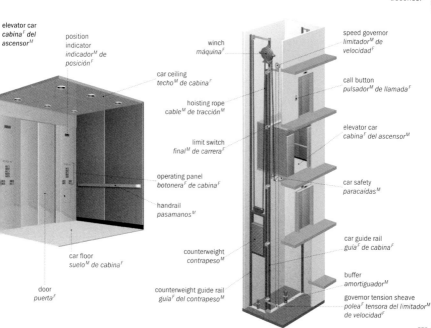

elevator car
cabina<sup>F</sup> del ascensor<sup>M</sup>

position indicator
indicador<sup>M</sup> de posición<sup>F</sup>

winch
máquina<sup>F</sup>

speed governor
limitador<sup>M</sup> de velocidad<sup>F</sup>

car ceiling
techo<sup>M</sup> de cabina<sup>F</sup>

call button
pulsador<sup>M</sup> de llamada<sup>F</sup>

hoisting rope
cable<sup>M</sup> de tracción<sup>M</sup>

limit switch
final<sup>M</sup> de carrera<sup>F</sup>

elevator car
cabina<sup>F</sup> del ascensor<sup>M</sup>

operating panel
botonera<sup>F</sup> de cabina<sup>F</sup>

car safety
paracaídas<sup>M</sup>

handrail
pasamanos<sup>M</sup>

car floor
suelo<sup>M</sup> de cabina<sup>F</sup>

counterweight
contrapeso<sup>M</sup>

car guide rail
guía<sup>F</sup> de cabina<sup>F</sup>

door
puerta<sup>F</sup>

counterweight guide rail
guía<sup>F</sup> del contrapeso<sup>M</sup>

buffer
amortiguador<sup>M</sup>

governor tension sheave
polea<sup>F</sup> tensora del limitador<sup>M</sup> de velocidad<sup>F</sup>

# traditional houses
*viviendas^F tradicionales*

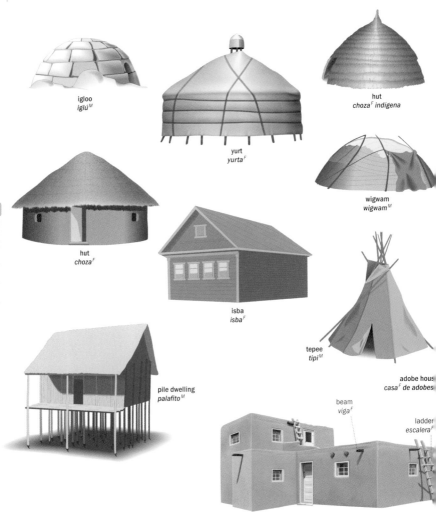

igloo
*iglú^M*

yurt
*yurta^F*

hut
*choza^F indígena*

wigwam
*wigwam^M*

hut
*choza^F*

isba
*isba^F*

tepee
*tipi^M*

adobe house
*casa^F de adobes*

pile dwelling
*palafito^M*

beam
*viga^F*

ladder
*escalera^F*

# city houses
*viviendas<sup>F</sup> urbanas*

two-storey house
*casa<sup>F</sup> de dos plantas<sup>M</sup>*

one-storey house
*casa<sup>F</sup> de una planta<sup>F</sup>*

semidetached house
*casas<sup>F</sup> pareadas*

town houses
*casas<sup>F</sup> adosadas*

condominiums
*viviendas<sup>F</sup> plurifamiliares*

high-rise apartment building
*bloque<sup>M</sup> de apartamentos<sup>M</sup>*

ARTS AND ARCHITECTURE

# sound stage
*plató<sup>M</sup> de rodaje<sup>M</sup>*

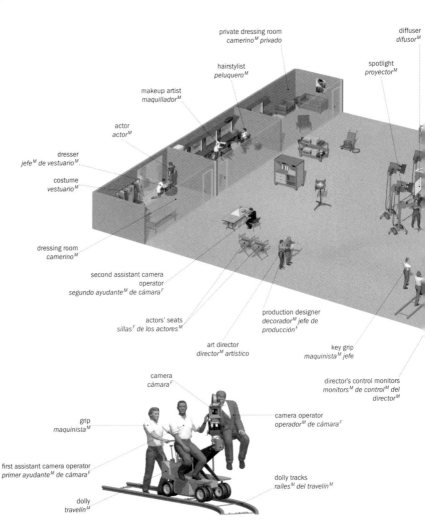

private dressing room
*camerino<sup>M</sup> privado*

diffuser
*difusor<sup>M</sup>*

hairstylist
*peluquero<sup>M</sup>*

spotlight
*proyector<sup>M</sup>*

makeup artist
*maquillador<sup>M</sup>*

actor
*actor<sup>M</sup>*

dresser
*jefe<sup>M</sup> de vestuario<sup>M</sup>*

costume
*vestuario<sup>M</sup>*

dressing room
*camerino<sup>M</sup>*

second assistant camera
operator
*segundo ayudante<sup>M</sup> de cámara<sup>F</sup>*

actors' seats
*sillas<sup>F</sup> de los actores<sup>M</sup>*

production designer
*decorador<sup>M</sup> jefe de
producción<sup>F</sup>*

art director
*director<sup>M</sup> artístico*

key grip
*maquinista<sup>M</sup> jefe*

camera
*cámara<sup>F</sup>*

director's control monitors
*monitors<sup>M</sup> de control<sup>M</sup> del
director<sup>M</sup>*

camera operator
*operador<sup>M</sup> de cámara<sup>F</sup>*

grip
*maquinista<sup>M</sup>*

first assistant camera operator
*primer ayudante<sup>M</sup> de cámara<sup>F</sup>*

dolly
*travelín<sup>M</sup>*

dolly tracks
*raíles<sup>M</sup> del travelín<sup>M</sup>*

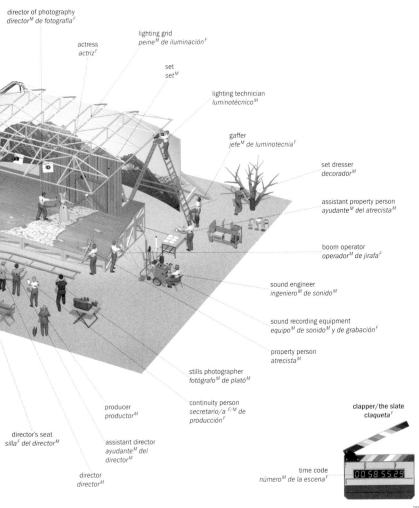

director of photography
director$^M$ de fotografía$^F$

lighting grid
peine$^M$ de iluminación$^F$

actress
actriz$^F$

set
set$^M$

lighting technician
luminotécnico$^M$

gaffer
jefe$^M$ de luminotecnia$^F$

set dresser
decorador$^M$

assistant property person
ayudante$^M$ del atrecista$^M$

boom operator
operador$^M$ de jirafa$^F$

sound engineer
ingeniero$^M$ de sonido$^M$

sound recording equipment
equipo$^M$ de sonido$^M$ y de grabación$^F$

property person
atrecista$^M$

stills photographer
fotógrafo$^M$ de plató$^M$

continuity person
secretario/a $^{F/M}$ de
producción$^F$

producer
productor$^M$

director's seat
silla$^F$ del director$^M$

assistant director
ayudante$^M$ del
director$^M$

director
director$^M$

clapper/the slate
claqueta$^F$

time code
número$^M$ de la escena$^F$

# theater
*teatro*<sup>M</sup>

ARTS AND ARCHITECTURE

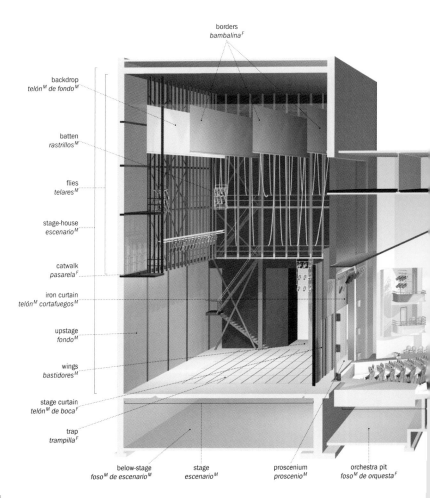

borders
*bambalina*<sup>F</sup>

backdrop
*telón*<sup>M</sup> *de fondo*<sup>M</sup>

batten
*rastrillos*<sup>M</sup>

flies
*telares*<sup>M</sup>

stage-house
*escenario*<sup>M</sup>

catwalk
*pasarela*<sup>F</sup>

iron curtain
*telón*<sup>M</sup> *cortafuegos*<sup>M</sup>

upstage
*fondo*<sup>M</sup>

wings
*bastidores*<sup>M</sup>

stage curtain
*telón*<sup>M</sup> *de boca*<sup>F</sup>

trap
*trampilla*<sup>F</sup>

below-stage
*foso*<sup>M</sup> *de escenario*<sup>M</sup>

stage
*escenario*<sup>M</sup>

proscenium
*proscenio*<sup>M</sup>

orchestra pit
*foso*<sup>M</sup> *de orquesta*<sup>F</sup>

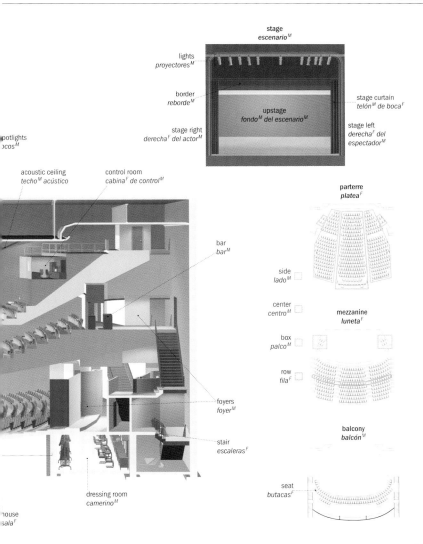

stage
escenario[M]

lights
proyectores[M]

border
reborde[M]

stage right
derecha[F] del actor[M]

upstage
fondo[M] del escenario[M]

stage curtain
telón[M] de boca[F]

stage left
derecha[F] del
espectador[M]

spotlights
ocos[M]

acoustic ceiling
techo[M] acústico

control room
cabina[F] de control[M]

bar
bar[M]

parterre
platea[F]

side
lado[M]

center
centro[M]

mezzanine
luneta[F]

box
palco[M]

row
fila[F]

foyers
foyer[M]

stair
escaleras[F]

balcony
balcón[M]

dressing room
camerino[M]

seat
butacas[F]

house
sala[F]

# movie theater
*cine*<sup>M</sup>

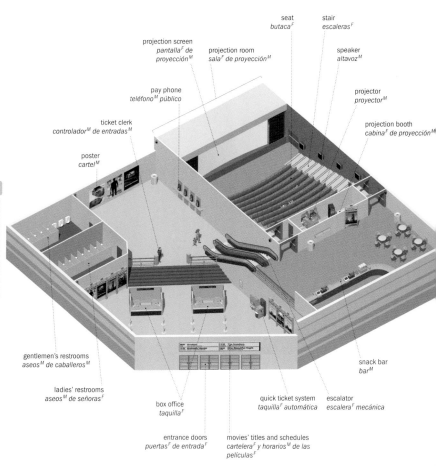

seat
*butaca*<sup>F</sup>

stair
*escaleras*<sup>F</sup>

projection screen
*pantalla*<sup>F</sup> *de proyección*<sup>M</sup>

projection room
*sala*<sup>F</sup> *de proyección*<sup>M</sup>

speaker
*altavoz*<sup>M</sup>

pay phone
*teléfono*<sup>M</sup> *público*

projector
*proyector*<sup>M</sup>

ticket clerk
*controlador*<sup>M</sup> *de entradas*<sup>M</sup>

projection booth
*cabina*<sup>F</sup> *de proyección*<sup>M</sup>

poster
*cartel*<sup>M</sup>

gentlemen's restrooms
*aseos*<sup>M</sup> *de caballeros*<sup>M</sup>

ladies' restrooms
*aseos*<sup>M</sup> *de señoras*<sup>F</sup>

snack bar
*bar*<sup>M</sup>

box office
*taquilla*<sup>F</sup>

quick ticket system
*taquilla*<sup>F</sup> *automática*

escalator
*escalera*<sup>F</sup> *mecánica*

entrance doors
*puertas*<sup>F</sup> *de entrada*<sup>F</sup>

movies' titles and schedules
*cartelera*<sup>F</sup> *y horarios*<sup>M</sup> *de las películas*<sup>F</sup>

# symphony orchestra
## orquesta<sup>F</sup> sinfónica

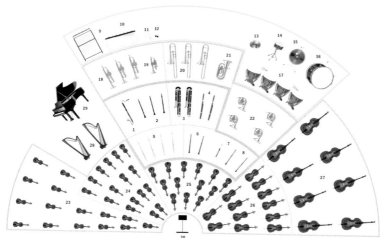

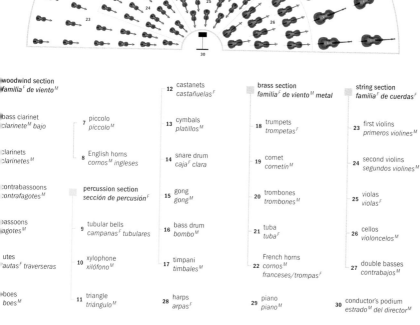

woodwind section
*familia<sup>F</sup> de viento<sup>M</sup>*

bass clarinet
*clarinete<sup>M</sup> bajo*

clarinets
*clarinetes<sup>M</sup>*

contrabassoons
*contrafagotes<sup>M</sup>*

bassoons
*fagotes<sup>M</sup>*

flutes
*flautas<sup>F</sup> traverseras*

oboes
*oboes<sup>M</sup>*

7 piccolo
*píccolo<sup>M</sup>*

8 English horns
*cornos<sup>M</sup> ingleses*

percussion section
*sección de percusión<sup>F</sup>*

9 tubular bells
*campanas<sup>F</sup> tubulares*

10 xylophone
*xilófono<sup>M</sup>*

11 triangle
*triángulo<sup>M</sup>*

12 castanets
*castañuelas<sup>F</sup>*

13 cymbals
*platillos<sup>M</sup>*

14 snare drum
*caja<sup>F</sup> clara*

15 gong
*gong<sup>M</sup>*

16 bass drum
*bombo<sup>M</sup>*

17 timpani
*timbales<sup>M</sup>*

28 harps
*arpas<sup>F</sup>*

brass section
*familia<sup>F</sup> de viento<sup>M</sup> metal*

18 trumpets
*trompetas<sup>F</sup>*

19 cornet
*cornetín<sup>M</sup>*

20 trombones
*trombones<sup>M</sup>*

21 tuba
*tuba<sup>F</sup>*

22 French horns
*cornos<sup>M</sup>
franceses/trompas<sup>F</sup>*

29 piano
*piano<sup>M</sup>*

string section
*familia<sup>F</sup> de cuerdas<sup>F</sup>*

23 first violins
*primeros violines<sup>M</sup>*

24 second violins
*segundos violines<sup>M</sup>*

25 violas
*violas<sup>F</sup>*

26 cellos
*violoncelos<sup>M</sup>*

27 double basses
*contrabajos<sup>M</sup>*

30 conductor's podium
*estrado<sup>M</sup> del director<sup>M</sup>*

# traditional musical instruments

*instrumentos<sup>M</sup> musicales tradicionales*

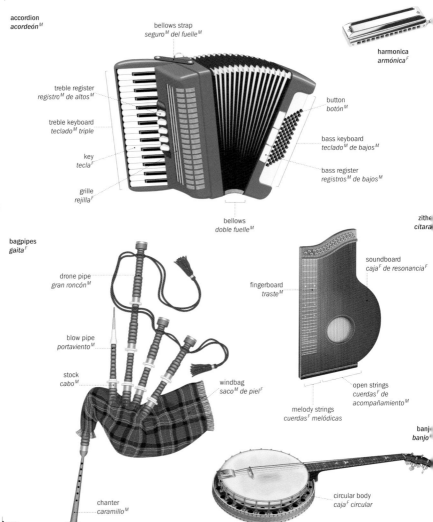

**accordion**
*acordeón<sup>M</sup>*

bellows strap
*seguro<sup>M</sup> del fuelle<sup>M</sup>*

**harmonica**
*armónica<sup>F</sup>*

treble register
*registro<sup>M</sup> de altos<sup>M</sup>*

treble keyboard
*teclado<sup>M</sup> triple*

key
*tecla<sup>F</sup>*

grille
*rejilla<sup>F</sup>*

button
*botón<sup>M</sup>*

bass keyboard
*teclado<sup>M</sup> de bajos<sup>M</sup>*

bass register
*registros<sup>M</sup> de bajos<sup>M</sup>*

bellows
*doble fuelle<sup>M</sup>*

**zither**
*cítara*

**bagpipes**
*gaita<sup>F</sup>*

drone pipe
*gran roncón<sup>M</sup>*

blow pipe
*portaviento<sup>M</sup>*

stock
*cabo<sup>M</sup>*

windbag
*saco<sup>M</sup> de piel<sup>F</sup>*

chanter
*caramillo<sup>M</sup>*

soundboard
*caja<sup>F</sup> de resonancia<sup>F</sup>*

fingerboard
*traste<sup>M</sup>*

open strings
*cuerdas<sup>F</sup> de acompañamiento<sup>M</sup>*

melody strings
*cuerdas<sup>F</sup> melódicas*

**banjo**
*banjo*

circular body
*caja<sup>F</sup> circular*

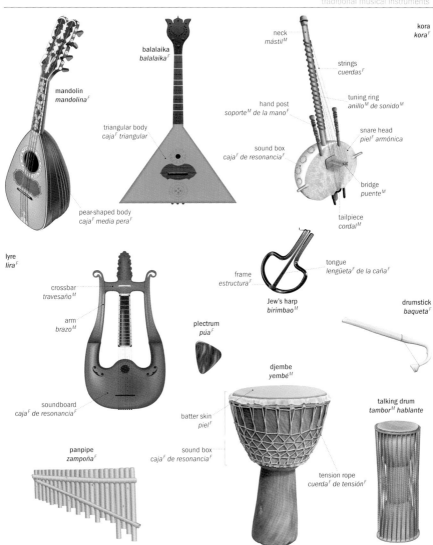

mandolin
*mandolina*<sup>F</sup>

pear-shaped body
*caja*<sup>F</sup> *media pera*<sup>F</sup>

balalaika
*balalaika*<sup>F</sup>

triangular body
*caja*<sup>F</sup> *triangular*

kora
*kora*<sup>F</sup>

neck
*mástil*<sup>M</sup>

strings
*cuerdas*<sup>F</sup>

hand post
*soporte*<sup>M</sup> *de la mano*<sup>F</sup>

tuning ring
*anillo*<sup>M</sup> *de sonido*<sup>M</sup>

sound box
*caja*<sup>F</sup> *de resonancia*<sup>F</sup>

snare head
*piel*<sup>F</sup> *armónica*

bridge
*puente*<sup>M</sup>

tailpiece
*cordal*<sup>M</sup>

lyre
*lira*<sup>F</sup>

crossbar
*travesaño*<sup>M</sup>

arm
*brazo*<sup>M</sup>

soundboard
*caja*<sup>F</sup> *de resonancia*<sup>F</sup>

frame
*estructura*<sup>F</sup>

tongue
*lengüeta*<sup>F</sup> *de la caña*<sup>F</sup>

Jew's harp
*birimbao*<sup>M</sup>

plectrum
*púa*<sup>F</sup>

drumstick
*baqueta*<sup>F</sup>

djembe
*yembé*<sup>M</sup>

batter skin
*piel*<sup>F</sup>

sound box
*caja*<sup>F</sup> *de resonancia*<sup>F</sup>

talking drum
*tambor*<sup>M</sup> *hablante*

tension rope
*cuerda*<sup>F</sup> *de tensión*<sup>F</sup>

panpipe
*zampoña*<sup>F</sup>

ARTS AND ARCHITECTURE

# musical notation
*notación<sup>F</sup> musical*

**staff**
*pentagrama<sup>M</sup>*

space
*espacio<sup>M</sup>*

line
*línea<sup>F</sup>*

ledger line
*línea<sup>F</sup> suplementaria*

**clefs**
*claves<sup>F</sup>*

treble clef
*clave<sup>F</sup> de sol*

bass clef
*clave<sup>F</sup> de fa*

C clef
*clave<sup>F</sup> de do*

**time signatures**
*compás<sup>M</sup>*

two-two time
*de dos mitades<sup>F</sup>*

three-four time
*de tres cuartos<sup>M</sup>*

four-four time
*de cuatro cuartos<sup>M</sup>*

bar line
*barra<sup>F</sup> de compás<sup>M</sup>*

repeat mark
*barra<sup>F</sup> de repetición<sup>F</sup>*

**intervals**
*intervalos<sup>M</sup>*

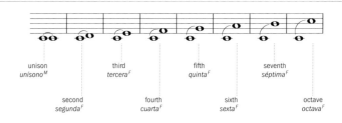

unison
*unísono<sup>M</sup>*

second
*segunda<sup>F</sup>*

third
*tercera<sup>F</sup>*

fourth
*cuarta<sup>F</sup>*

fifth
*quinta<sup>F</sup>*

sixth
*sexta<sup>F</sup>*

seventh
*séptima<sup>F</sup>*

octave
*octava<sup>F</sup>*

**scale**
*escala<sup>F</sup>*

C
*do (C)*

D
*re (D)*

E
*mi (E)*

F
*fa (F)*

G
*sol (G)*

A
*la (A)*

B
*si (B)*

C
*do (C)*

musical notation

rest symbols
*valores^M de los silencios^M*

whole rest
*silencio^M de redonda^F*

quarter rest
*silencio^M de negra^F*

sixteenth rest
*silencio^M de semicorchea^F*

sixty-fourth rest
*silencio^M de semifusa^F*

half rest
*silencio^M de blanca^F*

eighth rest
*silencio^M de corchea^F*

thirty-second rest
*silencio^M de fusa^F*

ornaments
*adornos^M*

appoggiatura
*apoyatura^F*

trill
*trino^M*

turn
*grupeto^M*

mordent
*mordente^M*

note symbols
*valores^M de las notas musicales*

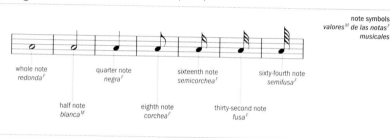

whole note
*redonda^F*

quarter note
*negra^F*

sixteenth note
*semicorchea^F*

sixty-fourth note
*semifusa^F*

half note
*blanca^M*

eighth note
*corchea^F*

thirty-second note
*fusa^F*

accidentals
*accidentales^M*

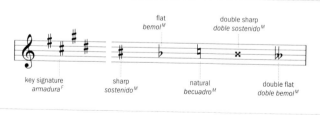

flat
*bemol^M*

double sharp
*doble sostenido^M*

key signature
*armadura^F*

sharp
*sostenido^M*

natural
*becuadro^M*

double flat
*doble bemol^M*

other signs
*otros signos^M*

chord
*acorde^M*

tie
*ligadura^F*

accent mark
*acento^M*

arpeggio
*arpegio^M*

fermata
*calderón^M*

299

# examples of instrumental groups
*ejemplos<sup>M</sup> de conjuntos<sup>M</sup> instrumentales*

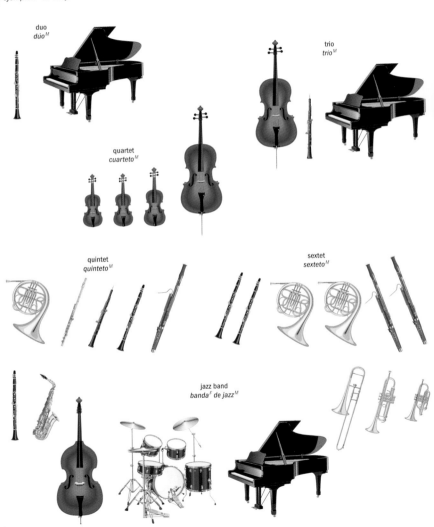

duo
*dúo<sup>M</sup>*

trio
*trio<sup>M</sup>*

quartet
*cuarteto<sup>M</sup>*

quintet
*quinteto<sup>M</sup>*

sextet
*sexteto<sup>M</sup>*

jazz band
*banda<sup>F</sup> de jazz<sup>M</sup>*

# stringed instruments
*instrumentos*$^M$ *de cuerda*$^F$

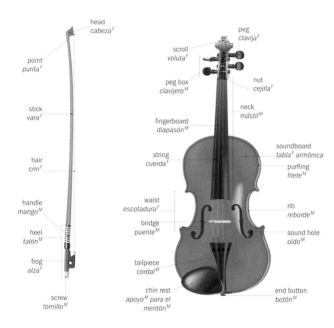

bow
*arco*$^M$

head
*cabeza*$^F$

point
*punta*$^F$

stick
*vara*$^F$

hair
*crin*$^F$

handle
*mango*$^M$

heel
*talón*$^M$

frog
*alza*$^F$

screw
*tornillo*$^M$

violin
*violín*$^M$

peg
*clavija*$^F$

scroll
*voluta*$^F$

peg box
*clavijero*$^M$

nut
*cejilla*$^F$

neck
*mástil*$^M$

fingerboard
*diapasón*$^M$

soundboard
*tabla*$^F$ *armónica*

string
*cuerda*$^F$

purfling
*filete*$^M$

waist
*escotadura*$^F$

bridge
*puente*$^M$

rib
*reborde*$^M$

sound hole
*oído*$^M$

tailpiece
*cordal*$^M$

chin rest
*apoyo*$^M$ *para el
mentón*$^M$

end button
*botón*$^M$

violin family
*familia*$^F$ *de los
violines*$^M$

double bass
*contrabajo*$^M$

cello
*violoncelo*$^M$

viola
*viola*$^F$

violin
*violín*$^M$

ARTS AND ARCHITECTURE

stringed instruments

harp
*arpa*<sup>F</sup>

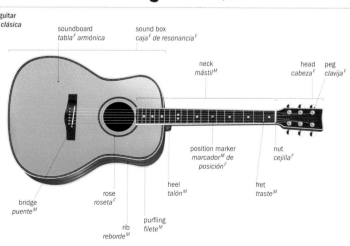

crown
*corona*<sup>F</sup>

tuning peg
*clavija*<sup>F</sup>

neck
*consola*<sup>F</sup>

shoulder
*hombrera*<sup>F</sup>

string
*cuerda*<sup>F</sup>

soundboard
*tabla*<sup>F</sup> *armónica*

pillar
*columna*<sup>F</sup>

sound box
*caja*<sup>F</sup> *de resonancia*<sup>F</sup>

pedal
*pedal*<sup>M</sup>

pedestal
*pedestal*<sup>M</sup>

foot
*pie*<sup>M</sup>

acoustic guitar
*guitarra*<sup>F</sup> *clásica*

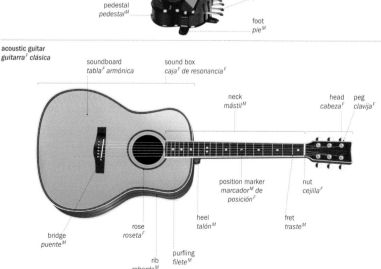

soundboard
*tabla*<sup>F</sup> *armónica*

sound box
*caja*<sup>F</sup> *de resonancia*<sup>F</sup>

neck
*mástil*<sup>M</sup>

head
*cabeza*<sup>F</sup>

peg
*clavija*<sup>F</sup>

position marker
*marcador*<sup>M</sup> *de posición*<sup>F</sup>

nut
*cejilla*<sup>F</sup>

heel
*talón*<sup>M</sup>

fret
*traste*<sup>M</sup>

bridge
*puente*<sup>M</sup>

rose
*roseta*<sup>F</sup>

rib
*reborde*<sup>M</sup>

purfling
*filete*<sup>M</sup>

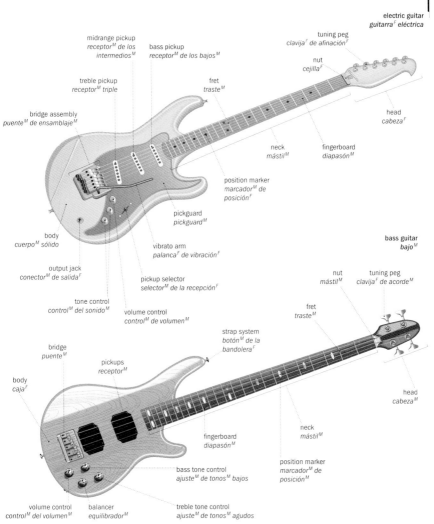

electric guitar
*guitarra^F eléctrica*

midrange pickup
*receptor^M de los intermedios^M*

bass pickup
*receptor^M de los bajos^M*

tuning peg
*clavija^F de afinación^F*

nut
*cejilla^F*

treble pickup
*receptor^M triple*

fret
*traste^M*

bridge assembly
*puente^M de ensamblaje^M*

head
*cabeza^F*

neck
*mástil^M*

fingerboard
*diapasón^M*

position marker
*marcador^M de posición^F*

body
*cuerpo^M sólido*

pickguard
*pickguard^M*

bass guitar
*bajo^M*

output jack
*conector^M de salida^F*

vibrato arm
*palanca^F de vibración^F*

nut
*mástil^M*

tuning peg
*clavija^F de acorde^M*

pickup selector
*selector^M de la recepción^F*

fret
*traste^M*

tone control
*control^M del sonido^M*

volume control
*control^M de volumen^M*

strap system
*botón^M de la bandolera^F*

bridge
*puente^M*

pickups
*receptor^M*

head
*cabeza^M*

body
*caja^F*

neck
*mástil^M*

fingerboard
*diapasón^M*

position marker
*marcador^M de posición^M*

bass tone control
*ajuste^M de tonos^M bajos*

volume control
*control^M del volumen^M*

balancer
*equilibrador^M*

treble tone control
*ajuste^M de tonos^M agudos*

# keyboard instruments
*instrumentos*<sup>M</sup> *de teclado*<sup>M</sup>

**upright piano**
*piano*<sup>M</sup> *vertical*

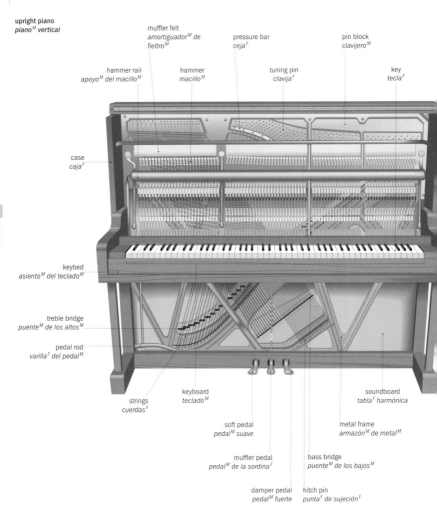

muffler felt
*amortiguador*<sup>M</sup> *de fieltro*<sup>M</sup>

pressure bar
*ceja*<sup>F</sup>

pin block
*clavijero*<sup>M</sup>

hammer rail
*apoyo*<sup>M</sup> *del macillo*<sup>M</sup>

hammer
*macillo*<sup>M</sup>

tuning pin
*clavija*<sup>F</sup>

key
*tecla*<sup>F</sup>

case
*caja*<sup>F</sup>

keybed
*asiento*<sup>M</sup> *del teclado*<sup>M</sup>

treble bridge
*puente*<sup>M</sup> *de los altos*<sup>M</sup>

pedal rod
*varilla*<sup>F</sup> *del pedal*<sup>M</sup>

strings
*cuerdas*<sup>F</sup>

keyboard
*teclado*<sup>M</sup>

soundboard
*tabla*<sup>F</sup> *harmónica*

soft pedal
*pedal*<sup>M</sup> *suave*

metal frame
*armazón*<sup>M</sup> *de metal*<sup>M</sup>

muffler pedal
*pedal*<sup>M</sup> *de la sordina*<sup>F</sup>

bass bridge
*puente*<sup>M</sup> *de los bajos*<sup>M</sup>

damper pedal
*pedal*<sup>M</sup> *fuerte*

hitch pin
*punta*<sup>F</sup> *de sujeción*<sup>F</sup>

ARTS AND ARCHITECTURE

organ
*órgano*$^M$

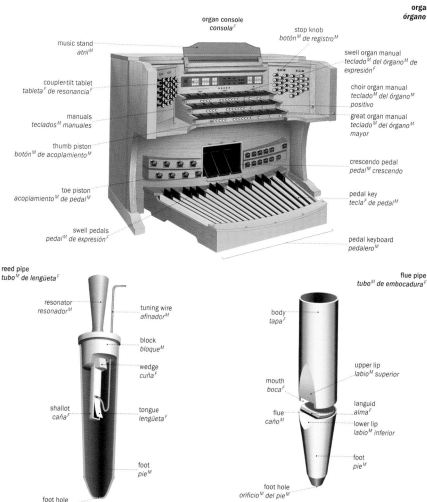

organ console
*consola*$^F$

music stand
*atril*$^M$

coupler-tilt tablet
*tableta*$^F$ *de resonancia*$^F$

manuals
*teclados*$^M$ *manuales*

thumb piston
*botón*$^M$ *de acoplamiento*$^M$

toe piston
*acoplamiento*$^M$ *de pedal*$^M$

swell pedals
*pedal*$^M$ *de expresión*$^F$

stop knob
*botón*$^M$ *de registro*$^M$

swell organ manual
*teclado*$^M$ *del órgano*$^M$ *de expresión*$^F$

choir organ manual
*teclado*$^M$ *del órgano*$^M$ *positivo*

great organ manual
*teclado*$^M$ *del órgano*$^M$ *mayor*

crescendo pedal
*pedal*$^M$ *crescendo*

pedal key
*tecla*$^F$ *de pedal*$^M$

pedal keyboard
*pedalero*$^M$

reed pipe
*tubo*$^M$ *de lengüeta*$^F$

resonator
*resonador*$^M$

tuning wire
*afinador*$^M$

block
*bloque*$^M$

wedge
*cuña*$^F$

shallot
*caña*$^F$

tongue
*lengüeta*$^F$

foot
*pie*$^M$

foot hole
*orificio*$^M$ *del pie*$^M$

flue pipe
*tubo*$^M$ *de embocadura*$^F$

body
*tapa*$^F$

upper lip
*labio*$^M$ *superior*

mouth
*boca*$^F$

flue
*caño*$^M$

languid
*alma*$^F$

lower lip
*labio*$^M$ *inferior*

foot
*pie*$^M$

foot hole
*orificio*$^M$ *del pie*$^M$

ARTS AND ARCHITECTURE

# wind instruments
*instrumentos^M de viento^M*

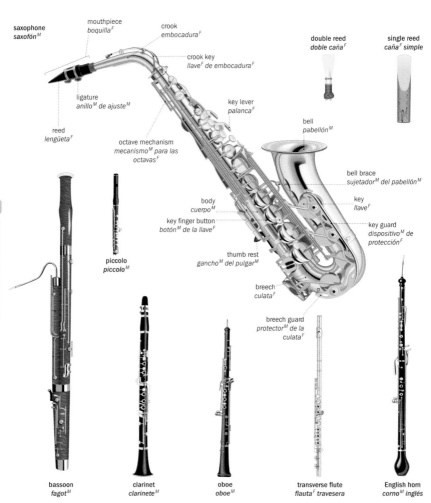

saxophone
*saxofón^M*

mouthpiece
*boquilla^F*

crook
*embocadura^F*

crook key
*llave^F de embocadura^F*

ligature
*anillo^M de ajuste^M*

reed
*lengüeta^F*

octave mechanism
*mecanismo^M para las octavas^F*

key lever
*palanca^F*

bell
*pabellón^M*

bell brace
*sujetador^M del pabellón^M*

body
*cuerpo^M*

key finger button
*botón^M de la llave^F*

key
*llave^F*

key guard
*dispositivo^M de protección^F*

thumb rest
*gancho^M del pulgar^M*

breech
*culata^F*

breech guard
*protector^M de la culata^F*

double reed
*doble caña^F*

single reed
*caña^F simple*

bassoon
*fagot^M*

clarinet
*clarinete^M*

oboe
*oboe^M*

piccolo
*piccolo^M*

transverse flute
*flauta^F travesera*

English horn
*corno^M inglés*

wind instruments

trumpet
*trompeta*<sup>F</sup>

key
*llave*<sup>F</sup>

little finger hook
*gancho*<sup>M</sup> *del meñique*<sup>M</sup>

bell
*pabellón*<sup>M</sup>

mouthpiece receiver
*empate*<sup>M</sup> *de la boquilla*<sup>F</sup>

mouthpipe
*tubo*<sup>M</sup>

ring
*anillo*<sup>M</sup>

mouthpiece
*boquilla*<sup>F</sup>

tuning slide
*corredera*<sup>F</sup> *de afinamiento*<sup>M</sup>

first valve slide
*primer pistón*<sup>M</sup> *móvil*

spit valve
*llave*<sup>F</sup> *para agua*<sup>F</sup>

third valve slide
*tercer pistón*<sup>M</sup> *móvil*

thumb hook
*gancho*<sup>M</sup> *del pulgar*<sup>M</sup>

valve
*pistón*<sup>M</sup>

valve casing
*tubo*<sup>M</sup> *del pistón*<sup>M</sup>

mute
*sordina*<sup>F</sup>

second valve slide
*segundo pistón*<sup>M</sup> *móvil*

cornet
*cornetín*<sup>M</sup>

French horn
*corno*<sup>M</sup>
*francés/trompa*<sup>F</sup>

bugle
*clarín*<sup>M</sup>

saxhorn
*bombardino*<sup>M</sup>

tuba
*tuba*<sup>F</sup>

trombone
*trombón*<sup>M</sup>

ARTS AND ARCHITECTURE

# percussion instruments
*instrumentos<sup>M</sup> de percusión<sup>F</sup>*

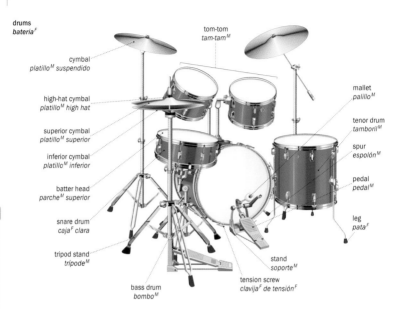

drums
*batería<sup>F</sup>*

tom-tom
*tam-tam<sup>M</sup>*

cymbal
*platillo<sup>M</sup> suspendido*

high-hat cymbal
*platillo<sup>M</sup> high hat*

superior cymbal
*platillo<sup>M</sup> superior*

inferior cymbal
*platillo<sup>M</sup> inferior*

batter head
*parche<sup>M</sup> superior*

snare drum
*caja<sup>F</sup> clara*

tripod stand
*trípode<sup>M</sup>*

bass drum
*bombo<sup>M</sup>*

tension screw
*clavija<sup>F</sup> de tensión<sup>F</sup>*

stand
*soporte<sup>M</sup>*

mallet
*palillo<sup>M</sup>*

tenor drum
*tamboril<sup>M</sup>*

spur
*espolón<sup>M</sup>*

pedal
*pedal<sup>M</sup>*

leg
*pata<sup>F</sup>*

kettledrum
*timbal<sup>M</sup>*

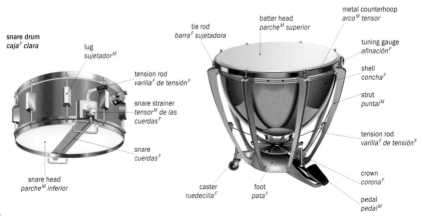

snare drum
*caja<sup>F</sup> clara*

lug
*sujetador<sup>M</sup>*

tension rod
*varilla<sup>F</sup> de tensión<sup>F</sup>*

snare strainer
*tensor<sup>M</sup> de las cuerdas<sup>F</sup>*

snare
*cuerdas<sup>F</sup>*

snare head
*parche<sup>M</sup> inferior*

tie rod
*barra<sup>F</sup> sujetadora*

batter head
*parche<sup>M</sup> superior*

metal counterhoop
*arco<sup>M</sup> tensor*

tuning gauge
*afinación<sup>F</sup>*

shell
*concha<sup>F</sup>*

strut
*puntal<sup>M</sup>*

tension rod
*varilla<sup>F</sup> de tensión<sup>F</sup>*

crown
*corona<sup>F</sup>*

pedal
*pedal<sup>M</sup>*

caster
*ruedecilla<sup>F</sup>*

foot
*pata<sup>F</sup>*

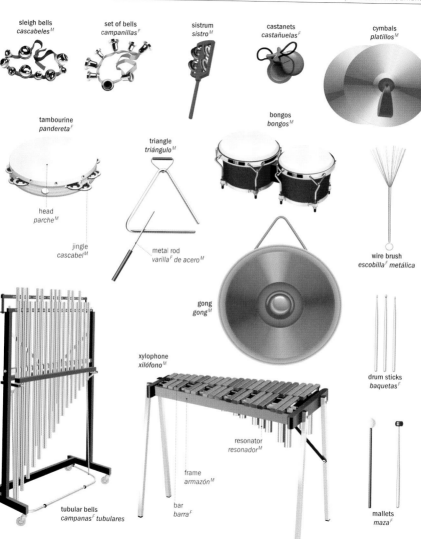

sleigh bells
*cascabeles*$^M$

set of bells
*campanillas*$^F$

sistrum
*sistro*$^M$

castanets
*castañuelas*$^F$

cymbals
*platillos*$^M$

tambourine
*pandereta*$^F$

triangle
*triángulo*$^M$

bongos
*bongos*$^M$

head
*parche*$^M$

jingle
*cascabel*$^M$

metal rod
*varilla*$^F$ *de acero*$^M$

wire brush
*escobilla*$^F$ *metálica*

gong
*gong*$^M$

drum sticks
*baquetas*$^F$

xylophone
*xilófono*$^M$

resonator
*resonador*$^M$

frame
*armazón*$^M$

tubular bells
*campanas*$^F$ *tubulares*

bar
*barra*$^F$

mallets
*maza*$^F$

# electronic instruments

*instrumentos* *electrónicos*

sequencer
*secuenciador* M

samp
muestreade

headphone jack
*toma* F *para auriculares* M

expander
*amplificador* M

function display
*display* M *de las
funciones* F

disk drive
*lector* M *de discos* M

synthesizer
*sintetizador* M

system buttons
*sistema* M *de botones* M

function display
*display* M *de funciones* F

program selector
*selector* M *de programa* M

voice edit buttons
*botones* M *para editar la ve*

volume control
*control* M *de volumen* M

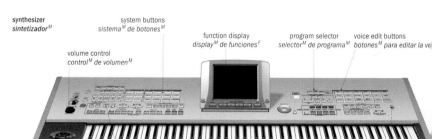

ARTS AND ARCHITECTURE

sequencer control
*control* M *de secuencias* F

keyboard
*teclado* M

USB port
*puerto* M USB

CD/DVD-ROM drive
*unidad* F CD/DVD-ROM

pitch and modulation switch
*modulación* F *del volumen* M *y del timbre* M *del sonido* M

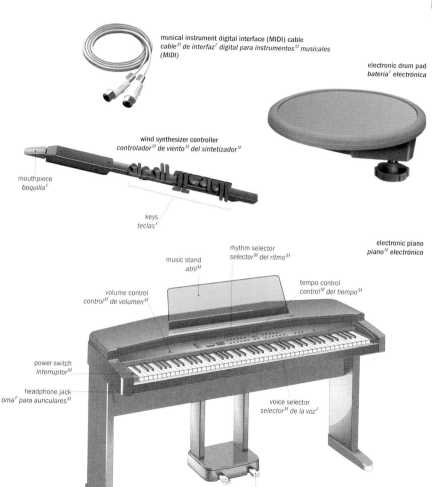

musical instrument digital interface (MIDI) cable
*cable*<sup>M</sup> *de interfaz*<sup>F</sup> *digital para instrumentos*<sup>M</sup> *musicales (MIDI)*

electronic drum pad
*batería*<sup>F</sup> *electrónica*

wind synthesizer controller
*controlador*<sup>M</sup> *de viento*<sup>M</sup> *del sintetizador*<sup>M</sup>

mouthpiece
*boquilla*<sup>F</sup>

keys
*teclas*<sup>F</sup>

electronic piano
*piano*<sup>M</sup> *electrónico*

rhythm selector
*selector*<sup>M</sup> *del ritmo*<sup>M</sup>

music stand
*atril*<sup>M</sup>

tempo control
*control*<sup>M</sup> *del tiempo*<sup>M</sup>

volume control
*control*<sup>M</sup> *de volumen*<sup>M</sup>

power switch
*interruptor*<sup>M</sup>

headphone jack
*oma*<sup>F</sup> *para auriculares*<sup>M</sup>

voice selector
*selector*<sup>M</sup> *de la voz*<sup>F</sup>

soft pedal
*pedal*<sup>M</sup> *de los bajos*<sup>M</sup>

damper pedal
*pedal*<sup>M</sup> *fuerte*

ARTS AND ARCHITECTURE

# writing instruments
*instrumentos[M] para escribir*

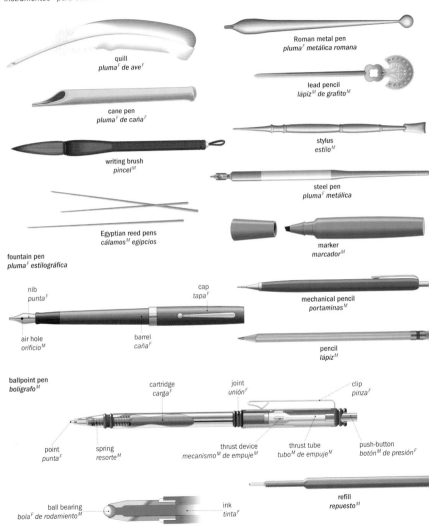

quill
*pluma[F] de ave[F]*

Roman metal pen
*pluma[F] metálica romana*

lead pencil
*lápiz[M] de grafito[M]*

cane pen
*pluma[F] de caña[F]*

stylus
*estilo[M]*

writing brush
*pincel[M]*

steel pen
*pluma[F] metálica*

Egyptian reed pens
*cálamos[M] egipcios*

marker
*marcador[M]*

fountain pen
*pluma[F] estilográfica*

nib
*punta[F]*

cap
*tapa[F]*

mechanical pencil
*portaminas[M]*

air hole
*orificio[M]*

barrel
*caña[F]*

pencil
*lápiz[M]*

ballpoint pen
*bolígrafo[M]*

cartridge
*carga[F]*

joint
*unión[F]*

clip
*pinza[F]*

point
*punta[F]*

spring
*resorte[M]*

thrust device
*mecanismo[M] de empuje[M]*

thrust tube
*tubo[M] de empuje[M]*

push-button
*botón[M] de presión[F]*

ball bearing
*bola[F] de rodamiento[M]*

ink
*tinta[F]*

refill
*repuesto[M]*

# newspaper
*periódico* M

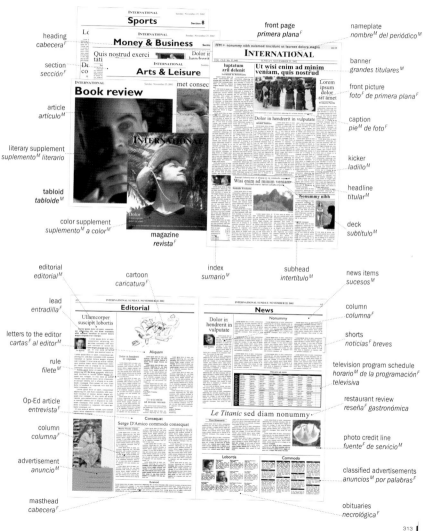

heading
*cabecera* F

section
*sección* F

article
*artículo* M

literary supplement
*suplemento* M *literario*

tabloid
*tabloide* M

color supplement
*suplemento* M *a color* M

magazine
*revista* F

front page
*primera plana* F

nameplate
*nombre* M *del periódico* M

banner
*grandes titulares* M

front picture
*foto* F *de primera plana* F

caption
*pie* M *de foto* F

kicker
*ladillo* M

headline
*titular* M

deck
*subtítulo* M

editorial
*editorial* M

cartoon
*caricatura* F

index
*sumario* M

subhead
*intertítulo* M

news items
*sucesos* M

lead
*entradilla* F

letters to the editor
*cartas* F *al editor* M

rule
*filete* M

Op-Ed article
*entrevista* F

column
*columna* F

advertisement
*anuncio* M

masthead
*cabecera* F

column
*columna* F

shorts
*noticias* F *breves*

television program schedule
*horario* M *de la programación* F *televisiva*

restaurant review
*reseña* F *gastronómica*

photo credit line
*fuente* F *de servicio* M

classified advertisements
*anuncios* M *por palabras* F

obituaries
*necrológica* F

# photography
*fotografía^F*

single-lens reflex (SLR) camera: front view
*cámara^F réflex monocular: vista^F frontal*

exposure adjustment knob
*botón^M de compensación^M de la exposición^F*

accessory shoe
*patín^M de los accesorios^M*

hot-shoe contact
*contacto^M central*

drive mode
*modo^M dispositivo^M*

control panel
*panel^M de controles^M*

command control dial
*selector^M de programa^M*

on-off switch
*interruptor^M de encendido/apagado*

shutter release button
*disparador^M*

self-timer indicator
*indicador^M de tiempo^M*

camera body
*caja^F*

lens release button
*botón^M de desbloqueo^M del objetivo^M*

objective lens
*objetivo^M*

exposure mode
*modalidad^F de exposició*

multiple exposure mode
*modalidad^F de exposición^F múltiple*

sensitivity
*sensibilidad^F*

remote control terminal
*terminal^M del control^M rem*

focus mode selector
*selector^M de focalización^F*

depth-of-field preview button
*botón^M de previsionado de profundidad^F de campo^M*

**lenses**
***objetivos^M***

telephoto lens
*teleobjetivo^M*

zoom lens
*objetivo^M zoom^M*

wide-angle lens
*objetivo^M gran angular^M*

macro lens
*objetivo^M macro*

**lens accessor**
***accesorios^M para el objetiv***

lens cap
*tapa^F del objetivo^M*

lens hood
*capuchón^M*

polarizing filter
*filtro^M de polarización^F*

digital reflex camera: camera back
*cámara*<sup>F</sup> *réflex digital: vista*<sup>F</sup> *posterior*

power switch
*conmutador*<sup>M</sup> *de alimentación*<sup>F</sup>

menu button
*botón*<sup>M</sup> *de selección*<sup>F</sup> *del menú*<sup>M</sup>

liquid crystal display
*pantalla*<sup>F</sup> *de cristal*<sup>M</sup> *líquido*

viewfinder
*visor*<sup>M</sup>

settings display button
*botón*<sup>M</sup> *de visualización*<sup>F</sup> *de ajustes*<sup>M</sup>

compact memory card
*tarjeta*<sup>F</sup> *de memoria*<sup>F</sup>

cover
*tapa*<sup>F</sup>

strap eyelet
*ojete*<sup>M</sup> *para la correa*<sup>F</sup>

multi-image jump button
*botón*<sup>M</sup> *de salto*<sup>M</sup> *de imágenes*<sup>F</sup>

video and digital terminals
*tomas*<sup>F</sup> *vídeo y digital*

image review button
*ón*<sup>M</sup> *de visualización*<sup>F</sup> *de imágenes*<sup>F</sup>

remote control terminal
*botón*<sup>M</sup> *de control*<sup>M</sup> *remoto*

index/enlarge button
*botón*<sup>M</sup> *de índice*<sup>M</sup>/*ampliación*<sup>F</sup>

erase button
*botón*<sup>M</sup> *de cancelación*<sup>F</sup>

four-way selector
*selector*<sup>M</sup> *cuadro-direccional*

eject button
*botón*<sup>M</sup> *de expulsión*<sup>F</sup>

**still cameras**
**cámaras<sup>F</sup> fijas**

Polaroid® camera
*cámara*<sup>F</sup> *Polaroid® Land*

medium-format SLR (6 x 6)
*cámara*<sup>F</sup> *reflex de formato*<sup>M</sup> *medio SLR (6x6)*

ultracompact camera
*aparato*<sup>M</sup> *ultracompacto*

compact camera
*aparato*<sup>M</sup> *compacto*

disposable camera
*cámara*<sup>F</sup> *desechable*

view camera
*cámara*<sup>F</sup> *de fuelle*<sup>M</sup>

COMMUNICATIONS AND OFFICE AUTOMATION

# broadcast satellite communication

*comunicación<sup>F</sup> vía satélite<sup>M</sup>*

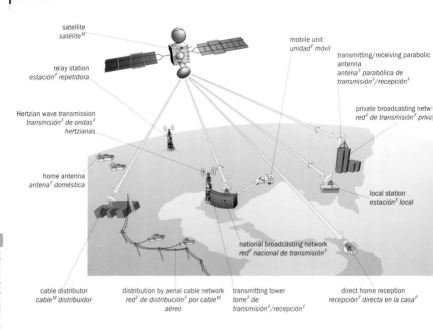

satellite
*satélite<sup>M</sup>*

relay station
*estación<sup>F</sup> repetidora*

mobile unit
*unidad<sup>F</sup> móvil*

transmitting/receiving parabolic antenna
*antena<sup>F</sup> parabólica de transmisión<sup>F</sup>/recepción<sup>F</sup>*

Hertzian wave transmission
*transmisión<sup>F</sup> de ondas<sup>F</sup> hertzianas*

private broadcasting netw
*red<sup>F</sup> de transmisión<sup>F</sup> priva*

home antenna
*antena<sup>F</sup> doméstica*

local station
*estación<sup>F</sup> local*

national broadcasting network
*red<sup>F</sup> nacional de transmisión<sup>F</sup>*

cable distributor
*cable<sup>M</sup> distribuidor*

distribution by aerial cable network
*red<sup>F</sup> de distribución<sup>F</sup> por cable<sup>M</sup> aéreo*

transmitting tower
*torre<sup>F</sup> de transmisión<sup>F</sup>/recepción<sup>F</sup>*

direct home reception
*recepción<sup>F</sup> directa en la casa<sup>F</sup>*

# telecommunication satellites

*satélites<sup>M</sup> de telecomunicaciones<sup>F</sup>*

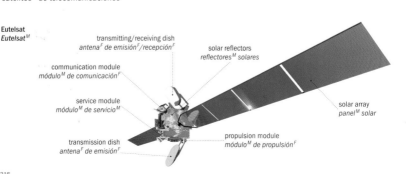

Eutelsat
*Eutelsat<sup>M</sup>*

transmitting/receiving dish
*antena<sup>F</sup> de emisión<sup>F</sup>/recepción<sup>F</sup>*

solar reflectors
*reflectores<sup>M</sup> solares*

communication module
*módulo<sup>M</sup> de comunicación<sup>F</sup>*

service module
*módulo<sup>M</sup> de servicio<sup>M</sup>*

solar array
*panel<sup>M</sup> solar*

transmission dish
*antena<sup>F</sup> de emisión<sup>F</sup>*

propulsion module
*módulo<sup>M</sup> de propulsión<sup>F</sup>*

# telecommunications by satellite
*telecomunicaciones^F vía satélite^M*

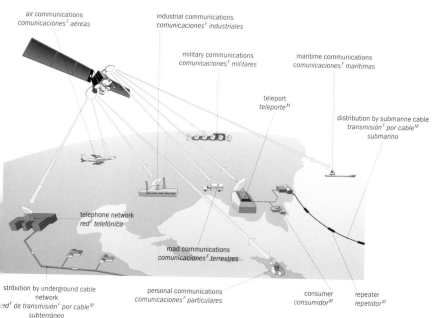

air communications
*comunicaciones^F aéreas*

industrial communications
*comunicaciones^F industriales*

military communications
*comunicaciones^F militares*

maritime communications
*comunicaciones^F maritimas*

teleport
*teleporte^M*

distribution by submarine cable
*transmisión^F por cable^M submarino*

telephone network
*red^F telefónica*

road communications
*comunicaciones^F terrestres*

stribution by underground cable
network
ed^F de transmisión^F por cable^M
subterráneo

personal communications
*comunicaciones^F particulares*

consumer
*consumidor^M*

repeater
*repetidor^M*

telecommunication satellites

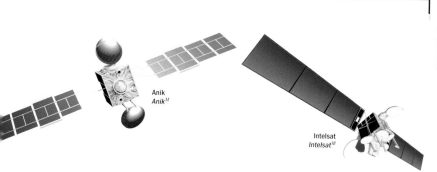

Anik
*Anik^M*

Intelsat
*Intelsat^M*

COMMUNICATIONS AND OFFICE AUTOMATION

317

# television
*televisión^F*

liquid crystal display (LCD) television
*televisor^M de cristal^M líquido*

plasma television
*televisor^M plasma^M*

cathode ray tube (CRT) television
*televisor^M con pantalla^F catódica*

cabinet
*caja^F*

screen
*pantalla^F*

power button
*botón^M de encendido*

tuning controls
*controles^M de sintonización^F*

remote control sensor
*sensor^M del mando^M a distancia*

picture tube
*tubo^M de pantalla^F*

funnel
*cono^M*

color selection filter
*filtro^M selector del color^M*

electron gun
*cañón^M de electrones^M*

base
*base^F*

neck
*cuello^M*

electron beam
*haz^M de electrones^M*

protective window
*ventana^F protectora*

screen
*pantalla^F*

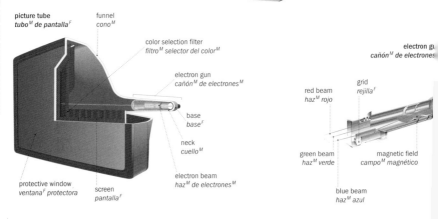

electron gun
*cañón^M de electrones*

grid
*rejilla^F*

red beam
*haz^M rojo*

green beam
*haz^M verde*

magnetic field
*campo^M magnético*

blue beam
*haz^M azul*

COMMUNICATIONS AND OFFICE AUTOMATION

318

television

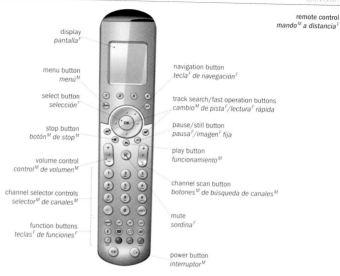

remote control
*mando*<sup>M</sup> *a distancia*<sup>F</sup>

display
*pantalla*<sup>F</sup>

menu button
*menú*<sup>M</sup>

select button
*selección*<sup>F</sup>

stop button
*botón*<sup>M</sup> *de stop*<sup>M</sup>

volume control
*control*<sup>M</sup> *de volumen*<sup>M</sup>

channel selector controls
*selector*<sup>M</sup> *de canales*<sup>M</sup>

function buttons
*teclas*<sup>F</sup> *de funciones*<sup>F</sup>

navigation button
*tecla*<sup>F</sup> *de navegación*<sup>F</sup>

track search/fast operation buttons
*cambio de pista*<sup>F</sup>/*lectura*<sup>F</sup> *rápida*

pause/still button
*pausa*<sup>F</sup>/*imagen*<sup>F</sup> *fija*

play button
*funcionamiento*<sup>M</sup>

channel scan button
*botones*<sup>M</sup> *de búsqueda de canales*<sup>M</sup>

mute
*sordina*<sup>F</sup>

power button
*interruptor*<sup>M</sup>

DVD recorder
*grabadora*<sup>F</sup> *DVD*

power button
*rruptor*<sup>M</sup> *de alimentación*<sup>F</sup>

channel selector
*selección*<sup>F</sup> *de canales*<sup>M</sup>

display
*pantalla*<sup>F</sup>

record button
*tecla*<sup>F</sup> *para grabar*

play button
*tecla*<sup>F</sup> *de lectura*<sup>F</sup>

stop button
*tecla*<sup>F</sup> *de parada*<sup>F</sup>

disc tray
*bandeja*<sup>F</sup> *de carga*<sup>F</sup>

disc compartment control
*control*<sup>M</sup> *de la bandeja*<sup>F</sup> *de carga*<sup>F</sup>

pause/still button
*pausa*<sup>F</sup>/*imagen*<sup>F</sup> *fija*

track search/fast operation buttons
*cambio*<sup>M</sup> *de pista*<sup>F</sup>/*lectura*<sup>F</sup> *rápida*

recording media
*soportes*<sup>M</sup> *para grabar*

ideocassette
*inta*<sup>F</sup> *de video*<sup>M</sup>

recording tape
*cinta*<sup>F</sup> *magnética*

reel
*bobina*<sup>F</sup>

digital versatile disc (DVD)
*disco*<sup>M</sup> *versátil digital (DVD)*

COMMUNICATIONS AND OFFICE AUTOMATION

319

**mini-DV camcorder: front view**
*videocámara$^F$ mini DV : vista$^F$ de frente*

zoom button
*tecla$^F$ de zoom$^M$*

recording mode
*modo$^M$ grabación$^F$*

electronic viewfinder
*visor$^M$ electrónico*

photoshot button
*tecla$^F$ foto$^F$*

zoom lens
*objetivo$^M$ zoom*

power/functions switch
*interruptor$^M$ alimentación$^F$/funciones$^F$*

terminal cover
*tapa$^F$ de conexión$^F$*

lamp
*lámpara$^F$*

hand strap
*correa$^F$ para la mano$^F$*

microphone
*micrófono$^M$*

**mini-DV camcorder: rear view**
*videocámara$^F$ mini DV : vista$^F$ posterior*

videotape operation controls
*mandos$^M$ de la cinta$^F$ de vídeo$^M$*

focus button
*botón$^M$ de enfoque$^M$*

nightshot button
*botón$^M$ de grabación$^F$ nocturna*

eyepiece
*ocular$^M$*

liquid crystal display
*pantalla$^F$ táctil LCD*

recording start/stop button
*tecla$^F$ de inicio/stop de grabación$^F$*

rechargeable battery pack
*pila$^F$ recargable*

card slot
*ranura$^F$ de la tarjeta$^F$ de memoria$^F$*

menu button
*tecla$^F$ de menú$^M$*

speaker
*altavoz$^M$*

backlighting button
*tecla$^F$ de contraluz$^M$*

widescreen/data code button
*tecla$^F$ pantalla$^F$ ancha/código$^M$ de datos$^M$*

television

**dish antenna**
*antena<sup>F</sup> parabólica*

**receiver**
*receptor<sup>M</sup>*

dish
*parábola<sup>M</sup>*

feedhorn
*alimentador<sup>M</sup>*

pole
*mástil<sup>M</sup>*

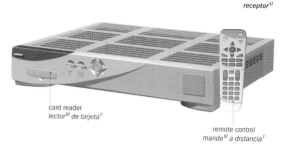

card reader
*lector<sup>M</sup> de tarjeta<sup>F</sup>*

remote control
*mando<sup>M</sup> a distancia<sup>F</sup>*

**home theater**
*home<sup>M</sup> theatre*

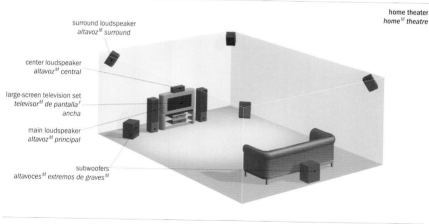

surround loudspeaker
*altavoz<sup>M</sup> surround*

center loudspeaker
*altavoz<sup>M</sup> central*

large-screen television set
*televisor<sup>M</sup> de pantalla<sup>F</sup> ancha*

main loudspeaker
*altavoz<sup>M</sup> principal*

subwoofers
*altavoces<sup>M</sup> extremos de graves<sup>M</sup>*

**videocassette recorder (VCR)**
*reproductor/grabador de video<sup>M</sup> VCR*

cassette compartment
*alojamiento<sup>M</sup> para la cinta<sup>F</sup>*

display
*indicador<sup>M</sup>*

power button
*interruptor<sup>M</sup>*

COMMUNICATIONS AND OFFICE AUTOMATION

# sound reproducing system
*equipo^M de alta fidelidad^F*

**ampli-tuner: front view**
*amplificador^M/sintonizador^M : vista^F frontal*

sound mode selector
*selector^M del modo^M audio*

sound mode lights
*indicadores^M del modo^M audio*

input lights
*indicadores^M de entrada^F*

tape recorder select button
*tecla^F de selección^F del grabador^M*

power button
*botón^M de encendido*

sound field control
*control^M del campo^M audio*

input select button
*tecla^F de selección^F de entrada^F*

loudspeaker system select buttons
*teclas^F de selección^F de los altavoces^M*

headphone jack
*toma^F para los auriculares^M*

tuning buttons
*teclas^F de selección^F de la sintonía^F*

display
*display^M*

volume control
*control^M del volumen^M*

preset tuning button
*tecla^F de selección^F sintonía^F*

memory button
*tecla^M memoria*

input selector
*selector^M de entrada^F*

balance control
*control^M de balance^M*

band select button
*tecla^F de selección^F de banda*

FM mode select button
*tecla^F de selección^F de modalidad^F FM*

bass tone control
*control^M de graves^M*

treble tone control
*control^M de agudos^M*

**ampli-tuner: back view**
*amplificador^M/sintonizador^M : vista^F posterior*

power cord
*cable^M de alimentación^F*

ground terminal
*conector^M de puesta^F de tierra^F*

cooling fan
*ventilador^M*

antenna terminals
*conectores^M de antenas^F*

input/output audio/video jacks
*tomas^F entrada^F/salida^F video^M*

loudspeaker terminals
*conector^M de altavoces^M*

switched outlet
*conmutador^M de corriente^F*

sound reproducing system

**cassette tape deck**
*pletina<sup>F</sup> de casete<sup>F</sup>*

counter reset button
*botón<sup>M</sup> de ajuste<sup>M</sup> a cero<sup>M</sup> del contador<sup>M</sup>*

play button
*botón<sup>M</sup> de reproducción<sup>F</sup>*

fast-forward button
*botón<sup>M</sup> de avance<sup>M</sup> rápido*

eject button
*botón<sup>M</sup> de expulsión<sup>F</sup>*

tape counter
*contador<sup>M</sup>*

tape selector
*selector<sup>M</sup> de tipo<sup>M</sup> de cinta<sup>F</sup>*

peak-level meter
*medidor<sup>M</sup> de altos niveles<sup>M</sup> de frecuencia<sup>F</sup>*

cassette holder
*alojamiento<sup>M</sup> de la casete<sup>F</sup>*

stop button
*botón<sup>M</sup> de stop<sup>M</sup>*

record muting button
*botón<sup>M</sup> de grabación<sup>F</sup> silenciosa*

rewind button
*botón<sup>M</sup> de rebobinado<sup>M</sup>*

record button
*botón<sup>M</sup> de inicio<sup>M</sup> de grabación<sup>F</sup>*

pause button
*botón<sup>M</sup> de pausa<sup>F</sup>*

recording level control
*botón<sup>M</sup> de nivel<sup>M</sup> de grabación<sup>F</sup>*

**compact disc player**
*lector<sup>M</sup> de disco<sup>M</sup> compacto*

power button
*interruptor<sup>M</sup>*

shuffle play
*lectura<sup>F</sup> aleatoria*

direct disc access buttons
*teclas<sup>F</sup> numéricas*

repeat button
*botón<sup>M</sup> de repetición<sup>F</sup>*

track search/fast operation buttons
*cambio<sup>M</sup> de pista<sup>F</sup>/lectura<sup>F</sup> rápida*

stop button
*parada<sup>F</sup>*

pause button
*pausa<sup>F</sup>*

play button
*lectura<sup>F</sup>*

disc skip
*cambio<sup>M</sup> de disco<sup>M</sup>*

headphone jack
*toma<sup>F</sup> para los auriculares<sup>M</sup>*

disc compartment
*alojamiento<sup>M</sup> para el disco<sup>M</sup>*

display
*indicador<sup>M</sup>*

disc compartment control
*botón<sup>M</sup> de control<sup>M</sup> del alojamiento<sup>M</sup> del disco<sup>M</sup>*

COMMUNICATIONS AND OFFICE AUTOMATION

**headphones**
*auriculares*<sup>M</sup>

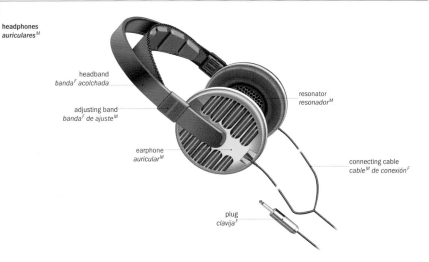

headband
*banda*<sup>F</sup> *acolchada*

resonator
*resonador*<sup>M</sup>

adjusting band
*banda*<sup>F</sup> *de ajuste*<sup>M</sup>

earphone
*auricular*<sup>M</sup>

connecting cable
*cable*<sup>M</sup> *de conexión*<sup>F</sup>

plug
*clavija*<sup>F</sup>

**loudspeakers**
*altavoz*<sup>M</sup>

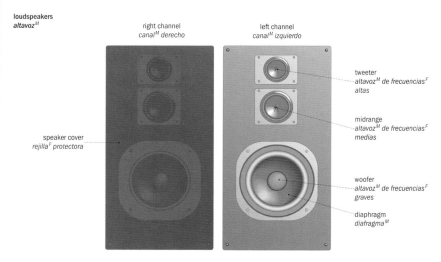

right channel
*canal*<sup>M</sup> *derecho*

left channel
*canal*<sup>M</sup> *izquierdo*

tweeter
*altavoz*<sup>M</sup> *de frecuencias*<sup>F</sup>
*altas*

midrange
*altavoz*<sup>M</sup> *de frecuencias*<sup>F</sup>
*medias*

speaker cover
*rejilla*<sup>F</sup> *protectora*

woofer
*altavoz*<sup>M</sup> *de frecuencias*<sup>F</sup>
*graves*

diaphragm
*diafragma*<sup>M</sup>

# mini stereo sound system
*mini-cadena<sup>F</sup> estéreo*

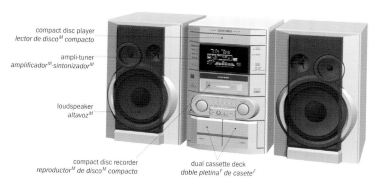

compact disc player
*lector de disco<sup>M</sup> compacto*

ampli-tuner
*amplificador<sup>M</sup>-sintonizador<sup>M</sup>*

loudspeaker
*altavoz<sup>M</sup>*

compact disc recorder
*reproductor<sup>M</sup> de disco<sup>M</sup> compacto*

dual cassette deck
*doble pletina<sup>F</sup> de casete<sup>F</sup>*

# portable sound systems
*sistemas<sup>M</sup> de sonido<sup>M</sup> portátiles*

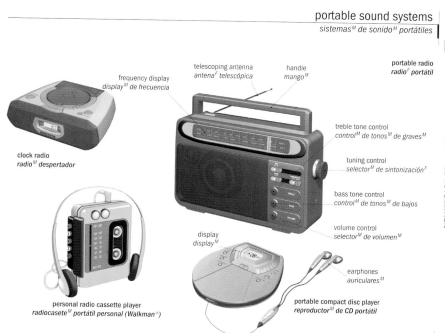

portable radio
*radio<sup>F</sup> portátil*

frequency display
*display<sup>M</sup> de frecuencia*

telescoping antenna
*antena<sup>F</sup> telescópica*

handle
*mango<sup>M</sup>*

treble tone control
*control<sup>M</sup> de tonos<sup>M</sup> de graves<sup>M</sup>*

tuning control
*selector<sup>M</sup> de sintonización<sup>F</sup>*

bass tone control
*control<sup>M</sup> de tonos<sup>M</sup> de bajos*

volume control
*selector<sup>M</sup> de volumen<sup>M</sup>*

clock radio
*radio<sup>M</sup> despertador*

display
*display<sup>M</sup>*

earphones
*auriculares<sup>M</sup>*

personal radio cassette player
*radiocasete<sup>M</sup> portátil personal (Walkman®)*

portable compact disc player
*reproductor<sup>M</sup> de CD portátil*

portable sound systems

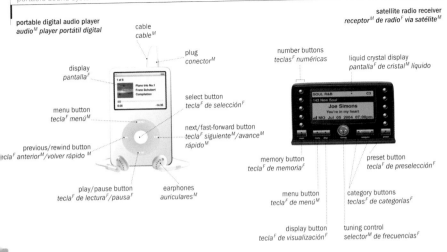

portable digital audio player
*audio^M player portátil digital*

cable
*cable^M*

plug
*conector^M*

display
*pantalla^F*

menu button
*tecla^F menú^M*

select button
*tecla^F de selección^F*

next/fast-forward button
*tecla^F siguiente^M/avance^M rápido^M*

previous/rewind button
*tecla^F anterior^M/volver rápido^M*

play/pause button
*tecla^F de lectura^F/pausa^F*

earphones
*auriculares^M*

satellite radio receiver
*receptor^M de radio^F vía satélite^M*

number buttons
*teclas^F numéricas*

liquid crystal display
*pantalla^F de cristal^M líquido*

memory button
*tecla^F de memoria^F*

preset button
*tecla^F de preselección^F*

menu button
*tecla^F de menú^M*

category buttons
*teclas^F de categorías^F*

display button
*tecla^F de visualización^F*

tuning control
*selector^M de frecuencias^F*

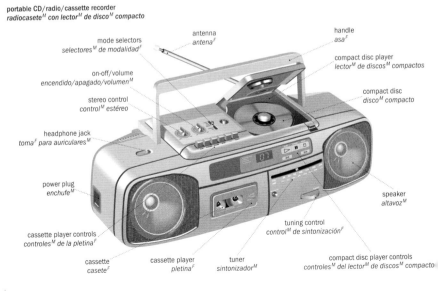

portable CD/radio/cassette recorder
*radiocasete^M con lector^M de disco^M compacto*

mode selectors
*selectores^M de modalidad^F*

antenna
*antena^F*

handle
*asa^F*

on-off/volume
*encendido/apagado/volumen^M*

compact disc player
*lector^M de discos^M compactos*

stereo control
*control^M estéreo*

compact disc
*disco^M compacto*

headphone jack
*toma^F para auriculares^M*

power plug
*enchufe^M*

speaker
*altavoz^M*

cassette player controls
*controles^M de la pletina^F*

cassette
*casete^F*

cassette player
*pletina^F*

tuner
*sintonizador^M*

tuning control
*control^M de sintonización^F*

compact disc player controls
*controles^M del lector^M de discos^M compacto*

COMMUNICATIONS AND OFFICE AUTOMATION

# communication by telephone
*comunicación$^F$ por teléfono$^M$*

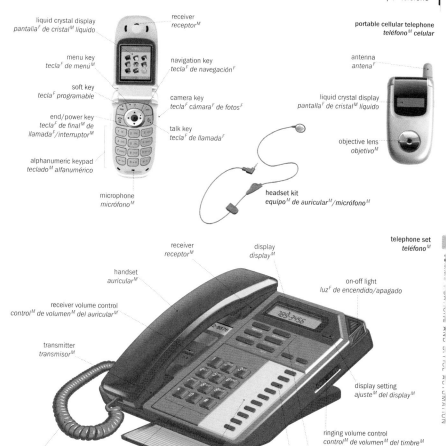

liquid crystal display
*pantalla$^F$ de cristal$^M$ líquido*

receiver
*receptor$^M$*

menu key
*tecla$^F$ de menú$^M$*

navigation key
*tecla$^F$ de navegación$^F$*

soft key
*tecla$^F$ programable*

camera key
*tecla$^F$ cámara$^F$ de fotos$^F$*

end/power key
*tecla$^F$ de final$^M$ de
llamada$^F$/interruptor$^M$*

talk key
*tecla$^F$ de llamada$^F$*

alphanumeric keypad
*teclado$^M$ alfanumérico*

microphone
*micrófono$^M$*

headset kit
*equipo$^M$ de auricular$^M$/micrófono$^M$*

portable cellular telephone
*teléfono$^M$ celular*

antenna
*antena$^F$*

liquid crystal display
*pantalla$^F$ de cristal$^M$ líquido*

objective lens
*objetivo$^M$*

telephone set
*teléfono$^M$*

receiver
*receptor$^M$*

display
*display$^M$*

on-off light
*luz$^F$ de encendido/apagado*

handset
*auricular$^M$*

receiver volume control
*control$^M$ de volumen$^M$ del auricular$^M$*

transmitter
*transmisor$^M$*

display setting
*ajuste$^M$ del display$^M$*

ringing volume control
*control$^M$ de volumen$^M$ del timbre$^M$*

function selectors
*selectores$^M$ de funciones$^F$*

handset cord
*cable$^M$ del auricular$^M$*

push buttons
*teclado$^M$*

telephone index
*agenda$^F$ telefónica*

memory button
*botón$^M$ de memoria$^F$*

automatic dialer index
*marcador$^M$ automático*

**digital answering machine**
*contestador^M numérico*

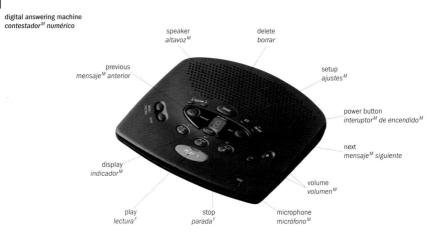

speaker
*altavoz^M*

delete
*borrar*

previous
*mensaje^M anterior*

setup
*ajustes^M*

power button
*interruptor^M de encendido^M*

next
*mensaje^M siguiente*

display
*indicador^M*

volume
*volumen^M*

play
*lectura^F*

stop
*parada^F*

microphone
*micrófono^M*

**facsimile (fax) machine**
*fax^M*

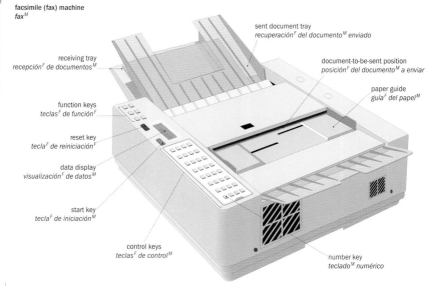

sent document tray
*recuperación^F del documento^M enviado*

receiving tray
*recepción^F de documentos^M*

document-to-be-sent position
*posición^F del documento^M a enviar*

paper guide
*guía^F del papel^M*

function keys
*teclas^F de función^F*

reset key
*tecla^F de reiniciación^F*

data display
*visualización^F de datos^M*

start key
*tecla^F de iniciación^M*

control keys
*teclas^F de control^M*

number key
*teclado^M numérico*

# personal computer
*ordenador^M personal*

video monitor
*monitor^M de vídeo^M*

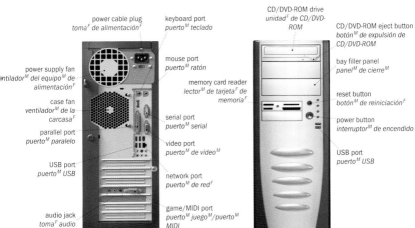

menu button
*botón^M de menú^M*

adjust buttons
*boutones^M de ajuste^M*

select button
*botón^M de selección^F*

power switch
*interruptor^M*

power indicator
*indicador^M de encendido*

tower case: back view
*ordenador^M : vista^F posterior*

tower case: front view
*ordenador^M : vista^F frontal*

power cable plug
*toma^F de alimentación^F*

keyboard port
*puerto^M teclado*

CD/DVD-ROM drive
*unidad^F de CD/DVD-ROM*

CD/DVD-ROM eject button
*botón^M de expulsión de CD/DVD-ROM*

mouse port
*puerto^M ratón*

power supply fan
*ntilador^M del equipo^M de alimentación^F*

bay filler panel
*panel^M de cierre^M*

memory card reader
*lector^M de tarjeta^F de memoria^F*

case fan
*ventilador^M de la carcasa^F*

reset button
*botón^M de reiniciación^F*

serial port
*puerto^M serial*

parallel port
*puerto^M paralelo*

power button
*interruptor^M de encendido*

video port
*puerto^M de vídeo^M*

USB port
*puerto^M USB*

network port
*puerto^M de red^F*

USB port
*puerto^M USB*

audio jack
*toma^F audio*

game/MIDI port
*puerto^M juego^M/puerto^M MIDI*

# input devices
*unidades[F] de entrada[F] de información[F]*

**keyboard and pictograms**
*teclado[M] y pictogramas[M]*

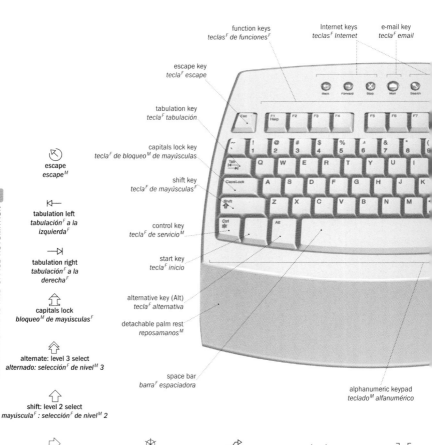

function keys
*teclas[F] de funciones[F]*

Internet keys
*teclas[F] Internet*

e-mail key
*tecla[F] email*

escape key
*tecla[F] escape*

tabulation key
*tecla[F] tabulación*

capitals lock key
*tecla[F] de bloqueo[M] de mayúsculas*

shift key
*tecla[F] de mayúsculas[F]*

control key
*tecla[F] de servicio[M]*

start key
*tecla[F] inicio*

alternative key (Alt)
*tecla[F] alternativa*

detachable palm rest
*reposamanos[M]*

space bar
*barra[F] espaciadora*

alphanumeric keypad
*teclado[M] alfanumérico*

escape
*escape[M]*

tabulation left
*tabulación[F] a la izquierda[F]*

tabulation right
*tabulación[F] a la derecha[F]*

capitals lock
*bloqueo[M] de mayúsculas[F]*

alternate: level 3 select
*alternado: selección[F] de nivel[M] 3*

shift: level 2 select
*mayúscula[F]: selección[F] de nivel[M] 2*

control: group select
*control[M]: selección[F] de grupo[M]*

control
*control[M]*

alternate
*alternativa[F]*

space
*espacio[M]*

nonbreaking space
*espacio[M] sin pausa*

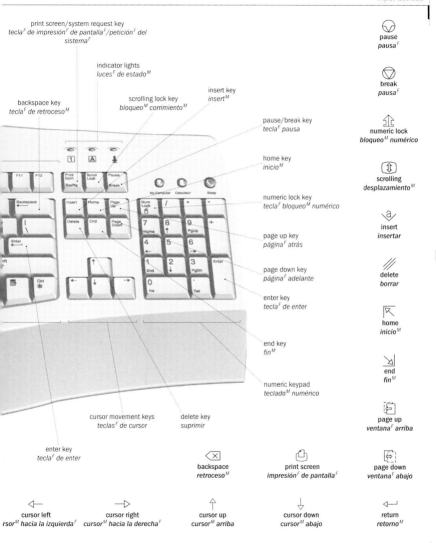

print screen/system request key
tecla$^F$ de impresión$^F$ de pantalla$^F$/petición$^F$ del sistema$^F$

indicator lights
luces$^F$ de estado$^M$

scrolling lock key
bloqueo$^M$ corrimiento$^M$

insert key
insert$^M$

backspace key
tecla$^F$ de retroceso$^M$

pause/break key
tecla$^F$ pausa

home key
inicio$^M$

numeric lock key
tecla$^F$ bloqueo$^M$ numérico

page up key
página$^F$ atrás

page down key
página$^F$ adelante

enter key
tecla$^F$ de enter

end key
fin$^M$

numeric keypad
teclado$^M$ numérico

cursor movement keys
teclas$^F$ de cursor

delete key
suprimir

enter key
tecla$^F$ de enter

pause
pausa$^F$

break
pausa$^F$

numeric lock
bloqueo$^M$ numérico

scrolling
desplazamiento$^M$

insert
insertar

delete
borrar

home
inicio$^M$

end
fin$^M$

page up
ventana$^F$ arriba

page down
ventana$^F$ abajo

backspace
retroceso$^M$

print screen
impresión$^F$ de pantalla$^F$

cursor left
rsor$^M$ hacia la izquierda$^F$

cursor right
cursor$^M$ hacia la derecha$^F$

cursor up
cursor$^M$ arriba

cursor down
cursor$^M$ abajo

return
retorno$^M$

COMMUNICATIONS AND OFFICE AUTOMATION

input devices

COMMUNICATIONS AND OFFICE AUTOMATION

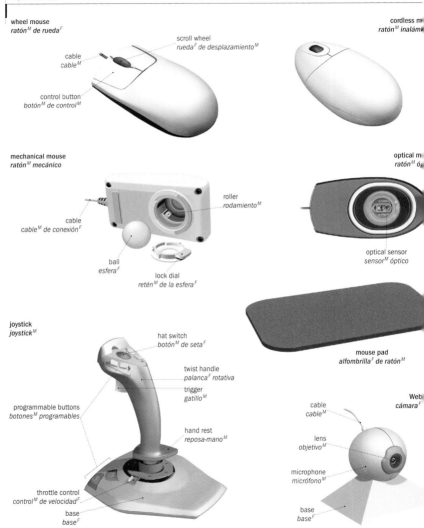

wheel mouse
*ratón$^M$ de rueda$^F$*

scroll wheel
*rueda$^F$ de desplazamiento$^M$*

cable
*cable$^M$*

control button
*botón$^M$ de control$^M$*

cordless m
*ratón$^M$ inalám*

mechanical mouse
*ratón$^M$ mecánico*

roller
*rodamiento$^M$*

cable
*cable$^M$ de conexión$^F$*

ball
*esfera$^F$*

lock dial
*retén$^M$ de la esfera$^F$*

optical m
*ratón$^M$ ó*

optical sensor
*sensor$^M$ óptico*

mouse pad
*alfombrilla$^F$ de ratón$^M$*

joystick
*joystick$^M$*

hat switch
*botón$^M$ de seta$^F$*

twist handle
*palanca$^F$ rotativa*

trigger
*gatillo$^M$*

programmable buttons
*botones$^M$ programables*

hand rest
*reposa-mano$^M$*

throttle control
*control$^M$ de velocidad$^F$*

base
*base$^F$*

Web
*cámara$^F$*

cable
*cable$^M$*

lens
*objetivo$^M$*

microphone
*micrófono$^M$*

base
*base$^F$*

## output devices
*unidades$^F$ de salida$^F$ de información$^F$*

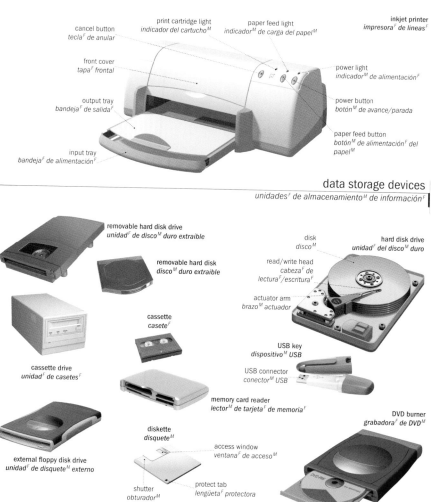

print cartridge light
*indicador del cartucho$^M$*

paper feed light
*indicador$^M$ de carga del papel$^M$*

inkjet printer
*impresora$^F$ de lineas$^F$*

cancel button
*tecla$^F$ de anular*

front cover
*tapa$^F$ frontal*

power light
*indicador$^M$ de alimentación$^F$*

output tray
*bandeja$^F$ de salida$^F$*

power button
*botón$^M$ de avance/parada*

input tray
*bandeja$^F$ de alimentación$^F$*

paper feed button
*botón$^M$ de alimentación$^F$ del papel$^M$*

## data storage devices
*unidades$^F$ de almacenamiento$^M$ de información$^F$*

removable hard disk drive
*unidad$^F$ de disco$^M$ duro extraible*

removable hard disk
*disco$^M$ duro extraible*

disk
*disco$^M$*

hard disk drive
*unidad$^F$ del disco$^M$ duro*

read/write head
*cabeza$^F$ de lectura$^F$/escritura$^F$*

actuator arm
*brazo$^M$ actuador*

cassette
*casete$^F$*

cassette drive
*unidad$^F$ de casetes$^F$*

USB key
*dispositivo$^M$ USB*

USB connector
*conector$^M$ USB*

memory card reader
*lector$^M$ de tarjeta$^F$ de memoria$^F$*

DVD burner
*grabadora$^F$ de DVD$^M$*

external floppy disk drive
*unidad$^F$ de disquete$^M$ externo*

diskette
*disquete$^M$*

access window
*ventana$^F$ de acceso$^M$*

shutter
*obturador$^M$*

protect tab
*lengüeta$^F$ protectora*

# Internet

*Internet*[M]

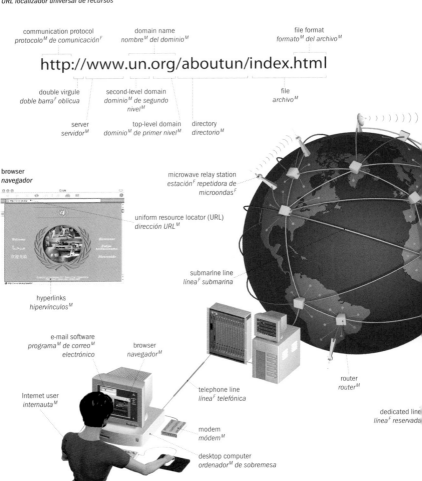

uniform resource locator (URL)
*URL localizador universal de recursos*

communication protocol
*protocolo*[M] *de comunicación*[F]

domain name
*nombre*[M] *del dominio*[M]

file format
*formato*[M] *del archivo*[M]

http://www.un.org/aboutun/index.html

double virgule
*doble barra*[F] *oblicua*

server
*servidor*[M]

second-level domain
*dominio*[M] *de segundo nivel*[M]

top-level domain
*dominio*[M] *de primer nivel*[M]

directory
*directorio*[M]

file
*archivo*[M]

browser
*navegador*

microwave relay station
*estación*[F] *repetidora de microondas*[F]

uniform resource locator (URL)
*dirección URL*[M]

hyperlinks
*hipervínculos*[M]

submarine line
*línea*[F] *submarina*

e-mail software
*programa*[M] *de correo*[M] *electrónico*

browser
*navegador*[M]

Internet user
*internauta*[M]

telephone line
*línea*[F] *telefónica*

modem
*módem*[M]

desktop computer
*ordenador*[M] *de sobremesa*

router
*router*[M]

dedicated line
*línea*[F] *reservada*

# Internet uses
*usos^M de Internet^M*

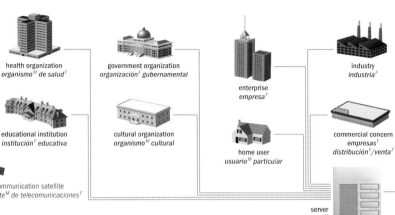

health organization
*organismo^M de salud^F*

government organization
*organización^F gubernamental*

enterprise
*empresa^F*

industry
*industria^F*

educational institution
*institución^F educativa*

cultural organization
*organismo^M cultural*

home user
*usuario^M particular*

commercial concern
*empresas^F*
*distribución^F/venta^F*

telecommunication satellite
*satélite^M de telecomunicaciones^F*

satellite earth station
*estación^F terrestre de telecomunicaciones^F*

server
*servidor^M*

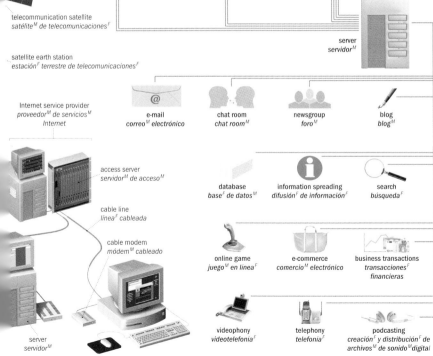

Internet service provider
*proveedor^M de servicios^M Internet*

access server
*servidor^M de acceso^M*

cable line
*línea^F cableada*

cable modem
*módem^M cableado*

e-mail
*correo^M electrónico*

chat room
*chat room^M*

newsgroup
*foro^M*

blog
*blog^M*

database
*base^F de datos^M*

information spreading
*difusión^F de información^F*

search
*búsqueda^F*

online game
*juego^M en línea^F*

e-commerce
*comercio^M electrónico*

business transactions
*transacciones^F financieras*

videophony
*videotelefonía^F*

telephony
*telefonía^F*

podcasting
*creación^F y distribución^F de archivos^M de sonido^M digital*

server
*servidor^M*

COMMUNICATIONS AND OFFICE AUTOMATION

335

# laptop computer
*ordenador^M portátil*

**laptop computer: front view**
*ordenador^M portátil: vista^F frontal*

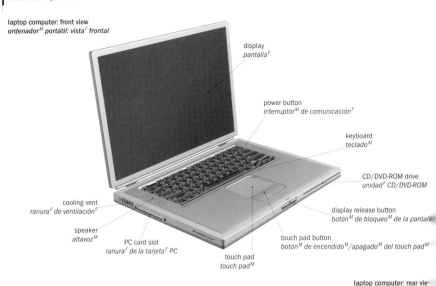

display
*pantalla^F*

power button
*interruptor^M de comunicación^F*

keyboard
*teclado^M*

CD/DVD-ROM drive
*unidad^F CD/DVD-ROM*

display release button
*botón^M de bloqueo^M de la pantalla*

touch pad button
*botón^M de encendido^M/apagado^M del touch pad^M*

touch pad
*touch pad^M*

cooling vent
*ranura^F de ventilación^F*

speaker
*altavoz^M*

PC card slot
*ranura^F de la tarjeta^F PC*

**laptop computer: rear view**
*ordenador^M portátil: vista^F posterior*

power adapter
*adaptador^M de corriente^F*

direct-current power cord
*cordón^M de alimentación^F de corriente^F continua*

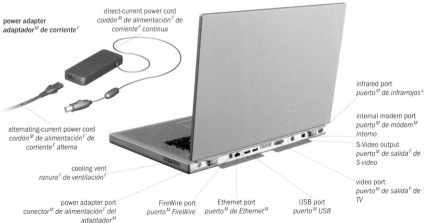

infrared port
*puerto^M de infrarrojos*

internal modem port
*puerto^M de módem^M interno*

S-Video output
*puerto^M de salida^F de S-video*

video port
*puerto^M de salida^F de TV*

alternating-current power cord
*cordón^M de alimentación^F de corriente^F alterna*

cooling vent
*ranura^F de ventilación^F*

power adapter port
*conector^M de alimentación^F del adaptador^M*

FireWire port
*puerto^M FireWire*

Ethernet port
*puerto^M de Ethernet^M*

USB port
*puerto^M USB*

# handheld computer/personal digital assistant (PDA)
*ordenador^M de bolsillo^M*

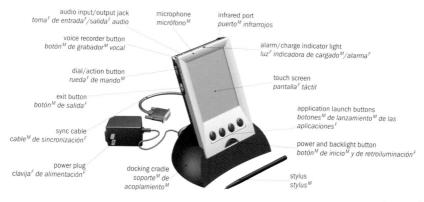

audio input/output jack
*toma^F de entrada^F/salida^F audio*

voice recorder button
*botón^M de grabador^M vocal*

dial/action button
*rueda^F de mando^M*

exit button
*botón^M de salida^F*

sync cable
*cable^M de sincronización^F*

power plug
*clavija^F de alimentación^F*

microphone
*micrófono^M*

infrared port
*puerto^M infrarrojos*

alarm/charge indicator light
*luz^F indicadora de cargado^M/alarma^F*

touch screen
*pantalla^F táctil*

application launch buttons
*botones^M de lanzamiento^M de las aplicaciones^F*

power and backlight button
*botón^M de inicio^M y de retroiluminación^F*

docking cradle
*soporte^M de acoplamiento^M*

stylus
*stylus^M*

## stationery
*artículos^M de escritorio^M*

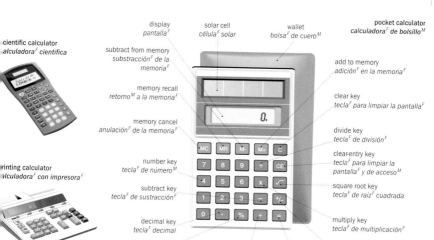

scientific calculator
*calculadora^F científica*

printing calculator
*calculadora^F con impresora^F*

display
*pantalla^F*

solar cell
*célula^F solar*

wallet
*bolsa^F de cuero^M*

pocket calculator
*calculadora^F de bolsillo^M*

subtract from memory
*substracción^F de la memoria^F*

memory recall
*retorno^M a la memoria^F*

memory cancel
*anulación^F de la memoria^F*

number key
*tecla^F de número^M*

subtract key
*tecla^F de sustracción^F*

decimal key
*tecla^F decimal*

percent key
*tecla^F de porcentaje^M*

add key
*tecla^F de adición^F*

equals key
*tecla^F de igualdad^F*

add to memory
*adición^F en la memoria^F*

clear key
*tecla^F para limpiar la pantalla^F*

divide key
*tecla^F de división^F*

clear-entry key
*tecla^F para limpiar la pantalla^F y de acceso^M*

square root key
*tecla^F de raíz^F cuadrada*

multiply key
*tecla^F de multiplicación^F*

change-sign key
*tecla^F de cambio^M de signo^M*

stationery

COMMUNICATIONS AND OFFICE AUTOMATION

**for time management**
*para el empleo<sup>M</sup> del tiempo<sup>M</sup>*

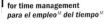

calendar pad
*calendario<sup>M</sup> de sobremesa*

electronic organizer
*agenda<sup>F</sup> electrónica*

tear-off calendar
*calendario<sup>M</sup> de sobremesa*

display
*pantalla<sup>F</sup>*

alphabetical keypad
*teclado<sup>M</sup> alfabético*

numeric keypad
*teclado<sup>M</sup> numérico*

appointment book
*agenda<sup>F</sup>*

self-stick note
*lámina<sup>F</sup> adhesiva*

memo pad
*libreta<sup>F</sup>*

**for correspondence**
*para la correspondencia<sup>F</sup>*

rubber stamp
*sello<sup>M</sup> de goma<sup>F</sup>*

numbering machine
*foliador<sup>M</sup>*

dater
*fechador<sup>M</sup>*

stamp pad
*cojín<sup>M</sup> para sellos<sup>M</sup>*

desk tray
*bandeja<sup>F</sup> de correspondencia<sup>F</sup>*

rotary file
*fichero<sup>M</sup> giratorio*

telephone index
*agenda<sup>F</sup> telefónica*

padded envelope
sobre<sup>M</sup> almohadillado

self-sealing flap
solapa<sup>F</sup> autoadhesiva

air bubbles
burbujas<sup>F</sup> de aire<sup>M</sup>

finger tip
dedil<sup>M</sup>

letter scale
balanza<sup>F</sup> para cartas<sup>F</sup>

moistener
rueda<sup>F</sup> humedecedora

letter opener
abrecartas<sup>M</sup>

**for filing**
*para archivar*

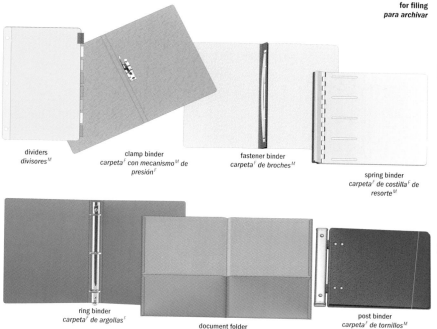

dividers
divisores<sup>M</sup>

clamp binder
carpeta<sup>F</sup> con mecanismo<sup>M</sup> de presión<sup>F</sup>

fastener binder
carpeta<sup>F</sup> de broches<sup>M</sup>

spring binder
carpeta<sup>F</sup> de costilla<sup>F</sup> de resorte<sup>M</sup>

ring binder
carpeta<sup>F</sup> de argollas<sup>F</sup>

document folder
carpeta<sup>F</sup> con guardas<sup>F</sup>

post binder
carpeta<sup>F</sup> de tornillos<sup>M</sup>

stationery

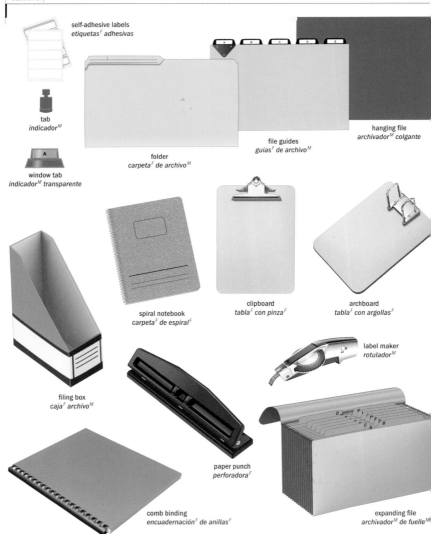

self-adhesive labels
*etiquetas*$^F$ *adhesivas*

tab
*indicador*$^M$

window tab
*indicador*$^M$ *transparente*

folder
*carpeta*$^F$ *de archivo*$^M$

file guides
*guías*$^F$ *de archivo*$^M$

hanging file
*archivador*$^M$ *colgante*

spiral notebook
*carpeta*$^F$ *de espiral*$^F$

clipboard
*tabla*$^F$ *con pinza*$^F$

archboard
*tabla*$^F$ *con argollas*$^F$

filing box
*caja*$^F$ *archivo*$^M$

label maker
*rotulador*$^M$

paper punch
*perforadora*$^F$

comb binding
*encuadernación*$^F$ *de anillas*$^F$

expanding file
*archivador*$^M$ *de fuelle*$^M$

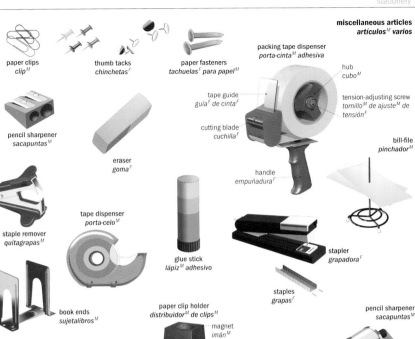

**miscellaneous articles**
*artículos* M *varios*

paper clips
*clip* M

thumb tacks
*chinchetas* F

paper fasteners
*tachuelas* F *para papel* M

packing tape dispenser
*porta-cinta* M *adhesiva*

hub
*cubo* M

tape guide
*guía* F *de cinta* F

tension-adjusting screw
*tornillo* M *de ajuste* M *de
tensión* F

pencil sharpener
*sacapuntas* M

cutting blade
*cuchilla* F

eraser
*goma* F

bill-file
*pinchador* M

handle
*empuñadura* F

staple remover
*quitagrapas* M

tape dispenser
*porta-celo* M

glue stick
*lápiz* M *adhesivo*

stapler
*grapadora* F

staples
*grapas* F

book ends
*sujetalibros* M

paper clip holder
*distribuidor* M *de clips* M

magnet
*imán* M

pencil sharpener
*sacapuntas* M

ulletin board
*blero* M *de anuncios* M

cutting head
*cabeza* F *cortadora*

waste basket
*papelera* F

waste basket
*papelera*

posting surface
*superficie* F *de fijación* F

paper shredder
*trituradora* F *de documentos* M

# road system
*sistema$^M$ de carreteras$^F$*

**cross section of a road**
*sección$^F$ transversal de una carretera$^F$*

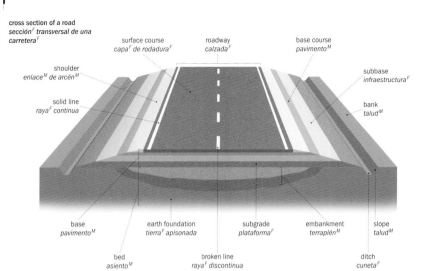

shoulder
*enlace$^M$ de arcén$^M$*

surface course
*capa$^F$ de rodadura$^F$*

roadway
*calzada$^F$*

base course
*pavimento$^M$*

subbase
*infraestructura$^F$*

solid line
*raya$^F$ continua*

bank
*talud$^M$*

base
*pavimento$^M$*

earth foundation
*tierra$^F$ apisonada*

subgrade
*plataforma$^F$*

embankment
*terraplén$^M$*

slope
*talud$^M$*

bed
*asiento$^M$*

broken line
*raya$^F$ discontinua*

ditch
*cuneta$^F$*

**examples of interchanges**
*ejemplos$^M$ de enlaces$^M$ de carreteras$^F$*

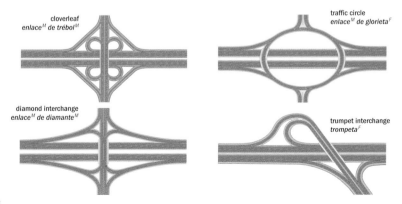

cloverleaf
*enlace$^M$ de trébol$^M$*

traffic circle
*enlace$^M$ de glorieta$^F$*

diamond interchange
*enlace$^M$ de diamante$^M$*

trumpet interchange
*trompeta$^F$*

TRANSPORT AND MACHINERY

**cloverleaf**
*enlace^M de trébol^M*

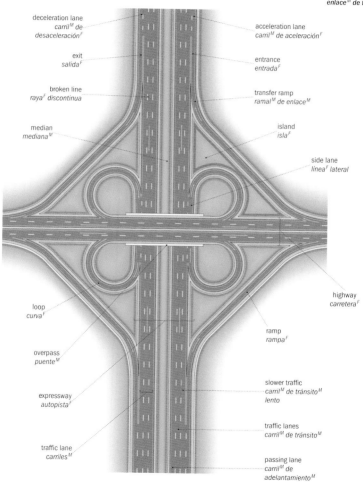

deceleration lane
*carril^M de
desaceleración^F*

exit
*salida^F*

broken line
*raya^F discontinua*

median
*mediana^M*

loop
*curva^F*

overpass
*puente^M*

expressway
*autopista^F*

traffic lane
*carriles^M*

acceleration lane
*carril^M de aceleración^F*

entrance
*entrada^F*

transfer ramp
*ramal^M de enlace^M*

island
*isla^F*

side lane
*línea^F lateral*

highway
*carretera^F*

ramp
*rampa^F*

slower traffic
*carril^M de tránsito^M
lento*

traffic lanes
*carril^M de tránsito^M*

passing lane
*carril^M de
adelantamiento^M*

TRANSPORT AND MACHINERY

# fixed bridges
*puentes<sup>M</sup> fijos*

**beam bridge**
*puente<sup>M</sup> de viga<sup>F</sup>*

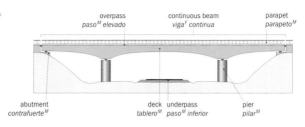

overpass
*paso<sup>M</sup> elevado*

continuous beam
*viga<sup>F</sup> continua*

parapet
*parapeto<sup>M</sup>*

abutment
*contrafuerte<sup>M</sup>*

deck
*tablero<sup>M</sup>*

underpass
*paso<sup>M</sup> inferior*

pier
*pilar<sup>M</sup>*

**suspension bridge**
*puente<sup>M</sup> colgante*

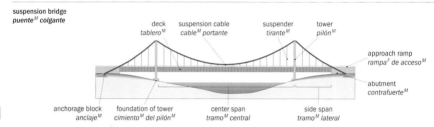

deck
*tablero<sup>M</sup>*

suspension cable
*cable<sup>M</sup> portante*

suspender
*tirante<sup>M</sup>*

tower
*pilón<sup>M</sup>*

approach ramp
*rampa<sup>F</sup> de acceso<sup>M</sup>*

abutment
*contrafuerte<sup>M</sup>*

anchorage block
*anclaje<sup>M</sup>*

foundation of tower
*cimiento<sup>M</sup> del pilón<sup>M</sup>*

center span
*tramo<sup>M</sup> central*

side span
*tramo<sup>M</sup> lateral*

**cantilever bridge**
*puente<sup>M</sup> cantilever*

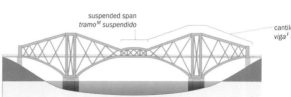

suspended span
*tramo<sup>M</sup> suspendido*

cantilever span
*viga<sup>F</sup> cantilever<sup>M</sup>*

# movable bridges
*puentes<sup>M</sup> móviles*

**swing bridge**
*puente<sup>M</sup> giratorio*

turntable
*tramo<sup>M</sup> giratorio*

TRANSPORT AND MACHINERY

movable bridges

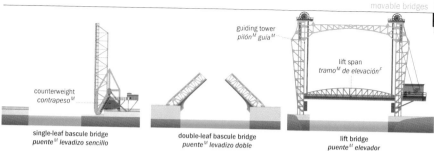

counterweight
contrapeso<sup>M</sup>

guiding tower
pilón<sup>M</sup> guía<sup>M</sup>

lift span
tramo<sup>M</sup> de elevación<sup>F</sup>

single-leaf bascule bridge
puente<sup>M</sup> levadizo sencillo

double-leaf bascule bridge
puente<sup>M</sup> levadizo doble

lift bridge
puente<sup>M</sup> elevador

## road tunnel
*túnel<sup>M</sup> de carretera<sup>F</sup>*

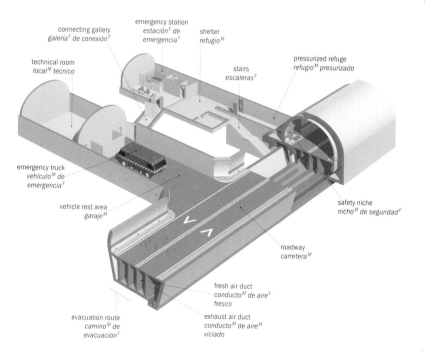

connecting gallery
galería<sup>F</sup> de conexión<sup>F</sup>

emergency station
estación<sup>F</sup> de
emergencia<sup>F</sup>

shelter
refugio<sup>M</sup>

technical room
local<sup>M</sup> técnico

stairs
escaleras<sup>F</sup>

pressurized refuge
refugio<sup>M</sup> presurizado

emergency truck
vehículo<sup>M</sup> de
emergencia<sup>F</sup>

vehicle rest area
garaje<sup>M</sup>

safety niche
nicho<sup>M</sup> de seguridad<sup>F</sup>

roadway
carretera<sup>M</sup>

evacuation route
camino<sup>M</sup> de
evacuación<sup>F</sup>

fresh air duct
conducto<sup>M</sup> de aire<sup>F</sup>
fresco

exhaust air duct
conducto<sup>M</sup> de aire<sup>M</sup>
viciado

TRANSPORT AND MACHINERY

# service station
*estación<sup>F</sup> de servicio<sup>M</sup>*

**gasoline pump**
*surtidor<sup>M</sup> de gasolina<sup>F</sup>*

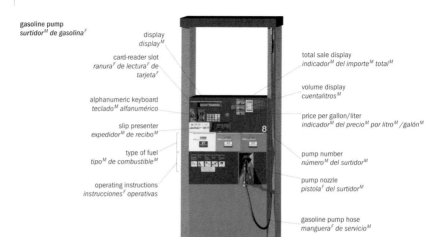

display
*display<sup>M</sup>*

card-reader slot
*ranura<sup>F</sup> de lectura<sup>F</sup> de tarjeta<sup>F</sup>*

alphanumeric keyboard
*teclado<sup>M</sup> alfanumérico*

slip presenter
*expedidor<sup>M</sup> de recibo<sup>M</sup>*

type of fuel
*tipo<sup>M</sup> de combustible<sup>M</sup>*

operating instructions
*instrucciones<sup>F</sup> operativas*

total sale display
*indicador<sup>M</sup> del importe<sup>M</sup> total<sup>M</sup>*

volume display
*cuentalitros<sup>M</sup>*

price per gallon/liter
*indicador<sup>M</sup> del precio<sup>M</sup> por litro<sup>M</sup> /galón<sup>M</sup>*

pump number
*número<sup>M</sup> del surtidor<sup>M</sup>*

pump nozzle
*pistola<sup>F</sup> del surtidor<sup>M</sup>*

gasoline pump hose
*manguera<sup>F</sup> de servicio<sup>M</sup>*

**service station**
*estación<sup>F</sup> de servicio<sup>M</sup>*

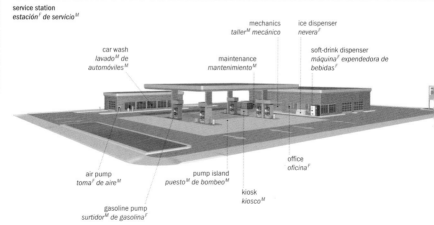

mechanics
*taller<sup>M</sup> mecánico*

ice dispenser
*nevera<sup>F</sup>*

car wash
*lavado<sup>M</sup> de automóviles<sup>M</sup>*

maintenance
*mantenimiento<sup>M</sup>*

soft-drink dispenser
*máquina<sup>F</sup> expendedora de bebidas<sup>F</sup>*

air pump
*toma<sup>F</sup> de aire<sup>M</sup>*

pump island
*puesto<sup>M</sup> de bombeo<sup>M</sup>*

office
*oficina<sup>F</sup>*

kiosk
*kiosco<sup>M</sup>*

gasoline pump
*surtidor<sup>M</sup> de gasolina<sup>F</sup>*

# automobile
*automóvil*[M]

sports car
*deportivo*[M]

**examples of bodies**
*ejemplos*[M] *de carrocerías*[F]

micro compact car
*automóvil*[M] *urbanita*

hatchback
*turismo*[M] *de tres*
*puertas*[F]

two-door sedan
*cupé*[M]

convertible
*descapotable*[M]

four-door sedan
*berlina*[F]

station wagon
*coche*[M] *familiar*

minivan
*monovolumen*[M]

sport-utility vehicle
*vehículo*[M] *todo terreno*[M]

pickup truck
*camioneta*[F]

limousine
*limusina*[F]

TRANSPORT AND MACHINERY

body
*carroceria*<sup>F</sup>

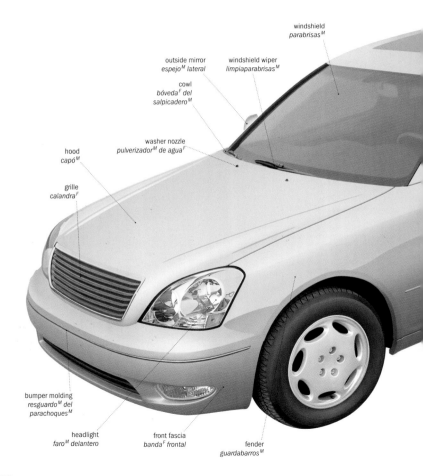

windshield
*parabrisas*<sup>M</sup>

outside mirror
*espejo*<sup>M</sup> *lateral*

windshield wiper
*limpiaparabrisas*<sup>M</sup>

cowl
*bóveda*<sup>F</sup> *del*
*salpicadero*<sup>M</sup>

washer nozzle
*pulverizador*<sup>M</sup> *de agua*<sup>F</sup>

hood
*capó*<sup>M</sup>

grille
*calandra*<sup>F</sup>

bumper molding
*resguardo*<sup>M</sup> *del*
*parachoques*<sup>M</sup>

headlight
*faro*<sup>M</sup> *delantero*

front fascia
*banda*<sup>F</sup> *frontal*

fender
*guardabarros*<sup>M</sup>

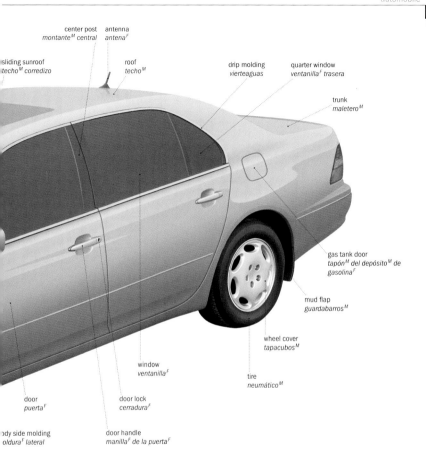

center post
*montante^M central*

antenna
*antena^F*

sliding sunroof
*techo^M corredizo*

roof
*techo^M*

drip molding
*vierteaguas*

quarter window
*ventanilla^F trasera*

trunk
*maletero^M*

gas tank door
*tapón^M del depósito^M de
gasolina^F*

mud flap
*guardabarros^M*

wheel cover
*tapacubos^M*

window
*ventanilla^F*

tire
*neumático^M*

door
*puerta^F*

door lock
*cerradura^F*

body side molding
*moldura^F lateral*

door handle
*manilla^F de la puerta^F*

**automobile systems: main parts**
*automóviles$^M$ : componentes$^M$ principales*

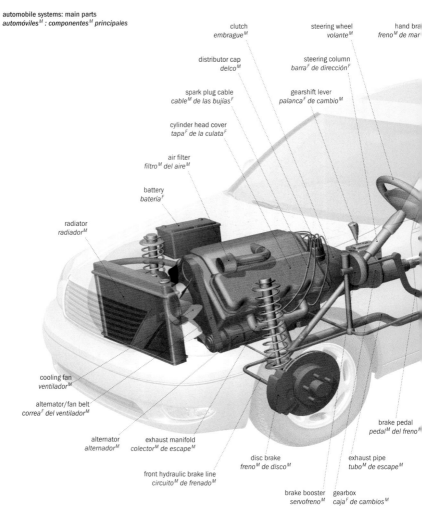

clutch
*embrague$^M$*

steering wheel
*volante$^M$*

hand bra
*freno$^M$ de mar*

distributor cap
*delco$^M$*

steering column
*barra$^F$ de dirección$^F$*

spark plug cable
*cable$^M$ de las bujías$^F$*

gearshift lever
*palanca$^F$ de cambio$^M$*

cylinder head cover
*tapa$^F$ de la culata$^F$*

air filter
*filtro$^M$ del aire$^M$*

battery
*batería$^F$*

radiator
*radiador$^M$*

cooling fan
*ventilador$^M$*

alternator/fan belt
*correa$^F$ del ventilador$^M$*

alternator
*alternador$^M$*

exhaust manifold
*colector$^M$ de escape$^M$*

disc brake
*freno$^M$ de disco$^M$*

front hydraulic brake line
*circuito$^M$ de frenado$^M$*

brake booster
*servofreno$^M$*

gearbox
*caja$^F$ de cambios$^M$*

exhaust pipe
*tubo$^M$ de escape$^M$*

brake pedal
*pedal$^M$ del freno$^M$*

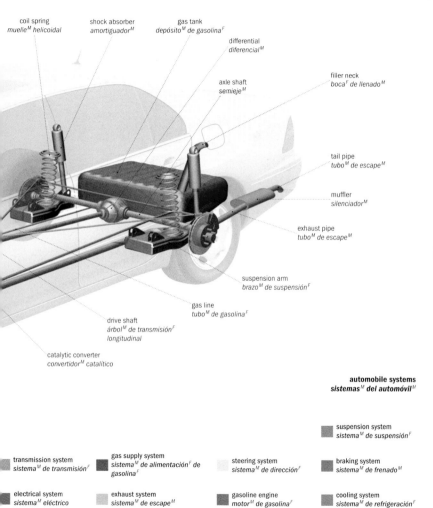

coil spring
*muelle^M helicoidal*

shock absorber
*amortiguador^M*

gas tank
*depósito^M de gasolina^F*

differential
*diferencial^M*

axle shaft
*semieje^M*

filler neck
*boca^F de llenado^M*

tail pipe
*tubo^M de escape^M*

muffler
*silenciador^M*

exhaust pipe
*tubo^M de escape^M*

suspension arm
*brazo^M de suspensión^F*

gas line
*tubo^M de gasolina^F*

drive shaft
*árbol^M de transmisión^F
longitudinal*

catalytic converter
*convertidor^M catalítico*

**automobile systems**
*sistemas^M del automóvil^M*

suspension system
*sistema^M de suspensión^F*

transmission system
*sistema^M de transmisión^F*

gas supply system
*sistema^M de alimentación^F de
gasolina^F*

steering system
*sistema^M de dirección^F*

braking system
*sistema^M de frenado^M*

electrical system
*sistema^M eléctrico*

exhaust system
*sistema^M de escape^M*

gasoline engine
*motor^M de gasolina^F*

cooling system
*sistema^M de refrigeración^F*

automobile

**headlights**
*faros*<sup>M</sup> *delanteros*

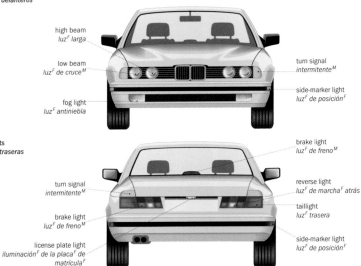

high beam
*luz*<sup>F</sup> *larga*

low beam
*luz*<sup>F</sup> *de cruce*<sup>M</sup>

fog light
*luz*<sup>F</sup> *antiniebla*

turn signal
*intermitente*<sup>M</sup>

side-marker light
*luz*<sup>F</sup> *de posición*<sup>F</sup>

**taillights**
*luces*<sup>F</sup> *traseras*

brake light
*luz*<sup>F</sup> *de freno*<sup>M</sup>

reverse light
*luz*<sup>F</sup> *de marcha*<sup>F</sup> *atrás*

taillight
*luz*<sup>F</sup> *trasera*

side-marker light
*luz*<sup>F</sup> *de posición*<sup>F</sup>

turn signal
*intermitente*<sup>M</sup>

brake light
*luz*<sup>F</sup> *de freno*<sup>M</sup>

license plate light
*iluminación*<sup>F</sup> *de la placa*<sup>F</sup> *de matrícula*<sup>F</sup>

**door**
*puerta*<sup>F</sup>

interior door handle
*tirador*<sup>M</sup> *de la puerta*<sup>F</sup>

assist grip
*asidero*<sup>M</sup>

outside mirror control
*control*<sup>M</sup> *del espejo*<sup>M</sup> *retrovisor exterior*

window regulator handle
*manivela*<sup>F</sup> *de la ventanilla*<sup>F</sup>

hinge
*bisagra*<sup>F</sup>

accessory pocket
*bolsillo*<sup>M</sup> *lateral*

window
*ventanilla*<sup>F</sup>

interior door lock button
*botón*<sup>M</sup> *del seguro*<sup>M</sup>

armrest
*soporte*<sup>M</sup> *para el brazo*<sup>M</sup>

lock
*cerradura*<sup>F</sup>

trim panel
*panel*<sup>M</sup> *de la puerta*<sup>F</sup>

inner door shell
*revestimiento*<sup>M</sup> *interior*

TRANSPORT AND MACHINERY

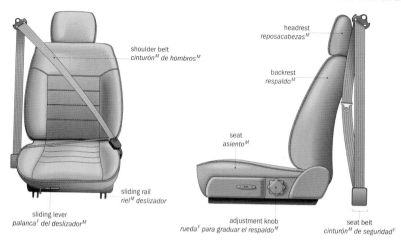

bucket seat: front view
*asiento*<sup>M</sup> : *vista*<sup>F</sup> *frontal*

bucket seat: side view
*asiento*<sup>M</sup> : *vista*<sup>F</sup> *lateral*

shoulder belt
*cinturón*<sup>M</sup> *de hombros*<sup>M</sup>

headrest
*reposacabezas*<sup>M</sup>

backrest
*respaldo*<sup>M</sup>

seat
*asiento*<sup>M</sup>

sliding rail
*riel*<sup>M</sup> *deslizador*

sliding lever
*palanca*<sup>F</sup> *del deslizador*<sup>M</sup>

adjustment knob
*rueda*<sup>F</sup> *para graduar el respaldo*<sup>M</sup>

seat belt
*cinturón*<sup>M</sup> *de seguridad*<sup>F</sup>

rear seat
*asiento*<sup>M</sup> *trasero*

armrest
*reposabrazo*<sup>M</sup>

webbing
*cinturón*<sup>M</sup> *subabdominal*

buckle
*enganche*<sup>M</sup>

bench seat
*asiento*<sup>M</sup>

TRANSPORT AND MACHINERY

automobile

## dashboard
*salpicadero*$^M$

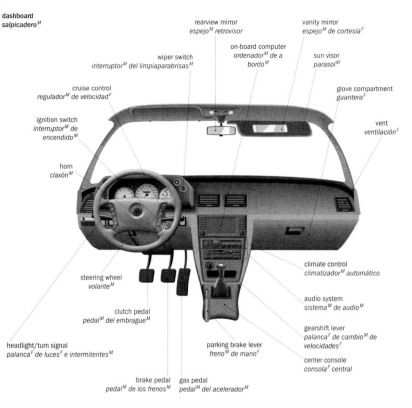

rearview mirror
*espejo*$^M$ *retrovisor*

vanity mirror
*espejo*$^M$ *de cortesía*$^F$

wiper switch
*interruptor*$^M$ *del limpiaparabrisas*$^M$

on-board computer
*ordenador*$^M$ *de a bordo*$^M$

sun visor
*parasol*$^M$

cruise control
*regulador*$^M$ *de velocidad*$^F$

glove compartment
*guantera*$^F$

ignition switch
*interruptor*$^M$ *de encendido*$^M$

vent
*ventilación*$^F$

horn
*claxón*$^M$

steering wheel
*volante*$^M$

climate control
*climatizador*$^M$ *automático*

clutch pedal
*pedal*$^M$ *del embrague*$^M$

audio system
*sistema*$^M$ *de audio*$^M$

gearshift lever
*palanca*$^F$ *de cambio*$^M$ *de velocidades*$^F$

headlight/turn signal
*palanca*$^F$ *de luces*$^F$ *e intermitentes*$^M$

parking brake lever
*freno*$^M$ *de mano*$^F$

center console
*consola*$^F$ *central*

brake pedal
*pedal*$^M$ *de los frenos*$^M$

gas pedal
*pedal*$^M$ *del acelerador*$^M$

## air bag restraint system
*sistema*$^M$ *de restricción*$^F$ *del airbag*$^M$

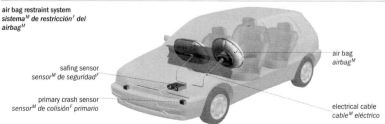

safing sensor
*sensor*$^M$ *de seguridad*$^F$

air bag
*airbag*$^M$

primary crash sensor
*sensor*$^M$ *de colisión*$^F$ *primario*

electrical cable
*cable*$^M$ *eléctrico*

TRANSPORT AND MACHINERY

**instrument panel**
*instrumentos$^M$ del salpicadero$^M$*

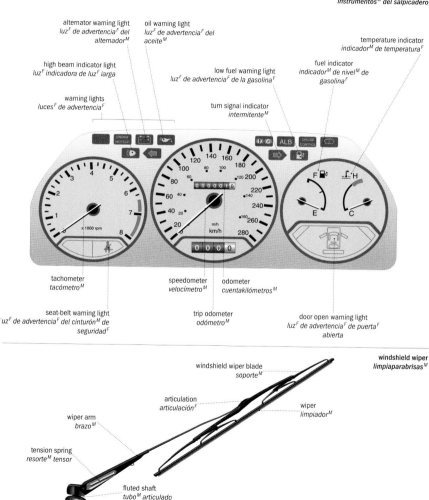

alternator warning light
*luz$^F$ de advertencia$^F$ del alternador$^M$*

oil warning light
*luz$^F$ de advertencia$^F$ del aceite$^M$*

temperature indicator
*indicador$^M$ de temperatura$^F$*

high beam indicator light
*luz$^F$ indicadora de luz$^F$ larga*

low fuel warning light
*luz$^F$ de advertencia$^F$ de la gasolina$^F$*

fuel indicator
*indicador$^M$ de nivel$^M$ de gasolina$^F$*

warning lights
*luces$^F$ de advertencia$^F$*

turn signal indicator
*intermitente$^M$*

tachometer
*tacómetro$^M$*

speedometer
*velocímetro$^M$*

odometer
*cuentakilómetros$^M$*

seat-belt warning light
*luz$^F$ de advertencia$^F$ del cinturón$^M$ de seguridad$^F$*

trip odometer
*odómetro$^M$*

door open warning light
*luz$^F$ de advertencia$^F$ de puerta$^F$ abierta*

**windshield wiper**
*limpiaparabrisas$^M$*

windshield wiper blade
*soporte$^M$*

articulation
*articulación$^F$*

wiper
*limpiador$^M$*

wiper arm
*brazo$^M$*

tension spring
*resorte$^M$ tensor*

fluted shaft
*tubo$^M$ articulado*

TRANSPORT AND MACHINERY

automobile

**accessories**
*accesorios*<sup>M</sup>

jumper cables
*cables*<sup>M</sup> *de*
*emergencia*<sup>F</sup>

black clamp
*pinza*<sup>F</sup> *negra*

floor mat
*alfombrilla*<sup>F</sup>

roller shade
*cortina*<sup>F</sup> *de enrollamiento*
*automático*

red clamp
*pinza*<sup>F</sup> *roja*

cable
*cable*<sup>M</sup>

ball mount
*enganche*<sup>M</sup> *de bola*<sup>F</sup>

hitch ball
*gancho*<sup>M</sup> *de arrastre*<sup>M</sup>

four-way lug wrench
*llave*<sup>F</sup> *en cruz*<sup>M</sup>

snow brush with scraper
*escoba*<sup>F</sup> *de nieve*<sup>F</sup> *con*
*rascador*<sup>M</sup>

ski rack
*porta-esqui*<sup>M</sup>

bike carrier
*portabicicletas*<sup>M</sup>

vehicle jack
*gato*<sup>M</sup>

sun visor
*parasol*<sup>M</sup>

handle
*manivela*<sup>F</sup>

car cover
*funda*<sup>F</sup> *de automóvil*<sup>M</sup>

child safety seat
*silla*<sup>F</sup> *de seguridad*<sup>F</sup> *para*
*niños*<sup>M</sup>

TRANSPORT AND MACHINERY

# brakes
*frenos*[M]

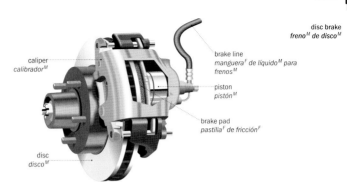

**disc brake**
*freno*[M] *de disco*[M]

caliper
*calibrador*[M]

brake line
*manguera*[F] *de líquido*[M] *para
frenos*[M]

piston
*pistón*[M]

brake pad
*pastilla*[F] *de fricción*[F]

disc
*disco*[M]

**drum brake**
*freno*[M] *de tambor*[M]

brake shoe
*zapata*[F]

anchor pin
*perno*[M] *de fijación*[F]

return spring
*resorte*[M] *de retorno*[M]

strut
*pistón*[M]

wheel stud
*espiga*[F]

wheel cylinder
*cilindro*[M] *de freno*[M]

backing plate
*plato*[M] *de retroceso*[M]

brake lining
*revestimiento*[M]

drum
*tambor*[M]

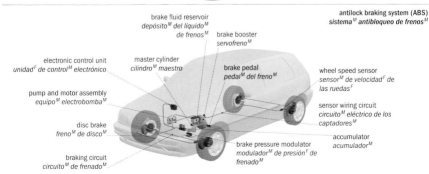

**antilock braking system (ABS)**
*sistema*[M] *antibloqueo de frenos*[M]

brake fluid reservoir
*depósito*[M] *del líquido*[M]
*de frenos*[M]

brake booster
*servofreno*[M]

electronic control unit
*unidad*[F] *de control*[M] *electrónico*

master cylinder
*cilindro*[M] *maestro*

brake pedal
*pedal*[M] *del freno*[M]

pump and motor assembly
*equipo*[M] *electrobomba*[M]

disc brake
*freno*[M] *de disco*[M]

braking circuit
*circuito*[M] *de frenado*[M]

brake pressure modulator
*modulador*[M] *de presión*[F] *de
frenado*[M]

wheel speed sensor
*sensor*[M] *de velocidad*[F] *de
las ruedas*[F]

sensor wiring circuit
*circuito*[M] *eléctrico de los
captadores*[M]

accumulator
*acumulador*[M]

# tire
*neumático*<sup>M</sup>

technical specifications
*especificaciones*<sup>F</sup> *técnicas*<sup>F</sup>

tread design
*dibujo*<sup>M</sup> *de la superficie*<sup>F</sup> *de*
*rodadura*<sup>F</sup>

rubbing strip
*banda*<sup>F</sup> *protectora*

rubber wall
*costado*<sup>M</sup>

bead
*moldura*<sup>F</sup>

**examples of tires**
*ejemplos*<sup>M</sup> *de neumáticos*<sup>M</sup>

performance tire
*neumático*<sup>M</sup> *de*
*rendimiento*<sup>M</sup>

all-season tire
*neumático*<sup>M</sup> *de todas las*
*estaciones*<sup>F</sup>

studded tire
*neumático*<sup>M</sup> *de tacos*<sup>M</sup>

winter tire
*neumático*<sup>M</sup> *de*
*invierno*<sup>M</sup>

touring tire
*neumático*<sup>M</sup> *de*
*turismo*<sup>M</sup>

# radiator
*radiador*<sup>M</sup>

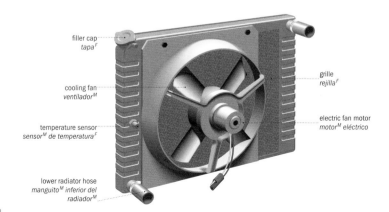

filler cap
*tapa*<sup>F</sup>

cooling fan
*ventilador*<sup>M</sup>

temperature sensor
*sensor*<sup>M</sup> *de temperatura*<sup>F</sup>

lower radiator hose
*manguito*<sup>M</sup> *inferior del*
*radiador*<sup>M</sup>

grille
*rejilla*<sup>F</sup>

electric fan motor
*motor*<sup>M</sup> *eléctrico*

TRANSPORT AND MACHINERY

## spark plug
*bujía*[F]

spline
*ranura*[F]

hex nut
*hexagonal*

spark plug body
*cuerpo*[M] *metálico de la bujía*[F]

spark plug terminal
*borne*[M]

center electrode
*electrodo*[M] *central*

insulator
*aislador*[M]

spark plug seat
*junta*[F]

ground electrode
*electrodo*[M] *de masa*[F]

spark plug gap
*espacio*[M] *para la chispa*[F]

## battery
*batería*[F]

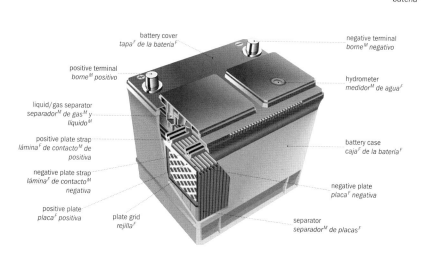

battery cover
*tapa*[F] *de la batería*[F]

positive terminal
*borne*[M] *positivo*

liquid/gas separator
*separador*[M] *de gas*[M] *y líquido*[M]

positive plate strap
*lámina*[F] *de contacto*[M] *de positiva*

negative plate strap
*lámina*[F] *de contacto*[M] *negativa*

positive plate
*placa*[F] *positiva*

plate grid
*rejilla*[F]

negative terminal
*borne*[M] *negativo*

hydrometer
*medidor*[M] *de agua*[F]

battery case
*caja*[F] *de la batería*[F]

negative plate
*placa*[F] *negativa*

separator
*separador*[M] *de placas*[F]

TRANSPORT AND MACHINERY

# gasoline engine
*motor^M de gasolina^F*

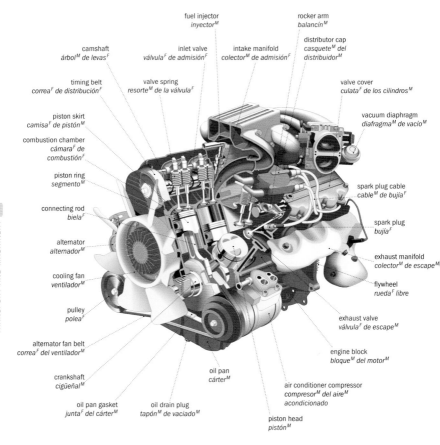

fuel injector
*inyector^M*

rocker arm
*balancín^M*

camshaft
*árbol^M de levas^F*

inlet valve
*válvula^F de admisión^F*

intake manifold
*colector^M de admisión^F*

distributor cap
*casquete^M del distribuidor^M*

timing belt
*correa^F de distribución^F*

valve spring
*resorte^M de la válvula^F*

valve cover
*culata^F de los cilindros^M*

piston skirt
*camisa^F de pistón^M*

vacuum diaphragm
*diafragma^M de vacío^M*

combustion chamber
*cámara^F de combustión^F*

piston ring
*segmento^M*

spark plug cable
*cable^M de bujía^F*

connecting rod
*biela^F*

spark plug
*bujía^F*

alternator
*alternador^M*

exhaust manifold
*colector^M de escape^M*

cooling fan
*ventilador^M*

flywheel
*rueda^F libre*

pulley
*polea^F*

exhaust valve
*válvula^F de escape^M*

alternator fan belt
*correa^F del ventilador^M*

engine block
*bloque^M del motor^M*

crankshaft
*cigüeñal^M*

oil pan
*cárter^M*

air conditioner compressor
*compresor^M del aire^M acondicionado*

oil pan gasket
*junta^F del cárter^M*

oil drain plug
*tapón^M de vaciado^M*

piston head
*pistón^M*

# camping trailers
*caravana^F*

**trailer**
*remolque^M*

roof vent
*ventanilla^F de ventilación^F del techo^M*

side vent
*respiradero^M lateral*

body
*carrocería^F*

sun visor
*parasol^M*

awning channel
*ranura^F para toldo^M*

propane gas cylinder
*tanque^M de gas^M propano^M*

grab handle
*asidero^M*

manual jack
*gato^M hidráulico*

outlet
*toma^F de corriente^M*

towing hitch
*enganche^M del remolque^M*

storage compartment
*compartimento^M para almacenamiento^M*

door
*puerta^F*

tow bar frame
*barra^F de remolque^M*

retractable step
*escalón^M retráctil*

tow safety chain
*cadena^F de seguridad^F*

landing gear
*amarre^M anterior retráctil*

lighting cable
*cable^M de alumbrado^M*

**tent trailer**
*caravana^F plegable*

roof
*techo^M*

canopy
*toldo^M*

bunk
*litera^F*

window
*ventana^F*

spare tire
*rueda^F de repuesto^M*

body
*carrocería^F*

stabilizer jack
*gato^M estabilizador*

screen door
*puerta^F mosquitera*

**motor home**
*autocaravana^M*

air conditioner
*aire^M acondicionado*

luggage rack
*portaequipajes^M*

ladder
*escalerilla^F*

# buses
*autobúses*<sup>M</sup>

school bus
*autobús*<sup>M</sup> *escolar*

outside mirror
*espejo*<sup>M</sup> *retrovisor exterior*

blind spot mirror
*retrovisor*<sup>M</sup> *de gran angular*<sup>M</sup>

blinking lights
*faros*<sup>M</sup> *intermitentes*

crossover mirror
*espejo*<sup>M</sup> *de cercanías*<sup>F</sup>

crossing arm
*barra*<sup>F</sup> *distanciadora*

city bus
*autobús*<sup>M</sup> *urbano*

air intake
*toma*<sup>F</sup> *de aire*<sup>M</sup>

two-leaf door
*puerta*<sup>F</sup> *de dos hojas*<sup>F</sup>

route sign
*indicador*<sup>M</sup> *de línea*<sup>F</sup>

coach
*autocar*<sup>M</sup>

engine air intake
*toma*<sup>F</sup> *de aire*<sup>M</sup> *del motor*<sup>M</sup>

entrance door
*puerta*<sup>F</sup> *de entrada*<sup>F</sup>

engine compartment
*compartimiento*<sup>M</sup> *motor*

baggage compartment
*maletero*<sup>M</sup>

TRANSPORT AND MACHINERY

double-decker bus
*autocar^M de dos
pisos^M*

upper deck
*piso^M superior*

route sign
*indicador^M de línea^F*

minibus
*minibús^M*

lift door
*puerta^F de la plataforma^F
elevadora*

blind spot mirror
*retrovisor^M gran
angular*

West Coast mirror
*espejo^M retrovisor*

handrail
*pasamano^M*

wheelchair lift
*-ataforma^F elevadora para
silla^F de ruedas^F*

platform
*plataforma^F*

entrance door
*puerta^F de entrada^F*

articulated bus
*autobús^M articulado*

articulated joint
*sección^F articulada*

rear rigid section
*remolque^M rígido
trasero*

front rigid section
*sección^F rígida de
tracción^F delantera*

# trucking
*camiones*<sup>M</sup>

**truck tractor**
*camión*<sup>M</sup> *tractor*<sup>M</sup>

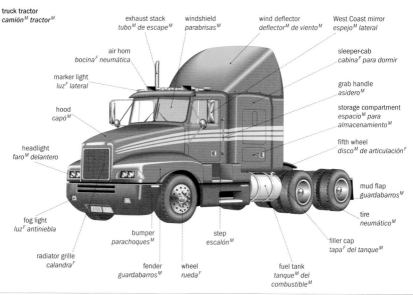

exhaust stack
*tubo*<sup>M</sup> *de escape*<sup>M</sup>

windshield
*parabrisas*<sup>M</sup>

wind deflector
*deflector*<sup>M</sup> *de viento*<sup>M</sup>

West Coast mirror
*espejo*<sup>M</sup> *lateral*

air horn
*bocina*<sup>F</sup> *neumática*

sleeper-cab
*cabina*<sup>F</sup> *para dormir*

marker light
*luz*<sup>F</sup> *lateral*

grab handle
*asidero*<sup>M</sup>

hood
*capó*<sup>M</sup>

storage compartment
*espacio*<sup>M</sup> *para*
*almacenamiento*<sup>M</sup>

headlight
*faro*<sup>M</sup> *delantero*

fifth wheel
*disco*<sup>M</sup> *de articulación*<sup>F</sup>

mud flap
*guardabarros*<sup>M</sup>

tire
*neumático*<sup>M</sup>

fog light
*luz*<sup>F</sup> *antiniebla*

bumper
*parachoques*<sup>M</sup>

step
*escalón*<sup>M</sup>

filler cap
*tapa*<sup>F</sup> *del tanque*<sup>M</sup>

radiator grille
*calandra*<sup>F</sup>

fender
*guardabarros*<sup>M</sup>

wheel
*rueda*<sup>F</sup>

fuel tank
*tanque*<sup>M</sup> *del*
*combustible*<sup>M</sup>

**examples of trucks**
*ejemplos*<sup>M</sup> *de camiones*<sup>M</sup>

tank body
*cisterna*<sup>F</sup>

tank truck
*camión*<sup>M</sup> *cisterna*<sup>F</sup>

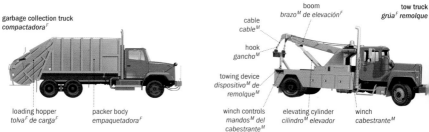

**garbage collection truck**
*compactadora*<sup>F</sup>

boom
*brazo*<sup>M</sup> *de elevación*<sup>F</sup>

tow truck
*grúa*<sup>F</sup> *remolque*

cable
*cable*<sup>M</sup>

hook
*gancho*<sup>M</sup>

towing device
*dispositivo*<sup>M</sup> *de*
*remolque*<sup>M</sup>

loading hopper
*tolva*<sup>F</sup> *de carga*<sup>F</sup>

packer body
*empaquetadora*<sup>F</sup>

winch controls
*mandos*<sup>M</sup> *del*
*cabestrante*<sup>M</sup>

elevating cylinder
*cilindro*<sup>M</sup> *elevador*

winch
*cabestrante*<sup>M</sup>

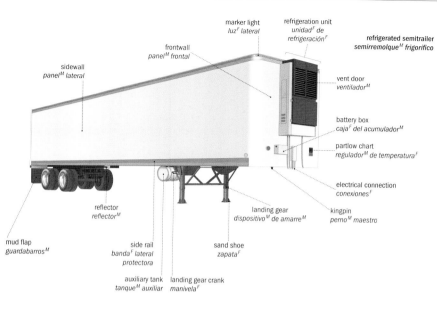

refrigerated semitrailer
*semirremolque* M *frigorífico*

marker light
*luz* F *lateral*

refrigeration unit
*unidad* F *de refrigeración* F

frontwall
*panel* M *frontal*

sidewall
*panel* M *lateral*

vent door
*ventilador* M

battery box
*caja* F *del acumulador* M

partlow chart
*regulador* M *de temperatura* F

electrical connection
*conexiones* F

kingpin
*perno* M *maestro*

landing gear
*dispositivo* M *de amarre* M

reflector
*reflector* M

mud flap
*guardabarros* M

side rail
*banda* F *lateral protectora*

sand shoe
*zapata* F

auxiliary tank
*tanque* M *auxiliar*

landing gear crank
*manivela* F

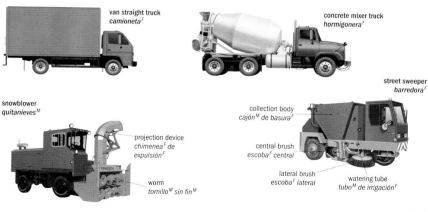

van straight truck
*camioneta* F

concrete mixer truck
*hormigonera* F

street sweeper
*barredora* F

snowblower
*quitanieves* M

projection device
*chimenea* F *de expulsión* F

worm
*tornillo* M *sin fin* M

collection body
*cajón* M *de basura* F

central brush
*escoba* F *central*

lateral brush
*escoba* F *lateral*

watering tube
*tubo* M *de irrigación* F

# motorcycle
*motocicleta<sup>F</sup>*

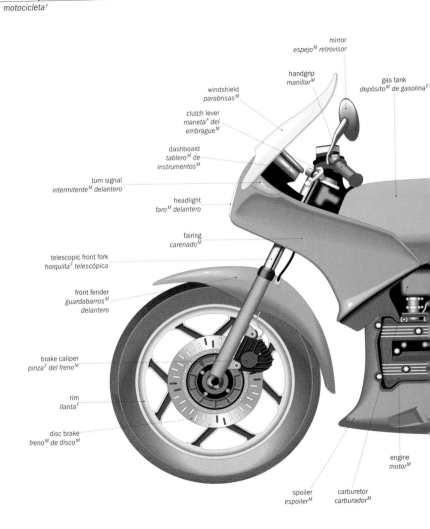

mirror
*espejo<sup>M</sup> retrovisor*

handgrip
*manillar<sup>M</sup>*

gas tank
*depósito<sup>M</sup> de gasolina<sup>F</sup>*

windshield
*parabrisas<sup>M</sup>*

clutch lever
*maneta<sup>F</sup> del
embrague<sup>M</sup>*

dashboard
*tablero<sup>M</sup> de
instrumentos<sup>M</sup>*

turn signal
*intermitente<sup>M</sup> delantero*

headlight
*faro<sup>M</sup> delantero*

fairing
*carenado<sup>M</sup>*

telescopic front fork
*horquilla<sup>F</sup> telescópica*

front fender
*guardabarros<sup>M</sup>
delantero*

brake caliper
*pinza<sup>F</sup> del freno<sup>M</sup>*

rim
*llanta<sup>F</sup>*

disc brake
*freno<sup>M</sup> de disco<sup>M</sup>*

engine
*motor<sup>M</sup>*

spoiler
*espoiler<sup>M</sup>*

carburetor
*carburador<sup>M</sup>*

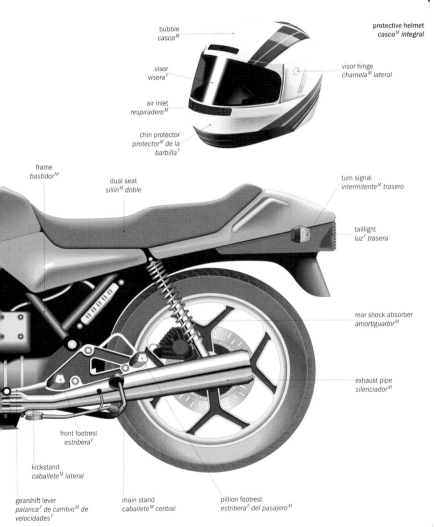

bubble
casco<sup>M</sup>

protective helmet
casco<sup>M</sup> integral

visor
visera<sup>F</sup>

visor hinge
charnela<sup>M</sup> lateral

air inlet
respiradero<sup>M</sup>

chin protector
protector<sup>M</sup> de la
barbilla<sup>F</sup>

frame
bastidor<sup>M</sup>

dual seat
sillín<sup>M</sup> doble

turn signal
intermitente<sup>M</sup> trasero

taillight
luz<sup>F</sup> trasera

rear shock absorber
amortiguador<sup>M</sup>

exhaust pipe
silenciador<sup>M</sup>

front footrest
estribera<sup>F</sup>

kickstand
caballete<sup>M</sup> lateral

gearshift lever
palanca<sup>F</sup> de cambio<sup>M</sup> de
velocidades<sup>F</sup>

main stand
caballete<sup>M</sup> central

pillion footrest
estribera<sup>F</sup> del pasajero<sup>M</sup>

motorcycle

**motorcycle dashboard**
*tablero<sup>M</sup> de instrumentos<sup>M</sup>*

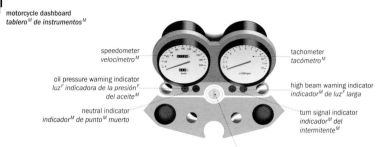

speedometer
*velocímetro<sup>M</sup>*

tachometer
*tacómetro<sup>M</sup>*

oil pressure warning indicator
*luz<sup>F</sup> indicadora de la presión<sup>F</sup> del aceite<sup>M</sup>*

high beam warning indicator
*indicador<sup>M</sup> de luz<sup>F</sup> larga*

neutral indicator
*indicador<sup>M</sup> de punto<sup>M</sup> muerto*

turn signal indicator
*indicador<sup>M</sup> del intermitente<sup>M</sup>*

ignition switch
*interruptor<sup>M</sup> de encendido<sup>M</sup>*

**motorcycle: view from above**
*motocicleta<sup>F</sup> : vista<sup>F</sup> desde lo alto<sup>M</sup>*

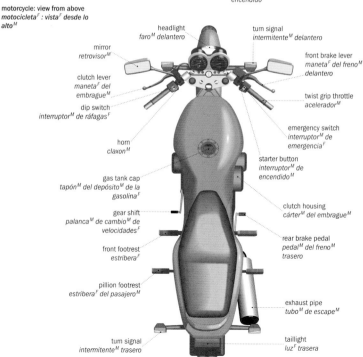

headlight
*faro<sup>M</sup> delantero*

turn signal
*intermitente<sup>M</sup> delantero*

mirror
*retrovisor<sup>M</sup>*

front brake lever
*maneta<sup>F</sup> del freno<sup>M</sup> delantero*

clutch lever
*maneta<sup>F</sup> del embrague<sup>M</sup>*

dip switch
*interruptor<sup>M</sup> de ráfagas<sup>F</sup>*

twist grip throttle
*acelerador<sup>M</sup>*

emergency switch
*interruptor<sup>M</sup> de emergencia<sup>F</sup>*

horn
*claxon<sup>M</sup>*

starter button
*interruptor<sup>M</sup> de encendido<sup>M</sup>*

gas tank cap
*tapón<sup>M</sup> del depósito<sup>M</sup> de la gasolina<sup>F</sup>*

gear shift
*palanca<sup>M</sup> de cambio<sup>M</sup> de velocidades<sup>F</sup>*

clutch housing
*cárter<sup>M</sup> del embrague<sup>M</sup>*

front footrest
*estribera<sup>F</sup>*

rear brake pedal
*pedal<sup>M</sup> del freno<sup>M</sup> trasero*

pillion footrest
*estribera<sup>F</sup> del pasajero<sup>M</sup>*

exhaust pipe
*tubo<sup>M</sup> de escape<sup>M</sup>*

turn signal
*intermitente<sup>M</sup> trasero*

taillight
*luz<sup>F</sup> trasera*

motorcycle

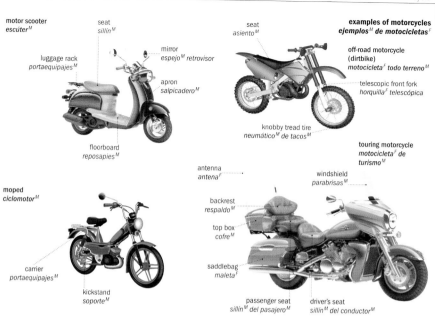

motor scooter
*escúter*<sup>M</sup>

seat
*sillín*<sup>M</sup>

mirror
*espejo*<sup>M</sup> *retrovisor*

luggage rack
*portaequipajes*<sup>M</sup>

apron
*salpicadero*<sup>M</sup>

floorboard
*reposapies*<sup>M</sup>

seat
*asiento*<sup>M</sup>

**examples of motorcycles**
**ejemplos*<sup>M</sup> *de motocicletas*<sup>F</sup>

**off-road motorcycle
(dirtbike)**
*motocicleta*<sup>F</sup> *todo terreno*<sup>M</sup>

telescopic front fork
*horquilla*<sup>F</sup> *telescópica*

knobby tread tire
*neumático*<sup>M</sup> *de tacos*<sup>M</sup>

**touring motorcycle**
*motocicleta*<sup>F</sup> *de*
*turismo*<sup>M</sup>

antenna
*antena*<sup>F</sup>

windshield
*parabrisas*<sup>M</sup>

moped
*ciclomotor*<sup>M</sup>

backrest
*respaldo*<sup>M</sup>

top box
*cofre*<sup>M</sup>

saddlebag
*maleta*<sup>F</sup>

carrier
*portaequipajes*<sup>M</sup>

kickstand
*soporte*<sup>M</sup>

passenger seat
*sillín*<sup>M</sup> *del pasajero*<sup>M</sup>

driver's seat
*sillín*<sup>M</sup> *del conductor*<sup>M</sup>

## 4 X 4 all-terrain vehicle
*quad*<sup>M</sup>

rear cargo rack
*portaequipajes*<sup>M</sup>
*posterior*

rear fender
*parachoques*<sup>M</sup>
*posterior*

muffler
*silenciador*<sup>M</sup>

seat
*sillín*<sup>M</sup>

gas tank
*depósito*<sup>M</sup> *de gasolina*<sup>F</sup>

handgrip
*manillar*<sup>M</sup>

bumper
*parachoques*<sup>M</sup>

front shock absorber
*amortiguador*<sup>M</sup>
*delantero*

gearshift lever
*palanca*<sup>F</sup> *de cambio*<sup>M</sup> *de*
*velocidades*<sup>F</sup>

TRANSPORT AND MACHINERY

# bicycle

bicicleta<sup>F</sup>

parts of a bicycle
partes<sup>F</sup> de una
bicicleta<sup>F</sup>

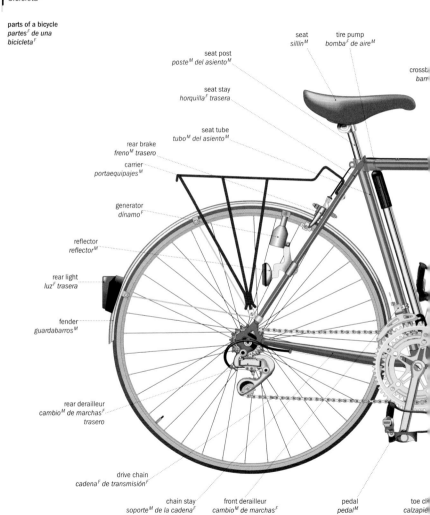

seat
sillín<sup>M</sup>

tire pump
bomba<sup>F</sup> de aire<sup>M</sup>

crossba
barr

seat post
poste<sup>M</sup> del asiento<sup>M</sup>

seat stay
horquilla<sup>F</sup> trasera

seat tube
tubo<sup>M</sup> del asiento<sup>M</sup>

rear brake
freno<sup>M</sup> trasero

carrier
portaequipajes<sup>M</sup>

generator
dínamo<sup>F</sup>

reflector
reflector<sup>M</sup>

rear light
luz<sup>F</sup> trasera

fender
guardabarros<sup>M</sup>

rear derailleur
cambio<sup>M</sup> de marchas<sup>F</sup>
trasero

drive chain
cadena<sup>F</sup> de transmisión<sup>F</sup>

chain stay
soporte<sup>M</sup> de la cadena<sup>F</sup>

front derailleur
cambio<sup>M</sup> de marchas<sup>F</sup>
delantero

pedal
pedal<sup>M</sup>

toe cl
calzapié

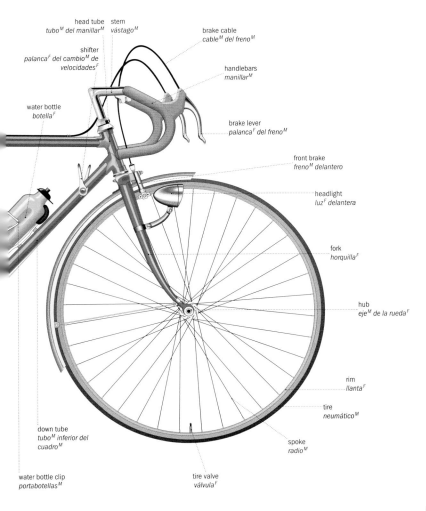

head tube
tubo<sup>M</sup> del manillar<sup>M</sup>

stem
vástago<sup>M</sup>

brake cable
cable<sup>M</sup> del freno<sup>M</sup>

shifter
palanca<sup>F</sup> del cambio<sup>M</sup> de
velocidades<sup>F</sup>

handlebars
manillar<sup>M</sup>

water bottle
botella<sup>F</sup>

brake lever
palanca<sup>F</sup> del freno<sup>M</sup>

front brake
freno<sup>M</sup> delantero

headlight
luz<sup>F</sup> delantera

fork
horquilla<sup>F</sup>

hub
eje<sup>M</sup> de la rueda<sup>F</sup>

rim
llanta<sup>F</sup>

tire
neumático<sup>M</sup>

down tube
tubo<sup>M</sup> inferior del
cuadro<sup>M</sup>

spoke
radio<sup>M</sup>

water bottle clip
portabotellas<sup>M</sup>

tire valve
válvula<sup>F</sup>

bicycle

TRANSPORT AND MACHINERY

**power train**
*transmisión$^F$ de cadena$^F$*

front derailleur
*cambio$^M$ de marchas$^F$ delantero*

chain guide
*guía$^F$ de la cadena$^F$*

shifter
*palanca$^F$ del cambio$^M$ de velocidades$^F$*

toe clip
*calapié$^M$*

freewheel
*piñón$^M$ libre*

chain
*cadena$^F$*

control cable
*cable$^M$ del cambio$^M$*

chain wheel A
*corona$^F$ externa de la cadena$^F$*

bottom bracket axle
*eje$^M$ del pedal$^M$*

rear derailleur
*cambio$^M$ de marchas$^F$ trasero*

chain wheel B
*corona$^F$ interna de la cadena$^F$*

jockey rollers
*poleas$^F$ de tensión$^F$*

pedal
*pedal$^M$*

crank
*manivela$^F$*

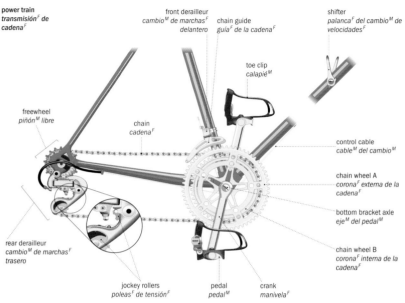

**accessories**
*accesorios$^M$*

lock
*candado$^M$ para bicicleta$^F$*

protective helmet
*casco$^M$ protector*

tool kit
*herramientas$^F$*

bicycle bag (pannier)
*cartera$^F$*

child carrier
*silla$^F$ porta-niño$^M$*

child's tricycle
*triciclo$^M$*

**examples of bicycles**
***ejemplos$^M$ de bicicletas$^F$***

BMX bike
*bicicleta$^F$ BMX*

mountain bike
*bicicleta$^F$ todo terreno$^M$*

Dutch bicycle
*bicicleta$^F$ holandesa*

road bicycle
*bicicleta$^F$ de carretera$^F$*

city bicycle
*bicicleta$^F$ de ciudad$^F$*

touring bicycle
*bicicleta$^F$ de turismo$^M$*

tandem bicycle
*tándem$^M$*

# passenger station
*estación<sup>F</sup> de ferrocarril<sup>M</sup>*

office
*oficina<sup>F</sup>*

indicator board
*tablero<sup>M</sup> de información<sup>F</sup>*

baggage cart
*carro<sup>M</sup> portaequipaje*

baggage locker
*taquillas<sup>F</sup> de consigna*
*automátic*

glassed roof
*techo<sup>M</sup> de vidrio<sup>M</sup>*

metal structure
*estructura<sup>F</sup> de metal<sup>M</sup>*

platform number
*indicador<sup>M</sup> de número<sup>M</sup> de*
*andén<sup>M</sup>*

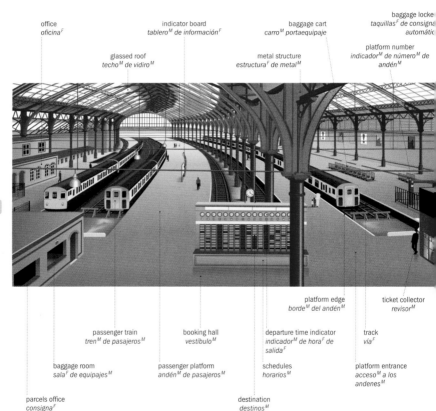

platform edge
*borde<sup>M</sup> del andén<sup>M</sup>*

ticket collector
*revisor<sup>M</sup>*

passenger train
*tren<sup>M</sup> de pasajeros<sup>M</sup>*

booking hall
*vestíbulo<sup>M</sup>*

departure time indicator
*indicador<sup>M</sup> de hora<sup>F</sup> de*
*salida<sup>F</sup>*

track
*vía<sup>F</sup>*

baggage room
*sala<sup>F</sup> de equipajes<sup>M</sup>*

passenger platform
*andén<sup>M</sup> de pasajeros<sup>M</sup>*

schedules
*horarios<sup>M</sup>*

platform entrance
*acceso<sup>M</sup> a los*
*andenes<sup>M</sup>*

parcels office
*consigna<sup>F</sup>*

destination
*destinos<sup>M</sup>*

# railroad station
*estación<sup>F</sup> de ferrocarril<sup>M</sup>*

passenger station
*estación<sup>F</sup> de ferrocarril<sup>M</sup>*

station platform
*andén<sup>M</sup>*

commuter train
*tren<sup>M</sup> suburbano*

main line
*vía<sup>F</sup> principal*

suburban commuter railroad
*vía<sup>F</sup> de tren<sup>M</sup> suburbano*

subsidiary track
*vía<sup>F</sup> subsidiaria*

bumper
*tope<sup>M</sup>*

level crossing
*paso<sup>M</sup> a nivel<sup>M</sup>*

platform shelter
*marquesina<sup>M</sup> del andén<sup>M</sup>*

footbridge
*pasarela<sup>F</sup>*

signal
*semáforo<sup>M</sup>*

parking
*estacionamiento<sup>M</sup>*

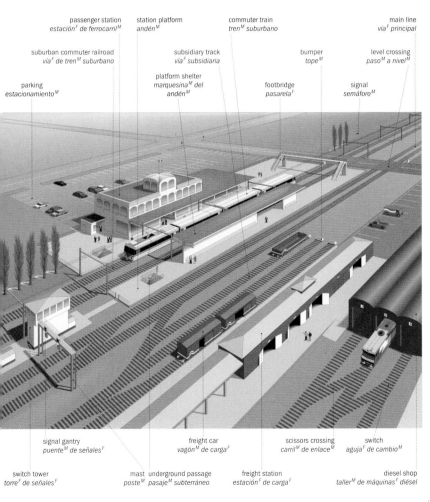

signal gantry
*puente<sup>M</sup> de señales<sup>F</sup>*

freight car
*vagón<sup>M</sup> de carga<sup>F</sup>*

scissors crossing
*carril<sup>M</sup> de enlace<sup>M</sup>*

switch
*aguja<sup>F</sup> de cambio<sup>M</sup>*

switch tower
*torre<sup>F</sup> de señales<sup>F</sup>*

mast
*poste<sup>M</sup>*

underground passage
*pasaje<sup>M</sup> subterráneo*

freight station
*estación<sup>F</sup> de carga<sup>F</sup>*

diesel shop
*taller<sup>M</sup> de máquinas<sup>F</sup> diésel*

TRANSPORT AND MACHINERY

375

# high-speed train
*tren<sup>M</sup> de alta velocidad<sup>F</sup>*

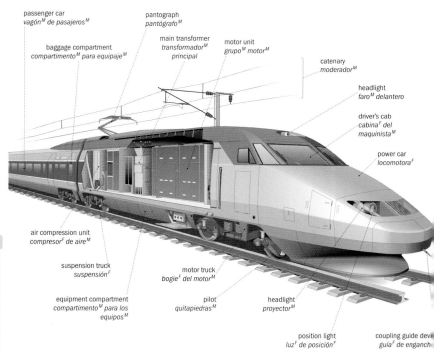

passenger car
*vagón<sup>M</sup> de pasajeros<sup>M</sup>*

baggage compartment
*compartimento<sup>M</sup> para equipaje<sup>M</sup>*

pantograph
*pantógrafo<sup>M</sup>*

main transformer
*transformador<sup>M</sup> principal*

motor unit
*grupo<sup>M</sup> motor<sup>M</sup>*

catenary
*moderador<sup>M</sup>*

headlight
*faro<sup>M</sup> delantero*

driver's cab
*cabina<sup>F</sup> del maquinista<sup>M</sup>*

power car
*locomotora<sup>F</sup>*

air compression unit
*compresor<sup>F</sup> de aire<sup>M</sup>*

suspension truck
*suspensión<sup>F</sup>*

equipment compartment
*compartimento<sup>M</sup> para los equipos<sup>M</sup>*

motor truck
*bogie<sup>F</sup> del motor<sup>M</sup>*

pilot
*quitapiedras<sup>M</sup>*

headlight
*proyector<sup>M</sup>*

position light
*luz<sup>F</sup> de posición<sup>F</sup>*

coupling guide devi
*guía<sup>F</sup> de enganch*

# types of passenger cars
*vagones<sup>M</sup> de pasajeros<sup>M</sup>*

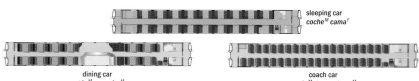

sleeping car
*coche<sup>M</sup> cama<sup>F</sup>*

dining car
*vagón<sup>M</sup> comedor<sup>M</sup>*

coach car
*vagón<sup>M</sup> de pasajeros<sup>M</sup>*

# diesel-electric locomotive
*locomotora<sup>F</sup> diésel eléctrica*

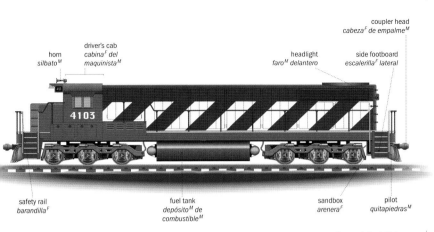

coupler head
*cabeza<sup>F</sup> de empalme<sup>M</sup>*

horn
*silbato<sup>M</sup>*

driver's cab
*cabina<sup>F</sup> del
maquinista<sup>M</sup>*

headlight
*faro<sup>M</sup> delantero*

side footboard
*escalerilla<sup>F</sup> lateral*

safety rail
*barandilla<sup>F</sup>*

fuel tank
*depósito<sup>M</sup> de
combustible<sup>M</sup>*

sandbox
*arenera<sup>F</sup>*

pilot
*quitapiedras<sup>M</sup>*

## examples of freight cars
*ejemplos<sup>M</sup> de vagones<sup>M</sup>*

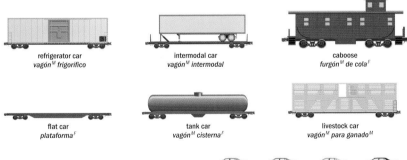

refrigerator car
*vagón<sup>M</sup> frigorífico*

intermodal car
*vagón<sup>M</sup> intermodal*

caboose
*furgón<sup>M</sup> de cola<sup>F</sup>*

flat car
*plataforma<sup>F</sup>*

tank car
*vagón<sup>M</sup> cisterna<sup>F</sup>*

livestock car
*vagón<sup>M</sup> para ganado<sup>M</sup>*

container car
*vagón<sup>M</sup> para contenedores<sup>M</sup>*

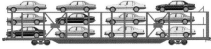

automobile car
*vagón<sup>M</sup> para automóviles<sup>M</sup>*

TRANSPORT AND MACHINERY

# subway
*metro* M

**subway station**
*estación* F *de metro* M

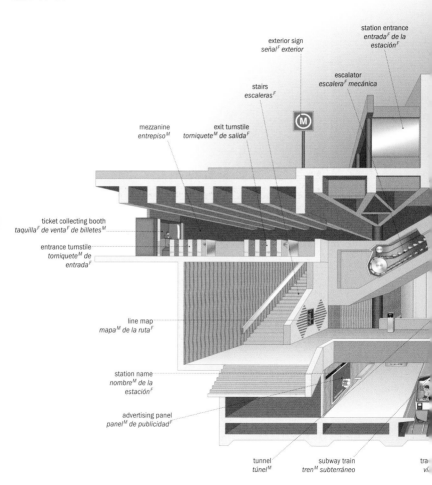

station entrance
*entrada* F *de la estación* F

exterior sign
*señal* F *exterior*

escalator
*escalera* F *mecánica*

stairs
*escaleras* F

mezzanine
*entrepiso* M

exit turnstile
*torniquete* M *de salida* F

ticket collecting booth
*taquilla* F *de venta* F *de billetes* M

entrance turnstile
*torniquete* M *de entrada* F

line map
*mapa* M *de la ruta* F

station name
*nombre* M *de la estación* F

advertising panel
*panel* M *de publicidad* F

tunnel
*túnel* M

subway train
*tren* M *subterráneo*

tra
ví

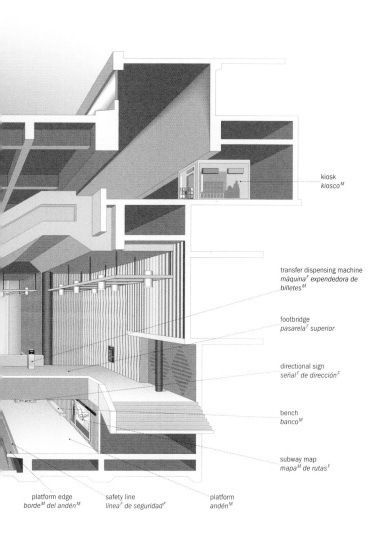

kiosk
*kiosco<sup>M</sup>*

transfer dispensing machine
*máquina<sup>F</sup> expendedora de billetes<sup>M</sup>*

footbridge
*pasarela<sup>F</sup> superior*

directional sign
*señal<sup>F</sup> de dirección<sup>F</sup>*

bench
*banco<sup>M</sup>*

subway map
*mapa<sup>M</sup> de rutas<sup>F</sup>*

platform edge
*borde<sup>M</sup> del andén<sup>M</sup>*

safety line
*línea<sup>F</sup> de seguridad<sup>F</sup>*

platform
*andén<sup>M</sup>*

TRANSPORT AND MACHINERY

**passenger car**
*vagón<sup>M</sup> de pasajeros<sup>M</sup>*

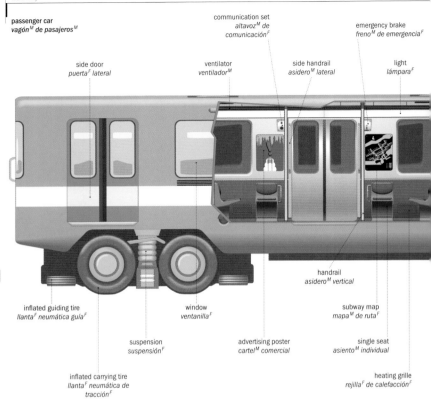

communication set
*altavoz<sup>M</sup> de comunicación<sup>F</sup>*

emergency brake
*freno<sup>M</sup> de emergencia<sup>F</sup>*

side door
*puerta<sup>F</sup> lateral*

ventilator
*ventilador<sup>M</sup>*

side handrail
*asidero<sup>M</sup> lateral*

light
*lámpara<sup>F</sup>*

handrail
*asidero<sup>M</sup> vertical*

inflated guiding tire
*llanta<sup>F</sup> neumática guía<sup>F</sup>*

window
*ventanilla<sup>F</sup>*

subway map
*mapa<sup>M</sup> de ruta<sup>F</sup>*

suspension
*suspensión<sup>F</sup>*

advertising poster
*cartel<sup>M</sup> comercial*

single seat
*asiento<sup>M</sup> individual*

inflated carrying tire
*llanta<sup>F</sup> neumática de tracción<sup>F</sup>*

heating grille
*rejilla<sup>F</sup> de calefacción<sup>F</sup>*

double sea
*asiento<sup>M</sup> doble*

**subway train**
*tren<sup>M</sup> subterráneo*

motor car
*vagón<sup>M</sup> máquina<sup>F</sup>*

trailer car
*coche<sup>M</sup> de tracción<sup>F</sup>*

motor car
*vagón<sup>M</sup> máquina<sup>F</sup>*

# harbor
*puerto*<sup>M</sup>

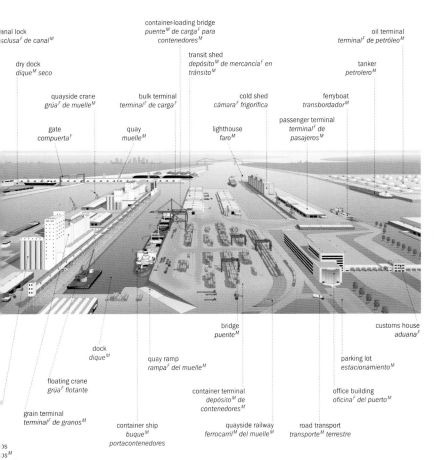

canal lock
*esclusa<sup>F</sup> de canal<sup>M</sup>*

dry dock
*dique<sup>M</sup> seco*

container-loading bridge
*puente<sup>M</sup> de carga<sup>F</sup> para
contenedores<sup>M</sup>*

transit shed
*depósito<sup>M</sup> de mercancía<sup>F</sup> en
tránsito<sup>M</sup>*

oil terminal
*terminal<sup>F</sup> de petróleo<sup>M</sup>*

tanker
*petrolero<sup>M</sup>*

quayside crane
*grúa<sup>F</sup> de muelle<sup>M</sup>*

bulk terminal
*terminal<sup>F</sup> de carga<sup>F</sup>*

cold shed
*cámara<sup>F</sup> frigorífica*

ferryboat
*transbordador<sup>M</sup>*

passenger terminal
*terminal<sup>F</sup> de
pasajeros<sup>M</sup>*

gate
*compuerta<sup>F</sup>*

quay
*muelle<sup>M</sup>*

lighthouse
*faro<sup>M</sup>*

bridge
*puente<sup>M</sup>*

customs house
*aduana<sup>F</sup>*

dock
*dique<sup>M</sup>*

quay ramp
*rampa<sup>F</sup> del muelle<sup>M</sup>*

parking lot
*estacionamiento<sup>M</sup>*

floating crane
*grúa<sup>F</sup> flotante*

container terminal
*depósito<sup>M</sup> de
contenedores<sup>M</sup>*

office building
*oficina<sup>F</sup> del puerto<sup>M</sup>*

grain terminal
*terminal<sup>F</sup> de granos<sup>M</sup>*

container ship
*buque<sup>M</sup>
portacontenedores*

quayside railway
*ferrocarril<sup>M</sup> del muelle<sup>M</sup>*

road transport
*transporte<sup>M</sup> terrestre*

os
os<sup>M</sup>

TRANSPORT AND MACHINERY

# examples of boats and ships
*ejemplos^M de barcos^M y embarcaciones^F*

drill ship
*barco^M perforador*

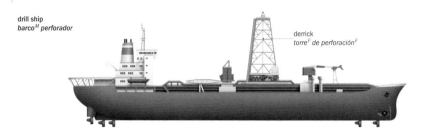

derrick
*torre^F de perforación^F*

bulk carrier
*buque^M de carga^F*

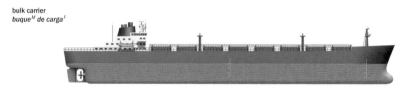

container ship
*carguero^M*
*portacontenedores*

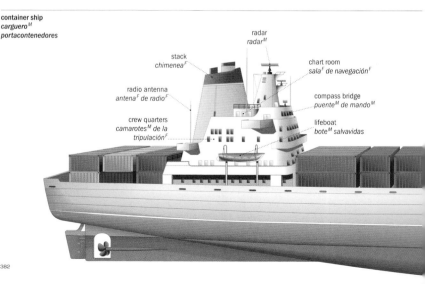

radar
*radar^M*

chart room
*sala^F de navegación^F*

stack
*chimenea^F*

compass bridge
*puente^M de mando^M*

radio antenna
*antena^F de radio^F*

lifeboat
*bote^M salvavidas*

crew quarters
*camarotes^M de la tripulación^F*

TRANSPORT AND MACHINERY

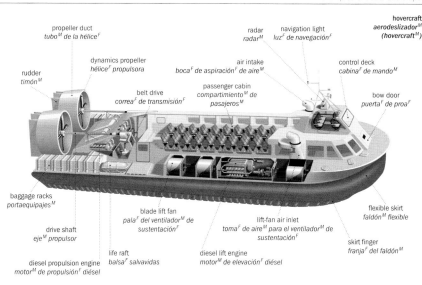

hovercraft
aerodeslizador^M
(hovercraft^M)

propeller duct
tubo^M de la hélice^F

dynamics propeller
hélice^F propulsora

rudder
timón^M

belt drive
correa^F de transmisión^F

passenger cabin
compartimiento^M de
pasajeros^M

air intake
boca^F de aspiración^F de aire^M

radar
radar^M

navigation light
luz^F de navegación^F

control deck
cabina^F de mando^M

bow door
puerta^F de proa^F

baggage racks
portaequipajes^M

blade lift fan
pala^F del ventilador^M de
sustentación^F

lift-fan air inlet
toma^F de aire^M para el ventilador^M de
sustentación^F

flexible skirt
faldón^M flexible

drive shaft
eje^M propulsor

life raft
balsa^F salvavidas

diesel lift engine
motor^M de elevación^F diésel

skirt finger
franja^F del faldón^M

diesel propulsion engine
motor^M de propulsión^F diésel

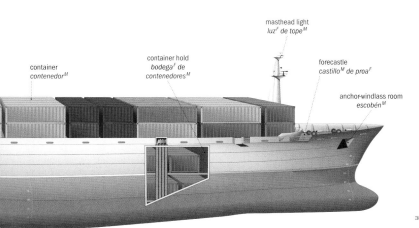

container
contenedor^M

container hold
bodega^F de
contenedores^M

masthead light
luz^F de tope^M

forecastle
castillo^M de proa^F

anchor-windlass room
escobén^M

examples of boats and ships

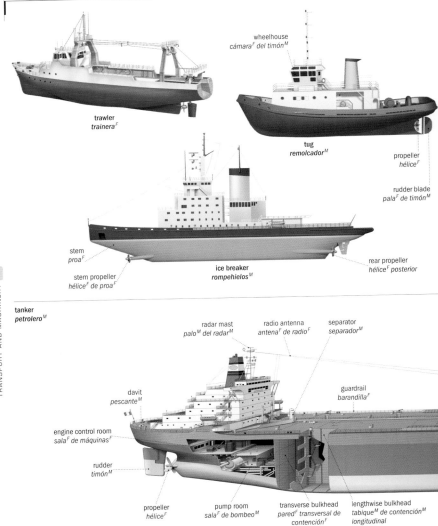

trawler
*trainera*[F]

wheelhouse
*cámara*[F] *del timón*[M]

tug
*remolcador*[M]

propeller
*hélice*[F]

rudder blade
*pala*[F] *de timón*[M]

stem
*proa*[F]

stem propeller
*hélice*[F] *de proa*[F]

ice breaker
*rompehielos*[M]

rear propeller
*hélice*[F] *posterior*

tanker
*petrolero*[M]

radar mast
*palo*[M] *del radar*[M]

radio antenna
*antena*[F] *de radio*[F]

separator
*separador*[M]

davit
*pescante*[M]

guardrail
*barandilla*[F]

engine control room
*sala*[F] *de máquinas*[F]

rudder
*timón*[M]

propeller
*hélice*[F]

pump room
*sala*[F] *de bombeo*[M]

transverse bulkhead
*pared*[F] *transversal de*
*contención*[F]

lengthwise bulkhead
*tabique*[M] *de contención*[M]
*longitudinal*

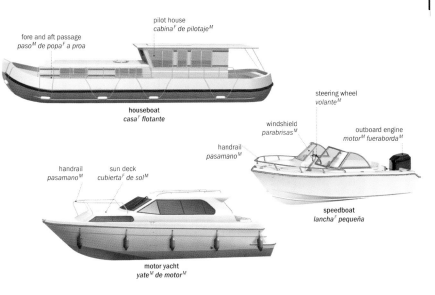

fore and aft passage
*paso^M de popa^F a proa*

pilot house
*cabina^F de pilotaje^M*

houseboat
*casa^F flotante*

steering wheel
*volante^M*

windshield
*parabrisas^M*

handrail
*pasamano^M*

outboard engine
*motor^M fueraborda^M*

speedboat
*lancha^F pequeña*

handrail
*pasamano^M*

sun deck
*cubierta^F de sol^M*

motor yacht
*yate^M de motor^M*

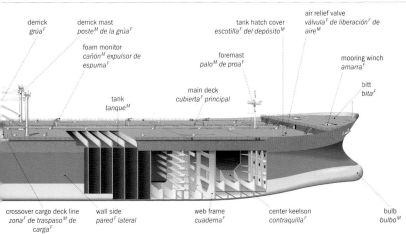

derrick
*grúa^F*

derrick mast
*poste^M de la grúa^F*

foam monitor
*cañón^M expulsor de
espuma^F*

tank hatch cover
*escotilla^F del depósito^M*

air relief valve
*válvula^F de liberación^F de
aire^M*

foremast
*palo^M de proa^F*

mooring winch
*amarra^F*

main deck
*cubierta^F principal*

bitt
*bita^F*

tank
*tanque^M*

crossover cargo deck line
*zona^F de traspaso^M de
carga^F*

wall side
*pared^F lateral*

web frame
*cuaderna^F*

center keelson
*contraquilla^F*

bulb
*bulbo^M*

**catamaran ferryboat**
*transbordador*[M]

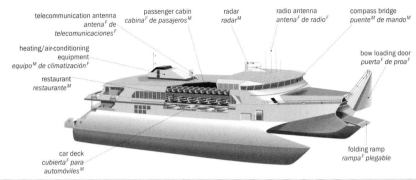

telecommunication antenna
*antena*[F] *de*
*telecomunicaciones*[F]

passenger cabin
*cabina*[F] *de pasajeros*[M]

radar
*radar*[M]

radio antenna
*antena*[F] *de radio*[F]

compass bridge
*puente*[M] *de mando*[M]

heating/air-conditioning
equipment
*equipo*[M] *de climatización*[F]

bow loading door
*puerta*[F] *de proa*[F]

restaurant
*restaurante*[M]

car deck
*cubierta*[F] *para*
*automóviles*[M]

folding ramp
*rampa*[F] *plegable*

**passenger liner**
*buque*[M] *trasatlántico*

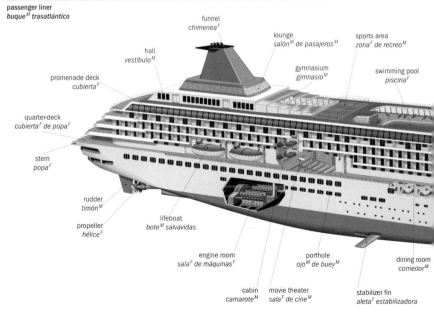

funnel
*chimenea*[F]

lounge
*salón*[M] *de pasajeros*[M]

sports area
*zona*[F] *de recreo*[M]

hall
*vestíbulo*[M]

gymnasium
*gimnasio*[O]

swimming pool
*piscina*[F]

promenade deck
*cubierta*[F]

quarter-deck
*cubierta*[F] *de popa*[F]

stern
*popa*[F]

rudder
*timón*[M]

propeller
*hélice*[F]

lifeboat
*bote*[M] *salvavidas*

engine room
*sala*[F] *de máquinas*[F]

porthole
*ojo*[M] *de buey*[M]

dining room
*comedor*[M]

cabin
*camarote*[M]

movie theater
*sala*[F] *de cine*[M]

stabilizer fin
*aleta*[F] *estabilizadora*

hydrofoil boat
*hidróptero*<sup>M</sup>

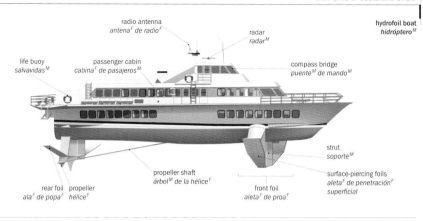

radio antenna
*antena*<sup>F</sup> *de radio*<sup>F</sup>

radar
*radar*<sup>M</sup>

life buoy
*salvavidas*<sup>M</sup>

passenger cabin
*cabina*<sup>F</sup> *de pasajeros*<sup>M</sup>

compass bridge
*puente*<sup>M</sup> *de mando*<sup>M</sup>

rear foil
*ala*<sup>F</sup> *de popa*<sup>F</sup>

propeller
*hélice*<sup>F</sup>

propeller shaft
*árbol*<sup>M</sup> *de la hélice*<sup>F</sup>

front foil
*aleta*<sup>F</sup> *de proa*<sup>F</sup>

strut
*soporte*<sup>M</sup>

surface-piercing foils
*aleta*<sup>F</sup> *de penetración*<sup>F</sup>
*superficial*

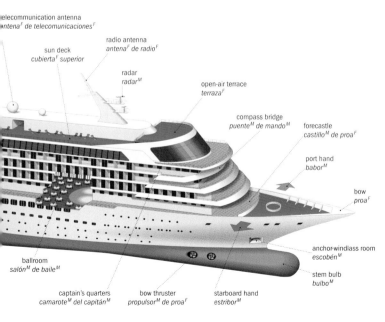

elecommunication antenna
*ntena*<sup>F</sup> *de telecomunicaciones*<sup>F</sup>

sun deck
*cubierta*<sup>F</sup> *superior*

radio antenna
*antena*<sup>F</sup> *de radio*<sup>F</sup>

radar
*radar*<sup>M</sup>

open-air terrace
*terraza*<sup>F</sup>

compass bridge
*puente*<sup>M</sup> *de mando*<sup>M</sup>

forecastle
*castillo*<sup>M</sup> *de proa*<sup>F</sup>

port hand
*babor*<sup>M</sup>

bow
*proa*<sup>F</sup>

ballroom
*salón*<sup>M</sup> *de baile*<sup>M</sup>

captain's quarters
*camarote*<sup>M</sup> *del capitán*<sup>M</sup>

bow thruster
*propulsor*<sup>M</sup> *de proa*<sup>F</sup>

starboard hand
*estribor*<sup>M</sup>

anchor-windlass room
*escobén*<sup>M</sup>

stem bulb
*bulbo*<sup>M</sup>

TRANSPORT AND MACHINERY

387

# airport
*aeropuerto*<sup>M</sup>

high-speed exit taxiway
*salida*<sup>F</sup> *de la pista*<sup>F</sup> *de alta velocidad*<sup>F</sup>

control tower cab
*cabina*<sup>F</sup> *de la torre*<sup>F</sup> *de control*<sup>M</sup>

control tower
*torre*<sup>F</sup> *de control*<sup>M</sup>

access road
*carretera*<sup>F</sup> *de acceso*<sup>M</sup>

taxiway
*pista*<sup>F</sup> *de rodaje*<sup>M</sup>

by-pass taxiway
*pista*<sup>F</sup> *de enlace*<sup>M</sup>

taxiway
*pista*<sup>F</sup> *de rodaje*<sup>M</sup>

apron
*pista*<sup>F</sup> *de estacionamiento*<sup>M</sup>

service road
*ruta*<sup>F</sup> *de servicio*<sup>M</sup>

maneuvering area
*pista*<sup>F</sup> *de estacionamiento*<sup>M</sup>

TRANSPORT AND MACHINERY

passenger terminal
*terminal^F de
pasajeros^M*

maintenance hangar
*hangar^M de
mantenimiento^M*

parking area
*parque^M de
estacionamiento^M*

TRANSPORT AND MACHINERY

telescopic corridor
*pasarela^F telescópico*

service area
*zona^F de servicio^M*

boarding walkway
*túnel^M de embarque^M*

taxiway line
*línea^F de pista^F*

radial passenger-loading area
*terminal^F satélite de pasajeros^M*

airport

passenger terminal
*terminal*$^M$ *de*
*pasajeros*$^M$

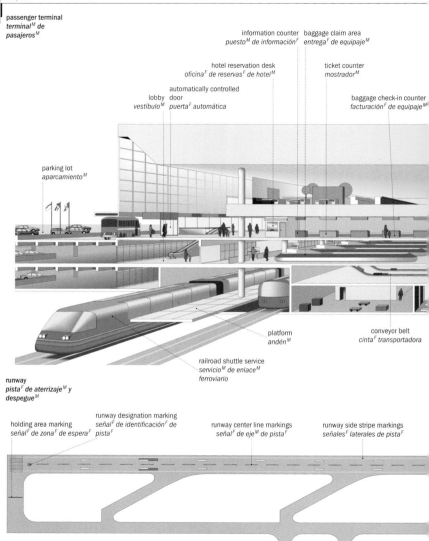

parking lot
*aparcamiento*$^M$

lobby
*vestíbulo*$^M$

automatically controlled
door
*puerta*$^F$ *automática*

hotel reservation desk
*oficina*$^F$ *de reservas*$^F$ *de hotel*$^M$

information counter
*puesto*$^M$ *de información*$^F$

baggage claim area
*entrega*$^F$ *de equipaje*$^M$

ticket counter
*mostrador*$^M$

baggage check-in counter
*facturación*$^F$ *de equipaje*$^M$

platform
*andén*$^M$

railroad shuttle service
*servicio*$^M$ *de enlace*$^M$
*ferroviario*

conveyor belt
*cinta*$^F$ *transportadora*

runway
*pista*$^F$ *de aterrizaje*$^M$ *y*
*despegue*$^M$

holding area marking
*señal*$^F$ *de zona*$^F$ *de espera*$^F$

runway designation marking
*señal*$^F$ *de identificación*$^F$ *de*
*pista*$^F$

runway center line markings
*señal*$^F$ *de eje*$^M$ *de pista*$^F$

runway side stripe markings
*señales*$^F$ *laterales de pista*$^F$

TRANSPORT AND MACHINERY

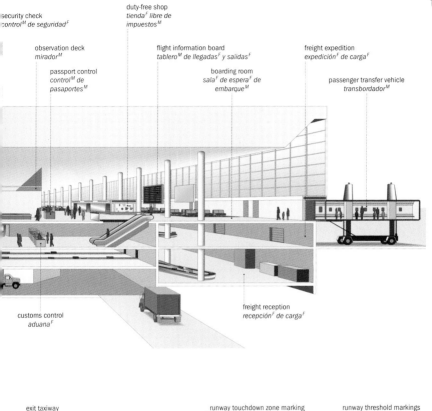

security check
*control* M *de seguridad* F

observation deck
*mirador* M

passport control
*control* M *de*
*pasaportes* M

duty-free shop
*tienda* F *libre de*
*impuestos* M

flight information board
*tablero* M *de llegadas* F *y salidas* F

boarding room
*sala* F *de espera* F *de*
*embarque* M

freight expedition
*expedición* F *de carga* F

passenger transfer vehicle
*transbordador* M

customs control
*aduana* F

freight reception
*recepción* F *de carga* F

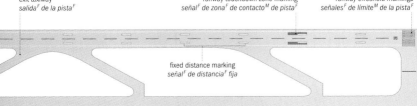

exit taxiway
*salida* F *de la pista* F

runway touchdown zone marking
*señal* F *de zona* F *de contacto* M *de pista* F

runway threshold markings
*señales* F *de límite* M *de la pista* F

fixed distance marking
*señal* F *de distancia* F *fija*

# long-range jet
*avión<sup>M</sup> turborreactor de pasajeros<sup>M</sup>*

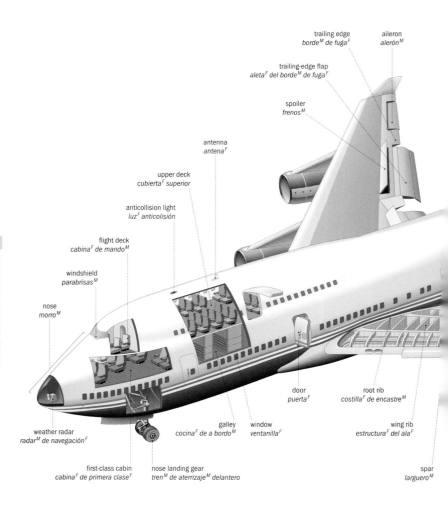

trailing edge
*borde<sup>M</sup> de fuga<sup>F</sup>*

aileron
*alerón<sup>M</sup>*

trailing-edge flap
*aleta<sup>F</sup> del borde<sup>M</sup> de fuga<sup>F</sup>*

spoiler
*frenos<sup>M</sup>*

antenna
*antena<sup>F</sup>*

upper deck
*cubierta<sup>F</sup> superior*

anticollision light
*luz<sup>F</sup> anticolisión*

flight deck
*cabina<sup>F</sup> de mando<sup>M</sup>*

windshield
*parabrisas<sup>M</sup>*

nose
*morro<sup>M</sup>*

weather radar
*radar<sup>M</sup> de navegación<sup>F</sup>*

first-class cabin
*cabina<sup>F</sup> de primera clase<sup>F</sup>*

nose landing gear
*tren<sup>M</sup> de aterrizaje<sup>M</sup> delantero*

galley
*cocina<sup>F</sup> de a bordo<sup>M</sup>*

window
*ventanilla<sup>F</sup>*

door
*puerta<sup>F</sup>*

root rib
*costilla<sup>F</sup> de encastre<sup>M</sup>*

wing rib
*estructura<sup>F</sup> del ala<sup>F</sup>*

spar
*larguero<sup>M</sup>*

TRANSPORT AND MACHINERY

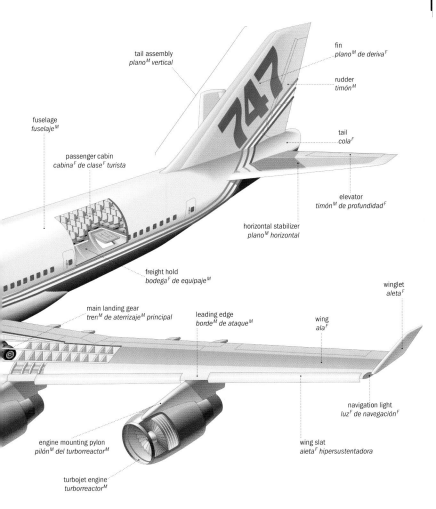

tail assembly
*plano$^M$ vertical*

fin
*plano$^M$ de deriva$^F$*

rudder
*timón$^M$*

fuselage
*fuselaje$^M$*

tail
*cola$^F$*

passenger cabin
*cabina$^F$ de clase$^F$ turista*

elevator
*timón$^M$ de profundidad$^F$*

horizontal stabilizer
*plano$^M$ horizontal*

freight hold
*bodega$^F$ de equipaje$^M$*

winglet
*aleta$^F$*

main landing gear
*tren$^M$ de aterrizaje$^M$ principal*

leading edge
*borde$^M$ de ataque$^M$*

wing
*ala$^F$*

navigation light
*luz$^F$ de navegación$^F$*

engine mounting pylon
*pilón$^M$ del turborreactor$^M$*

wing slat
*aieta$^F$ hipersustentadora*

turbojet engine
*turborreactor$^M$*

# examples of airplanes
*ejemplos<sup>M</sup> de aviones<sup>M</sup>*

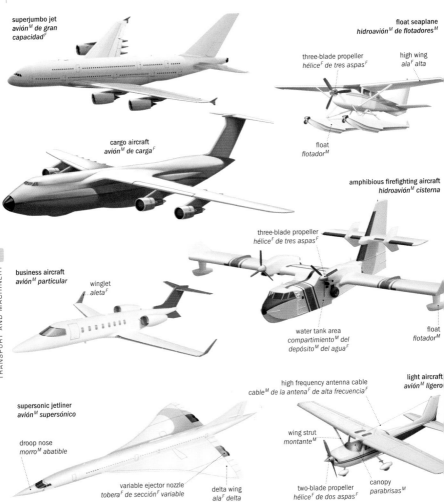

superjumbo jet
*avión<sup>M</sup> de gran capacidad<sup>F</sup>*

float seaplane
*hidroavión<sup>M</sup> de flotadores<sup>M</sup>*

three-blade propeller
*hélice<sup>F</sup> de tres aspas<sup>F</sup>*

high wing
*ala<sup>F</sup> alta*

float
*flotador<sup>M</sup>*

cargo aircraft
*avión<sup>M</sup> de carga<sup>F</sup>*

amphibious firefighting aircraft
*hidroavión<sup>M</sup> cisterna*

three-blade propeller
*hélice<sup>F</sup> de tres aspas<sup>F</sup>*

business aircraft
*avión<sup>M</sup> particular*

winglet
*aleta<sup>F</sup>*

water tank area
*compartimiento<sup>M</sup> del depósito<sup>M</sup> del agua<sup>F</sup>*

float
*flotador<sup>M</sup>*

high frequency antenna cable
*cable<sup>M</sup> de la antena<sup>F</sup> de alta frecuencia<sup>F</sup>*

light aircraft
*avión<sup>M</sup> ligero*

supersonic jetliner
*avión<sup>M</sup> supersónico*

wing strut
*montante<sup>M</sup>*

droop nose
*morro<sup>M</sup> abatible*

variable ejector nozzle
*tobera<sup>F</sup> de sección<sup>F</sup> variable*

delta wing
*ala<sup>F</sup> delta*

two-blade propeller
*hélice<sup>F</sup> de dos aspas<sup>F</sup>*

canopy
*parabrisas<sup>M</sup>*

TRANSPORT AND MACHINERY

# movements of an airplane
*movimientos<sup>M</sup> de un avión<sup>M</sup>*

pitch
*cabeceo<sup>M</sup>*

yaw
*guiñada<sup>F</sup>*

roll
*oscilación<sup>F</sup>*

# helicopter
*helicóptero<sup>M</sup>*

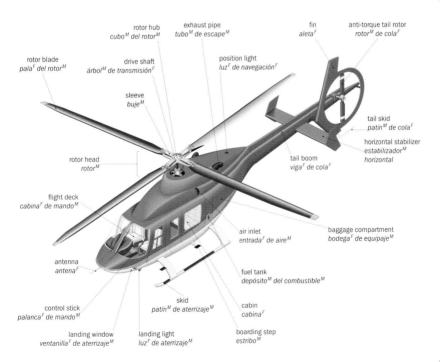

rotor hub
*cubo<sup>M</sup> del rotor<sup>M</sup>*

exhaust pipe
*tubo<sup>M</sup> de escape<sup>M</sup>*

fin
*aleta<sup>F</sup>*

anti-torque tail rotor
*rotor<sup>M</sup> de cola<sup>F</sup>*

rotor blade
*pala<sup>F</sup> del rotor<sup>M</sup>*

drive shaft
*árbol<sup>M</sup> de transmisión<sup>F</sup>*

position light
*luz<sup>F</sup> de navegación<sup>F</sup>*

sleeve
*buje<sup>M</sup>*

tail skid
*patín<sup>M</sup> de cola<sup>F</sup>*

horizontal stabilizer
*estabilizador<sup>M</sup>
horizontal*

rotor head
*rotor<sup>M</sup>*

tail boom
*viga<sup>F</sup> de cola<sup>F</sup>*

flight deck
*cabina<sup>F</sup> de mando<sup>M</sup>*

air inlet
*entrada<sup>F</sup> de aire<sup>M</sup>*

baggage compartment
*bodega<sup>F</sup> de equipaje<sup>M</sup>*

antenna
*antena<sup>F</sup>*

fuel tank
*depósito<sup>M</sup> del combustible<sup>M</sup>*

control stick
*palanca<sup>F</sup> de mando<sup>M</sup>*

skid
*patín<sup>M</sup> de aterrizaje<sup>M</sup>*

cabin
*cabina<sup>F</sup>*

landing window
*ventanilla<sup>F</sup> de aterrizaje<sup>M</sup>*

landing light
*luz<sup>F</sup> de aterrizaje<sup>M</sup>*

boarding step
*estribo<sup>M</sup>*

TRANSPORT AND MACHINERY

# material handling
*manejo*$^M$ *de materiales*$^M$

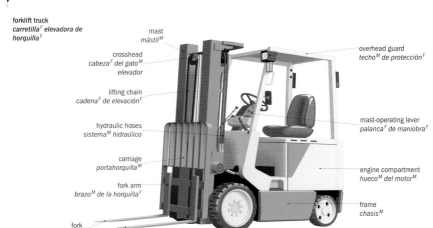

**forklift truck**
*carretilla*$^F$ *elevadora de*
*horquilla*$^F$

mast
*mástil*$^M$

crosshead
*cabeza*$^F$ *del gato*$^M$
*elevador*

lifting chain
*cadena*$^F$ *de elevación*$^F$

hydraulic hoses
*sistema*$^M$ *hidraúlico*

carriage
*portahorquilla*$^M$

fork arm
*brazo*$^M$ *de la horquilla*$^F$

fork
*horquilla*$^F$

overhead guard
*techo*$^M$ *de protección*$^F$

mast-operating lever
*palanca*$^F$ *de maniobra*$^F$

engine compartment
*hueco*$^M$ *del motor*$^M$

frame
*chasis*$^M$

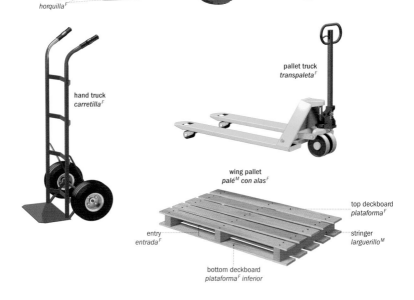

hand truck
*carretilla*$^F$

pallet truck
*transpaleta*$^F$

wing pallet
*palé*$^M$ *con alas*$^F$

top deckboard
*plataforma*$^F$

stringer
*larguerillo*$^M$

entry
*entrada*$^F$

bottom deckboard
*plataforma*$^F$ *inferior*

TRANSPORT AND MACHINERY

# cranes
*grúas*[F]

tower crane
*grúa*[F] *torre*[F]

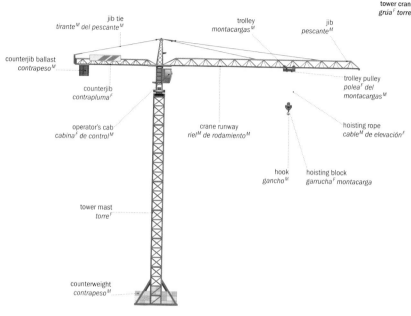

jib tie
*tirante*[M] *del pescante*[M]

trolley
*montacargas*[M]

jib
*pescante*[M]

counterjib ballast
*contrapeso*[M]

counterjib
*contrapluma*[F]

trolley pulley
*polea*[F] *del montacargas*[M]

operator's cab
*cabina*[F] *de control*[M]

crane runway
*riel*[M] *de rodamiento*[M]

hoisting rope
*cable*[M] *de elevación*[F]

hook
*gancho*[M]

hoisting block
*garrucha*[F] *montacarga*

tower mast
*torre*[F]

counterweight
*contrapeso*[M]

truck crane
*grúa*[F] *móvil*

telescopic boom
*brazo*[M] *telescópico*

elevating cylinder
*cilindro*[M] *elevador*

operator's cab
*cabina*[F] *de mando*[M]

outrigger
*estabilizador*[M]

# bulldozer
*bulldozer*[M]

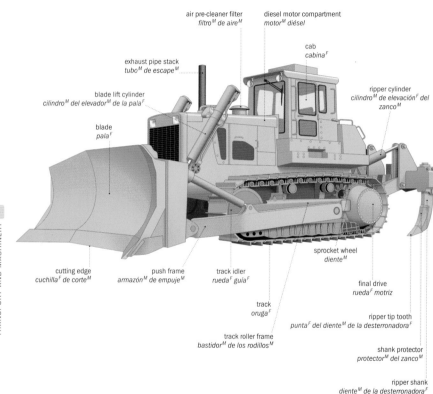

air pre-cleaner filter
*filtro*[M] *de aire*[M]

diesel motor compartment
*motor*[M] *diésel*

cab
*cabina*[F]

exhaust pipe stack
*tubo*[M] *de escape*[M]

ripper cylinder
*cilindro*[M] *de elevación*[F] *del zanco*[M]

blade lift cylinder
*cilindro*[M] *del elevador*[M] *de la pala*[F]

blade
*pala*[F]

cutting edge
*cuchilla*[F] *de corte*[M]

push frame
*armazón*[M] *de empuje*[M]

track idler
*rueda*[F] *guía*[F]

sprocket wheel
*diente*[M]

final drive
*rueda*[F] *motriz*

track
*oruga*[F]

ripper tip tooth
*punta*[F] *del diente*[M] *de la desterronadora*[F]

track roller frame
*bastidor*[M] *de los rodillos*[M]

shank protector
*protector*[M] *del zanco*[M]

ripper shank
*diente*[M] *de la desterronadora*[F]

crawler tractor
**tractor*[M] de orugas*[F]

blade
**pala*[F]

ripper
**zanco*[M]

# wheel loader
*cargadora<sup>f</sup>-retroexcavadora<sup>f</sup>*

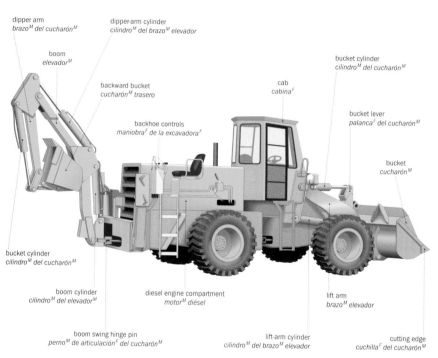

dipper arm
*brazo<sup>M</sup> del cucharón<sup>M</sup>*

dipper-arm cylinder
*cilindro<sup>M</sup> del brazo<sup>M</sup> elevador*

boom
*elevador<sup>M</sup>*

backward bucket
*cucharón<sup>M</sup> trasero*

backhoe controls
*maniobra<sup>f</sup> de la excavadora<sup>f</sup>*

bucket cylinder
*cilindro<sup>M</sup> del cucharón<sup>M</sup>*

cab
*cabina<sup>f</sup>*

bucket cylinder
*cilindro<sup>M</sup> del cucharón<sup>M</sup>*

bucket lever
*palanca<sup>f</sup> del cucharón<sup>M</sup>*

bucket
*cucharón<sup>M</sup>*

bucket cylinder
*cilindro<sup>M</sup> del cucharón<sup>M</sup>*

boom cylinder
*cilindro<sup>M</sup> del elevador<sup>M</sup>*

diesel engine compartment
*motor<sup>M</sup> diésel*

lift arm
*brazo<sup>M</sup> elevador*

boom swing hinge pin
*perno<sup>M</sup> de articulación<sup>f</sup> del cucharón<sup>M</sup>*

lift-arm cylinder
*cilindro<sup>M</sup> del brazo<sup>M</sup> elevador*

cutting edge
*cuchilla<sup>f</sup> del cucharón<sup>M</sup>*

**front-end loader**
*cargador<sup>M</sup> delantero*

**wheel tractor**
*tractor<sup>M</sup> de ruedas<sup>f</sup>*

**backhoe**
*excavadora<sup>f</sup>*

# scraper
*raspador*<sup>M</sup>

gooseneck
*cuello*<sup>M</sup> *de ganso*<sup>M</sup>

steering cylinder
*cilindro*<sup>M</sup> *de dirección*<sup>F</sup>

elevator
*elevador*<sup>M</sup>

tractor engine compartment
*motor*<sup>M</sup> *del tractor*<sup>M</sup>

draft tube
*barra*<sup>F</sup> *de arrastre*<sup>M</sup>

bowl
*contenedor*<sup>M</sup>

cutting edge
*cuchilla*<sup>F</sup> *de corte*<sup>M</sup>

draft arm
*brazo*<sup>M</sup> *de arrastre*<sup>M</sup>

# hydraulic shovel
*pala*<sup>F</sup> *hidráulica*

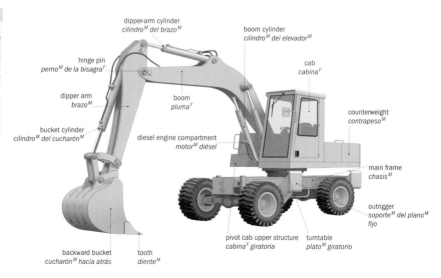

dipper-arm cylinder
*cilindro*<sup>M</sup> *del brazo*<sup>M</sup>

boom cylinder
*cilindro*<sup>M</sup> *del elevador*<sup>M</sup>

hinge pin
*perno*<sup>M</sup> *de la bisagra*<sup>F</sup>

cab
*cabina*<sup>F</sup>

dipper arm
*brazo*<sup>M</sup>

boom
*pluma*<sup>F</sup>

counterweight
*contrapeso*<sup>M</sup>

bucket cylinder
*cilindro*<sup>M</sup> *del cucharón*<sup>M</sup>

diesel engine compartment
*motor*<sup>M</sup> *diésel*

main frame
*chasis*<sup>M</sup>

outrigger
*soporte*<sup>M</sup> *del plano*<sup>M</sup> *fijo*

backward bucket
*cucharón*<sup>M</sup> *hacia atrás*

tooth
*diente*<sup>M</sup>

pivot cab upper structure
*cabina*<sup>F</sup> *giratoria*

turntable
*plato*<sup>M</sup> *giratorio*

TRANSPORT AND MACHINERY

## grader
*niveladora^F*

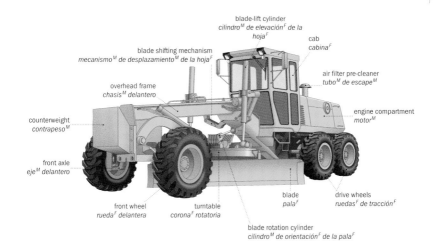

blade-lift cylinder
*cilindro^M de elevación^F de la hoja^F*

cab
*cabina^F*

blade shifting mechanism
*mecanismo^M de desplazamiento^M de la hoja^F*

air filter pre-cleaner
*tubo^M de escape^M*

overhead frame
*chasis^M delantero*

engine compartment
*motor^M*

counterweight
*contrapeso^M*

front axle
*eje^M delantero*

front wheel
*rueda^F delantera*

turntable
*corona^F rotatoria*

blade
*pala^F*

drive wheels
*ruedas^F de tracción^F*

blade rotation cylinder
*cilindro^M de orientación^F de la pala^F*

## dump truck
*volcadora^F*

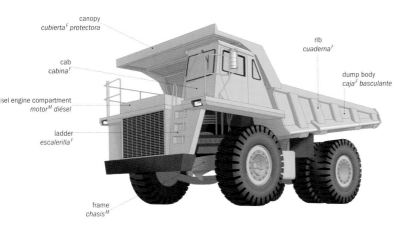

canopy
*cubierta^F protectora*

rib
*cuaderna^F*

cab
*cabina^F*

dump body
*caja^F basculante*

sel engine compartment
*motor^M diésel*

ladder
*escalerilla^F*

frame
*chasis^M*

# production of electricity from geothermal energy

*producción<sup>F</sup> de electricidad<sup>F</sup> por energía<sup>F</sup> geotérmica*

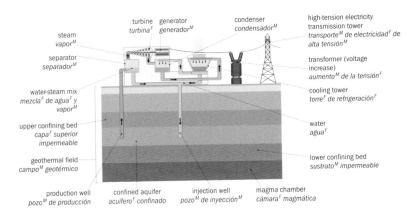

turbine
*turbina<sup>F</sup>*

generator
*generador<sup>M</sup>*

condenser
*condensador<sup>M</sup>*

high-tension electricity transmission tower
*transporte<sup>M</sup> de electricidad<sup>F</sup> de alta tensión<sup>M</sup>*

steam
*vapor<sup>M</sup>*

separator
*separador<sup>M</sup>*

transformer (voltage increase)
*aumento<sup>M</sup> de la tensión<sup>F</sup>*

water-steam mix
*mezcla<sup>F</sup> de agua<sup>F</sup> y vapor<sup>M</sup>*

cooling tower
*torre<sup>F</sup> de refrigeración<sup>F</sup>*

upper confining bed
*capa<sup>F</sup> superior impermeable*

water
*agua<sup>F</sup>*

geothermal field
*campo<sup>M</sup> geotérmico*

lower confining bed
*sustrato<sup>M</sup> impermeable*

production well
*pozo<sup>M</sup> de producción*

confined aquifer
*acuífero<sup>F</sup> confinado*

injection well
*pozo<sup>M</sup> de inyección<sup>M</sup>*

magma chamber
*cámara<sup>F</sup> magmática*

## thermal energy

*energía<sup>F</sup> térmica*

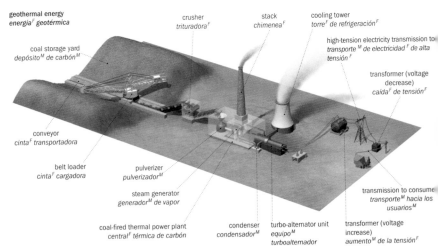

geothermal energy
*energía<sup>F</sup> geotérmica*

crusher
*trituradora<sup>F</sup>*

stack
*chimenea<sup>F</sup>*

cooling tower
*torre<sup>F</sup> de refrigeración<sup>F</sup>*

coal storage yard
*depósito<sup>M</sup> de carbón<sup>M</sup>*

high-tension electricity transmission to
*transporte<sup>M</sup> de electricidad<sup>F</sup> de alta tensión<sup>F</sup>*

transformer (voltage decrease)
*caída<sup>F</sup> de tensión<sup>F</sup>*

conveyor
*cinta<sup>F</sup> transportadora*

belt loader
*cinta<sup>F</sup> cargadora*

pulverizer
*pulverizador<sup>M</sup>*

steam generator
*generador<sup>M</sup> de vapor*

transmission to consume
*transporte<sup>M</sup> hacia los usuarios<sup>M</sup>*

coal-fired thermal power plant
*central<sup>F</sup> térmica de carbón<sup>M</sup>*

condenser
*condensador<sup>M</sup>*

turbo-alternator unit
*equipo<sup>M</sup> turboalternador*

transformer (voltage increase)
*aumento<sup>M</sup> de la tensión<sup>F</sup>*

ENERGY

# oil
*petróleo*<sup>M</sup>

surface prospecting
*prospección*<sup>F</sup> *terrestre*

seismographic recording
*registro*<sup>M</sup> *sísmico*

petroleum trap
*trampa*<sup>F</sup> *petrolífera*

shock wave
*onda*<sup>F</sup> *de choque*<sup>M</sup>

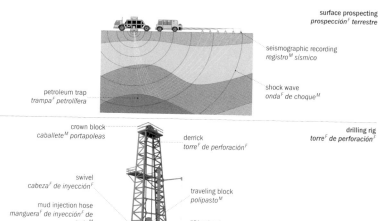

crown block
*caballete*<sup>M</sup> *portapoleas*

derrick
*torre*<sup>F</sup> *de perforación*<sup>F</sup>

drilling rig
*torre*<sup>F</sup> *de perforación*<sup>F</sup>

swivel
*cabeza*<sup>F</sup> *de inyección*<sup>F</sup>

traveling block
*polipasto*<sup>M</sup>

mud injection hose
*manguera*<sup>F</sup> *de inyección*<sup>F</sup> *de
lodo*<sup>M</sup>

lifting hook
*gancho*<sup>M</sup> *de tracción*<sup>F</sup>

drilling drawworks
*torno*<sup>M</sup> *de perforación*<sup>F</sup>

rotary system
*sistema*<sup>M</sup> *rotativo*

kelly
*vástago*<sup>M</sup> *de arrastre*<sup>M</sup>

substructure
*estructura*<sup>F</sup> *inferior*

rotary table
*mesa*<sup>F</sup> *rotatoria*

vibrating mudscreen
*tamiz*<sup>M</sup> *vibratorio para lodos*<sup>M</sup>

anticline
*anticlinal*<sup>M</sup>

drill pipe
*tubo*<sup>M</sup> *de perforación*<sup>F</sup>

mud pit
*depósito*<sup>M</sup> *de lodos*<sup>M</sup>

drill collar
*collar*<sup>M</sup> *de perforación*<sup>F</sup>

mud pump
*bomba*<sup>F</sup> *para lodos*<sup>M</sup>

bit
*barrena*<sup>F</sup>

gas
*gas*<sup>M</sup>

engine
*motor*<sup>M</sup>

oil
*petróleo*<sup>M</sup>

impervious rock
*roca*<sup>F</sup> *impermeable*

ENERGY

oil

**floating-roof tank**
*tanque^M de techo^M pontón*

ground
*conexión^F eléctrica a tierra^F*

stairs
*escalera^F*

bottom deck
*cubierta^F inferior*

manhole
*boca^F de acceso^M*

floating roof
*tapa^F flotante*

top deck
*cubierta^F superior*

sealing ring
*anillo^M sellador*

ladder
*escalerilla^F*

shell
*casco^M*

drain valve
*válvula^F de vaciado^M*

thermometer
*termómetro^M*

filling inlet
*válvula^F de llenado^M*

**crude-oil pipeline**
*oleoducto^M para crudo^M*

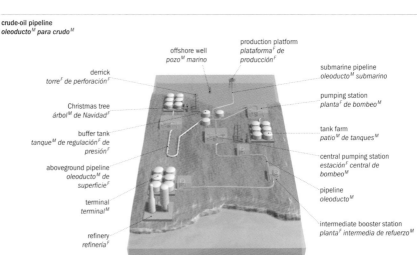

offshore well
*pozo^M marino*

production platform
*plataforma^F de producción^F*

derrick
*torre^F de perforación^F*

submarine pipeline
*oleoducto^M submarino*

Christmas tree
*árbol^M de Navidad^F*

pumping station
*planta^F de bombeo^M*

buffer tank
*tanque^M de regulación^F de presión^F*

tank farm
*patio^M de tanques^M*

aboveground pipeline
*oleoducto^M de superficie^F*

central pumping station
*estación^F central de bombeo^M*

terminal
*terminal^M*

pipeline
*oleoducto^M*

refinery
*refinería^F*

intermediate booster station
*planta^F intermedia de refuerzo^M*

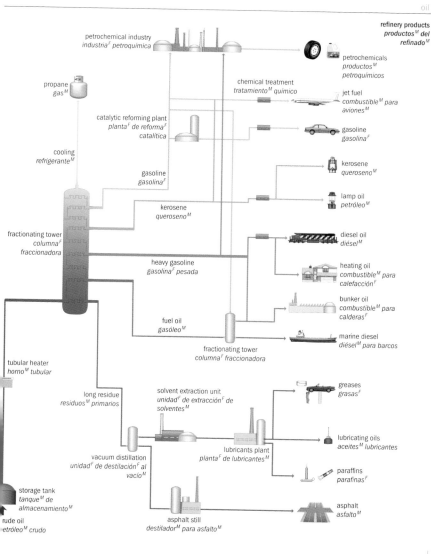

refinery products
*productos*$^M$ *del*
*refinado*$^M$

petrochemical industry
*industria*$^F$ *petroquímica*

petrochemicals
*productos*$^M$
*petroquímicos*

propane
*gas*$^M$

chemical treatment
*tratamiento*$^M$ *químico*

jet fuel
*combustible*$^M$ *para*
*aviones*$^M$

catalytic reforming plant
*planta*$^F$ *de reforma*$^F$
*catalítica*

gasoline
*gasolina*$^F$

cooling
*refrigerante*$^M$

gasoline
*gasolina*$^F$

kerosene
*queroseno*$^M$

lamp oil
*petróleo*$^M$

fractionating tower
*columna*$^F$
*fraccionadora*

kerosene
*queroseno*$^M$

diesel oil
*diésel*$^M$

heavy gasoline
*gasolina*$^F$ *pesada*

heating oil
*combustible*$^M$ *para*
*calefacción*$^F$

bunker oil
*combustible*$^M$ *para*
*calderas*$^F$

fuel oil
*gasóleo*$^M$

marine diesel
*diésel*$^M$ *para barcos*

fractionating tower
*columna*$^F$ *fraccionadora*

tubular heater
*horno*$^M$ *tubular*

long residue
*residuos*$^M$ *primarios*

solvent extraction unit
*unidad*$^F$ *de extracción*$^F$ *de*
*solventes*$^M$

greases
*grasas*$^F$

lubricating oils
*aceites*$^M$ *lubricantes*

lubricants plant
*planta*$^F$ *de lubricantes*$^M$

vacuum distillation
*unidad*$^F$ *de destilación*$^F$ *al*
*vacío*$^M$

paraffins
*parafinas*$^F$

storage tank
*tanque*$^M$ *de*
*almacenamiento*$^M$

crude oil
*petróleo*$^M$ *crudo*

asphalt still
*destilador*$^M$ *para asfalto*$^M$

asphalt
*asfalto*$^M$

ENERGY

# hydroelectric complex
*complejo<sup>M</sup> hidroeléctrico*

ENERGY

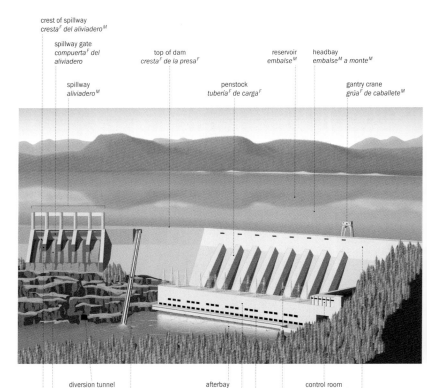

crest of spillway
*cresta<sup>F</sup> del aliviadero<sup>M</sup>*

spillway gate
*compuerta<sup>F</sup> del
aliviadero*

top of dam
*cresta<sup>F</sup> de la presa<sup>F</sup>*

reservoir
*embalse<sup>M</sup>*

headbay
*embalse<sup>M</sup> a monte<sup>M</sup>*

spillway
*aliviadero<sup>M</sup>*

penstock
*tubería<sup>F</sup> de carga<sup>F</sup>*

gantry crane
*grúa<sup>F</sup> de caballete<sup>M</sup>*

diversion tunnel
*túnel<sup>M</sup> de desvío<sup>M</sup>*

afterbay
*embalse<sup>M</sup> de
compensación<sup>F</sup>*

control room
*sala<sup>F</sup> de control<sup>M</sup>*

spillway chute
*canal<sup>M</sup> del aliviadero<sup>M</sup>*

power plant
*central<sup>F</sup> eléctrica*

bushing
*boquilla<sup>F</sup>*

training wall
*muro<sup>M</sup> de
encauzamiento<sup>M</sup>*

log chute
*rebosadero<sup>M</sup>*

machine hall
*sala<sup>F</sup> de máquinas<sup>F</sup>*

dam
*presa<sup>F</sup>*

cross section of a hydroelectric power plant
*sección^F transversal de una central^F*
*hidroeléctrica*

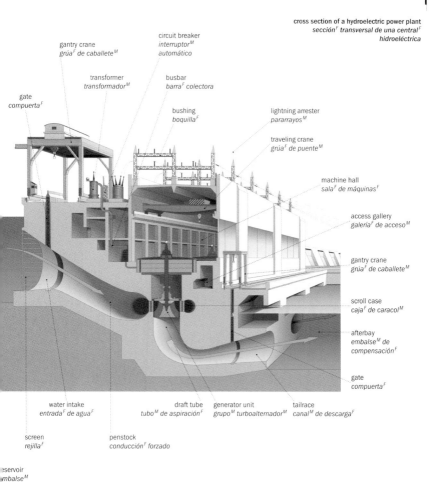

gantry crane
*grúa^F de caballete^M*

circuit breaker
*interruptor^M*
*automático*

transformer
*transformador^M*

busbar
*barra^F colectora*

gate
*compuerta^F*

bushing
*boquilla^F*

lightning arrester
*pararrayos^M*

traveling crane
*grúa^F de puente^M*

machine hall
*sala^F de máquinas^F*

access gallery
*galería^F de acceso^M*

gantry crane
*grúa^F de caballete^M*

scroll case
*caja^F de caracol^M*

afterbay
*embalse^M de*
*compensación^F*

gate
*compuerta^F*

water intake
*entrada^F de agua^F*

draft tube
*tubo^M de aspiración^F*

generator unit
*grupo^M turboalternador^M*

tailrace
*canal^M de descarga^F*

screen
*rejilla^F*

penstock
*conducción^F forzado*

reservoir
*embalse^M*

# production of electricity from nuclear energy

*producción<sup>F</sup> de electricidad<sup>F</sup> por energía<sup>F</sup> nuclear*

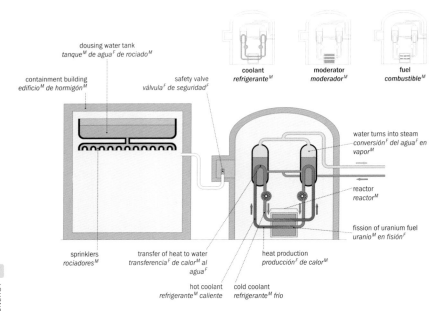

dousing water tank
*tanque<sup>M</sup> de agua<sup>F</sup> de rociado<sup>M</sup>*

coolant
*refrigerante<sup>M</sup>*

moderator
*moderador<sup>M</sup>*

fuel
*combustible<sup>M</sup>*

containment building
*edificio<sup>M</sup> de hormigón<sup>M</sup>*

safety valve
*válvula<sup>F</sup> de seguridad<sup>F</sup>*

water turns into steam
*conversión<sup>F</sup> del agua<sup>F</sup> en vapor<sup>M</sup>*

reactor
*reactor<sup>M</sup>*

fission of uranium fuel
*uranio<sup>M</sup> en fisión<sup>F</sup>*

sprinklers
*rociadores<sup>M</sup>*

transfer of heat to water
*transferencia<sup>F</sup> de calor<sup>M</sup> al agua<sup>F</sup>*

heat production
*producción<sup>F</sup> de calor<sup>M</sup>*

hot coolant
*refrigerante<sup>M</sup> caliente*

cold coolant
*refrigerante<sup>M</sup> frío*

ENERGY

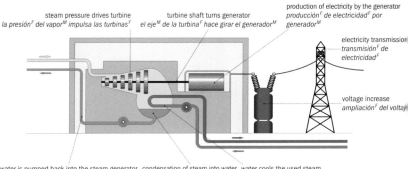

steam pressure drives turbine
*la presión<sup>F</sup> del vapor<sup>M</sup> impulsa las turbinas<sup>F</sup>*

turbine shaft turns generator
*el eje<sup>M</sup> de la turbina<sup>F</sup> hace girar el generador<sup>M</sup>*

production of electricity by the generator
*producción<sup>F</sup> de electricidad<sup>F</sup> por generador<sup>M</sup>*

electricity transmission
*transmisión<sup>F</sup> de electricidad<sup>F</sup>*

voltage increase
*ampliación<sup>F</sup> del voltaj...*

water is pumped back into the steam generator
*el agua<sup>F</sup> regresa al generador<sup>M</sup> de vapor<sup>M</sup>*

condensation of steam into water
*el vapor<sup>M</sup> se condensa en agua<sup>F</sup>*

water cools the used steam
*el agua<sup>F</sup> enfría el vapor<sup>M</sup> utilizado*

## fuel bundle
*elemento<sup>M</sup> de combustible<sup>M</sup>*

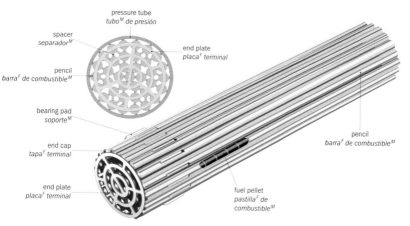

pressure tube
*tubo<sup>M</sup> de presión*

spacer
*separador<sup>M</sup>*

end plate
*placa<sup>F</sup> terminal*

pencil
*barra<sup>F</sup> de combustible<sup>M</sup>*

bearing pad
*soporte<sup>M</sup>*

end cap
*tapa<sup>F</sup> terminal*

end plate
*placa<sup>F</sup> terminal*

pencil
*barra<sup>F</sup> de combustible<sup>M</sup>*

fuel pellet
*pastilla<sup>F</sup> de
combustible<sup>M</sup>*

## nuclear reactor
*carga<sup>F</sup> del reactor<sup>M</sup> nuclear*

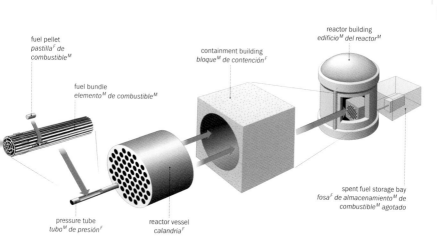

fuel pellet
*pastilla<sup>F</sup> de
combustible<sup>M</sup>*

fuel bundle
*elemento<sup>M</sup> de combustible<sup>M</sup>*

containment building
*bloque<sup>M</sup> de contención<sup>F</sup>*

reactor building
*edificio<sup>M</sup> del reactor<sup>M</sup>*

spent fuel storage bay
*fosa<sup>F</sup> de almacenamiento<sup>M</sup> de
combustible<sup>M</sup> agotado*

pressure tube
*tubo<sup>M</sup> de presión<sup>F</sup>*

reactor vessel
*calandria<sup>F</sup>*

ENERGY

# solar cell
*célula<sup>F</sup> solar*

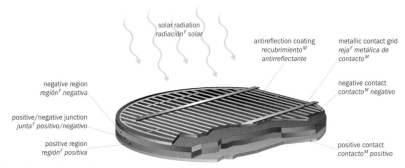

solar radiation
*radiación<sup>F</sup> solar*

antireflection coating
*recubrimiento<sup>M</sup>
antirreflectante*

metallic contact grid
*reja<sup>F</sup> metálica de
contacto<sup>M</sup>*

negative region
*región<sup>F</sup> negativa*

negative contact
*contacto<sup>M</sup> negativo*

positive/negative junction
*junta<sup>F</sup> positivo/negativo*

positive region
*región<sup>F</sup> positiva*

positive contact
*contacto<sup>M</sup> positivo*

# flat-plate solar collector
*colector<sup>M</sup> solar plano*

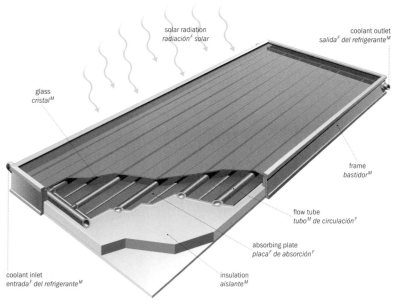

solar radiation
*radiación<sup>F</sup> solar*

coolant outlet
*salida<sup>F</sup> del refrigerante<sup>M</sup>*

glass
*cristal<sup>M</sup>*

frame
*bastidor<sup>M</sup>*

flow tube
*tubo<sup>M</sup> de circulación<sup>F</sup>*

absorbing plate
*placa<sup>F</sup> de absorción<sup>F</sup>*

coolant inlet
*entrada<sup>F</sup> del refrigerante<sup>M</sup>*

insulation
*aislante<sup>M</sup>*

ENERGY

## solar-cell system
*sistema^M de células^F solares*

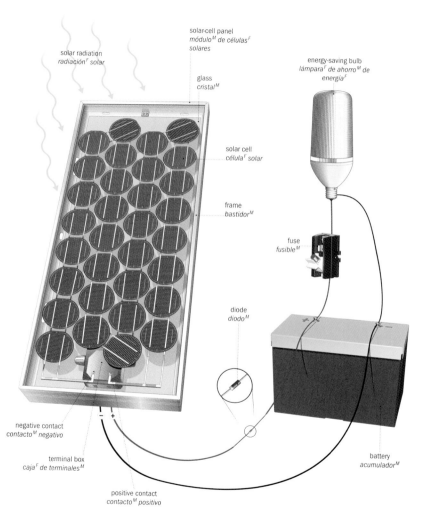

solar radiation
*radiación^F solar*

solar-cell panel
*módulo^M de células^F*
*solares*

glass
*cristal^M*

energy-saving bulb
*lámpara^F de ahorro^M de*
*energía^F*

solar cell
*célula^F solar*

frame
*bastidor^M*

fuse
*fusible^M*

diode
*diodo^M*

negative contact
*contacto^M negativo*

terminal box
*caja^F de terminales^M*

positive contact
*contacto^M positivo*

battery
*acumulador^M*

# windmill

*molino$^M$ de viento$^M$*

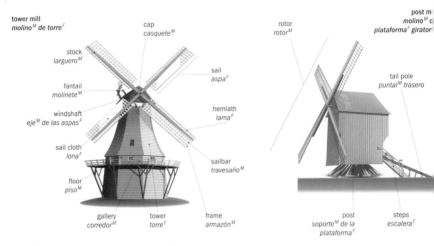

**tower mill**
*molino$^M$ de torre$^F$*

stock
*larguero$^M$*

fantail
*molinete$^M$*

windshaft
*eje$^M$ de las aspas$^F$*

sail cloth
*lona$^F$*

floor
*piso$^M$*

gallery
*corredor$^M$*

tower
*torre$^F$*

cap
*casquete$^M$*

sail
*aspa$^F$*

hemlath
*lama$^F$*

sailbar
*travesaño$^M$*

frame
*armazón$^M$*

rotor
*rotor$^M$*

**post m**
*molino$^M$ c*
*plataforma$^F$ girator*

tail pole
*puntal$^M$ trasero*

post
*soporte$^M$ de la*
*plataforma$^F$*

steps
*escalera$^F$*

# wind turbines and electricity production

*turbinas$^F$ de viento$^M$ y producción$^F$ eléctrica*

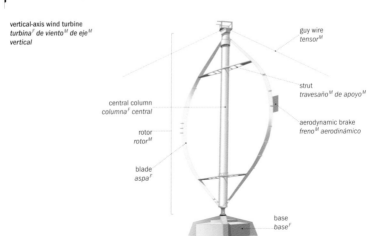

**vertical-axis wind turbine**
*turbina$^F$ de viento$^M$ de eje$^M$*
*vertical*

central column
*columna$^F$ central*

rotor
*rotor$^M$*

blade
*aspa$^F$*

guy wire
*tensor$^M$*

strut
*travesaño$^M$ de apoyo$^M$*

aerodynamic brake
*freno$^M$ aerodinámico*

base
*base$^F$*

ENERGY

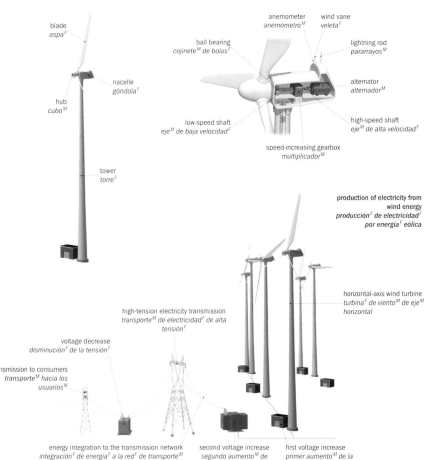

horizontal-axis wind turbine
*turbina*$^F$ *de viento*$^M$ *de eje*$^M$
*horizontal*

blade
*aspa*$^F$

nacelle
*góndola*$^F$

hub
*cubo*$^M$

tower
*torre*$^F$

nacelle cross-section
*sección*$^F$ *transversal de la*
*góndola*$^F$

anemometer
*anemómetro*$^M$

wind vane
*veleta*$^F$

ball bearing
*cojinete*$^M$ *de bolas*$^F$

lightning rod
*pararrayos*$^M$

alternator
*alternador*$^M$

low-speed shaft
*eje*$^M$ *de baja velocidad*$^F$

high-speed shaft
*eje*$^M$ *de alta velocidad*$^F$

speed-increasing gearbox
*multiplicador*$^M$

production of electricity from
wind energy
*producción*$^F$ *de electricidad*$^F$
*por energía*$^F$ *eólica*

horizontal-axis wind turbine
*turbina*$^F$ *de viento*$^M$ *de eje*$^M$
*horizontal*

high-tension electricity transmission
*transporte*$^M$ *de electricidad*$^F$ *de alta*
*tensión*$^F$

voltage decrease
*disminución*$^F$ *de la tensión*$^F$

transmission to consumers
*transporte*$^M$ *hacia los*
*usuarios*$^M$

energy integration to the transmission network
*integración*$^F$ *de energía*$^F$ *a la red*$^F$ *de transporte*$^M$

second voltage increase
*segundo aumento*$^M$ *de*
*tensión*$^F$

first voltage increase
*primer aumento*$^M$ *de la*
*tensión*$^F$

ENERGY

# matter
*materia*[F]

atom
*átomo*[M]

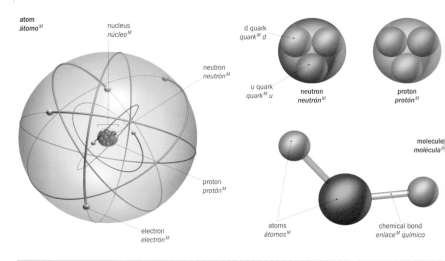

nucleus
*núcleo*[M]

neutron
*neutrón*[M]

d quark
*quark*[M] *d*

u quark
*quark*[M] *u*

neutron
*neutrón*[M]

proton
*protón*[M]

molecule
*molécula*[F]

proton
*protón*[M]

electron
*electrón*[M]

atoms
*átomos*[M]

chemical bond
*enlace*[M] *químico*

states of matter
*estados*[M] *de la materia*[F]

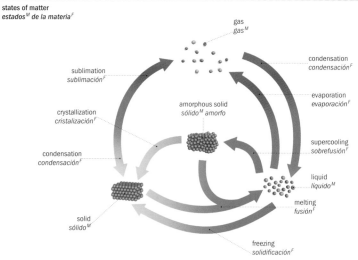

gas
*gas*[M]

sublimation
*sublimación*[F]

condensation
*condensación*[F]

evaporation
*evaporación*[F]

crystallization
*cristalización*[F]

amorphous solid
*sólido*[M] *amorfo*

supercooling
*sobrefusión*[F]

condensation
*condensación*[F]

liquid
*líquido*[M]

melting
*fusión*[F]

solid
*sólido*[M]

freezing
*solidificación*[F]

matter

**nuclear fission**
*fisión[F] nuclear*

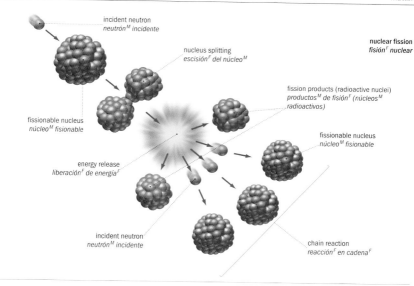

incident neutron
*neutrón[M] incidente*

nucleus splitting
*escisión[F] del núcleo[M]*

fission products (radioactive nuclei)
*productos[M] de fisión[F] (núcleos[M] radioactivos)*

fissionable nucleus
*núcleo[M] fisionable*

fissionable nucleus
*núcleo[M] fisionable*

energy release
*liberación[F] de energía[F]*

incident neutron
*neutrón[M] incidente*

chain reaction
*reacción[F] en cadena[F]*

**heat transfer**
*transmisión[F] de calor[M]*

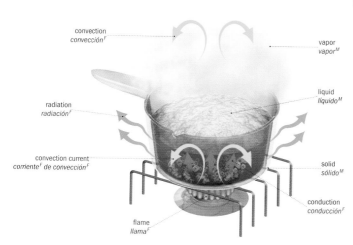

convection
*convección[F]*

vapor
*vapor[M]*

radiation
*radiación[F]*

liquid
*líquido[M]*

convection current
*corriente[F] de convección[F]*

solid
*sólido[M]*

conduction
*conducción[F]*

flame
*llama[F]*

SCIENCE

# magnetism
*magnetismo*<sup>M</sup>

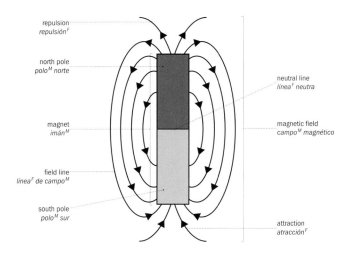

repulsion
*repulsión*<sup>F</sup>

north pole
*polo*<sup>M</sup> *norte*

magnet
*imán*<sup>M</sup>

field line
*línea*<sup>F</sup> *de campo*<sup>M</sup>

south pole
*polo*<sup>M</sup> *sur*

neutral line
*línea*<sup>F</sup> *neutra*

magnetic field
*campo*<sup>M</sup> *magnético*

attraction
*atracción*<sup>F</sup>

# parallel electrical circuit
*circuito*<sup>M</sup> *eléctrico en paralelo*<sup>M</sup>

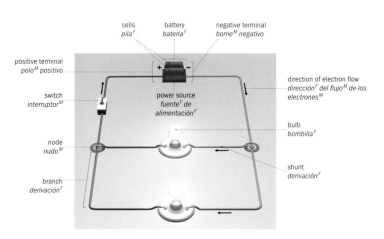

cells
*pila*<sup>F</sup>

battery
*batería*<sup>F</sup>

negative terminal
*borne*<sup>M</sup> *negativo*

positive terminal
*polo*<sup>M</sup> *positivo*

switch
*interruptor*<sup>M</sup>

power source
*fuente*<sup>F</sup> *de alimentación*<sup>F</sup>

direction of electron flow
*dirección*<sup>F</sup> *del flujo*<sup>M</sup> *de los electrones*<sup>M</sup>

node
*nudo*<sup>M</sup>

branch
*derivación*<sup>F</sup>

bulb
*bombilla*<sup>F</sup>

shunt
*derivación*<sup>F</sup>

SCIENCE

# dry cells
*pilas<sup>F</sup> secas*

## carbon-zinc cell
*pila<sup>F</sup> de carbón<sup>M</sup>-cinc<sup>M</sup>*

sealing plug
*tapa<sup>F</sup> de cierre<sup>M</sup>*

positive terminal
*borne<sup>M</sup> positivo*

washer
*arandela<sup>F</sup>*

top cap
*tapa<sup>F</sup> superior*

electrolytic separator
*separador<sup>M</sup> electrolítico*

jacket
*funda<sup>F</sup>*

carbon rod (cathode)
*varilla<sup>F</sup> de carbón<sup>M</sup>
(cátodo<sup>M</sup>)*

depolarizing mix
*sustancia<sup>F</sup> despolarizante*

zinc can (anode)
*caja<sup>F</sup> de cinc<sup>M</sup>
(ánodo<sup>M</sup>)*

bottom cap
*tapa<sup>F</sup> inferior*

negative terminal
*polo<sup>M</sup> negativo*

## alkaline manganese-zinc cell
*pila<sup>F</sup> alcalina de manganeso<sup>M</sup>-cinc<sup>M</sup>*

zinc-electrolyte mix (anode)
*mezcla<sup>F</sup> de cinc<sup>M</sup> y electrolito<sup>M</sup>
(ánodo<sup>M</sup>)*

sealing material
*material<sup>M</sup> de cierre<sup>M</sup>*

electron collector
*colector<sup>M</sup> de electrones<sup>M</sup>*

steel casing
*encofrado<sup>M</sup> metálico*

separator
*separador<sup>M</sup>*

manganese mix (cathode)
*mezcla<sup>F</sup> de manganeso<sup>M</sup> (cátodo<sup>M</sup>)*

sealing plug
*tapa<sup>F</sup> de sellado<sup>M</sup>*

bottom cap
*tapa<sup>F</sup> inferior*

direction of electron flow
*dirección<sup>F</sup> de flujo<sup>M</sup> de electrones<sup>M</sup>*

# electronics
*electrónica<sup>F</sup>*

SCIENCE

## printed circuit board
*tarjeta<sup>F</sup> de circuito<sup>M</sup>
impreso*

ceramic capacitor
*condensador<sup>M</sup> de cerámica<sup>F</sup>*

electrolytic capacitors
*condensadores<sup>M</sup> electrolíticos*

plastic film capacitor
*condensador<sup>M</sup> de
película<sup>F</sup> plástica*

packaged integrated
circuit
*placa<sup>F</sup> de circuito<sup>M</sup>
impreso*

printed circuit
*circuito<sup>M</sup> impreso*

resistors
*resistencias<sup>F</sup>*

dual-in-line package
*caja<sup>F</sup> de doble fila<sup>F</sup> de conexiones<sup>F</sup>*

## packaged integrated circuit
*placa<sup>F</sup> de circuito<sup>M</sup> impreso*

integrated circuit
*circuito<sup>M</sup> integrado*

lid
*tapa<sup>F</sup>*

wire
*hilo<sup>M</sup>*

connection pin
*clavija<sup>F</sup> de conexión<sup>F</sup>*

# electromagnetic spectrum
*espectro ᴹ electromagnético*

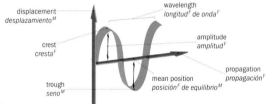

microwaves
*microondas ᶠ*

ultraviolet radiation
*radiación ᶠ ultravioleta*

radio waves
*ondas ᶠ radio*

infrared radiation
*radiación ᶠ infrarroja*

X-rays
*rayos ᴹ X*

gamma rays
*rayos ᴹ gamma*

visible light
*luz ᶠ visible*

# wave
*onda ᶠ*

displacement
*desplazamiento ᴹ*

wavelength
*longitud ᶠ de onda ᶠ*

amplitude
*amplitud ᶠ*

crest
*cresta ᶠ*

propagation
*propagación ᶠ*

trough
*seno ᴹ*

mean position
*posición ᶠ de equilibrio ᴹ*

# color synthesis
*síntesis ᶠ de los colores ᴹ*

SCIENCE

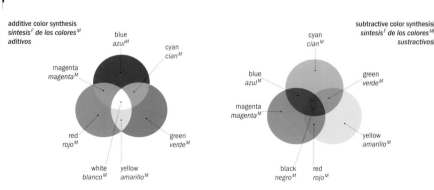

**additive color synthesis**
*síntesis ᶠ de los colores ᴹ aditivos*

blue
*azul ᴹ*

cyan
*cian ᴹ*

magenta
*magenta ᴹ*

red
*rojo ᴹ*

green
*verde ᴹ*

white
*blanco ᴹ*

yellow
*amarillo ᴹ*

**subtractive color synthesis**
*síntesis ᶠ de los colores ᴹ sustractivos*

cyan
*cian ᴹ*

blue
*azul ᴹ*

green
*verde ᴹ*

magenta
*magenta ᴹ*

yellow
*amarillo ᴹ*

black
*negro ᴹ*

red
*rojo ᴹ*

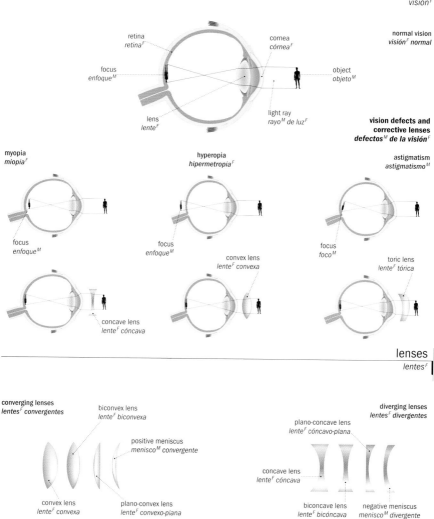

# vision
*visión<sup>F</sup>*

**normal vision**
*visión<sup>F</sup> normal*

retina
*retina<sup>F</sup>*

cornea
*córnea<sup>F</sup>*

focus
*enfoque<sup>M</sup>*

object
*objeto<sup>M</sup>*

lens
*lente<sup>F</sup>*

light ray
*rayo<sup>M</sup> de luz<sup>F</sup>*

**vision defects and corrective lenses**
*defectos<sup>M</sup> de la visión<sup>F</sup>*

myopia
*miopía<sup>F</sup>*

hyperopia
*hipermetropía<sup>F</sup>*

astigmatism
*astigmatismo<sup>M</sup>*

focus
*enfoque<sup>M</sup>*

focus
*enfoque<sup>M</sup>*

focus
*foco<sup>M</sup>*

convex lens
*lente<sup>F</sup> convexa*

toric lens
*lente<sup>F</sup> tórica*

concave lens
*lente<sup>F</sup> cóncava*

# lenses
*lentes<sup>F</sup>*

**converging lenses**
*lentes<sup>F</sup> convergentes*

biconvex lens
*lente<sup>F</sup> biconvexa*

positive meniscus
*menisco<sup>M</sup> convergente*

convex lens
*lente<sup>F</sup> convexa*

plano-convex lens
*lente<sup>F</sup> convexo-plana*

**diverging lenses**
*lentes<sup>F</sup> divergentes*

plano-concave lens
*lente<sup>F</sup> cóncavo-plana*

concave lens
*lente<sup>F</sup> cóncava*

biconcave lens
*lente<sup>F</sup> bicóncava*

negative meniscus
*menisco<sup>M</sup> divergente*

SCIENCE

# pulsed ruby laser
*láser<sup>M</sup> de rubí<sup>M</sup> pulsado*

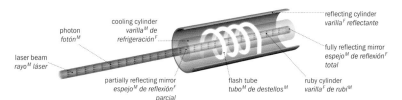

reflecting cylinder
*varilla<sup>F</sup> reflectante*

photon
*fotón<sup>M</sup>*

cooling cylinder
*varilla<sup>M</sup> de refrigeración<sup>F</sup>*

fully reflecting mirror
*espejo<sup>M</sup> de reflexión<sup>F</sup> total*

laser beam
*rayo<sup>M</sup> láser*

partially reflecting mirror
*espejo<sup>M</sup> de reflexión<sup>F</sup> parcial*

flash tube
*tubo<sup>M</sup> de destellos<sup>M</sup>*

ruby cylinder
*varilla<sup>F</sup> de rubí<sup>M</sup>*

# prism binoculars
*prismáticos<sup>M</sup> binoculares*

eyepiece
*ocular<sup>M</sup>*

focusing ring
*anillo<sup>M</sup> de enfoque<sup>M</sup>*

lens system
*sistema<sup>M</sup> de lentes<sup>F</sup>*

central focusing wheel
*rueda<sup>F</sup> central de enfoque<sup>M</sup>*

Porro prism
*prisma<sup>M</sup> de Porro*

hinge
*bisagra<sup>F</sup>*

bridge
*puente<sup>M</sup>*

objective lens
*objetivo<sup>M</sup>*

body
*tubo<sup>M</sup>*

# telescopic sight
*visor<sup>M</sup> telescópico*

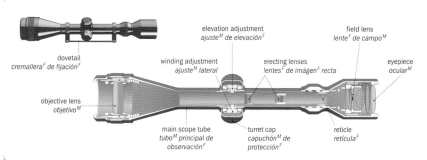

elevation adjustment
*ajuste<sup>M</sup> de elevación<sup>F</sup>*

field lens
*lente<sup>F</sup> de campo<sup>M</sup>*

dovetail
*cremallera<sup>F</sup> de fijación<sup>F</sup>*

winding adjustment
*ajuste<sup>M</sup> lateral*

erecting lenses
*lentes<sup>F</sup> de imágen<sup>F</sup> recta*

eyepiece
*ocular<sup>M</sup>*

objective lens
*objetivo<sup>M</sup>*

main scope tube
*tubo<sup>M</sup> principal de observación<sup>F</sup>*

turret cap
*capuchón<sup>M</sup> de protección<sup>F</sup>*

reticle
*retícula<sup>F</sup>*

SCIENCE

# magnifying glass and microscopes
*lupa* y *microscopios*

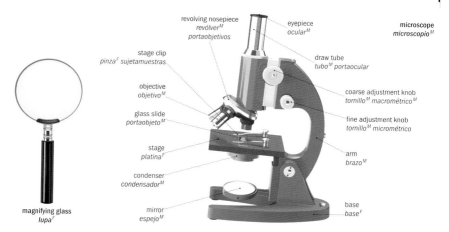

microscope
*microscopio*

revolving nosepiece
*revólver*
*portaobjetivos*

eyepiece
*ocular*

draw tube
*tubo portaocular*

stage clip
*pinza sujetamuestras*

coarse adjustment knob
*tornillo macrométrico*

objective
*objetivo*

fine adjustment knob
*tornillo micrométrico*

glass slide
*portaobjeto*

stage
*platina*

arm
*brazo*

condenser
*condensador*

mirror
*espejo*

base
*base*

magnifying glass
*lupa*

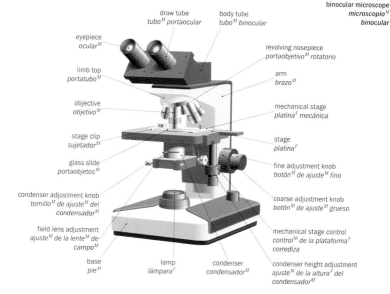

binocular microscope
*microscopio*
*binocular*

draw tube
*tubo portaocular*

body tube
*tubo binocular*

eyepiece
*ocular*

revolving nosepiece
*portaobjetivo rotatorio*

limb top
*portatubo*

arm
*brazo*

objective
*objetivo*

mechanical stage
*platina mecánica*

stage clip
*sujetador*

stage
*platina*

glass slide
*portaobjetos*

fine adjustment knob
*botón de ajuste fino*

condenser adjustment knob
*tornillo de ajuste del*
*condensador*

coarse adjustment knob
*botón de ajuste grueso*

field lens adjustment
*ajuste de la lente de*
*campo*

mechanical stage control
*control de la plataforma*
*corrediza*

base
*pie*

lamp
*lámpara*

condenser
*condensador*

condenser height adjustment
*ajuste de la altura del*
*condensador*

# measurement of weight
*medición<sup>F</sup> del peso<sup>M</sup>*

beam balance
*balanza<sup>F</sup> de astil<sup>M</sup>*

beam
*astil<sup>M</sup>*

pan
*platillo<sup>M</sup>*

weight
*pesa<sup>F</sup>*

steelyard
*báscula<sup>F</sup> romana*

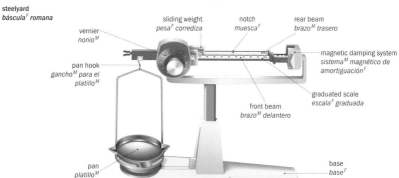

sliding weight
*pesa<sup>F</sup> corrediza*

notch
*muesca<sup>F</sup>*

rear beam
*brazo<sup>M</sup> trasero*

vernier
*nonio<sup>M</sup>*

pan hook
*gancho<sup>M</sup> para el
platillo<sup>M</sup>*

magnetic damping system
*sistema<sup>M</sup> magnético de
amortiguación<sup>F</sup>*

graduated scale
*escala<sup>F</sup> graduada*

front beam
*brazo<sup>M</sup> delantero*

pan
*platillo<sup>M</sup>*

base
*base<sup>F</sup>*

Roberval's balance
*balanza<sup>F</sup> de Roberval*

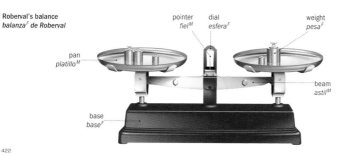

pointer
*fiel<sup>M</sup>*

dial
*esfera<sup>F</sup>*

weight
*pesa<sup>F</sup>*

pan
*platillo<sup>M</sup>*

beam
*astil<sup>M</sup>*

base
*base<sup>F</sup>*

SCIENCE

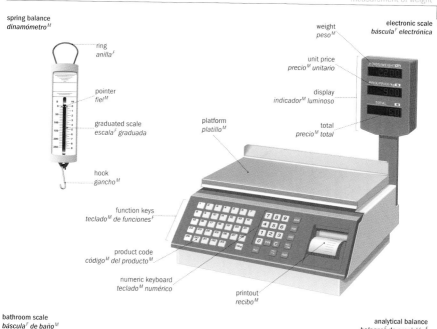

spring balance
*dinamómetro* M

ring
*anilla* F

pointer
*fiel* M

graduated scale
*escala* F *graduada*

hook
*gancho* M

weight
*peso* M

unit price
*precio* M *unitario*

display
*indicador* M *luminoso*

total
*precio* M *total*

electronic scale
*báscula* F *electrónica*

platform
*platillo* M

function keys
*teclado* M *de funciones* F

product code
*código* M *del producto* M

numeric keyboard
*teclado* M *numérico*

printout
*recibo* M

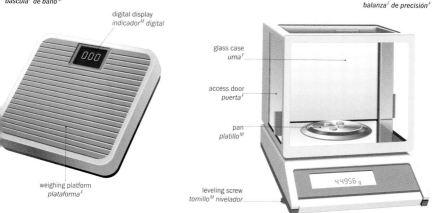

bathroom scale
*báscula* F *de baño* M

digital display
*indicador* M *digital*

weighing platform
*plataforma* F

analytical balance
*balanza* F *de precisión* F

glass case
*urna* F

access door
*puerta* F

pan
*platillo* M

leveling screw
*tornillo* M *nivelador*

SCIENCE

# measurement of temperature

*medición[F] de la temperatura[F]*

thermometer
*termómetro[M]*

Fahrenheit scale
*escala[F] Fahrenheit*

Celsius scale
*escala[F] Celsius*

temperature measured in
Fahrenheit
*grados[M] F*

temperature measured in
Celsius
*grados[M] C*

alcohol column
*columna[F] de alcohol[M]*

alcohol bulb
*cubeta[F] de alcohol[M]*

clinical thermomete
*termómetro[M] clínic*

capillary tube
*tubo[M] capilar*

expansion chamber
*cámara[F] de expansión[F]*

scale
*escala[F] de temperaturas[F]*

stem
*tubo[M] de cristal[M]*

column of mercury
*columna[F] de mercurio[M]*

mercury bulb
*cubeta[F] de mercurio[M]*

constriction
*estrechamiento[M]*

# measurement of time

*medición[F] del tiempo[M]*

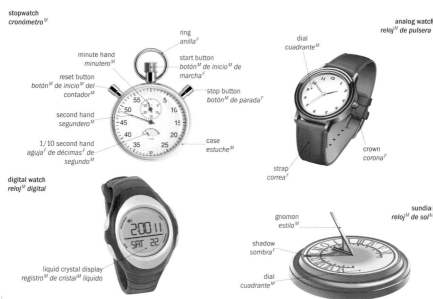

stopwatch
*cronómetro[M]*

ring
*anilla[F]*

minute hand
*minutero[M]*

start button
*botón[M] de inicio[M] de marcha[F]*

reset button
*botón[M] de inicio[M] del contador[M]*

stop button
*botón[M] de parada[F]*

second hand
*segundero[M]*

1/10 second hand
*aguja[F] de décimas[F] de segundo[M]*

case
*estuche[M]*

analog watch
*reloj[M] de pulsera*

dial
*cuadrante[M]*

crown
*corona[F]*

strap
*correa[F]*

digital watch
*reloj[M] digital*

liquid crystal display
*registro[M] de cristal[M] líquido*

sundia
*reloj[M] de sol*

gnomon
*estilo[M]*

shadow
*sombra[F]*

dial
*cuadrante[M]*

SCIENCE

# measurement of length
*medición<sup>F</sup> de la longitud<sup>F</sup>*

ruler
*regla<sup>F</sup> graduada*

scales
*escala<sup>F</sup> graduada*

# measurement of thickness
*medición<sup>F</sup> del espesor<sup>M</sup>*

vernier caliper
*escala<sup>F</sup> graduada de vernier<sup>M</sup>, pico<sup>M</sup> de rey<sup>M</sup>*

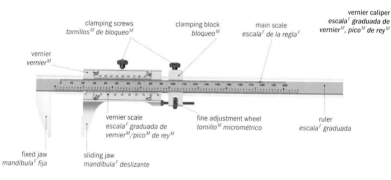

clamping screws
*tornillos<sup>M</sup> de bloqueo<sup>M</sup>*

clamping block
*bloqueo<sup>M</sup>*

main scale
*escala<sup>F</sup> de la regla<sup>F</sup>*

vernier
*vernier<sup>M</sup>*

vernier scale
*escala<sup>F</sup> graduada de vernier<sup>M</sup>/pico<sup>M</sup> de rey<sup>M</sup>*

fine adjustment wheel
*tornillo<sup>M</sup> micrométrico*

ruler
*escala<sup>F</sup> graduada*

fixed jaw
*mandíbula<sup>F</sup> fija*

sliding jaw
*mandíbula<sup>F</sup> deslizante*

micrometer caliper
*micrómetro<sup>M</sup>*

anvil
*tope<sup>M</sup> fijo*

spindle
*tope<sup>M</sup> móvil*

finely threaded screw
*rosca<sup>F</sup>*

ratchet knob
*husillo<sup>M</sup>*

lock nut
*tuerca<sup>F</sup> de bloqueo<sup>M</sup>*

thimble
*tambor<sup>M</sup>*

frame
*cuerpo<sup>M</sup>*

SCIENCE

# international system of units
*sistema^M internacional de unidades^F de medida^F*

**unit of frequency**
***unidad^F de medida^F de frecuencia^F***

## Hz
hertz
*hercio^M*

**unit of electric potential difference**
***unidad^F de medida^F de la diferencia^F de potencial^M eléctrico***

## V
volt
*voltio^M , volt^M*

**unit of electric charge**
***unidad^F de medida^F de carga^F eléctrica***

## C
coulomb
*culombio^M*

**unit of energy**
***unidad^F de medida^F energía^F***

## J
joule
*julio^M*

**unit of power**
***unidad^F de medida^F de potencia^F eléctrica***

## W
watt
*vatio^M*

**unit of force**
***unidad^F de medida^F de fuerza^F***

## N
newton
*newton^M*

**unit of electric resistance**
***unidad^F de medida^F de resistencia^F eléctrica***

## Ω
ohm
*ohmnio^M/ohm^M*

**unit of electric current**
***unidad^F de medida^F de corriente^F eléctrica***

## A
ampere
*amperio^M*

**unit of length**
***unidad^F de medida^F de longitud^F***

## m
meter
*metro^M*

**unit of mass**
***unidad^F de medida^F de masa^F***

## kg
kilogram
*kilogramo^M*

**unit of temperature**
***unidad^F de medida^F de la temperatura^F***

## °C
degree Celsius
*grado^M Celsius*

**unit of thermodynamic temperature**
***unidad^F de medida^F de temperatura termodinámica***

## K
kelvin
*kelvin^M*

**unit of amount of substance**
***unidad^F de medida^F de cantidad^F de materia^F***

## mol
mole
*mole^M*

**unit of radioactivity**
***unidad^F de medida^F de radioactividad^F***

## Bq
becquerel
*becquerel^M*

**unit of pressure**
***unidad^F de medida^F de presión^F***

## Pa
pascal
*pascal^M*

**unit of luminous intensity**
***unidad^F de medida^F de intensidad^F luminosa***

## cd
candela
*candela^F*

# biology
*biología^F*

male
*masculino^M*

female
*femenino^M*

Rh+
blood factor RH positive
*factor^M RH positivo*

Rh-
blood factor RH negative
*factor^M RH negativo*

death
*muerte^F*

★
birth
*nacimiento^M*

# mathematics
*matemáticas*[F]

minus/negative
*resta*[F]

plus/positive
*suma*[F]

multiplied by
*multiplicación*[F]

divided by
*división*[F]

equals
*igual a*

≠
is not equal to
*no es igual a*

is approximately equal to
*casi igual a*

⌣
is equivalent to
*equivalente a*

≡
is identical to
*idéntico a*

≢
is not identical to
*no es idéntico a*

±
plus or minus
*más*[M] *o menos*[M]

≤
is less than or equal to
*igual o menor que*

>
is greater than
*mayor que*

≥
is greater than or equal to
*igual o mayor que*

<
is less than
*menor que*

∅
empty set
*conjunto*[M] *vacío*

∪
union of two sets
*unión*[F]

∩
intersection of two sets
*intersección*[F]

⊂
is included in/is a subset of
*inclusión*[F]

%
percent
*porcentaje*[M]

∈
is an element of
*pertenece a*

∉
is not an element of
*no pertenece a*

Σ
sum
*suma*[F]

√
square root of
*raíz*[F] *cuadrada de*

½
fraction
*fracción*[M]

∞
infinity
*infinito*[M]

∫
integral
*integral*

!
factorial
*factorial*

---

**Roman numerals**
*números*[M] **romanos**

I
one
*uno*

V
five
*cinco*

X
ten
*diez*

L
fifty
*cincuenta*

C
one hundred
*cien*

D
five hundred
*quinientos*

M
one thousand
*mil*

SCIENCE

# geometry
*geometría* F

○
degree
*grado* M

'
minute
*minuto* M

"
second
*segundo* M

π
pi
*pi* M

⊥
perpendicular
*perpendicular* F

‖
is parallel to
es paralelo a

⫲
is not parallel to
no es paralelo a

∟
right angle
*ángulo* M *recto*

∠
obtuse angle
*ángulo* M *obtuso*

∠
acute angle
*ángulo* M *agudo*

# geometrical shapes
*formas* F *geométricas*

**examples of angles**
*ejemplos* M *de ángulos* M

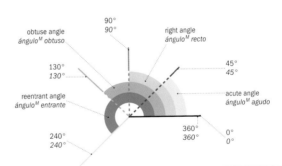

obtuse angle
*ángulo* M *obtuso*

90°
90°

right angle
*ángulo* M *recto*

130°
130°

45°
45°

reentrant angle
*ángulo* M *entrante*

acute angle
*ángulo* M *agudo*

240°
240°

360°
360°

0°
0°

**plane surfaces**
*superficies* F

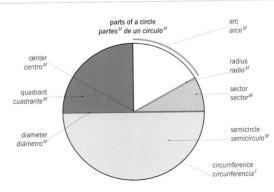

parts of a circle
*partes* M *de un círculo* M

arc
*arco* M

center
*centro* M

radius
*radio* M

quadrant
*cuadrante* M

sector
*sector* M

diameter
*diámetro* M

semicircle
*semicírculo* M

circumference
*circunferencia* F

SCIENCE

## polygons
### *polígonos* [M]

triangle
*triángulo* [M]

square
*cuadrado* [M]

rectangle
*rectángulo* [M]

rhombus
*rombo* [M]

trapezoid
*trapecio* [M]

parallelogram
*paralelogramo* [M]

quadrilateral
*cuadrilátero* [M]

regular pentagon
*pentágono* [M] *regular*

regular hexagon
*hexágono* [M] *regular*

regular heptagon
*heptágono* [M] *regular*

regular octagon
*octágono* [M] *regular*

regular nonagon
*nonágono* [M] *regular*

regular decagon
*decágono* [M] *regular*

regular hendecagon
*endecágono* [M] *regular*

regular dodecagon
*dodecágono* [M] *regular*

## solids
### *cuerpos* [M] *sólidos* [M]

helix
*hélice* [F]

torus
*toro* [M]

hemisphere
*hemisferio* [M]

sphere
*esfera* [F]

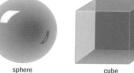

cube
*cubo* [M]

cone
*cono* [M]

pyramid
*pirámide* [M]

cylinder
*cilindro* [M]

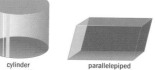

parallelepiped
*paralelepípedo* [M]

regular octahedron
*octaedro* [M] *regular*

SCIENCE

# agglomeration
*conurbación^F*

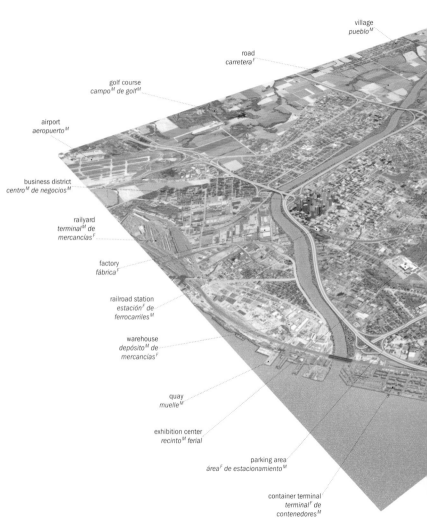

village
*pueblo^M*

road
*carretera^F*

golf course
*campo^M de golf^M*

airport
*aeropuerto^M*

business district
*centro^M de negocios^M*

railyard
*terminal^M de
mercancías^F*

factory
*fábrica^F*

railroad station
*estación^F de
ferrocarriles^M*

warehouse
*depósito^M de
mercancías^F*

quay
*muelle^M*

exhibition center
*recinto^M ferial*

parking area
*área^F de estacionamiento^M*

container terminal
*terminal^F de
contenedores^M*

SOCIETY

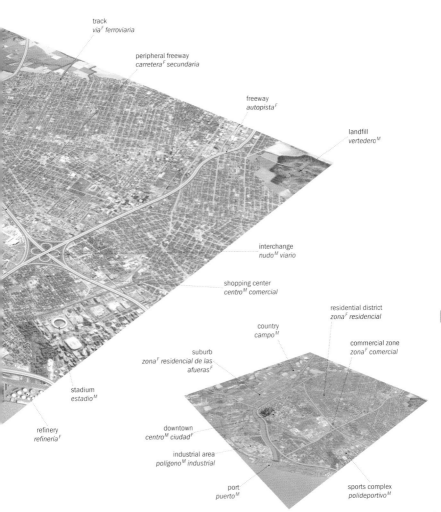

track
*vía*<sup>F</sup> *ferroviaria*

peripheral freeway
*carretera*<sup>F</sup> *secundaria*

freeway
*autopista*<sup>F</sup>

landfill
*vertedero*<sup>M</sup>

interchange
*nudo*<sup>M</sup> *viario*

shopping center
*centro*<sup>M</sup> *comercial*

residential district
*zona*<sup>F</sup> *residencial*

country
*campo*<sup>M</sup>

commercial zone
*zona*<sup>F</sup> *comercial*

suburb
*zona*<sup>F</sup> *residencial de las afueras*<sup>F</sup>

stadium
*estadio*<sup>M</sup>

refinery
*refinería*<sup>F</sup>

downtown
*centro*<sup>M</sup> *ciudad*<sup>F</sup>

industrial area
*polígono*<sup>M</sup> *industrial*

port
*puerto*<sup>M</sup>

sports complex
*polideportivo*<sup>M</sup>

SOCIETY

431

# downtown
*centro^M ciudad^F*

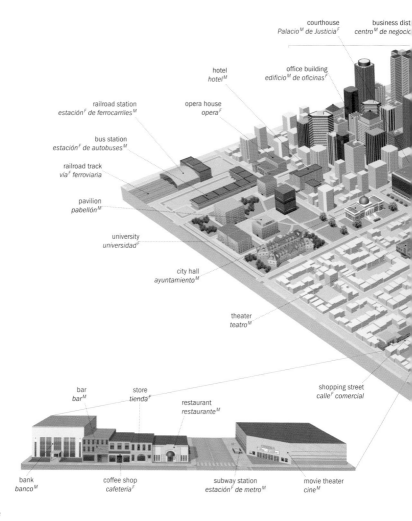

courthouse
*Palacio^M de Justicia^F*

business dist
*centro^M de negocio*

hotel
*hotel^M*

office building
*edificio^M de oficinas^F*

railroad station
*estación^F de ferrocarriles^M*

opera house
*opera^F*

bus station
*estación^F de autobuses^M*

railroad track
*vía^F ferroviaria*

pavilion
*pabellón^M*

university
*universidad^F*

city hall
*ayuntamiento^M*

theater
*teatro^M*

shopping street
*calle^F comercial*

bar
*bar^M*

store
*tienda^F*

restaurant
*restaurante^M*

bank
*banco^M*

coffee shop
*cafetería^F*

subway station
*estación^F de metro^M*

movie theater
*cine^M*

SOCIETY

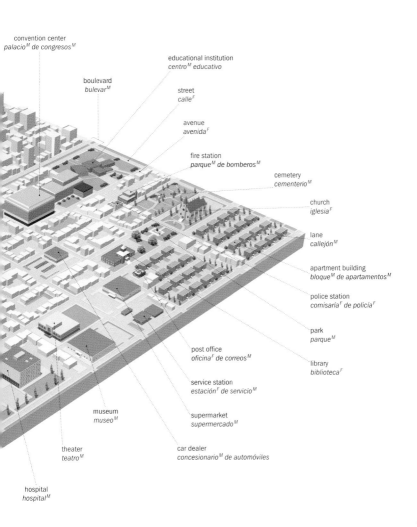

convention center
*palacio* M *de congresos* M

educational institution
*centro* M *educativo*

boulevard
*bulevar* M

street
*calle* F

avenue
*avenida* F

fire station
*parque* M *de bomberos* M

cemetery
*cementerio* M

church
*iglesia* F

lane
*callejón* M

apartment building
*bloque* M *de apartamentos* M

police station
*comisaría* F *de policía* F

park
*parque* M

library
*biblioteca* F

post office
*oficina* F *de correos* M

service station
*estación* F *de servicio* M

museum
*museo* M

supermarket
*supermercado* M

theater
*teatro* M

car dealer
*concesionario* M *de automóviles*

hospital
*hospital* M

# cross section of a street

*vista<sup>F</sup> transversal de una calle<sup>F</sup>*

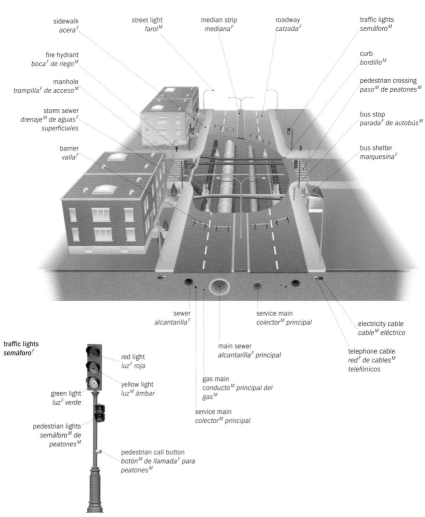

sidewalk
*acera<sup>F</sup>*

street light
*farol<sup>M</sup>*

median strip
*mediana<sup>F</sup>*

roadway
*calzada<sup>F</sup>*

traffic lights
*semáforo<sup>M</sup>*

fire hydrant
*boca<sup>F</sup> de riego<sup>M</sup>*

curb
*bordillo<sup>M</sup>*

manhole
*trampilla<sup>F</sup> de acceso<sup>M</sup>*

pedestrian crossing
*paso<sup>M</sup> de peatones<sup>M</sup>*

storm sewer
*drenaje<sup>M</sup> de aguas<sup>F</sup>
superficiales*

bus stop
*parada<sup>F</sup> de autobús<sup>M</sup>*

barrier
*valla<sup>F</sup>*

bus shelter
*marquesina<sup>F</sup>*

sewer
*alcantarilla<sup>F</sup>*

service main
*colector<sup>M</sup> principal*

electricity cable
*cable<sup>M</sup> eléctrico*

main sewer
*alcantarilla<sup>F</sup> principal*

telephone cable
*red<sup>F</sup> de cables<sup>M</sup>
telefónicos*

traffic lights
**semáforo<sup>F</sup>**

red light
*luz<sup>F</sup> roja*

gas main
*conducto<sup>M</sup> principal del
gas<sup>M</sup>*

yellow light
*luz<sup>M</sup> ámbar*

green light
*luz<sup>F</sup> verde*

service main
*colector<sup>M</sup> principal*

pedestrian lights
*semáforo<sup>M</sup> de
peatones<sup>M</sup>*

pedestrian call button
*botón<sup>M</sup> de llamada<sup>F</sup> para
peatones<sup>M</sup>*

SOCIETY

# office building
*edificio<sup>M</sup> de oficinas<sup>F</sup>*

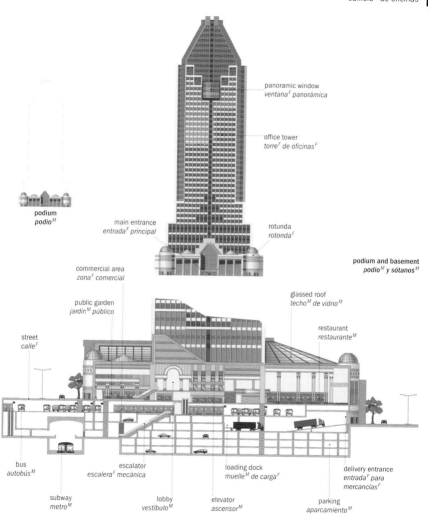

panoramic window
*ventana<sup>F</sup> panorámica*

office tower
*torre<sup>F</sup> de oficinas<sup>F</sup>*

podium
*podio<sup>M</sup>*

main entrance
*entrada<sup>F</sup> principal*

rotunda
*rotonda<sup>F</sup>*

podium and basement
*podio<sup>M</sup> y sótanos<sup>M</sup>*

commercial area
*zona<sup>F</sup> comercial*

public garden
*jardín<sup>M</sup> público*

glassed roof
*techo<sup>M</sup> de vidrio<sup>M</sup>*

restaurant
*restaurante<sup>M</sup>*

street
*calle<sup>F</sup>*

SOCIETY

bus
*autobús<sup>M</sup>*

escalator
*escalera<sup>F</sup> mecánica*

loading dock
*muelle<sup>M</sup> de carga<sup>F</sup>*

delivery entrance
*entrada<sup>F</sup> para mercancías<sup>F</sup>*

subway
*metro<sup>M</sup>*

lobby
*vestíbulo<sup>M</sup>*

elevator
*ascensor<sup>M</sup>*

parking
*aparcamiento<sup>M</sup>*

# shopping center
*centro<sup>M</sup> comercial*

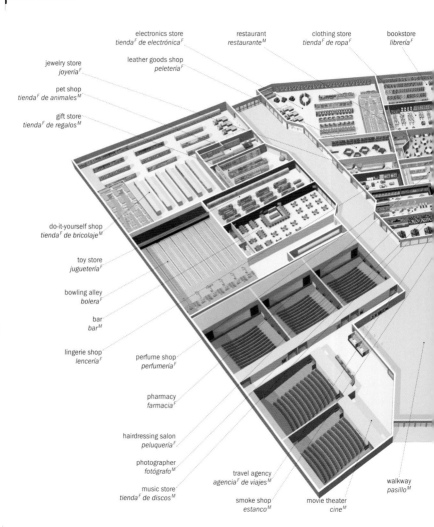

electronics store
*tienda<sup>F</sup> de electrónica<sup>F</sup>*

restaurant
*restaurante<sup>M</sup>*

clothing store
*tienda<sup>F</sup> de ropa<sup>F</sup>*

bookstore
*librería<sup>F</sup>*

leather goods shop
*peletería<sup>F</sup>*

jewelry store
*joyería<sup>F</sup>*

pet shop
*tienda<sup>F</sup> de animales<sup>M</sup>*

gift store
*tienda<sup>F</sup> de regalos<sup>M</sup>*

do-it-yourself shop
*tienda<sup>F</sup> de bricolaje<sup>M</sup>*

toy store
*juguetería<sup>F</sup>*

bowling alley
*bolera<sup>F</sup>*

bar
*bar<sup>M</sup>*

lingerie shop
*lencería<sup>F</sup>*

perfume shop
*perfumería<sup>F</sup>*

pharmacy
*farmacia<sup>F</sup>*

hairdressing salon
*peluquería<sup>F</sup>*

photographer
*fotógrafo<sup>M</sup>*

travel agency
*agencia<sup>F</sup> de viajes<sup>M</sup>*

music store
*tienda<sup>F</sup> de discos<sup>M</sup>*

smoke shop
*estanco<sup>M</sup>*

movie theater
*cine<sup>M</sup>*

walkway
*pasillo<sup>M</sup>*

SOCIETY

shopping center

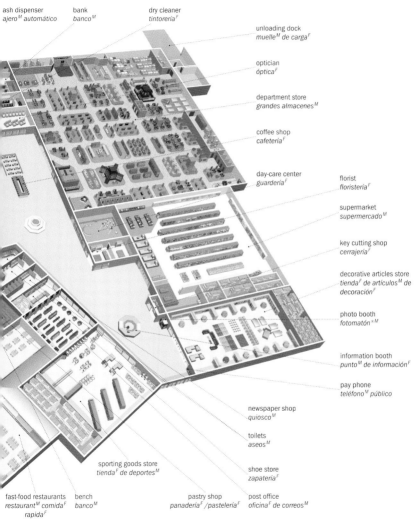

ash dispenser
*ajero* M *automático*

bank
*banco* M

dry cleaner
*tintorería* F

unloading dock
*muelle* M *de carga* F

optician
*óptica* F

department store
*grandes almacenes* M

coffee shop
*cafetería* F

day-care center
*guardería* F

florist
*floristería* F

supermarket
*supermercado* M

key cutting shop
*cerrajería* F

decorative articles store
*tienda* F *de artículos* M *de decoración* F

photo booth
*fotomatón* * M

information booth
*punto* M *de información* F

pay phone
*teléfono* M *público*

newspaper shop
*quiosco* M

toilets
*aseos* M

sporting goods store
*tienda* F *de deportes* M

shoe store
*zapatería* F

fast-food restaurants
*restaurant* M *comida* F
*rapida* F

bench
*banco* M

pastry shop
*panadería* F /*pastelería* F

post office
*oficina* F *de correos* M

SOCIETY

# restaurant

*restaurante*<sup>M</sup>

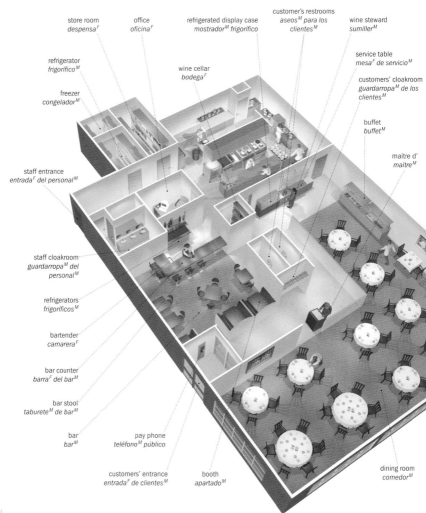

store room
*despensa*<sup>F</sup>

office
*oficina*<sup>F</sup>

refrigerated display case
*mostrador*<sup>M</sup> *frigorífico*

customer's restrooms
*aseos*<sup>M</sup> *para los clientes*<sup>M</sup>

wine steward
*sumiller*<sup>M</sup>

refrigerator
*frigorífico*<sup>M</sup>

wine cellar
*bodega*<sup>F</sup>

service table
*mesa*<sup>F</sup> *de servicio*<sup>M</sup>

freezer
*congelador*<sup>M</sup>

customers' cloakroom
*guardarropa*<sup>M</sup> *de los clientes*<sup>M</sup>

buffet
*buffet*<sup>M</sup>

staff entrance
*entrada*<sup>F</sup> *del personal*<sup>M</sup>

maitre d'
*maitre*<sup>M</sup>

staff cloakroom
*guardarropa*<sup>M</sup> *del personal*<sup>M</sup>

refrigerators
*frigoríficos*<sup>M</sup>

bartender
*camarera*<sup>F</sup>

bar counter
*barra*<sup>F</sup> *del bar*<sup>M</sup>

bar stool
*taburete*<sup>M</sup> *de bar*<sup>M</sup>

bar
*bar*<sup>M</sup>

pay phone
*teléfono*<sup>M</sup> *público*

customers' entrance
*entrada*<sup>F</sup> *de clientes*<sup>M</sup>

booth
*apartado*<sup>M</sup>

dining room
*comedor*<sup>M</sup>

# hotel
*hotel*<sup>M</sup>

**reception level**
*nivel*<sup>M</sup> *de la*
*recepción*<sup>F</sup>

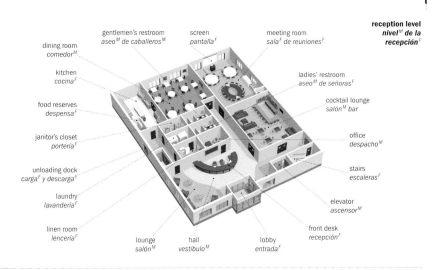

gentlemen's restroom
*aseo*<sup>M</sup> *de caballeros*<sup>M</sup>

screen
*pantalla*<sup>F</sup>

meeting room
*sala*<sup>F</sup> *de reuniones*<sup>F</sup>

dining room
*comedor*<sup>M</sup>

kitchen
*cocina*<sup>F</sup>

food reserves
*despensa*<sup>F</sup>

janitor's closet
*portería*<sup>F</sup>

unloading dock
*carga*<sup>F</sup> *y descarga*<sup>F</sup>

laundry
*lavandería*<sup>F</sup>

linen room
*lencería*<sup>F</sup>

ladies' restroom
*aseo*<sup>M</sup> *de señoras*<sup>F</sup>

cocktail lounge
*salón*<sup>M</sup> *bar*

office
*despacho*<sup>M</sup>

stairs
*escaleras*<sup>F</sup>

elevator
*ascensor*<sup>M</sup>

front desk
*recepción*<sup>F</sup>

lounge
*salón*<sup>M</sup>

hall
*vestíbulo*<sup>M</sup>

lobby
*entrada*<sup>F</sup>

**hotel rooms**
*habitación*<sup>F</sup> *de hotel*<sup>M</sup>

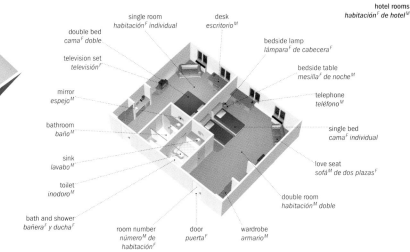

single room
*habitación*<sup>F</sup> *individual*

desk
*escritorio*<sup>M</sup>

double bed
*cama*<sup>F</sup> *doble*

bedside lamp
*lámpara*<sup>F</sup> *de cabecera*<sup>F</sup>

television set
*televisión*<sup>F</sup>

bedside table
*mesilla*<sup>F</sup> *de noche*<sup>M</sup>

mirror
*espejo*<sup>M</sup>

telephone
*teléfono*<sup>M</sup>

bathroom
*baño*<sup>M</sup>

single bed
*cama*<sup>F</sup> *individual*

sink
*lavabo*<sup>M</sup>

love seat
*sofá*<sup>M</sup> *de dos plazas*<sup>F</sup>

toilet
*inodoro*<sup>M</sup>

double room
*habitación*<sup>M</sup> *doble*

bath and shower
*bañera*<sup>F</sup> *y ducha*<sup>F</sup>

room number
*número*<sup>M</sup> *de
habitación*<sup>F</sup>

door
*puerta*<sup>F</sup>

wardrobe
*armario*<sup>M</sup>

SOCIETY

# court
*tribunal* M

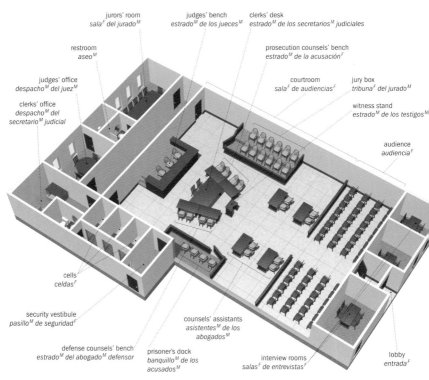

jurors' room
*sala* F *del jurado* M

judges' bench
*estrado* M *de los jueces* M

clerks' desk
*estrado* M *de los secretarios* M *judiciales*

restroom
*aseo* M

prosecution counsels' bench
*estrado* M *de la acusación* F

judges' office
*despacho* M *del juez* M

courtroom
*sala* F *de audiencias* F

jury box
*tribuna* F *del jurado* M

clerks' office
*despacho* M *del secretario* M *judicial*

witness stand
*estrado* M *de los testigos* M

audience
*audiencia* F

cells
*celdas* F

security vestibule
*pasillo* M *de seguridad* F

counsels' assistants
*asistentes* M *de los abogados* M

defense counsels' bench
*estrado* M *del abogado* M *defensor*

prisoner's dock
*banquillo* M *de los acusados* M

interview rooms
*salas* F *de entrevistas* F

lobby
*entrada* F

# examples of currency abbreviations
*ejemplos* M *de abreviaciones* F *de monedas* F

| | cent *centavo* M | | euro *euro* M | | peso *peso* M | | pound *libra* F |
|---|---|---|---|---|---|---|---|

$ 
dollar
*dólar* M

¢
cent
*centavo* M

Rs
rupee
*rupia* F

€
euro
*euro* M

₪
new shekel
*nuevo shekel* M

₱
peso
*peso* M

¥
yen
*yen* M

£
pound
*libra* F

## money and modes of payment
*dinero$^M$ y modos$^M$ de pago$^M$*

coin: obverse
*moneda$^F$ : anverso$^M$*

initials of the issuing bank
*iniciales$^F$ del banco$^M$ emisor*

banknote: front
*billete$^M$ : recto$^M$*

security thread
*hilo$^M$ de seguridad$^F$*

hologram foil strip
*banda$^F$ holográfica metalizada*

date
*fecha$^F$*

official signature
*firma$^F$ oficial*

watermark
*filigrana$^F$*

edge
*canto$^M$*

color shifting ink
*tinta$^F$ de color$^M$ cambiante*

portrait
*retrato$^M$*

serial number
*número$^M$ de serie$^F$*

coin: reverse
*moneda$^F$ : reverso$^M$*

banknote: back
*billete$^M$ : verso$^M$*

flag of the European Union
*bandera$^F$ de la Unión$^F$ Europea*

serial number
*número$^M$ de serie$^F$*

outer ring
*cordoncillo$^M$*

denomination
*valor$^M$*

motto
*lema$^M$*

denomination
*valor$^M$*

name of the currency
*nombre$^M$ de la moneda$^F$*

magnetic stripe
*banda$^F$ magnética*

cardholder's signature
*firma$^F$ del titular$^M$*

credit card
*tarjeta$^F$ de crédito$^M$*

checks
*cheques$^M$*

card number
*número$^M$ de la tarjeta$^F$*

traveler's check
*cheque$^M$ de viaje$^M$*

cardholder's name
*nombre$^M$ del titular$^M$*

expiration date
*fecha$^F$ de vencimiento$^M$*

SOCIETY

# bank
*banco^M*

cash dispenser
*cajero^M automático*

professional training office
*oficina^F de formación profesional*

waiting area
*zona^F de espera^F*

insurance services
*servicios^M de seguros^M*

brochure rack
*expositor^M de folletos^M*

photocopier
*fotocopiadora^F*

financial services
*servicios^M financieros*

information desk
*información^F*

conference room
*sala^F de conferencias^F*

automatic teller
machine (ATM)
*cajero^M automático*

reception desk
*recepción^F*

loan services
*servicios^M de crédito^M*

operation keys
*teclas^F de operación^F*

deposit slot
*ranura^F de depósito^M*

meeting room
*sala^F de reuniones^F*

display
*pantalla^F*

card reader slot
*lector^M de tarjeta^F*

transaction record slot
*ranura^F de registro^M de la transacción^F*

alphanumeric keyboard
*teclado^M alfanumérico*

security grille
*reja^F de seguridad^F*

bill presenter
*emisión^F de billetes^M*

passbook update slot
*ranura^F de puesta^F al día^F de la cartilla^F*

lobby
*entrada*

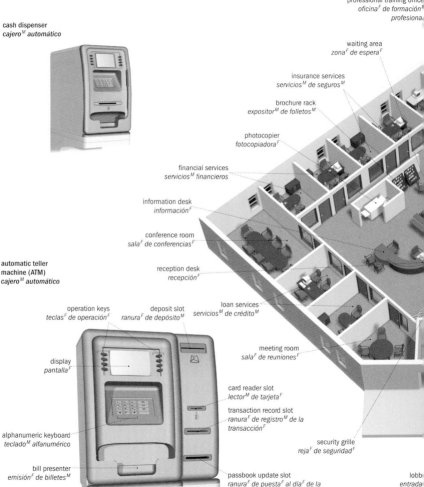

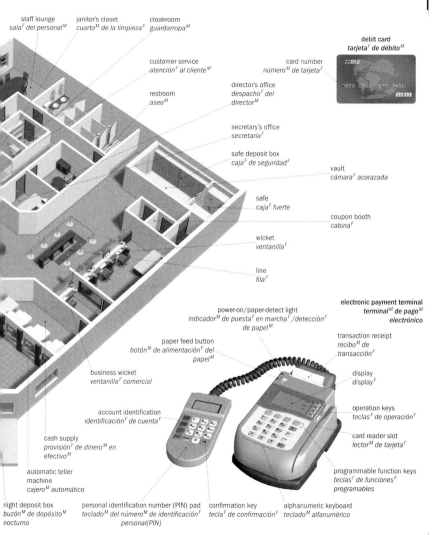

staff lounge
*sala<sup>F</sup> del personal<sup>M</sup>*

janitor's closet
*cuarto<sup>M</sup> de la limpieza<sup>F</sup>*

cloakroom
*guardarropa<sup>M</sup>*

debit card
*tarjeta<sup>F</sup> de débito<sup>M</sup>*

customer service
*atención<sup>F</sup> al cliente<sup>M</sup>*

card number
*número<sup>M</sup> de tarjeta<sup>F</sup>*

director's office
*despacho<sup>F</sup> del
director<sup>M</sup>*

restroom
*aseo<sup>M</sup>*

secretary's office
*secretaría<sup>F</sup>*

safe deposit box
*caja<sup>F</sup> de seguridad<sup>F</sup>*

vault
*cámara<sup>F</sup> acorazada*

safe
*caja<sup>F</sup> fuerte*

coupon booth
*cabina<sup>F</sup>*

wicket
*ventanilla<sup>F</sup>*

line
*fila<sup>F</sup>*

power-on/paper-detect light
*indicador<sup>M</sup> de puesta<sup>F</sup> en marcha<sup>F</sup> /detección<sup>F</sup>
de papel<sup>M</sup>*

electronic payment terminal
*terminal<sup>M</sup> de pago<sup>M</sup>
electrónico*

paper feed button
*botón<sup>M</sup> de alimentación<sup>F</sup> del
papel<sup>M</sup>*

transaction receipt
*recibo<sup>M</sup> de
transacción<sup>F</sup>*

business wicket
*ventanilla<sup>F</sup> comercial*

display
*display<sup>F</sup>*

account identification
*identificación<sup>F</sup> de cuenta<sup>F</sup>*

operation keys
*teclas<sup>F</sup> de operación<sup>F</sup>*

cash supply
*provisión<sup>F</sup> de dinero<sup>M</sup> en
efectivo<sup>M</sup>*

card reader slot
*lector<sup>M</sup> de tarjeta<sup>F</sup>*

automatic teller
machine
*cajero<sup>M</sup> automático*

programmable function keys
*teclas<sup>F</sup> de funciones<sup>F</sup>
programables*

night deposit box
*buzón<sup>M</sup> de depósito<sup>M</sup>
nocturno*

personal identification number (PIN) pad
*teclado<sup>M</sup> del número<sup>M</sup> de identificación<sup>F</sup>
personal(PIN)*

confirmation key
*tecla<sup>F</sup> de confirmación<sup>F</sup>*

alphanumeric keyboard
*teclado<sup>M</sup> alfanumérico*

SOCIETY

# school
*colegio* [M]

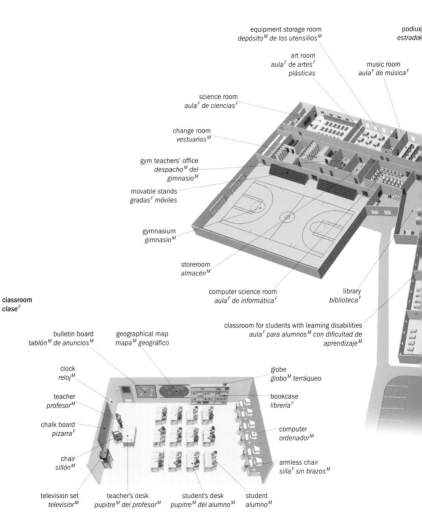

equipment storage room
*depósito* [M] *de los utensilios* [M]

podiu|
estrado|

art room
*aula* [F] *de artes* [F]
*plásticas*

music room
*aula* [F] *de música* [F]

science room
*aula* [F] *de ciencias* [F]

change room
*vestuarios* [M]

gym teachers' office
*despacho* [M] *del*
*gimnasio* [M]

movable stands
*gradas* [F] *móviles*

gymnasium
*gimnasio* [M]

storeroom
*almacén* [M]

computer science room
*aula* [F] *de informática* [F]

library
*biblioteca* [F]

classroom for students with learning disabilities
*aula* [F] *para alumnos* [M] *con dificultad de*
*aprendizaje* [M]

classroom
*clase* [F]

bulletin board
*tablón* [M] *de anuncios* [M]

geographical map
*mapa* [M] *geográfico*

clock
*reloj* [M]

globe
*globo* [M] *terráqueo*

teacher
*profesor* [M]

bookcase
*librería* [F]

chalk board
*pizarra* [F]

computer
*ordenador* [M]

chair
*sillón* [M]

armless chair
*silla* [F] *sin brazos* [M]

television set
*televisior* [M]

teacher's desk
*pupitre* [M] *del profesor* [M]

student's desk
*pupitre* [M] *del alumno* [M]

student
*alumno* [M]

SOCIETY

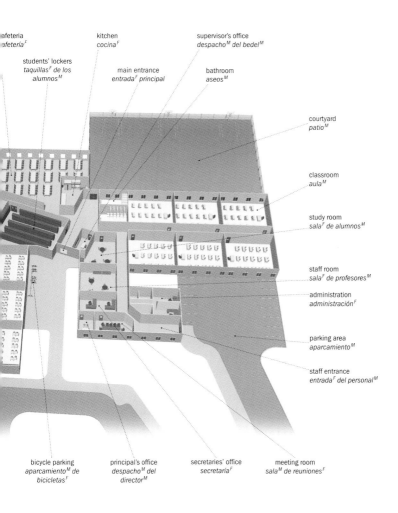

cafeteria
*cafetería*<sup>F</sup>

students' lockers
*taquillas*<sup>F</sup> *de los*
*alumnos*<sup>M</sup>

kitchen
*cocina*<sup>F</sup>

main entrance
*entrada*<sup>F</sup> *principal*

supervisor's office
*despacho*<sup>M</sup> *del bedel*<sup>M</sup>

bathroom
*aseos*<sup>M</sup>

courtyard
*patio*<sup>M</sup>

classroom
*aula*<sup>M</sup>

study room
*sala*<sup>F</sup> *de alumnos*<sup>M</sup>

staff room
*sala*<sup>F</sup> *de profesores*<sup>M</sup>

administration
*administración*<sup>F</sup>

parking area
*aparcamiento*<sup>M</sup>

staff entrance
*entrada*<sup>F</sup> *del personal*<sup>M</sup>

bicycle parking
*aparcamiento*<sup>M</sup> *de*
*bicicletas*<sup>F</sup>

principal's office
*despacho*<sup>M</sup> *del*
*director*<sup>M</sup>

secretaries' office
*secretaría*<sup>F</sup>

meeting room
*sala*<sup>M</sup> *de reuniones*<sup>F</sup>

SOCIETY

445

# Catholic church

*iglesia^F*

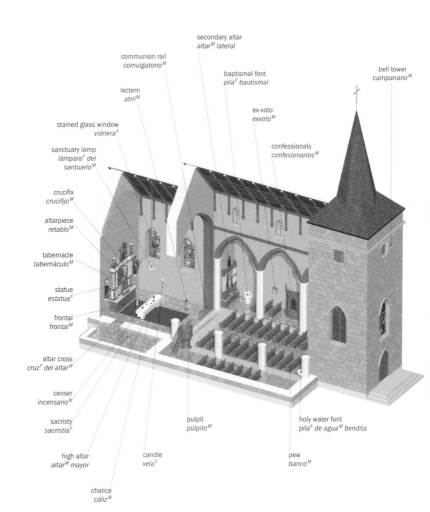

secondary altar
*altar^M lateral*

communion rail
*comulgatorio^M*

baptismal font
*pila^F bautismal*

bell tower
*campanario^M*

lectern
*atril^M*

ex-voto
*exvoto^M*

stained glass window
*vidriera^F*

confessionals
*confesionarios^M*

sanctuary lamp
*lámpara^F del
santuario^M*

crucifix
*crucifijo^M*

altarpiece
*retablo^M*

tabernacle
*tabernáculo^M*

statue
*estatua^F*

frontal
*frontal^M*

altar cross
*cruz^F del altar^M*

censer
*incensario^M*

sacristy
*sacristía^F*

pulpit
*púlpito^M*

holy water font
*pila^F de agua^M bendita*

high altar
*altar^M mayor*

candle
*vela^F*

pew
*banco^M*

chalice
*cáliz^M*

# synagogue
*sinagoga<sup>F</sup>*

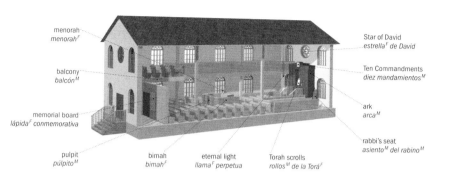

menorah
*menorah<sup>F</sup>*

balcony
*balcón<sup>M</sup>*

memorial board
*lápida<sup>F</sup> conmemorativa*

pulpit
*púlpito<sup>M</sup>*

bimah
*bimah<sup>F</sup>*

eternal light
*llama<sup>F</sup> perpetua*

Torah scrolls
*rollos<sup>M</sup> de la Torá<sup>F</sup>*

Star of David
*estrella<sup>F</sup> de David*

Ten Commandments
*diez mandamientos<sup>M</sup>*

ark
*arca<sup>M</sup>*

rabbi's seat
*asiento<sup>M</sup> del rabino<sup>M</sup>*

# mosque
*mezquita<sup>F</sup>*

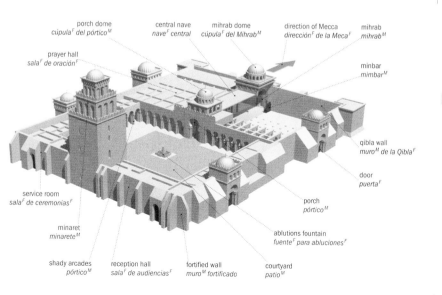

porch dome
*cúpula<sup>F</sup> del pórtico<sup>M</sup>*

central nave
*nave<sup>F</sup> central*

mihrab dome
*cúpula<sup>F</sup> del Mihrab<sup>M</sup>*

direction of Mecca
*dirección<sup>F</sup> de la Meca<sup>F</sup>*

mihrab
*mihrab<sup>M</sup>*

prayer hall
*sala<sup>F</sup> de oración<sup>F</sup>*

minbar
*mimbar<sup>M</sup>*

qibla wall
*muro<sup>M</sup> de la Qibla<sup>F</sup>*

door
*puerta<sup>F</sup>*

service room
*sala<sup>F</sup> de ceremonias<sup>F</sup>*

porch
*pórtico<sup>M</sup>*

minaret
*minarete<sup>M</sup>*

ablutions fountain
*fuente<sup>F</sup> para abluciones<sup>F</sup>*

shady arcades
*pórtico<sup>M</sup>*

reception hall
*sala<sup>F</sup> de audiencias<sup>F</sup>*

fortified wall
*muro<sup>M</sup> fortificado*

courtyard
*patio<sup>M</sup>*

SOCIETY

# flags
*banderas*<sup>F</sup>

## Americas
*Américas*<sup>F</sup>

1 Canada
*Canadá*<sup>M</sup>

2 United States of America
*Estados*<sup>M</sup> *Unidos de
América*<sup>F</sup>

3 Mexico
*México*<sup>M</sup>

4 Honduras
*Honduras*<sup>M</sup>

5 Guatemala
*Guatemala*<sup>F</sup>

6 Belize
*Belice*<sup>M</sup>

7 El Salvador
*El Salvador*<sup>M</sup>

8 Nicaragua
*Nicaragua*<sup>F</sup>

9 Costa Rica
*Costa Rica*<sup>F</sup>

10 Panama
*Panamá*<sup>M</sup>

11 Colombia
*Colombia*<sup>F</sup>

12 Venezuela
*Venezuela*<sup>F</sup>

13 Guyana
*Guyana*<sup>F</sup>

14 Suriname
*Surinam*<sup>M</sup>

15 Ecuador
*Ecuador*<sup>M</sup>

16 Peru
*Perú*<sup>M</sup>

17 Brazil
*Brasil*<sup>M</sup>

18 Bolivia
*Bolivia*<sup>F</sup>

19 Paraguay
*Paraguay*<sup>M</sup>

20 Chile
*Chile*<sup>M</sup>

21 Argentina
*Argentina*<sup>F</sup>

22 Uruguay
*Uruguay*<sup>M</sup>

## Caribbean Islands
*islas*<sup>F</sup> *del Caribe*<sup>M</sup>

23 The Bahamas
*Bahamas*<sup>F</sup>

24 Cuba
*Cuba*<sup>F</sup>

25 Jamaica
*Jamaica*<sup>F</sup>

26 Haiti
*Haiti*<sup>M</sup>

SOCIETY

flags

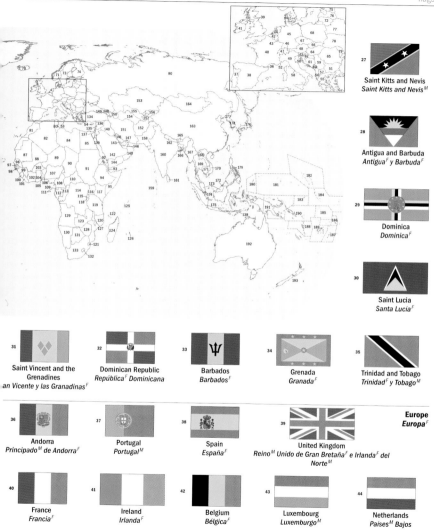

27 Saint Kitts and Nevis
*Saint Kitts and Nevis$^M$*

28 Antigua and Barbuda
*Antigua$^F$ y Barbuda$^F$*

29 Dominica
*Dominica$^F$*

30 Saint Lucia
*Santa Lucía$^F$*

SOCIETY

31 Saint Vincent and the Grenadines
*San Vicente y las Granadinas$^F$*

32 Dominican Republic
*República$^F$ Dominicana*

33 Barbados
*Barbados$^F$*

34 Grenada
*Granada$^F$*

35 Trinidad and Tobago
*Trinidad$^F$ y Tobago$^M$*

36 Andorra
*Principado$^M$ de Andorra$^F$*

37 Portugal
*Portugal$^M$*

38 Spain
*España$^F$*

39 United Kingdom
*Reino$^M$ Unido de Gran Bretaña$^F$ e Irlanda$^F$ del Norte$^M$*

Europe
*Europa$^F$*

40 France
*Francia$^F$*

41 Ireland
*Irlanda$^F$*

42 Belgium
*Bélgica$^F$*

43 Luxembourg
*Luxemburgo$^M$*

44 Netherlands
*Países$^M$ Bajos*

flags

45 Germany
*Alemania*[F]

46 Liechtenstein
*Liechtenstein*[M]

47 Switzerland
*Suiza*[F]

48 Austria
*Austria*[F]

49 Italy
*Italia*[F]

50 San Marino
*República*[F] *de San Marino*[M]

51 Bulgaria
*Bulgaria*[F]

52 Monaco
*Principado*[M] *de Mónaco*[M]

53 Malta
*Malta*[F]

54 Cyprus
*Chipre*[M]

55 Greece
*Grecia*[F]

56 Albania
*Albania*[F]

57 The Former Yugoslav Republic of Macedonia
*Antigua República*[F] *Yugoslava de Macedonia*[F]

58 Holy See (Vatican City)
*Ciudad*[F] *del Vaticano*[M]

59 Serbia
*Serbia*[F]

60 Montenegro
*Montenegro*[M]

61 Bosnia and Herzegovina
*Bosnia-Herzegovina*[F]

62 Croatia
*Croacia*[F]

63 Slovenia
*Eslovenia*[F]

64 Hungary
*Hungria*[F]

65 Romania
*Rumania*[F]

66 Slovakia
*Eslovaquia*[F]

67 Czech Republic
*República*[F] *Checa*

68 Poland
*Polonia*[F]

69 Denmark
*Dinamarca*[F]

70 Iceland
*Islandia*[F]

71 Norway
*Noruega*[F]

72 Lithuania
*Lituania*[F]

73 Sweden
*Suecia*[F]

74 Finland
*Finlandia*[F]

75 Estonia
*Estonia*[F]

76 Latvia
*Letonia*[F]

77 Belarus
*Bielorrusia*[F]

78 Ukraine
*Ucrania*[F]

79 Moldova
*Moldavia*[F]

80 Russia
*Federación*[F] *Rusa*

SOCIETY

flags

**Africa**
*África* F

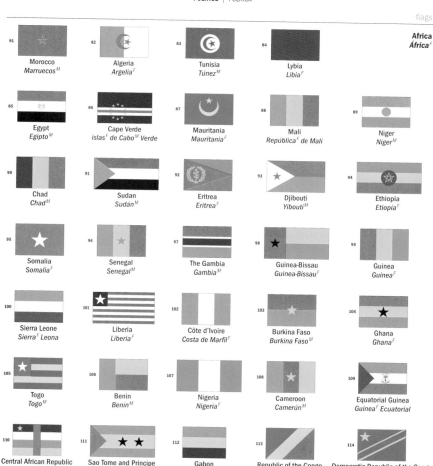

81 Morocco
*Marruecos* M

82 Algeria
*Argelia* F

83 Tunisia
*Túnez* M

84 Lybia
*Libia* F

85 Egypt
*Egipto* M

86 Cape Verde
*islas* F *de Cabo* M *Verde*

87 Mauritania
*Mauritania* F

88 Mali
*República* F *de Mali*

89 Niger
*Niger* M

90 Chad
*Chad* M

91 Sudan
*Sudán* M

92 Eritrea
*Eritrea* F

93 Djibouti
*Yibouti* M

94 Ethiopia
*Etiopía* F

95 Somalia
*Somalia* F

96 Senegal
*Senegal* M

97 The Gambia
*Gambia* M

98 Guinea-Bissau
*Guinea-Bissau* F

99 Guinea
*Guinea* F

100 Sierra Leone
*Sierra* F *Leona*

101 Liberia
*Liberia* F

102 Côte d'Ivoire
*Costa de Marfil* F

103 Burkina Faso
*Burkina Faso* M

104 Ghana
*Ghana* F

105 Togo
*Togo* M

106 Benin
*Benin* M

107 Nigeria
*Nigeria* F

108 Cameroon
*Camerún* M

109 Equatorial Guinea
*Guinea* F *Ecuatorial*

110 Central African Republic
*República* F
*Centroafricana*

111 Sao Tome and Principe
*Santo Tomé y Principe* M

112 Gabon
*Gabón* M

113 Republic of the Congo
*Congo* M

114 Democratic Republic of the Congo
*República* F *Democrática del*
*Congo* M

115 Rwanda
*Ruanda* M

116 Uganda
*Uganda* F

117 Kenya
*Kenia* F

118 Burundi
*Burundi* M

119 Tanzania
*Tanzania* F

SOCIETY

flags

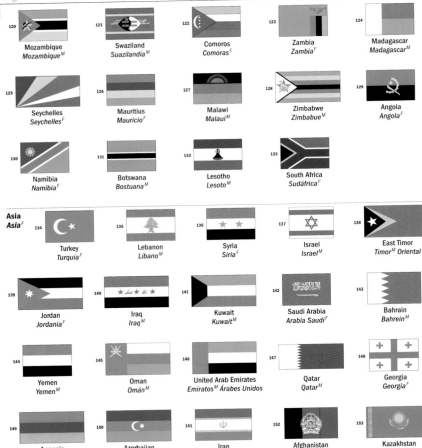

120 Mozambique
*Mozambique*<sup>M</sup>

121 Swaziland
*Suazilandia*<sup>M</sup>

122 Comoros
*Comoras*<sup>F</sup>

123 Zambia
*Zambia*<sup>F</sup>

124 Madagascar
*Madagascar*<sup>M</sup>

125 Seychelles
*Seychelles*<sup>F</sup>

126 Mauritius
*Mauricio*<sup>F</sup>

127 Malawi
*Malaui*<sup>M</sup>

128 Zimbabwe
*Zimbabue*<sup>M</sup>

129 Angola
*Angola*<sup>F</sup>

130 Namibia
*Namibia*<sup>F</sup>

131 Botswana
*Bostuana*<sup>M</sup>

132 Lesotho
*Lesoto*<sup>M</sup>

133 South Africa
*Sudáfrica*<sup>F</sup>

**Asia**
*Asia*<sup>F</sup>

134 Turkey
*Turquía*<sup>F</sup>

135 Lebanon
*Líbano*<sup>M</sup>

136 Syria
*Siria*<sup>F</sup>

137 Israel
*Israel*<sup>M</sup>

138 East Timor
*Timor*<sup>M</sup> *Oriental*

139 Jordan
*Jordania*<sup>F</sup>

140 Iraq
*Iraq*<sup>M</sup>

141 Kuwait
*Kuwait*<sup>M</sup>

142 Saudi Arabia
*Arabia Saudí*<sup>F</sup>

143 Bahrain
*Bahrein*<sup>M</sup>

144 Yemen
*Yemen*<sup>M</sup>

145 Oman
*Omán*<sup>M</sup>

146 United Arab Emirates
*Emiratos*<sup>M</sup> *Árabes Unidos*

147 Qatar
*Qatar*<sup>M</sup>

148 Georgia
*Georgia*<sup>F</sup>

149 Armenia
*Armenia*<sup>F</sup>

150 Azerbaijan
*Azerbaiyán*<sup>M</sup>

151 Iran
*Irán*<sup>M</sup>

152 Afghanistan
*Afganistán*<sup>M</sup>

153 Kazakhstan
*Kazajistán*<sup>M</sup>

154 Turkmenistan
*Turkmenistán*<sup>M</sup>

155 Uzbekistan
*Uzbekistán*<sup>M</sup>

156 Kyrgyzstan
*Kirguizistán*<sup>M</sup>

157 Tajikistan
*Tajikistán*<sup>M</sup>

158 Pakistan
*Pakistán*<sup>M</sup>

SOCIETY

**159** Maldives
*Maldivas*[F]

**160** India
*India*[F]

**161** Sri Lanka
*Sri Lanka*[M]

**162** Nepal
*Nepal*[M]

**163** China
*China*[F]

**164** Mongolia
*Mongolia*[F]

**165** Bhutan
*Bután*[M]

**166** Bangladesh
*Bangladesh*[M]

**167** Burma
*Myanmar*[M]

**168** Laos
*Laos*[M]

**169** Thailand
*Tailandia*[F]

**170** Vietnam
*Vietnam*[M]

**171** Cambodia
*Camboya*[F]

**172** Brunei
*Brunei*[M]

**173** Malaysia
*Malasia*[F]

**174** Singapore
*Singapur*[M]

**175** Indonesia
*Indonesia*[F]

**176** Japan
*Japón*[M]

**177** North Korea
*República*[F] *Democrática Popular de Corea*[F]

**178** South Korea
*República*[F] *de Corea*[F]

**179** Philippines
*Filipinas*[F]

**180** Palau
*Palau*[M]

**181** Federated States of Micronesia
*Micronesia*[F]

**Oceania and Polynesia**
*Oceanía*[F] *y Polinesia*[F]

**182** Marshall Islands
*Islas*[F] *Marshall*

**183** Nauru
*Nauru*[M]

**184** Kiribati
*Kiribati*[M]

**185** Tuvalu
*Tuvalu*[M]

**186** Samoa
*Samoa*[F]

**187** Tonga
*Tonga*[M]

**188** Vanuatu
*Vanuatu*[M]

**189** Fiji
*Fiji*[F]

**190** Solomon Islands
*Islas Salomón*[F]

**191** Papua New Guinea
*Papúa Nueva Guinea*[F]

**192** Australia
*Australia*[F]

**193** New Zealand
*Nueva Zelanda*[F]

SOCIETY

# fire prevention
*prevención<sup>F</sup> de incendios<sup>M</sup>*

**fire-fighting materials**
**material<sup>M</sup> de lucha<sup>F</sup> contra los incendios<sup>M</sup>**

**firefighter**
*bombero<sup>M</sup>*

**smoke detector**
*detector<sup>M</sup> de humo<sup>M</sup>*

base
*base<sup>F</sup>*

cover
*tapa<sup>F</sup>*

test button
*botón<sup>M</sup> de ensayo<sup>M</sup>*

indicator light
*testigo<sup>M</sup> luminoso*

helmet
*casco<sup>M</sup>*

compressed-air cylinder
*bombona<sup>F</sup> de aire<sup>M</sup> comprimido*

full face mask
*máscara<sup>F</sup>*

self-contained breathing apparatus
*aparato<sup>M</sup> de respiración<sup>F</sup> autónomo*

air-supply tube
*tubo<sup>M</sup> de aire<sup>M</sup>*

pressure demand regulator
*regulador<sup>M</sup> de presión<sup>F</sup>*

**portable fire extinguisher**
*extintor<sup>M</sup> portátil*

trigger
*disparador<sup>M</sup>*

pin
*clavija<sup>F</sup>*

hose
*manguera<sup>F</sup>*

tank
*tanque<sup>M</sup>*

mandown alarm
*avisador<sup>M</sup> de alarma<sup>F</sup>*

turnouts
*vestido<sup>M</sup> ignífugo y impermeable*

pike pole
*pica<sup>F</sup>*

hatchet
*hacha<sup>F</sup>*

**fire hose**
*manguera<sup>F</sup> de incendios<sup>M</sup>*

**fire hydrant**
*boca<sup>F</sup> de riego<sup>M</sup>*

rubber boot
*botas<sup>F</sup> de caucho<sup>M</sup>*

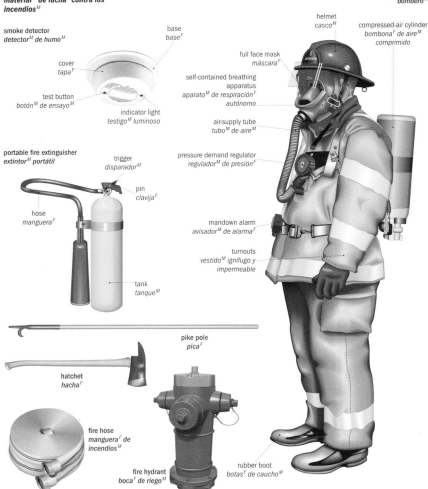

SOCIETY

**fire trucks**
*camiones$^M$ de*
*bomberos$^M$*

pumper
*autobomba$^M$ tanque*

control panel
*tablero$^M$ de*
*operaciones$^F$*

control wheel
*volante$^M$ de control$^M$*

deluge gun
*cañón$^M$ lanza agua$^F$*

spotlight
*faro$^M$ reflector*

suction hose
*manguera$^F$ de*
*aspiración$^F$*

fitting
*conector$^M$*

light bar
*puente$^M$ de luces$^F$*

horn
*sirena$^F$*

loudspeaker
*altavoz$^M$*

hydrant intake
*toma$^F$ para la boca$^F$ de*
*riego$^M$*

rear step
*peldaño$^M$ posterior*

storage compartment
*compartimiento$^M$ de*
*almacenamiento$^M$*

hydrant intake
*toma$^F$ para la boca$^F$ de*
*riego$^M$*

water pressure gauge
*manómetro$^M$*

grab handle
*asidero$^M$*

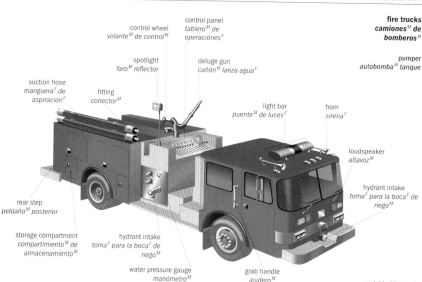

**aerial ladder truck**
*autoescalera$^M$*

ladder pipe nozzle
*escalera$^F$ con boquilla$^F$*
*telescópica*

telescopic boom
*elevador$^M$ telescópico*

oscillating light
*faro$^M$ de destello$^M$*

elevating cylinder
*cilindro$^M$ elevador*

turntable mounting
*plataforma$^F$ giratoria*

tower ladder
*escalera$^F$ telescópica*

top ladder
*tope$^M$ de la escalera$^F$*

spotlight
*faro$^M$ reflector*

storage compartment
*compartimiento$^M$ de*
*almacenamiento$^M$*

outrigger
*gato$^M$*

SOCIETY

455

# crime prevention
*prevención^F de la criminalidad^F*

**police officer**
*agente^M de policía^F*

cap
*gorra^F*

badge
*insignia^F*

shoulder strap
*hombrera^F*

rank insignia
*insignia^F de grado^M*

identification badge
*placa^F de identificación^F*

uniform
*uniforme^M*

**duty belt**
*cinturón^M de servicio^M*

microphone
*micrófono^M*

latex glove case
*funda^F de guantes^M de látex^M*

handcuff case
*estuche^M de las esposas^F*

pistol
*pistola^F*

pepper spray
*aerosol^M de pimienta^F*

ammunition pouch
*cartuchera^F*

walkie-talkie
*walkie-talkie^M*

holster
*pistolera^F*

baton holder
*gancho^M para la porra^F*

expandable baton
*porra^F*

flashlight
*linterna^F*

SOCIETY

dashboard equipment
*equipamiento<sup>M</sup> del
salpicadero<sup>M</sup>*

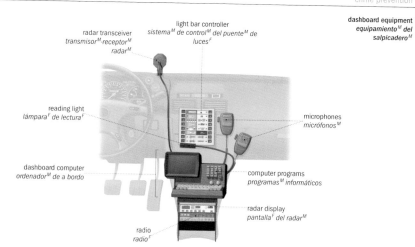

radar transceiver
*transmisor<sup>M</sup>-receptor<sup>M</sup>
radar<sup>M</sup>*

light bar controller
*sistema<sup>M</sup> de control<sup>M</sup> del puente<sup>M</sup> de
luces<sup>F</sup>*

reading light
*lámpara<sup>F</sup> de lectura<sup>F</sup>*

microphones
*micrófonos<sup>M</sup>*

dashboard computer
*ordenador<sup>M</sup> de a bordo*

computer programs
*programas<sup>M</sup> informáticos*

radar display
*pantalla<sup>F</sup> del radar<sup>M</sup>*

radio
*radio<sup>F</sup>*

police car
*coche<sup>M</sup> de policía<sup>F</sup>*

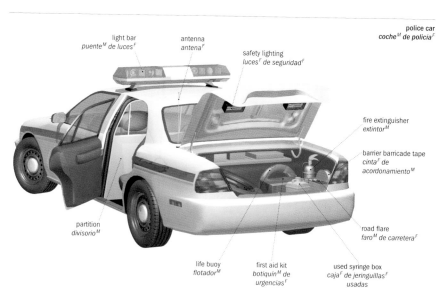

light bar
*puente<sup>M</sup> de luces<sup>F</sup>*

antenna
*antena<sup>F</sup>*

safety lighting
*luces<sup>F</sup> de seguridad<sup>F</sup>*

fire extinguisher
*extintor<sup>M</sup>*

barrier barricade tape
*cinta<sup>F</sup> de
acordonamiento<sup>M</sup>*

partition
*divisorio<sup>M</sup>*

road flare
*faro<sup>M</sup> de carretera<sup>F</sup>*

life buoy
*flotador<sup>M</sup>*

first aid kit
*botiquín<sup>M</sup> de
urgencias<sup>F</sup>*

used syringe box
*caja<sup>F</sup> de jeringuillas<sup>F</sup>
usadas*

SOCIETY

# ear protection
*protección<sup>F</sup> para los oídos<sup>M</sup>*

safety earmuffs
*cascos<sup>M</sup> de seguridad<sup>F</sup>*

headband
*diadema<sup>F</sup>*

earplugs
*tapones<sup>M</sup> para los oídos<sup>M</sup>*

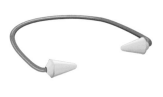

foam cushion
*protector<sup>M</sup> de espuma<sup>F</sup>*

# eye protection
*protección<sup>F</sup> para los ojos<sup>M</sup>*

safety glasses
*gafas<sup>F</sup> de seguridad<sup>F</sup>*

safety goggles
*gafas<sup>F</sup> protectoras*

# head protection
*protección<sup>F</sup> para la cabeza<sup>F</sup>*

SOCIETY

hard hat
*casco<sup>M</sup> de seguridad<sup>F</sup>*

rib
*refuerzo<sup>M</sup>*

peak
*visera<sup>F</sup>*

suspension band
*banda<sup>F</sup> de suspensión<sup>F</sup>*

headband
*cinta<sup>F</sup>*

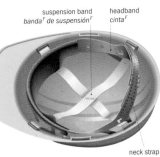

neck strap
*correa<sup>F</sup> para el cuello<sup>M</sup>*

# respiratory system protection
*protección<sup>F</sup> para el sistema<sup>M</sup> respiratorio*

respirator
*máscara<sup>F</sup> antigás*

facepiece
*sección<sup>F</sup> frontal*

visor
*careta<sup>F</sup>*

head harness
*correas<sup>F</sup>*

cartridge
*cartucho<sup>M</sup>*

inhalation valve
*válvula<sup>F</sup> de inhalación<sup>F</sup>*

filter cover
*tapa<sup>F</sup> del filtro<sup>M</sup>*

exhalation valve
*válvula<sup>F</sup> de exhalación<sup>F</sup>*

half-mask respirator
*máscara<sup>F</sup> para el
polvo<sup>M</sup>*

operating mask
*mascarilla<sup>F</sup> de cirujano<sup>M</sup>*

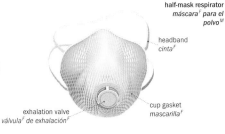

headband
*cinta<sup>F</sup>*

exhalation valve
*válvula<sup>F</sup> de exhalación<sup>F</sup>*

cup gasket
*mascarilla<sup>F</sup>*

# foot protection
*protección<sup>F</sup> para los pies<sup>M</sup>*

safety boot
*bota<sup>F</sup> de seguridad<sup>F</sup>*

reinforced toe
*tope<sup>M</sup>*

toe guard
*puntera<sup>F</sup> protectora*

SOCIETY

# first aid equipment
*equipo<sup>M</sup> de primeros auxilios<sup>M</sup>*

**stethoscope**
*fonendoscopio<sup>M</sup>*

Y-tube
*tubo<sup>M</sup> en Y*

sound receiver
*receptor<sup>M</sup> del sonido<sup>M</sup>*

branch clip
*muelle<sup>M</sup>*

earpiece
*auricular<sup>M</sup>*

flexible tube
*tubo<sup>M</sup> flexible*

branch
*rama<sup>F</sup>*

latex glove
*guantes<sup>M</sup> de látex<sup>M</sup>*

**syringe**
*jeringuilla*

bevel
*bisel<sup>M</sup>*

needle
*aguja<sup>F</sup>*

needle hub
*portaagujas<sup>M</sup>*

Luer-Lock tip
*jeringuilla<sup>F</sup> de Luer-Lock*

tip protector
*capuchón<sup>M</sup>*

hollow barrel
*cilindro<sup>M</sup>*

rubber bulb
*pera<sup>F</sup> de goma<sup>F</sup>*

finger flange
*pestaña<sup>F</sup> de arrojo<sup>M</sup>*

scale
*escala<sup>F</sup>*

thumb rest
*apoyo<sup>M</sup> del pulgar<sup>M</sup>*

plunger
*émbolo<sup>M</sup>*

syringe for irrigation
*jeringuilla<sup>F</sup> de irrigación<sup>F</sup>*

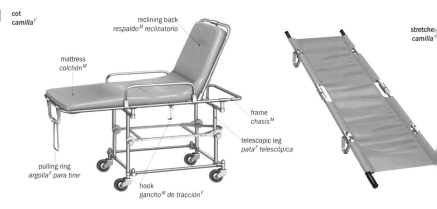

cot
*camilla<sup>F</sup>*

reclining back
*respaldo<sup>M</sup> reclinatorio*

mattress
*colchón<sup>M</sup>*

stretcher
*camilla*

frame
*chasis<sup>M</sup>*

telescopic leg
*pata<sup>F</sup> telescópica*

pulling ring
*argolla<sup>F</sup> para tirar*

hook
*gancho<sup>M</sup> de tracción<sup>F</sup>*

SOCIETY

# first aid kit
*botiquín[M] de primeros auxilios[M]*

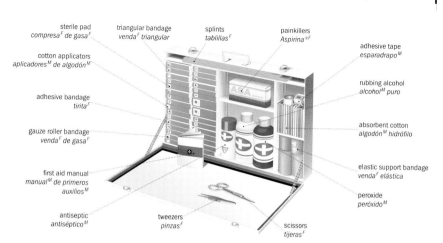

sterile pad
*compresa[F] de gasa[F]*

triangular bandage
*venda[F] triangular*

splints
*tablillas[F]*

painkillers
*Aspirina[*F]*

adhesive tape
*esparadrapo[M]*

cotton applicators
*aplicadores[M] de algodón[M]*

rubbing alcohol
*alcohol[M] puro*

adhesive bandage
*tirita[F]*

gauze roller bandage
*venda[F] de gasa[F]*

absorbent cotton
*algodón[M] hidrófilo*

first aid manual
*manual[M] de primeros auxilios[M]*

elastic support bandage
*venda[F] elástica*

peroxide
*peróxido[M]*

antiseptic
*antiséptico[M]*

tweezers
*pinzas[F]*

scissors
*tijeras[F]*

# clinical thermometers
*termómetros[M] clínicos*

digital thermometer
*termómetro[M] digital*

mercury thermometer
*termómetro[M] de mercurio[M]*

# blood pressure monitor
*tensiómetro[M]*

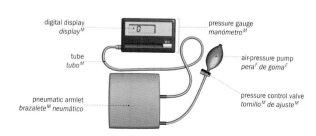

digital display
*display[M]*

pressure gauge
*manómetro[M]*

tube
*tubo[M]*

air-pressure pump
*pera[F] de goma[F]*

pneumatic armlet
*brazalete[M] neumático*

pressure control valve
*tornillo[M] de ajuste[M]*

SOCIETY

461

# hospital
*hospital*<sup>M</sup>

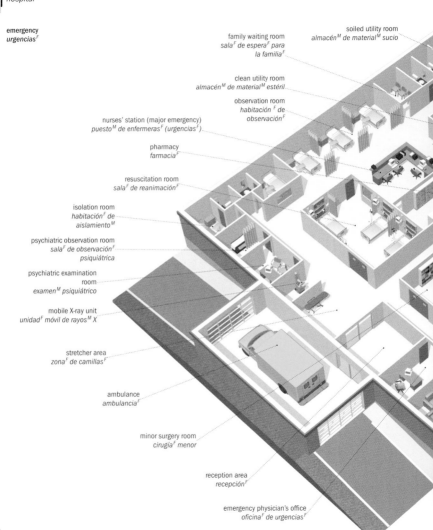

emergency
*urgencias*<sup>F</sup>

family waiting room
*sala*<sup>F</sup> *de espera*<sup>F</sup> *para
la familia*<sup>F</sup>

soiled utility room
*almacén*<sup>M</sup> *de material*<sup>M</sup> *sucio*

clean utility room
*almacén*<sup>M</sup> *de material*<sup>M</sup> *estéril*

observation room
*habitación*<sup>F</sup> *de
observación*<sup>F</sup>

nurses' station (major emergency)
*puesto*<sup>M</sup> *de enfermeras*<sup>F</sup> *(urgencias*<sup>F</sup>*)*

pharmacy
*farmacia*<sup>F</sup>

resuscitation room
*sala*<sup>F</sup> *de reanimación*<sup>F</sup>

isolation room
*habitación*<sup>F</sup> *de
aislamiento*<sup>M</sup>

psychiatric observation room
*sala*<sup>F</sup> *de observación*<sup>F</sup>
*psiquiátrica*

psychiatric examination
room
*examen*<sup>M</sup> *psiquiátrico*

mobile X-ray unit
*unidad*<sup>F</sup> *móvil de rayos*<sup>M</sup> *X*

stretcher area
*zona*<sup>F</sup> *de camillas*<sup>F</sup>

ambulance
*ambulancia*<sup>F</sup>

minor surgery room
*cirugía*<sup>F</sup> *menor*

reception area
*recepción*<sup>F</sup>

emergency physician's office
*oficina*<sup>F</sup> *de urgencias*<sup>F</sup>

SOCIETY

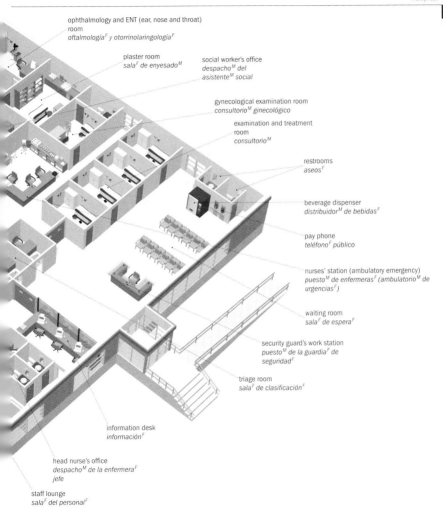

ophthalmology and ENT (ear, nose and throat)
room
*oftalmología<sup>F</sup> y otorrinolaringología<sup>F</sup>*

plaster room
*sala<sup>F</sup> de enyesado<sup>M</sup>*

social worker's office
*despacho<sup>M</sup> del
asistente<sup>M</sup> social*

gynecological examination room
*consultorio<sup>M</sup> ginecológico*

examination and treatment
room
*consultorio<sup>M</sup>*

restrooms
*aseos<sup>F</sup>*

beverage dispenser
*distribuidor<sup>M</sup> de bebidas<sup>F</sup>*

pay phone
*teléfono<sup>F</sup> público*

nurses' station (ambulatory emergency)
*puesto<sup>M</sup> de enfermeras<sup>F</sup> (ambulatorio<sup>M</sup> de
urgencias<sup>F</sup>)*

waiting room
*sala<sup>F</sup> de espera<sup>F</sup>*

security guard's work station
*puesto<sup>M</sup> de la guardia<sup>F</sup> de
seguridad<sup>F</sup>*

triage room
*sala<sup>F</sup> de clasificación<sup>F</sup>*

information desk
*información<sup>F</sup>*

head nurse's office
*despacho<sup>M</sup> de la enfermera<sup>F</sup>
jefe*

staff lounge
*sala<sup>F</sup> del personal<sup>F</sup>*

hospital

**patient room**
*habitación^M de un paciente^M*

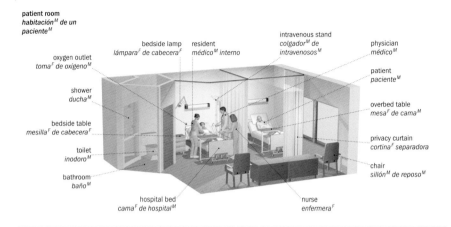

oxygen outlet
*toma^F de oxígeno^M*

bedside lamp
*lámpara^F de cabecera^F*

resident
*médico^M interno*

intravenous stand
*colgador^M de intravenosos^M*

physician
*médico^M*

shower
*ducha^M*

patient
*paciente^M*

bedside table
*mesilla^F de cabecera^F*

overbed table
*mesa^F de cama^M*

toilet
*inodoro^M*

privacy curtain
*cortina^F separadora*

bathroom
*baño^M*

chair
*sillón^M de reposo^M*

hospital bed
*cama^F de hospital^M*

nurse
*enfermera^F*

**operating suite**
*bloque^M de cirugía^F*

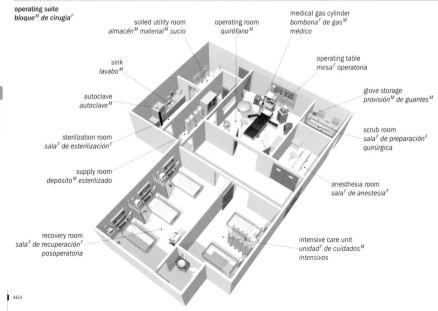

soiled utility room
*almacén^M material^M sucio*

operating room
*quirófano^M*

medical gas cylinder
*bombona^F de gas^M médico*

sink
*lavabo^M*

operating table
*mesa^F operatoria*

autoclave
*autoclave^M*

glove storage
*provisión^F de guantes^M*

sterilization room
*sala^F de esterilización^F*

scrub room
*sala^F de preparación^F quirúrgica*

supply room
*depósito^M esterilizado*

anesthesia room
*sala^F de anestesia^F*

recovery room
*sala^F de recuperación^F posoperatoria*

intensive care unit
*unidad^F de cuidados^M intensivos*

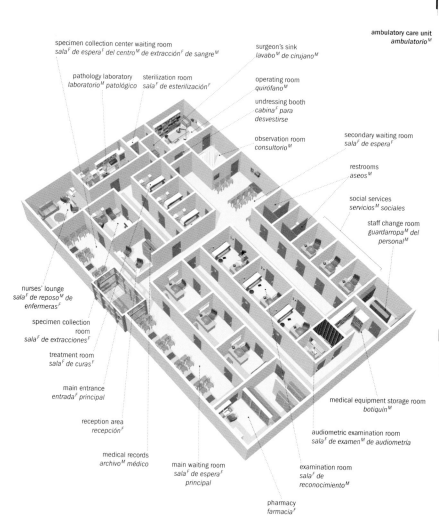

ambulatory care unit
*ambulatorio* M

specimen collection center waiting room
*sala* F *de espera* F *del centro* M *de extracción* F *de sangre* M

surgeon's sink
*lavabo* M *de cirujano* M

pathology laboratory
*laboratorio* M *patológico*

sterilization room
*sala* F *de esterilización* F

operating room
*quirófano* M

undressing booth
*cabina* F *para
desvestirse*

observation room
*consultorio* M

secondary waiting room
*sala* F *de espera* F

restrooms
*aseos* M

social services
*servicios* M *sociales*

staff change room
*guardarropa* M *del
personal* M

nurses' lounge
*sala* F *de reposo* M *de
enfermeras* F

specimen collection
room
*sala* F *de extracciones* F

treatment room
*sala* F *de curas* F

main entrance
*entrada* F *principal*

reception area
*recepción* F

medical records
*archivo* M *médico*

main waiting room
*sala* F *de espera* F
*principal*

medical equipment storage room
*botiquín* M

audiometric examination room
*sala* F *de examen* M *de audiometría*

examination room
*sala* F *de
reconocimiento* M

pharmacy
*farmacia* F

# walking aids
*auxiliares*<sup>M</sup> *ortopédicos para caminar*

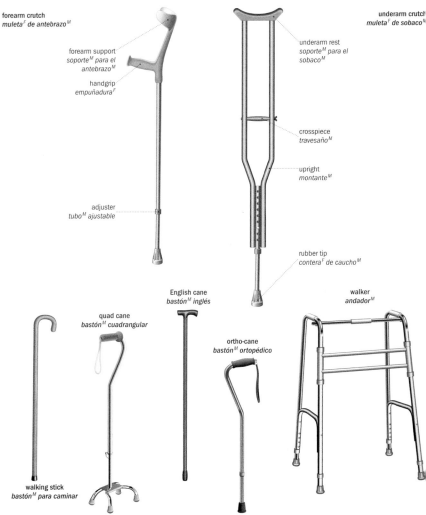

**forearm crutch**
*muleta*<sup>F</sup> *de antebrazo*<sup>M</sup>

forearm support
soporte<sup>M</sup> para el
antebrazo<sup>M</sup>

handgrip
empuñadura<sup>F</sup>

adjuster
tubo<sup>M</sup> ajustable

**underarm crutch**
*muleta*<sup>F</sup> *de sobaco*<sup>M</sup>

underarm rest
soporte<sup>M</sup> para el
sobaco<sup>M</sup>

crosspiece
travesaño<sup>M</sup>

upright
montante<sup>M</sup>

rubber tip
contera<sup>F</sup> de caucho<sup>M</sup>

**English cane**
*bastón*<sup>M</sup> *inglés*

**walker**
*andador*<sup>M</sup>

**quad cane**
*bastón*<sup>M</sup> *cuadrangular*

ortho-cane
bastón<sup>M</sup> ortopédico

**walking stick**
*bastón*<sup>M</sup> *para caminar*

# wheelchair
*silla<sup>F</sup> de ruedas<sup>F</sup>*

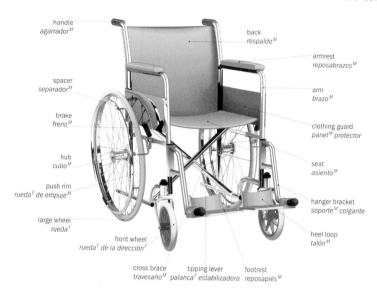

handle
*agarrador<sup>M</sup>*

back
*respaldo<sup>M</sup>*

armrest
*reposabrazos<sup>M</sup>*

spacer
*separador<sup>M</sup>*

arm
*brazo<sup>M</sup>*

brake
*freno<sup>M</sup>*

clothing guard
*panel<sup>M</sup> protector*

hub
*cubo<sup>M</sup>*

seat
*asiento<sup>M</sup>*

push rim
*rueda<sup>F</sup> de empuje<sup>M</sup>*

hanger bracket
*soporte<sup>M</sup> colgante*

large wheel
*rueda<sup>F</sup>*

heel loop
*talón<sup>M</sup>*

front wheel
*rueda<sup>F</sup> de la dirección<sup>F</sup>*

cross brace
*travesaño<sup>M</sup>*

tipping lever
*palanca<sup>F</sup> estabilizadora*

footrest
*reposapiés<sup>M</sup>*

# forms of medications
*formas<sup>F</sup> farmacéuticas de medicamentos<sup>M</sup>*

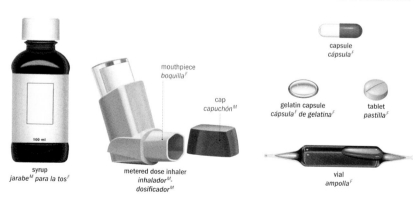

capsule
*cápsula<sup>F</sup>*

mouthpiece
*boquilla<sup>F</sup>*

cap
*capuchón<sup>M</sup>*

gelatin capsule
*cápsula<sup>F</sup> de gelatina<sup>F</sup>*

tablet
*pastilla<sup>F</sup>*

100 ml

syrup
*jarabe<sup>M</sup> para la tos<sup>F</sup>*

metered dose inhaler
*inhalador<sup>M</sup>.
dosificador<sup>M</sup>*

vial
*ampolla<sup>F</sup>*

SOCIETY

467

# dice and dominoes
*dados M y dominós M*

ordinary die
*dado M común*

poker die
*dado M de póquer M*

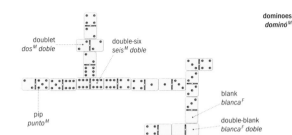

dominoes
*dominó M*

doublet
*dos M doble*

double-six
*seis M doble*

blank
*blanca F*

double-blank
*blanca F doble*

pip
*punto M*

# cards
*baraja F*

symbols
*símbolos M*

heart
*corazón M*

diamond
*diamante M*

club
*trébol M*

spade
*espada F*

joker
*comodín M*

ace
*as M*

king
*rey M*

queen
*reina F*

jack
*jota F*

standard poker hands
*manos F de póquer M*

high card
*cartas F altas*

one pair
*un par M*

two pairs
*dobles pares M*

three-of-a-kind
*trío M*

straight
*escalera F*

flush
*color M*

full house
*full M*

four-of-a-kind
*póquer M*

straight flush
*escalera F de color M*

royal flush
*escalera F real*

# board games
*juegos^M de mesa^F*

## backgammon
*backgammon^M*

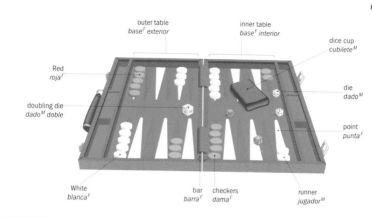

outer table
*base^F exterior*

inner table
*base^F interior*

dice cup
*cubilete^M*

Red
*roja^F*

die
*dado^M*

doubling die
*dado^M doble*

point
*punta^F*

White
*blanca^F*

bar
*barra^F*

checkers
*dama^F*

runner
*jugador^M*

## snakes and ladders
*serpientes^F y escalas^F*

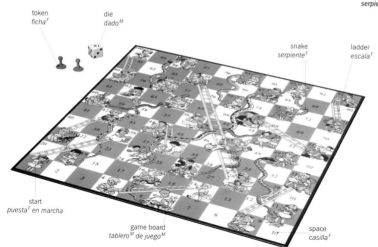

token
*ficha^F*

die
*dado^M*

snake
*serpiente^F*

ladder
*escala^F*

start
*puesta^F en marcha*

game board
*tablero^M de juego^M*

space
*casilla^F*

board games

### chess
*ajedrez*<sup>M</sup>

chessboard
*tablero*<sup>M</sup> *de ajedrez*<sup>M</sup>

queen's side
*lado*<sup>M</sup> *de la reina*<sup>F</sup>

king's side
*lado*<sup>M</sup> *del rey*<sup>M</sup>

Black
*negras*<sup>F</sup>

white square
*escaque*<sup>M</sup> *blanco*

black square
*escaque*<sup>M</sup> *negro*

chess notation
*notación*<sup>F</sup> *del ajedrez*<sup>M</sup>

White
*blancas*<sup>F</sup>

chess pieces
*piezas*<sup>F</sup>

pawn
*peón*<sup>M</sup>

rook
*torre*<sup>F</sup>

bishop
*alfil*<sup>M</sup>

knight
*caballo*<sup>M</sup>

king
*rey*<sup>M</sup>

queen
*reina*<sup>F</sup>

types of movements
*tipos*<sup>M</sup> *de movimientos*<sup>M</sup>

diagonal movement
*movimiento*<sup>M</sup> *diagonal*

vertical movement
*movimiento*<sup>M</sup> *vertical*

square movement
*movimiento*<sup>M</sup> *en ángulo*<sup>M</sup>

horizontal movement
*movimiento*<sup>M</sup> *horizontal*

### go
*go (sun-tse)*<sup>M</sup>

board
*tablero*<sup>M</sup>

handicap spot
*obstáculo*<sup>M</sup>

center
*centro*<sup>M</sup>

black stone
*piedra*<sup>F</sup> *negra*

white stone
*piedra*<sup>F</sup> *blanca*

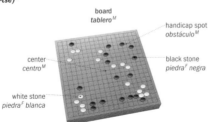

**major motions**
*principales movimientos*<sup>M</sup>

connection
*conexión*<sup>F</sup>

capture
*captura*<sup>F</sup>

contact
*contacto*<sup>M</sup>

### checkers
*damas*<sup>F</sup>

checker
*dama*<sup>F</sup>

checkerboard
*tablero*<sup>M</sup> *de damas*<sup>F</sup>

SPORTS AND GAMES

# video entertainment system
*videojuego*[M]

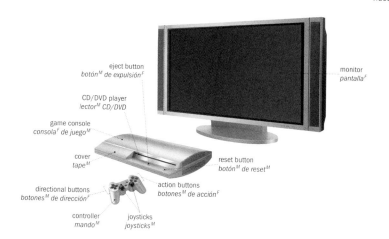

eject button
*botón*[M] *de expulsión*[F]

monitor
*pantalla*[F]

CD/DVD player
*lector*[M] *CD/DVD*

game console
*consola*[F] *de juego*[M]

cover
*tape*[M]

reset button
*botón*[M] *de reset*[M]

directional buttons
*botones*[M] *de dirección*[F]

action buttons
*botones*[M] *de acción*[F]

controller
*mando*[M]

joysticks
*joysticks*[M]

# darts
*juego*[M] *de dardos*[M]

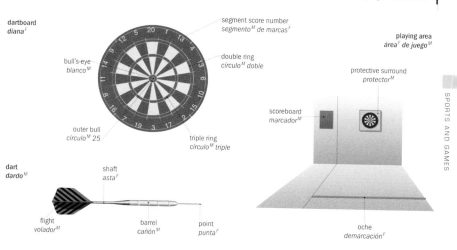

dartboard
*diana*[F]

segment score number
*segmento*[M] *de marcas*[F]

playing area
*área*[F] *de juego*[M]

bull's-eye
*blanco*[M]

double ring
*círculo*[M] *doble*

protective surround
*protector*[M]

scoreboard
*marcador*[M]

outer bull
*círculo*[M] *25*

triple ring
*círculo*[M] *triple*

dart
*dardo*[M]

shaft
*asta*[F]

flight
*volador*[M]

barrel
*cañón*[M]

point
*punta*[F]

oche
*demarcación*[F]

# arena
estadio<sup>M</sup>

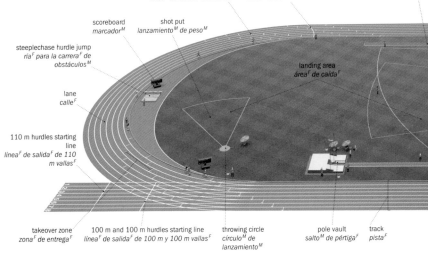

200 m starting line
línea<sup>F</sup> de salida<sup>F</sup> de 200 m

5,000 m starting line
línea<sup>F</sup> de salida<sup>F</sup> de 5.000 m

long jump and triple jump
salto<sup>M</sup> de longitud<sup>F</sup> y triple
salto<sup>M</sup>

scoreboard
marcador<sup>M</sup>

shot put
lanzamiento<sup>M</sup> de peso<sup>M</sup>

steeplechase hurdle jump
ría<sup>F</sup> para la carrera<sup>F</sup> de
obstáculos<sup>M</sup>

landing area
área<sup>F</sup> de caída<sup>F</sup>

lane
calle<sup>F</sup>

110 m hurdles starting
line
línea<sup>F</sup> de salida<sup>F</sup> de 110
m vallas<sup>F</sup>

takeover zone
zona<sup>F</sup> de entrega<sup>F</sup>

100 m and 100 m hurdles starting line
línea<sup>F</sup> de salida<sup>F</sup> de 100 m y 100 m vallas<sup>F</sup>

throwing circle
círculo<sup>M</sup> de
lanzamiento<sup>M</sup>

pole vault
salto<sup>M</sup> de pértiga<sup>F</sup>

track
pista<sup>F</sup>

## equipment
equipamiento<sup>M</sup>

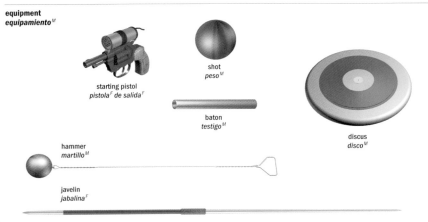

starting pistol
pistola<sup>F</sup> de salida<sup>F</sup>

shot
peso<sup>M</sup>

baton
testigo<sup>M</sup>

discus
disco<sup>M</sup>

hammer
martillo<sup>M</sup>

javelin
jabalina<sup>F</sup>

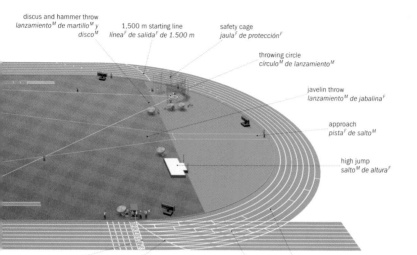

discus and hammer throw
*lanzamiento$^M$ de martillo$^M$ y disco$^M$*

1,500 m starting line
*línea$^F$ de salida$^F$ de 1.500 m*

safety cage
*jaula$^F$ de protección$^F$*

throwing circle
*círculo$^M$ de lanzamiento$^M$*

javelin throw
*lanzamiento$^M$ de jabalina$^F$*

approach
*pista$^F$ de salto$^M$*

high jump
*salto$^M$ de altura$^F$*

finish line
*llegada$^F$*

10,000 m and 4 x 400 m relay starting line
*línea$^F$ de salida$^F$ de 10.000 m y de relevos$^M$ de 4 x 400 m*

800 m starting line
*línea$^F$ de salida$^F$ 800 m*

400 m, 400 m hurdles, 4 x 100 m relay starting line
*línea$^F$ de salida$^F$ de 400 m, 400 m vallas$^F$ y relevos$^M$ de 4x100 m*

athlete: starting block
**atleta$^F$ : taco$^M$ de salida$^F$**

singlet
*camiseta$^F$*

number
*número$^M$ dorsal*

shorts
*pantalón$^M$*

pedal
*soporte$^M$ del pie$^M$*

track shoe
*zapatilla$^F$*

notch
*ranura$^F$*

starting line
*línea$^F$ de salida$^F$*

anchor
*tornillo$^M$ de anclaje$^M$*

lane line
*línea$^F$ de la calle$^F$*

rack
*cremallera$^F$*

spike
*tacos$^M$*

block
*taco$^M$*

base
*pedestal$^M$*

# baseball

*béisbol*<sup>M</sup>

**player positions**
*posición*<sup>F</sup> *de los jugadores*<sup>M</sup>

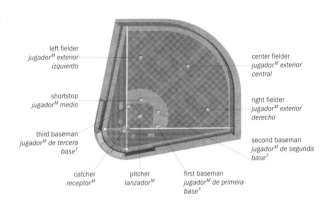

left fielder
*jugador*<sup>M</sup> *exterior izquierdo*

center fielder
*jugador*<sup>M</sup> *exterior central*

shortstop
*jugador*<sup>M</sup> *medio*

right fielder
*jugador*<sup>M</sup> *exterior derecho*

third baseman
*jugador*<sup>M</sup> *de tercera base*<sup>F</sup>

second baseman
*jugador*<sup>M</sup> *de segunda base*<sup>F</sup>

catcher
*receptor*<sup>M</sup>

pitcher
*lanzador*<sup>M</sup>

first baseman
*jugador*<sup>M</sup> *de primera base*<sup>F</sup>

**field**
*campo*<sup>M</sup>

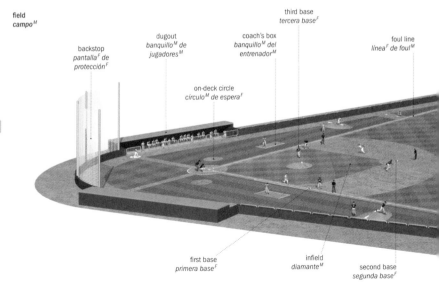

third base
*tercera base*<sup>F</sup>

dugout
*banquillo*<sup>M</sup> *de jugadores*<sup>M</sup>

coach's box
*banquillo*<sup>M</sup> *del entrenador*<sup>M</sup>

foul line
*línea*<sup>F</sup> *de foul*<sup>M</sup>

backstop
*pantalla*<sup>F</sup> *de protección*<sup>F</sup>

on-deck circle
*círculo*<sup>M</sup> *de espera*<sup>F</sup>

first base
*primera base*<sup>F</sup>

infield
*diamante*<sup>M</sup>

second base
*segunda base*<sup>F</sup>

SPORTS AND GAMES

pitch
*lanzamiento*<sup>M</sup>

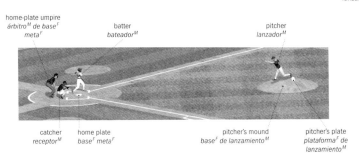

home-plate umpire
*árbitro*<sup>M</sup> *de base*<sup>F</sup>
*meta*<sup>F</sup>

batter
*bateador*<sup>M</sup>

pitcher
*lanzador*<sup>M</sup>

catcher
*receptor*<sup>M</sup>

home plate
*base*<sup>F</sup> *meta*<sup>F</sup>

pitcher's mound
*base*<sup>F</sup> *de lanzamiento*<sup>M</sup>

pitcher's plate
*plataforma*<sup>F</sup> *de
lanzamiento*<sup>M</sup>

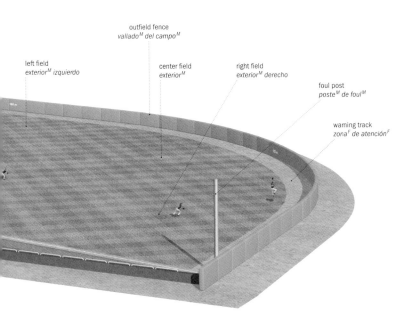

outfield fence
*vallado*<sup>M</sup> *del campo*<sup>M</sup>

left field
*exterior*<sup>M</sup> *izquierdo*

center field
*exterior*<sup>M</sup>

right field
*exterior*<sup>M</sup> *derecho*

foul post
*poste*<sup>M</sup> *de foul*<sup>M</sup>

warning track
*zona*<sup>F</sup> *de atención*<sup>F</sup>

baseball

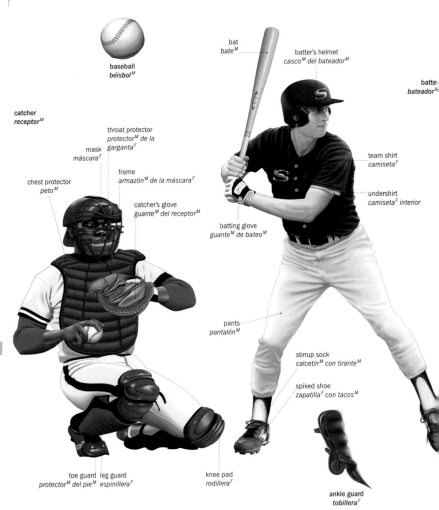

bat
*bate*<sup>M</sup>

batter's helmet
*casco*<sup>M</sup> *del bateador*<sup>M</sup>

baseball
*béisbol*<sup>M</sup>

batte
*bateador*<sup>M</sup>

catcher
*receptor*<sup>M</sup>

throat protector
*protector*<sup>M</sup> *de la*
*garganta*<sup>F</sup>

mask
*máscara*<sup>F</sup>

team shirt
*camiseta*<sup>F</sup>

frame
*armazón*<sup>M</sup> *de la máscara*<sup>F</sup>

undershirt
*camiseta*<sup>F</sup> *interior*

chest protector
*peto*<sup>M</sup>

catcher's glove
*guante*<sup>M</sup> *del receptor*<sup>M</sup>

batting glove
*guante*<sup>M</sup> *de bateo*<sup>M</sup>

pants
*pantalón*<sup>M</sup>

stirrup sock
*calcetín*<sup>M</sup> *con tirante*<sup>M</sup>

spiked shoe
*zapatilla*<sup>F</sup> *con tacos*<sup>M</sup>

toe guard   leg guard
*protector*<sup>M</sup> *del pie*<sup>M</sup>  *espinillera*<sup>F</sup>

knee pad
*rodillera*<sup>F</sup>

ankle guard
*tobillera*<sup>F</sup>

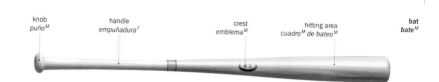

knob
puño M

handle
empuñadura F

crest
emblema M

hitting area
cuadro M de bateo M

bat
bate M

cross section of a baseball
corte M de la pelota F de
béisbol M

cork ball
bola F de corcho M

yarn
bola F de hilo M

cover
forro M

stitches
costura F

web
canasta F

fielder's glove
guante M de recogida F

strap
trabilla F

thumb
pulgar M

finger
dedo M

palm
palma F

heel
talón M

lace
cordón M

softball
softball M

softball glove
guante M de softball M

softball bat
bate M de softball M

softball
pelota de softball M

SPORTS AND GAMES

# cricket
*cricket*^M

cricket player: batsman
*jugador*^M *de criquet*^M :
*bateador*^M

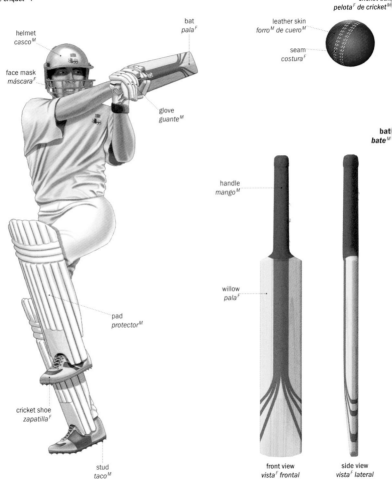

bat
*pala*^F

helmet
*casco*^M

face mask
*máscara*^F

glove
*guante*^M

cricket ball
*pelota*^F *de cricket*^M

leather skin
*forro*^M *de cuero*^M

seam
*costura*^F

bat
*bate*^M

handle
*mango*^M

willow
*pala*^F

pad
*protector*^M

cricket shoe
*zapatilla*^F

stud
*taco*^M

front view
*vista*^F *frontal*

side view
*vista*^F *lateral*

field
campo^M

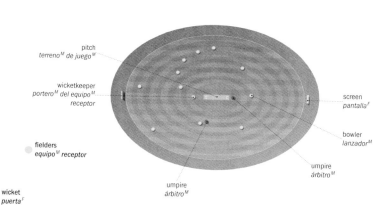

pitch
terreno^M de juego^M

wicketkeeper
portero^M del equipo^M
receptor

screen
pantalla^F

bowler
lanzador^M

umpire
árbitro^M

fielders
equipo^M receptor

umpire
árbitro^M

wicket
puerta^F

bail
travesaño^M

stump
estaca^F

pitch
terreno^M de juego^M

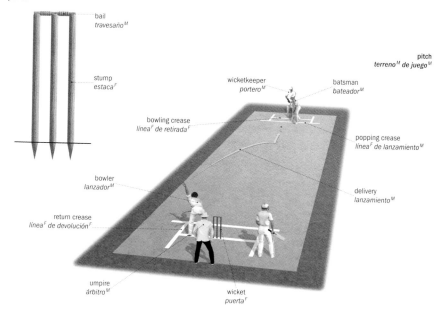

wicketkeeper
portero^M

batsman
bateador^M

bowling crease
línea^F de retirada^F

popping crease
línea^F de lanzamiento^M

bowler
lanzador^M

delivery
lanzamiento^M

return crease
línea^F de devolución^F

umpire
árbitro^M

wicket
puerta^F

# soccer

*fútbol*$^M$

**soccer player**
*futbolista*$^{M/F}$

team shirt
*camiseta*$^F$ *del equipo*$^M$

goalkeeper's gloves
*guantes*$^M$ *del portero*$^M$

shorts
*pantalones*$^M$

interchangeable studs
*tacos*$^M$ *de rosca*$^F$

soccer shoe
*bota*$^F$ *de fútbol*$^M$

shin guard
*espinillera*$^F$

sock
*calcetín*$^M$

soccer ball
*balón*$^M$ *de fútbol*$^M$

**playing field**
*campo*$^M$

center flag
*banderín*$^M$ *de línea*$^M$ *de centro*$^M$

penalty spot
*punto*$^M$ *de penalti*$^M$

goal area
*área*$^F$ *pequeña*

goal
*portería*$^F$

penalty area
*área*$^F$ *de penalti*$^M$

penalty marker
*línea*$^F$ *de área*$^F$ *de penalti*$^M$

penalty arc
*semicírculo*$^M$ *del área*$^F$

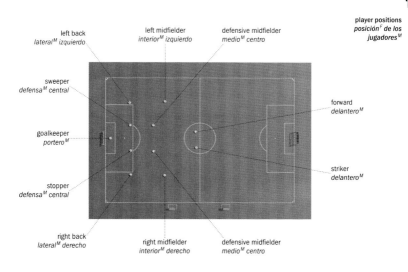

left back
*lateral<sup>M</sup> izquierdo*

left midfielder
*interior<sup>M</sup> izquierdo*

defensive midfielder
*medio<sup>M</sup> centro*

sweeper
*defensa<sup>M</sup> central*

forward
*delantero<sup>M</sup>*

goalkeeper
*portero<sup>M</sup>*

striker
*delantero<sup>M</sup>*

stopper
*defensa<sup>M</sup> central*

right back
*lateral<sup>M</sup> derecho*

right midfielder
*interior<sup>M</sup> derecho*

defensive midfielder
*medio<sup>M</sup> centro*

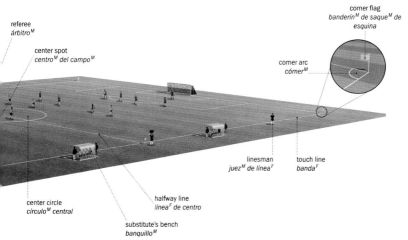

referee
*árbitro<sup>M</sup>*

center spot
*centro<sup>M</sup> del campo<sup>M</sup>*

corner flag
*banderín<sup>M</sup> de saque<sup>M</sup> de esquina*

corner arc
*córner<sup>M</sup>*

linesman
*juez<sup>M</sup> de línea<sup>F</sup>*

touch line
*banda<sup>F</sup>*

center circle
*círculo<sup>M</sup> central*

halfway line
*línea<sup>F</sup> de centro*

substitute's bench
*banquillo<sup>M</sup>*

SPORTS AND GAMES

# rugby
*rugby*<sup>M</sup>

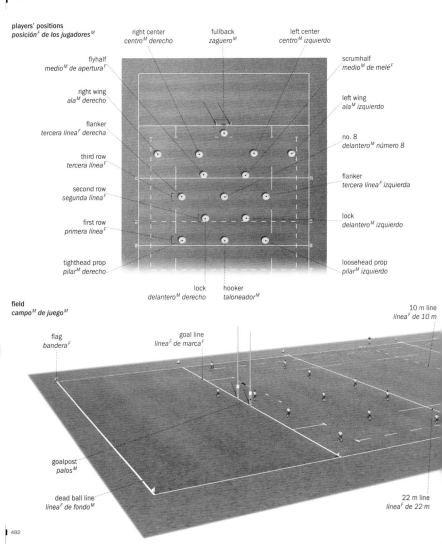

**players' positions**
*posición<sup>F</sup> de los jugadores<sup>M</sup>*

right center
*centro<sup>M</sup> derecho*

fullback
*zaguero<sup>M</sup>*

left center
*centro<sup>M</sup> izquierdo*

flyhalf
*medio<sup>M</sup> de apertura<sup>F</sup>*

scrumhalf
*medio<sup>M</sup> de melé<sup>F</sup>*

right wing
*ala<sup>M</sup> derecho*

left wing
*ala<sup>M</sup> izquierdo*

flanker
*tercera línea<sup>F</sup> derecha*

no. 8
*delantero<sup>M</sup> número 8*

third row
*tercera línea<sup>F</sup>*

flanker
*tercera línea<sup>F</sup> izquierda*

second row
*segunda línea<sup>F</sup>*

lock
*delantero<sup>M</sup> izquierdo*

first row
*primera línea<sup>F</sup>*

tighthead prop
*pilar<sup>M</sup> derecho*

loosehead prop
*pilar<sup>M</sup> izquierdo*

lock
*delantero<sup>M</sup> derecho*

hooker
*taloneador<sup>M</sup>*

**field**
*campo<sup>M</sup> de juego<sup>M</sup>*

10 m line
*línea<sup>F</sup> de 10 m*

flag
*bandera<sup>F</sup>*

goal line
*línea<sup>F</sup> de marca<sup>F</sup>*

goalpost
*palos<sup>M</sup>*

dead ball line
*línea<sup>F</sup> de fondo<sup>M</sup>*

22 m line
*línea<sup>F</sup> de 22 m*

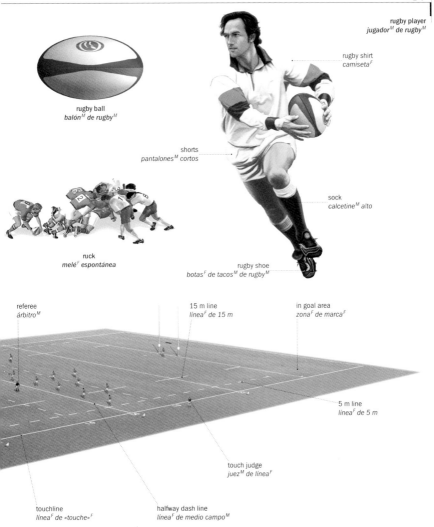

rugby player
*jugador*<sup>M</sup> *de rugby*<sup>M</sup>

rugby shirt
*camiseta*<sup>F</sup>

rugby ball
*balón*<sup>M</sup> *de rugby*<sup>M</sup>

shorts
*pantalones*<sup>M</sup> *cortos*

sock
*calcetine*<sup>M</sup> *alto*

ruck
*melé*<sup>F</sup> *espontánea*

rugby shoe
*botas*<sup>F</sup> *de tacos*<sup>M</sup> *de rugby*<sup>M</sup>

referee
*árbitro*<sup>M</sup>

15 m line
*línea*<sup>F</sup> *de 15 m*

in goal area
*zona*<sup>F</sup> *de marca*<sup>F</sup>

5 m line
*línea*<sup>F</sup> *de 5 m*

touch judge
*juez*<sup>M</sup> *de línea*<sup>F</sup>

touchline
*línea*<sup>F</sup> *de «touche»*<sup>F</sup>

halfway dash line
*línea*<sup>F</sup> *de medio campo*<sup>M</sup>

SPORTS AND GAMES

483

# American football

*fútbol*$^M$ *americano*

**scrimmage: defense**
*melé*$^F$*: defensa*$^F$

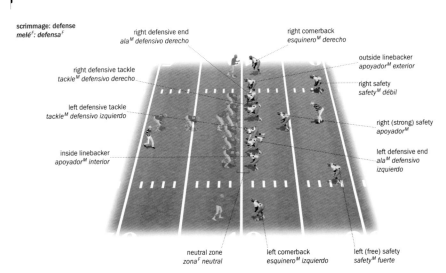

right defensive end
*ala*$^M$ *defensivo derecho*

right cornerback
*esquinero*$^M$ *derecho*

outside linebacker
*apoyador*$^M$ *exterior*

right defensive tackle
*tackle*$^M$ *defensivo derecho*

right safety
*safety*$^M$ *débil*

left defensive tackle
*tackle*$^M$ *defensivo izquierdo*

right (strong) safety
*apoyador*$^M$

inside linebacker
*apoyador*$^M$ *interior*

left defensive end
*ala*$^M$ *defensivo izquierdo*

neutral zone
*zona*$^F$ *neutral*

left cornerback
*esquinero*$^M$ *izquierdo*

left (free) safety
*safety*$^M$ *fuerte*

**playing field for American football**
*campo*$^M$ *de juego*$^M$ *de fútbol*$^M$ *americano*

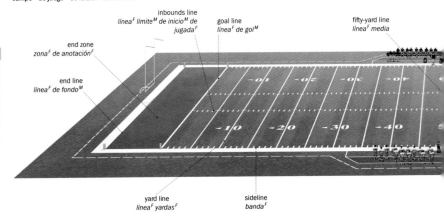

inbounds line
*línea*$^F$ *límite*$^M$ *de inicio*$^M$ *de jugada*$^F$

goal line
*línea*$^F$ *de gol*$^M$

fifty-yard line
*línea*$^F$ *media*

end zone
*zona*$^F$ *de anotación*$^F$

end line
*línea*$^F$ *de fondo*$^M$

yard line
*línea*$^F$ *yardas*$^F$

sideline
*banda*$^F$

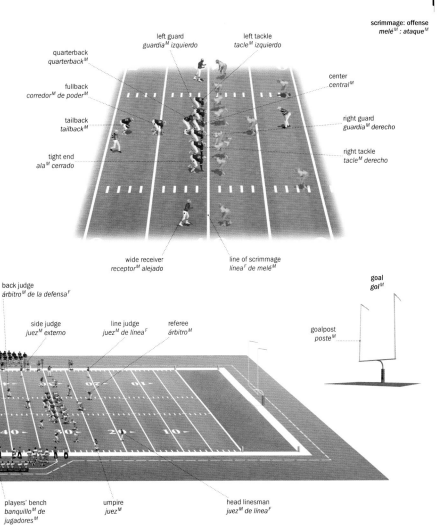

scrimmage: offense
*melé*$^M$ : *ataque*$^M$

left guard
*guardia*$^M$ *izquierdo*

left tackle
*tacle*$^M$ *izquierdo*

quarterback
*quarterback*$^M$

center
*central*$^M$

fullback
*corredor*$^M$ *de poder*$^M$

tailback
*tailback*$^M$

right guard
*guardia*$^M$ *derecho*

tight end
*ala*$^M$ *cerrado*

right tackle
*tacle*$^M$ *derecho*

wide receiver
*receptor*$^M$ *alejado*

line of scrimmage
*línea*$^F$ *de melé*$^M$

goal
*gol*$^M$

back judge
*árbitro*$^M$ *de la defensa*$^F$

side judge
*juez*$^M$ *externo*

line judge
*juez*$^M$ *de línea*$^F$

referee
*árbitro*$^M$

goalpost
*poste*$^M$

players' bench
*banquillo*$^M$ *de jugadores*$^M$

umpire
*juez*$^M$

head linesman
*juez*$^M$ *de línea*$^F$

American football

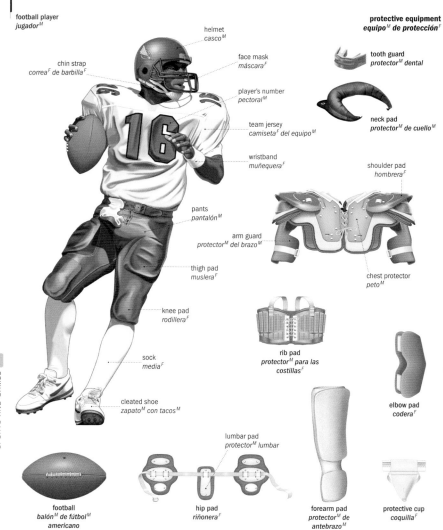

football player
*jugador*<sup>M</sup>

protective equipment
*equipo*<sup>M</sup> *de protección*<sup>F</sup>

helmet
*casco*<sup>M</sup>

face mask
*máscara*<sup>F</sup>

chin strap
*correa*<sup>F</sup> *de barbilla*<sup>F</sup>

player's number
*pectoral*<sup>M</sup>

team jersey
*camiseta*<sup>F</sup> *del equipo*<sup>M</sup>

wristband
*muñequera*<sup>F</sup>

pants
*pantalón*<sup>M</sup>

arm guard
*protector*<sup>M</sup> *del brazo*<sup>M</sup>

thigh pad
*muslera*<sup>F</sup>

knee pad
*rodillera*<sup>F</sup>

sock
*media*<sup>F</sup>

cleated shoe
*zapato*<sup>M</sup> *con tacos*<sup>M</sup>

tooth guard
*protector*<sup>M</sup> *dental*

neck pad
*protector*<sup>M</sup> *de cuello*<sup>M</sup>

shoulder pad
*hombrera*<sup>F</sup>

chest protector
*peto*<sup>M</sup>

rib pad
*protector*<sup>M</sup> *para las
costillas*<sup>F</sup>

elbow pad
*codera*<sup>F</sup>

lumbar pad
*protector*<sup>M</sup> *lumbar*

football
*balón*<sup>M</sup> *de fútbol*<sup>M</sup>
*americano*

hip pad
*riñonera*<sup>F</sup>

forearm pad
*protector*<sup>M</sup> *de
antebrazo*<sup>M</sup>

protective cup
*coquilla*<sup>F</sup>

SPORTS AND GAMES

# volleyball
*voleibol*[M]

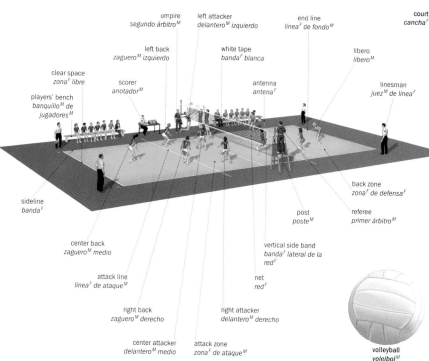

court
*cancha*[F]

umpire
*segundo árbitro*[M]

left attacker
*delantero*[M] *izquierdo*

end line
*línea*[F] *de fondo*[M]

left back
*zaguero*[M] *izquierdo*

white tape
*banda*[F] *blanca*

libero
*libero*[M]

clear space
*zona*[F] *libre*

scorer
*anotador*[M]

antenna
*antena*[F]

linesman
*juez*[M] *de línea*[F]

players' bench
*banquillo*[M] *de
jugadores*[M]

sideline
*banda*[F]

back zone
*zona*[F] *de defensa*[F]

post
*poste*[M]

referee
*primer árbitro*[M]

center back
*zaguero*[M] *medio*

vertical side band
*banda*[F] *lateral de la
red*[F]

attack line
*línea*[F] *de ataque*[M]

net
*red*[F]

right back
*zaguero*[M] *derecho*

right attacker
*delantero*[M] *derecho*

center attacker
*delantero*[M] *medio*

attack zone
*zona*[F] *de ataque*[M]

volleyball
*voleibol*[M]

## techniques
*técnicas*[F]

tip
*toque*[M]

bump
*rebote*[M]

serve
*saque*[M]

# basketball
*baloncesto*<sup>M</sup>

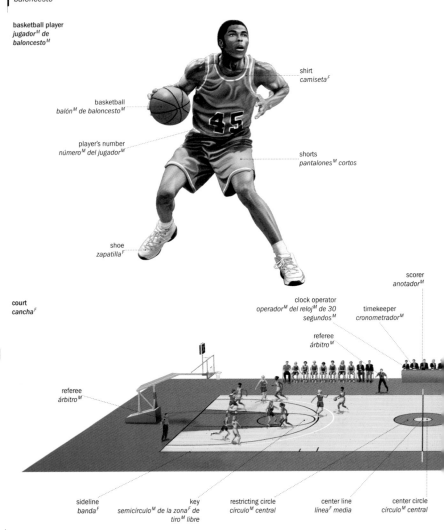

basketball player
*jugador*<sup>M</sup> *de*
*baloncesto*<sup>M</sup>

shirt
*camiseta*<sup>F</sup>

basketball
*balón*<sup>M</sup> *de baloncesto*<sup>M</sup>

player's number
*número*<sup>M</sup> *del jugador*<sup>M</sup>

shorts
*pantalones*<sup>M</sup> *cortos*

shoe
*zapatilla*<sup>F</sup>

scorer
*anotador*<sup>M</sup>

court
*cancha*<sup>F</sup>

clock operator
*operador*<sup>M</sup> *del reloj*<sup>M</sup> *de 30 segundos*<sup>M</sup>

timekeeper
*cronometrador*<sup>M</sup>

referee
*árbitro*<sup>M</sup>

referee
*árbitro*<sup>M</sup>

sideline
*banda*<sup>F</sup>

key
*semicírculo*<sup>M</sup> *de la zona*<sup>F</sup> *de tiro*<sup>M</sup> *libre*

restricting circle
*círculo*<sup>M</sup> *central*

center line
*línea*<sup>F</sup> *media*

center circle
*círculo*<sup>M</sup> *central*

player positions
*posiciones*^M *de los*
*jugadores*^M

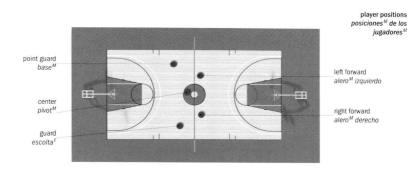

point guard
*base*^M

center
*pívot*^M

guard
*escolta*^F

left forward
*alero*^M *izquierdo*

right forward
*alero*^M *derecho*

backstop
*canasta*^F

backboard
*tablero*^M

rim
*aro*^M

net
*red*^F

coach
*entrenador*^M

assistant coach
*entrenador*^M *adjunto*

trainer
*preparador*^M

backboard support
*soporte*^M *del tablero*^M

basket
*canasta*^F

padded upright
*poste*^M *con*
*protecciones*^M

padded base
*base*^F *con*
*protecciones*^F

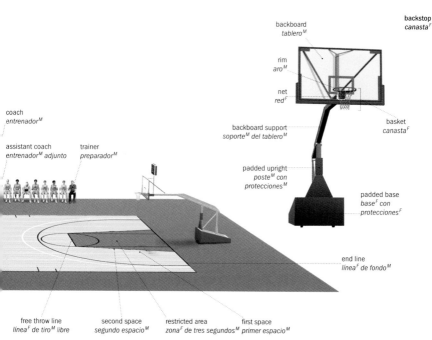

end line
*línea*^F *de fondo*^M

free throw line
*línea*^F *de tiro*^M *libre*

second space
*segundo espacio*^M

restricted area
*zona*^F *de tres segundos*^M

first space
*primer espacio*^M

# tennis
*tenis*$^M$

**court**
*cancha*$^F$

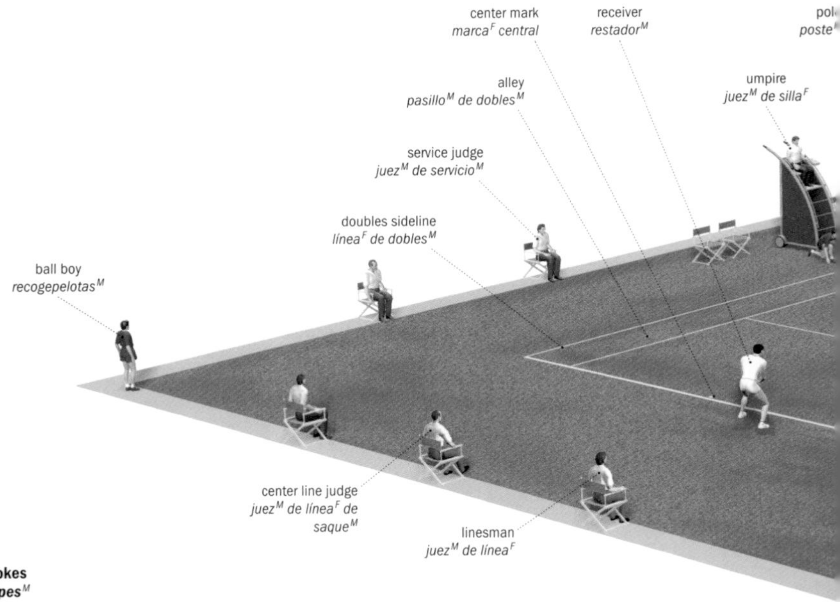

center mark
*marca*$^F$ *central*

receiver
*restador*$^M$

pol
*poste*

alley
*pasillo*$^M$ *de dobles*$^M$

umpire
*juez*$^M$ *de silla*$^F$

service judge
*juez*$^M$ *de servicio*$^M$

doubles sideline
*línea*$^F$ *de dobles*$^M$

ball boy
*recogepelotas*$^M$

center line judge
*juez*$^M$ *de línea*$^F$ *de saque*$^M$

linesman
*juez*$^M$ *de línea*$^F$

**strokes**
*golpes*$^M$

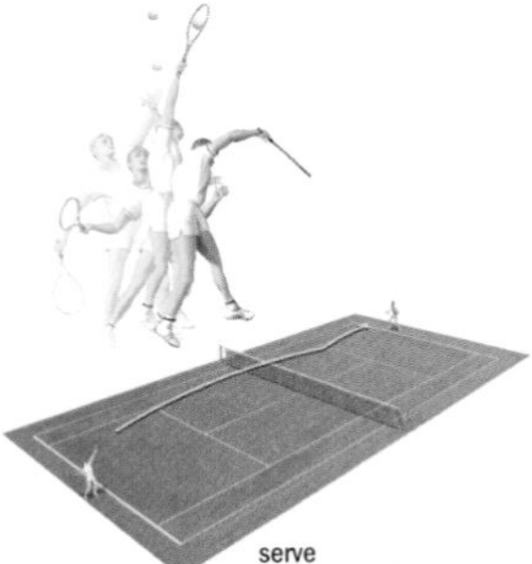

serve
*de servicio*$^M$

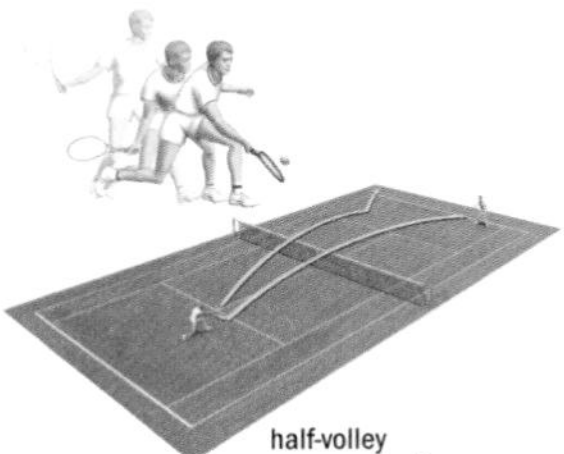

half-volley
*media volea*$^F$

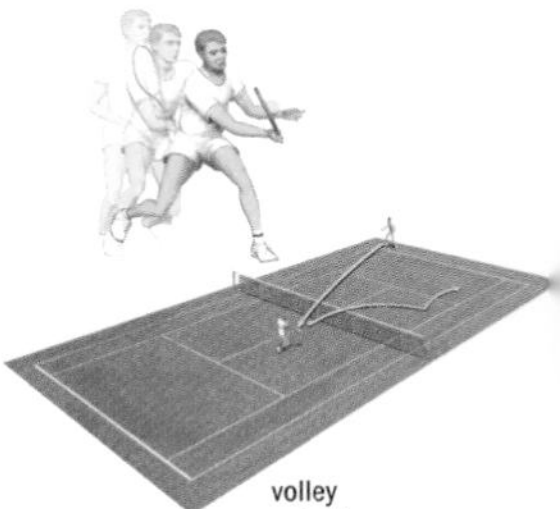

volley
*volea*$^F$

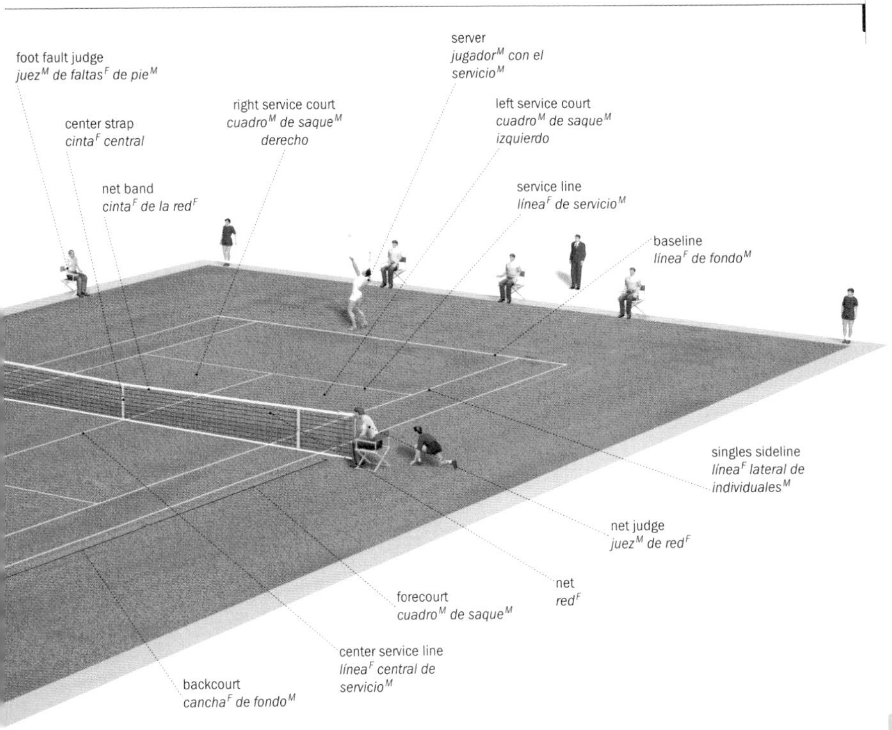

foot fault judge
*juez^M de faltas^F de pie^M*

center strap
*cinta^F central*

net band
*cinta^F de la red^F*

server
*jugador^M con el
servicio^M*

right service court
*cuadro^M de saque^M
derecho*

left service court
*cuadro^M de saque^M
izquierdo*

service line
*línea^F de servicio^M*

baseline
*línea^F de fondo^M*

singles sideline
*línea^F lateral de
individuales^M*

net judge
*juez^M de red^F*

net
*red^F*

forecourt
*cuadro^M de saque^M*

center service line
*línea^F central de
servicio^M*

backcourt
*cancha^F de fondo^M*

lob
*globo^M*

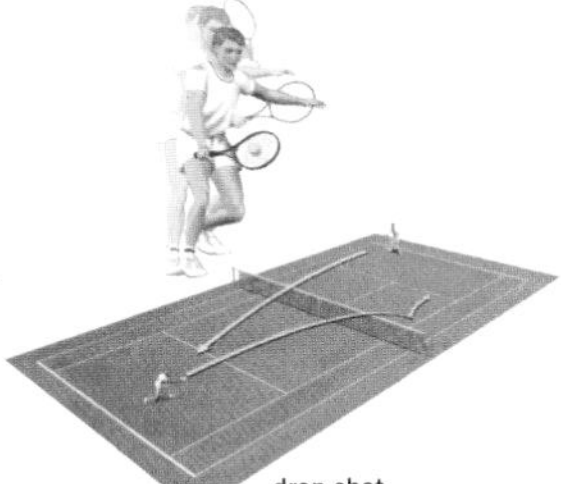

drop shot
*dejada^F*

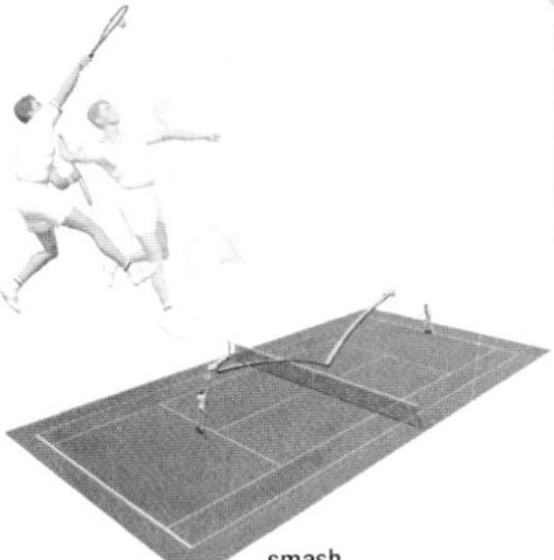

smash
*smash^M*

tennis

tennis racket
*raqueta<sup>F</sup> de tenis<sup>M</sup>*

frame
*bastidor<sup>M</sup>*

stringing
*cordaje<sup>M</sup>*

head
*cabeza<sup>F</sup>*

shoulder
*hombro<sup>M</sup>*

throat
*garganta<sup>F</sup>*

shaft
*mango<sup>M</sup>*

handle
*empuñadura<sup>F</sup>*

butt
*puño<sup>M</sup>*

tennis ball
*pelota<sup>F</sup> de tenis<sup>M</sup>*

polo shirt
*polo<sup>M</sup>*

tennis player
*tenista<sup>M/F</sup>*

wristband
*muñequera<sup>F</sup>*

tennis skirt
*falda<sup>M</sup>*

sock
*calcetín<sup>M</sup>*

tennis shoe
*zapatilla<sup>F</sup> de tenis<sup>M</sup>*

scoreboard
*marcador<sup>M</sup>*

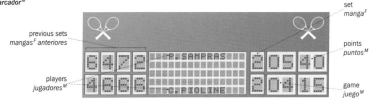

set
*manga<sup>F</sup>*

previous sets
*mangas<sup>F</sup> anteriores*

points
*puntos<sup>M</sup>*

players
*jugadores<sup>M</sup>*

game
*juego<sup>M</sup>*

playing surfaces
*superficies<sup>F</sup> de juego<sup>M</sup>*

grass
*hierba<sup>F</sup>*

clay
*tierra<sup>F</sup> batida*

hard surface (cement)
*superficie<sup>F</sup> dura (cemento<sup>M</sup>)*

synthetic surface
*superficie<sup>F</sup> sintética*

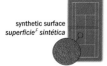

# table tennis
*tenis*<sup>M</sup> *de mesa*<sup>F</sup>

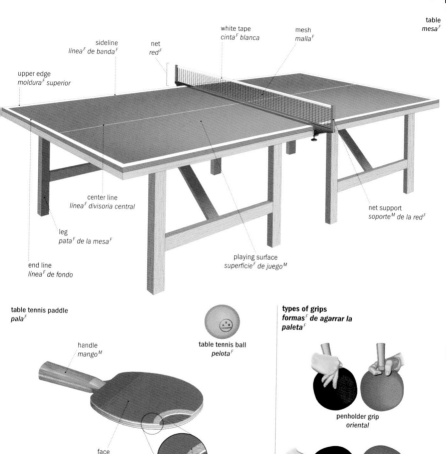

table
*mesa*<sup>F</sup>

white tape
*cinta*<sup>F</sup> *blanca*

mesh
*malla*<sup>F</sup>

sideline
*línea*<sup>F</sup> *de banda*<sup>F</sup>

net
*red*<sup>F</sup>

upper edge
*moldura*<sup>F</sup> *superior*

center line
*línea*<sup>F</sup> *divisoria central*

net support
*soporte*<sup>M</sup> *de la red*<sup>F</sup>

leg
*pata*<sup>F</sup> *de la mesa*<sup>F</sup>

end line
*línea*<sup>F</sup> *de fondo*

playing surface
*superficie*<sup>F</sup> *de juego*<sup>M</sup>

table tennis paddle
*pala*<sup>F</sup>

table tennis ball
*pelota*<sup>F</sup>

types of grips
**formas**<sup>F</sup> **de agarrar la**
**paleta**<sup>F</sup>

handle
*mango*<sup>M</sup>

penholder grip
*oriental*

face
*cara*<sup>F</sup>

blade
*paleta*<sup>F</sup>

covering
*revestimiento*<sup>M</sup>

shake-hands grip
*occidental*

SPORTS AND GAMES

# badminton

*bádminton*<sup>M</sup>

**court**
*cancha*<sup>F</sup>

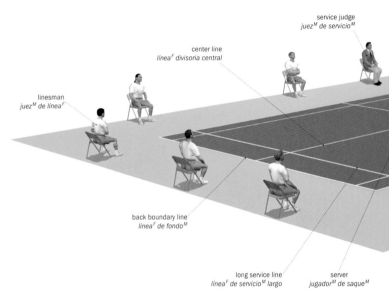

service judge
*juez*<sup>M</sup> *de servicio*<sup>M</sup>

center line
*línea*<sup>F</sup> *divisoria central*

linesman
*juez*<sup>M</sup> *de línea*<sup>F</sup>

back boundary line
*línea*<sup>F</sup> *de fondo*<sup>M</sup>

long service line
*línea*<sup>F</sup> *de servicio*<sup>M</sup> *largo*

server
*jugador*<sup>M</sup> *de saque*<sup>M</sup>

**badminton racket**
*raqueta*<sup>F</sup> *de bádminton*<sup>M</sup>

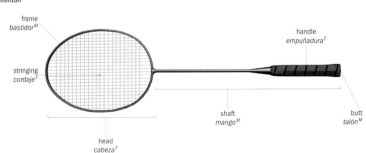

frame
*bastidor*<sup>M</sup>

handle
*empuñadura*<sup>F</sup>

stringing
*cordaje*<sup>F</sup>

shaft
*mango*<sup>M</sup>

butt
*talón*<sup>M</sup>

head
*cabeza*<sup>F</sup>

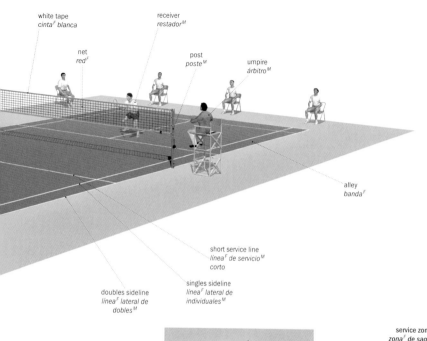

white tape
cinta<sup>F</sup> blanca

receiver
restador<sup>M</sup>

net
red<sup>F</sup>

post
poste<sup>M</sup>

umpire
árbitro<sup>M</sup>

alley
banda<sup>F</sup>

short service line
línea<sup>F</sup> de servicio<sup>M</sup>
corto

singles sideline
línea<sup>F</sup> lateral de
individuales<sup>M</sup>

doubles sideline
línea<sup>F</sup> lateral de
dobles<sup>M</sup>

service zones
zona<sup>F</sup> de saque

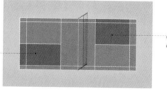

singles service court
cuadro<sup>M</sup> de servicio<sup>M</sup> de
individuales<sup>M</sup>

doubles service court
cuadro<sup>M</sup> de servicio<sup>M</sup> de dobles<sup>M</sup>

synthetic shuttlecock
volante<sup>M</sup> sintético

feathered shuttlecock
volante<sup>M</sup> de plumas<sup>F</sup>

feather crown
penacho<sup>M</sup> de plumas<sup>F</sup>

cork tip
corcho<sup>M</sup>

# gymnastics
*gimnasia*<sup>F</sup>

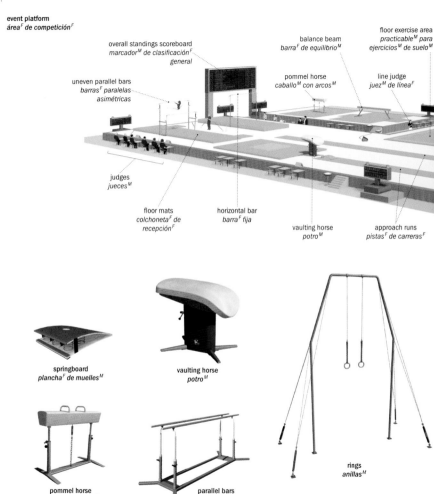

**event platform**
*área*<sup>F</sup> *de competición*<sup>F</sup>

overall standings scoreboard
*marcador*<sup>M</sup> *de clasificación*<sup>F</sup>
*general*

balance beam
*barra*<sup>F</sup> *de equilibrio*<sup>M</sup>

floor exercise area
*practicable*<sup>M</sup> *para
ejercicios*<sup>M</sup> *de suelo*<sup>M</sup>

uneven parallel bars
*barras*<sup>F</sup> *paralelas
asimétricas*

pommel horse
*caballo*<sup>M</sup> *con arcos*<sup>M</sup>

line judge
*juez*<sup>M</sup> *de línea*<sup>F</sup>

judges
*jueces*<sup>M</sup>

floor mats
*colchoneta*<sup>F</sup> *de
recepción*<sup>F</sup>

horizontal bar
*barra*<sup>F</sup> *fija*

vaulting horse
*potro*<sup>M</sup>

approach runs
*pistas*<sup>F</sup> *de carreras*<sup>F</sup>

springboard
*plancha*<sup>F</sup> *de muelles*<sup>M</sup>

vaulting horse
*potro*<sup>M</sup>

rings
*anillas*<sup>M</sup>

pommel horse
*caballo*<sup>M</sup> *con aros*<sup>M</sup>

parallel bars
*barras*<sup>F</sup> *paralelas*

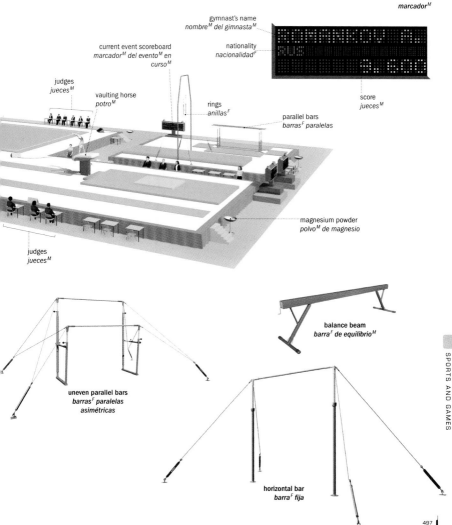

scoreboard
*marcador*$^M$

gymnast's name
*nombre*$^M$ *del gimnasta*$^M$

nationality
*nacionalidad*$^F$

current event scoreboard
*marcador*$^M$ *del evento*$^M$ *en curso*$^M$

score
*jueces*$^M$

judges
*jueces*$^M$

vaulting horse
*potro*$^M$

rings
*anillas*$^F$

parallel bars
*barras*$^F$ *paralelas*

magnesium powder
*polvo*$^M$ *de magnesio*

judges
*jueces*$^M$

uneven parallel bars
*barras*$^F$ *paralelas asimétricas*

balance beam
*barra*$^F$ *de equilibrio*$^M$

horizontal bar
*barra*$^F$ *fija*

# boxing
*boxeo*<sup>M</sup>

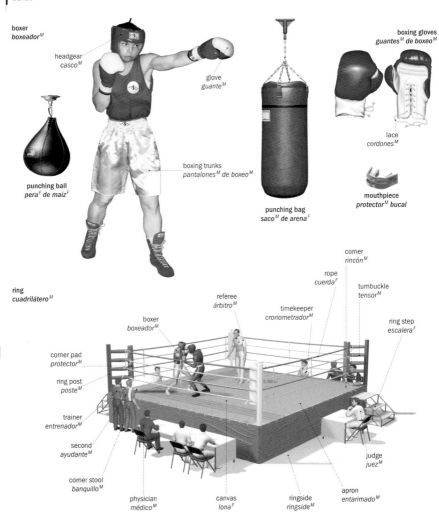

boxer
*boxeador*<sup>M</sup>

headgear
*casco*<sup>M</sup>

glove
*guante*<sup>M</sup>

boxing gloves
*guantes*<sup>M</sup> *de boxeo*<sup>M</sup>

lace
*cordones*<sup>M</sup>

boxing trunks
*pantalones*<sup>M</sup> *de boxeo*<sup>M</sup>

punching ball
*pera*<sup>F</sup> *de maíz*<sup>F</sup>

mouthpiece
*protector*<sup>M</sup> *bucal*

punching bag
*saco*<sup>M</sup> *de arena*<sup>F</sup>

corner
*rincón*<sup>M</sup>

rope
*cuerda*<sup>F</sup>

turnbuckle
*tensor*<sup>M</sup>

ring
*cuadrilátero*<sup>M</sup>

referee
*árbitro*<sup>M</sup>

timekeeper
*cronometrador*<sup>M</sup>

ring step
*escalera*<sup>F</sup>

boxer
*boxeador*<sup>M</sup>

corner pad
*protector*<sup>M</sup>

ring post
*poste*<sup>M</sup>

trainer
*entrenador*<sup>M</sup>

second
*ayudante*<sup>M</sup>

judge
*juez*<sup>M</sup>

corner stool
*banquillo*<sup>M</sup>

physician
*médico*<sup>M</sup>

canvas
*lona*<sup>F</sup>

ringside
*ringside*<sup>M</sup>

apron
*entarimado*<sup>M</sup>

SPORTS AND GAMES

# judo
*judo^M*

scorers and timekeepers
*anotadores^M y cronometradores^M*

mat
*tatami^M*

medical team
*equipo^M médico*

safety area
*zona^F de seguridad^F*

contestant
*uke (defensor^M)*

danger area
*área^F de peligro^M*

contest area
*zona^F de combate^M*

referee
*judoka^M neutral*

judge
*juez^M*

scoreboard
*marcador^M*

judogi
*traje^M de judo (judoji^M)*

jacket
*kimono^M*

**examples of holds and throws**
*ejemplos^M de llaves^F*

holding
*inmovilización^F*

stomach throw
*proyección^F en circulo^M*

sweeping hip throw
*proyección^F primera de cadera^F*

major outer reaping throw
*osoto-gari (gran siega^F) exterior*

major inner reaping throw
*gran siega^F interior*

naked strangle
*estrangulación^F*

arm lock
*inmovilización^F de brazo^M*

one-arm shoulder throw
*proyección^F por encima del hombro^M con una mano^F*

trousers
*pantalón^M*

belt
*cinturón^M*

SPORTS AND GAMES

499

# weightlifting
*halterofilia*<sup>F</sup>

barbell
*barra*<sup>F</sup> *con pesas*<sup>F</sup>

wristband
*muñequera*<sup>F</sup>

weightlifting belt
*cinturón*<sup>M</sup>

sleeveless jersey
*camiseta*<sup>F</sup> *sin mangas*<sup>F</sup>

trunks
*pantalón*<sup>M</sup>

knee wrap
*rodillera*<sup>F</sup>

strap
*correa*<sup>F</sup>

weightlifting shoe
*zapatilla*<sup>F</sup>

clean and jerk
*envión*<sup>M</sup>

snatch
*arranque*<sup>M</sup>

# fitness equipment
*aparatos*<sup>M</sup> *de ejercicios*<sup>M</sup>

SPORTS AND GAMES

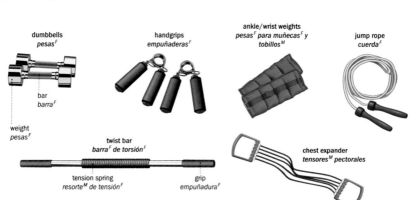

dumbbells
*pesas*<sup>F</sup>

handgrips
*empuñaderas*<sup>F</sup>

ankle/wrist weights
*pesas*<sup>F</sup> *para muñecas*<sup>F</sup> *y
tobillos*<sup>M</sup>

jump rope
*cuerda*<sup>F</sup>

bar
*barra*<sup>F</sup>

weight
*pesas*<sup>F</sup>

twist bar
*barra*<sup>F</sup> *de torsión*<sup>F</sup>

chest expander
*tensores*<sup>M</sup> *pectorales*

tension spring
*resorte*<sup>M</sup> *de tensión*<sup>F</sup>

grip
*empuñadura*<sup>F</sup>

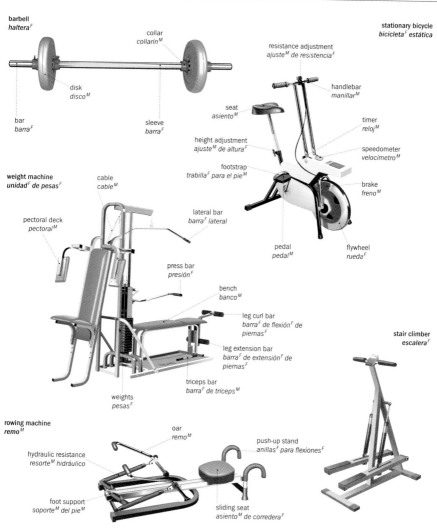

barbell
*haltera*<sup>F</sup>

collar
*collarín*<sup>M</sup>

disk
*disco*<sup>M</sup>

bar
*barra*<sup>F</sup>

sleeve
*barra*<sup>F</sup>

stationary bicycle
*bicicleta*<sup>F</sup> *estática*

resistance adjustment
*ajuste*<sup>M</sup> *de resistencia*<sup>F</sup>

handlebar
*manillar*<sup>M</sup>

seat
*asiento*<sup>M</sup>

timer
*reloj*<sup>M</sup>

height adjustment
*ajuste*<sup>M</sup> *de altura*<sup>F</sup>

speedometer
*velocímetro*<sup>M</sup>

footstrap
*trabilla*<sup>F</sup> *para el pie*<sup>M</sup>

brake
*freno*<sup>M</sup>

weight machine
*unidad*<sup>F</sup> *de pesas*<sup>F</sup>

cable
*cable*<sup>M</sup>

lateral bar
*barra*<sup>F</sup> *lateral*

pectoral deck
*pectoral*<sup>M</sup>

pedal
*pedal*<sup>M</sup>

flywheel
*rueda*<sup>F</sup>

press bar
*presión*<sup>F</sup>

bench
*banco*<sup>M</sup>

leg curl bar
*barra*<sup>F</sup> *de flexión*<sup>F</sup> *de piernas*<sup>F</sup>

stair climber
*escalera*<sup>F</sup>

leg extension bar
*barra*<sup>F</sup> *de extensión*<sup>F</sup> *de piernas*<sup>F</sup>

triceps bar
*barra*<sup>F</sup> *de tríceps*<sup>M</sup>

weights
*pesas*<sup>F</sup>

rowing machine
*remo*<sup>M</sup>

oar
*remo*<sup>M</sup>

push-up stand
*anillas*<sup>F</sup> *para flexiones*<sup>F</sup>

hydraulic resistance
*resorte*<sup>M</sup> *hidráulico*

foot support
*soporte*<sup>M</sup> *del pie*<sup>M</sup>

sliding seat
*asiento*<sup>M</sup> *de corredera*<sup>F</sup>

SPORTS AND GAMES

501

# billiards
*billar^M*

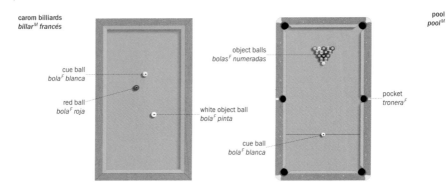

**carom billiards**
*billar^M francés*

**pool**
*pool^M*

cue ball
*bola^F blanca*

red ball
*bola^F roja*

white object ball
*bola^F pinta*

object balls
*bolas^F numeradas*

pocket
*tronera^F*

cue ball
*bola^F blanca*

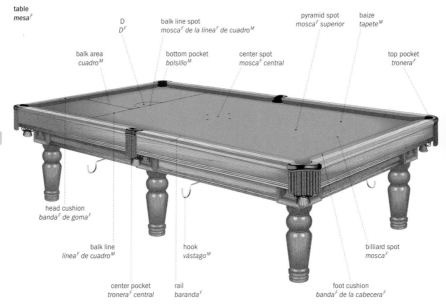

**table**
*mesa^F*

D
*D^F*

balk line spot
*mosca^F de la línea^F de cuadro^M*

pyramid spot
*mosca^F superior*

baize
*tapete^M*

balk area
*cuadro^M*

bottom pocket
*bolsillo^M*

center spot
*mosca^F central*

top pocket
*tronera^F*

head cushion
*banda^F de goma^F*

balk line
*línea^F de cuadro^M*

hook
*vástago^M*

billiard spot
*mosca^F*

center pocket
*tronera^F central*

rail
*baranda^F*

foot cushion
*banda^F de la cabecera^F*

SPORTS AND GAMES

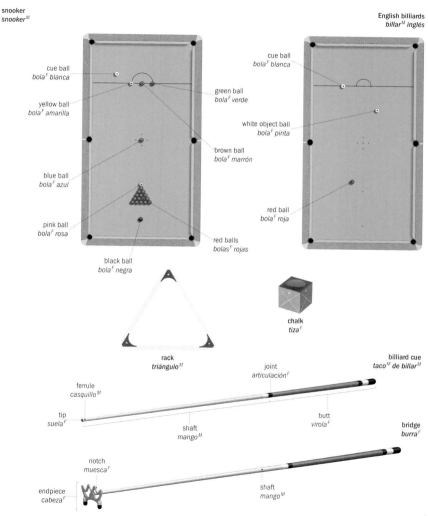

snooker
*snooker*<sup>M</sup>

English billiards
*billar*<sup>M</sup> *inglés*

cue ball
*bola*<sup>F</sup> *blanca*

green ball
*bola*<sup>F</sup> *verde*

yellow ball
*bola*<sup>F</sup> *amarilla*

cue ball
*bola*<sup>F</sup> *blanca*

white object ball
*bola*<sup>F</sup> *pinta*

brown ball
*bola*<sup>F</sup> *marrón*

blue ball
*bola*<sup>F</sup> *azul*

pink ball
*bola*<sup>F</sup> *rosa*

red ball
*bola*<sup>F</sup> *roja*

red balls
*bolas*<sup>F</sup> *rojas*

black ball
*bola*<sup>F</sup> *negra*

rack
*triángulo*<sup>M</sup>

chalk
*tiza*<sup>F</sup>

billiard cue
*taco*<sup>M</sup> *de billar*<sup>M</sup>

joint
*articulación*<sup>F</sup>

ferrule
*casquillo*<sup>M</sup>

tip
*suela*<sup>F</sup>

shaft
*mango*<sup>M</sup>

butt
*virola*<sup>F</sup>

bridge
*burra*<sup>F</sup>

notch
*muesca*<sup>F</sup>

endpiece
*cabeza*<sup>F</sup>

shaft
*mango*<sup>M</sup>

SPORTS AND GAMES

503

# golf
*accesorios^M de golf^M*

course
*campo^M de golf^M*

green
*green^M*

hole
*zona^F del hoyo^M*

cart path
*vereda^F*

clubhouse
*casa^F club^M*

fairway
*pista^F*

practice green
*green^M de entrenamiento^M*

parking
*aparcamiento^M*

pond
*estanque^M*

sand bunker
*foso^M de arena^F*

trees
*árboles^M*

rough
*maleza^F*

teeing ground
*punto^M de salida^F*

water hazard
*trampa^F de agua^F*

par 5 hole
*hoyo^M de par 5*

water hazard
*fosa^F de agua^F*

fairway
*fairway^M*

teeing ground
*colina^F de salida^F*

green
*green^M*

natural environment
*ambiente^M natural*

sand bunker
*trampas^F de arena^F*

rough
*rough^M*

hole
*hoyo^M*

removable flagpole
*banderín^M móvil*

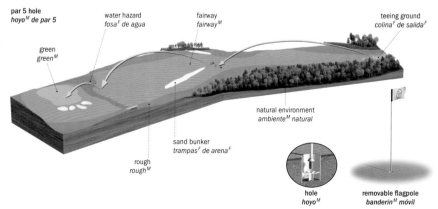

SPORTS AND GAMES

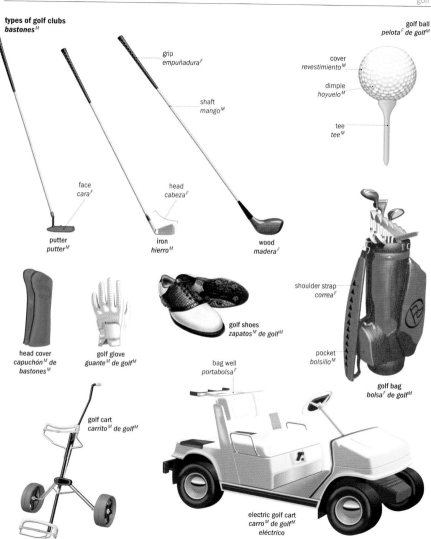

**types of golf clubs**
*bastones*<sup>M</sup>

grip
*empuñadura*<sup>F</sup>

shaft
*mango*<sup>M</sup>

face
*cara*<sup>F</sup>

head
*cabeza*<sup>F</sup>

putter
*putter*<sup>M</sup>

iron
*hierro*<sup>M</sup>

wood
*madera*<sup>F</sup>

golf ball
*pelota*<sup>F</sup> *de golf*<sup>M</sup>

cover
*revestimiento*<sup>M</sup>

dimple
*hoyuelo*<sup>M</sup>

tee
*tee*<sup>M</sup>

head cover
*capuchón*<sup>M</sup> *de
bastones*<sup>M</sup>

golf glove
*guante*<sup>M</sup> *de golf*<sup>M</sup>

golf shoes
*zapatos*<sup>M</sup> *de golf*<sup>M</sup>

shoulder strap
*correa*<sup>F</sup>

pocket
*bolsillo*<sup>M</sup>

golf bag
*bolsa*<sup>F</sup> *de golf*<sup>M</sup>

bag well
*portabolsa*<sup>F</sup>

golf cart
*carrito*<sup>M</sup> *de golf*<sup>M</sup>

electric golf cart
*carro*<sup>M</sup> *de golf*<sup>M</sup>
*eléctrico*

SPORTS AND GAMES

505

# ice hockey
*hockey^M sobre hielo^M*

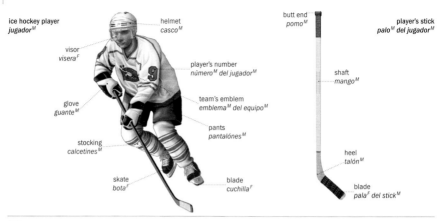

**ice hockey player**
*jugador^M*

helmet
*casco^M*

visor
*visera^F*

player's number
*número^M del jugador^M*

glove
*guante^M*

team's emblem
*emblema^M del equipo^M*

pants
*pantalónes^M*

stocking
*calcetines^M*

skate
*bota^F*

blade
*cuchilla^F*

butt end
*pomo^M*

**player's stick**
*palo^M del jugador^M*

shaft
*mango^M*

heel
*talón^M*

blade
*pala^F del stick^M*

**rink**
*pista^F*

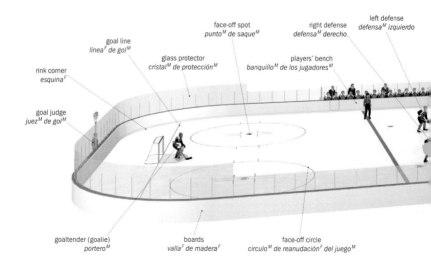

face-off spot
*punto^M de saque^M*

right defense
*defensa^M derecho*

left defense
*defensa^M izquierdo*

goal line
*línea^F de gol^M*

glass protector
*cristal^M de protección^M*

players' bench
*banquillo^M de los jugadores^M*

rink corner
*esquina^F*

goal judge
*juez^M de gol^M*

goaltender (goalie)
*portero^M*

boards
*valla^F de madera^F*

face-off circle
*círculo^M de reanudación^F del juego^M*

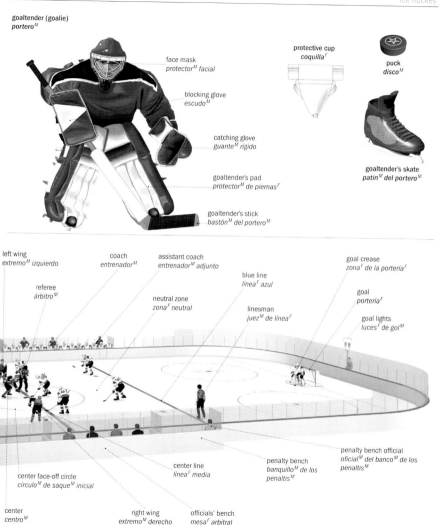

goaltender (goalie)
*portero*<sup>M</sup>

face mask
*protector*<sup>M</sup> *facial*

blocking glove
*escudo*<sup>M</sup>

catching glove
*guante*<sup>M</sup> *rígido*

goaltender's pad
*protector*<sup>M</sup> *de piernas*<sup>F</sup>

goaltender's stick
*bastón*<sup>M</sup> *del portero*<sup>M</sup>

protective cup
*coquilla*<sup>F</sup>

puck
*disco*<sup>M</sup>

goaltender's skate
*patín*<sup>M</sup> *del portero*<sup>M</sup>

left wing
*extremo*<sup>M</sup> *izquierdo*

referee
*árbitro*<sup>M</sup>

coach
*entrenador*<sup>M</sup>

assistant coach
*entrenador*<sup>M</sup> *adjunto*

neutral zone
*zona*<sup>F</sup> *neutral*

blue line
*línea*<sup>F</sup> *azul*

linesman
*juez*<sup>M</sup> *de línea*<sup>F</sup>

goal crease
*zona*<sup>F</sup> *de la portería*<sup>F</sup>

goal
*portería*<sup>F</sup>

goal lights
*luces*<sup>F</sup> *de gol*<sup>M</sup>

center face-off circle
*círculo*<sup>M</sup> *de saque*<sup>M</sup> *inicial*

center line
*línea*<sup>F</sup> *media*

penalty bench
*banquillo*<sup>M</sup> *de los penaltis*<sup>M</sup>

penalty bench official
*oficial*<sup>M</sup> *del banco*<sup>M</sup> *de los penaltis*<sup>M</sup>

center
*centro*<sup>M</sup>

right wing
*extremo*<sup>M</sup> *derecho*

officials' bench
*mesa*<sup>F</sup> *arbitral*

SPORTS AND GAMES

# speed skating
*patinaje$^M$ de velocidad$^F$*

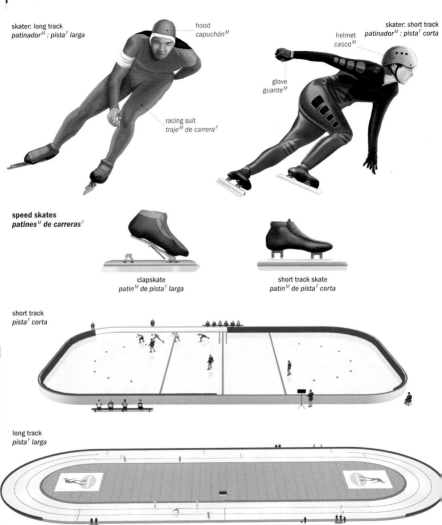

skater: long track
*patinador$^M$ : pista$^F$ larga*

hood
*capuchón$^M$*

skater: short track
*patinador$^M$ : pista$^F$ corta*

helmet
*casco$^M$*

glove
*guante$^M$*

racing suit
*traje$^M$ de carrera$^F$*

**speed skates**
*patines$^M$ de carreras$^F$*

clapskate
*patin$^M$ de pista$^F$ larga*

short track skate
*patin$^M$ de pista$^F$ corta*

short track
*pista$^F$ corta*

long track
*pista$^F$ larga*

## figure skating
*patinaje<sup>M</sup> artístico*

**figure skate**
*patín<sup>M</sup> para figuras<sup>F</sup>*

lining
*forro<sup>M</sup>*

hook
*corchete<sup>M</sup>*

tongue
*lengüeta<sup>F</sup>*

backstay
*contrafuerte<sup>M</sup>*

lace
*cordón<sup>M</sup>*

boot
*bota<sup>F</sup>*

eyelet
*ojal<sup>M</sup>*

heel
*tacón<sup>M</sup>*

dance blade
*cuchilla<sup>F</sup> de baile<sup>M</sup>*

sole
*suela<sup>F</sup>*

free skating blade
*cuchilla<sup>F</sup> de patinaje<sup>M</sup> artístico*

stanchion
*montante<sup>M</sup>*

edge
*canto<sup>M</sup>*

blade
*hoja<sup>F</sup> de cuchilla<sup>F</sup>*

toe pick
*dientes<sup>M</sup>*

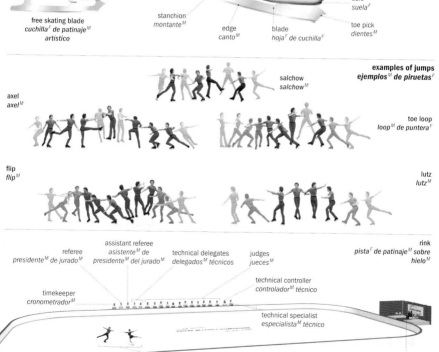

**examples of jumps**
*ejemplos<sup>M</sup> de piruetas<sup>F</sup>*

salchow
*salchow<sup>M</sup>*

axel
*axel<sup>M</sup>*

toe loop
*loop<sup>M</sup> de puntera<sup>F</sup>*

flip
*flip<sup>M</sup>*

lutz
*lutz<sup>M</sup>*

**rink**
*pista<sup>F</sup> de patinaje<sup>M</sup> sobre hielo<sup>M</sup>*

assistant referee
*asistente<sup>M</sup> de presidente<sup>M</sup> del jurado<sup>M</sup>*

referee
*presidente<sup>M</sup> de jurado<sup>M</sup>*

technical delegates
*delegados<sup>M</sup> técnicos*

judges
*jueces<sup>M</sup>*

technical controller
*controlador<sup>M</sup> técnico*

timekeeper
*cronometrador<sup>M</sup>*

technical specialist
*especialista<sup>M</sup> técnico*

pair
*pareja<sup>F</sup>*

coaches
*entrenadores<sup>M</sup>*

SPORTS AND GAMES

509

# alpine skiing
*esquí<sup>M</sup> alpino*

**alpine skier**
*esquiador<sup>M</sup> alpino*

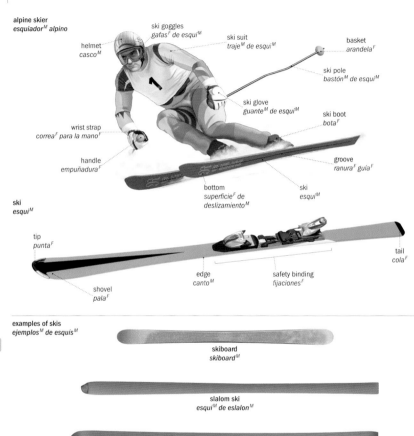

ski goggles
*gafas<sup>F</sup> de esquí<sup>M</sup>*

helmet
*casco<sup>M</sup>*

ski suit
*traje<sup>M</sup> de esquí<sup>M</sup>*

basket
*arandela<sup>F</sup>*

ski pole
*bastón<sup>M</sup> de esquí<sup>M</sup>*

ski glove
*guante<sup>M</sup> de esquí<sup>M</sup>*

ski boot
*bota<sup>F</sup>*

wrist strap
*correa<sup>F</sup> para la mano<sup>F</sup>*

groove
*ranura<sup>F</sup> guía<sup>F</sup>*

handle
*empuñadura<sup>F</sup>*

bottom
*superficie<sup>F</sup> de
deslizamiento<sup>M</sup>*

ski
*esquí<sup>M</sup>*

**ski**
*esquí<sup>M</sup>*

tip
*punta<sup>F</sup>*

tail
*cola<sup>F</sup>*

edge
*canto<sup>M</sup>*

safety binding
*fijaciones<sup>F</sup>*

shovel
*pala<sup>F</sup>*

**examples of skis**
*ejemplos<sup>M</sup> de esquis<sup>M</sup>*

skiboard
*skiboard<sup>M</sup>*

slalom ski
*esquí<sup>M</sup> de eslalon<sup>M</sup>*

giant slalom ski
*esquí<sup>M</sup> de eslalon<sup>M</sup> gigante*

downhill and super-G ski
*esquí<sup>M</sup> de descenso<sup>M</sup>/eslalon<sup>M</sup>*

alpine skiing

**technical events**
*pruebas*<sup>F</sup>

ski boot
*botas*<sup>F</sup> *para esquiar*

downhill
*descenso*<sup>M</sup>

super giant (super-G)
slalom
*eslalon*<sup>M</sup> *supergigante*

giant slalom
*eslalon*<sup>M</sup> *gigante*

special slalom
*eslalon*<sup>M</sup> *especial*

inner boot
*botín*<sup>M</sup> *interior*

upper cuff
*guarnición*<sup>F</sup>

upper
*alto*<sup>M</sup> *de caña*<sup>F</sup>

tongue
*lengüeta*<sup>F</sup>

upper shell
*bota*<sup>F</sup> *externa*

upper strap
*correa*<sup>F</sup> *de ajuste*<sup>M</sup>

buckle
*hebilla*<sup>F</sup>

adjusting catch
*ajustador*<sup>M</sup> *de la bota*<sup>F</sup>

hinge
*pivote*<sup>M</sup>

sole
*suela*<sup>F</sup> *rígida*

lower shell
*contrafuerte*<sup>M</sup>

safety binding
*fijación*<sup>F</sup> *de seguridad*<sup>F</sup> *del esquí*<sup>M</sup>

manual release
*desenganchador*<sup>M</sup> *manual*

brake pedal
*placa*<sup>F</sup> *de freno*<sup>M</sup>

antifriction pad
*placa*<sup>F</sup> *antifricción*

setting indicator
*indicador*<sup>M</sup> *de ajuste*<sup>M</sup>

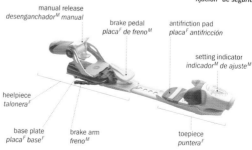

heelpiece
*talonera*<sup>F</sup>

base plate
*placa*<sup>F</sup> *base*<sup>F</sup>

brake arm
*freno*<sup>M</sup>

toepiece
*puntera*<sup>F</sup>

SPORTS AND GAMES

# ski resort

*estación<sup>F</sup> de esquí*

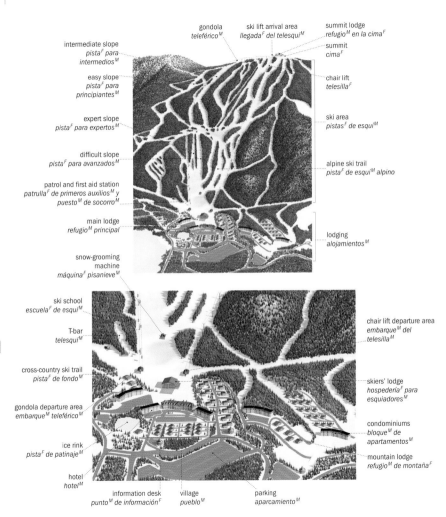

gondola
*teleférico<sup>M</sup>*

ski lift arrival area
*llegada<sup>F</sup> del telesquí<sup>M</sup>*

summit lodge
*refugio<sup>M</sup> en la cima<sup>F</sup>*

summit
*cima<sup>F</sup>*

intermediate slope
*pista<sup>F</sup> para
intermedios<sup>M</sup>*

easy slope
*pista<sup>F</sup> para
principiantes<sup>M</sup>*

chair lift
*telesilla<sup>F</sup>*

expert slope
*pista<sup>F</sup> para expertos<sup>M</sup>*

ski area
*pistas<sup>F</sup> de esquí<sup>M</sup>*

difficult slope
*pista<sup>F</sup> para avanzados<sup>M</sup>*

alpine ski trail
*pista<sup>F</sup> de esquí<sup>M</sup> alpino*

patrol and first aid station
*patrulla<sup>F</sup> de primeros auxilios<sup>M</sup> y
puesto<sup>M</sup> de socorro<sup>M</sup>*

main lodge
*refugio<sup>M</sup> principal*

lodging
*alojamientos<sup>M</sup>*

snow-grooming
machine
*máquina<sup>F</sup> pisanieve<sup>M</sup>*

ski school
*escuela<sup>F</sup> de esquí<sup>M</sup>*

T-bar
*telesquí<sup>M</sup>*

chair lift departure area
*embarque<sup>M</sup> del
telesilla<sup>M</sup>*

cross-country ski trail
*pista<sup>F</sup> de fondo<sup>M</sup>*

skiers' lodge
*hospedería<sup>F</sup> para
esquiadores<sup>M</sup>*

gondola departure area
*embarque<sup>M</sup> teleférico<sup>M</sup>*

condominiums
*bloque<sup>M</sup> de
apartamentos<sup>M</sup>*

ice rink
*pista<sup>F</sup> de patinaje<sup>M</sup>*

mountain lodge
*refugio<sup>M</sup> de montaña<sup>F</sup>*

hotel
*hotel<sup>M</sup>*

information desk
*punto<sup>M</sup> de información<sup>F</sup>*

village
*pueblo<sup>M</sup>*

parking
*aparcamiento<sup>M</sup>*

SPORTS AND GAMES

# snowboarding
*snowboard*<sup>M</sup>

snowboarder
*snowboarder*<sup>M</sup>

helmet
*casco*<sup>M</sup>

coveralls
*traje*<sup>M</sup> *de esquí*<sup>M</sup>

goggles
*gafas*<sup>F</sup> *de esquí*<sup>M</sup>

shin guard
*tobillera*<sup>F</sup>

snowboard
*snowboard*<sup>M</sup>

glove
*guante*<sup>M</sup>

hard boot
*bota*<sup>F</sup> *rígida*

flexible boot
*bota*<sup>F</sup> *blanda*

freestyle snowboard
*tabla*<sup>F</sup> *de freestyle*<sup>M</sup>

alpine snowboard
*tabla*<sup>F</sup> *alpina*

# ski jumping
*técnica*<sup>F</sup> *de salto*<sup>M</sup>

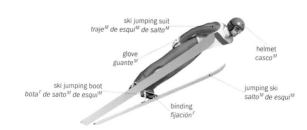

ski jumper
*saltador*<sup>M</sup>

ski jumping suit
*traje*<sup>M</sup> *de esquí*<sup>M</sup> *de salto*<sup>M</sup>

glove
*guante*<sup>M</sup>

helmet
*casco*<sup>M</sup>

ski jumping boot
*bota*<sup>F</sup> *de salto*<sup>M</sup> *de esquí*<sup>M</sup>

binding
*fijación*<sup>F</sup>

jumping ski
*salto*<sup>M</sup> *de esquí*<sup>M</sup>

# cross-country skiing
*esquí<sup>M</sup> de fondo<sup>M</sup>*

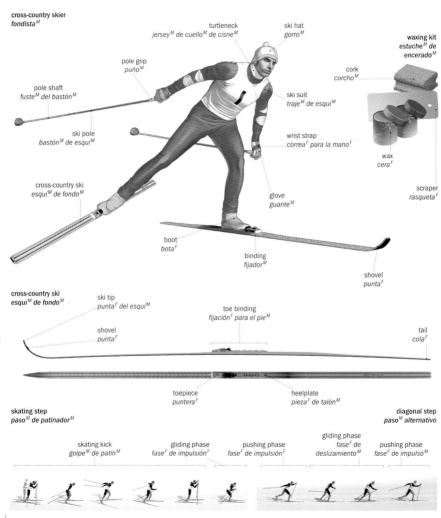

**cross-country skier**
*fondista<sup>M</sup>*

turtleneck
*jersey<sup>M</sup> de cuello<sup>M</sup> de cisne<sup>M</sup>*

ski hat
*gorro<sup>M</sup>*

**waxing kit**
*estuche<sup>M</sup> de encerado<sup>M</sup>*

pole grip
*puño<sup>M</sup>*

cork
*corcho<sup>M</sup>*

pole shaft
*fuste<sup>M</sup> del bastón<sup>M</sup>*

ski suit
*traje<sup>M</sup> de esquí<sup>M</sup>*

ski pole
*bastón<sup>M</sup> de esquí<sup>M</sup>*

wrist strap
*correa<sup>F</sup> para la mano<sup>F</sup>*

wax
*cera<sup>F</sup>*

cross-country ski
*esquí<sup>M</sup> de fondo<sup>M</sup>*

scraper
*rasqueta<sup>F</sup>*

glove
*guante<sup>M</sup>*

boot
*bota<sup>F</sup>*

binding
*fijador<sup>M</sup>*

shovel
*punta<sup>F</sup>*

**cross-country ski**
*esquí<sup>M</sup> de fondo<sup>M</sup>*

ski tip
*punta<sup>F</sup> del esquí<sup>M</sup>*

toe binding
*fijación<sup>F</sup> para el pie<sup>M</sup>*

tail
*cola<sup>F</sup>*

shovel
*punta<sup>F</sup>*

toepiece
*puntera<sup>F</sup>*

heelplate
*pieza<sup>F</sup> de talón<sup>M</sup>*

**skating step**
*paso<sup>M</sup> de patinador<sup>M</sup>*

**diagonal step**
*paso<sup>M</sup> alternativo*

skating kick
*golpe<sup>M</sup> de patín<sup>M</sup>*

gliding phase
*fase<sup>F</sup> de impulsión<sup>F</sup>*

pushing phase
*fase<sup>F</sup> de impulsión<sup>F</sup>*

gliding phase
*fase<sup>F</sup> de deslizamiento<sup>M</sup>*

pushing phase
*fase<sup>F</sup> de impulso<sup>M</sup>*

# curling
*curling^M*

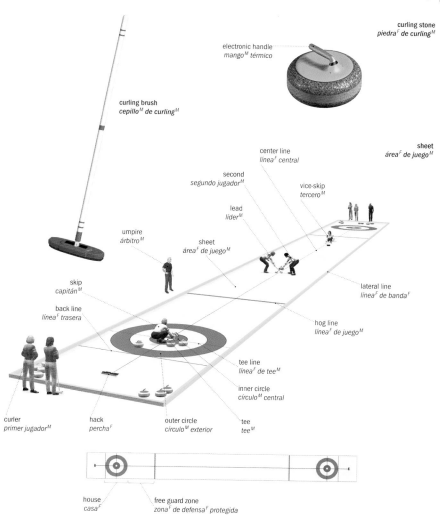

curling stone
*piedra^F de curling^M*

electronic handle
*mango^M térmico*

curling brush
*cepillo^M de curling^M*

sheet
*área^F de juego^M*

center line
*línea^F central*

second
*segundo jugador^M*

vice-skip
*tercero^M*

lead
*líder^M*

umpire
*árbitro^M*

sheet
*área^F de juego^M*

lateral line
*línea^F de banda^F*

skip
*capitán^M*

back line
*línea^F trasera*

hog line
*línea^F de juego^M*

tee line
*línea^F de tee^M*

inner circle
*círculo^M central*

curler
*primer jugador^M*

hack
*percha^F*

outer circle
*círculo^M exterior*

tee
*tee^M*

house
*casa^F*

free guard zone
*zona^F de defensa^F protegida*

515

# swimming
*natación<sup>F</sup>*

**starting block**
**plataforma<sup>F</sup> de salida<sup>F</sup>**

swimsuit
*traje<sup>M</sup> de baño<sup>M</sup>*

cap
*gorro<sup>M</sup> de baño<sup>M</sup>*

platform
*plataforma<sup>F</sup> de salida<sup>F</sup>*

swimming goggles
*gafas<sup>F</sup> de baño<sup>M</sup>*

starting grip (backstroke)
*asidero<sup>M</sup> : (espalda<sup>F</sup>)*

referee
*árbitro<sup>M</sup>*

starter
*juez<sup>M</sup> de salida<sup>F</sup>*

stroke judge
*juez<sup>M</sup> de brazado<sup>M</sup>*

false start rope
*cuerda<sup>F</sup> de salida<sup>F</sup>*
*falsa*

finish wall
*muro<sup>M</sup> de llegada<sup>F</sup>*

lane timekeeper
*cronometrador<sup>M</sup> de*
*calle<sup>F</sup>*

lane
*calle<sup>F</sup>*

starting block
*podio<sup>M</sup> de salida<sup>F</sup>*

chief timekeeper
*jefe<sup>M</sup> de*
*cronometradores<sup>M</sup>*

placing judge
*juez<sup>M</sup> de llegada<sup>F</sup>*

**types of strokes**
*estilos^M de natación^F*

front crawl
*crol^M*

butterfly stroke
*mariposa*

breaststroke
*braza^F*

backstroke
*espalda*

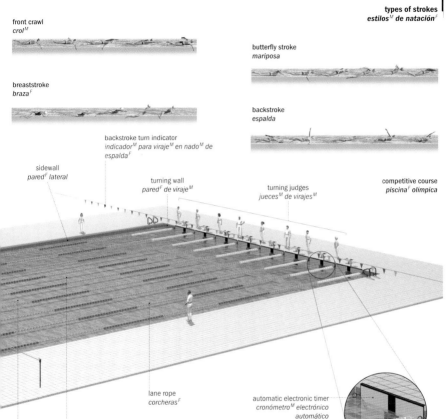

backstroke turn indicator
*indicador^M para viraje^M en nado^M de espalda^F*

sidewall
*pared^F lateral*

turning wall
*pared^F de viraje^M*

turning judges
*jueces^M de virajes^M*

competitive course
*piscina^F olímpica*

lane rope
*corcheras^F*

automatic electronic timer
*cronómetro^M electrónico automático*

bottom line
*línea^F del fondo^M de la piscina^F*

swimming pool
*piscina^F*

# diving
*saltos*$^M$

## starting positions
*posiciones*$^F$ *de salto*$^M$

reverse
*salto*$^M$ *inverso*

inward
*salto*$^M$ *interior*

backward
*salto*$^M$ *de espalda*$^F$

forward
*salto*$^M$ *frontal*

armstand
*salto*$^M$ *en equilibrio*$^M$

## flights
*saltos*$^M$

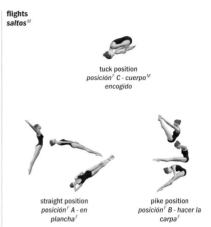

tuck position
*posición*$^F$ *C - cuerpo*$^M$
*encogido*

straight position
*posición*$^F$ *A - en*
*plancha*$^F$

pike position
*posición*$^F$ *B - hacer la*
*carpa*$^F$

## diving installations
*torre*$^F$ *de saltos*$^M$

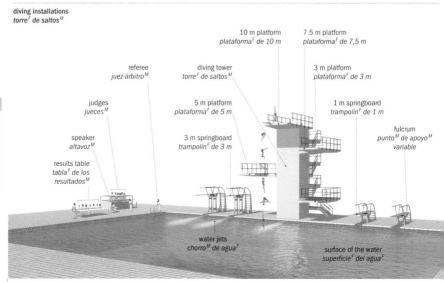

10 m platform
*plataforma*$^F$ *de 10 m*

7.5 m platform
*plataforma*$^F$ *de 7,5 m*

referee
*juez-árbitro*$^M$

diving tower
*torre*$^F$ *de saltos*$^M$

3 m platform
*plataforma*$^F$ *de 3 m*

judges
*jueces*$^M$

5 m platform
*plataforma*$^F$ *de 5 m*

1 m springboard
*trampolín*$^F$ *de 1 m*

speaker
*altavoz*$^M$

3 m springboard
*trampolín*$^F$ *de 3 m*

fulcrum
*punto*$^M$ *de apoyo*$^M$
*variable*

results table
*tabla*$^F$ *de los*
*resultados*$^M$

water jets
*chorro*$^M$ *de agua*$^F$

surface of the water
*superficie*$^F$ *del agua*$^F$

# sailboard
*windsurf*[M]

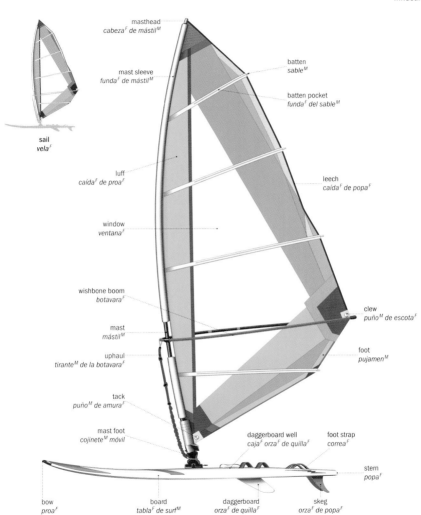

sail
*vela*[F]

masthead
*cabeza*[F] *de mástil*[M]

batten
*sable*[M]

mast sleeve
*funda*[F] *de mástil*[M]

batten pocket
*funda*[F] *del sable*[M]

luff
*caída*[F] *de proa*[F]

leech
*caída*[F] *de popa*[F]

window
*ventana*[F]

wishbone boom
*botavara*[F]

clew
*puño*[M] *de escota*[F]

mast
*mástil*[M]

uphaul
*tirante*[M] *de la botavara*[F]

foot
*pujamen*[M]

tack
*puño*[M] *de amura*[F]

mast foot
*cojinete*[M] *móvil*

daggerboard well
*caja*[F] *orza*[F] *de quilla*[F]

foot strap
*correa*[F]

stern
*popa*[F]

bow
*proa*[F]

board
*tabla*[F] *de surf*[M]

daggerboard
*orza*[F] *de quilla*[F]

skeg
*orza*[F] *de popa*[F]

SPORTS AND GAMES

519

# sailing
*vela*[F]

**sailboat**
**velero**[M]

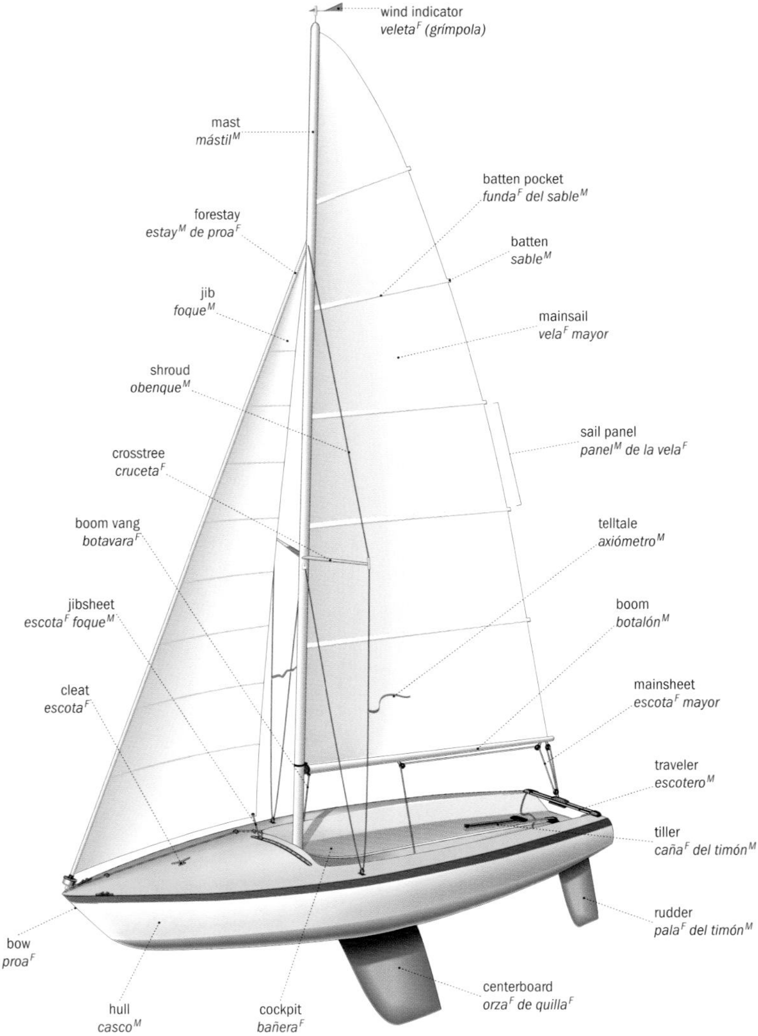

wind indicator
*veleta*[F] *(grímpola)*

mast
*mástil*[M]

batten pocket
*funda*[F] *del sable*[M]

forestay
*estay*[M] *de proa*[F]

batten
*sable*[M]

jib
*foque*[M]

mainsail
*vela*[F] *mayor*

shroud
*obenque*[M]

sail panel
*panel*[M] *de la vela*[F]

crosstree
*cruceta*[F]

boom vang
*botavara*[F]

telltale
*axiómetro*[M]

jibsheet
*escota*[F] *foque*[M]

boom
*botalón*[M]

cleat
*escota*[F]

mainsheet
*escota*[F] *mayor*

traveler
*escotero*[M]

tiller
*caña*[F] *del timón*[M]

rudder
*pala*[F] *del timón*[M]

bow
*proa*[F]

centerboard
*orza*[F] *de quilla*[F]

hull
*casco*[M]

cockpit
*bañera*[F]

sailing

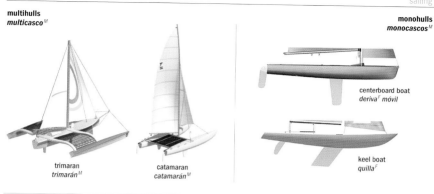

**multihulls**
*multicasco* $^M$

**monohulls**
*monocascos* $^M$

centerboard boat
*deriva* $^F$ *móvil*

keel boat
*quilla* $^F$

trimaran
*trimarán* $^M$

catamaran
*catamarán* $^M$

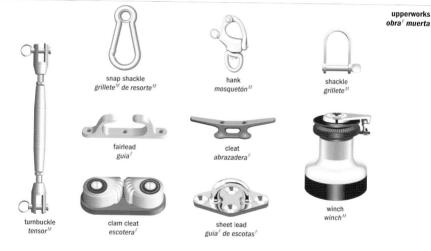

**upperworks**
*obra* $^F$ *muerta*

snap shackle
*grillete* $^M$ *de resorte* $^M$

hank
*mosquetón* $^M$

shackle
*grillete* $^M$

fairlead
*guía* $^F$

cleat
*abrazadera* $^F$

winch
*winch* $^M$

turnbuckle
*tensor* $^M$

clam cleat
*escotera* $^F$

sheet lead
*guía* $^F$ *de escotas* $^F$

traveler
*barra* $^F$ *de escotas* $^F$

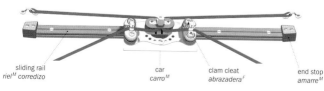

sliding rail
*riel* $^M$ *corredizo*

car
*carro* $^M$

clam cleat
*abrazadera* $^F$

end stop
*amarre* $^M$

SPORTS AND GAMES

# road racing
*ciclismo<sup>M</sup> por carretera<sup>F</sup>*

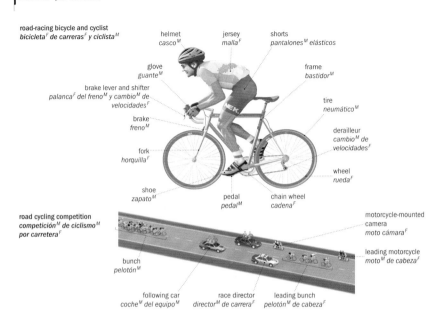

**road-racing bicycle and cyclist**
*bicicleta<sup>F</sup> de carreras<sup>F</sup> y ciclista<sup>M</sup>*

helmet
*casco<sup>M</sup>*

jersey
*malla<sup>F</sup>*

shorts
*pantalones<sup>M</sup> elásticos*

glove
*guante<sup>M</sup>*

frame
*bastidor<sup>M</sup>*

brake lever and shifter
*palanca<sup>F</sup> del freno<sup>M</sup> y cambio<sup>M</sup> de velocidades<sup>F</sup>*

tire
*neumático<sup>M</sup>*

brake
*freno<sup>M</sup>*

derailleur
*cambio<sup>M</sup> de velocidades<sup>F</sup>*

fork
*horquilla<sup>F</sup>*

wheel
*rueda<sup>F</sup>*

shoe
*zapato<sup>M</sup>*

pedal
*pedal<sup>M</sup>*

chain wheel
*cadena<sup>F</sup>*

**road cycling competition**
*competición<sup>M</sup> de ciclismo<sup>M</sup> por carretera<sup>F</sup>*

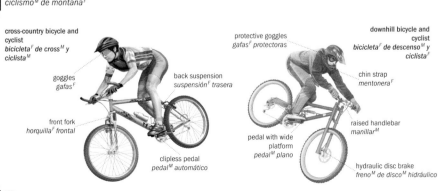

motorcycle-mounted camera
*moto cámara<sup>F</sup>*

leading motorcycle
*moto<sup>M</sup> de cabeza<sup>F</sup>*

bunch
*pelotón<sup>M</sup>*

following car
*coche<sup>M</sup> del equipo<sup>M</sup>*

race director
*director<sup>M</sup> de carrera<sup>F</sup>*

leading bunch
*pelotón<sup>M</sup> de cabeza<sup>F</sup>*

# mountain biking
*ciclismo<sup>M</sup> de montaña<sup>F</sup>*

**cross-country bicycle and cyclist**
*bicicleta<sup>F</sup> de cross<sup>M</sup> y ciclista<sup>M</sup>*

**downhill bicycle and cyclist**
*bicicleta<sup>F</sup> de descenso<sup>M</sup> y ciclista<sup>F</sup>*

protective goggles
*gafas<sup>F</sup> protectoras*

goggles
*gafas<sup>F</sup>*

back suspension
*suspensión<sup>F</sup> trasera*

chin strap
*mentonera<sup>F</sup>*

front fork
*horquilla<sup>F</sup> frontal*

raised handlebar
*manillar<sup>M</sup>*

clipless pedal
*pedal<sup>M</sup> automático*

pedal with wide platform
*pedal<sup>M</sup> plano*

hydraulic disc brake
*freno<sup>M</sup> de disco<sup>M</sup> hidráulico*

SPORTS AND GAMES

# personal watercraft
*moto<sup>F</sup> acuática*

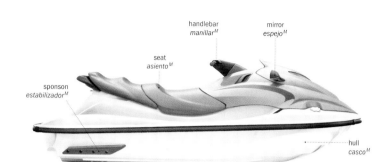

handlebar
*manillar<sup>M</sup>*

mirror
*espejo<sup>M</sup>*

seat
*asiento<sup>M</sup>*

sponson
*estabilizador<sup>M</sup>*

hull
*casco<sup>M</sup>*

# snowmobile
*moto<sup>M</sup> nieve*

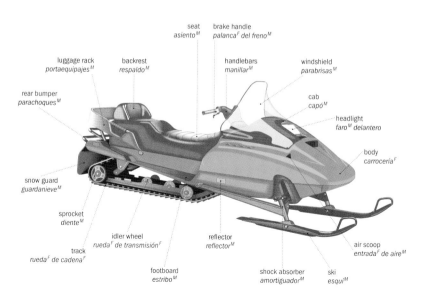

seat
*asiento<sup>M</sup>*

brake handle
*palanca<sup>F</sup> del freno<sup>M</sup>*

luggage rack
*portaequipajes<sup>M</sup>*

backrest
*respaldo<sup>M</sup>*

handlebars
*manillar<sup>M</sup>*

windshield
*parabrisas<sup>M</sup>*

rear bumper
*parachoques<sup>M</sup>*

cab
*capó<sup>M</sup>*

headlight
*faro<sup>M</sup> delantero*

body
*carrocería<sup>F</sup>*

snow guard
*guardanieve<sup>M</sup>*

sprocket
*diente<sup>M</sup>*

idler wheel
*rueda<sup>F</sup> de transmisión<sup>F</sup>*

reflector
*reflector<sup>M</sup>*

air scoop
*entrada<sup>F</sup> de aire<sup>M</sup>*

track
*rueda<sup>F</sup> de cadena<sup>F</sup>*

footboard
*estribo<sup>M</sup>*

shock absorber
*amortiguador<sup>M</sup>*

ski
*esquí<sup>M</sup>*

SPORTS AND GAMES

# car racing
*carreras<sup>F</sup> de coches<sup>M</sup>*

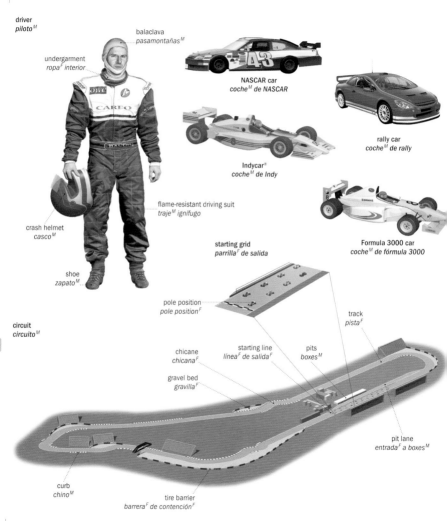

driver
*piloto<sup>M</sup>*

balaclava
*pasamontañas<sup>M</sup>*

undergarment
*ropa<sup>F</sup> interior*

NASCAR car
*coche<sup>M</sup> de NASCAR*

rally car
*coche<sup>M</sup> de rally*

Indycar®
*coche<sup>M</sup> de Indy*

flame-resistant driving suit
*traje<sup>M</sup> ignífugo*

crash helmet
*casco<sup>M</sup>*

Formula 3000 car
*coche<sup>M</sup> de fórmula 3000*

shoe
*zapato<sup>M</sup>*

starting grid
*parrilla<sup>F</sup> de salida*

pole position
*pole position<sup>F</sup>*

track
*pista<sup>F</sup>*

circuit
*circuito<sup>M</sup>*

chicane
*chicana<sup>F</sup>*

starting line
*línea<sup>F</sup> de salida<sup>F</sup>*

pits
*boxes<sup>M</sup>*

gravel bed
*gravilla<sup>F</sup>*

pit lane
*entrada<sup>F</sup> a boxes<sup>M</sup>*

curb
*chino<sup>M</sup>*

tire barrier
*barrera<sup>F</sup> de contención<sup>F</sup>*

Formula 1° car
*coche*<sup>M</sup> *de Fórmula*<sup>F</sup> *1*

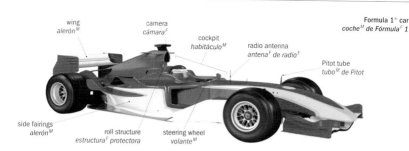

wing
*alerón*<sup>M</sup>

camera
*cámara*<sup>F</sup>

cockpit
*habitáculo*<sup>M</sup>

radio antenna
*antena*<sup>F</sup> *de radio*<sup>F</sup>

Pitot tube
*tubo*<sup>M</sup> *de Pitot*

side fairings
*alerón*<sup>M</sup>

roll structure
*estructura*<sup>F</sup> *protectora*

steering wheel
*volante*<sup>M</sup>

# motorcycling
*motocicleta*<sup>F</sup>

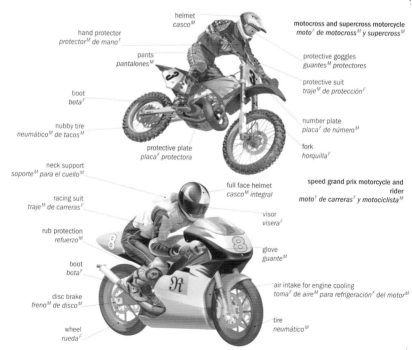

helmet
*casco*<sup>M</sup>

hand protector
*protector*<sup>M</sup> *de mano*<sup>F</sup>

pants
*pantalones*<sup>M</sup>

boot
*bota*<sup>F</sup>

nubby tire
*neumático*<sup>M</sup> *de tacos*<sup>M</sup>

protective plate
*placa*<sup>F</sup> *protectora*

**motocross and supercross motorcycle**
*moto*<sup>F</sup> *de motocross*<sup>M</sup> *y supercross*<sup>M</sup>

protective goggles
*guantes*<sup>M</sup> *protectores*

protective suit
*traje*<sup>M</sup> *de protección*<sup>F</sup>

number plate
*placa*<sup>F</sup> *de número*<sup>M</sup>

fork
*horquilla*<sup>F</sup>

neck support
*soporte*<sup>M</sup> *para el cuello*<sup>M</sup>

racing suit
*traje*<sup>M</sup> *de carreras*<sup>F</sup>

rub protection
*refuerzo*<sup>M</sup>

boot
*bota*<sup>F</sup>

disc brake
*freno*<sup>M</sup> *de disco*<sup>M</sup>

wheel
*rueda*<sup>F</sup>

full face helmet
*casco*<sup>M</sup> *integral*

**speed grand prix motorcycle and rider**
*moto*<sup>F</sup> *de carreras*<sup>F</sup> *y motociclista*<sup>M</sup>

visor
*visera*<sup>F</sup>

glove
*guante*<sup>M</sup>

air intake for engine cooling
*toma*<sup>F</sup> *de aire*<sup>M</sup> *para refrigeración*<sup>F</sup> *del motor*<sup>M</sup>

tire
*neumático*<sup>M</sup>

# skateboarding
*skateboard*<sup>M</sup>

skateboard
*monopatín*<sup>M</sup>

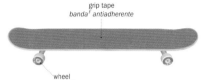

tail
*cola*<sup>F</sup>

truck
*bloqueo*<sup>M</sup> *eje*<sup>M</sup>

nose
*punta*<sup>F</sup>

grip tape
*banda*<sup>F</sup> *antiadherente*

wheel
*rueda*<sup>F</sup>

skateboarder
*monopatín*<sup>M</sup>

knee pad
*rodillera*<sup>F</sup>

elbow pad
*codera*<sup>F</sup>

helmet
*casco*<sup>M</sup>

coping
*coping*<sup>M</sup>

ramp
*medio tubo*<sup>M</sup>

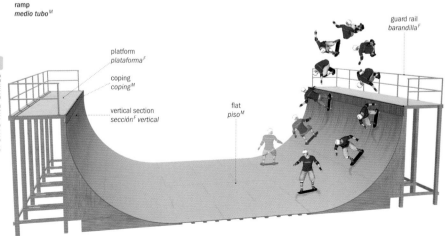

platform
*plataforma*<sup>F</sup>

coping
*coping*<sup>M</sup>

vertical section
*sección*<sup>F</sup> *vertical*

flat
*piso*<sup>M</sup>

guard rail
*barandilla*<sup>F</sup>

# in-line skating
*patinaje<sup>M</sup> en línea<sup>F</sup>*

acrobatic skate
*patín<sup>M</sup> acrobático*

inner boot
*botín<sup>M</sup> interior*

upper shell
*bota<sup>F</sup> externa*

frame
*bastidor<sup>M</sup>*

wheel
*rueda<sup>F</sup>*

skater
*patinadora<sup>F</sup>*

helmet
*casco<sup>M</sup>*

elbow pad
*codera<sup>F</sup>*

knee pad
*rodillera<sup>F</sup>*

wrist guard
*muñequera<sup>F</sup>*

in-line speed skate
*patín<sup>M</sup> en línea<sup>F</sup>*

in-line hockey skate
*patín en línea<sup>F</sup> de hockey<sup>M</sup>*

in-line skate
*patín<sup>M</sup> en línea<sup>F</sup>*

upper shell
*bota<sup>F</sup> externa*

inner boot
*botín<sup>M</sup> interior*

adjusting buckle
*hebilla<sup>F</sup> de ajuste<sup>M</sup>*

boot
*bota<sup>F</sup>*

axle
*eje<sup>M</sup>*

heel stop
*freno<sup>M</sup> trasero*

wheel
*rueda<sup>F</sup>*

truck
*bogie<sup>M</sup>*

SPORTS AND GAMES

527

# camping
*acampada*<sup>F</sup>

## examples of tents
**ejemplos** <sup>M</sup> **de tiendas** <sup>F</sup> **de campaña** <sup>F</sup>

rainfly
*doble techo* <sup>M</sup>

two-person tent
*tienda* <sup>F</sup> *para dos*

door
*puerta* <sup>F</sup>

canopy
*toldo* <sup>M</sup> *delantero*

guy line
*viento* <sup>M</sup>

stake
*estaquilla* <sup>F</sup>

strainer
*fiador* <sup>M</sup>

elastic strainer
*fiador* <sup>M</sup> *elástico*

zipper
*cierre* <sup>M</sup>

inner tent
*tienda* <sup>F</sup> *interior*

family tent
**tienda** <sup>F</sup> **de campaña** <sup>F</sup> **tamaño** <sup>M</sup>
**familiar**

window canopy
*toldo* <sup>M</sup> *de ventana* <sup>F</sup>

living room
*cuarto* <sup>M</sup> *de estar*

guy line
*viento* <sup>M</sup>

elastic strainer
*fiador* <sup>M</sup> *elástico*

bedroom
*dormitorio* <sup>M</sup>

sewn-in floor
*piso* <sup>M</sup> *cosido*

wall
*muro* <sup>M</sup>

stake loop
*presilla* <sup>F</sup> *de estaquilla* <sup>F</sup>

canvas divider
*lona* <sup>F</sup> *de separación* <sup>F</sup>

frame
*armadura* <sup>F</sup>

screen window
*ventana* <sup>F</sup>*-mosquitero* <sup>M</sup>

wagon tent
**tienda** <sup>F</sup> **tipo** <sup>M</sup> **vagón** <sup>M</sup>

wall tent
**tienda** <sup>F</sup> **rectangular**

SPORTS AND GAMES

camping

pup tent
*tienda$^F$ de campaña$^F$
clásica*

rainfly
*doble toldo$^M$*

roof pole
*palo$^M$ de la tienda$^F$*

elastic strainer
*fiador$^M$ elástico*

inner tent
*tienda$^F$ interior*

door
*puerta$^F$*

stake loop
*presilla$^F$ de estaquilla$^F$*

sewn-in floor
*piso$^M$ cosido*

stake
*estaquilla$^F$*

one-person tent
*tienda$^F$ unipersonal*

dome tent
*tienda$^F$ tipo$^M$ domo$^M$*

pop-up tent
*tienda$^F$ tipo$^M$ iglú$^M$*

lantern
*linterna$^F$*

burner frame
*armazón$^M$ del
quemador$^M$*

globe
*globo$^M$*

pressure regulator
*regulador$^M$ de presión$^F$*

pump
*bomba$^F$*

leakproof cap
*tapón$^M$ hermético*

tank
*tanque$^M$*

propane or butane accessories
*equipos$^M$ de gas$^M$*

heater
*calentador$^M$*

double-burner camp stove
*cocina$^F$ de campo$^M$*

burner
*quemador$^M$*

tank
*bombona$^F$ de gas$^M$*

wire support
*parrilla$^F$ estabilizadora*

single-burner camp stove
*hornillo$^M$*

control valve
*válvula$^F$ de control$^M$*

SPORTS AND GAMES

camping

**examples of sleeping bags**
*ejemplos<sup>M</sup> de sacos<sup>M</sup> de dormir*

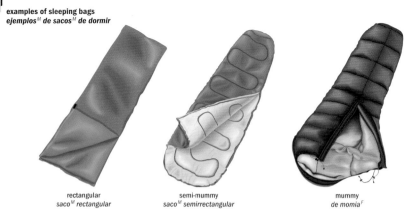

rectangular
*saco<sup>M</sup> rectangular*

semi-mummy
*saco<sup>M</sup> semirrectangular*

mummy
*de momia<sup>F</sup>*

**bed and mattress**
*camas<sup>F</sup> y colchonetas<sup>F</sup>*

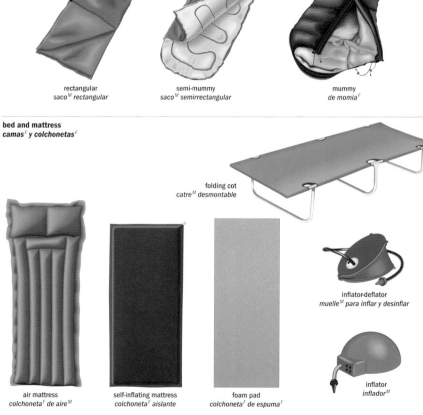

folding cot
*catre<sup>M</sup> desmontable*

inflator-deflator
*muelle<sup>M</sup> para inflar y desinflar*

inflator
*inflador<sup>M</sup>*

air mattress
*colchoneta<sup>F</sup> de aire<sup>M</sup>*

self-inflating mattress
*colchoneta<sup>F</sup> aislante*

foam pad
*colchoneta<sup>F</sup> de espuma<sup>F</sup>*

SPORTS AND GAMES

## cutlery set
*cuberteria*<sup>F</sup>

cooking set
***utensilios*<sup>M</sup> *de cocina*<sup>F</sup>**

belt loop
*presilla*<sup>F</sup>

sheath
*funda*<sup>F</sup>

knife
*cuchillo*<sup>M</sup>

spoon
*cuchara*<sup>F</sup>

fork
*tenedor*<sup>M</sup>

plate
*plato*<sup>M</sup>

saucepan
*cazuela*<sup>F</sup>

handle
*mango*<sup>M</sup>

frying pan
*sartén*<sup>F</sup>

coffee pot
*cafetera*<sup>F</sup>

cup
*taza*<sup>F</sup>

camping equipment
***equipamiento*<sup>M</sup> *para acampar***

Swiss Army knife
*navaja*<sup>F</sup> *multiusos suiza*

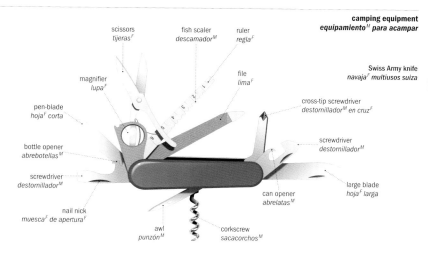

scissors *tijeras*<sup>F</sup>

fish scaler *descamador*<sup>M</sup>

ruler *regla*<sup>F</sup>

file *lima*<sup>F</sup>

magnifier *lupa*<sup>F</sup>

pen-blade *hoja*<sup>F</sup> *corta*

cross-tip screwdriver *destornillador*<sup>M</sup> *en cruz*<sup>F</sup>

screwdriver *destornillador*<sup>M</sup>

bottle opener *abrebotellas*<sup>M</sup>

screwdriver *destornillador*<sup>M</sup>

nail nick *muesca*<sup>F</sup> *de apertura*<sup>F</sup>

awl *punzón*<sup>M</sup>

can opener *abrelatas*<sup>M</sup>

large blade *hoja*<sup>F</sup> *larga*

corkscrew *sacacorchos*<sup>M</sup>

SPORTS AND GAMES

camping

backpack
*mochila*<sup>F</sup>

top flap
*solapa*<sup>F</sup>

shoulder strap
*espaldera*<sup>F</sup>

tightening buckle
*hebilla*<sup>F</sup> *de regulación*<sup>F</sup>

side compression strap
*correa*<sup>F</sup> *de compresión*<sup>F</sup>

front compression strap
*correa*<sup>F</sup> *de cierre*<sup>M</sup>

strap loop
*pasador*<sup>M</sup>

hip belt
*cinturón*<sup>M</sup>

folding shovel
*pala*<sup>F</sup> *plegable*

hurricane lamp
*lámpara*<sup>F</sup> *de petróleo*<sup>M</sup>

vacuum bottle
*termo*<sup>M</sup>

bottle
*botella*<sup>F</sup> *del termo*<sup>M</sup>

stopper
*tapón*<sup>M</sup>

cup
*taza*<sup>F</sup>

canteen
*cantimplora*<sup>F</sup>

cooler
*nevera*<sup>F</sup>

SPORTS AND GAMES

water carrier
*termo*<sup>M</sup> *con llave*<sup>F</sup> *de servicio*<sup>M</sup>

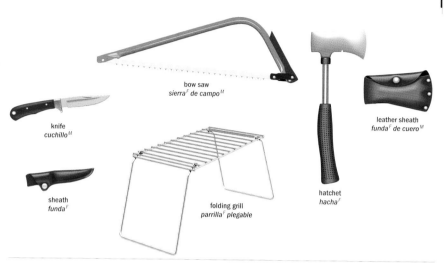

bow saw
*sierra* $^F$ *de campo* $^M$

leather sheath
*funda* $^F$ *de cuero* $^M$

knife
*cuchillo* $^M$

sheath
*funda* $^F$

folding grill
*parrilla* $^F$ *plegable*

hatchet
*hacha* $^F$

magnetic compass
*brújula* $^F$ *magnética*

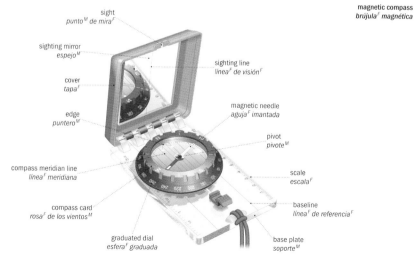

sight
*punto* $^M$ *de mira* $^F$

sighting mirror
*espejo* $^M$

sighting line
*línea* $^F$ *de visión* $^F$

cover
*tapa* $^F$

magnetic needle
*aguja* $^F$ *imantada*

edge
*puntero* $^M$

pivot
*pivote* $^M$

compass meridian line
*línea* $^F$ *meridiana*

scale
*escala* $^F$

compass card
*rosa* $^F$ *de los vientos* $^M$

baseline
*línea* $^F$ *de referencia* $^F$

graduated dial
*esfera* $^F$ *graduada*

base plate
*soporte* $^M$

# hunting
*caza*<sup>F</sup>

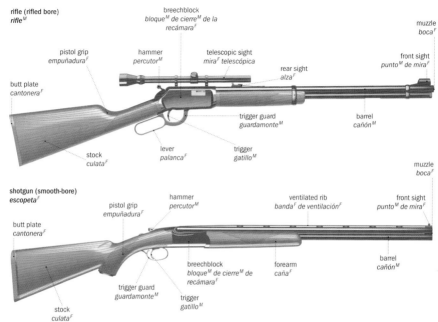

**rifle (rifled bore)**
*rifle*<sup>M</sup>

breechblock
*bloque*<sup>M</sup> *de cierre*<sup>M</sup> *de la recámara*<sup>F</sup>

muzzle
*boca*<sup>F</sup>

pistol grip
*empuñadura*<sup>F</sup>

hammer
*percutor*<sup>M</sup>

telescopic sight
*mira*<sup>F</sup> *telescópica*

rear sight
*alza*<sup>F</sup>

front sight
*punto*<sup>M</sup> *de mira*<sup>F</sup>

butt plate
*cantonera*<sup>F</sup>

trigger guard
*guardamonte*<sup>M</sup>

barrel
*cañón*<sup>M</sup>

stock
*culata*<sup>F</sup>

lever
*palanca*<sup>F</sup>

trigger
*gatillo*<sup>M</sup>

**shotgun (smooth-bore)**
*escopeta*<sup>F</sup>

muzzle
*boca*<sup>F</sup>

hammer
*percutor*<sup>M</sup>

ventilated rib
*banda*<sup>F</sup> *de ventilación*<sup>F</sup>

front sight
*punto*<sup>M</sup> *de mira*<sup>F</sup>

pistol grip
*empuñadura*<sup>F</sup>

butt plate
*cantonera*<sup>F</sup>

breechblock
*bloque*<sup>M</sup> *de cierre*<sup>M</sup> *de recámara*<sup>F</sup>

forearm
*caña*<sup>F</sup>

barrel
*cañón*<sup>M</sup>

trigger guard
*guardamonte*<sup>M</sup>

trigger
*gatillo*<sup>M</sup>

stock
*culata*<sup>F</sup>

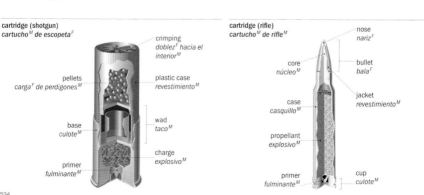

**cartridge (shotgun)**
*cartucho*<sup>M</sup> *de escopeta*<sup>F</sup>

crimping
*doblez*<sup>F</sup> *hacia el interior*<sup>M</sup>

pellets
*carga*<sup>F</sup> *de perdigones*<sup>M</sup>

plastic case
*revestimiento*<sup>M</sup>

base
*culote*<sup>M</sup>

wad
*taco*<sup>M</sup>

primer
*fulminante*<sup>M</sup>

charge
*explosivo*<sup>M</sup>

**cartridge (rifle)**
*cartucho*<sup>M</sup> *de rifle*<sup>M</sup>

nose
*nariz*<sup>F</sup>

core
*núcleo*<sup>M</sup>

bullet
*bala*<sup>F</sup>

case
*casquillo*<sup>M</sup>

jacket
*revestimiento*<sup>M</sup>

propellant
*explosivo*<sup>M</sup>

primer
*fulminante*<sup>M</sup>

cup
*culote*<sup>M</sup>

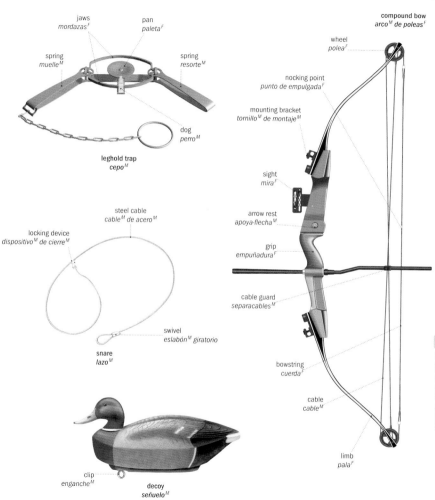

jaws
mordazas<sup>F</sup>

pan
paleta<sup>F</sup>

spring
muelle<sup>M</sup>

spring
resorte<sup>M</sup>

dog
perro<sup>M</sup>

leghold trap
cepo<sup>M</sup>

compound bow
arco<sup>M</sup> de poleas<sup>F</sup>

wheel
polea<sup>F</sup>

nocking point
punto de empulgada<sup>F</sup>

mounting bracket
tornillo<sup>M</sup> de montaje<sup>M</sup>

sight
mira<sup>F</sup>

arrow rest
apoya-flecha<sup>M</sup>

grip
empuñadura<sup>F</sup>

cable guard
separacables<sup>M</sup>

bowstring
cuerda<sup>F</sup>

cable
cable<sup>M</sup>

limb
pala<sup>F</sup>

steel cable
cable<sup>M</sup> de acero<sup>M</sup>

locking device
dispositivo<sup>M</sup> de cierre<sup>M</sup>

swivel
eslabón<sup>M</sup> giratorio

snare
lazo<sup>M</sup>

clip
enganche<sup>M</sup>

decoy
señuelo<sup>M</sup>

SPORTS AND GAMES

535

# fishing
*pesca^F*

## flyfishing
**pesca^F con mosca^F**

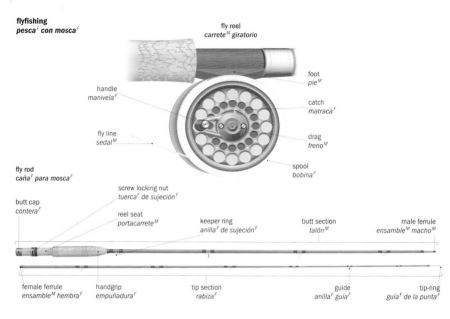

fly reel
*carrete^M giratorio*

foot
*pie^M*

handle
*manivela^F*

catch
*matraca^F*

fly line
*sedal^M*

drag
*freno^M*

spool
*bobina^F*

## fly rod
**caña^F para mosca^F**

screw locking nut
*tuerca^F de sujeción^F*

butt cap
*contera^F*

reel seat
*portacarrete^M*

keeper ring
*anilla^F de sujeción^F*

butt section
*talón^M*

male ferrule
*ensamble^M macho^M*

female ferrule
*ensamble^M hembra^F*

handgrip
*empuñadura^F*

tip section
*rabiza^F*

guide
*anilla^F guía^F*

tip-ring
*guía^F de la punta^F*

## artificial fly
**mosca^F artificial**

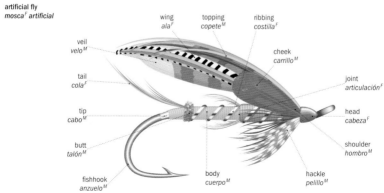

wing
*ala^F*

topping
*copete^M*

ribbing
*costilla^F*

veil
*velo^M*

cheek
*carrillo^M*

tail
*cola^F*

joint
*articulación^F*

tip
*cabo^M*

head
*cabeza^F*

butt
*talón^M*

shoulder
*hombro^M*

fishhook
*anzuelo^M*

body
*cuerpo^M*

hackle
*pelillo^M*

**casting**
*pesca<sup>F</sup> de lanzado<sup>M</sup>*

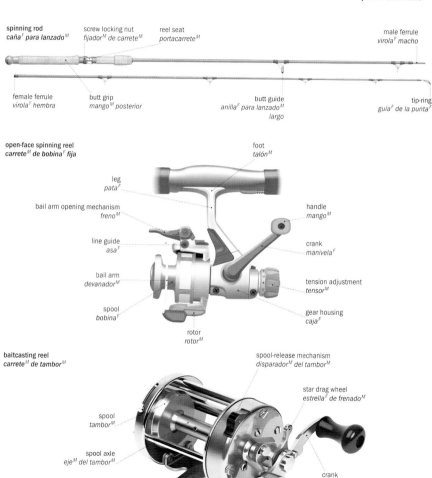

spinning rod
*caña<sup>F</sup> para lanzado<sup>M</sup>*

screw locking nut
*fijador<sup>M</sup> de carrete<sup>M</sup>*

reel seat
*portacarrete<sup>M</sup>*

male ferrule
*virola<sup>F</sup> macho*

female ferrule
*virola<sup>F</sup> hembra*

butt grip
*mango<sup>M</sup> posterior*

butt guide
*anilla<sup>F</sup> para lanzado<sup>M</sup> largo*

tip-ring
*guía<sup>F</sup> de la punta<sup>F</sup>*

open-face spinning reel
*carrete<sup>M</sup> de bobina<sup>F</sup> fija*

foot
*talón<sup>M</sup>*

leg
*pata<sup>F</sup>*

bail arm opening mechanism
*freno<sup>M</sup>*

handle
*mango<sup>M</sup>*

line guide
*asa<sup>F</sup>*

crank
*manivela<sup>F</sup>*

bail arm
*devanador<sup>M</sup>*

tension adjustment
*tensor<sup>M</sup>*

spool
*bobina<sup>F</sup>*

gear housing
*caja<sup>F</sup>*

rotor
*rotor<sup>M</sup>*

baitcasting reel
*carrete<sup>M</sup> de tambor<sup>M</sup>*

spool-release mechanism
*disparador<sup>M</sup> del tambor<sup>M</sup>*

star drag wheel
*estrella<sup>F</sup> de frenado<sup>M</sup>*

spool
*tambor<sup>M</sup>*

spool axle
*eje<sup>M</sup> del tambor<sup>M</sup>*

crank
*manivela<sup>F</sup>*

stand
*pie<sup>M</sup>*

SPORTS AND GAMES

537

fishing

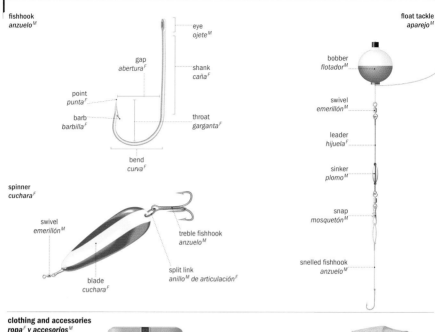

**fishhook**
*anzuelo*<sup>M</sup>

eye
*ojete*<sup>M</sup>

gap
*abertura*<sup>F</sup>

shank
*caña*<sup>F</sup>

point
*punta*<sup>F</sup>

barb
*barbilla*<sup>F</sup>

throat
*garganta*<sup>F</sup>

bend
*curva*<sup>F</sup>

**float tackle**
*aparejo*<sup>M</sup>

bobber
*flotador*<sup>M</sup>

swivel
*emerillón*<sup>M</sup>

leader
*hijuela*<sup>F</sup>

sinker
*plomo*<sup>M</sup>

snap
*mosquetón*<sup>M</sup>

snelled fishhook
*anzuelo*<sup>M</sup>

**spinner**
*cuchara*<sup>F</sup>

swivel
*emerillón*<sup>M</sup>

treble fishhook
*anzuelo*<sup>M</sup>

split link
*anillo*<sup>M</sup> *de articulación*<sup>F</sup>

blade
*cuchara*<sup>F</sup>

**clothing and accessories**
*ropa*<sup>F</sup> *y accesorios*<sup>M</sup>

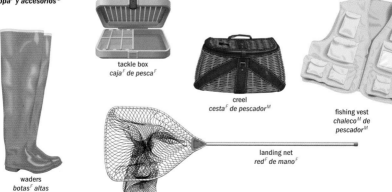

tackle box
*caja*<sup>F</sup> *de pesca*<sup>F</sup>

creel
*cesta*<sup>F</sup> *de pescador*<sup>M</sup>

fishing vest
*chaleco*<sup>M</sup> *de*
*pescador*<sup>M</sup>

landing net
*red*<sup>F</sup> *de mano*<sup>F</sup>

waders
*botas*<sup>F</sup> *altas*

# English Index

balcony door 189
baling 49
balk area 502
balk line 502
balk line spot 502
Balkan Peninsula 18
ball 332
ball bearing 312, 413
ball boy 490
ball mount 356
ball peen 220
ball sports 474
ball-cock supply valve 196
ball-peen hammer 220
ballerina slipper 241
ballpoint pen 312
ballroom 387
balsamic vinegar 141
Baltic Sea 18
baluster 191
balustrade 283
bamboo shoot 125
banana 136
band ring 264
band select button 322
Bangladesh 453
bangle 264
banister 191
banjo 296
bank 342, 432, 437, 442
banknote 441
banknote, back 441
banknote, front 441
banner 313
banquette 201
baptismal font 446
bar 273, 293, 309, 432, 436, 438, 469, 500, 501
bar counter 438
bar frame 207
bar line 298
bar nose 235
bar stool 201, 438
barb 538
Barbados 449
barbell 500, 501
barber comb 268
barbican 282
Barbuda 449
Barents Sea 18
bark 63
barley 61, 143
barley: spike 61
barn 122
barometric pressure 39
barometric tendency 39
barrel 269, 270, 312, 471, 534
barrel vault 281
barrette 268
barrier 205, 434
barrier barricade tape 457
barrier beach 35
bartender 438
bartizan 282
basaltic layer 26
base 54, 179, 180, 192, 199, 206, 227, 229, 269, 283, 318, 332, 342, 412, 421, 422, 454, 473, 534
base cabinet 164
base course 342
base of splat 200
base plate 227, 511, 533
baseball 474, 476
baseball, cross section 477
baseboard 191
baseline 491, 533

basement 182, 435
basement window 183
basic source of food 45
basil 142
basilic vein 102
basin wrench 216
basket 178, 181, 211, 212, 489, 510
basket weave pattern 190
basketball 488
basketball player 488
basmati rice 147
bass 160
bass bridge 304
bass clarinet 295
bass clef 298
bass drum 295, 308
bass guitar 303
bass keyboard 296
bass pickup 303
bass register 296
Bass Strait 15
bass tone control 303, 322, 325
bassoon 306
bassoons 295
baster 173
bat 476, 477, 478
bath 194, 439
bath brush 267
bath sheet 267
bath towel 267
bathing wrap 260
bathrobe 256
bathroom 188, 189, 195, 439, 445, 464
bathroom scale 423
bathroom skylight 189
bathtub 189, 195
baton 472
baton holder 456
batsman 478, 479
batten 292, 519, 520
batten pocket 519, 520
batter 475, 476
batter head 308
batter skin 297
batter's helmet 476
battery 221, 350, 359, 411, 416
battery box 365
battery case 359
battery cover 359
battery pack 228
batting glove 476
battlement 282
bay 5, 24
bay filler panel 329
Bay of Bengal 19
bayonet base 199
beach 35
bead 358
beak 90
beaker 171
beam 283, 288, 422
beam balance 422
beam bridge 344
bean bag chair 201
bean thread cellophane noodles 147
beans 130, 131
bearing pad 409
beater 176
beater ejector 176
beaters 176
Beaufort Sea 16
beauty care 121

beaver 82
becquerel 426
bed 204, 342, 530
bed chamber 280
bedrock 27, 54
bedroom 189, 528
bedside lamp 439, 464
bedside table 439, 464
beech 64
beechnut 133
beef cubes 152
beef, cuts 152
beer 120
beer mug 165
beet 129
begonia 56
Belarus 450
belfry 284, 285
Belgian endive 127
Belgium 449
Belize 448
bell 306, 307
bell bottoms 254
bell brace 306
bell tower 285, 446
bellows 296
bellows strap 296
bells 309
belly 83
below-stage 292
belt 225, 246, 248, 499
belt drive 383
belt highway 25
belt loader 402
belt loop 246, 248, 531
bench 201, 379, 437, 501
bench seat 353
bend 273, 538
Bengal, Bay 19
Benin 451
beret 239
bergamot 134
bergère 200
bergschrund 30
Bering Sea 14
Bering Strait 16
Bermuda shorts 254
berries 132
berry fruit 59
bevel 460
bevel square 225
beverage can 163
beverage dispenser 463
Bhutan 453
bib 260, 261
bib necklace 264
biceps brachii 96
biceps femoris 97
biconcave lens 419
biconvex lens 419
bicycle 370
bicycle bag (pannier) 372
bicycle parking 445
bicycle, accessories 372
bicycle, parts 370
bicycles, examples 373
bidet 195
bikini 259
bikini briefs 247
bilberries 132
bill 78
bill compartment 274
bill presenter 442
bill-file 341
billfold 275
billhook 234

billiard cue 503
billiard spot 502
billiards 502
billiards, carom 502
billiards, English 503
bills, examples 79
bimah 447
binding 238, 513, 514
binocular microscope 421
biology 426
biosphere 44
biosphere, structure 44
biparous cyme 57
birch 64
bird 78
bird of prey 79
bird's eye chile 139
bird's nest fern 52
bird, morphology 78
birds 78
birds, examples 80
birth 426
bishop 470
bison 84
bit 221, 403
bits 228
bitt 385
bitter melon 128
bivalve shell 73
bivalve shell, anatomy 73
bivalve shell, morphology 73
Black 470
black 418
black ball 503
black beans 131
black bear 89
black clamp 356
black currants 132
black gram beans 131
black mustard 138
black pepper 138
black pollock 161
black radishes 129
black rye bread 144
black salsify 129
Black Sea 14, 18, 19
black square 470
black stone 470
black tea 148
black-eyed peas 130
blackberries 132
blade 52, 55, 167, 169, 177, 180, 198, 216, 219, 221, 226, 227, 229, 235, 270, 271, 398, 401, 412, 413, 493, 506, 509, 538
blade close stop 270
blade injector 271
blade lift cylinder 398
blade lift fan 383
blade locking bolt 227
blade rotation cylinder 401
blade shifting mechanism 401
blade tilting lock 227
blade tilting mechanism 227
blade-lift cylinder 401
blank 468
blanket 204
blanket sleepers 261
blastodisc 79
blazer 254
blender 176
blending 176
blending attachment 176
blind spot mirror 362, 363
blinking lights 362
block 215, 305, 473

blocking glove 507
blog 335
blood circulation 102
blood circulation, schema 103
blood factor RH negative 426
blood factor RH positive 426
blood pressure monitor 461
blood sausage 156
blood vessel 104, 114
blood, composition 104
blow pipe 296
blowhole 90
blucher oxford 240
blue 418
blue ball 503
blue beam 318
blue line 507
blue mussels 157
blue-veined cheeses 151
blueberries 132
bluefish 160
blusher brush 266
BMX bike 373
boa 77
board 470, 519
board games 469
boarding room 391
boarding step 395
boarding walkway 389
boards 506
boater 238
boats 382
bobber 538
bobby pin 268
bobeche 207
bodies, examples 347
body 118, 180, 208, 228, 303, 305, 306, 348, 361, 420, 523, 536
body care 267
body flap 13
body of fcmix 109
body of nail 114
body side molding 349
body suit 255, 258
body temperature control unit 10
body tube 421
bodysuit 260
bok choy 126
bole 63
bolero 254
Bolivia 448
bolster 167, 169, 204
bolt 222, 223, 224
bolts 223
bongos 309
boning knife 169
bony fish 74
bony fishes 159
book ends 341
bookcase 444
booking hall 374
bookstore 436
boom 364, 399, 400, 520
boom cylinder 399, 400
boom operator 291
boom swing hinge pin 399
boom vang 520
booster parachute 12
booster seat 205
boot 241, 509, 514, 525, 527
bootee 240
bootees 260
booth 438
borage 142
bordeaux glass 165

552

ENGLISH INDEX

ENGLISH INDEX

## U

u quark 414
U.S. habitation module 11
U.S. laboratory 11
udon noodles 147
Uganda 451
Ukraine 450
ulna 98
ulnar nerve 108
ultracompact camera 315
ultraviolet radiation 418
umbel 57
umbo 73
umbra shadow 4, 5
umbrella pine 65
umbrella stand 273
umbrellas 273
umbrellas and stick 273
Umbriel 3
umpire 479, 485, 487, 490, 495, 515
unbleached flour 144
under tail covert 78
underarm crutch 466
underarm portfolio 275
underarm rest 466
undergarment 524
underground 281
underground cable network 317
underground chamber 278
underground flow 45
underground passage 375
underground stem 54
underlay 190
underpass 344
undershirt 476
underwater light 184
underwear 247, 258
underwire 259
undressing booth 465
uneven parallel bars 496, 497
ungulate mammals 83
ungulate mammals, examples of 84
unicellulars 66
uniform 456
uniform resource locator 334
uniform resource locator (URL) 334
union of two sets 427
union suit 247
uniparous cyme 57
unisex headgear 239
unisex shoes 242
unison 298
unit of amount of substance 426
unit of electric charge 426
unit of electric current 426
unit of electric potential difference 426
unit of electric resistance 426
unit of energy 426
unit of force 426
unit of frequency 426
unit of length 426
unit of luminous intensity 426
unit of mass 426
unit of power 426
unit of pressure 426
unit of radioactivity 426
unit of temperature 426
unit of thermodynamic temperature 426
unit price 423
United Arab Emirates 452

United Kingdom 449
United States of America 448
univalve shell 73
univalve shell, morphology 73
university 432
unleavened bread 145
unloading dock 437, 439
up and over garage door 286
uphaul 519
upholstery nozzle 209
upper 511
upper blade guard 227
upper bowl 181
upper confining bed 402
upper cuff 511
upper deck 363, 392
upper edge 493
upper eyelid 75, 87, 119
upper lateral lobe 62
upper lateral sinus 62
upper lip 116, 305
upper lobe 105
upper mandible 78
upper mantle 26
upper shell 511, 527
upper strap 511
upper tail covert 78
upperworks 521
upright 184, 466
upright piano 304
upright suitcase 277
upright vacuum cleaner 209
upstage 292, 293
Ural Mountains 18
Uranus 2, 3
urban map 25
ureter 107
urethra 107, 112
urinary bladder 107, 111, 112
urinary meatus 111
urinary system 107
URL 334
uropod 71
Uruguay 448
USB connector 333
USB key 333
USB port 310, 329, 336
used syringe box 457
usual terms 57, 58, 59
utensils for cutting, examples 169
utensils, kitchen 169
utensils, set 173
uterovesical pouch 112
uterus 112, 113
utility case 276
uvula 116, 117
Uzbekistan 452

## V

V-neck 244, 250
V-neck cardigan 250
vacuole 50, 66
vacuum bottle 532
vacuum cleaner attachments 209
vacuum cleaner, cylinder 209
vacuum cleaner, upright 209
vacuum coffee maker 181
vacuum diaphragm 360
vacuum distillation 405
vagina 112, 113
valley 29, 32
valve 60, 73, 307
valve casing 307

valve cover 360
valve seat shaft 196
valve spring 360
vamp 240, 263
van straight truck 365
vane 213
vanilla extract 140
vanity cabinet 195
vanity mirror 354
Vanuatu 453
vapor 415
variable ejector nozzle 394
vastus lateralis 96, 97
vastus medialis 96
vault 284, 443
vaulting horse 496, 497
veal cubes 152
vegetable bowl 166
vegetable brush 173
vegetable garden 122, 182
vegetable kingdom 50
vegetable sponge 267
vegetables 120, 124
vegetables, bulb 124
vegetables, fruit 128
vegetables, inflorescent 127
vegetables, leaf 126
vegetables, root 129
vegetables, stalk 125
vegetables, tuber 124
vegetation 44
vegetation regions 44
vehicle jack 356
vehicle rest area 345
veil 536
vein 55
veins 102
velarium 281
Velcro closure 260
velvet-band choker 264
Venezuela 448
venom canal 76
venom gland 76
venom-conducting tube 76
venomous snake, morphology 76
vent 354
vent brush 268
vent door 365
ventilated rib 534
ventilating circuit 194
ventilating grille 209
ventilator 380
ventral abdominal artery 71
ventral nerve cord 71
Venus 2, 3
verbena 148
vermicelli 147
vermiform appendix 106
vernal equinox 38
vernier 422, 425
vernier caliper 425
vernier scale 425
Versailles parquet 190
vertebral body 110
vertebral column 98, 109
vertebral shield 76
vertical cord lift 208
vertical ground movement 27
vertical movement 470
vertical pivoting window 287
vertical pupil 76
vertical section 526

vertical seismograph 27
vertical side band 487
vertical-axis wind turbine 412
vest 244, 255
vestibular nerve 116
vestibule 116, 280
vial 467
vibrating mudscreen 403
vibrato arm 303
vice-skip 515
Victoria, Lake 20
video and digital terminals 315
video entertainment system 471
video monitor 329
video port 329, 336
videocassette 319
videocassette recorder (VCR) 321
videophony 335
videotape operation controls 320
Vietnam 453
view camera 315
viewfinder 315
village 430, 512
vine shoot 62
vine stock 62
vinyl grip sole 261
viola 301
violas 295
violet 56
violin 301
violin family 301
viper 77
visceral ganglion 73
visceral pleura 105
vision 419
vision defects 419
visor 367, 459, 506, 525
visor hinge 367
Vistula River 18
vitelline membrane 79
vitreous body 119
vocal cord 105
voice edit buttons 310
voice recorder button 337
voice selector 311
volcanic bomb 28
volcanic island 33
volcanic lake 32
volcano 26, 28
volcano during eruption 28
volcanoes, examples 28
Volga River 18
volley 490
volleyball 487
volt 426
voltage decrease 413
voltage increase 408
voltage tester 217
volume 328
volume control 303, 310, 311, 319, 322, 325
volume display 346
volute 200
volva 52
vulture 80
vulva 94, 113

## W

wad 534
waders 538
wadi 36
wading bird 79
waffle iron 178
wagon tent 528
waist 93, 95, 240, 301
waist belt 205
waistband 246, 247, 249
waistband extension 246
waiter's corkscrew 170
waiting area 442
waiting room 463
wakame 123
walk 83
walk-in closet 189
walker 466
walkie-talkie 456
walking aids 466
walking leg 67
walking stick 273, 466
walkway 436
wall 5, 58, 184, 528
wall cabinet 164
wall cloud 43
wall lantern 207
wall sconce 207
wall side 385
wall tent 528
wallet 275, 337
walnut 64, 133
walnut, section 60
waning gibbous 5
wapiti (elk) 84
wardrobe 189, 203, 439
warehouse 430
warm air 41
warm temperate climates 40
warm-air baffle 192
warming plate 181
warning lights 355
warning plate 228
warning track 475
wasabi 141
wash tower 214
washcloth 267
washer 194, 417
washer nozzle 348
washer, front-loading 212
washer, top-loading 212
washers 222
wasp-waisted corset 259
Wassily chair 200
waste basket 341
waste layers 47
waste pipe 196
waste stack 194
waste water 48
waste, selective sorting 49
water 402
water bottle 371
water bottle clip 371
water carrier 532
water chestnut 124
water cools the used steam 408
water dispenser 211
water goblet 165
water hazard 504
water hose 214
water intake 407
water is pumped back into the steam generator 408
water jets 518

# Índice español

ÍNDICE ESPAÑOL